"By its ambitious depth and breadth, this book is a major undertaking. A great read for the general public interested in the region at the heart of Eurasia. The book is a 'must read' for decision-makers in the public and private sector directly or indirectly involved with Central Asia."

Philippe Le Houérou, *Chairman of the French Development Agency, former Vice-President of the World Bank and CEO of International Finance Corporation*

"The author takes readers to the deep history from the Silk Road to the Soviet era, and discusses economic and political challenges after independence, including complicated issues of transport, energy and water for the landlocked countries separated by mountainous terrain, and how the region can cultivate cooperation between them and with international partners."

Takehiko Nakao, *former President of Asian Development Bank*

"Djoomart Otorbaev draws our attention and to a region that has always been a bridge between East and West. What is its potential? What opportunities for cooperation are opening up? Pursuing these questions and enhancing our knowledge about the Central Asian region is indeed a worthwhile pursuit."

Professor Dr Horst Köhler, *former President of Germany*

"The book is essential reading for anyone who wants to learn something about Central Asia."

Václav Klaus, *former Prime Minister and President of the Czech Republic*

"This insightful and absorbing work actually poses the most important question of our time – the question of the connectivity and interdependence of our world."

Petar Stoyanov, *former President of the Republic of Bulgaria*

"This book is very valuable source for politicians and business people not only locally but worldwide."

Valdis Zatlers, *former President of Latvia*

"As one of the most prominent experts about this part of the world, Otorbaev takes us on a journey through the past and leads to perhaps the most important crossroads on the way to the future development of the whole world, with precise instructions about what each turn at that crossroad entails."

Boris Tadić, *former President of Serbia*

"Djoomart Otorbaev, combining the skills of an accomplished prime minister, economist/analyst, and international banker, offers an attractive and feasible economic future for his native Kyrgyzstan and all Central Asia."

S. Frederick Starr, *Chairman Central Asia-Caucasus Institute, Washington*

"Until recently, there was no in-depth description of the Central Asian region in the post-Soviet period, written by a real insider. Djoomart Otorbaev's book makes up for this deficiency. A gifted, effective modern leader for an emerging country. I do not doubt that the book will be an excellent guide for a wide range of readers."

Ehud Barak, *former Prime Minister of Israel*

"I consider such a book to be a vital contribution coming at a crucial moment."

Amre Moussa, *former Secretary-General of the Arab League and former Minister of Foreign Affairs, Egypt*

Central Asia's Economic Rebirth in the Shadow of the New Great Game

This volume describes the unique development of Central Asia as defined by its landlocked geography. Particular attention is paid to the achievements and challenges of the region's post-Soviet economic and political transformation, as well as to its relationship with the participants in the New Great Game – Russia, China and the West. Located as it is in the geographical centre of booming Asia, and with the opportunity to become a key logistics bridge connecting the world's largest economies, Central Asia is well placed for rapid development. However, the region faces a range of complex problems that are explained and analysed in the volume. The Eurasian powers that encircle Central Asia look certain to become the engines of global economic growth, but how will this affect the region? Will Central Asia join the powerful locomotive of history, or will it remain on the side-lines?

Djoomart Otorbaev is a former Prime Minister of the Kyrgyz Republic (2014–15). He also worked as a Senior Adviser in the European Bank for Reconstruction and Development, based in London (2006–11). He is an honorary member and invited speaker at numerous boards and forums on development and investment.

Europa Regional Perspectives

Providing in-depth analysis with a global reach, this series from Europa examines a wide range of contemporary political, economic, developmental and social issues in regional perspective. Intended to complement the Europa Regional Surveys of the World series, Europa Regional Perspectives will be a valuable resource for academics, students, researchers, policymakers, business people and anyone with an interest in current world affairs with an emphasis on regional issues.

While the Europa World Year Book and its associated Regional Surveys inform on and analyse contemporary economic, political and social developments, the Editors considered the need for more in-depth volumes written and/or edited by specialists in their field, in order to delve into particular regional situations. Volumes in the series are not constrained by any particular template, but may explore recent political, economic, international relations, social, defence, or other issues in order to increase knowledge. Regions are thus not specifically defined, and volumes may focus on small or large group of countries, regions or blocs.

Catalonia, Scotland and the EU
Visions of Independence and Integration
Niklas Bremberg and Richard Gillespie

Social Welfare Issues in Southern Europe
Edited by Maria Brown and Michael Briguglio

Constructive Competition in the Caspian Sea Region?
An Alternative Image
Agha Bayramov

The Nordic, Baltic and Visegrád Small Powers in Europe
A Dance with Giants for Survival and Prosperity
Hilmar Þór Hilmarsson

Central Asia's Economic Rebirth in the Shadow of the New Great Game
Djoomart Otorbaev

For more information about this series, please visit: www.routledge.com/Europa-Regional-Perspectives/book-series/ERP.

Central Asia's Economic Rebirth in the Shadow of the New Great Game

Djoomart Otorbaev

Routledge
Taylor & Francis Group
LONDON AND NEW YORK

Designed cover image: © Shutterstock

First published 2023
by Routledge
4 Park Square, Milton Park, Abingdon, Oxon OX14 4RN

and by Routledge
605 Third Avenue, New York, NY 10158

Routledge is an imprint of the Taylor & Francis Group, an informa business

British Library Cataloguing in Publication Data
A catalogue record for this book is available from the British Library

Library of Congress Cataloging-in-Publication Data
A catalog record has been requested for this book

ISBN: 978-1-032-41992-3 (hbk)
ISBN: 978-1-032-41989-3 (pbk)
ISBN: 978-1-003-36072-8 (ebk)

DOI: 10.4324/9781003360728

Typeset in Times New Roman
by Taylor & Francis Books

Dedicated to the people without whom I would not exist.
To: Akima Djoldosheva, Kaip Otorbaev and Maria Nanaeva.

Contents

Figures

Tables

Foreword

I am honoured to provide my personal comments on this volume about the future of the landlocked countries of Central Asia. I comment on these countries at a moment when the details we hear from their neighbourhood deal with geopolitical strategies, imperialist ambitions and, alas, those of one of the most cruel wars of recent history. In such circumstances, apart from humanitarian support to the millions of victims, the proper attitude for the "man in the street" that I am now is to remain silent and pray for peace and help to all those working for an early settlement, particularly of the conflict between Russia and Ukraine as it affects all the world's process of development.

I see, nevertheless, a modest justification for making a few comments about the work that Djoomart Otorbaev is boldly undertaking, to reflect on the future of Central Asia in the context of the long-term perspectives of developing countries. This is a very hard job for economists, but it is certainly one of the most useful, as it is the best way to provide a reasonable vision of the future and restore hope. I can imagine of course that many observers could see such reflections as futile – to say the least – in view of the present environment and the precarious situation of many of these countries. That being said, let me tell you that in my country, we used to say "C'est la nuit qu'il est beau de croire à la lumière". (It is at night that it is beautiful to believe in the light.) It is this humble conviction which has decided me to offer a few comments on the author's views on the future transformation of Central Asia. Having been myself associated, at the beginning of the 1960s, with the first footsteps of the European Union, I believe that Central Asia can also surprise the world with a similar miracle! One knows well its two secrets: cooperation and solidarity on the one hand, and mutual reconciliation and peace on the other hand. I believe that those in charge, today, of the historical responsibility of Central Asia could find in this book inspiration for similar achievements. Two additional suggestions seem to me of the highest importance: instead of continuing to conduct their consultative processes in a bilateral way, the potential partners would enormously benefit from the creation suggested in conclusion of a new multilateral Advisory Council composed of Central Asia, China and the European Union. I warmly hope that this book could contribute towards convincing their leaders to identify the extraordinary opportunities for progress and the critical responsibilities they face for the future of their region and the wellbeing not only of their part of the world, but also for the care of all the planet.

Michel Camdessus, former Managing Director of the International Monetary Fund, and former Governor of the Banque de France.

Preface

Naturally, I wanted to write a book with reflections on realities that are as fresh as possible. But I realise that this goal is unattainable. The modern world is developing exponentially, and writing and publishing a book takes a long time. And so it happened. As I was preparing the book, the world changed.

Work on the book was in full swing when, on 24 February 2022, Russia launched its special military operation in Ukraine. Obviously, I would need to describe the implications for the future of Central Asia, so I waited until the very last minute before sending the final version of the book to the publisher. I was waiting for this operation to end so that my readers could better understand how the world, and my region along with it, would change. But unfortunately, the war continues without an end in sight. Now, one thing is clear – the Western world and Russia have had fundamental quarrels for a long time. There is nothing good in this fact, neither for the world order nor for Central Asia. Politically, the region's countries took a neutral position in response, not supporting either side. At the same time, none of the countries has recognised the so-called Donetsk and Lugansk People's Republics, nor will they recognise them. The President of Kazakhstan, Kassym-Jomart Tokayev, stated this unequivocally in the presence of Vladimir Putin at the St. Petersburg International Economic Summit in June 2022.

Naturally, Russia's economic and political isolation will greatly affect the position of the Central Asian region. The predicted sharp decline of at least 9 per cent in the Russian economy in 2022 (World Bank, 2022) will negatively affect mutual trade and investment. According to World Bank estimates from June 2022, Uzbekistan's GDP growth in 2022 will reach 4.3 per cent, and Kazakhstan's 2 per cent. The other countries are expected to decline – Tajikistan's GDP will decrease by 0.4 per cent, and the Kyrgyz Republic's by 2 per cent (World Bank, 2022). There will also be a sharp decline in remittances from migrants in Russia to the Kyrgyz Republic, Tajikistan and Uzbekistan.

The region has suddenly found itself between a rock and a hard place. Efforts by the countries to comply with sanctions against Russia may displease Moscow. At the same time, Central Asia is trying to take into account

Russia's interests, for which it may fall under secondary sanctions. A weak Russia will have a negative impact on the whole region. Likely, countries will focus on damage limitation by recalibrating their foreign policy. They are also busy exploring new opportunities that are opening up. For example, in June 2022, in St Petersburg, the President of Kazakhstan stated: "The Eurasian Economic Union should pursue an active trade policy with a wide coverage of the markets of Asia and the Middle East. Kazakhstan could play a useful role here as a kind of buffer market." The countries of the region want to show that they are open to trade and that they are good neighbours and effective partners.

Here it is worth mentioning the Eurasian railway bridge connecting Asia and Europe through the territories of Central Asia and Russia, which is described in detail in the book. According to the China National Railway Group, China–Europe rail freight traffic amounted to 1.46 million TEU in 2021, accounting for 4.45 per cent of the total sea container traffic between Asia and Europe of 32.8 million TEU. Experts believe the traffic on the China–Europe rail network will fall sharply in 2022, wiping out years of growth (Wishnick, 2022). In the best-case scenario, it may take up to three years to restore the volume of traffic to pre-crisis levels. Rail trade between China and Europe is forecast to decline by at least 35 per cent, as 90 per cent of the cargo before the Russian invasion went on the northern route through Russia and Belarus (Knowler, 2022).

On top of everything else, relations between China and the EU remain frigid and tense. The long-awaited China–EU summit in April 2022 did not cause optimism for traders and logisticians. On the contrary, Josep Borrell, EU High Commissioner for Foreign Affairs and Security Affairs, described it by saying "[it] was not really a dialogue – maybe a dialogue of the deaf" (Lau, 2022).

One of the options for restoring East–West transportation could be a southern route from China through Central Asia to the Caspian Sea region, Iran, Turkey and further to Europe. Testing out such an option has already begun. On 13 April 2022, a new multimodal service began, including rail transit from Xi'an through Kazakhstan, sea delivery over the Caspian Sea to Baku, and then rail transit to Poti in Georgia, followed by shipment via the Black Sea to European ports.

It is in the interests of the countries of Central Asia for the Russian–Ukrainian conflict to end and for the regional and world economy to function normally again. But as is often the case in history, politics prevails over common sense for a time. Let's hope that in this case, this won't be for too long.

It is, of course, beyond the scope of this volume to give a full and complete study of Central Asia: for example, I decided not to include a detailed analysis of previous research conducted by scholars. The views expressed and any errors within are my own. The book is my subjective perception of the processes in the region and around it.

References

Knowler, G., 2022. Falling China-Europe rail volumes may take years to recover: rail executives. [Online] Available at: https://www.joc.com/rail-intermodal/international-rail/falling-china-europe-rail-volumes-may-take-years-recover-rail-executives_20220406.html [Accessed July 2022].

Lau, S., 2022. China Direct: What next after EU summit? — Indo-Pacific plans from Prague — Good job, Viktor. [Online] Available at: https://www.politico.eu/newsletter/china-direct/what-next-after-eu-summit-indo-pacific-plans-from-prague-good-job-viktor/ [Accessed July 2022].

Wishnick, E., 2022. China's Belt and Road Loses a Notch and Gains a Bump. [Online] Available at: https://chinaobservers.eu/chinas-belt-and-road-loses-a-notch-and-gains-a-bump/ [Accessed July 2022].

World Bank, 2022. Stagflation Risk Rises Amid Sharp Slowdown in Growth. [Online] Available at: https://www.worldbank.org/en/news/press-release/2022/06/07/stagflation-risk-rises-amid-sharp-slowdown-in-growth-energy-markets [Accessed July 2022].

Acknowledgements

This will be my second book published in English by a well-known publisher. The first book was co-authored with V. V. Lelevkin and D.C. Schram and titled *Physics of Non-equilibrium Plasmas.* It was published in Amsterdam by the North-Holland Publishing Company in 1992. I think that there are few authors who first publish in physics and then in political economy. But this fact once again shows that my life has consisted of two different parts – during the Soviet times and after the country's disintegration. In Soviet times, I lived the life of a physicist, reaching the rank of professor at 34. After that, I became a businessman, economist, and politician in a newly born country – the independent Kyrgyz Republic.

Why did all this happen, and how did it become possible? As the years went by, it became evident that I made my most important decisions based on my father's advice when I was fourteen. I asked him who I should become in the future. He replied that the profession you choose is not so important. The only important thing is to always try to be among clever people.

Generally speaking, in making the most critical decisions in my life, I always followed this advice. To list all the cases, I would have to write a separate book. So I will explain here just one example of the first time I applied this advice.

Here one should make a slight digression into the past. In Soviet times, the most respected people were people of science, especially those who worked in mathematics and the natural sciences. It is easy to explain. At that time, the Soviet Union was in a tough arms race with the United States. And although the military budgets of these two countries differed significantly, and not in favour of the Soviets, there was approximate military parity between the two. I explain this by the fact that in the Soviet Union, there was a unique system for finding talent to work in defence. In high school, prominent students in mathematics, physics and chemistry were selected. At 13–14, they were offered a place at specialised schools. Then the most promising ones were invited to study at boarding schools in three cities – Moscow, Leningrad and Novosibirsk. In these schools, leading scientists gave in-depth lectures and held intensive seminars for these students.

After graduating, the young talents were enrolled in the country's leading universities. Successful graduates received prestigious and highly paid jobs in research institutes, which, as a rule, dealt with defence. Additionally, they received free apartments and residence permits in major Soviet cities. But the highlight was that the graduates could travel abroad, a privilege that was totally inaccessible to ordinary Soviet citizens. No less important was the scientists' high social status, as the whole country was proud of these people. Films, theatrical productions, books and songs were all dedicated to those role models.

As I was a high school student during this time, it became clear to me that to be among clever people, I must be either a mathematician or a physicist. So I ended up becoming a student at the Faculty of Physics at Leningrad State University.

To my surprise, the thing that I most had to work on during my first year of study wasn't physics or mathematics. It was English. One of the main priorities of the faculty was for the graduates to read, write and speak English to be able to communicate with our foreign colleagues.

After graduating from university and getting my doctorate, I became a scientist and attended numerous international conferences. So I ended up among clever people not only in my country but around the world. As a physicist, I have attended hundreds of scientific conferences and travelled to dozens of countries around the world. And so it seemed that the exciting life of a professor was ahead of me. But everything turned out completely different.

The disintegration of the Soviet Union in 1991 posed a huge dilemma for my personal and professional life – to remain a physicist but live and work abroad or to return home to start doing something completely different since funding for science had ceased. I decided to go home, which is how my second life began.

Now I don't regret this choice for a minute, as my work in economics and politics in the last twenty-five years gave me the privilege to communicate and to work with many prominent personalities. These include current and former heads of state and government, heads of international financial institutions and great thinkers.

I had to meet and work with them regularly on official and informal occasions, at open and non-public venues, whether in annual global forums or periodic professional discussions. Regular business contacts became a bridge to good camaraderie. They were supported not only by official communication but also by personal phone calls and sometimes by joint family dinners. Numerous collaborative projects, meetings of various formats and friendly communication with them allowed me to get to know my new colleagues and friends well and understand their business and life principles.

Mostly, these are soft and intelligent people who listen more than they speak. If they talk, it is deep and sincere. They are supporters of balance, not extremes. They prefer quiet and practical actions, do not make loud statements and do not give empty promises. They play for the long haul and avoid populist decisions. They build bridges and never burn them down. All these are universal rules for any successful person, even more so for a prominent leader.

Here I will only give their names without mentioning their positions since they are widely known. And since this book is no longer related to physics, I will allow myself to list only people who were associated with the second part of my life. I wrote this book under the influence of each of these personalities. I want to thank them for their input.[1]

Current and former Presidents (in alphabetical order): Sali Berisha, Laura Chinchilla, Joaquim Chissano, Emil Constantinescu, Igor Dodon, Tsakhia Elbegorj, Recep Tayyip Erdoğan, Ashraf Ghani, Ameenah Gurib-Fakim, Abdullah Gül, Ivo Josipovic, Islam Karimov, Hamid Karzai, Vaclav Klaus, Horst Köhler, Petru Lucinschi, Dmitry Medvedev, Rexhep Meidani, Bujar Nishani, Punsalmaagiin Ochirbat, Rosen Plevneliev, Fidel Ramos, Jose Ramos-Horta, Rosalia Arteaga Serrano, Petar Stoyanov, Boris Tadic, Kassym-Jomart Tokayev, Alejandro Toledo, Dioncounda Traoré, Danilo Turk, Vaira Vike-Freiberga, Filip Vujanovic, Vladimir Voronin, Viktor Yushchenko, Valdis Zatlers.

Current and former Prime Ministers: Fakhruddin Ahmed, Norovyn Altankhuyag, Shaukat Aziz, Ehud Barak, Ahmet Davutoğlu, Jan Fisher, Chiril Gaburici, Yegor Gaidar, Zinaida Greceanii, Giorgi Kvirikashvili, Zlatko Lagumdzija, Yves Leterme, Li Keqiang, Karim Massimov, Peter Medgyessy, Mahathir Mohamad, Michail Myasnikovich, Raila Odinga, Kokhir Rasulzoda, Sergey Rumas, Bakytzhan Sagintayev, Tigran Sargsyan, Essam Sharaf, Sergey Sidorsky, Fuad Siniora.

Current and former Ministers and Governors: Aleksi Aleksishvili, Murodali Alimardon, Baldanjav Ariunsan, Rustam Azimov, Ali Babacan, Levon Barkhudaryan, Kakha Bendukidze, Luvsanvandan Bold, Bekir Bozdag, Hikmet Cetin, Tigran Davtyan, Benita Ferrero-Waldner, Jacob Frenkel, Sergey Glaziev, Koba Gvenetadze, Nematullo Hikmatullozoda, Erlan Idrissov, Oraz Jandosov, Mikheil Janelidze, Kairat Kelimbetov, Grzegorz Kołodko, Jan Kubis, Haruhiko Kuroda, Valeriu Lazar, Tzipi Livni, Irakli Managadze, Grigori Marchenko, Rashid Meredov, Amre Moussa, Mustapha Nabli, Vladimir Norov, Roberto de Ocampo, Stefan Odagiu, Erbol Orynbayev, Sanjaasurengin Oyun, Tsedevdamba Oyungerel, Lundeg Purevsuren, Sharif Rahimzoda, Davlatali Said, Abdujabbor Shirinov, Mehmet Simsek, Yashar Yakish, Cevdet Yilmaz.

Current and former heads and deputy heads of International Financial Institutions: Erik Berglof, Michel Camdessus, Suma Chakrabarti, Enrique Garcia, Jean-Daniel Gerber, Philippe Le Houérou, Jin Liqun, Gautam Kaji, Shigeo Katsu, Jean Lemierre, Justin Yifu Lin, Johannes Linn, Bindu Lohani, Rajat Nag, Takehiko Nakao, Ismail Serageldin, Zhang Wencai, Zhao Xiaoyu.

In my life, I have met many bright personalities from academia. Here I would like to mention a few of them, which had a particularly great influence on me: Hu Biliang, Masood Ahmed, Anders Aslund, Harinder Kohli and Frederick Starr.

After acquaintance with this pretty long list, the reader can see that I tried hard to follow my father's advice to be among clever people. How lucky must the person who had such a father.

In preparation for writing this book, I received a great deal of advice and guidance from Anders Åslund and Frederick Starr, for which I am very grateful. Ken Murphy helped me with the formulation of the most important elements of the book.

Many of the results of the book were part of a course of lectures that I deliver as a visiting professor at the Belt and Road School of Beijing Normal University. I am grateful to the leadership of this school and the University for the invitation.

Since English is not my native language, I needed help preparing the book. Timothy and Esther Johnson have provided invaluable editing support, and my special thanks go to them.

I am lucky in life with good people, and I was lucky again with Cathy Hartley, Senior Editor at Routledge, who gave me invaluable support in making the book a reality.

I must express my gratitude to my family members, to my wife and children for their support and patience.

Note

1 I am not giving a list of top politicians and bright personalities from my country, the Kyrgyz Republic, all of which I personally know.

Introduction

Central Asia, the subject of this book, is not so well known to the general public. It is as if an area the size of the European Union does not exist. Central Asia is certainly not featured on the popular weather forecasts of the world's leading countries such as CNN or the BBC.

The single most essential geographic feature of Central Eurasia is its lack of access to the ocean. The landlocked countries of Eurasia include the five countries of Central Asia, the countries of the South Caucasus – Azerbaijan and Armenia, as well as Afghanistan and Mongolia. This book will deal only with those countries located east of the Caspian Sea – Kazakhstan, the Kyrgyz Republic (also known as Kyrgyzstan), Tajikistan, Turkmenistan and Uzbekistan – hereafter referred to simply as "Central Asia".

These five countries collectively cover an area of 4,003,451 km^2. According to the latest UN estimates, the current population of Central Asia is approximately 76 million, of which about 34 million live in Uzbekistan, 19 million in Kazakhstan, 10 million in Tajikistan, 7 million in the Kyrgyz Republic and 6 million in Turkmenistan (Worldometer, 2022). By comparison, the total area of the 27 member states of the European Union (EU) is 4,233,255.3 km^2, and its population is about 447 million people.

The term The Great Game, presented in the book's title, is widely used in the relevant literature to describe the competition between great powers for political dominance over regions and territories. Only a few know that the term was first introduced to describe the events of the 19th century when the British and Russian empires fought for influence in Central Asia (Fromkin, 1980). This process sometimes uses other terms, such as "the grand chessboard" coined by Zbigniew Brzezinski in the 1990s and again referring to Central Asia (Brzezinski, 1997). But what about competition between the great powers in modern Central Asia? This will also be discussed in the book.

For any landlocked country, its neighbours are essential. In the south-east lies the People's Republic of China, in the north, the Russian Federation, in the south-east, Afghanistan, Pakistan, and India, to the west lie Iran, the countries of the South Caucasus (Armenia, Azerbaijan and Georgia) and Turkey. Some of these countries are becoming the main centres of economic

DOI: 10.4324/9781003360728-1

and political power in the 21st century. In less than thirty years, they will produce more than half of the world's gross domestic product (GDP) (ADB, 2011). It is no longer North America or Europe, but a resurgent Asia which is becoming the engine of global economic growth. Whether Central Asia can join the powerful locomotives of current economic expansion will determine its future fate.

Forward or Backwards

Is such a shift in the centre of gravity of global economic power surprising or unique? Historians and economists unequivocally say it is neither. Figure A.1 shows a graph from the data provided in (Maddison, 2006) illustrating the economic history of the world, and showing the share of the largest economic powers in world GDP since the first year of our era. Until about 1820, when the industrial revolution led to an unprecedented rise in labour productivity, the bulk of the world's GDP was produced in Asia. Figure A.1 shows that over the past 20 centuries, Asia only ceased being a dominant world economic zone within the last 200 years.

Figure A.2 shows the evolution of the centre of gravity of the world economy, provided by the McKinsey Global Institute analysis using data from the University of Groningen (Dobbs et al., 2012). According to this data, it appears that the current global geopolitical and economic transformation is just a return to the "good old days" for Asia.

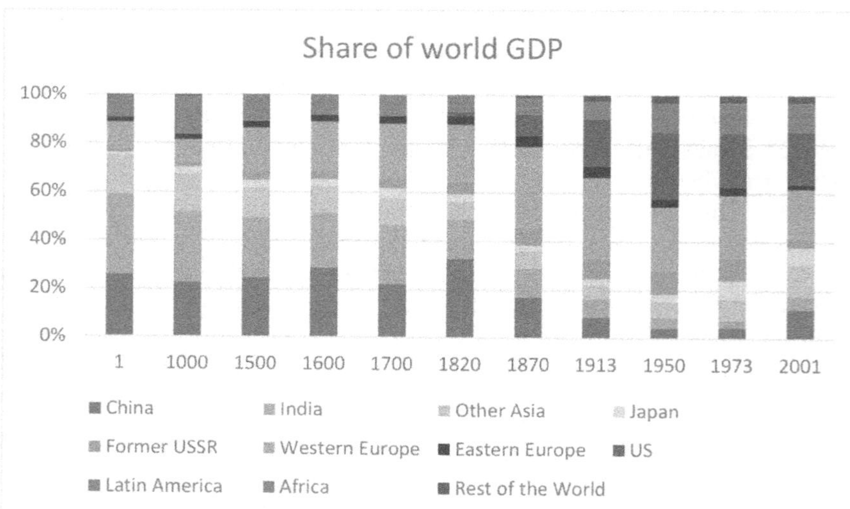

Figure A.1 Share of the largest economic powers in world GDP
Source: Dobbs et al. (2012).

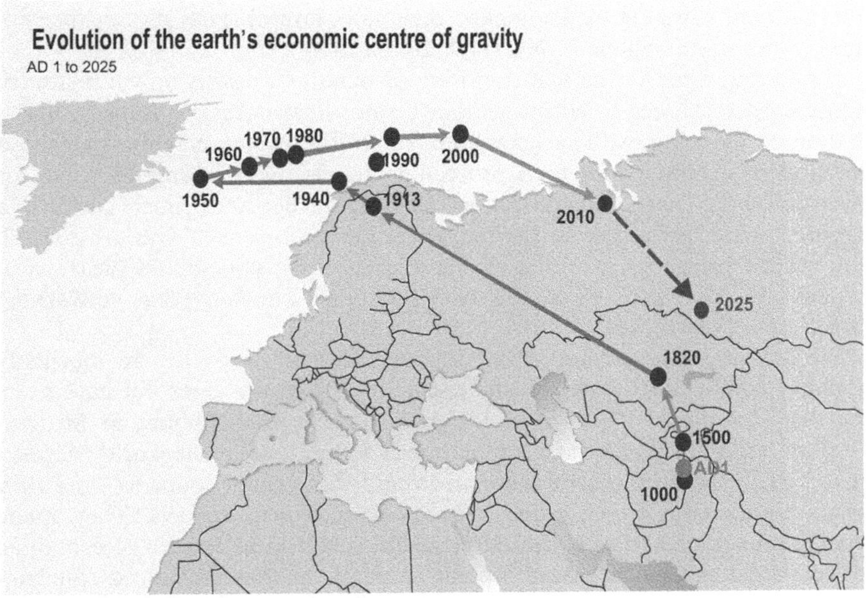

Figure A.2 Evolution of the centre of gravity of the world economy
Source: Dobbs et al. (2012).

The renewed centres of world economic power surrounding Central Asia are now becoming the engine of the "Asian economic miracle". But what effect will this have on Central Asia? Will this region join the "powerful locomotive" of world history in the 21st century, or will it remain on the side-lines of history? The answer, as history teaches us, is that either option is possible.

During the Golden Age of Central Asia, between 800 and 1200 AD, the region was the centre of world development in fundamental areas such as mathematics, astronomy, geography, geology and medicine. As Frederick Starr writes in his in-depth study: "Rarely in history has a more impressive group of polymaths appeared at one place and time" (Starr, 2015: 15).

However, before and after this Golden Age, the region found itself on the periphery of world civilisation. What happened here? Where can one find the answer to such a radical metamorphosis?

The answer to this riddle is found in just one word: connectivity. Politics is a product of history, and history is a product of geography. The unusual geography of Central Asia shaped its complex history (Onion et al., 2017). As a landlocked region, it is one of the least connected areas in the world.

Approximately 40 per cent of the world's GDP is produced in territories within 100 kilometres of an ocean coast (United Nations, 2007). Less than 7 per cent of the world's population lives in landlocked countries (SurferToday.com, 2022). Doing business and trading effectively without access to the sea is complicated and the capital for growth is limited. For example, international shipping in landlocked regions is several times more expensive than in maritime regions (UNCTAD, 2021).

If someone lives by the sea, travelling or making a deal is only a matter of jumping into a boat. In countries that do not have access to the sea, it is a matter of agreeing with a neighbour (or with several neighbours) about entering its territory and then proceeding to organise a complex route for your travel or cargo transportation. Everything becomes much easier if a country has direct access to the sea. As it has been said: if you are coastal, you should please the world; if you are landlocked, you should please your neighbours. In Central Asia, this reality requires knowing what networking and connectivity mean.

What is the fate of landlocked regions? Is it a recipe for an inevitably hopeless future? Fortunately, history teaches us that this does not have to be the case. Landlocked European countries such as Luxembourg or Switzerland are among the ten most interconnected countries in the world (Altman et al., 2019). More powerful states surround these small countries, and they became successful by choosing suitable development models. They made tremendous efforts to establish effective links with local centres of economic power, which is why they have become some of the most advanced countries in the world. There is no reason why Central Asia cannot do the same.

Unique Geography

Central Asia lies at the heart of the Eurasian continent, which is convenient for developing short land communication routes between the centres of economic power. That said, unlike waterways, land routes have several fundamental drawbacks. The presence of high mountains and deep valleys significantly complicates any logistics plans and, therefore, determines the low transit potential of the region. None of the Central Asian rivers flows to the ocean and instead feed into inland waters, the Caspian or Aral Seas. Thus, unlike, for example, China or Europe, no natural water transport corridors can connect this region with the outside world.

The complex mountain ranges may help to explain the region's geographic and logistical paradoxes. For example, nature separated Tajikistan and Pakistan with the Wakhan corridor, which is less than 15 km wide (Dunning, 2021). Even this narrow strip of land means that to deliver goods from Pakistan to Tajikistan, loads must first be transported through the Suez Canal to the Black Sea ports, then shipped to Tajikistan by rail, overcoming several states' complex and bureaucratic customs posts.

But it is precisely the mountains that made the territory of Central Asia inhabitable. Glaciers on mountain peaks provide water to the surrounding areas when it is needed for tillage in spring and summer. Natural water arteries and artificial canals irrigate numerous oases along their path. Where water is scarce, the land turns into deserts, such as the Kyzylkum in Uzbekistan and Kazakhstan, the Karakum in Turkmenistan, the Registan Desert in Afghanistan and the Taklamakan Desert in China. That is why Central Asia may become one of the first regions on Earth to feel the effects of climate change.

Due to global warming, glaciers are experiencing huge losses in mass and area. Along the Tien Shan, the most extensive mountain range in Central Asia, glaciers have lost 27 per cent of their mass and 18 per cent of their area over the past 50 years (Farinotti et al., 2015). An international research team has calculated that about half of Tien Shan's glaciers could be depleted by the 2050s (Kirby, 2015). If environmentalists' estimates are correct, by 2050 Central Asia will lose two-thirds of its glaciers and therefore two-thirds of its water. How can agriculture, a sector which employs more than half of the population, hope to develop? Why build giant hydroelectric power plants for which there will not be enough water? The problem of climate change in Central Asia is not just a theoretical problem, but a dangerous reality. Countries must start fighting this global menace now.

How far are the borders of Central Asia from the four nearest oceans? The southernmost borders of Turkmenistan are 1,000 km from the closest shores of the Indian Ocean (Arabian Sea). The easternmost ranges of the Kazakh Altai are located 2,650 km from the Pacific Ocean (Bohai Bay of the Yellow Sea). From the northernmost point in Kazakhstan to the Arctic Ocean (Gulf of Ob) is 1,300 km. While the distance from the farthest west of Kazakhstan to the Sea of Azov, which connects to the Black Sea and beyond may be only 400 km, to measure the distance to the oceans or the open seas, the distances are even bigger – the Atlantic is 3,500 km away. To the Pacific Ocean, it exceeds 3,000 km.

The land route from China's leading trade hub Guangzhou to Europe's key distribution centre Duisburg is 9,000 kilometres, comparable to the distance from the US West Coast to China. The distance from the Kyrgyz capital Bishkek to Guangzhou is about 4,200 kilometres, close to the distance between the east and west coasts of the US. The distance between Bishkek and Duisburg (6,000 kilometres) is the same as that between Duisburg and New York. That is why, until recently, few people thought about the possibility of delivering goods by land between China and Europe through Central Asia.

Efficient ground transportation by rail or road over comparable distances exists elsewhere. However, as a rule, they are within a particular country, such as the US, Russia, or China. On the other hand, the modern Silk Road is a transit route that crosses many borders. The existence of borders is a source of fragmentation in supply chains, significantly increasing transport costs and delivery times. It is probably why the creation of a customs union on the territory of the former Soviet Union facilitated the creation of a highly efficient Eurasian railway bridge, which will be discussed in detail in a dedicated chapter.

Historical Overview

Central Asia has always occupied a strategic place in the heart of Eurasia. It is located at the crossroads of long-standing trade routes between Asia and

Europe, the most famous of which is the legendary Silk Road. However, during the region's history, it has long suffered from isolation and the presence of an inferiority complex formed by its unique landlocked status. Over the past two millennia, the region's central location has ensured its direct trade links with all the great powers of the Eurasian continent: China, India, Russia, Europe and the countries of Western Asia. However, the region was not just a transit crossroads, facilitating the movement of trade flows. The Great Silk Road was a network of logistic routes connecting the East with the West through the territory of many different countries. Historians date the beginning of the Silk Road from the moment described in the literature when the Chinese Han Dynasty opened trade with the West in 130 BC. Traders actively used its routes until 1453 AD, when the Ottoman Empire imposed a ban on transit trade (Onion et al., 2017).

The origin of the term "Central Asia" dates back to a German polymath, geographer, naturalist and explorer, Alexander von Humboldt (1769–1859), whose masterpiece "Central Asia" (Humboldt, 1843) gave the world the name. An interesting side note is that he dedicated the book to Russian Tsar Nicholas I, in what he called "an unavoidable step, as the expedition [to the Russian Empire] was accomplished at his expense" (De Terra, 1955: 188). At the end of the 19th century, a student of Humboldt, the renowned German geographer and geologist Ferdinand von Richthofen (1833–1905) offered the first scientific definition of this vast territory. He proposed an appellation reflecting the main reason for the flourishing of the region's economy – the Silk Road. In creating this definition, Richthofen was inspired by the writings of the great ancient Greek historian and geographer Ptolemy (AD 125–151), who described that during the Han Dynasty, Chinese silk was one of the most precious and expensive goods shipped across Central Asia's steppes to the West. Although it was obvious that there were many types of trade, Richthofen preferred to refer to silk specifically, as it had long been considered the magical gift of the East.

Richthofen understood the importance of Central Asia as described in Humboldt's book, which he then interpreted in his own way, defining this vast region as follows (Richthofen, 1877):

> First, it is an area where an ancient puddle without an outlet connects to the continent, in other words, the long-standing existence of this puddle is the most fully developed special phenomenon which was caused by the nature of having no outlet: from the Tibetan Plateau in the south to the Altai Mountains in the north and from the Pamir Watershed in the west to a watershed of an enormous Chinese river and Khingan Mountains in the east. Second, rivers around that area run into the sea and flow into the ocean-like parts of land such as the Caspian and Aral Seas. Third, mountain pass areas, where there were no outlets in the past, were either partially turned into water areas or vice versa. These areas still maintain a considerable degree of uniqueness in Central Asia and have not yet

> completely lost their characteristics. So these areas do not belong entirely to this area, nor do they belong to that area. Fourth, in island separated from the continent by a port without water.
>
> (Kwon, 2018: 4)

On the one hand, the region's central location created an opportunity to trade with all neighbouring states and provided the shortest transit of goods through to third countries. On the other hand, it was open to aggressive attacks from all sides by neighbouring powers. Regular conquests and the subsequent departure of the invaders led to political fragmentation or even a complete power vacuum. Most historians believe the four main power centres (from the north, south, east and west of the region) influenced Central Asia's development. In terms of historical progress, these influences have been both positive and negative.

1 In the north, vast steppes gave geographical advantages to tribes and peoples with high mobility. Nomadic peoples such as the Huns and Mongols using horse-drawn vehicles were regular invaders. Later, Russian merchants began to penetrate the region. As the Russian Empire consolidated and expanded eastward, it also moved south. Central Asia was not of particular interest to the Russians at that time since their ultimate goal was to advance to the seas. Their path through this territory to the Indian Ocean was soon blocked by the British, who occupied Afghanistan and were alarmed that the Russians might reach the "pearl" of their empire – India. The expansion of the Russian Empire into Central Asia took place in the 19th century. They annexed Kazakh lands in the 1840s and Kyrgyz territories in the 1860s. After a series of military campaigns against the Kokand and Khiva khanates, as well as the Emirate of Bukhara, Russia-occupied parts of modern Uzbekistan in the 1860s and 1870s. After that, the territory of Turkmenistan was annexed in the 1880s, and the Pamirs and other regions (modern Tajikistan) in the 1890s. Russia's borders expanded to Afghanistan and areas of direct British influence. By the 1890s, the accession of Central Asia was complete. It came about that Russia dominated Central Asia and attempted to project its power as far south as the modern borders of Afghanistan and Iran (Morrison, 2020).
2 The history of invasions from the West begins with the campaigns of Alexander the Great (356 BC–323 BC) in the 4th century BC. After the departure of the Greeks, there were invasions by Persian and Arab conquerors, which had a significant impact, especially on the southern parts of Central Asia. Here one should mention the Battle of Talas (modern Kyrgyzstan) – a military clash between the Abbasid Caliphate and the Chinese Tang Dynasty. In July 751 AD, their forces met in the Talas river valley to gain control of Central Asia and the Silk Road. The defeat in the battle marked the end of the Tang's westward expansion. Two

Arab empires, the Umayyads and Abbasids, which brought Islam to the region, governed for more than a century. The Arab conquest of the land between the rivers Oxus (Amu Darya) and Jaksart (Syr Darya), which today includes all or part of Kazakhstan, the Kyrgyz Republic, Tajikistan and Uzbekistan, took place in the 7th and 8th centuries (Encyclopedia.com, 2019). In subsequent periods of history, counteracting Russian influence, both Turkey and Iran attempted to increase their role in supporting local political elites.

3 South Asia's demographic and cultural influence spread from the south, mainly through the territory of modern Afghanistan. For example, Babur (1483–1530), who was emperor (1526–1530) and founder of the Mughal dynasty of northern India, brought many enlighteners, artisans and enslaved people from India to the territory of the modern Fergana valley, which was his historical homeland (Spear, 2022). However, this influence remained limited, tempered by domestic troubles in South Asia, the rugged terrain of Afghanistan, and the British occupation of India. Later, given the impact of Russia in Central Asia and its desire to advance to the Indian Ocean, Britain, at significant cost, had no choice but to occupy Afghanistan.

4 In the East, the region has maintained various relationships with Chinese empires throughout history. The Han (202 BC–9 AD, 25–220 AD), Tang (618–907 AD) and Ming (1368–1644) dynasties at various times conquered large parts of the Fergana Valley and the Tarim Basin. Evidence of China's extensive ties with Central Asia is that the great Chinese poet Li Bai (701–762) was born in Suyab (the city of Tokmok in the modern Kyrgyz Republic), where his father was either an official or engaged in business. Later, the Qing dynasty (1644–1911) tried to consolidate Chinese control over these territories, especially in later periods. However, the Middle Kingdom could not hold onto these territories owing to its weakness.

A brief overview of Central Asia's history demonstrates how the development of seemingly new trade routes crossing the region is just the restoration of ancient pathways that have connected the area with the world's centres of economic power for centuries. A thorough investigation of the geography of any territory will help to understand the features of its history. An analysis of history allows one to interpret its civilisational and political story. But perhaps more importantly, such research helps to predict the development of these territories, for example, when planning the expansion of their economic infrastructure.

The Formation of Modern Borders

The modern borders of the Central Asian states developed through two stages of delimitation that occurred in the past two centuries. The first division of territory occurred at the end of the 19th century when the Russian empire and the Qing and British empires negotiated peace treaties. On 10 September 1885, the Russian and British empires resolved the so-called Afghan crisis through diplomacy, which became the peak point in the "Great Game" between them to possess the territories of South and Central Asia. Thus, the parties managed to avoid turning the cold war into a military conflict. They established a border between Russian Turkestan (now the sovereign states of Central Asia) and Afghanistan, then dependent on Great Britain. Thus, within a day, two empires divided the united Central Asia, which had existed for centuries, into two parts.

In 1871, taking advantage of an uprising of the Dungans and Uighurs that began in Xinjiang, Russian troops entered the territory of western China. They occupied the Ili Sultanate, located in the upper reaches of the Ili River. The occupation lasted for ten years (1871–1881). According to the St Petersburg Treaty with China in 1881, the Ili region was returned to China by the Russian government. Nevertheless, Russia had managed to open its consulates in Ili (Kulja), Tarbagatai (Chuguchak), Kashgar and Urga. The modern borders of the countries of Central Asia and China are the borders fixed by the Tarbagatai Treaty of 7 October 1864 between the Russian Empire and Qing Empire of China, which determined most of their borders.

In the 1920s and 1930s, the second and final stage of the so-called national-territorial delimitation of the Soviet Central Asian states, which exist within these borders to this day, took place.

First Challenges After Independence

The dissolution of the Soviet Union in 1991 was a massive shock for the nations of Central Asia. Taken as a whole, it is remarkable that the transition to independence and the fundamental change in economic systems both within and between the countries of Central Asia were relatively peaceful. Some exceptions were the tragic events in Tajikistan, which faced a bloody civil war in the 1990s. However, some long-standing problems were exacerbated during this period, especially in water and energy management in upstream and downstream countries. What was previously controlled by the Union of Soviet Socialist Republics (USSR) had to be decided in new negotiation processes between independent nations. It is noteworthy that each country chose unique options for developing their economies, which greatly differed and continue to do so to this day.

The "parades of sovereignties" underestimated the complementarity of regional ties built during the Soviet era. It is also easy to grasp how there was a lack of knowledge about the principles of the functioning of a modern market economy. These restrictions have led to many systemic crises in the region, which will be discussed in dedicated chapters. The loss of direct control and the massive drop in subsidies from Moscow led to confusion among the countries' political elites. The main reason for the "administrative chaos" was the lack of trust between the leaders of recently "fraternal countries". Consequently, immediately after the disintegration of the Soviet Union, the economies of all countries encountered difficulties. The standard of living of most of the population declined, and the poverty rate increased rapidly.

The problems in the region in the 1990s escalated soon after gaining independence because the Central Asian countries found themselves in a vacuum of interest from powerful foreign partners.

Russia did not have the resources to implement an effective foreign policy. The country struggled with internal problems and the risks of further disintegration and was forced to beg for new loans from the International Monetary Fund (OECD, 2013). The economic crisis of the 1990s in Russia was so deep that its economy only returned to pre-crisis levels again in 2007 (Grinkevich & Mityaev, 2008).

China was not yet strong enough to act in the region and was absorbed in the development of its economy and the fight against poverty. Besides, Deng Xiaoping's instructions were still in force, as he formulated a policy of maximum caution in international affairs in the phrase "Hide your strength, bide your time". During these years, China was not particularly active in Central Asia. Gradually, people began to trade with each other, and the states were busy with the important work of demarcating and delimiting their borders, which were successfully completed.

The emergence of the independent states of Central Asia provided unique opportunities for the West to try to draw them into their orbit of interest, gain access to rich energy resources, and help establish energy and transportation routes through the region. One of the most notable investment projects is the pipeline delivery of crude oil from hydrocarbon-rich Kazakhstan to Western markets, which will be addressed in detail in Chapter 9.

Collectively, the efforts of the West have focused on supporting the establishment of democratic governance, a market economy, and regional economic integration. Despite the strong rhetoric, the West viewed the region as a relatively low-priority area. Its involvement in achieving better stability, security, prosperity and governance remained limited. This changed after 11 September 2001, when a new policy put forward by the US and the West began to take shape. The previous decade's political and economic reform programmes ceased to be a priority. Instead, military and security cooperation came to the fore. Support for US military operations in Afghanistan and reliance on access to regional military installations took precedence over advancing political and economic reforms and human rights. In Western strategy, Central Asia immediately changed from an area of secondary interest to a place with a higher priority.

As part of the Western strategy, the representatives of various development agencies began operating in the region on a bilateral and multilateral basis. International financial institutions such as the International Monetary Fund (IMF), the World Bank (WB) and the Asian Development Bank (ADB) had a significant influence on the rapid transformation of the economies of

Central Asia from planned to market principles. These institutions supported the newly independent states by offering financial and advisory services.

The countries of Central Asia had ancient historical and ethnic ties with the states of Western Asia, especially Turkey, Azerbaijan and Iran, with whom they speak the same (Turkic or Persian) languages. Turkey was the first to recognise the Turkic-speaking countries of the region (Kazakhstan, the Kyrgyz Republic, Turkmenistan and Uzbekistan) as independent states, and Iran was the first to recognise Tajikistan. The romantic idea of restoring ancient Turkestan, stretching from the Kyrgyz mountains to the European continent, has re-emerged among the Turkic-speaking countries (Otorbaev, 2021). For economic and logistical reasons, this could not take place overnight, however, the emergence of independent nations in Central Asia opened up opportunities for reviving trade and restoring former political and economic ties with Iran, the Caucasian countries, and Turkey. The unexpected fall of the Iron Curtain once again brought the region to a pivotal crossroads connecting Europe and Asia. As in the days of the Silk Road, a new opportunity arose for the area to become a land bridge between East and West. However, for the Central Asian countries to play a decisive role in a Eurasian land bridge and once again determine their destiny, it is necessary to ensure close cooperation with each other.

Today and the Future

In recent years, Central Asia has entered a dynamic renewal phase driven by a combination of three factors. First, the most significant development in domestic and regional politics were political and economic reforms in Uzbekistan, the region's most populous country. Since 2016, President Shavkat Mirziyoyev has decisively transformed this country. In 2019, *The Economist* declared Uzbekistan as the world's most improved country (The Economist, 2019). Crucially, the countries' leaders began regular meetings for the first time after a long break, outlining specific plans for regional cooperation.

Two other factors relate to the area of international cooperation. These are the Russia-led Eurasian Economic Union (EAEU) and China's Belt and Road Initiative (BRI). The two global projects are expected to bring tangible social and economic benefits by facilitating trade and investment, developing infrastructure, and efficient exchange of labour, goods and capital.

What awaits our region in the near future? In April 2022, in its World Economic Outlook (WEO), the International Monetary Fund presented a scenario for the development of the world economy for the next five years (IMF, 2022a). Where are the countries of Central Asia in this forecast? Figure A.3 shows the dynamics of GDP growth until 2027, and Figure A.4 shows GDP per capita in purchasing power parity in the region. Growth is expected in both indicators, but is it sufficient?

The economies of the Caucasus and Central Asia (CCA) are predicted to grow by 2.5 per cent in 2022 and 4.2 per cent in 2023 (IMF, 2022b).

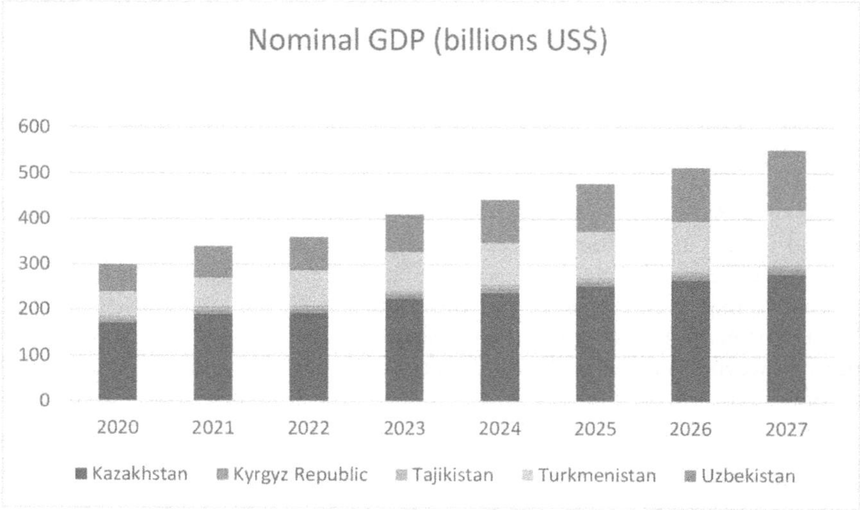

Figure A3 GDP growth for Central Asian countries
Source: IMF (2022a).

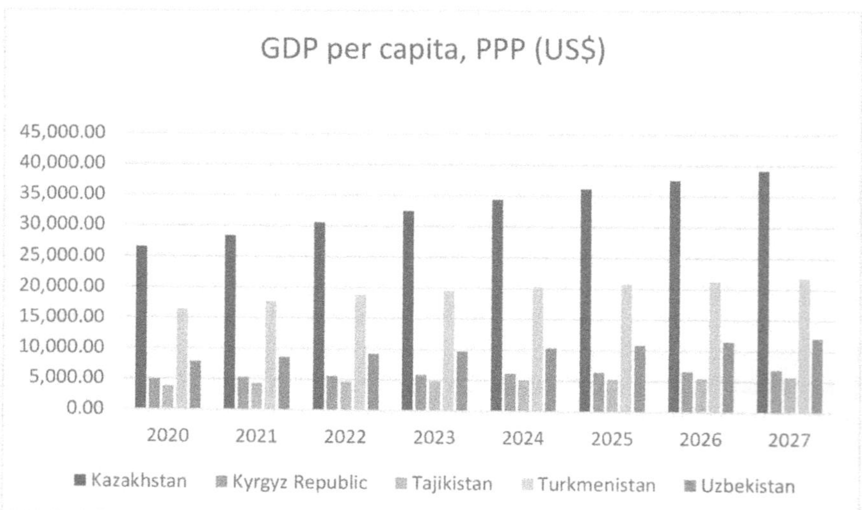

Figure A4 Changes in GDP per capita in purchasing power parity for Central Asian countries
Source: IMF (2022a).

However, considering these forecasts, it must be said that this growth is not enough. The unworthy thing is that in five years, two countries will still have a GDP per capita at purchasing power parity of around $5,000, and Kazakhstan will only reach the level that Aruba or the Bahamas are currently at. This analysis shows that the current evolutionary path and economic model will not lead the region to accelerated economic growth.

Currently, the combined GDP of Central Asia, which is exceptionally rich in natural resources, is less than the GDP of the tiny cities of Singapore or Hong Kong, which have no resources, but an educated and hard-working population. How can we make sure that the equally well-educated people of Central Asia reach this level? New ideas and actions are needed to outpace the average growth of the global economy. But how can new ideas for a decisive leap forward be found? Should we look for a new model of economic growth? Finding ways to accelerate Central Asia's progress towards the future will be the primary focus of this book.

The first condition on the path to the accelerated development of Central Asia should be regional cooperation. That is why the Fourth Consultative Meeting of the Heads of State, which took place on 21 July 2022, in the city of Cholpon-Ata in the Kyrgyz Republic, was a major step in this direction. All the leaders of the Central Asian countries took part in the meeting, indicating that the countries are striving for closer cooperation. The meeting had several important features. Like all previous meetings, it was held without any foreign actors. One of the most active participants was Uzbekistan, which is usually reluctant to participate in other associations in the post-Soviet space; the country is not a member of the Collective Security Treaty Organization or the EAEU. The participation of Turkmenistan is unique, as the country always emphasises its neutral status. Economic issues are becoming increasingly important. At this meeting, specific decisions were made on the joint construction of the China–Kyrgyz Republic–Uzbekistan railway and the Kambarata hydroelectric power station in the Kyrgyz Republic, and investments in the East–West and North–South railway corridors. By strengthening intra-regional ties, Central Asia will become economically and politically much stronger, which will be beneficial to everyone and above all to the peoples who inhabit the region.

This book is about hope. Despite the complex geography and history, there is hope that Central Asia will once again become a prosperous region and be a place known not only for the beauty of its nature and hospitality, but also a place talent will not run away from, and rather would be drawn to. A place where scientific discoveries and inventions will be generated, new minds will form bright ideas, and new skills will create unique masterpieces. There is little chance that Central Asia will return to the global economic and creative dominance that it had during the Golden Days of the Great Silk Road. That era in the region is long gone, but development in other parts of the world has not stopped. There is hope that these changes could brighten Central Asia's present and its future. Central Asia has reason to hope for much more than what its peoples see right now. The realisation of these hopes depends on communication and relationships with its neighbours and the rest of the world, but most importantly, it depends on the people living here, their minds, knowledge, creativity and perseverance in achieving goals.

Outline of this Book

The countries of Central Asia face many problems – both individually and as a region – on the path to their future. Based on an analysis of thirty years of their development as independent countries, this book describes the main challenges and opportunities in balancing their internal interactions and external relations with powerful neighbours. The book's main idea is that the region has unique opportunities and significant potential to accelerate its economic and social development, something which can only be achieved through effective regional cooperation and proactive collaboration with its powerful neighbours.

The current state of development of the region and its prospects for the future cannot be understood without knowing its rich history, which for thousands of years has been associated with the cooperation and coexistence of various ethnic groups and their neighbours. Therefore, Chapter 1 offers a brief look at the region's rich history. Despite the harsh geographical conditions that prevented efficient trade, Central Asia was the most developed part of the ancient world. The region became a world leader in economic development, trade, technology, manufacturing and intellectual life during a period commonly referred to as its Golden Age (1100–1600 AD). The medieval history of Central Asia is the history of the struggle for control over trade along the Great Silk Road. At that time, the region was open, ready and able to learn from others and adapt to innovation.

Chapter 2 provides a comparative overview of the demographic, economic and social development of the post-Soviet republics after independence, and analyses the causes of their successes and failures. Globalisation calls for proactive cooperation with the centres of economic power, including powerful neighbours, whether close to home or further afield. The high level of education of the region's population points to making advanced technologies of the 21st century a priority for the development of the region. The final section of Chapter 2 is devoted to a brief analysis of current trends in the competition between capitalism and socialism.

Chapter 3 analyses the economic development of the region since its countries gained independence. All countries experienced a time of upheaval in the painful transition from a planned to a market economy. In the 1990s, the standard of living of the countries' populations fell sharply. Then, after a decade of difficult reforms, the first phase of socio-economic transformation in the region was largely complete. Between 2000 and 2020, the economy of the region grew faster than the world average, leading to higher household incomes and reduced poverty. This happened mainly due to rising energy prices. The most impressive growth in per capita income was observed in Kazakhstan and Turkmenistan, which are both countries that export large volumes of oil and gas to outside markets.

Chapter 3 describes the features of regional demographic processes. Despite economic difficulties, favourable demographic trends were observed in all countries, albeit to varying degrees. This chapter also describes the dynamics of human capital development. Countries have been able to maintain their education, health and social support systems at a relatively high level by prioritising funding for these areas.

Within the discussion of health issues, the global issue of tuberculosis is raised. Even compared to less conservative estimates of deaths by a coronavirus, tuberculosis is still the bigger killer. Why then did the coronavirus bring the whole world to its knees? Why has humanity sacrificed a colossal $17 trillion of global GDP to the fight against the coronavirus? And why does humanity only spend about $10 billion annually to fight tuberculosis? The frank answer to these questions is that the world is an unfair place and that coronavirus claimed disproportionately more victims in wealthy countries.

The oil boom in the 2000s boosted wages in Russia and created opportunities to attract migrant workers from three main countries: the Kyrgyz Republic, Tajikistan, and Uzbekistan. This trend was caused by the radically different demographic situations in these countries. While Russia has seen a demographic decline that was exceptionally sharp in the 1990s, the Kyrgyz Republic, Tajikistan, and Uzbekistan experienced large population growth. This demographic complementarity can be called a win-win situation since the lack of labour force in some countries is compensated by its surplus in others. External migration issues, which are of paramount importance for several countries in the region, are discussed in detail in Chapter 3.

Difficult geographical conditions complicate domestic and foreign trade. Due to long distances, low economic density and complex trade regimes, trade costs are high. Until recently, internal trade in the region was underdeveloped. The main reason for this was that the most populous country, Uzbekistan, located in the geographical centre of Central Asia, did not welcome trade with its neighbours for political reasons. Things changed about six years ago when the new president of Uzbekistan came to power. Before this, independence had provided for a big change in the development of foreign trade. Since 2000, all countries have shown impressive growth in foreign trade, especially in hydrocarbon-rich countries. The lack of diversification remains the main shortcoming of the current export structure. All five countries are focused on relatively narrow product groups. These are principally commodities – crude oil, natural gas, ferrous and non-ferrous metals, cotton and wheat. The volume of exports of industrial goods and services with higher value-added remains insignificant. Trade prospects in Central Asia offer great opportunities due to the region's proximity to major Asian markets, its location at the centre of the rapidly integrating Eurasian economic space, and the potential for greater intra-regional economic integration. However, overly "thick" borders remain a serious obstacle to both domestic and foreign trade and transit.

The economic development of any territory is determined not only by the presence of modern roads or railways, power plants or power lines, but also by the quality of the business environment and investment climate. For a comparative analysis of the quality of doing business and the investment climate in different countries, it is advisable to refer to the ratings compiled by recognised international institutions. The positions of the countries of Central Asia on these indicators are analysed in Chapter 3. The two main reasons for the inflow of foreign direct investment (FDI) into the countries of Central Asia are the availability of natural resources and their blossoming markets. Over the past twenty years, rising world prices for energy and other commodities have been an important driver for these investments. FDI stocks increased in all five countries, benefitting directly or indirectly from the commodity boom. Labour-intensive production and infrastructure received a much smaller share of FDI, while agriculture received almost nothing. It is shown that the participation of Central Asian producers in global supply chains is limited mainly to the supply of natural resources and labour.

The instruments of foreign economic relations between the countries of Central Asia and major economic centres remain limited. These include direct financial flows, official development assistance, transport and transit services, external migration and remittances. The region's financial markets are underdeveloped – except for the financial sector in Kazakhstan, similar systems in other countries of Central Asia are not yet integrated into global financial markets. Going forward, the countries of the region need to better take into account the interconnectedness of various sectors of the economy, pursue a prudent monetary policy, stabilise the exchange rate, reduce the dollarisation of the economy, stimulate the growth of consumer lending and increase limited lending to small and medium-sized businesses.

The situation with sovereign debt, discussed in Chapter 3, deserves special attention. The structure of external borrowing differs significantly amongst the countries. The sovereign debt structure of the Kyrgyz Republic, Tajikistan and Uzbekistan is dominated by obligations to China and international financial institutions, as they offer concessional financing. At the same time, Kazakhstan and Turkmenistan mainly raise their finances from the capital markets and state institutions of China, often backed by hydrocarbon contracts. The good news is that so far the countries of the region have succeeded, on the one hand, in attracting significant funds, and, on the other hand, in maintaining their debt levels at a sustainable level.

One of the goals of this book is to show that the future growth of Central Asia will be linked to its cooperation with the centres of world economic power. After gaining independence, governments began to look for ways to enter international markets. But what have they achieved in thirty years of independence? Who are the leading economic players and why have they started trading and investing in the region? Various analysts often refer to Central Asia in the context of the "great game" and its rivalry for regional dominance between Russia, China, India and the collective West. Many speculate that a rapidly growing China is using its economic power to oust other competitors and become a major economic and political player in this strategically important region. But the answer to the question of who is more active can be obtained not by reasoning, but by comparing economic and financial data. Chapter 4 provides a comparison of the trade and FDI with Central Asia of five powers, namely Russia, China, the EU, the US, and India.

It is essential to understand the impact of infrastructure development on the region's economic growth. Despite the difficult economic situation after post-independence, the countries of Central Asia have implemented several large-scale infrastructure projects. Governments have invested in building pipelines to export hydrocarbons, laying new electrical networks, building roads and expanding rail networks. Recently, there has been an active investment in digital infrastructure. Chapter 5 provides an overview of the current state of infrastructure in various sectors of the Central Asian economy and a comparison with similar indicators in other countries and continents. The analysis shows that, despite its strategic position at the crossroads of Europe and Asia, Central Asia remains poorly connected to the rest of the world. Given the relevance of the development of the digital agenda in the region and the current trends in the global market, the telecommunications sector in Central Asia should attract private, primarily foreign, investment to meet its infrastructure needs. So far, there is no visible interest on the part of western companies to invest in this sector. At the same time, the region's closest neighbours – China, Russia and India – are trying to actively invest in digital technologies and communications.

All great civilisations have successfully developed thanks to efficient access to logistics. The great civilisations of antiquity were primarily river and sea-based. They were at the crossroads of world transport routes, which led to their accelerated economic and cultural development. When describing the efficiency of supply chains, we introduce the concept of transport resistance. Its value is the time spent on the road, multiplied by the material costs required to transport goods from point A to point B. This indicator was used – implicitly or explicitly – in the history of mankind to determine optimal logistics routes. In regions that do not have access to the ocean, the problem of building efficient logistics is especially acute. The features of the organisation of the region's logistics are discussed in Chapter 6. Particular attention is paid to the history of railway transport in Central Asia, both in Soviet times and in the period after independence, where railways have demonstrated their effectiveness.

Until recently, the countries of Central Asia were unable to make use of their transit potential. Naturally, immediately after gaining independence, they began to look for ways out of this "stagnant" situation, which the region had been placed in by geographical and historical realities. Before our very eyes, a real Eurasian railway revolution is taking place, a revolution which only began its journey some ten years ago. If everything goes according to objective economic laws, Central Asia will soon connect East and West, North and South through its territory with highly efficient railway bridges. It will also become a transit hub for new transport routes connecting all four parts of the world. If these ambitious projects are successfully implemented, Central Asia's transformation into a dynamically developing region is not far off. The economic revival of the new Great Silk Road draws near. Chapter 7 is devoted to the formation and development of the Eurasian railway revolution. Expanding its transit potential, Central Asia has every opportunity to become a part of the macro-regional transport and logistics system. Creating a diversified transport and communication system will allow the region to realise its transport and transit potential, provide a multiplier effect for the sustainable development of the most dynamic and stable region, and turn it into a logistics hub.

Given prospects for the use of rail transport in further strengthening transit trade between Asia and Europe and, therefore, its impact on the development of Central Asia, one cannot help but dwell on the impressive results of new technological solutions in this field. The absolute leader in this area is Central Asia's neighbour, China. From the data presented in Chapter 8, one can conclude that China is noticeably ahead of all its competitors. Will we see the results of the railway technological revolution in our region before our eyes? Considering China's impressive achievements in developing the domestic rail network and its desire to keep up with the times, the answer is probably affirmative.

In Soviet times, when the region was part of a single country, its energy system was uniquely configured. This system had a powerful synergistic effect and worked successfully for many decades. Within this framework, five countries were divided into two clusters. One cluster includes downstream countries with low hydropower potential but significant hydrocarbon resources – Kazakhstan, Uzbekistan and Turkmenistan. Another cluster, which included the Kyrgyz Republic and Tajikistan, did not have large reserves of hydrocarbons, but their upstream location meant that they had ample glacier freshwater resources and significant hydropower potential. Chapter 9 discusses the problems of interaction between the region's countries on energy issues. The harmonisation of the use of this energy, including its export to powerful neighbours with enormous needs for it, is essential for the successful development of the region. Chapter 9 examines the role of climate change on the region's development prospects and which priorities Central Asia could consider to achieve carbon neutrality. The presence of enormous gas reserves and the significant potential for developing a green economy through investments in electricity generation through hydro, solar and wind energy could greatly reduce the dependence on fossil fuels for generating energy. Perhaps the countries of the region should appeal to the international community for additional support for green development in exchange for greater responsibility for climate change mitigation in the region.

Water has been the principal means for the peoples of Central Asia for centuries, connecting them physically, economically and culturally. The deserving topic of water is paid special attention in Chapter 10. Due to Central Asia's natural features and geographical location, it is one of the largest regions in the world in terms of water resources. For the entire region, where people have directed the main water flows to the fields for land irrigation, the history of water and land relations is the history of the development of irrigation systems. The primary sources of tension between the countries of Central Asia are seasonal competition for the flow of large rivers and the high cost of maintaining upstream reservoirs. Climate change will only exacerbate these tensions. Data from national meteorological agencies indicate an increase in annual precipitation in winter and a decrease in summer, resulting in an increase in both floods and droughts. The task of strengthening trust between countries through practical dialogue and mutual incentives is of paramount importance.

Good governance and effective public administration are essential for sustainable economic growth. Chapter 11 presents the evolution of governance indicators in the countries of Central Asia from the mid-1990s to the present. Indicators are provided for six indicators of governance quality: voice and accountability, political stability and absence of violence, government effectiveness, regulatory quality, the rule of law, and anti-corruption. The analysis shows that further systematic work is needed to strengthen Central Asia's current political and economic institutions, which are still underdeveloped. The institutional development of all countries should be based on the rule of law, the fight against corruption, building responsible public administration, ensuring the transparency of the state apparatus and the democratisation of society and the state. The creation of such institutions will no doubt be challenging, but such work must not stop.

The book is mainly devoted to Central Asia's problems, challenges and prospects for economic development. However, it would be wrong to bypass the socio-political processes taking place there. Chapters 12 and 13 comment on interstate tensions in the Fergana Valley, the civil war in Tajikistan, and the recent political developments in the Kyrgyz Republic, Kazakhstan and Uzbekistan.

Almost a quarter of the entire population of Central Asia lives in the Fergana Valley, which covers just 5 per cent of the area. The valley feeds the whole population of the region and depends on the tributaries of the Syr Darya to irrigate its exceptionally fertile lands. Its territory lies within three states – the Kyrgyz Republic, Tajikistan and Uzbekistan. For millennia, people have found ways to negotiate the division of pastures and water use, regardless of nationality. They moved freely, traded and made friends with each other. The growing scarcity of resources, namely the lack of water, land and pastures, combined with the rapid population growth and disputes over borders, has contributed to the growing tension and instability in the valley. Both in Soviet times and especially in the post-Soviet period, clashes at the boundaries of states are regularly recorded since significant sections of the borders have not yet been demarcated or delimited. Chapter 12 describes the complex inter-ethnic processes in the Fergana Valley and options for resolving conflicts.

A tragic page in Tajikistan's recent history was the civil war, which reached its worst from July 1992 to July 1993, when the country was divided in two between government forces and the United Tajik Opposition (UTO). Chapter 13 describes how between 35,000 and 157,000 people were killed in the clashes, according to various estimates. War destroyed the economy of Tajikistan. It lasted more than five years and ended thanks to international efforts, primarily by Russia, Iran and neighbouring Uzbekistan. Chapter 13 explains that the cause of all three recent revolutions in the Kyrgyz Republic were not poverty or unemployment but injustice. Since the first days of the Kyrgyz Republic's independence, public trust in the government has been repeatedly undermined by systemic corruption, electoral fraud, and the state's dependence on informal institutions, including criminal structures. According to a well-known conspiracy, the US organised the first Kyrgyz "Tulip" Revolution in 2005. According to some media reports, the second revolution of 2010 was provoked by Russia, dissatisfied with the policies of the country's second president. As for the third and most recent revolution, its "external organiser" has not yet been found or appointed. Perhaps it is time to re-think the popular theories of "colour revolutions". There are few people who believe that revolutions only take place for internal reasons. The latest experience of revolution in the country shows that this possibility might not be so far from the truth.

Chapter 13 also addresses the protests that erupted across Kazakhstan on 2 January 2022. These quickly escalated into riots in all major cities. Although the initial trigger was the doubling of fuel prices, protesters soon demanded the dissolution of parliament and a fresh round of elections. Moreover, they demanded that former President, Nursultan Nazarbayev, leave the political scene. According to most experts, the protests were caused by people's fatigue with the dominance of the Nazarbayev family in power and business, the country's oligarchic rule, and the absence of fair elections, free press and political competition. As is further described in Chapter 13 what was new is that in the past, the political upheavals in the post-Soviet space mostly took place in the relatively poor states of Georgia, Ukraine, Armenia, Moldova, and Kyrgyzstan. For the first time, nationwide protests were held in what, by post-Soviet standards, is a prosperous country. Thus we can see that it is not only poverty and desolation but the injustice that brings people to the streets.

On 1 July 2022, in response to a package of planned constitutional changes, protests and violence erupted in Uzbekistan's autonomous Republic of Karakalpakstan. The first version of the new constitution was supposed to deprive Karakalpakstan of the status of a sovereign republic and equate it to an ordinary province. The inhabitants, primarily ethnic Karakalpaks, took this as a blow to their identity, as they felt that the proposed changes would deprive them of their last insignia. In protest, people took to the streets, where they clashed with the police and security forces. The main reasons for the current protests are poverty, unemployment and climate change. Besides this, the residents suffer from health problems associated with water shortages and the drying up of the Aral Sea. Chapter 13 later explains how Uzbekistan is set apart among the five countries of Central Asia since it had statehood before the arrival of the Russian Empire. Uzbek people understand state power and what the unity of the country means. The nation has a responsible elite that will not tolerate the undermining of their country. The most recent lesson learned will be the necessary impetus for the country's ongoing reforms and progress. Everyone needs a peaceful and prosperous Uzbekistan, not least its own inhabitants.

The book's final chapters analyse the most crucial external processes around Central Asia. Among them are the creation of the Eurasian Economic Union (EAEU), the Chinese-led Belt and Road Initiative (BRI), and the developments in neighbouring Afghanistan. Chapter 14 describes the EAEU, which, along with Russia, Belarus and Armenia, includes two countries in Central Asia – Kazakhstan and the Kyrgyz Republic. Additionally, in December 2020, the heads of the member states of the EAEU decided to grant the Republic of Uzbekistan observer state status to the EAEU. Many observers still express fair criticism of the functioning of the EAEU. For example, they compare its development with that of the EU. Here it is worth recognising that the history and time of their formation, the economic scale and the quality of their members differ greatly. If one union includes only developing economies, then the backbone of the other is made up of the most developed countries. It is more appropriate to compare the EAEU with similar unions that include developing economies, such as ASEAN, MERCOSUR, the Gulf Cooperation Council, or the South African Customs Union. As described in Chapter 14, the new economic reality of the post-Soviet space is only now emerging. Its institutions have been established and are functioning. A joint labour market is being formed, and social protection and pension systems are beginning to bear fruit. The EAEU is a single market for foreign investors. Much more work needs to be done to bring the practice of the union closer to best practices in other parts of the world. The economic achievements of the countries participating in the EAEU will be decisive for the union's future.

For Central Asians, it is essential to understand what is happening after almost a decade since the launch of the Belt and Road Initiative. In September 2013, in his speech in the Kazakhstani capital of Astana, Chinese President Xi Jinping announced the "Silk Road Economic Belt" to deepen cooperation and expand development in the Eurasian region. It will form a vast network of roads, railways, oil and gas pipelines, power grids, transmission and communication networks, various industrial clusters and service networks. Ideally, they will form an integrated land area stretching from the Pacific to the Atlantic oceans and establish a direct land link between the two major global economic powers, China and Europe. The construction of this intercontinental infrastructure will be the basis for regional economic integration to strengthen the free flow of goods, labour and capital, creating, in the long run, a single Eurasian market. How have the Central Asian countries received the initiative? What mistakes have been made in its implementation? Chapter 15 describes the historical reasons for the emergence of the new Silk Road, China's prospects for interaction with the Central Asian countries, and the opportunities and threats that stand in the way of closer cooperation. This chapter also details the role of China's soft power in spreading the country's positive image abroad. Investments in human capital and high-quality development are of utmost importance in planning future economic and humanitarian relations between China and Central Asia.

Continuing the problem of discussing China's interaction with the countries of Central Asia, Chapter 16 discusses the issues of Chinese loans to Central Asia and beyond. These days, China's loans to developing countries exceed those of all other lenders combined, so it is crucial to understand the debt situation in detail. This chapter analyses various forms of borrowing provided by China, specific data, and recommendations for countries in the region.

Afghanistan is of particular interest to Central Asia since, until the middle of the 19th century, it was an integral part of greater Central Asia. Its northern border was the dividing line that separated the Russian and British empires in the 19th century. After American troops' withdrawal from the country in August 2021 and the coming to power of the Taliban, the government of Afghanistan has remained unrecognised by the international community. Chapter 17 discusses that the first step in rebuilding a country must be attracting foreign investment and creating jobs. At the same time, the list of potential investors is minimal. Most experts agree that China could be the first country to become a significant investor, but China is in no hurry to invest for security reasons. Two large infrastructure projects related to Central and South Asia may acquire special significance. These are the construction of the Kabul Corridor railway in Afghan territory from Termez in Uzbekistan to the Pakistani city of Peshawar via Mazar-i-Sharif and Kabul, and the TAPI gas pipeline, named after the four countries through which it will pass: Turkmenistan, Afghanistan, Pakistan and India. These projects are currently on hold as the Afghan government needs to be recognised for the projects to go ahead. Now the new Afghan government must do everything possible to achieve such a status.

The conclusion presents the main findings that follow from the book. The engine of world economic development will be the Eurasian centres of world economic power located on the edge of Central Asia. But how will this affect our region? Will the region join the powerful locomotive of history, or will it remain on the side-lines? History teaches us that both options are eminently possible. The main conclusion is that the people of Central Asia must set ambitious goals and achieve them with their talent and tireless work. Being located in the geographical centre of booming Asia and having the opportunity to become a key logistics bridge connecting the world's largest economies, the region is well placed for rapid development, but Central Asia faces a range of complex problems that only its inhabitants can solve.

References

ADB, 2011. *Asia 2050: Realizing the Asian Century*, Manila: Asian Development Bank.

Altman, S. A., Ghemawat, P. & Bastian, P., 2019. *How Globalized Are Individual Countries and Regions?. In: DHL Global Connectedness Index 2018*. Bonn: Deutsche Post DHL Group, pp. 34–61.

Brzezinski, Z., 1997. *The Grand Chessboard: American Primacy and Its Geostrategic Imperatives.* New York: Basic Books.

De Terra, H., 1955. *Humboldt; the Life and Times of Alexander von Humboldt, 1769–1859*. New York: Knopf.

Dobbs, R. *et al.*, 2012. Urban world: Cities and the rise of the consuming class. [Online] Available at: https://www.mckinsey.com/featured-insights/urbanization/urban-world-cities-and-the-rise-of-the-consuming-class [Accessed July 2022].

Dunning, S., 2021. China is protecting its thin corridor to the Afghan heartland. [Online] Available at: https://foreignpolicy.com/2021/08/14/china-afghanistan-wakhan-corridor-imperial-ambitions/ [Accessed July 2022].

Encyclopedia.com, 2019. Central Asia, Islam in. [Online] Available at: https://www.encyclopedia.com/religion/encyclopedias-almanacs-transcripts-and-maps/central-asia-islam [Accessed July 2022].

Farinotti, D. *et al.*, 2015. Substantial glacier mass loss in the Tien Shan over the past 50 years. *Nature Geoscience*, 8 (9), pp. 716–722.

Fromkin, D., 1980. The great game in Asia. *Foreign Affairs*, 58 (4), pp. 936–952.

Grinkevich, V. & Mityaev, O., 2008. Ekonomicheskoe razvitie Rossii za poslednie vosem' let. [Online] Available at: https://ria.ru/20080228/100224681.html [Accessed July 2022].

Humboldt, A. V., 1843. *Asie Centrale.* Paris: Gide.

IMF, 2022a. World economic outlook database. [Online] Available at: https://www.imf.org/en/Publications/WEO/weo-database/2022/April [Accessed July 2022].

IMF, 2022b. *Regional Economic Outlook. Middle East and Central Asia: Divergent Recoveries in Turbulent Times*, Washington, DC: International Monetary Fund.

Kirby, A., 2015. Central Asia's glaciers may lose half their ice by mid-century. [Online] Available at: https://theenergymix.com/2015/08/21/central-asias-glaciers-may-lose-half-their-ice-by-mid-century/ [Accessed July 2022].

Kwon, Y.-. P., 2018. The original concept of the Silk Road and Richthofen's humanistic ideas. *Acta Via Serica*, 3 (2), pp. 1–22.

Maddison, A., 2006. *The World Economy: Volume 1: A Millennial Perspective and Volume 2: Historical Statistics.* Paris: OECD Publishing.

Morrison, A., 2020. *The Russian Conquest of Central Asia: A Study in Imperial Expansion, 1814–1914*. Cambridge: Cambridge University Press.

OECD, 2013. Rossiya: modernizaciya ekonomiki. [Online] Available at: https://www.oecd.org/countries/russia/Russia-Modernising-the-Economy-RU.pdf [Accessed July 2022].

Onion, A., Sullivan, M. & Mullen, M., 2017. History: Silk Road. [Online] Available at: https://www.history.com/topics/ancient-middle-east/silk-road [Accessed July 2022].

Otorbaev, D., 2021. A more perfect turkic union? [Online] Available at: https://www.project-syndicate.org/commentary/organization-of-turkic-states-great-power-reaction-by-djoomart-otorbaev-2021-12 [Accessed July 2022].

Richthofen, F. F. v., 1877. *Band 1, Einleitender Theil. In: China: Ergebnisse eigener Reisen und darauf gegründeter Studien*. Berlin: Verlag von Dietrich Reimer.

Spear, T. P., 2022. Encyclopedia Britannica: Bābur. [Online] Available at: https://www.britannica.com/biography/Babur [Accessed July 2022].

Starr, S. F., 2015. *Lost Enlightenment: Central Asia's Golden Age from the Arab Conquest to Tamerlane*. Princeton, NJ: Princeton University Press.

SurferToday.com, 2022. The complete list of landlocked countries. [Online] Available at: https://www.surfertoday.com/environment/the-complete-list-of-landlocked-countries [Accessed July 2022].

The Economist, 2019. Which nation improved the most in 2019?. [Online] Available at: https://www.economist.com/leaders/2019/12/21/which-nation-improved-the-most-in-2019 [Accessed July 2022].

UNCTAD, 2021. Review of Maritime Transport 2021 - Chapter 3: Freight rates, maritime transport costs and their impact on prices. [Online] Available at: https://unctad.org/system/files/official-document/rmt2021ch3_en.pdf [Accessed July 2022].

United Nations, 2007. Percentage of total population living in coastal areas. [Online] Available at: https://www.un.org/esa/sustdev/natlinfo/indicators/methodology_sheets/oceans_seas_coasts/pop_coastal_areas.pdf [Accessed July 2022].

Worldometer, 2022. Population. [Online] Available at: https://www.worldometers.info/population/ [Accessed July 2022].

Part I

Great History is Behind Us

1 The Silk Road

Connecting Cultures, Creating Trust

Introduction

This chapter suggests that the history of state independence in Central Asia, which is only thirty years old, cannot be understood without first understanding the patterns of the emergence and flourishing of the Great Silk Road: what happened a thousand years ago during the golden age of Central Asia. Understanding the positive and negative lessons of distant history described in this chapter are essential for understanding the region's future. Despite Central Asia's harsh geography that impedes effective trade and economic development, it is paradoxical, but true, that for a rather long period of its history, this region was the most developed part of our world (Starr, 2013).

During what is commonly referred to as the Golden Age of Central Asia (1100–1600), the region was a world leader in economic development, trade, technology, manufacturing, and intellectual life. Central Asia was open, willing, and able to learn from others, adapt, and to innovate. This period is also known as the time of the Great Silk Road.

History

Historians believe that the Silk Road arose during the Han Dynasty in China (206 BC to 220 AD). When Emperor Wu sent his envoy Zhang Qian to establish contact with Central Asia in 138 BC, the reports of his travels contained detailed information about the peoples and lands that lay to the west of the Middle Kingdom. Indeed, the transportation of goods and services along these routes had been happening much earlier (Onion et al., 2017). According to archaeological data, there was a so-called "Lapis Lazuli Road" in the 3rd century BC, a route along which this prized blue gem was transported from the Badakhshan region of modern-day Afghanistan and Tajikistan for considerable distances to the west and south, all the way from Mesopotamia to India. From the end of the 2nd century BC, another such road, the "Jade Road" came to operate. Gems from Central Asia were traded eastwards, where they would be exchanged for silk from China (Frankopan, 2015).

DOI: 10.4324/9781003360728-3

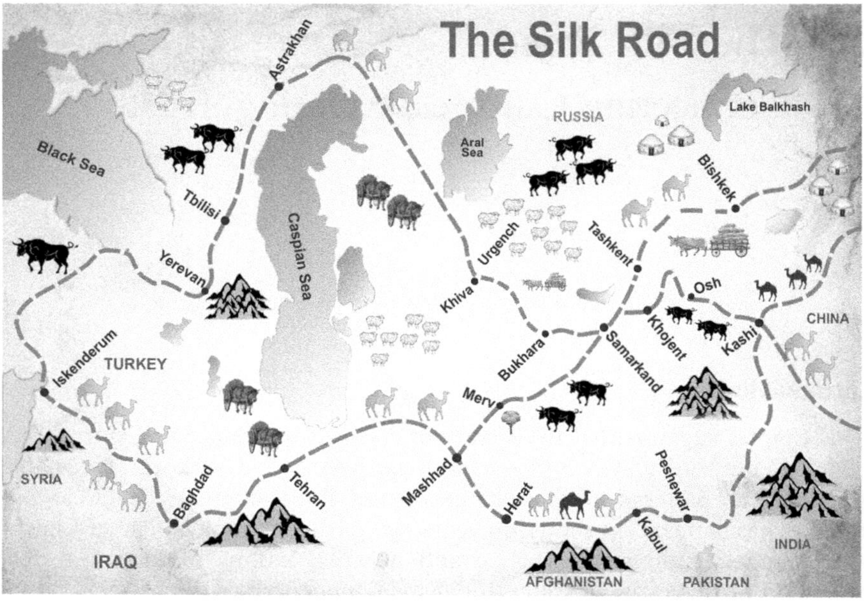

Figure 1.1 The ancient Silk Road

In this way the first so-called "caravan routes" appeared, on which merchants used horses and camels to transport their goods vast distances across Central Asia.

These two caravan routes for lapis lazuli and jade began to merge in the middle of the 1st century BC. Badakhshan lapis lazuli found its way to China, and clothing made from Chinese silk spread to Persia and the Indus Valley. At the same time, trade went through a long chain of intermediaries, such that the Chinese and the Europeans were not in direct contact. For this reason, historians have tended to focus on the movement of goods and technologies and not people. To give an idea of the scale of trade along the Silk Road, the number of camels in the caravans crossing the Taklamakan Desert in Northwest China at any given point varied from 3 to 300. Trade intensified during the Tang dynasty in China (618 to 907 AD), reflecting a growing appetite for Central Asian clothes and products (BBC, 2009).

Silk was the main and most noteworthy item transported along the transcontinental route. However, it was by no means the only commodity seen on the Silk Road. Khuttal horses made their way from modern-day Tajikistan to China where they were highly valued. Gold and silver, semi-precious stones and glassware, leather and wool, carpets and cotton fabrics, exotic fruit such as watermelons and peaches, fat-tailed sheep and hunting dogs, leopards, and lions were all exported from Central Asia. In the opposite direction from China, caravans brought porcelain and metal utensils, lacquerware and cosmetics, tea, and rice. The most popular goods transported from east to west were rare spices or luxury items that required unique technology. Perhaps the most significant of these was paper, which was invented in China in the 2nd century BC. Paper production in Europe would only begin at the end of the 14th century (Boulnois, 2004).

The intensity of trade relations decreased after the expulsion of the Romans from the Middle East and the beginning of the Arab conquests in the 7th century (Swietochowski & Collins, 1999). It should be noted that there are few periods in the region's history when a single state has controlled the multiple trade routes that make up the Silk Road. These exceptions include the Turkic Khaganate in the last third of the 6th century, and the Chinese Tang Empire from the 7th to the first half of the 8th century. Later, all the western routes of the Great Silk Road would come under the control of the Umayyad and Abbasid Arab caliphates after the historic defeat of the Chinese troops in July 751 AD in the Battle of Talas, in an area on the present Kyrgyz-Kazakh border. During the Byzantine-Sasanian War in the sixth–seventh centuries before this, the rulers of Persia (known as the Sassanids) blocked the caravan routes through Central Asia to cause maximum damage to the economy of Byzantium. Because of this, caravans from China and Central Asia began to bypass the realm of the Sassanids, travelling via the Caspian Sea and the North Caucasus, instead of around the south of the sea. Difficulties with the delivery of goods also arose in the early Arab period, especially after the defeat of the Chinese army in the Battle of Talas in 751 AD, which forced the Chinese empire to withdraw from Central Asia.

New conditions for the revival of overland trade along the ancient routes appeared with the formation of the Mongol Empire in the 13th century, within which almost the entire length of the Great Silk Road ran. With the assistance of the Mongols, European travellers such as Marco Polo, Carpini, and Rubruck freely made their way to East Turkestan (in modern-day Western China) and back to Europe. Due to the sheer length of these trade routes, it was challenging to unite them under single control. As is often seen across history, there was a "division of the world" between several major powers or associations of states. While the Timurid Empire (also known as Tamerlane) controlled the Silk Road in the last third of the 14th century, the western section of the Great Silk Road in the 14th–15th centuries was under the control of the Venetians and the Genoese, who had acquired fortified trading posts along the shores of the Black Sea.

By the 15th century, trade on the Silk Road fell into decline for two principal reasons. Firstly, active maritime trade development began in Europe and China, which led to significant geographical discoveries. The Age of Discovery or Age of Exploration was a period largely coinciding with the Age of Sailing, from the 15th to the 17th centuries, when European navigators began to explore other parts of the world. The efficiency of maritime transportation was aided by technological advances, such as the use of the magnetic compass and developments in ship design. The growing interest of

Chinese traders in maritime transportation can be seen, in particular, by the famous voyages of the enormous fleet of Admiral Zheng He (Zhèng Hé) to Southeast Asia, the Persian Gulf and the coast of Africa in the early 15th century. The second reason for the decline of the Silk Road was a surge in political instability and turbulence due to multiple military conflicts in Central Asia in this same period.

In the 14th and 15th centuries, maritime trade between the east and west therefore became more appealing than caravan routes overland. Such routes had always been dangerous, because the vast territory was governed by uncontrolled tribes who might rob caravans or levy taxes from them. Transporting goods by sea was more popular for reasons of security and speed. The sea route from the Persian Gulf to China took just 150 days, while the caravan route from Tana (Azov) in the west to Khanbalik (Beijing) in the east took closer to 300 days. One ship could carry as much cargo as a vast caravan of 1,000 pack animals.

The well-known English historian Arnold Toynbee summarises the decline of the Silk Road well (Toynbee, 1948: 70): "during the life of Babur, the center of the world suddenly moved to Seville, Lisbon and further to England. Steppe ports - caravanserais - were put out of action, as sailboats forced out the camel and horse". Looking at the past, Toynbee goes on to pose a pertinent question for the future: "now, when steamboats are being replaced by airplanes, we can ask the question, is the center of the world going to make the jump again?".

As a result of these geopolitical and geoeconomic factors, the Great Silk Road had ceased to exist by the 16th century. However, some segments of the Silk Road, such as the caravan trade between Central Asia and China, continued to function for a long time afterwards.

Economics and Finance

In the heyday of the Great Silk Road, the trade volume between east and west reached enormous proportions. The great Chinese and Roman empires were geographically distant from each other but enjoyed active trade with one other along this important route. For such huge trading operations to succeed, traders and merchants needed to constantly develop economic and financial mechanisms that could cope with the rapid development of the route.

Merchants actively used gold and silver coins in cash payments for goods. They especially appreciated the coins minted in "prestigious" and "respected" countries. For example, in the early Middle Ages, along the entirety of the Silk Road, up to and including China, gold Byzantine coins and silver Sasanian and Arab coins were particularly valued in transactions. Despite the active use of such coins, the merchants along the Silk Road did not have enough of them for satisfactory trade. Therefore, more complex mechanisms were widely deployed, such as bartering, or in other words, the exchange of goods for other goods, where cash was only used to pay the contractual difference in the cost of the transported goods (Asia Society, n.d.).

Since it was dangerous to transport large amounts of money over long distances, an innovative banking system was developed. Silk Road merchants invented the "cheque", which means "document" or "receipt" in Persian (Lektsia.com, 2022). Before embarking on a journey, the merchant would hand over his cash to a reputable money changer, who played the role of a banker, in exchange for a unique receipt. The merchant could present this cheque in any city along the route where a trusted representative of this banker would exchange it for cash, minus a service fee. This system could only work effectively if money changers from far-flung Silk Road cities personally trusted each other as members of the same cultural, ethnic, or religious community. This system came into active use around the 10th century, when trade along the Silk Road was mainly controlled by Muslim and Jewish bankers (Foltz, 1999).

Security and Property

The protection of merchants' property and the security of trade were of paramount importance to the effective functioning of the Great Silk Road. To minimise risks, merchants sought not to do business alone, but in confessional and ethnic groups. For their own safety and the safety of their cargo on their dangerous journeys from city to city, merchants would travel in large caravans. They would be accompanied by hundreds, and at times thousands of armed men familiar with the particular area, local laws, and customs. It is known, for example, that under Timur (Tamerlane) in the late 14th century, when the caravan trade was already in decline, caravans from China came to Samarkand in modern-day Uzbekistan in groups of up to 800.

While merchants could protect themselves from petty robbers through basic self-defence, they had less control over rulers' whims and fancies or over the attacks of powerful hostile tribes. It was however in the interest of both state formations and nomadic associations to preserve and maintain trade and communication since rulers received substantial income from customs duties levied in cities along the caravan routes. To avoid losing these revenues, the rulers of many territories adopted strict laws to ensure the safety of trade caravans. For example, under Timur, the province in which a merchant was robbed was obliged to compensate the merchant for losses twice over and also to pay a fivefold fine to Timur himself. In addition, the local tribes along the Great Silk Road needed many of the goods being transported, so it was in their own interest to maintain the trade. So even without being able to offer anything in return, local tribes were forced to be content with collecting customs duties.

Given the high risks, merchants rarely moved along the entire length of the Great Silk Road. They instead exchanged goods in intermediary trading cities, such as Nishapur, Khorezm and Samarkand. The risk to traders paid off in high profits. A medieval Arabic proverb said that a merchant travels from Arabia to China with 1,000 dirhams and returns with 1,000 dinars (a dinar was about 20 dirhams).

The Great Silk Road made it possible for nomadic tribes to find their place in the peaceful division of labour. These tribes would act as guides for merchant caravans through the deserts and steppes, charging them for their help and security. The Silk Road became a unique manifestation of long-term, mutually beneficial cooperation between settled and nomadic peoples. Given the active development of territories and trade caravans, this business remained highly profitable for centuries.

New Technologies

The Great Silk Road introduced many people to new or previously unknown goods, technologies, and inventions. Historians believe that Europe benefited most from importing new goods and technologies as a form of mutually beneficial exchange with Asia (Beck, 2022). Silk fabrics improved the personal hygiene of Europeans, and doctors used spices to make medicines and preserve products. Paper, made according to instructions from China and Central Asia, began to replace parchment and papyrus, reducing the cost of replicating handwritten books. After buying the first paper from merchants from the East, Europeans would much later begin to make it themselves.

Merchants not only sell goods but also the technology necessary for their manufacture. For example, silk was initially produced only in China, but in the 1st–2nd centuries, sericulture (the production of raw silk) penetrated East Turkestan and entered Iran in the 5th century. In the 6th century, the emperor of Byzantium successfully established sericulture in Greece, by persuading traveller monks to secretly bring him silkworm eggs in a hollow staff, according to legend. During the era of the Silk Road, it must be noted that not all technologies were adopted by the Europeans: for example, damask weapons or porcelain utensils.

Some new products appeared thanks to the unique joint creativity of different civilisations along the entire length of the Great Silk Road. Gunpowder was discovered in China in the 9th century, and in the 14th century, other inventors created firearms based on it, although the exact place and time of the invention of these firearms are not known – historians attribute this variously to China, the Arab countries, or to Europe. Knowledge of new types of weapons quickly spread along the Silk Road, and, in the 15th century, guns began to be used everywhere from Europe to China.

The Great Silk Road opened up opportunities for the East to get acquainted with many new Western goods and technologies. For example, when the Chinese traveller Zhang Qian returned from Central Asia, he brought back to his homeland information about Fergana argamaks: a tall and hardy breed of horse which did not exist in China. Additionally, when trade along the Silk Road was beginning to develop, the Chinese took alfalfa seeds from Central Asia, which serves as a high-calorie feed for horses. They also received grapes; before this, the Chinese knew nothing about grapes or grape wine. Later, through caravan trade, the Chinese mastered the cultivation of hitherto unknown vegetable crops such as beans, onions, cucumbers, and carrots, among others. From Central Asia, technical inventions such as the screw, the pressure pump and the crankshaft spread worldwide.

Most historians agree that the West learned many industrial innovations because of contact made possible via the Silk Road. At the same time, the East adopted many agricultural technologies, pointing towards the technological superiority of the East over the West, which was only outpaced in the 18th and 19th centuries (Anievas & Nişancioğlu, 2015).

Conclusion

The medieval history of Central Asia represents the struggle for control over trade routes along the Great Silk Road. The emerging caravanserais combined the functions of both hotels and warehouses, and in their place, cities later flourished, thanks to the same traffic. Important cities sprung up along the route such as Tabriz, Ormuz, Bukhara, Samarkand, Khorezm, Otrar, Kashgar, Turpan, Khotan, and Dunhuang. From the incoming taxes and duties, as well as the funds for renting premises, entrepreneurs built fortresses and cities where military garrisons were located. The Great Silk Road contributed to the rapid development of science and technology, promoted interethnic and interfaith relations, and contributed to the exchange of cultural values. Arnold Toynbee wrote that Fergana in the heart of Central Asia, under the rule of Babur in the early 16th century "was the center of the world, and the Turks in Babur's time were the central clan in the family of nations" (Toynbee, 1948: 69). It is many years since Central Asia occupied this central position and the new states of Central Asia emerged only thirty years ago. They are still in a transition period that will continue for some time. Like any teenager, their immediate future will be a period of formation and some self-doubt. But an understanding of the great history of the region will undoubtedly help these young states to believe in their bright future.

References

Anievas, A. & Nişancioğlu, K., 2015. *Origins of the Great Divergence over the Longue Durée: Rethinking the 'Rise of the West'. In: How the West Came to Rule: The Geopolitical Origins of Capitalism*. London: Pluto Press, pp. 245–273.

Asia Society, n.d. Belief Systems Along the Silk Road. [Online] Available at: https://asiasociety.org/education/belief-systems-along-silk-road [Accessed July 2022].

BBC, 2009. BBC Radio 4 - In Our Time, The Silk Road. [Online] Available at: https://www.bbc.co.uk/programmes/b00p315t [Accessed July 2022].

Beck, E., 2022. Silk Road. [Online] Available at: https://www.historycrunch.com/silk-road.html#/ [Accessed July 2022].

Boulnois, L., 2004. *Silk Road: Monks, Warriors & Merchants on the Silk Road.* Hong Kong: Odyssey.

Foltz, R., 1999. *Religion and Overland Trade in Asia, 1000 BC to AD 1400.* s.l.: Encarta Historical Essays.

Frankopan, P., 2015. *The Silk Roads: A New History of the World.* London: Bloomsbury.

Lektsia.com, 2022. Ponyatie cheka i ego funktsii. [Online] Available at: https://lektsia.com/3x62c6.html.

Onion, A., Sullivan, M. & Mullen, M., 2017. History: Silk Road. [Online] Available at: https://www.history.com/topics/ancient-middle-east/silk-road [Accessed July 2022].

Starr, S. F., 2013. *Lost Enlightenment: Central Asia's Golden Age from the Arab Conquest to Tamerlane.* Princeton, NJ: Princeton University Press.

Swietochowski, T. & Collins, B. C., 1999. *Historical Dictionary of Azerbaijan.* Lanham, MD: Scarecrow Press.

Toynbee, A., 1934. *A Study of History.* s.l.: Oxford University Press.

Toynbee, A., 1948. *Civilization on Trial.* New York: Oxford University Press.

2 Thirty Years after the Soviet Union

How Did It All Begin?

The independent development of the Central Asian countries began after the collapse of the Soviet Union in 1991. More than thirty years have passed since then, which is a long enough period to look back and analyse what has happened during this time of independent development. What do the fifteen "fraternal" countries that set off on an independent voyage in 1991 have in common, and how do they differ now? What mistakes did they make, and what problems did each country face in their separate development? Which countries have been more successful on their own, and which have had less success in this regard? What valuable lessons can humanity learn from these countries' unique and unprecedented transition from one reality to a completely different one?

The year 2021 marked the 30th anniversary of the collapse of the Soviet Union. It is vital to understand the fundamental consequences of what happened in 1991, when the Soviet Union, a powerful multi-nation country, collapsed like a house of cards. New states, including five in Central Asia, gained independence and began to exist separately from each other. How is it that a geopolitical earthquake of such a colossal scale unexpectedly occurred, which in 2005 Russian President Vladimir Putin later would call "the greatest geopolitical catastrophe of the century" (AP News, 2018).

George F. Kennan, who was one of the key architects of American strategy during the Cold War, said that he found it "hard to think of any event more strange and startling, and at first glance inexplicable, than the sudden and total disintegration and disappearance… of the great power known successively as the Russian Empire and then the Soviet Union" (Aron, 2012: 5). Another eminent historian, François Furet, admitted that "the manner in which first the Soviet Union and then its empire fell apart remains mysterious" (Aron, 2012: 5). To unravel this mystery, it is first necessary to understand what kind of country the Soviet Union was shortly before its disintegration, and from there we can begin to understand why it collapsed.

In the 1960s and 1970s, the growth of the Soviet economy began to slow after a long period of impressive development. The real problems came in the

DOI: 10.4324/9781003360728-4

1980s, characterised by a sudden worsening of the economic situation, which proved *catastrophic*; the country was not able to recover. The Soviet economic strategy involved a focus on oil exports: the share of oil exports in the country's foreign trade was more than 50 per cent in those years. This one-sided focus of the Soviet economy towards exporting hydrocarbons turned out to be a tragic mistake. By the mid-1980s, world oil prices had plummeted. For reference, in 1980 hydrocarbons on the world market peaked at $35 per barrel (which, adjusted for inflation today, would be about $118). By 1986, this had fallen to just $10 (about $25 in today's money) or less (Golovnin & Grinberg, 2021). Such a sharp fall in oil prices practically paralysed the Soviet economy.

Although the Soviet Union possessed vast territories with ideal conditions for harvesting crops, it bought huge amounts of grain and other foodstuffs abroad, and instead sold what it understood as its more strategic resources, like oil, gas or metals. The Leninist-Stalinist idea of collective farming did not stand the test of time and had long since collapsed. The products manufactured by Soviet industrial enterprises were of poor quality and could not stand up to competition in the global market. The arms race with the United States conducted by the Soviet leadership devastated the state treasury, and one of the final nails in the coffin of the Soviet budget came from the reckless financing by the Soviet government's programme to counter President Ronald Reagan's US Strategic Defense Initiative (SDI).

There is a popular conspiracy theory about the political cause of the sharp drop in world crude oil prices in the mid-1980s. The theory suggests that there was a secret agreement between the United States and Saudi Arabia to weaken the Soviet Union through a strategic game to lower world oil prices. In 2014, Ronald Reagan's son Michael explicitly stated the existence of such a plan: "how Ronald Reagan defeated the Soviet Union… He did it without firing a shot, as we know, but he had a super weapon – oil" (Reagan, 2014). Since the early 1980s, the Saudi Arabian government has controlled oil prices by reducing production. But after a visit to Saudi Arabia by CIA Director William Casey in September 1985, the country began to "unexpectedly" increase oil production, while keeping prices low. Its production rose from 2 million to 10 million barrels per day in just four months, while prices fell from $32 to $10 per barrel. It was a mortal blow to the revenues of the Soviet state budget, which was almost entirely dependent on oil exports. In 1986, its budget lost more than $20 billion, or about 7.5 per cent of the country's annual income.

Many were perplexed, but the economy of Saudi Arabia also suffered due to the low oil prices. So why did they do it? To explain this "paradox", it is important to note that up to 80 per cent of Saudi oil was, in those days, sold to foreign markets through the American companies Texaco, Exxon, Mobil and Chevron. These companies had to listen to the American government's opinions while simultaneously satisfying the Saudi government's requests. After the oil crisis of 1985–1986, the Soviet Union plunged into a deep recession and it proved enough for the Soviet economy to collapse. In 1986, Soviet foreign loans amounted to about $30 billion, and by 1989 they had reached $50 billion.

The tragic mistake of the country's political leadership was that high prices for hydrocarbons caused the country to be over-reliant on their oil revenues. The state failed to prioritise advanced innovative developments, which had previously ensured their leading positions in scientific and technological advancement. Excessive military spending and financial support of their allies worldwide, for example for the war in Afghanistan (1979–1989), had become exorbitant in budget expenditures. A voluntarist anti-alcohol campaign began in the same years, which caused a sharp decline in budget revenues (Aneculaesei, 2020).

With the republics' essential distinction in terms of ties with Russia, their geographical and historical features, relations with the outside world, and their neighbours, it is not difficult to imagine the complexity of their civilised divorce. Recalling events of the period in the Baltics, Moldova, the South Caucasus and Central Asia, we can acknowledge that the split was painful and somewhat turbulent. However, except for the conflict over Nagorno-Karabakh, the countries were able to avoid major interethnic clashes. In addition, realising the inefficiency of the Soviet economic model, all the republics decided to develop their countries on the principles of a market economy, with which they were unfamiliar. Although this gave them a fresh start, they were entering new waters.

The geographical and historical characteristics of the post-Soviet republics split the new states naturally into four groups: firstly, the three Baltic republics, Lithuania, Latvia and Estonia, which had joined the Soviet Union following the Second World War; secondly, the three republics that border the Russian Federation to the west – Ukraine, Belarus and Moldova; thirdly, the three republics of the South Caucasus – Azerbaijan, Armenia and Georgia; and finally, on the country's southern borders, the five Central Asian republics formed a group – Kazakhstan, the Kyrgyz Republic, Tajikistan, Turkmenistan, and Uzbekistan. Standing independently, the Russian Federation is the largest of all post-Soviet countries.

Different Demographics

Before analysing the economic development of the post-Soviet countries, let us turn to their demographics. Here we should note that the great historical and cultural diversification of the former Russian Empire and then the Soviet Union affected their demographics. There was a largely urbanised European population in the country's western regions, and, in the southern areas of Central Asia, the people of Asian traditions lived primarily in rural areas. These features determined the dynamics of the demographic processes which have become the most critical feature of the development of post-Soviet countries. They developed unevenly and influenced different countries' economic and social development as well as their migration processes.

It should be noted that in 1989 the population of the Soviet Union was the third largest in the world and exceeded the population of the United States. From 1979 to 1989, the country's population grew by 24 million people from 262 million to 286 million (Statista, 1991). However, with the dissolution of this single country and the aggravation of economic problems, the demographic situation in the newly independent countries began to change. Figure 2.1 shows the change in the population in the post-Soviet republics during the years of independence, from 1991 to 2018. The data were taken from the Maddison Project Database of Groningen University, and includes statistics for all post-Soviet countries (Bolt & Luiten van Zanden, 2020).

The countries of Central Asia, together with Azerbaijan, experienced population growth. At the same time, all other countries saw a decline in their populations. The two extremes demonstrate the importance of the processes taking place in different countries: between 1991 and 2021, the population of Tajikistan increased by 80 per cent (UN: Population Division, 2022), while the population of Latvia decreased by 40 per cent (Official Statistics of Latvia, 2022). Alongside these population changes, the demographics of 14 out of 15 republics between 1989 and 2010 became more mono-ethnic. Only in Russia did the share of ethnic Russians fall – from 81.57 per cent to 80.9 per cent (Denisenko, et al., 2018).

Since 1993, Russia's population has consistently declined. In 1991, its population was 148.4 million, but by 2009 this figure had dropped to 142.8 million. Even the significant immigration of ethnic Russians observed in the

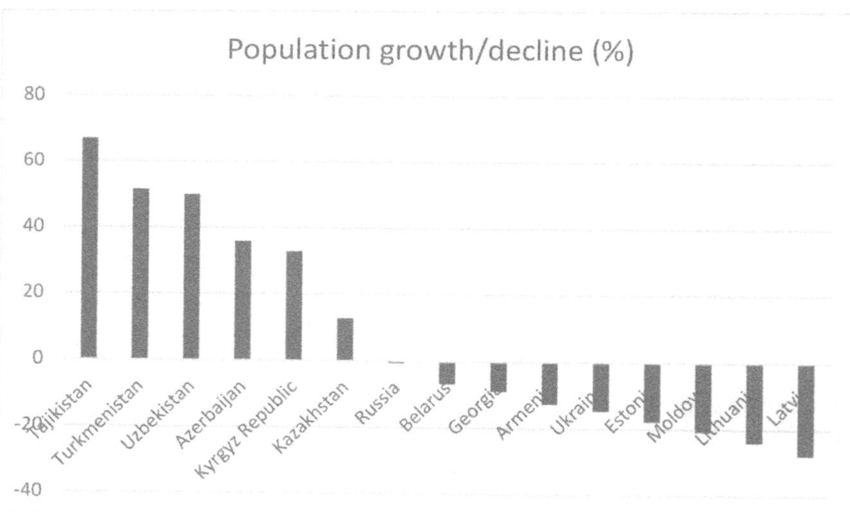

Figure 2.1 Population change in the post-Soviet republics between 1991 and 2018
Source: Bolt and Luiten van Zanden (2020).

1990s and 2000s from other post-Soviet republics to Russia did not help compensate for the natural decline in the population. The country's population stabilised for a few years in the late 2000s and 2010s, but in 2019 it began to decline again (Bolt & Luiten van Zanden, 2020).

Among the former republics, the population of the Baltic countries, and of Moldova and Ukraine, decreased significantly. The population of Estonia in 2021 decreased by 13 per cent, Latvia by 27 per cent, Lithuania by 27 per cent, Moldova by 21 per cent, and Ukraine by 15 per cent. These statistics were affected by both negative natural growth and migration outflow. In Lithuania, where the population decreased by 700,000 people over 30 years to 2.8 million, the outflow of the Russian-speaking population in the 1990s was replaced in the 21st century by the departure of residents to work elsewhere in Europe. According to UN forecasts, if the current trend continues, the population of Lithuania could be as low as 1.5 million people by the end of the century (Filippenok, et al., 2021).

Statistics also show that while the populations of the Baltics, Russia, Ukraine and Belarus are gradually ageing, in the countries of Central Asia, there is a large percentage of children under the age of 14. This group accounts for 35 per cent of the population in Turkmenistan, 34 per cent in Tajikistan, and 31 per cent in Kyrgyzstan. For comparison, in Russia this figure is 16 per cent, in Ukraine and Belarus it is 15 per cent, and in both Latvia and Lithuania – 14 per cent.

Economic Decline and Growth

In 1991, the lack of trust, the ruling elite's lack of knowledge in handling territories, the lack of understanding of the principles of a market economy, and the romantic but premature desire to become "truly independent" became the main reasons for the collapse of the Soviet Union, the collapse of the administrative-command system, and the "parade of sovereignties" (a series of declarations of sovereignty of varying degrees by the Soviet republics, from 1988–1991) that followed (History.com, 2022). Since then, the further rupture of economic ties and centralised supply chains led to a halt in industrial enterprises, a sharp economic downturn, rising unemployment and endemic poverty. The newly independent entities have had to quickly learn how to survive in their new realities.

The main problem of Soviet socialism was that the country's model of a command economy did not encourage economic reproduction. Within this framework, the authorities were not able to create a system of incentives to increase labour productivity due to lack of motivation on the part of the workers. The state failed to build institutions of private property and arouse interest in individual initiatives.

In 1990, the Soviet economy ranked second in the world for GDP (Central Intelligence Agency, 2019). According to the International Monetary Fund (IMF), the US' Gross National Product (GNP) in 1990 was $5.23 trillion, the Soviet Union $2.66 trillion, Japan $1.91 trillion, and Germany $0.95 trillion (Central Intelligence Agency, 2020). The population of the Soviet Union in 1990 was 288.6 million; in the same year, the US had a population of 249.6 million. The number of employable people in 1989 amounted to 152.3 million, and the Soviet Union had the third highest number of employable people in the world (Central Intelligence Agency, 2019).

The UN estimates (UNSD, 2019) that in 1990, the Soviet Union's share in the world GDP, in 2015 constant prices, was 4.6 per cent, while in 2019, the percentage of the total GDP of the fifteen former Soviet republics dropped to about 2.6 per cent. Based on purchasing power parity (PPP), we are able to compare the GDP of different countries adjusted for exchange rates. The share of GDP at PPP of all Soviet republics in the world economy in 1990 stayed at 4.7 per cent (3 per cent of that share was Russia).

It is noteworthy that even when they coexisted in a single country, the republics showed different economic growth rates, and their per capita incomes differed greatly. Figure 2.1 shows GDP per capita in terms of PPP in 1990. This data is from the University of Groningen's Maddison Project Database in 2011, and is gathered from post-Soviet countries using historical data and estimates (Bolt & Luiten van Zanden, 2020).

For example, it can be seen that GDP per capita in terms of PPP was 3.6 times greater in Estonia than in Tajikistan. This indicator in all the Baltic countries exceeded Russia. However, it was on Russian territory that the leading research institutes and the main capacities of the military-industrial complex were located. The country's main commodity, crude oil, was also extracted and exported. Except for Kazakhstan, all the Central Asian republics had the lowest per capita incomes. The republics began their sovereign path into the uncertain future from these varying starting positions.

Figures 2.2–2.5 show the evolution of GDP per capita in terms of PPP (World Bank, 2022a). The graphs are divided into four parts following the geographical location of these countries – the Baltic countries, the Western post-Soviet countries, the countries of the South Caucasus and the countries of Central Asia. The dynamics of the Russian economy are shown in Figure 2.5 alongside the Central Asian economies. These graphs show that the Baltic countries demonstrated the most impressive per capita economic growth, although it should be noted that they had better starting positions (Figure 2.1).

GDP per capita at PPP at the current price in US$ in most of the post-Soviet countries was in decline until 1996–1999 (World Bank, 2022a), and then there was also a slowdown in 2009 due to the global financial crisis. In 2015–2016, the per capita GDP of the oil-dependent countries of the region (Russia, Kazakhstan, Azerbaijan, and Belarus) decreased. This was mainly associated with the anti-Russian sanctions imposed by Western governments and the subsequent devaluation of almost all national currencies, led by the Russian rouble. Finally, the most recent synchronous decline occurred in 2020 amid the Coronavirus pandemic (World Bank, 2022b).

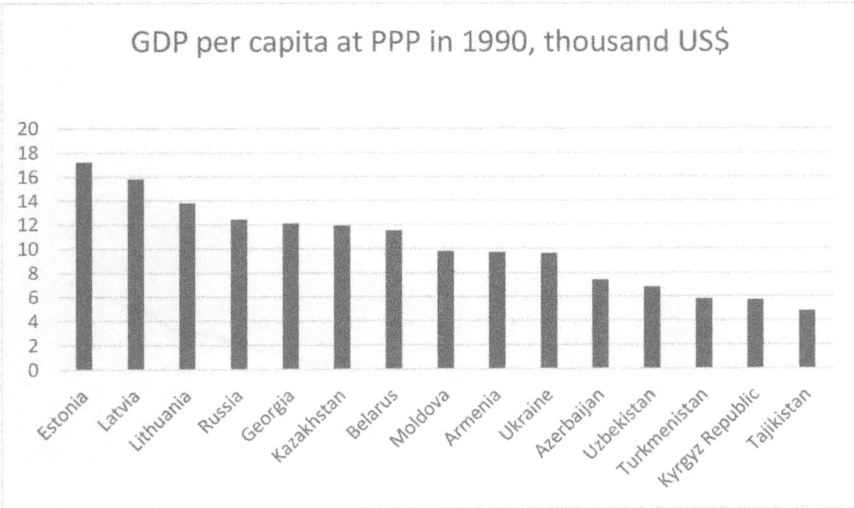

Figure 2.2 GDP per capita at PPP for post-Soviet countries in 1990
Source: World Bank (2022a).

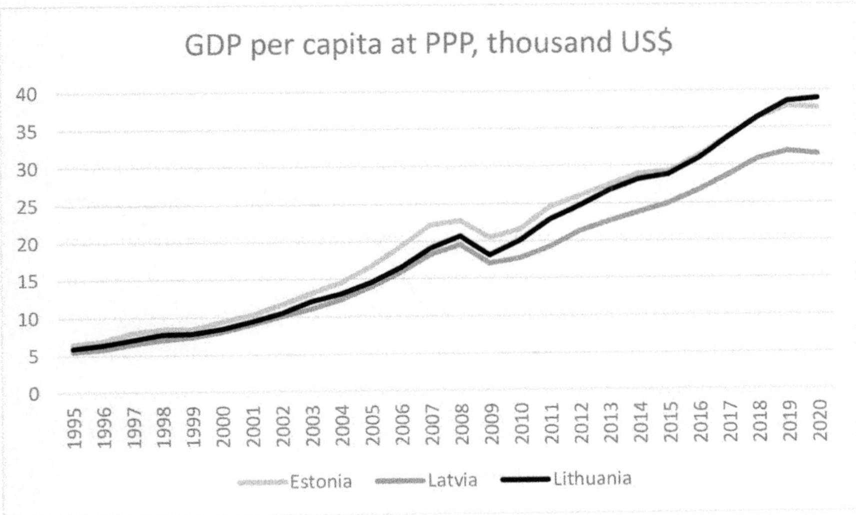

Figure 2.3 GDP per capita at PPP for Estonia, Latvia and Lithuania
Source: World Bank (2022a).

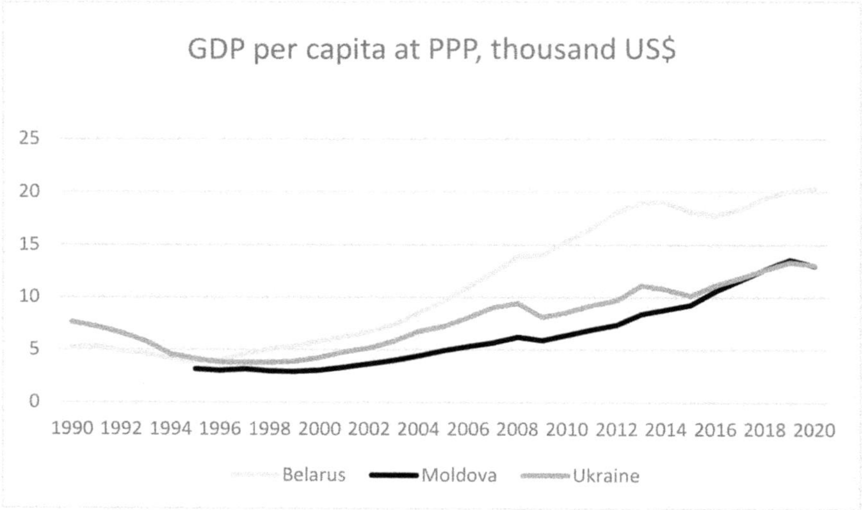

Figure 2.4 GDP per capita at PPP for Belarus, Moldova and Ukraine
Source: World Bank (2022a).

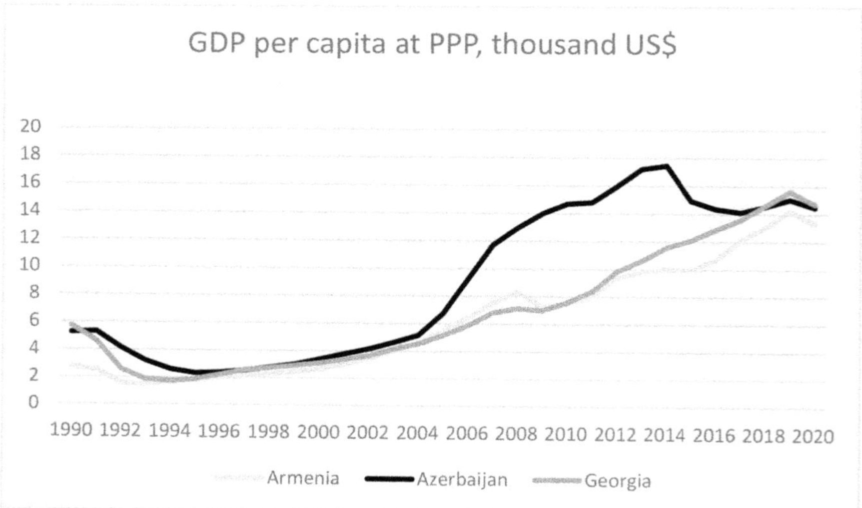

Figure 2.5 GDP per capita at PPP for Armenia, Azerbaijan and Georgia
Source: World Bank (2022a).

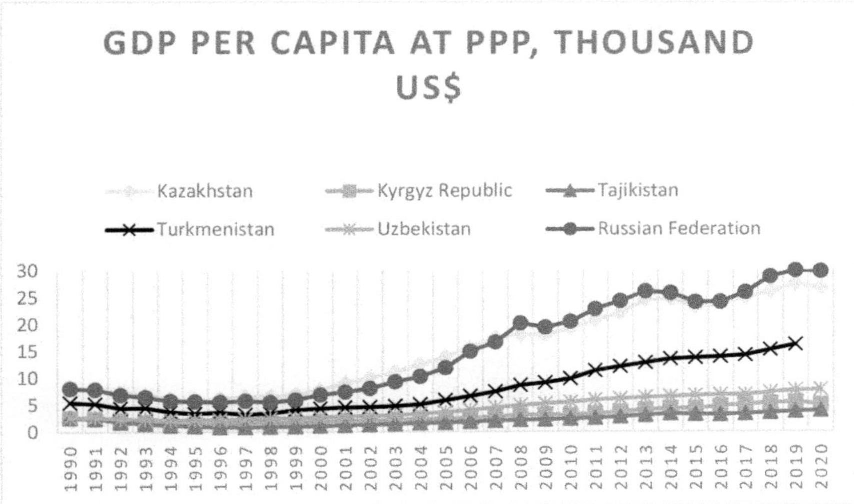

Figure 2.6 GDP per capita at PPP for Central Asia countries and Russia
Source: World Bank (2022a).

From Figure 2.6, the changes in GDP per capita in terms of PPP for Russia and Kazakhstan are very similar. Although the structure of their economies is very different, their almost identical characteristics seem to be because the main income-generating item for both countries is the export of hydrocarbons.

According to the same data from the World Bank (World Bank, 2022a), by 2020, compared to 1991, the economy of the Central Asian countries per capita in terms of PPP has shown substantial growth: in Kazakhstan by 3.2 times, in Turkmenistan by 3 times, Uzbekistan by 2.9 times, almost 2 times in the Kyrgyz Republic and nearly 1.5 times in Tajikistan. This growth has been seen despite the fact that the population level in all of these countries, except Kazakhstan, has greatly increased.

Trade Dynamics

The dynamics of foreign trade deserve special attention. Figures 2.7–2.9 compare absolute trade figures for twelve of the ex-Soviet countries, excluding the Baltics, between 2000 and 2020 (CIS Stat, 2022). The countries are divided into three groups according to their trade volume. The figures show that impressive trade growth has occurred over the past twenty years. Moreover, the volume of trade has increased for countries both exporting and importing hydrocarbons. This increase can be linked, among other things, to the increase in world prices for raw materials seen since the 2000s.

Over twenty years, trade turnover has greatly increased in former-Soviet countries' exporters of raw materials. In Azerbaijan this has increased by 8.5

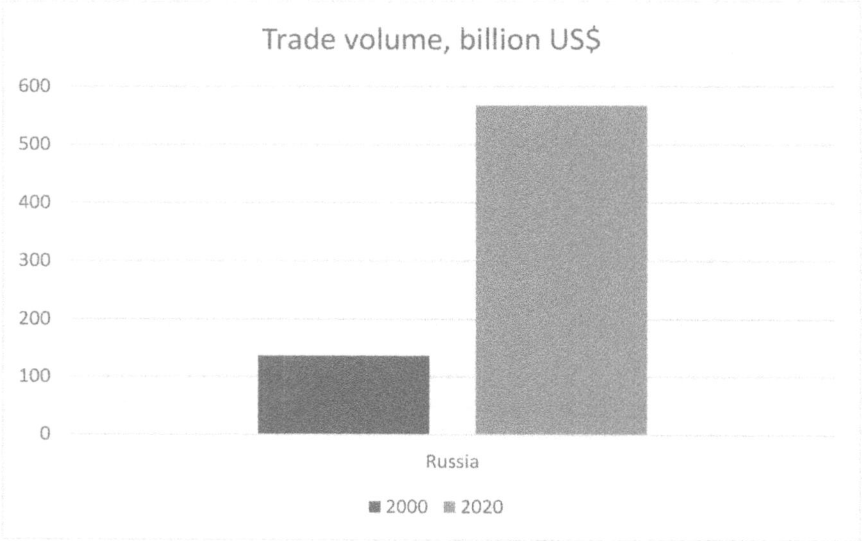

Figure 2.7 Change in the volume of international trade in Armenia, the Kyrgyz Republic, Moldova and Tajikistan in 2000 and 2020
Source: CIS Stat (2022).

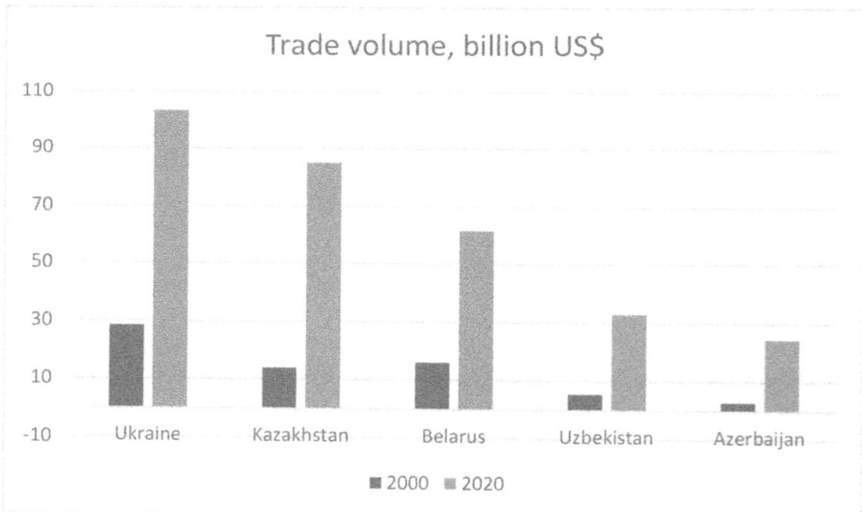

Figure 2.8 Change in the volume of international trade in Azerbaijan, Belarus, Kazakhstan, Ukraine and Uzbekistan in 2000 and 2020
Source: CIS Stat (2022).

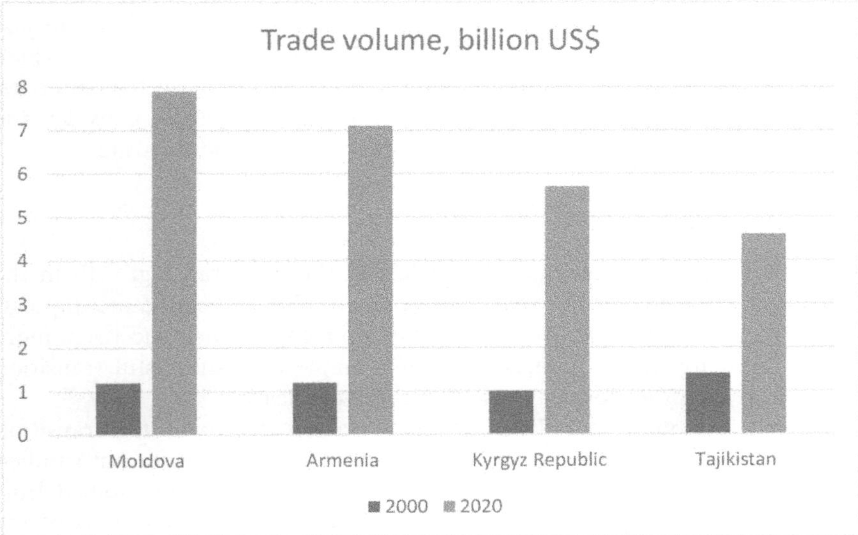

Figure 2.9 Change in the volume of international trade in Russia in 2000 and 2020
Source: CIS Stat (2022).

times, Kazakhstan by 6.1 times, and Russia by 4.1 times. It is striking that similar figures were also observed in countries which are not rich in natural resources. For example, in Moldova, the increase was by 6.6, in Armenia by 5.9, and in the Kyrgyz Republic by 5.7. If exports dominated the first group of countries for obvious reasons, then imports increased markedly in countries from the second group.

This was due to a strengthening in the economic activity and the growth of incomes of the population in the countries exporting raw materials. This in turn led to labour migration to these countries, primarily Russia, by workers from other post-Soviet countries. The absence of a visa regime, lack of language barrier, and a similar mentality allowed incoming workers to easily integrate and settle in new countries. During these years those migrants' remittances to their countries began to snowball, thereby increasing imports. Given the large inflow of foreign currency into these countries, significant imports did not affect the balance of payments. Therefore, with the growth of imports in these countries, there was no devaluation of national currencies, and they even often strengthened.

Such unusual dynamics of the flow of labour resources between the post-Soviet countries can be described as a "win-win" situation, since all participants in the process benefitted from the process. Although the Soviet Union collapsed, the ties between the peoples inhabiting its former republics did not break, but rather embraced a new reality.

After 1991, the newly formed countries chose different political, economic, and social transformation strategies. They can be divided into groups and although there are various variants we could consider, the division into just two groups seems to be the most obvious: the three Baltic countries, which have integrated into the European Union, and the other twelve countries, which have not joined any other significant bloc. Let us consider the development of these two groups in the post-Soviet period separately.

Baltic Route to Europe

Since the Baltic countries have demonstrated the most rapid growth in the post-Soviet period and improved their population's well-being quite impressively, it is essential to look into the main components of their success in more detail. Their impressive progress sets an example of a successful transition from which the other former Soviet republics can learn.

It could be argued that there are three main reasons why the transition process was so successful. First, the peoples of these countries have rallied around the prospect of a long-awaited return to Europe. They joined European institutions, and these expectations became the primary basis of the nations' political and economic consensus. Secondly, the geographic proximity of the Baltic States to Europe, and their Scandinavian and other neighbours' willingness to support their peoples' aspirations to reintegrate into Europe had a significant impact. Much financial, technical and advisory assistance followed. Many European companies have begun to invest in them, creating new jobs and generating much-needed taxes. Thirdly, at various periods in their history, for example, from 1918 to 1940, the Baltic countries were independent and they already had solid state institutions, which was not the case in the other Soviet republics. There was a broad consensus to join NATO and the EU, and all three countries joined the two institutions in 2004.

To fulfil the conditions for EU accession as quickly as possible, the countries' governments undertook tough economic reforms, often using draconian principles for running their economies, known as "shock therapy" (Geohistory.today, 2016). The state-building process was part of a broader programme of modernisation that included abandoning the basic principles of the Soviet legacy. Another critical factor in the growth is their geographical location. Since Soviet times, they have used their transport accessibility effectively, and lots of trade from nearby countries was directed to Baltic ports such as Klaipeda, Riga and Tallinn. Post-Soviet countries, including Russia and Belarus, still use the Baltic ports for their foreign trade operations. Despite the problems that still exist today, it is evident that the economies of the Baltic countries are the strongest and most stable in the entire post-Soviet space.

However, not everything went smoothly. Despite the positive economic results and impressive growth in the well-being of their citizens, public opinion polls conducted in all three countries showed that respondents, especially after 2005, were generally dissatisfied with their standard of living, the state of the economy and democracy (Fabrykant, 2018). People noted high levels of unemployment, low wages (especially compared to other EU countries), high levels of corruption and mass migration. The considerable expectations that came with joining European structures have affected and continue to affect the nations' outlook. There is nothing unusual in the survey results, as the principle "no pain, no gain" always applies.

After gaining independence, the population of all three Baltic republics began to decline rapidly for three main reasons. Firstly, the population's income level fell due to high inflation and the end of government subsidies. Healthcare was mainly privatised and became much more expensive as a result and, therefore, is often inaccessible to the poor meaning that, the death rate has also risen. Secondly, many factories built during Soviet times quickly became uncompetitive and subsequently ceased to operate. As a result, unemployment rose sharply, and people began to leave their respective countries. Thirdly, citizens had the opportunity to work in Europe, where income levels were several times higher. Many, especially young people, took advantage of this, resulting in large-scale emigration to other European countries.

Depopulation is still one of the most severe problems in the region. Since independence, the populations of Estonia, Latvia, and Lithuania have contracted by 13 per cent, 27 per cent, and 27 per cent, respectively (World Population Review, 2022). As early as the 1990s, the Russian-speaking population began to leave these countries en masse. Since 1990, the combined population of Latvia, Lithuania and Estonia has declined by 25 per cent, from 7.9 million to less than 6 million by 2020. This has happened both against the backdrop of natural population decline and due to the active emigration of the indigenous population to the countries of Western Europe and the Russian-speaking population to Russia. Latvia and Lithuania occupy the first two places of per capita emigration in the European Union. It is paradoxical but true – the citizens of the Baltic countries at first fought hard for the existence of independent states, and then, when they had achieved their goals, they began to leave them.

Lithuania and Latvia have the worst mortality rates in the EU. Estonia also has an excess of deaths over births. As a result, the employable population emigrates while pensioners and children, who may soon have no one to support them, remain in the country. Experts believe that by 2050, more than half of the inhabitants of the Baltic countries will be out of the working age range of 15 to 64 years old (Varpina, 2018).

Soon after gaining independence, the service sector began to take a dominant position in the economy of the Baltic states. Today, services constitute more than 73 per cent of Latvia's GDP, over 60 per cent of Lithuania's and about 70 per cent of Estonia's. For such an economic model to work successfully, the authorities must constantly stimulate domestic consumption. Demand needs to be supported through the efficient operation of joint ventures with foreign capital, remittances from migrants and large EU subsidies.

From 2004 to 2020, Latvia received more than 15 billion euros in subsidies from the EU, Lithuania more than 19 billion, and Estonia more than 10 billion. Like other developed regions, the Baltic countries are experiencing population decline, accompanied by an ageing society. In addition, being among the less developed members of the EU, Estonia, Latvia and Lithuania are experiencing a large external migration, further exacerbating the negative demographic trends.

Twelve Countries in Freefall

While the Baltic countries fell under the effective tutelage of the West, the remaining twelve countries began to live independently, and their political elites chose very different strategies for economic transformation. It is important to note here that, with a few exceptions, the former leaders of the communist parties of the republics came to power. They each had their own, sometimes radically different, ideas about the development of their countries. Over time, all the leaders have changed, the last being the former President of Kazakhstan, Nursultan Nazarbayev, who left his post in March 2019.

Despite the different development models in almost all countries in the early 1990s, their economies fell sharply. From 1990–1991, the scale of economic decline was at its height in the South Caucasus – in Armenia there was a 21.1 per cent decline, in Azerbaijan – 22.6 per cent, and in Georgia – 43.1 per cent. The minimum economic drop was recorded in Turkmenistan, where it fell by 1.3 per cent and in Uzbekistan by 2.1 per cent, while in Kyrgyzstan, there was actually a slight economic growth of 1.1 per cent, although this figure is due to a technical correction.

During the initial stages of the transition from a planned to a market economy, several countries such as Russia, Armenia, Georgia, Kyrgyzstan, Moldova, and Ukraine chose a liberal model of economic reform with the limited regulatory role of the state. For example, these countries carried out the large-scale privatisation of state property. The authorities have moved forward with slower reforms in several other countries, such as in Belarus, Tajikistan, Turkmenistan, and Uzbekistan. The state has played a bigger role in shaping markets in these countries and, further, these countries have seen a change in the models of economic transformation.

After the countries gained independence, the most critical choice was the state's role in economic activity. Immediately after independence, the essential choice was between maintaining or eliminating the state's leading role in economic activity. Many have reasonably argued that the state's dominant position in economic activity led to the collapse of the Soviet economy. It is for this reason that it was necessary to transfer the states' assets into private hands.

In the early 2000s, the state's role in the economy increased in Russia, Azerbaijan, Turkmenistan and Kazakhstan. In all these countries, the export of hydrocarbons has played, and continues to play, a dominant role. Most of the enterprises operating in these sectors have remained in state hands. In

Belarus and Uzbekistan, where there was significant industrial potential during the Soviet era, the authorities supported state-owned enterprises for quite a long time, which quickly enough showed their non-competitiveness. On the other hand, new private owners have not consistently demonstrated their effectiveness, for example, in Armenia, Georgia, Kyrgyzstan, Moldova and Ukraine, where rapid privatisation has occurred.

Moreover, the massive privatisation of large assets has led to dangerous trends. For example, privatisation in Russia and Ukraine led to a class of oligarchs which began to intervene in, and even influence, the political processes. In Ukraine, there is still a confrontation between state institutions and several oligarchic structures. In early November 2021, President of Ukraine Volodymyr Zelensky announced that he had signed a law to prevent threats to national security associated with the influence of oligarchs (Jushkov, 2021). According to him, now, "all economic players will be equal before the law and will not be able to buy political privileges for themselves".

The geographical location and the presence of natural resources dictated the different economic development models of the post-Soviet countries. The most important of these were hydrocarbons, which some countries offered to international markets. Nature and geography divided all countries into oil and gas exporters – Russia, Azerbaijan, Kazakhstan, Turkmenistan, Uzbekistan; and their importers – the Baltic countries, Armenia, Belarus, Georgia, Kyrgyzstan, Moldova, Tajikistan and Ukraine.

The first group of countries showed more favourable economic growth, especially from 2000 to 2013, due to rising energy prices. At the same time, having no similar export earnings, the countries from the second group were forced to attract external loans, primarily from global financial institutions such as the International Monetary Fund (IMF) and the World Bank. Given the possibility of free movement, these years began an active flow of labour resources from countries with low incomes and surplus labour resources to countries that needed to attract migrants (primarily to Russia). This trend continues and even intensifies at present.

The republics are actively exporting their labour, primarily the Kyrgyz Republic and Tajikistan, where the ratio of incoming remittances to GDP is at the highest level in the world at around 30 per cent. This indicator is also high in Armenia, Georgia and Moldova, and in 2020 ranged from 10 to 16 per cent of GDP.

The availability of natural resources is not by itself enough to develop successful states. Moreover, the concept of the resource curse, sometimes called "the resource trap" or "the paradox of plenty", has taken root in modern political science (The Natural Resource Governance Institute, 2015). When resource-rich countries lose their motivation for innovative development, over-reliance on their resource revenue is dangerous in the long run. Countries such as Angola, Nigeria, Sudan or the Democratic Republic of the Congo are often cited as examples of countries who have fallen into this trap (Theconversation.com, 2021).

All post-Soviet countries that are rich in hydrocarbons try to avoid resource dependence by creating specialised sovereign funds (for example, national welfare funds and future generation funds), where their governments accumulate the primary export earnings. The financial resources of such funds are not spent on current needs but are collected to cover future government spending. According to the Sovereign Wealth Fund Institute rating (SWFI, 2022), the top five funds include the State Pension Fund of Norway, the China Investment Corporation, the Investment Authority of Abu-Dhabi, Hong Kong Monetary Authority Investment Portfolio, and Kuwait Investment Authority. The Russian National Welfare Fund ranks 14th (RIA Novosti, 2021).

Countries lacking natural resources and actively supporting external sovereign borrowing are at the other end of the spectrum. The problem of the post-Soviet countries' sovereign debts will be discussed in more detail in Chapter 3. However, here we present data on the integral government debt to GDP in the countries of Central Asia and the South Caucasus. Figure 2.10 shows the changes from the 2000s to the present day and a forecast until 2027 (International Monetary Fund, 2022). The figure shows that the region's average stock of sovereign debt reached 70 per cent of GDP in the early 2000s and then decreased dramatically almost threefold over five to six years. In some countries, this indicator greatly exceeded that figure: in Moldova in 1998, it reached 160 per cent of GDP, in the Kyrgyz Republic in 2000 – 125 per cent of GDP, and in Tajikistan in 2000 – 110 per cent of GDP.

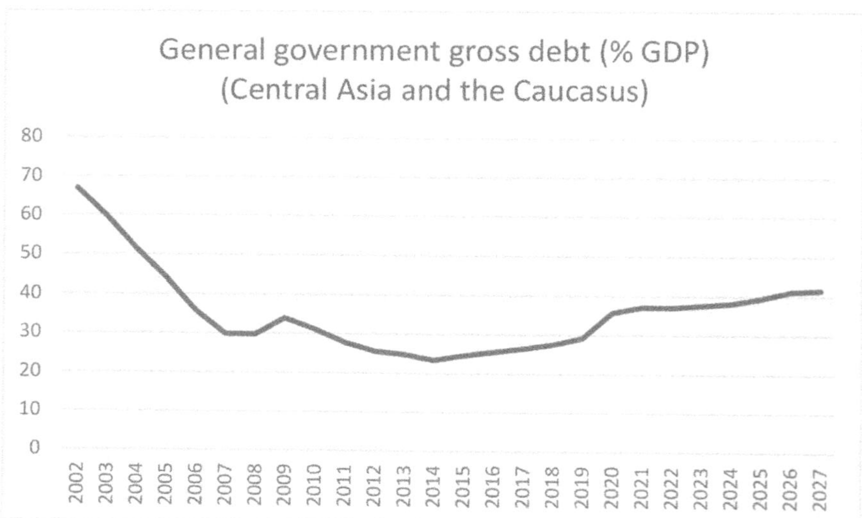

Figure 2.10 Sovereign debt in Central Asia and South Caucasus countries from the 2000s to the present day, and a forecast until 2027

Source: International Monetary Fund (2022).

The sovereign debt-to-GDP ratio in the region reached its lowest point around 2014 and began to rise gradually, most noticeably in 2020. Such trends were associated with an economic slowdown due to the introduction of anti-Russian sanctions and the weakening of national currencies in 2014, and the onset of the Coronavirus pandemic in 2020.

Capitalism or Socialism?

The debate about whether socialism or capitalism is best for humanity has lasted almost two centuries. Politicians, scientists, and practitioners have written numerous articles and books on this topic, and many dissertations have been defended exploring the theme. Both "defeated" socialism and "victorious" capitalism have experienced several fundamental upheavals as the world has moved forward. Watching the evolution of the post-Soviet countries in a market economy, or, more simply, under capitalism, one begins to think about the state of competition between the two global socio-political systems.

In the early 1990s, after the collapse of the Soviet Union, it seemed that this question was answered – liberal capitalism finally and irrevocably won. It is therefore no surprise that the well-known American political scientist and economist Francis Fukuyama formulated his famous thesis about the end of history in his articles and books (Fukuyama, 2006). Perhaps what he theorised would have happened if it had not been for two major events – a severe blow to the foundations of capitalism in 2008–2009 and the rapid growth of socialist China.

The demise of the Soviet Union clearly showed the failure of the socialist system, at least in its Soviet guise. The country failed to modernise its economy and compete with advanced countries, maintain a decent standard of living for its citizens, and give young people hope for the future. The tragic story of the Soviet Union teaches us that though classic socialism worked well in the fair distribution of resources, it was inefficient in earning wealth, and this became the main reason for the country's collapse.

At the same time, capitalism has shown its exceptional vitality and adaptability, quickly responding to a changing world and modernising its fundamental aspects and values. If we compare the capitalism of Karl Marx's time to the capitalism of the 21st century, it is easy to find similarities. No one can dispute that capitalism has lifted hundreds of millions of people out of poverty over the past two centuries, increased the length and quality of their lives, transformed and improved educational standards, and fostered profound and massive innovations that have improved the well-being of large numbers of people. Over time, capitalism has undergone modernisation and transformed variously like a kind of living organism. Currently, looking at North or South America, Asia or Europe, its standard features are not easy to identify but, although many different forms of capitalism exist, its basic ideology has remained the same: as formulated by Scottish economist Adam

Smith in 1776 in his work *An Inquiry into the Nature and Causes of the Wealth of Nations*, capitalism is characterised by "leaving economic decisions to free play self-regulating market forces" (Smith, 1977: 18).

However, the history of capitalism has been full of failures and even catastrophes. In our fast-paced times, its shortcomings have become even more apparent. Prioritising short-term profit for a limited number of people without considering the destruction of nature and the interests of ordinary citizens shows that the long-term well-being of both societies and the environment has been threatened. As a result, in many developed countries, capitalism has contributed to a significant increase in inequality, and the gap between the wealth of the richest and poorest people is widening, as measured by the Gini coefficient (World Bank, 2022c). This is especially noticeable in the US, where the poorest people have not seen real income growth since 1980, while the incomes of the super-rich have grown by about 6 per cent each year (Roser & Ortiz-Ospina, 2013). In other words, the fortunes of billionaires are constantly increasing, while since the beginning of this century, the average household income has grown very little.

In 2007–2008, capitalism was close to collapse. Its crisis became even more evident in 2020–2021 as the world grappled with the Coronavirus pandemic and the potentially catastrophic effects of climate change. Global upheavals, growing economic and political instability, and sharply increased inequality and polarisation worldwide have contributed to a growing dissatisfaction with the status quo. In a survey conducted by global public relations consultancy firm Edelman in 2020, 57 per cent of people agreed with the statement that "capitalism, as it exists today, does more harm than good in the world" (Edelman Trust Barometer, 2020: 12). Measured by indicators such as rising global inequality and environmental damage, "the performance of Western capitalism in recent decades has been deeply problematic", as Michael Jacobs and Mariana Mazzucato wrote in their book *Rethinking Capitalism* (Jacobs & Mazzucato, 2016: 11).

Capitalism remains the undisputed leader in the efficiency of earning individual and collective wealth. Only one country is left in the modern world that still denies this – North Korea. However, there has been a lot of criticism of capitalism regarding the fair distribution of wealth.

The debate about which system is better – capitalism or socialism – revolves around how a country's national wealth is created and distributed among its citizens. The Soviet Union, as a socialist country, first introduced the basic principles of fairly distributing national wealth and bringing less developed and less privileged regions to a reasonable level of development. That is why the primary beneficiary of the Great October Socialist Revolution was the poorest region of the Soviet Union, Central Asia. At the beginning of the last century, it was an almost empty vast, poor, and landlocked part of the world where the big powers were fighting for dominance. But during the days of the Soviet Union, the region was dramatically changed.

We can legitimately compare the five republics of Central Asia and compare these countries with their closest neighbour – Afghanistan, which has been part of Greater Central Asia for many centuries. The difference is enormous. This post-Soviet region is not rich, but its citizens are educated and ambitious. It is stable and developing. No one argues that its full literacy, adequate health care and reliable social protection system are the legacies of Soviet socialism.

In recent years, a real turnaround in our understanding of the balance between capitalism and socialism has taken place in China, tirelessly building "socialism with Chinese characteristics". It has become the world's second-largest economy within an unprecedentedly short space of time. The modern history of China is the history of the new socialism. It is a story of earning wealth through market economic principles, with the distribution of accumulated wealth along socialistic principles where, in this case, the rich and powerful help the less privileged. The results of the development of socialist China are unprecedented and truly impressive. In 2020, China's GDP reached 15.7 trillion dollars, an increase of 1,500 times compared to 1952. In 1960, China's GDP per capita was $89, and by 2020 it had reached $10,500. From 1948 to 2020, China's total foreign trade rose from $907 billion to $4.65 trillion, at an average annual growth rate of nearly 14 per cent. In the early years of the founding of the People's Republic of China, 80 per cent of the Chinese were illiterate, and the average length of schooling was only 1.6 years. In 1949, there were only 205 universities with fewer than 120,000 students, and overall enrolment was only 0.26 per cent. By 2020, the average length of study has increased to 10.8 years. By the end of 2020, the number of general education institutions of higher education reached 2,738, with 32.85 million students studying on campuses, ranking first in the world. As a result, poverty in the country has been quickly overcome due to the efforts of the whole society.

By comparison, in the US, the wealthiest country in the world, in 2020 37.2 million people or 11.4 per cent of the total population, lived in poverty, which is about 3.3 million more than in 2019. Of these, the vast majority are unemployed without access to education and health services, and we see crime thriving in this group.

How did China achieve such success? What are the characteristics of Chinese socialism? Does China's social and political practice have something in common with classic Marxist-Leninist socialism? From the point of view of earning personal wealth, Chinese socialism is entirely different to Soviet socialism. According to open-source data, as of August 2020, in dollar terms, China has produced 257 billionaires in just a year, or five a week, adding to this figure the existing 621 billionaires (Li, 2020).

But how do Chinese billionaires and millionaires differ from American ones? What else can they do for the "socialist" distribution of accumulated wealth among other community members, following socialist principles? They pay high taxes and create jobs, increasing national wealth and helping others, but this is the not the extent of their fundamentals. Many have recently chosen a different path in distributing their wealth. To explore and analyse this concept further, it is pertinent to explore one example from Inner Mongolia, one of China's poorest provinces.

The well-known Kubuqi International Desert Forum in Inner Mongolia's Ordos has taken place every two years since 2013 and provides a platform "dedicated to promoting desertification control" (Kubuqi International Desert Forum, 2019). The Kubuqi desert is located about 800 kilometres to the west of Beijing. Living and maintaining decent lives and successful businesses in this remote and arid area is challenging, and the poverty level has always been much higher than the country's average. Desertification affects about 2 billion people worldwide, mostly in developing countries. Almost all previous efforts to control desertification in this region of China were not successful. However, the Kubuqi Desert Project, which began thirty years ago, has succeeded in containing one of the largest deserts in China, roughly the size of Israel. It has also turned one-third of the desert (an area of almost 6,000 square kilometres) into green pastures (Kubuqi International Desert Forum, 2019).

As to the other critical issue of climate change, over the past thirty years the project has increased annual precipitation in Kubuqi from 100 millimetres to more than 400 millimetres of rain. This is mainly due to its 53 per cent plantation coverage, a fundamental change facilitating ecological sustainability. As a result, one of the most successful land reclamation projects globally can now be found not in a coastal area, but in the Kubuqi desert. This unique project also proved that at least three components should be part of successful desertification – support from the local communities and the government, technology, and capital.

It is surprising to some that this unique and complex project was supported and financed not by the state but by a private company with its own resources. Since 1988, Elion, a Chinese private company, has invested more than 40 billion yuan (or $5.9 billion) in the Kubuqi desert-greening project, helping to lift about 102,000 local farmers and herders out of poverty. Additionally, Elion has invested heavily in plantations as well as in research and development. Their scientists and engineers have invented and applied more than 100 technologies to ensure the plants survive in the harsh environment and to ensure sustainable green restoration.

The project was a straightforward demonstration of the fundamental qualities of socialism – those characteristics which were important in the Soviet Union. Societies must develop harmoniously, and stronger entities (provinces, cities, enterprises, people) should help the less privileged. It is hoped that the Kubuqi model's remarkable results will not remain the exclusive example for long, but that it will inspire other leaders from both private sector players and governments worldwide.

This unique case was not only a demonstration of the social responsibility of Chinese business leaders but also a vivid example of how to fight climate change on the planet, including by investing private capital. Additionally, although this case study explored an example surrounding climate change, the lessons from it are applicable to many sectors of a country's development. No matter what country we live in and what principles we follow, everyone needs to work together to fight climate change, poverty and inequality and make our world a better, greener, and fairer place to live, and this example in China could serve as inspiration to many.

When discussing the future of our planet and civilisation, we can conclude that the real test of the quality of socio-political systems will be the effectiveness of mobilising public and private funds to combat climate change and other issues that affect a country's well-being.

The sustainable fight for the survival of our planet against irreversible climate change will lead to the introduction of new taxes, an increase in existing ones, for the well-being of all citizens. There will have to be a natural drift towards more equitable principles for the redistribution of national wealth. The convergence of capitalism with socialism may occur naturally along the path of humanity's movement towards sustainable development.

References

Aneculaesei, C., 2020. Destroying Tradition: The Soviet Anti-Alcohol Campaigns. [Online] Available at: https://historyofyesterday.com/destroying-tradition-the-soviet-anti-alcohol-campaigns-e6fec177135d [Accessed July 2022].

AP News, 2018. Putin: If he could, he'd try to prevent 1991 USSR collapse. [Online] Available at: https://apnews.com/article/d36b368c6ad44bb2b8e883fc8d800514.

Aron, L., 2012. *Roads to the Temple: Truth, Memory, Ideas, and Ideals in the Making of the Russian Revolution, 1987–1991*. New Haven: Yale University Press.

Bolt, Jutta, Luiten van Zanden, Jan, 2020. *Maddison Style Estimates of the Evolution of the World Economy. A New 2020 Update*, Groningen: Maddison Project Database.

Central Intelligence Agency, 2019. *The 1991 CIA World Factbook*. s.l.: Good Press.

Central Intelligence Agency, 2020. *The 1990 CIA World Factbook*. s.l.: Good Press.

CIS Stat, 2022. Interstate Statistical Committee of the CIS. [Online] Available at: http://www.cisstat.org/eng/index.htm [Accessed July 2022].

Denisenko, M., Dmitriev, R. & Elizarov, V. eds., 2018. *Demograficheskoe pazvitie postcovetskogo prostranstva*. Moscow: Moscow State University.

Edelman Trust Barometer, 2020. *Edelman Trust Barometer 2020*, s.l.: Global Report.

Fabrykant, M., 2018. National Identity in the Contemporary Baltics: Comparative Quantitative Analysis. *Journal of Baltic Studies*, 49 (3), pp. 305–331.

Filippenok, A., Creegan, J. & Antipova, A., 2021. RBK: Proval na zapade i bum na vostoke. Kak menjalos' naselenie byvshego SSSR. [Online] Available at: https://www.rbc.ru/society/09/12/2021/61af3dab9a7947c72ecf6ff5 [Accessed July 2022].

Fukuyama, F., 2006. *The End of History and the Last Man*. New York: Free Press.

Geohistory.today, 2016. Four Reformers in Russia's Shock Therapy. [Online] Available at: https://geohistory.today/russia-shock-therapy [Accessed July 2022].

Golovnin, M. & Grinberg, R., 2021. Outcomes of 30 Years of Economic Transformation in the Post-Soviet Space: Light and Shadows. *Outlines of Global Transformations: Politics, Economics, Law*, 14 (5), pp. 6–29.

History.com, 2022. Collapse of the Soviet Union. [Online] Available at: https://www.history.com/topics/cold-war/fall-of-soviet-union [Accessed July 2022].

International Monetary Fund, 2022. World Economic Outlook Databases. [Online] Available at: https://www.imf.org/en/Publications/SPROLLS/world-economic-outlook-databases#sort=%40imfdate%20descending [Accessed July 2022].

Jacobs, M. & Mazzucato, M., 2016. *Rethinking Capitalism: Economics and Policy for Sustainable and Inclusive Growth*. S.l.: John Wiley & Sons.

Jushkov, M., 2021. RBK: Zelenskij podpisal «zakon ob oligarhah». [Online] Available at: https://www.rbc.ru/politics/05/11/2021/61853aed9a79476737c59c7f [Accessed July 2022].

Kubuqi International Desert Forum, 2019. Kubuqi International Desert Forum. [Online] Available at: http://en.kubuqiforum.org/ [Accessed July 2022].

Li, J., 2020. China is rapidly producing new billionaires despite Covid-19. [Online] Available at: https://qz.com/1919974/china-created-a-record-number-of-billionaires-despite-covid-19/ [Accessed July 2022].

Official Statistics of Latvia, 2022. Demographics of Latvia. [Online] Available at: https://stat.gov.lv/en/statistics-themes/population [Accessed July 2022].

Reagan, M., 2014. Putin, Petroleum and Pantyhose. [Online] Available at: https://townhall.com/columnists/michaelreagan/2014/03/06/putin-petroleum-and-pantyhose-n1804878 [Accessed 5 July 2022].

RIA Novosti, 2021. Fondy nacional'nogo blagosostojanija v stranah mira. [Online] Available at: https://ria.ru/20210603/blagosostoyanie-1735494319.html [Accessed July 2022].

Roser, M. & Ortiz-Ospina, E., 2013. Income Inequality. [Online] Available at: https://ourworldindata.org/income-inequality [Accessed July 2022].

Smith, A., 1977. *An Inquiry into the Nature and Causes of the Wealth of Nations*. Chicago: University of Chicago Press.

Statista, 1991. Total population of select ethnicities and nationalities in the Soviet Union in 1979 and 1989. [Online] Available at: https://www.statista.com/statistics/1248304/population-ussr-by-ethnicity-cold-war/ [Accessed July 2022].

SWFI, 2022. Top 100 Largest Sovereign Wealth Fund Rankings by Total Assets. [Online] Available at: https://www.swfinstitute.org/fund-rankings/sovereign-wealth-fund [Accessed July 2022].

The Natural Resource Governance Institute, 2015. *NRGI Reader - The Resource Curse*, New York: The Natural Resource Governance Institute.

Theconversation.com, 2021. Is the resource curse hard-baked into African economies? China's approach hints that it may not be. [Online] Available at: https://theconversation.com/is-the-resource-curse-hard-baked-into-african-economies-chinas-approach-hints-that-it-may-not-be-167397 [Accessed July 2022].

UN: Population Division, 2022. Countrymeters: Naselenie Tadzhikistana. [Online] Available at: https://countrymeters.info/ru/Tajikistan [Accessed July 2022].

UNSD, 2019. UNdata: GDP by Type of Expenditure at current prices. [Online] Available at: http://data.un.org/Data.aspx?d=SNAAMA&f=grID%3a101%3bcurrID%3aUSD%3bpcFlag%3a0#SNAAMA [Accessed July 2022].

Varpina, Z., 2018. Countries of old men? Demographic challenges in Estonia. [Online] Available at: https://baltic.fes.de/fileadmin/user_upload/documents/FES_Countries_of_old_men_final.pdf [Accessed July 2022].

World Bank, 2022a. DataBank: World Development Indicators. [Online] Available at: https://databank.worldbank.org/source/world-development-indicators# [Accessed July 2022].

World Bank, 2022b. GDP per capita, PPP (constant 2017 international $) - Ukraine, Armenia, Azerbaijan, Belarus, Estonia, Georgia, Kazakhstan, Kyrgyz Republic,

Latvia, Lithuania, Moldova, Russian Federation, Tajikistan, Turkmenistan, Uzbekistan. [Online] Available at: https://data.worldbank.org/indicator/NY.GDP.PCAP.PP.KD?locations=UA-AM-AZ-BY-EE-GE-KZ-KG-LV-LT-MD-RU-TJ-TM-UZ [Accessed July 2022].

World Bank, 2022c. Data: Gini Index. [Online] Available at: https://data.worldbank.org/indicator/SI.POV.GINI [Accessed July 2022].

World Population Review, 2022. 2022 World Population by Country. [Online] Available at: https://worldpopulationreview.com/.

Part II

Post-Soviet Transformation

3 Economic Transformation

Introduction

More than thirty years have passed since the former Soviet republics became independent states in 1991, when they began a rapid programme of economic change. As such, the period is long enough to look back on and begin to more accurately assess the complex issues that each of the five countries of Central Asia has faced, some of which they have already overcome. The formation of new states became especially difficult because none of them, except perhaps Uzbekistan, had any state-building experience. The nations built state institutions and developed a new market model for economic transformation from scratch. At that time, none of the post-Soviet countries expected to continue building their future based on the socialist principles of a planned economy, through which a single decision-making centre in Moscow had controlled the economy of all the republics. Most leaders of post-Soviet countries and their elites reasonably believed that the defeat of the Soviet Union in economic competition with the West was due to the inefficiency of the socialist governance model. Additional difficulties in the construction of states were created by the so-called "Parade of Sovereignties" when new countries, not trusting their neighbours, decided to develop their economies separately. Many leaders of these new states quickly but short-sightedly rejected the basic principles of the socialist planned economy, such as collective ownership of the means of production, central planning, and the emphasis on equality and economic security.

It is ironic that the leaders of the new republics unconsciously followed the words of one of the founders of the Soviet state, Vladimir Lenin, who in 1900 famously wrote in his article for the *Iskra* newspaper: "Before uniting, and in order to unite, we must first decisively and definitely disengage" (Lenin, 1900). The essence of this phrase was that any institution would be strong only when people with common goals and interests unite, but that to reach this level, it was first necessary to "disengage" from those who do not share the principles of the new institution.

The republics' disengagement with each other led to the rupture of economic ties between enterprises, the suspension of entire industries, mass unemployment, and a rapid increase in poverty. The post-Soviet countries

DOI: 10.4324/9781003360728-6

avoided chaos and unrest only because each former state's institutions continued to operate and the people demonstrated unbelievable adaptability to the new conditions. The "Parade of Sovereignties" led countries to choose different models for their economic development. In Central Asia, Kazakhstan and the Kyrgyz Republic selected a model of liberal market economy, trying to carry out privatisation as quickly as possible based on "shock therapy" principles. Tajikistan, Turkmenistan and Uzbekistan decided to keep many of the principles of socialist planning. They privatised only small and medium-sized enterprises while the state continued to play an essential role in economic development and employment.

The dynamics of demography determined the development models of each of the post-Soviet states. This differed greatly in different geographic regions. In the Baltic countries, Ukraine, Belarus, Moldova and Russia, population growth first stopped and then began to fall. In the republics of the South Caucasus, except for Azerbaijan, similar processes took place. However, in the countries of Central Asia, the population began to grow again after a slight decline. This healthy trend continues today, albeit at a different rate. Compared with Soviet times, the structure of the economy of all the republics has dramatically changed. The migration of labour flows occurred from agriculture to the services sector, while the share of the industry remains about the same. The rapid population growth in rural areas caused internal migration to the cities and urbanisation. In general, one can note the favourable development of the demographic situation with a constant flow of young people into the labour market, contributing to the development of the regional economy. Because of the importance of demography in this region, this chapter will discuss these trends in detail.

We will also discuss the key trends in the development of human capital. The population of Central Asia in Soviet times had a high level of education, access to reliable health care services and a social safety net. Despite tremendous economic difficulties during the period of transition, especially during the 1990s, all countries maintained these achievements. Governments have prioritised funding for education and health care in formulating state budgets, which has allowed these countries to maintain a satisfactory level of human capital quality, significantly higher than in other countries with a similar per capita income.

In the early 2000s, hydrocarbon prices began to rise quickly and had a profound impact on the economies and demographics of the Central Asian nations. Countries producing hydrocarbons needed additional labour, but their population, primarily in Russia, had fallen significantly during the 1990s. On the other hand, due to the rapid population growth in the countries of Central Asia, the market began to experience a surplus in the labour force. As a result, the flow of migrant workers from Central Asia to Russia was, in purely demographic terms, a win-win situation. The absence of a visa regime between the countries and knowledge of the Russian language by migrants led to mass labour migration from one region to another. According to various estimates, up to ten million migrants currently work in Russia, mainly from Central Asia. Collectively, they send home a large sum of money to support their relatives. The remittance flows from Russia to the Kyrgyz Republic and Tajikistan are currently estimated to be around 30 per cent of GDP, one of the world's highest (TheGlobalEconomy, 2020a). This chapter focuses on external labour migration and analyses the dynamics of remittance flows between Russia and Central Asia.

Trade is of fundamental importance for developing an economy, creating jobs and growing income. We will devote special attention to analysing the dynamics of trade flows. The region of Central Asia is in a geographically disadvantageous position with no access to the sea, which is perhaps why, according to various international ratings, the region's countries are in the worst places in terms of ease of international trade. But the area has a positive domestic and foreign trade dynamic associated mainly with exporting oil, gas and metals. The negative feature of the region's trade is the lack of diversification, as the main exported products are crude oil from Kazakhstan and natural gas from Turkmenistan. Thus, there is an urgent need to diversify exports focusing on value-added goods. To reduce the expenses of delivering modern goods to large markets, governments must minimise transaction costs and develop hard and soft infrastructure in transportation.

In addition to geographic circumstances, the sustainability of logistics depends not only on hard infrastructures, such as the quality and quantity of roads, but also on the availability of convenient soft infrastructures, such as lower barriers to cross-border flows of goods and services, and the speed of customs procedures, including simplified legislation, etc. Therefore, the next part of the chapter deals with the problems of improving business conduct in the region's countries. The main emphasis is on the ratings provided by reputable international institutions. The countries of Central Asia are still lagging behind the world leaders in many indicators, for example, the "Trading across Borders" indicator (Doing Business, 2019). Therefore, governments will need to put in significant effort to make conducting business easier and to reduce the cost of a trade.

Along with active trade, attracting the right investments is necessary for the effective economic transformation of any country. Investments create jobs, fill government budgets with direct and indirect taxes, and strengthen national currencies. Investment falls into two categories: direct investment, which bypasses public institutions and goes directly to the private sector, and public investment, which goes to government budgets. These can be grants or loans from public institutions – the governments of donor countries or international financial institutions (IFIs). How investment is attracted to the countries of Central Asia is described in the closing section of this chapter.

Economy

For many centuries, the economic development of Central Asia was hindered by its isolation and the consequent "peripheral syndrome" since the region had no access to the sea and was far from the economic core. However, it was not always so isolated. During the golden age of the Great Silk Road, Central Asia flourished when the area was the very bridge that connected the centres of world civilisation.

After gaining independence in 1991, the new countries of Central Asia experienced a painful transition from a planned economy to a market economy. After all, the basic principles of their planned economies consisted of broad subsidisation of transportation, energy resources, free education, health care and social support for the population. This differed fundamentally from the basic principles of a market economy. Price liberalisation forced households and state-owned companies to face international prices for goods and services. This "shock therapy" required fundamental changes in the sectoral structure of the economy, which led to rapid economic decline and increased unemployment and poverty in the short to mid-term.

The collapse of the central planning system, severe disruption to the organisational arrangements governing production and trade, and the new customs barriers that arose on the new borders between the independent republics meant that many enterprises stopped working altogether. As a result, the standard of living sharply plunged in all countries of Central Asia (Figure 3.1). By 2000, GDP per capita had fallen by more than 218 per cent of its 1990 value in the Kyrgyz Republic (Data Commons, 2022a), and by 360 per cent in Tajikistan (Data Commons, 2022b), where a civil war further aggravated the situation.

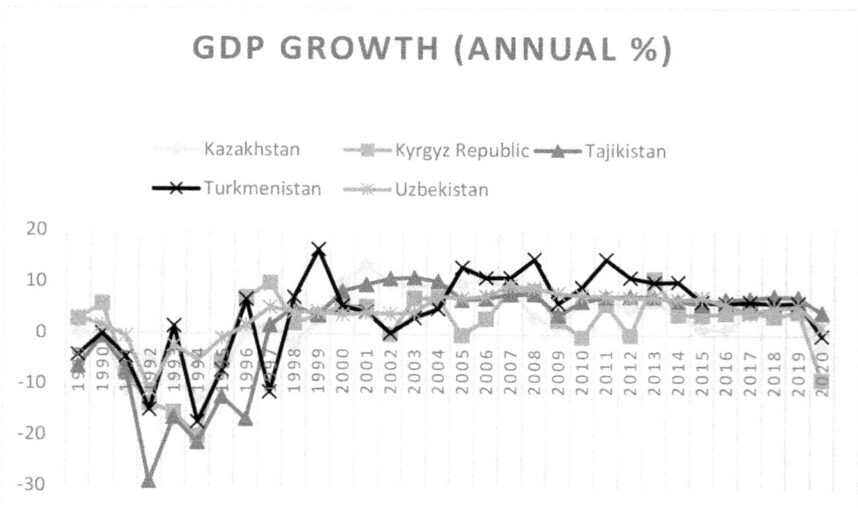

Figure 3.1 GDP growth in Central Asian countries (1989–2019)
Source: Data Commons (2022a; 2022b).

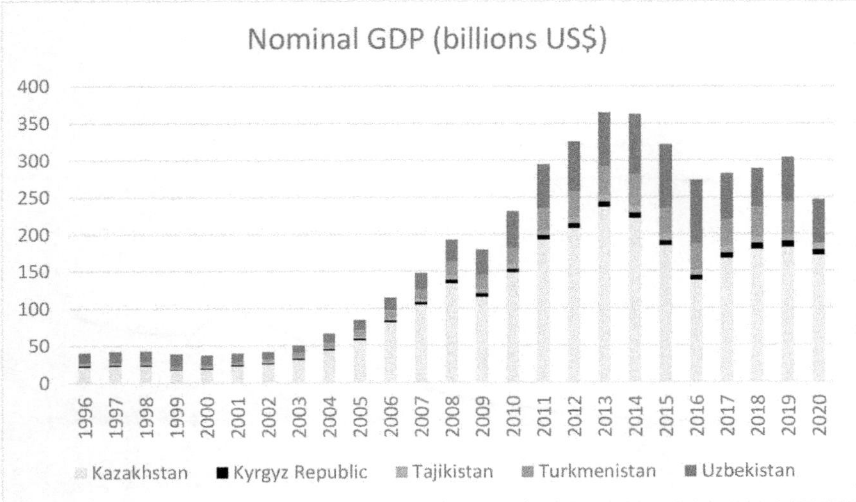

Figure 3.2 Nominal GDP in Central Asian countries (1996–2020)
Source: World Bank (2022c).

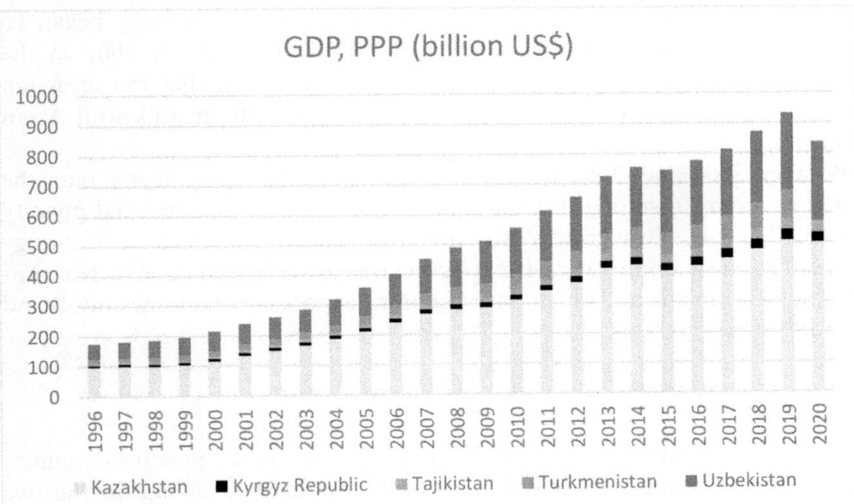

Figure 3.3 GDP at PPP in Central Asia (1996–2020)
Source: World Bank (2022c).

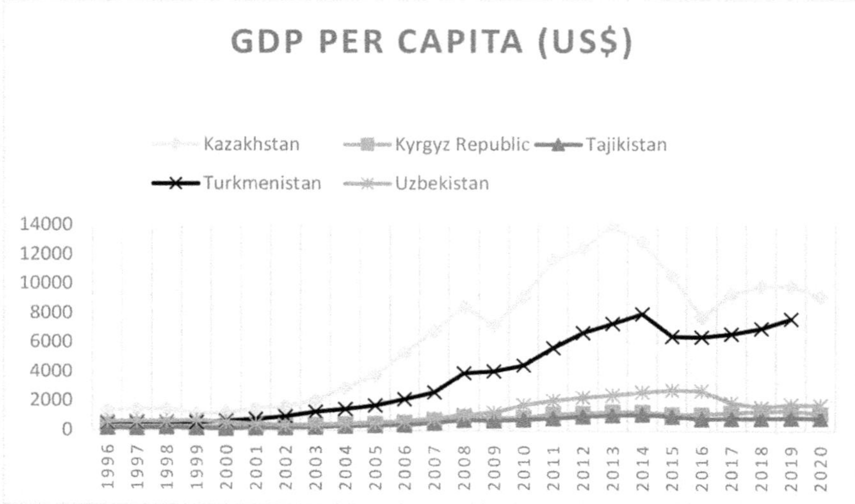

Figure 3.4 GDP per capita in Central Asia by country (1996–2020)
Source: World Bank (2022c).

In the period of about ten years leading up to 2000, the major socio-economic transformations of the region's countries in the transition to a market economy were all but complete, and against the backdrop of a rapid increase in world prices for hydrocarbons, the economy of each country began to grow. However, GDP per capita reached 1990 levels only by 2006 in the Kyrgyz Republic and by 2007 in Tajikistan, highlighting that the recession was more profound and drawn out in the poorest of the five Central Asian countries.

Between 2000 and 2020, the Central Asian economy grew faster than the global economy, resulting in higher household incomes and reduced poverty (Figure 3.1–3.4). This growth was driven primarily by increases in energy prices. The most impressive per capita income growth happened in Kazakhstan and Turkmenistan, which have begun to export large volumes of oil and gas to external markets.

Demographics

An important driver of long-term economic growth is the positive dynamics of population change. Figures 3.5–3.7 show population change in the five Central Asian countries over the past half-century. As of early 2022, their collective population has more than doubled in size and reached a total of 76 million. This is equivalent to about 1 per cent of the global population (Worldometer, 2022a). The population of Central Asia is very young, with every third resident in the region aged 15 or under (World Bank, 2021a). Only 3 per cent of the population in Tajikistan and 8 per cent of the population in Kazakhstan is over 65 years old (World Bank, 2021b). The median age in Central Asia is less than twenty-eight years old (Worldometer, 2022a). In addition, the region is set for further growth; according to some estimates, by 2050, the region's population will exceed 100 million people (Worldometer, 2022a).

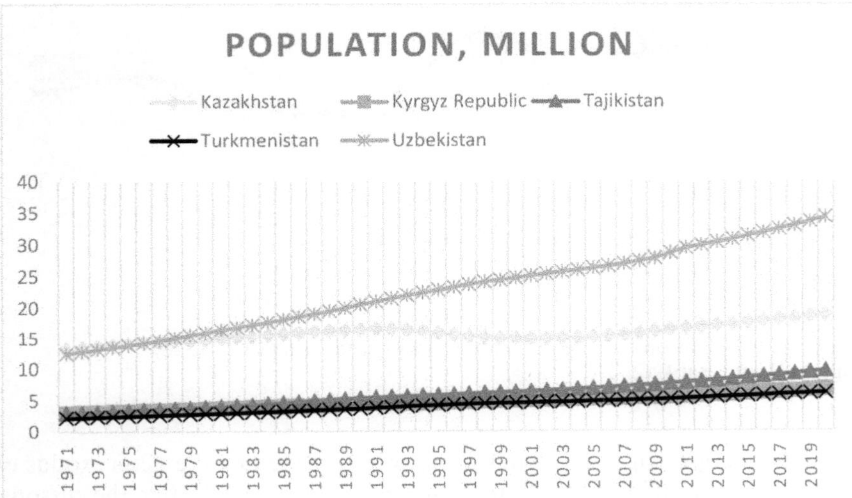

Figure 3.5 Population change in Central Asia by country (1971–2019)

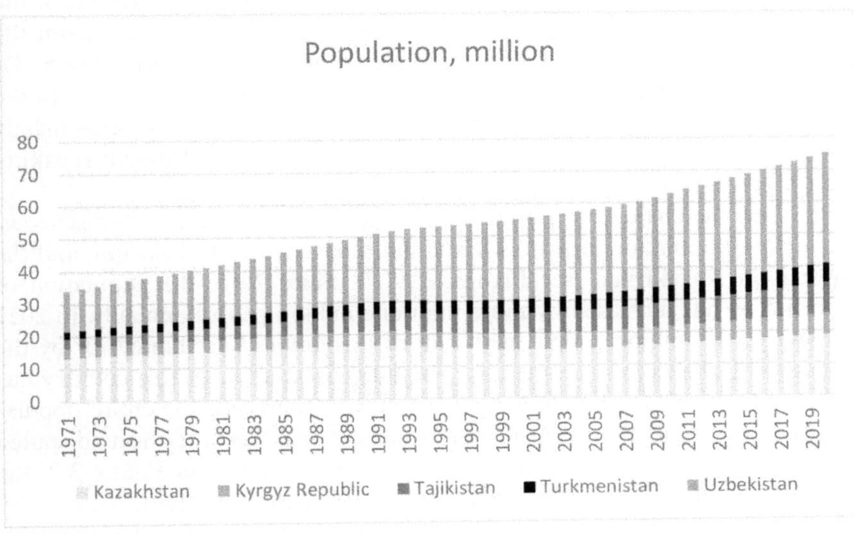

Figure 3.6 Total population change in Central Asian countries (1971–2019)
Source: World Bank (2022c).

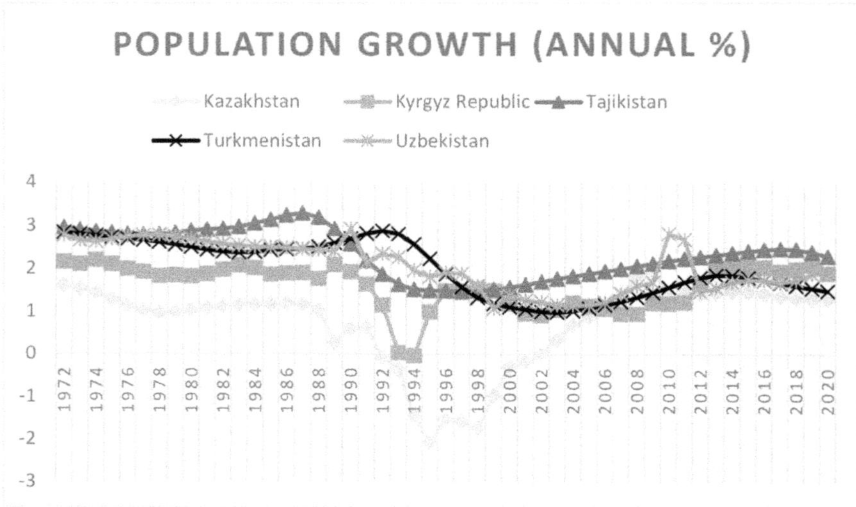

Figure 3.7 Population change in Central Asian countries (1972–2020)
Source: World Bank (2022c).

Population growth in the area was not even affected by the mass exodus of the Russian-speaking population in the early 1990s, right after the dissolution of the Soviet Union. A sharp drop in living standards and uncertainty about the future caused their departure, mainly to Russia. In those years and still today, the Russian government actively encouraged the relocation of the Russian-speaking population to Russia, offering various benefits – from the provision of free housing to the payment of monetary compensation. Of course, this is related to Russia's significant challenges in connection with the ageing and decline of its population. Figure 3.7 shows that this process mainly affected Kazakhstan and the Kyrgyz Republic, where most Russian-speaking citizens in Central Asia lived and still live.

However, the changes in population in the region are quite heterogeneous. The highest population growth is found in Tajikistan and Uzbekistan, and the lowest is in Kazakhstan (see Figure 3.5–3.7). Since 2015, the population of Central Asia has increased by more than one million people annually. In 2021 it grew by 1.17 million people, with half of this amount accounted for by the increase in Uzbekistan's population. The total population of this country has increased by 7 million people over 10 years, which exceeds the entire population of Kyrgyzstan or Turkmenistan. Tajikistan has become the undisputed leader in population growth in the last decade. As shown in Figure 3.7, the number of its citizens increases annually by more than 2 per cent.

Population growth is a positive phenomenon for the nation's development, strengthening its human resources base and expanding the economy. However, in countries with a poor economy, population growth can lead to increased poverty and unemployment, overpopulation, and a shortage of resources such as land and water.

In this regard, it is vital to also investigate the data surrounding life expectancy. As seen from Figure 3.8, it has a clear upward trend except for a transitional recession around or immediately after 1991. It is noteworthy that the positive changes to life expectancy happened during an unprecedently challenging decade – from the 1990s to the 2000s, when the region experienced a sharp economic decline, falling living standards, rising unemployment and poverty (Figure 3.8). This overall positive trend is because the standards of education, health care and social security that existed in the Soviet era were maintained, although to a lesser extent, during the years after independence.

An equally important trend has been the steady decline in the infant mortality rate in all countries of Central Asia (Figure 3.9). This happened although even in the Soviet Union health support in the republics was a state priority and supported by the central governments through large subsidies from Moscow. When the countries gained independence, such subsidies ceased. In addition, despite the de facto collapse of their economies and the cessation of centralised budgetary support, all countries managed to retain the staff of medical institutions and continue training medical personnel in educational institutions. Despite financial difficulties, the state authorities gave priority to the purchase of modern medical equipment and medicines. Naturally, in these years, new medical technologies and discoveries took

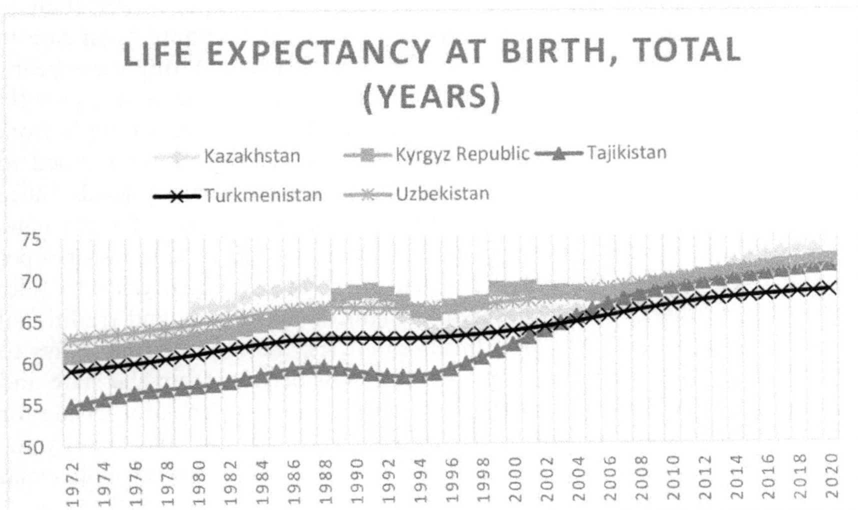

Figure 3.8 Life expectancy at birth in Central Asian countries (1972–2020)
Source: World Bank (2022c).

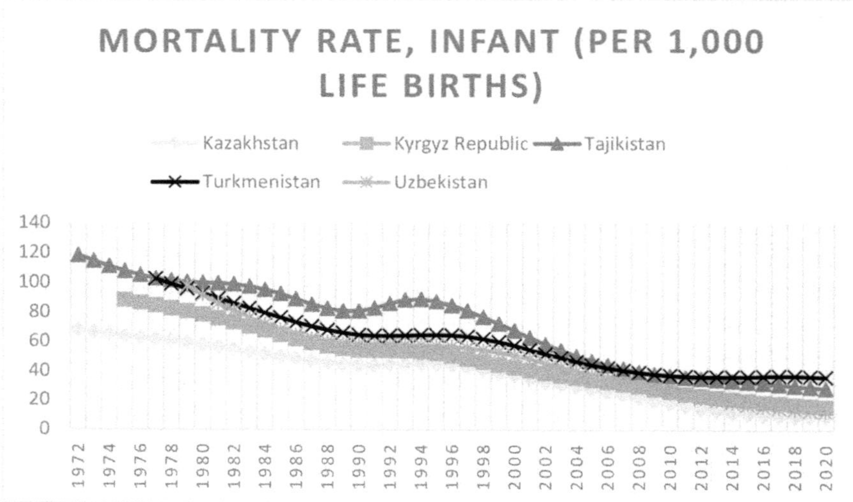

Figure 3.9 Infant mortality rates in Central Asian countries, 1972–2020
Source: World Bank (2022c).

place in developed countries, which brought many important innovations to the medical practice across the globe.

Experts have long recognised the trend that fertility rates decline as social welfare improves. The birth rate in rich countries is much lower than in developing countries. This theory applies well to the declining birth rate in the countries of Central Asia from the 1970s until 1990. During these years, the Soviet Union and its republics experienced sustainable economic growth. However, in all countries of Central Asia, this theory ceased to apply from the 1990s until the mid-2000s (Figure 3.10). The fertility rate continued to fall despite the economy's sharp decline and increase in poverty levels. Since the mid-2000s, the birth rate began stabilising at an average of three newborns per woman. In Tajikistan, it was higher and averaged 3.5 newborns per woman. Experts attribute such abnormal birth rates in these years to state support for mothers, the availability of reliable medical care, and traditional values in Central Asian families. In all countries, there are various ways to support birth rates. Authorities provide payment benefits from the state and local budgets; for non-working mothers, there is an allowance for caring for a child up to the age of one year. Working mothers may also qualify for specific maternity benefits. There is support for large families through social benefits for family members and mothers.

It is also interesting to analyse the correlation between fertility rates (Figure 3.10) and urbanisation rates (Figure 3.11–3.12). During the Soviet period until 1991, fertility and urbanisation in Central Asia aligned with generally accepted norms. With an increase in the level of urbanisation, the

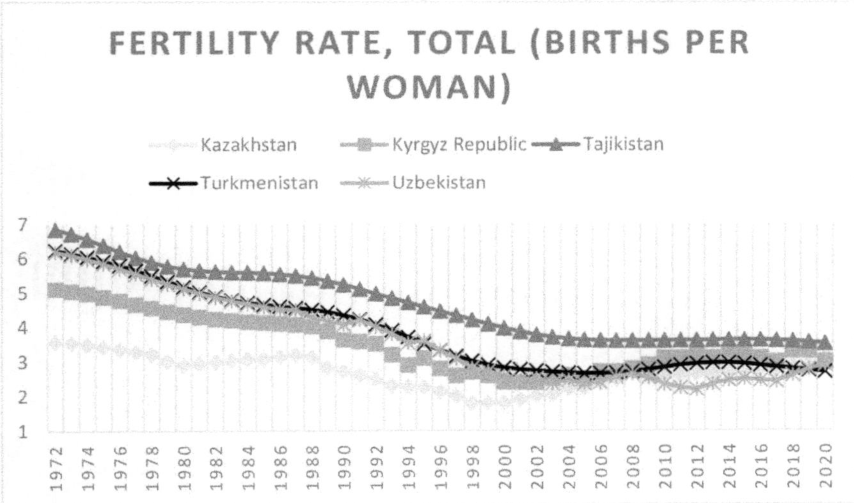

Figure 3.10 Fertility rate (births per woman) in Central Asia by country (1972–2020)
Source: World Bank (2022c).

birth rate decreased. Women in cities are more educated and career-oriented. Besides this in urban areas, the age of marriage is higher, meaning families are often started later, so the age of marriage in cities is also higher. In addition, in cities, the number of children in families is less than in rural areas.

But again, with the advent of independence of the region's countries, these generally accepted standards started to look different. Since the 2000s, the rapid growth of the urban population has not led to a further drop in the birth rate. This can be accounted for by the same reasons for the birth rate – state support for families with children, the availability of reliable medical care, and traditional family values in the region.

Figure 3.12 shows that the total urbanisation level of the region has more than doubled in fifty years. But one can observe an uneven distribution of the level of urbanisation among the countries (Figure 3.12). If in Kazakhstan it approaches 60 per cent, in Tajikistan it stays below the 30 per cent mark.

Another critical demographic parameter for predicting economic development is the dependency ratio, which measures the number of dependants under the age of fifteen and over sixty-five compared to the total working-age population aged fifteen to sixty-five. Figure 3.13 shows that during the 1970s, there was a fall in this ratio, reflecting the time gap between the fall in child mortality and the subsequent decline in the fertility rate. This increased the proportion of children in the total population. This ratio has decreased in all countries of Central Asia as the baby boomer generation, caused by a delayed decline in fertility, has become part of the working population.

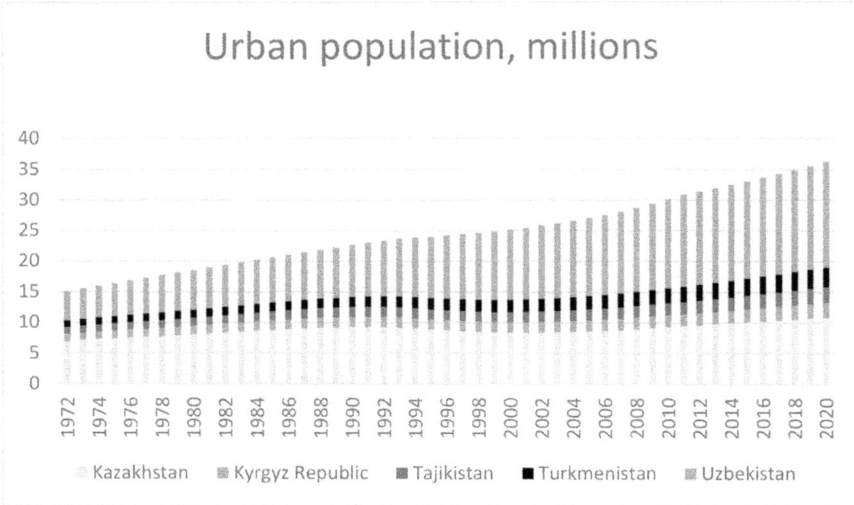

Figure 3.11 Urbanisation in Central Asian countries (1972–2020)

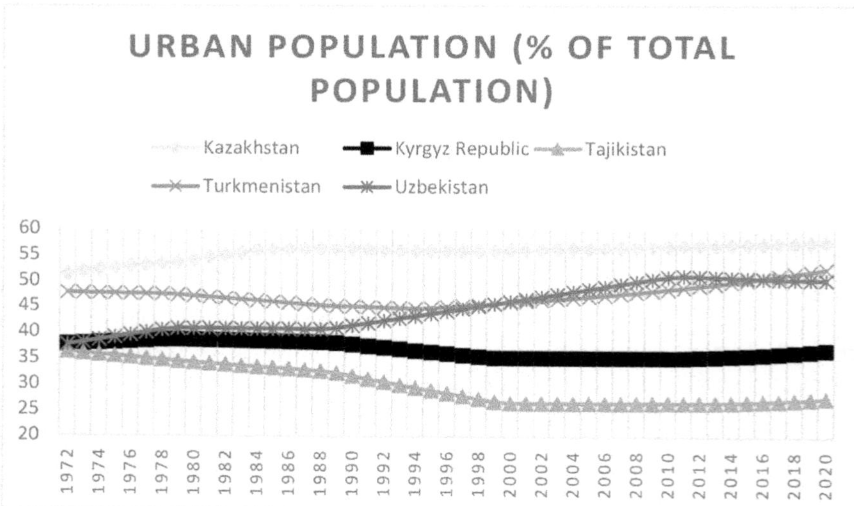

Figure 3.12 Urban population in Central Asian countries as a percentage (1972–2020)

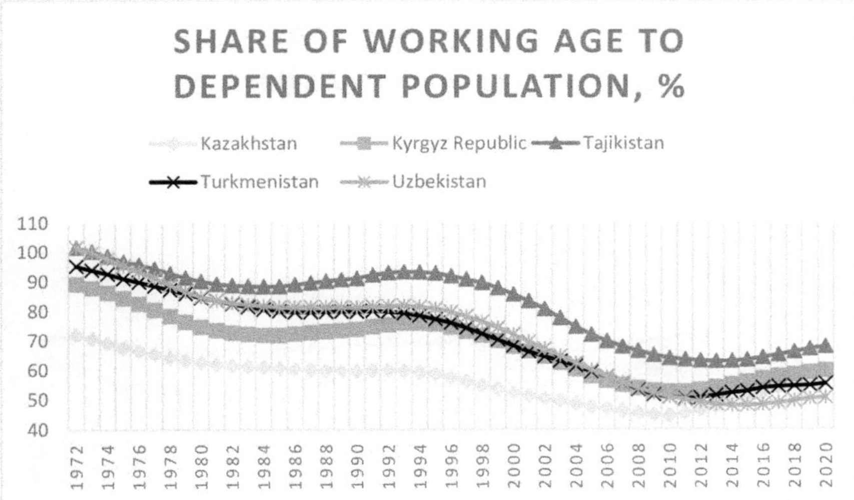

Figure 3.13 Age dependency ratio in Central Asian countries (1972–2020)
Source: World Bank (2022a).

As a result, the increase in the proportion of the working-age population meant fewer dependants in need of support. The resources saved are known as a "demographic dividend". As the baby boomer generation ages, the demographic transition is giving way to dependence on old age. It is a turning point that Kazakhstan reached in the early 2010s. For the other four Central Asian countries, this ratio has declined significantly since the 1970s, and it is predicted that the demographics will reach their lowest point around 2040. It should increase in all four countries, except Kazakhstan, until around 2050. Therefore, all four Central Asian countries should expect to benefit from the demographic dividend over the next twenty-five years.

A higher dependency ratio makes the economy less responsive to stimulative measures. Figures 3.13–3.14 show that, so far, the dependency ratios for the countries of Central Asia are higher than in a few other selected countries, including high-income ones. Data show the proportion of dependants per 100 working-age population (World Bank, 2022a). However, according to UN calculations, after 2025, this indicator in the countries of Central Asia will decrease and remain below the global average at about the same level as in other middle-income countries (United Nations, Department of Economic and Social Affairs, 2019). Unlike Central Asia, developed countries and some of Central Asia's prominent neighbours and trading partners, such as China and Russia, are rapidly ageing. Even if there is a decline in global and regional demand, which could slow growth in Central Asia over the next few years, positive demographic dynamics will mitigate the negative effect of such a slowdown.

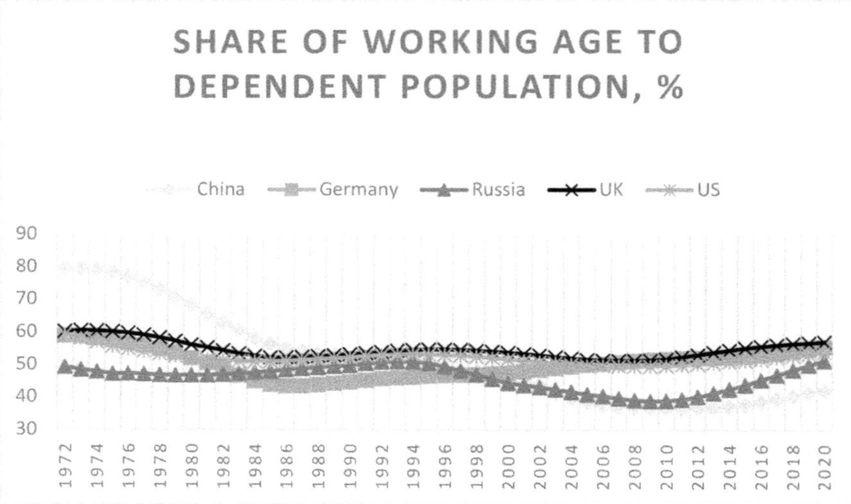

Figure 3.14 Age dependency ratio in a few select countries (1972–2020)
Source: World Bank (2022a).

Human Capital

When discussing the demographic features of the countries of Central Asia, it can be seen that some characteristics that did not quite fit into the generally accepted demographic trends. For example, the increase in the urban population which accompanied rapid economic growth has not led to a drop in the birth rate. This has already been accounted for by a variety of factors, but perhaps one more factor can be added – the relatively high human capital of the population in comparison with other places with similar GDP per capita. As a result, when planning a family, parents make conscious decisions.

The so-called Human Capital Index (HCI) is measured using a methodology developed by the World Bank. The index measures which countries are best in mobilising their citizens' economic and professional potential. It estimates how much capital each country loses through lack of education and health care (World Bank, 2018). Figure 3.15 shows the dynamics of this index for the countries of Central Asia compared to Mexico and Serbia, which have about the same GDP per capita as Kazakhstan, and Zambia and Myanmar, which have about the same GDP per capita as the Kyrgyz Republic. Figure 3.15 shows that the HCI in the countries of Central Asia exceeds their values in countries with similar household incomes. The exception is the former socialist country of Serbia, where it turned out to be close to the value of HCI in Kazakhstan.

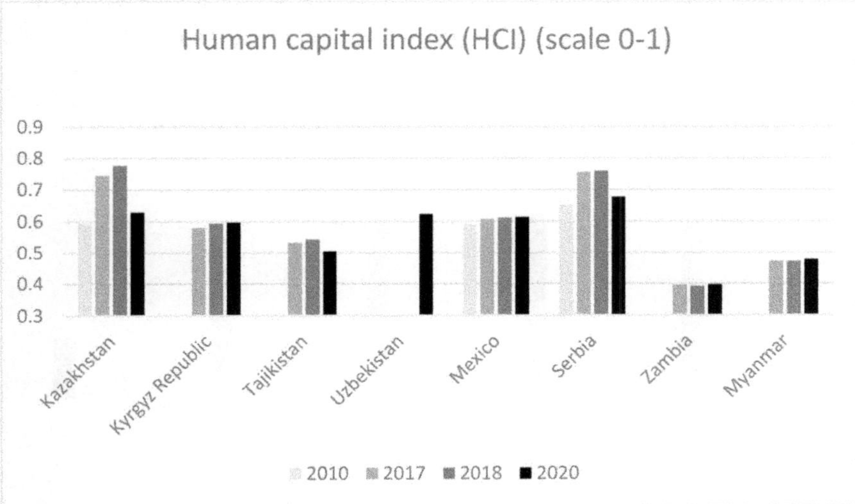

Figure 3.15 Human Capital Index in Central Asia and a few select countries
Source: World Bank (2018).

This section addresses issues related to building an adequate human capital base in Central Asia. The two main components of human capital, education and health, will be briefly discussed.

Education

We have already mentioned that the Soviet system greatly improved primary and secondary education access in the region. School attendance was universally compulsory for all children, from the age of six or seven. Consequently, at the time of the countries' independence, the level of education was high. The education level in the region at the time of independence was close to that of Western European countries.

After independence, education indicators deteriorated somewhat due to the decline and sharp fall in government spending. Figure 3.16 shows the dynamics of change in the percentage of the population aged 15+ with no education. The data was taken from the well-known education database Barro-Lee Education Data (Barro & Lee, 2013). Figure 3.16 shows data for both Central Asian countries and Germany. Surprisingly, there were significantly fewer illiterate people in the region than in wealthy Germany (probably due to the presence of migrants). Despite the somewhat different rate of the restoration of full access to education in other countries, it reached the level that existed during the Soviet Union in a reasonably short time. Presently, primary and secondary education enrolment rates are on par with, and sometimes exceed, those of developed countries.

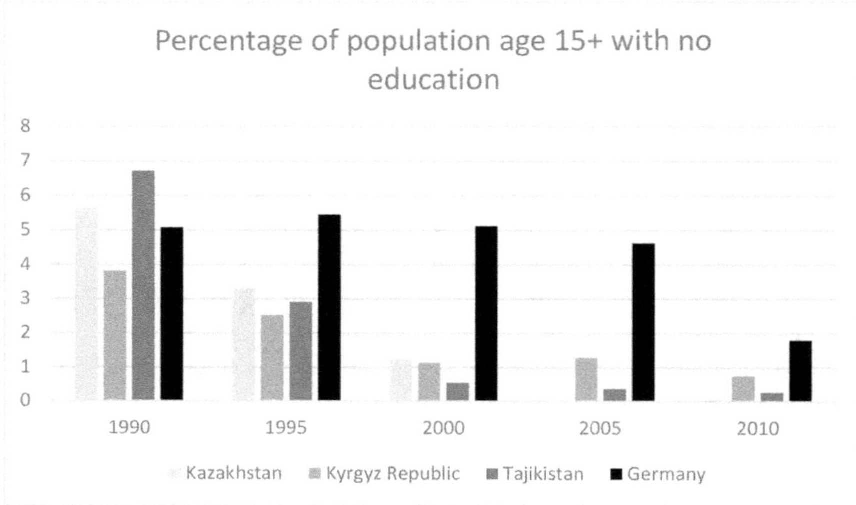

Figure 3.16 Change in the percentage of the population aged 15+ with no education in Central Asian countries compared to Germany
Source: Barro and Lee (2013).

Despite severe economic difficulties, governments continued to prioritise spending on education. Figure 3.17, based on available data, shows government expenditures on education as a percentage of GDP in Central Asian countries, as well as, for comparison, similar data for Afghanistan and Germany. Note that in the case of Turkmenistan, data is only available for 2012, which is 3.05 per cent of GDP (World Bank, 2020a). It is easy to see that spending on education is on the same level as in Germany, at least as a percentage of GDP. In the case of the Kyrgyz Republic and Uzbekistan, they even exceed the level of Germany and the OECD average of 5 per cent. As a result of significant educational investments, according to the World Bank, all citizens receive at least a secondary education and are literate upon leaving school. The countries of Central Asia can be proud of these facts.

While government expenditure in Central Asia in the sphere of education may be more than in some other countries, it is also important to mention that the quality of education leaves much to be desired. There are considerable differences in teacher qualifications between urban and rural areas in all countries. Competent budgeting is lacking, monitoring and evaluation remain weak, and there is no system of appropriate incentives. As a result, the level of training of students falls short. Figures 3.18–3.19 show student performance in terms of reading quality and math comprehension for Kazakhstan and the Kyrgyz Republic. The two countries agreed to conduct these studies under the well-known PISA programme, the OECD's Program for International Student Assessment, which measures fifteen-year-olds' ability to use their reading, mathematics and science knowledge and skills to

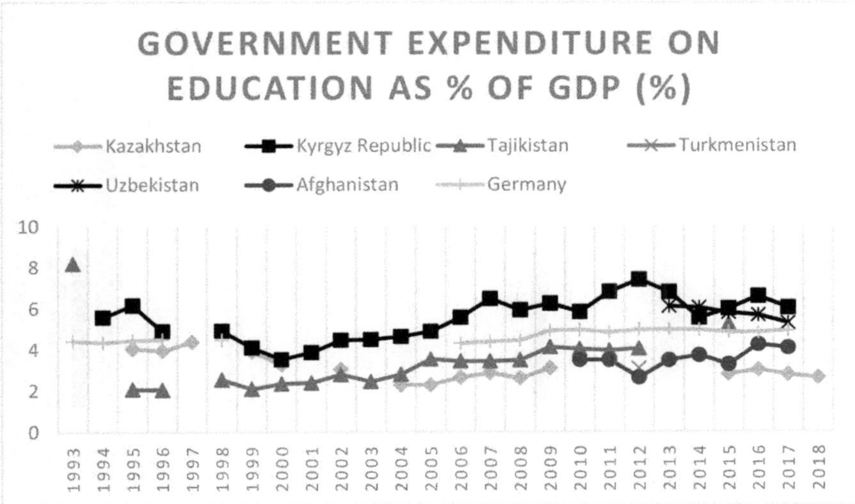

Figure 3.17 Government expenditures on education as a percentage of GDP in Central Asia and a few selected countries
Source: World Bank (2020a).

meet real-life challenges (OECD, 2018). Note that countries may opt in or opt out of this study, so a full set of data is unavailable. For comparison, similar results are shown for Germany as well as Georgia, a post-Soviet country, which, like the Kyrgyz Republic, spends approximately $800 per student annually (KG Analytics Intellectual Fund, 2022). From the figures presented, Georgian students received higher scores, almost on par with Kazakhstan, which spends about three times more annually per student (World Bank, 2020b). But students from all these countries are still far behind students in Germany (Figure 3.18–3.19).

A particular study conducted by the World Bank in 2014 revealed quite a curious feature in terms of the impact of language of study on education. "Students in Kyrgyz- and Uzbek-language schools were 40 percentage points more likely than their Russian-educated peers to fall below this [PISA learning assessments] threshold" (World Bank, 2014a). This trend is continuing and has become even starker in recent years. The reason is that teachers who teach in Russian are considered more educated and literate. They tended to graduate from higher-quality universities and strive toward continued professional development. In addition, many parents prefer to send their children to a Russian-instruction school. Such schools are typically considered to provide better education and also provide opportunities for better employment for Russian-speaking school graduates both in their homeland and in Russia or Kazakhstan. In the region, knowledge of Russian is considered prestigious, and more ambitious young people try to learn it. This is perhaps similar to how English proficiency is perceived in continental

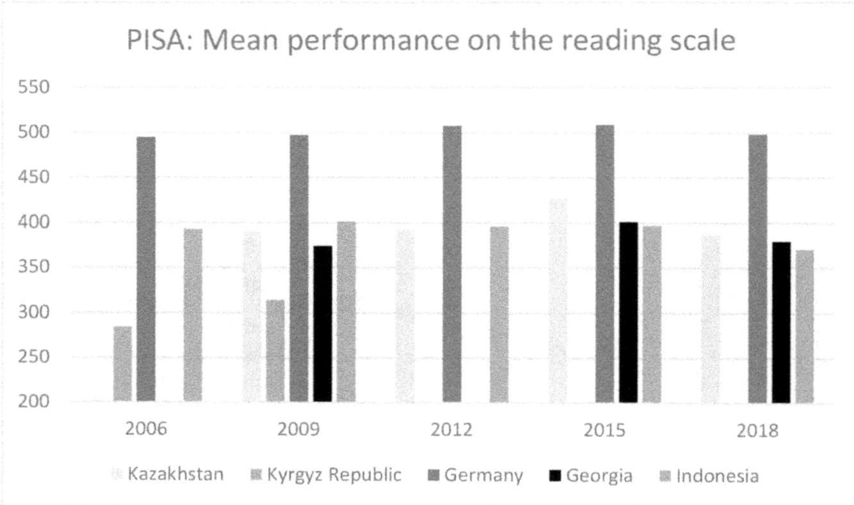

Figure 3.18 Students' reading performance for Kazakhstan, the Kyrgyz Republic, Germany and Georgia (2006–2018)
Source: World Bank (2020b).

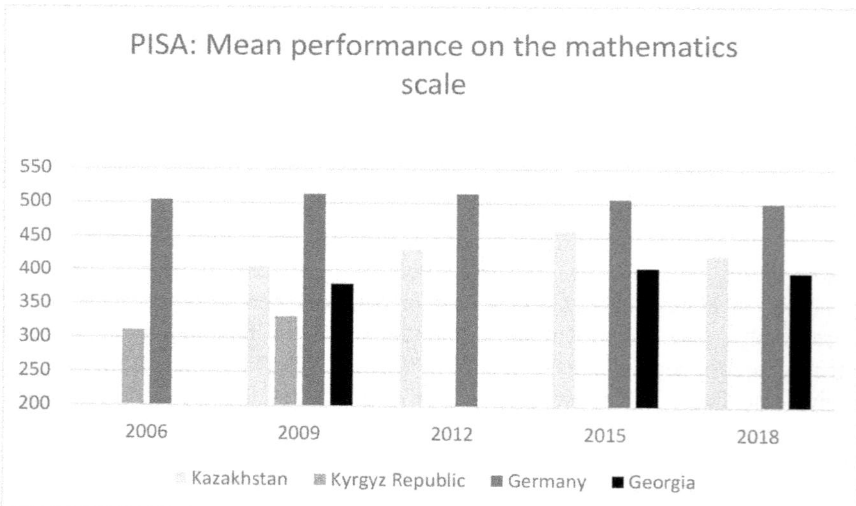

Figure 3.19 Students' mathematics performance in Kazakhstan, the Kyrgyz Republic, Germany and Georgia (2006–2018)
Source: World Bank (2020b).

Europe: a competitive advantage. It can also be suggested that through the Russian language, the youth of Central Asia have better access to the achievements of modern science and culture and, of course, to the Internet. Similar trends are taking place in Russian-language schools in Kazakhstan, Tajikistan, and Uzbekistan, both in cities and rural areas.

In recent years, there has been an important trend in the region's countries that young people seek education not in universities but in vocational colleges, increasing the chances of finding a job. In the 1990s, most young people tried to enter universities, regardless of the quality of the individual institution. It was believed that receiving vocational training was not so prestigious. However, now that people see that finding a job after vocational training has become much easier, the situation has completely changed over the past decade and many more are entering vocational establishments.

Regarding the development of higher education, private and non-governmental educational institutions are gaining more and more authority and influence. Leaders in higher education in Central Asia include Nazarbayev University and KIMEP University in Kazakhstan, and the American University of Central Asia (AUCA) in the Kyrgyz Republic. They moved away from the Soviet standards of higher education and switched to the principles of Western liberal education. A particular programme of the government of Kazakhstan in operation is Bolashak, which finances the education of young Kazakhstanis in the world's best universities. For almost thirty years since the implementation of the programme, the number of programme graduates has exceeded 11,000 (Murat, 2021).

Despite the high level of commitment to education across the region and the reforms already in place, the demand to improve human capital is enormous. Central Asia still has a long way to go before it can fulfil its aspirations to achieve the desired educational results close to those of developed countries. Visible improvements over the last two decades are a reason for hope for faster progress towards this goal. Persistent efforts must continue to reform the education system and attract private investment in this area.

Health Care

Issues of health care were discussed earlier in the chapter concerning demographic trends. We noted positive trends with a steady increase in life expectancy (Figure 3.8), a decrease in the number of newborn deaths (Figure 3.9) and a consistently high birth rate (Figure 3.10). These indicators' short-term negative trends were observed in the early 1990s but quickly corrected, so the health indicators in all countries of Central Asia quickly surpassed their pre-independence levels. Kazakhstan and the Kyrgyz Republic will achieve the Millennium Development Goals (MDGs) targets to reduce infant and under-five mortality. Kazakhstan will soon reach the target for maternal mortality rates too.

In addition to the graphs presented, we will also show the dynamics of change in the indicator "births attended by skilled health staff (% of total)" in the countries of Central Asia (Figure 3.20). Even during the most challenging times immediately after the collapse of the Soviet Union, when health care was practically unfunded, this indicator remained close to 100 per cent in all countries, except for Tajikistan, which also quickly reached 100 per cent.

The most challenging health problem in the countries of Central Asia is associated with a relatively high incidence of Tuberculosis. Given the critical importance of combating this disease, we will analyse global trends in the fight against this disease in a separate section.

Public spending on health care has grown continuously since the early 1990s. However, relative to GDP, it has been stable, ranging in 2020 from 2 per cent of GDP in Kazakhstan to 7 per cent of GDP in Tajikistan (Figure 3.21) (World Bank, 2022b). These expenditures remain at about the same level for most countries in Central and Eastern Europe (about 4.5 per cent of GDP on average) but well below European countries, which exceed 8 per cent of GDP. For comparison, Figure 3.21 shows Germany's public health spending evolution. It still has steady growth, and in 2020, it reached almost 12 per cent of GDP (World Bank, 2022b).

As a result of the low level of public spending on health, out-of-pocket expenditures paid by households as co-payments (flat fees for accessing healthcare) and informal payments have increased (Wagstaff, et al., 2019). In 2019, they accounted for 34 per cent of all health spending in Kazakhstan, 46 per cent in the Kyrgyz Republic, 58 per cent in Uzbekistan, 71 per cent in Tajikistan, and 77 per cent in Turkmenistan (World Bank, World Health

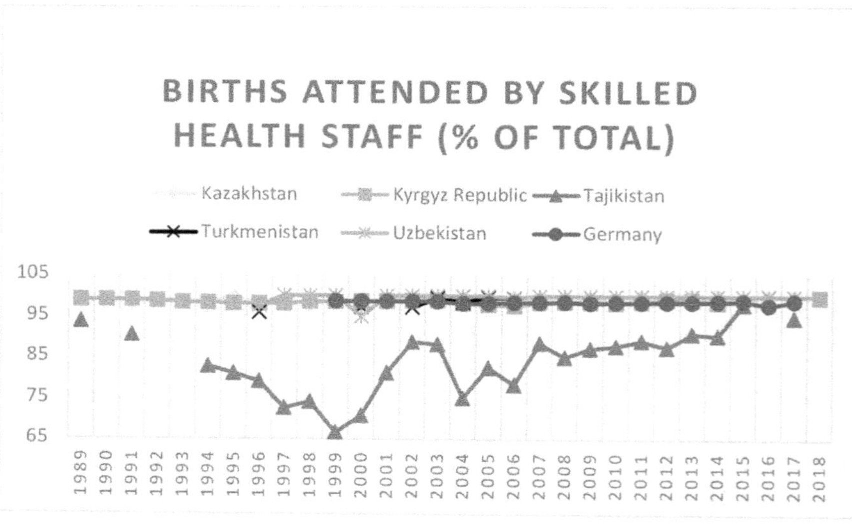

Figure 3.20 Births attended by skilled health staff in Central Asia and Germany (1989–2017)

Source: World Bank (2022c).

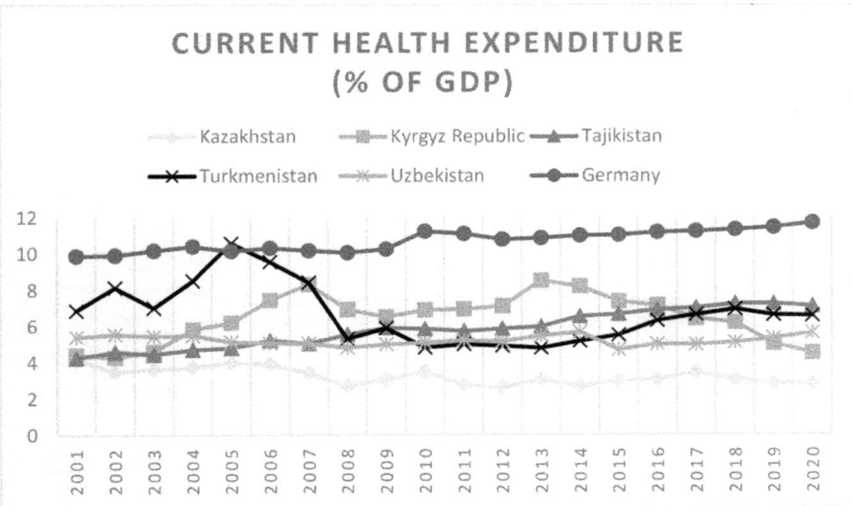

Figure 3.21 Public spending on health care in Central Asia and Germany (2001–2020)
Source: World Bank (2022b).

Organization, 2022). This share was significantly higher than in most countries of Eastern Europe – 21 per cent, and the countries of the Eurozone – 15 per cent. The concept of co-payment was included in the legislation as an official source of health care financing and is now part of the national legislation of Central Asian countries.

Many experts believe that the Kyrgyz Republic is a regional leader in health system reforms, having started radical reforms in the sector as early as the mid-1990s. The authorities planned reforms for the next two decades. It is the only country in Central Asia that has introduced a mandatory health insurance system, covering about 74 per cent of the population in 2016. The reports of various international organisations noted that the current system provides better financial protection for the people than in other countries (Jakab, et al., 2018). In 1996, a mandatory health insurance fund was created in Kazakhstan but abolished in 1998 (Wickham, et al., 1999).

Before independence, all Central Asian countries practised expensive and inefficient Soviet health care systems. Each hospital operated autonomously with its budgets, staff, laboratories and administrative structures. During this time, the number of hospital beds per 1,000 members of the population was about 50 per cent higher than in EU countries. This proportion has declined rapidly and is currently slightly below the EU average in all countries except Kazakhstan, where the numbers are still higher (World Bank, World Health Organization, 2019). In Kazakhstan, the number of beds per 1,000 members of the population in 2014 was 6.1, in Tajikistan – 4.7, in the Kyrgyz

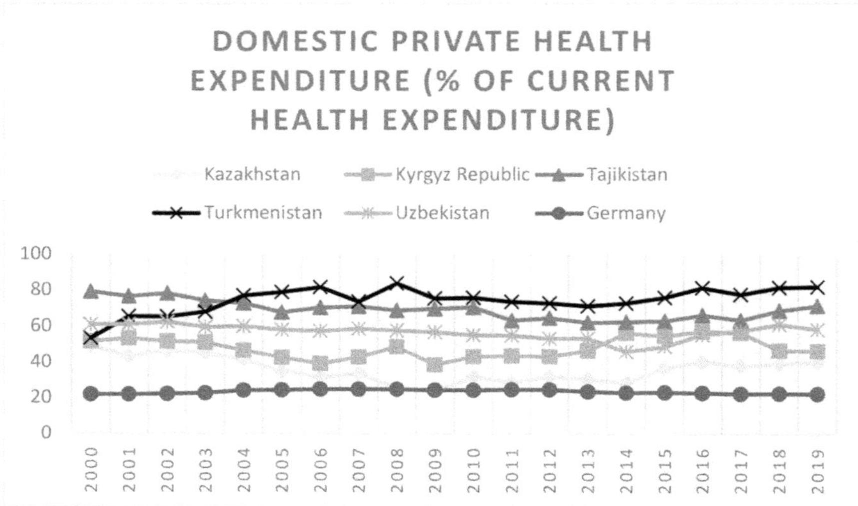

Figure 3.22 The share of current health expenditures funded from domestic private sources in Central Asia and Germany (2000–2019)
Source: WHO (2022a).

Republic – 4.4, in Turkmenistan and Uzbekistan – 4.0. For comparison, in the Eurozone, the number of beds per 1000 was 4.3 (World Bank, World Health Organization, 2019).

An essential feature in developing the healthcare system in recent years has been the growth of private medicine. Given the emergence of a higher-income population, the market began offering them better medical services than state medical institutions. Now such institutions are developing everywhere. Figure 3.22 shows the dynamics of the share of current health expenditures funded from domestic private sources, including funds from households, corporations, and non-profit organisations. Such expenditures can be prepaid to voluntary health insurance or paid directly to healthcare providers. The data presented are taken from the World Health Organization Global Health Expenditure database (WHO, 2022a). Since the beginning of the 2000s, private medical expenses in all Central Asian countries have been consistently high, exceeding the corresponding level in developed countries several times (for comparison, Figure 3.22 demonstrates the case of Germany).

Why is the world panicking about the coronavirus and not about tuberculosis?

What would be the answer to the following quiz question: "Which disease is the biggest infectious killer, caused by bacteria and affecting the lungs? It is spread through the air when people cough or sneeze. A person needs to inhale only a few germs to become infected. What disease is it?" Nine out of ten people will probably say today that it is the coronavirus disease. However, it is not. It is … tuberculosis. And indeed, it is the most prolific killer in the world even today.

Here we discuss the most dangerous disease, which is still claiming numerous lives of people not only in Central Asia but throughout the world. The disease is tuberculosis. Although the disease is gradually receding, even in 2020, more than 50,000 people die from this disease every year in Central Asia (WHO, 2021a). For comparison, official figures show that just over 18,000 people have died from the coronavirus disease in the region in more than two years (Worldometer, 2022b).

Deterioration in health care funding, and poor veterinary control of cattle, together with the cross-border transmission in Central Asia, have contributed to an almost doubling of the incidence of tuberculosis (TB) between 1990 and 2002 (WHO, 2021a). However, Central Asian countries' efforts enabled them to reverse this trend in the early 2000s through better case detection and adoption of effective treatment. As a result, the incidence of tuberculosis has fallen sharply and is now closer to the average for upper-middle-income countries (Figure 3.23). The same graph shows the dynamics of the development of tuberculosis in Germany.

The highest number of deaths from tuberculosis in Central Asia in 2020 was observed in the Kyrgyz Republic – annually, 105 per 100,000 population. In comparison, about 3,000 people died from coronavirus in this country in two years, corresponding to an annual death rate of 22 per 100,000 (Worldometer, 2022b), which is five times less than deaths from tuberculosis (World Bank, World Health Organization, 2020).

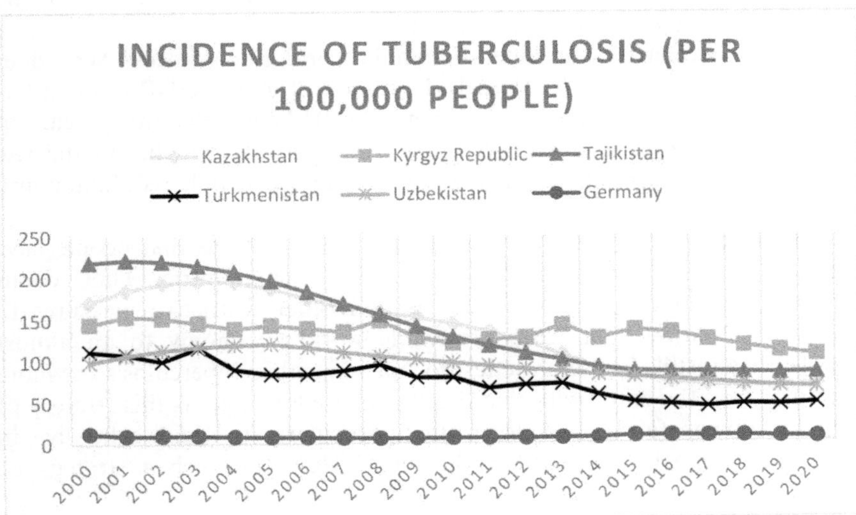

Figure 3.23 Incidence of tuberculosis in Central Asia and Germany (2000–2020)
Source: WHO (2021a).

Let us now consider the situation with the development of tuberculosis around the world and compare it with the impact of the coronavirus pandemic. The World Health Organization estimates that nearly 15 million people were killed either by coronavirus or by its effects on overwhelmed health systems in the past two years, more than double the official death toll of over 6 million. Most fatalities were in Southeast Asia, Europe, and the Americas (WHO, 2022b). If it is true, then the annual death toll from that pandemic would be 192 people per 100,000 population, which is a vast number. What are the other main causes of death nowadays?

The 2019 World Health Statistics report of the World Health Organization (WHO) shows the following mortality rates per 100,000 population. Deaths due to road traffic incidents were 18.2 per 100,000, due to homicide was 6.4, the suicide mortality rate was 10.6, and the rate attributed to exposure to unsafe water, sanitation, and hygiene services was 11.7. The highest mortality rate was due to the "disease of the poor", tuberculosis. In 2020, the world's average mortality rate from that disease was 127 per 100,000 (World Bank, World Health Organization, 2020). However, sub-Saharan Africa remains at 220 deaths per 100,000, which is more than coronavirus.

For many decades, perhaps even centuries, tuberculosis was the most common cause of death worldwide. The WHO estimates that 1.8 billion people, or close to one-quarter of the world's population, are infected with Mycobacterium tuberculosis, the bacteria that cause tuberculosis. 5 to 15 per cent of these people will fall ill with the active tuberculosis disease. In 2020, 10 million people, mainly from poor communities, fell sick from tuberculosis, and 1.5 million died (WHO, 2021b). Why has humanity panicked about coronavirus, even though tuberculosis has claimed more lives over many generations throughout the same period?

Why has coronavirus brought the whole world to its knees? Why does humanity "agree" to lose a colossal $17 trillion of global GDP in the aftermath of coronavirus (Cutler & Summers, 2020)? Why, after thirty years of poverty reduction, did humanity "agree" that poverty will be on the rise again, as the World Bank estimates up to 100 million people risk falling into extreme poverty?

In my opinion, the honest answer to those questions is that people have begun to die more often, not everywhere, but in rich countries. Those countries have introduced tough lockdowns and other restrictive measures to protect their citizens, bringing the whole world's economy to an almost complete standstill. Those societies do not remember tuberculosis anymore since they won the battle with that deadly disease long ago. Is this strategy of hard lockdowns fair to everyone else, particularly to those who live in developing countries, who suffer the most? How can such a strategy be justified? Is this just egoism or even cynicism?

It is not only disastrous socio-economic or financial damage that coronavirus has brought to humanity. It almost wholly diverts the attention of medical communities from fighting tuberculosis and other deadly "diseases of the poor". It is not just a diversion of scientific attention. The lockdowns, particularly across developing countries, have raised insurmountable barriers to patients who must travel to obtain diagnoses or drugs. According to the WHO, more than 120 countries have reported a drop in tuberculosis patients visiting clinics since the pandemic began, threatening hard-fought gains achieved against the disease during the last couple of years.

Calculations show that a lockdown of 3 months followed by an extended recovery of 10 months might result in 1.4 million tuberculosis deaths and an additional 6.3 million tuberculosis cases from 2020 to 2025 (Hashem, et al., 2022). It now seems likely that the indicated time frames will last much longer.

The pandemic is also shrinking the supply of diagnostic tests and drugs against tuberculosis, malaria, AIDS, and other killers, as pharmaceutical companies make more expensive medicines to detect and fight coronavirus. There are numerous examples of the sheer cynicism of companies that are preparing to produce more costly drugs for coronavirus instead of desperately needed drugs against other "diseases of the poor".

As it is well known, ending the tuberculosis epidemic by 2030 is among the health targets of the Sustainable Development Goals adopted by all UN Member States in 2015. Humanity should act quickly and decisively if it is committed to accomplishing these UN goals. During the pandemic, we have observed a shocking fact that those who live in poverty die of infectious diseases disproportionally more often. We must work hard to stop this terrible injustice. The coronavirus crisis should bring humanity back to the realisation that the time has come to defeat tuberculosis and other infectious diseases forever.

Severe crises are known to create opportunities for fundamental reform. To achieve victory over infectious diseases, all must finally decide how to defeat global poverty and inequality. Society must show its best qualities by being united and being able to deliver a complete and final victory over tuberculosis as soon as possible.

External Migration

The oil boom that began in the 2000s boosted wages in Russia and Kazakhstan and created opportunities in the labour markets of these two countries to fill the labour gap in their domestic markets by attracting migrants from Kyrgyzstan, Tajikistan and Uzbekistan. While Russia experienced a significant demographic decline, which was particularly sharp in the 1990s, the Kyrgyz Republic, especially Tajikistan and Uzbekistan, experienced substantial population growth. These countries' radically different demographic situations, therefore, created an opportunity for mass labour migration.

At the end of 2020, the Russian Ministry of Internal Affairs announced that the number of migrants during the pandemic decreased from 9–11 million to about 6 million (Kurnosova & Lisicyna, 2020). Then it began to recover gradually, and in September 2021, the Ministry estimated the number of foreign migrants at 7 million people (RBK, 2021), most of which were from Central Asia.

The type of employment undertaken by migrants from the Kyrgyz Republic, Tajikistan and Uzbekistan in Russia is quite different. Kyrgyz nationals mainly work in the services sector, where approximately 60 per cent of citizens of both sexes are employed. This is largely because most Kyrgyz migrants already have a sufficient command of Russian when they first arrive in Russia. According to the Asian Development Bank, about 60 per cent of those who come from Tajikistan work in construction and only 17 per cent in trade and services (Asian Development Bank, 2020). Uzbekistan's citizens work mainly in construction, housing and communal services, transport and logistics, retail and wholesale trade, and catering (Degot'kova, 2022).

Such complementarity in demographics can, in purely demographic terms, be called a win-win situation since some countries' lack of labour force on one hand was compensated by a surplus in others on the other. This complementarity has eased the situation in the labour market of the migrants' countries of origin and provided significant material support for their population through remittances. In Tajikistan and the Kyrgyz Republic, migrant remittances have become even greater in number than export figures.

However, despite the undeniable short and medium-term benefits, labour outflow is associated with a drain of skilled workers from these countries in the long term. Such migration creates social risks and costs, including poor

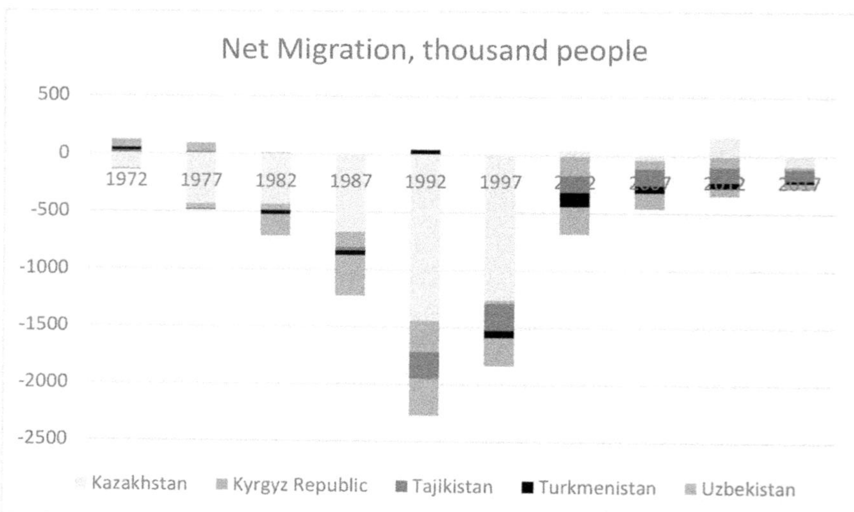

Figure 3.24 Net migration from the countries of Central Asia (1972–2017)
Source: World Bank (2022c).

living conditions for migrants, limited labour protections, safety at work, and inadequate childcare for their families at home in Russia.

Considering the features of net migration from the countries of Central Asia (Figure 3.24), we can see the large outflow of the population in the late 1980s and throughout the 1990s (World Bank, 2022c). During these years, about 10 million people left the region. It was mainly the Russian-speaking population, which after the collapse of the Soviet Union, emigrated permanently to the Russian Federation. Many who left were members of the middle class and the intelligentsia. They worked in state and educational institutions, at industrial enterprises, and occupied pedagogical, technical and engineering positions. This drain of qualified personnel further exacerbated the sharp decline in the Central Asia region's economies.

Remittances

Remittances are an essential source of external financing in the countries of Central Asia. This echoes the growing importance of remittances worldwide, where remittance flows exceeded 5 per cent of GDP in 54 countries in 2020 (TheGlobalEconomy, 2020a). The World Bank estimates that remittance flows to low and middle-income countries (LMICs) will reach $589 billion in 2021, up 7.3 per cent from the previous year. Remittances currently account for more than three times that of official development assistance and, excluding China, are more than 50 per cent higher than the contribution of foreign direct investment to GDP (Ratha, 2021). Remittances to Central Asia mainly come from Russia, as the citizens of these countries quickly settle in Russia, due to the shared history and culture. In addition, the absence of a visa regime and pre-existing knowledge of the language facilitate migrants' assimilation into their new country. Due to the ageing of its population, Russia must attract labour from abroad for many years to come.

Figures 3.25–3.26 show the total volumes of remittances and their relation to GDP in five Central Asian countries (World Bank, 2022c). According to this indicator, Uzbekistan ranks twenty-third in the world among countries with a population of more than one million, and the Kyrgyz Republic and Tajikistan rank second and third worldwide (TheGlobalEconomy, 2020a). The volumes of remittances are so high that they exceed the state budgets in these two countries.

In May 2022, the World Bank published its study on remittance flows to Low and Middle Income Countries or LMICs (World Bank, 2022e). The top five countries where the inflow of remittances makes up the highest share of GDP include two countries in Central Asia. The list is as follows – Lebanon (54 per cent), Tonga (44 per cent), Tajikistan (34 per cent), Kyrgyz Republic (33 per cent) and Samoa (32 per cent).

Estimates show that remittance flows to the countries of Central Asia, the primary source of which is Russia, will likely decrease by about 1.6 per cent in 2022 (World Bank, 2022e), depending on the scale of the war in Ukraine.

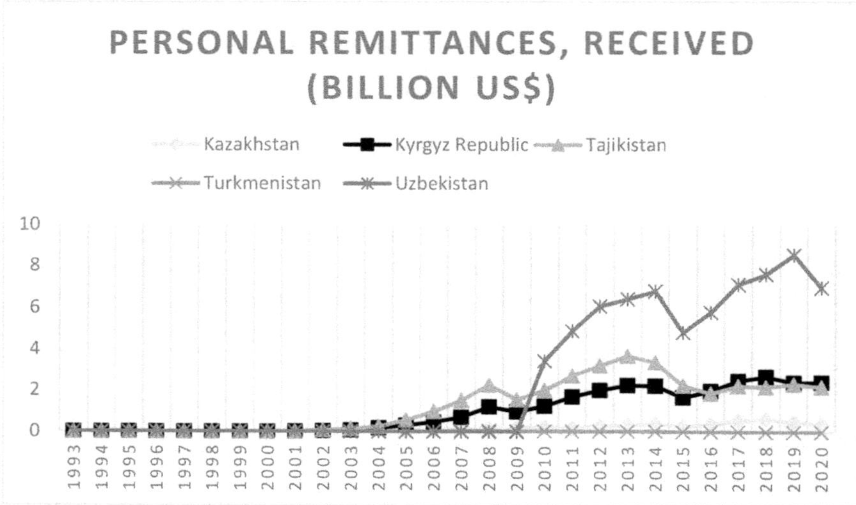

Figure 3.25 A total volume of remittances to Central Asian countries (1993–2020)
Source: World Bank (2022c).

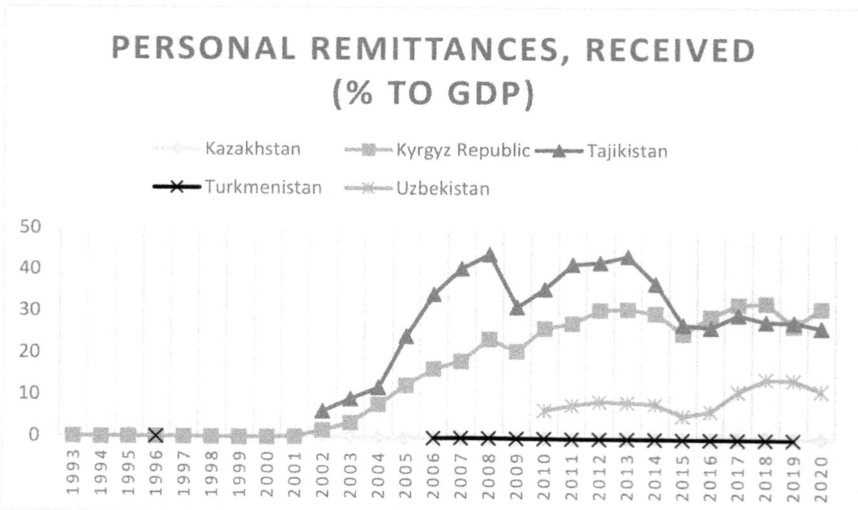

Figure 3.26 Remittances to Central Asian countries as a percentage of GDP (1993–2020)
Source: World Bank (2022c).

This decline, combined with rising food, fertiliser and oil prices, is likely to increase food security risks and exacerbate poverty in many of these countries.

Migrant remittances are highly dependent on their host countries' economic situation and the exchange rate of the respective currencies. From Figure 3.25–3.26, it can be seen that the remittances, especially to Tajikistan and Uzbekistan, experienced drops in 2008, 2014 and 2020, which were associated with the global financial crisis, the imposition of Western sanctions against Russia, and the onset of the coronavirus pandemic, respectively. During these years, the Russian economy declined with a subsequent severe ruble devaluation against major international currencies. The more stable remittances from Kyrgyz migrants are explained by the fact that most Kyrgyz people fluent in Russian work in the services sector, which is more resistant to external shocks. In addition, once the Kyrgyz Republic joined the Eurasian Economic Union (EAEU) in 2015, Kyrgyz migrants received equal labour rights to Russian citizens.

The tendencies of external migration from the relatively prosperous Kazakhstan deserve particular mention. According to the World Bank, the net population outflow from Kazakhstan in the 5 years to 2017 amounted to approximately 90,000 people (World Bank, 2022c). If one takes into account the large number of so-called oralmans (in Kazakh "returner"), that is, ethnic Kazakhs arriving from neighbouring countries for permanent residence, then the total number of those who left the country becomes much higher. From 1991 to 1 January 2020, 313,256 families or 1,057,280 ethnic Kazakhs returned to their historical homeland and received the status of Oralman (Kunafin, 2020).

It is alarming that representatives of technical specialists, economists and teachers are leaving the country in large numbers. Statisticians recorded an increase in the outflow of highly qualified Kazakhstanis over the past few years. For example, for 9 months of 2017, 11,900 people arrived in the country for permanent residence, study, or work. At the same time, significantly more people, or 28,200, left Kazakhstan for the very same reasons (Finprom, 2017). Around 73 per cent of migrants permanently leaving Kazakhstan are ethnically Russian. In 2019, amendments to Russia's migration legislation allowed Kazakhstani citizens to obtain permanent residence permits upon arrival (Pravo i Status, 2020).

It is also interesting to look at the trends in outgoing remittances from the countries of Central Asia themselves (Figure 3.27). Central Asian migrants also find work in neighbouring Kazakhstan. Most migrants go to Kazakhstan from the Kyrgyz Republic and Uzbekistan. A shared border, convenient logistics, ethnic proximity, and the absence of a language barrier make migration there easy. Although Kazakhstan has stricter migration laws than Russia, and workers earn slightly lower wages than in Russia, the flow of workers and remittances from Kazakhstan remains high (Figure 3.27). It is worth noting that the figure of two to four billion dollars in annual transfers from Kazakhstan is a gross understatement since the wages received in cash by seasonal workers in agriculture are not possible to be tracked and counted.

Some remittances from the Kyrgyz Republic to neighbouring countries are also due to some migrants in seasonal agricultural work in the Kyrgyz part of the Ferghana Valley.

In connection with the sanctions of Western countries against Russia, the fall of its economy and increased inflation there, in March 2022 the World Bank (WB) gave a pessimistic forecast of remittances from Russia to the countries of Central Asia (Ratha & Kim, 2022). According to their calculations, the Kyrgyz Republic and Tajikistan would suffer especially hard since in the first three-quarters of 2021, respectively, 83 and 58 per cent of all external migrants from these countries worked in Russia. Estimates from the WB show that in 2022, remittances to the Kyrgyz Republic would fall by 33 per cent and in Tajikistan by 22 per cent, compared to a year earlier. Since Uzbekistan receives 55 per cent of all migrant remittances from Russia, the decline in remittances could reach 21 per cent.

However, the statistics of July 2022 refuted the pessimistic predictions. According to the Russian Ministry of Internal Affairs, in the second quarter of 2022, a record number of labour migrants entered Russia over the past six years. In April–June of this year, their number reached 3.12 million people, of which 87.3 per cent were from Central Asian countries (Kommersant.ru, 2022). Following the statistics of the National Bank of the Kyrgyz Republic, remittances from Russia in June 2022 increased to a record $303 million. The

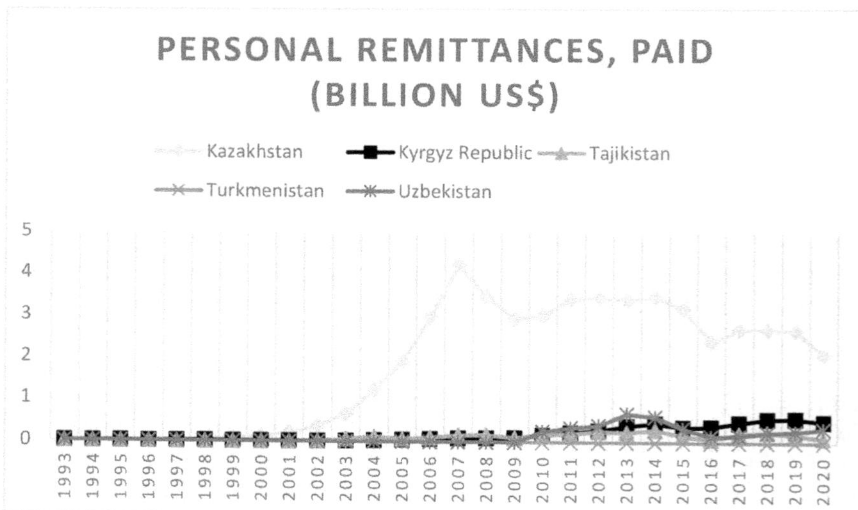

Figure 3.27 A total volume of remittances from Central Asian countries
Source: World Bank (2022c).

previous monthly maximum was recorded in November 2021, amounting to $289 million (Tazabek, 2022). This growth was affected by the strengthening of the ruble against the currency of the Central Asian countries.

The long-term effects of migration from Central Asia are more negative than positive. In social terms, migration leads to a brain drain when the talented and skilled people from Central Asia leave "temporarily" for study or internship, and do not return. This in turn worsens the social structure of the countries. Economically, migration makes the region, especially Tajikistan, Kyrgyzstan and Uzbekistan, more vulnerable to external shocks and reduces pressure on governments to incentivise the creation of more jobs at home.

Changes in Economic Structure

High natural resource prices have attracted large volumes of foreign direct investment (FDI) to the region, primarily in the oil and gas industry and transport infrastructure. It has led to a rapid increase in exports and an improvement in the balance of payments. Countries that did not have significant hydrocarbon deposits, such as the Kyrgyz Republic and Tajikistan, benefitted from rising energy prices indirectly through increased remittances from their labour migrants employed in resource-rich countries, primarily in Russia.

Three decades of intensive, first negative, and then positive economic changes have led to severe structural transformations in each Central Asian nation. The oil, gas, mining, logistics and other services sectors became the critical engines of economic growth and the economy's largest sectors. The production structure has changed since independence (Figure 3.28–3.30). In particular, the share of services as a percentage of GDP, which was marginal during the Soviet era, rose (except for in Kazakhstan), while the share of GDP from agriculture fell. The people laid off as a result of this moved to the countryside, and there were massive closures of industrial companies and weakening social security nets due to a sharp decline in government revenue. Many turned to subsistence farming to earn a living. However, after some time, people began to move to the cities and were employed mainly in the services sector. Such trends have become most visible in the region's poorest countries, the Kyrgyz Republic and Tajikistan (Figure 3.28–3.30). The figures presented also show that the lowest share of agriculture in GDP is in Kazakhstan, and the highest is in Tajikistan and Uzbekistan, where a significant part of the population lives in the fertile Ferghana Valley and is still engaged in food production.

An active export policy has allowed the countries of Central Asia to open to international trade. They are now connected to the global economy through multiple channels, including active trade in goods and services, FDI, labour migration and migrant remittances. A positive functional correlation has emerged between the economic performance of countries and the intensity of their external relations. However, specialisation in the export of natural resources and labour increased the dependence of these countries'

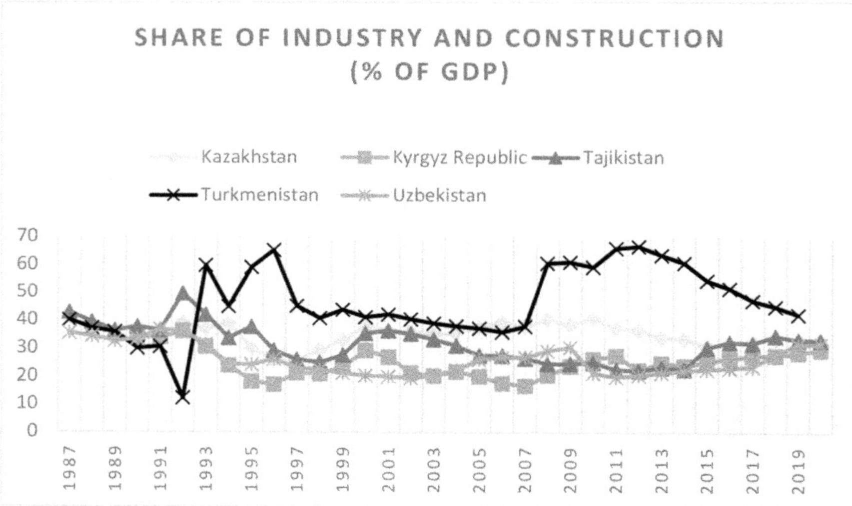

Figure 3.28 Industry and construction's share as a percentage of GDP in Central Asian countries (1987–2019)

Source: World Bank (2022c).

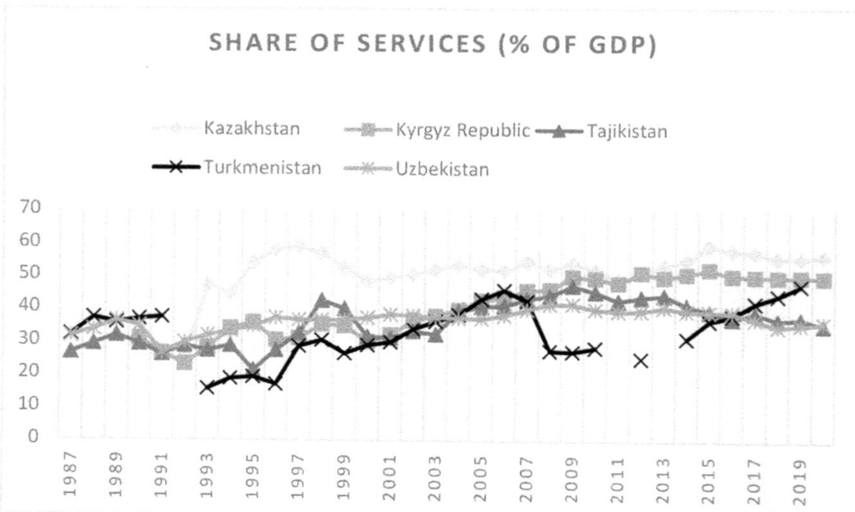

Figure 3.29 Share of services as a percentage of GDP in Central Asian countries (1987–2019)

Source: World Bank (2022c).

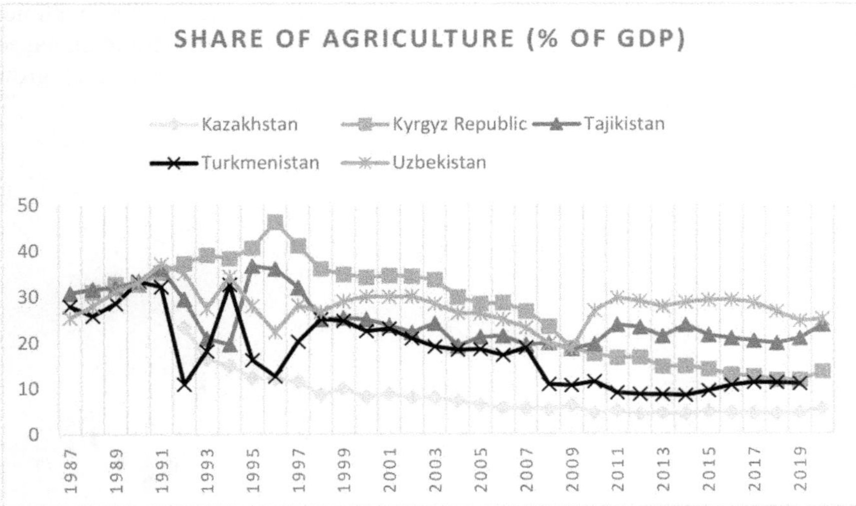

Figure 3.30 Agriculture's share of GDP (as a percentage) in Central Asian countries (1987–2019)
Source: World Bank (2022c).

economies on a limited number of world markets. Economic diversification is now high on the investment policy agenda in these countries.

Even though the incomes of the population have increased significantly over the past two decades, and the proportion of the population below the poverty line has declined, hard work is required to reduce poverty further, overcome existing inequalities, and strengthen national social security systems.

Trade

External Trade

Efficient trade is essential to economic growth, which is why the quality of supply chains is so important. Due to difficult geographic conditions, conducting domestic and foreign business in the landlocked region of Central Asia is expensive. Trade costs increase due to long distances, low economic density, and sometimes complicated regulatory environments and trade regimes. The World Bank estimates that delivery to domestic markets in Central Asia will cost 80–150 per cent of the value of goods sold, compared to 20 per cent in the EU countries (World Bank, 2014b).

Until 1991, Central Asia was part of the unified Soviet economic space, where there were no borders and a relatively efficient trade logistics system. At the same time, most of the manufactured products shipped to the north-west, to the European part of Russia. The collapse of the Soviet Union caused a rupture of economic ties, a sharp drop in GDP, and increased unemployment and poverty in all countries of Central Asia. Trading volumes fell at least twofold (Figure 3.31–3.32). The volume of foreign trade managed to return to previous levels only ten years later and then began to grow quickly, most significantly in the case of Kazakhstan.

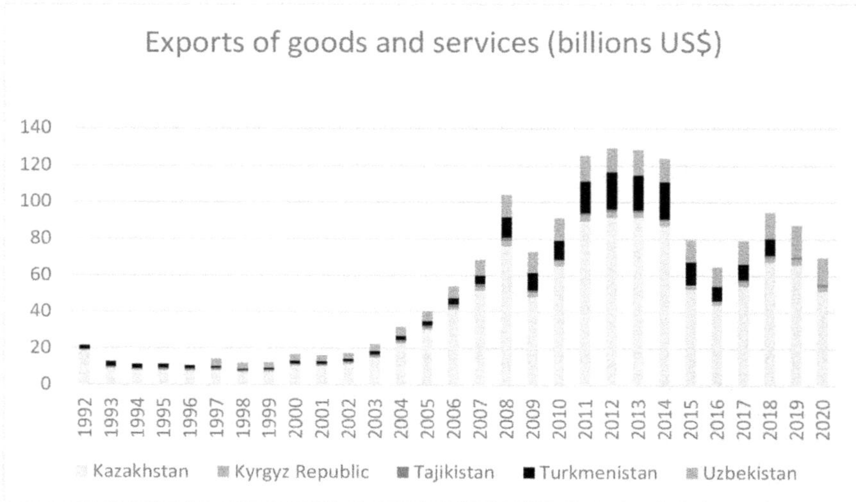

Figure 3.31 Exports of goods and services in Central Asian countries (1992–2020)
Source: World Bank (2022c).

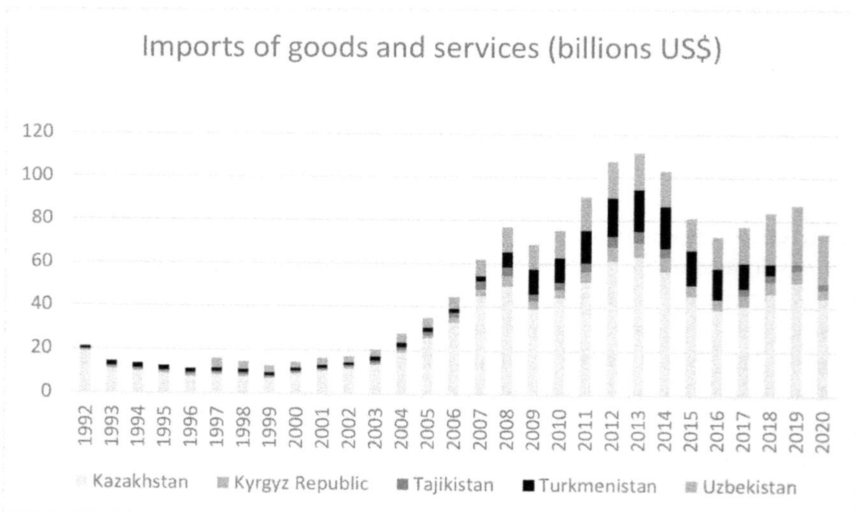

Figure 3.32 Imports of goods and services in Central Asian countries (1992–2020)
Source: World Bank (2022c).

Trade growth has been driven mainly by rising prices for hydrocarbons and metals. Efficient oil and gas pipelines were built, making it possible to export crude oil and gas to the European and Chinese markets. However, if one looks at the trade to GDP dynamics, since the 2010s, this indicator has been decreasing (Figure 3.33–3.34). This was due to both GDP growth and insufficiently efficient logistics supply chains because the quality of both hard and soft transport infrastructure was unsatisfactory.

Now the Central Asian region trades mainly with China, Russia, and the countries of the European Union. Its exports are concentrated primarily on hydrocarbons and metals. As the area is highly dependent on quality export-import supply chains through pipeline, rail, or road networks, providing high-quality logistics is paramount for the region, and for this reason control over logistics costs is critical for the region's wellbeing. Since Central Asia sits between China, Russia, and Europe, which has minimal internal transport resistance, it needs to take measures to improve its standards for providing efficient trade and transit. Otherwise, high costs will make such trade unreliable and unprofitable.

Observing the dynamics of exports and imports, the openness of the economies of the Central Asian countries is evident. If we compare the volumes of foreign trade operations to GDP (Figure 3.29–3.30), they correspond to the average world level. The average export to GDP ratio for 2020 based on 158 countries was 38.72 per cent. The highest value was in Luxembourg – 204.69 per cent and the lowest was in Sudan – 0.44 per cent

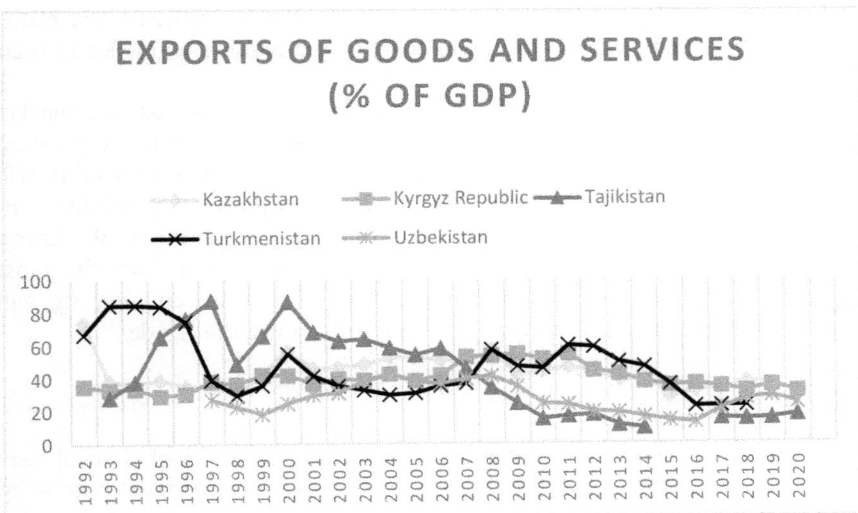

Figure 3.33 Exports of goods and services as a percentage of GDP in Central Asian countries (1992–2020)
Source: World Bank (2022c).

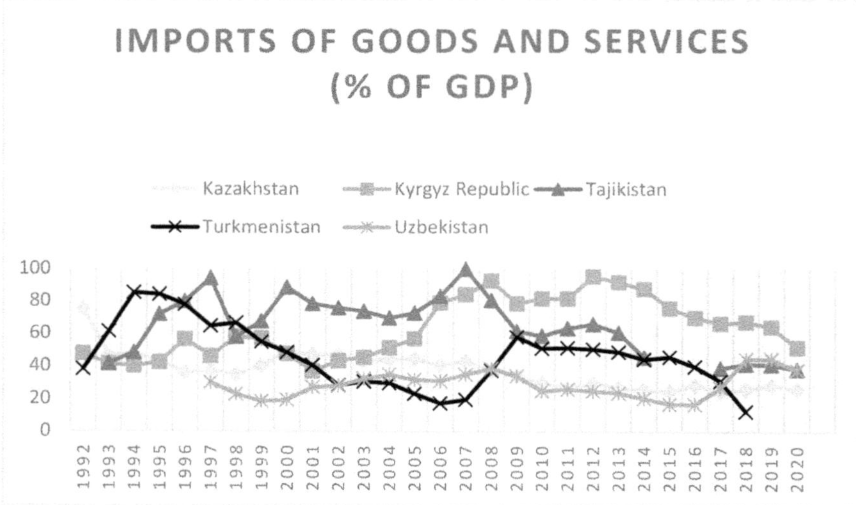

Figure 3.34 Imports of goods and services as a percentage of GDP in Central Asian countries (1992–2020)
Source: World Bank (2022c).

(TheGlobalEconomy, 2020b). The average import to GDP ratio for 2020 based on 158 countries was 43.98 per cent. The highest value was in Hong Kong – 174.92 per cent, and the lowest was in Sudan – 0.35 per cent (TheGlobalEconomy, 2020c). These figures are not poor, considering the transport resistance and the high logistical costs of the region's countries in their foreign trade.

Systematic work to reduce transport resistance would increase the market size and make the region more attractive for investors who want to produce goods for sale both within the area and beyond. The following section will analyse the quality of formal and informal trade in post-independence Central Asia. The main foreign economic partners of the countries of Central Asia are its neighbours – China and Russia. Since trade with the most important trade partners will be analysed in a separate chapter, we will confine ourselves here to describing the features of internal trade.

Internal Trade

Until 2016, internal trade between the independent countries of Central Asia had hardly developed. The main reason for this was that the most populated country in the region – Uzbekistan – did not welcome trade relationships with its neighbours. Located in the geographical centre of Central Asia and sharing borders with all four other states, for various political reasons its borders were closed for trade and even for the passage of people.

Before 2016, just 10 per cent of the Central Asian countries' trade was with neighbouring countries across the region, compared to 47 per cent in the much more diversified East Asia and the Pacific region (Lord, 2015) and about 60 per cent in the EU (European Commission, 2021).

This abnormal situation began to change rapidly due to the new economic policy of openness of the new leadership of Uzbekistan in 2016. Between 2017 and 2018, Uzbekistan's imports from Kazakhstan increased by $569 million, or by over 53 per cent. Total trade with Kyrgyzstan jumped from $242 million to $462 million the same year, with Turkmenistan from $159 million to $274 million. Trade with Tajikistan sharply increased from $124 million to $287 million (Bhutia, 2019).

In 2021, the official bilateral trade volume between Kazakhstan and Uzbekistan grew by another 33 per cent and reached $4.3 billion. The two countries' presidents agreed to increase the trade volume to $5 billion soon and then to $10 billion (The Astana Times, 2022). Uzbekistan is now the leading trading partner of Kazakhstan in Central Asia.

According to official data from the National Statistical Committee of Kyrgyzstan, from 2016 to 2019, Uzbekistan tripled its exports to Kyrgyzstan – from $67 million to $200 million. During this time, Kyrgyzstan's exports to Uzbekistan increased from $125 million to $138 million. According to Uzbek statisticians, the difference is many times greater, and exports to Kyrgyzstan reached $645 million. In 2019 the total trade volume between the countries was $792 million. Uzbek president Shavkat Mirziyoyev has repeatedly stated his plans to bring trade with Kyrgyzstan to $1 billion a year. Here it is necessary to comment on the discrepancies in the figures for mutual trade. The Uzbek data deserve a higher level of confidence since the statistical work in this country has been at a high level since Soviet times (Popov, 2013).

Apart from the officially reported growth in internal trade in the region, it is worth emphasising that these figures do not reflect the full extent of this growth (Kaiser, 1997) since there is a massive amount of uncontrolled trade between countries at the household level (Murzakulova, et al., 2019). It is easy to see this by visiting neighbouring countries' borders and customs points, for example at the popular Dostuk-Dostlik crossing point between Osh in the Kyrgyz Republic and Andijan in Uzbekistan. According to official data, 10,000–12,000 people cross the border daily through this point with "goods for personal consumption", which are mainly commercial (Jeraliev, 2018).

Following Uzbekistan's liberalisation of the border, customs and trade regimes in 2016, the Kyrgyz Republic and Uzbekistan agreed to open six of the seventeen checkpoints that had previously been in operation in Soviet times. Overall, following the opening of these checkpoints, the flow of people between the countries increased dramatically. While 3 million people crossed this border in 2017, in 2018, this number rose more than threefold to reach 9.3 million (Gazeta.uz, 2018).

A similar picture at an even larger scale can be seen at the border and customs checkpoint of Chernyaevka between the cities of Tashkent in Uzbekistan and Shymkent in Kazakhstan (Turaeva, 2018). Officials from the Saryagash region of Kazakhstan, where Chernyaevka is located, say that after improving relations between the two countries and the creation of favourable conditions for crossing the border have led to a significant increase in the number of Uzbek residents visiting Kazakhstan. Before 2016, 6,000 people crossed the border every day, while since 2018, it has been about 27,000 people (Isa, 2018).

"In total, over 10,000 citizens cross the border between Uzbekistan and Tajikistan every day, and the number of people wishing to visit Uzbekistan or Tajikistan is growing daily," the Tajik border troops said in a statement made in April 2018 (Asiaplustj.info, 2018). Four years on, this figure has doubled. "According to our data, about 20,000 people cross the Tajik-Uzbek border daily. It is a very significant number. The regime of free movement of goods and services has been ensured. The frequency of air and road transportation has increased significantly. We agreed to consider the possibility of opening passenger rail transportation between the capitals and other cities of our countries soon," said Tajik president Emomali Rahmon in June 2022 (Avesta, 2020). The two countries' most active border and customs points are currently between Tursunzade and Sariosiyo, and Penjikent and Samarkand.

According to the data from the State Security Service of Uzbekistan, more than 40 million people and 1.7 million vehicles passed through any of the border checkpoints in 2018, which is twice as much as in the previous year (Gazeta.uz, 2018). In the same year, 9.3 million people crossed the border with Kyrgyzstan (3 million in 2017), 20 million (13.8 million in 2017) with Kazakhstan, 5.7 million (1.2 million in 2017) with Tajikistan, 952.6 thousand (574.1 thousand in 2017) with Turkmenistan, and 227.8 thousand (115.9 thousand in 2017) with Afghanistan. Additionally, 4 million people (3.4 million in 2017) passed aviation checkpoints (Gazeta.uz, 2018). For the first time in many years, people were free to visit and, therefore, trade with neighbouring countries. There is no doubt that such freedom of movement and trade will lead to an increase in trust between people, more active business, and then to mutual investment.

The diversity of the Central Asian countries' economies in terms of size, economic structure, and resource availability will benefit from trade based on comparative advantage. Gravity model studies that examine actual and potential trade between the countries of Central Asia show that they trade with each other at levels still below their full potential, indicating the presence of artificial barriers to intra-regional trade (Baier & Standaert, 2020).

How Difficult is it to Trade?

In all previous Ease of Doing Business rankings and the latest one of 2020, countries in Central Asia scored particularly low on the Trading Across

Borders indicator (Doing Business, 2019). Figure 3.35 demonstrates the dynamics of this index over the past five years. Larger numbers indicate stronger performance. The indices for all five countries are at a deficient level. For example, back in 2015, the Kyrgyz Republic ranked 182nd, Kazakhstan – 186th, Tajikistan – 188th, and Uzbekistan – 189th out of 189 countries. But by 2020, the countries' positions had visibly improved – the Kyrgyz Republic was in 89th place, Kazakhstan – 105th, Tajikistan – 141st, and Uzbekistan – 152nd. For comparison, Afghanistan was 177th. This increase in trade was facilitated by more active regional trade in connection with the opening of Uzbekistan and the establishment of new international transport corridors. Nevertheless, these ratings reflect that the countries of Central Asia continue to be in unfavourable conditions for international trade and there is room for growth.

For many years, the World Bank has been conducting studies on the quality of foreign trade, evaluating them by the average time required for exports and imports. Figures 3.36–3.39 show such indicators for Central Asia and some other countries, conducted by the Doing Business methodology used by the World Bank from 2016–2020.

The results differ from the best practices not by a few percentages but by hundreds of per cent. This is, in part, due to the geographic remoteness of markets and poor hard infrastructure, but not only this. The poor results are also related to the poor quality of the soft infrastructure, namely the complicated regulatory framework, bureaucratic barriers and corruption at border crossings. Figures 3.38–3.39 demonstrate this. In the region's

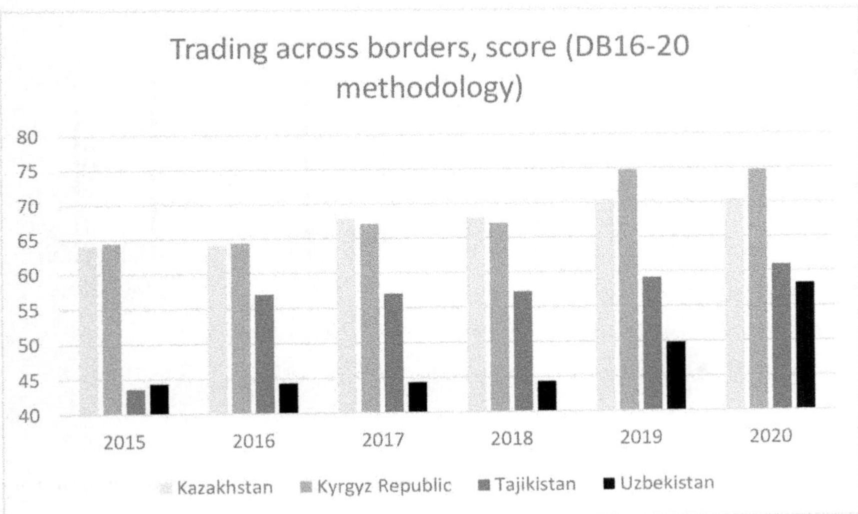

Figure 3.35 Trading across borders indicator in Central Asian countries (2015–2020)
Source: Doing Business (2019).

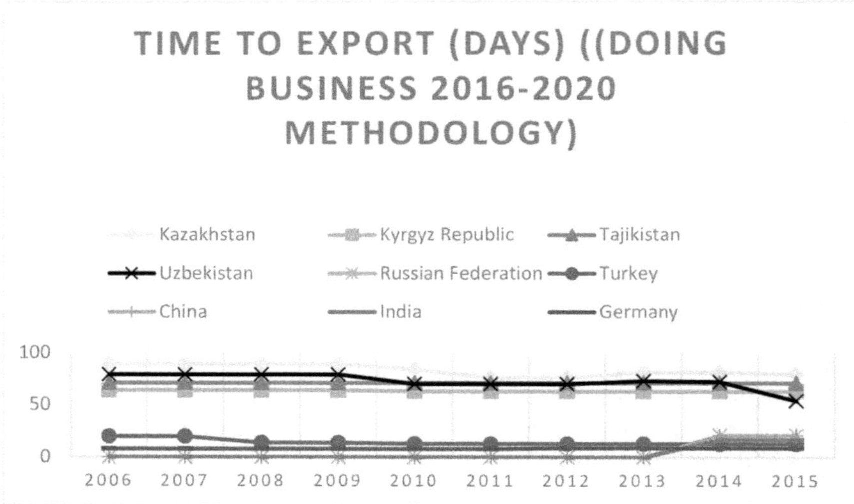

Figure 3.36 Time to export indicator in Central Asia and a few select countries (2006–2015)

Source: Doing Business (2019).

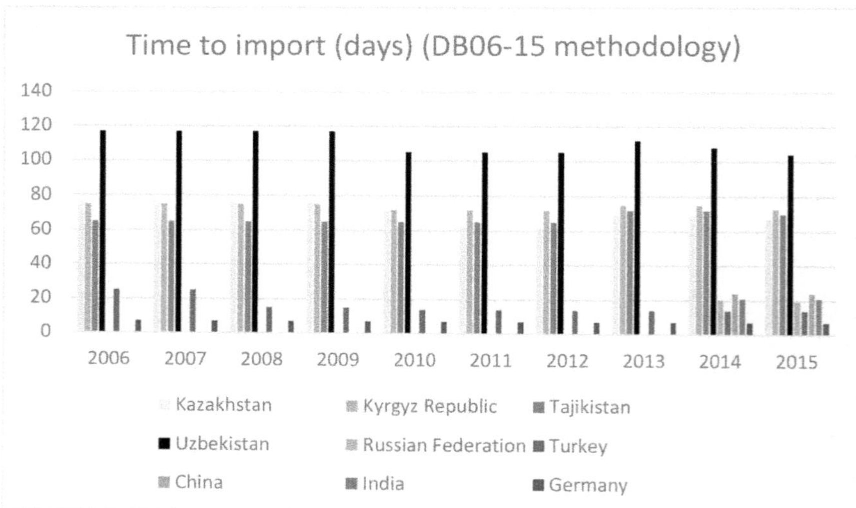

Figure 3.37 Time to import indicator in Central Asia and a few select countries (2006–2015)

Source: Doing Business (2019).

countries, border crossing times (Figure 3.38) and border crossing costs (Figure 3.39) are too high. Border compliance means the time and cost associated with complying with a country's customs regulations, other regulatory checks and the processing of the crossing.

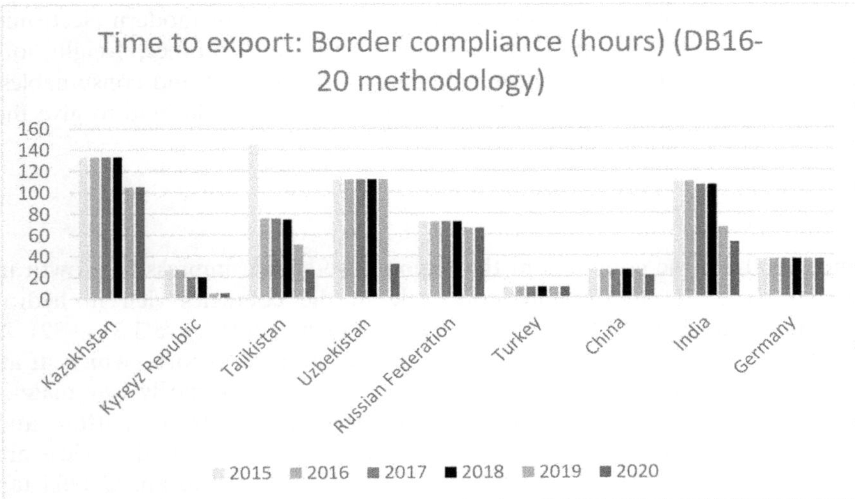

Figure 3.38 Time to export indicator (border compliance) in Central Asia and a few select countries (2015–2020)
Source: Doing Business (2019).

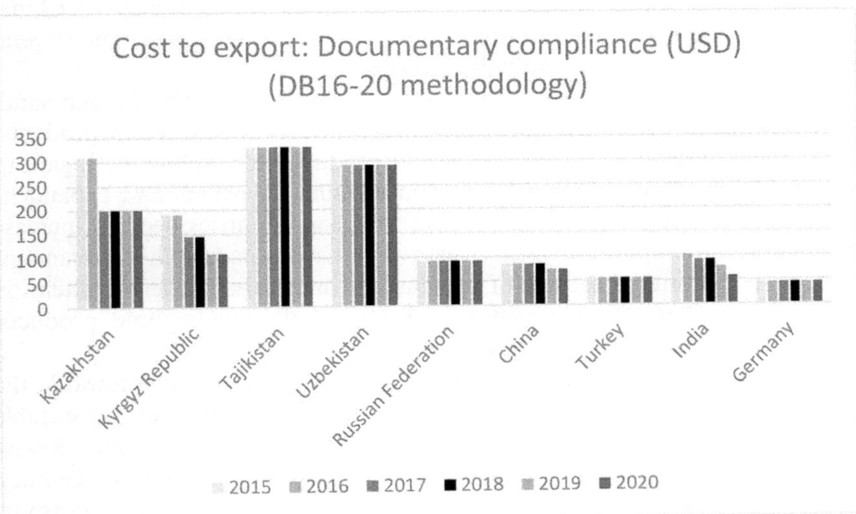

Figure 3.39 Time to export indicator (documentary compliance) in Central Asia and a few select countries (2015–2020)
Source: Doing Business (2019).

Nevertheless, in several countries in the region, positive trends are visible, such as in the case of border crossings in the Kyrgyz Republic. From the figures presented, it can be seen that large and systematic work will be required to reduce transaction costs and improve the region's competitiveness in foreign trade. One positive change on the horizon which will help with this is a customs union mechanism. Within the framework of modern electronic procedures, new techniques for customs clearance, insurance, freight forwarding and storage of goods, maintenance of equipment and consumables, and the hospitality industry will be launched, which should help to give the region that competitive edge it requires.

Conclusion

Since 2000, all the countries in the region have shown impressive growth in foreign trade. It is especially noticeable in the countries rich in hydrocarbons – Kazakhstan, Uzbekistan, and Turkmenistan (Figure 3.31–3.32). A significant shortcoming is the lack of diversification of exports, which in all five countries focused on narrow commodity groups, primarily raw materials – crude oil, natural gas, ferrous and non-ferrous metals, cotton, and wheat. Exports of higher value-added manufactured goods and services are low. The exception here is the export of cars from Kazakhstan, Uzbekistan and the provision of tourist services in the Kyrgyz Republic. There is practically no export of high-tech goods.

Imports to the countries of Central Asia consist mainly of manufactured goods, transport, engineering, and construction services. Unsurprisingly, exports are concentrated in a few wealthy neighbouring markets – China, Russia and the EU. Trade volumes with Turkey, Iran, Korea, and several other Asian countries are gradually growing.

How badly does Central Asia need trade diversification? On the one hand, more significant horizontal differentiation (the number of types of products) and vertical differentiation (the quality of products), will allow the region to consolidate trade relations with its main economic partners and expand its sales markets. On the other hand, Central Asian countries need to increase production and exports in areas where they have a competitive advantage, such as in the critical sectors of oil, gas and minerals. Particular attention should be paid to the production and export of manufactured products, which are characterised by high capital intensity.

The countries should develop high-tech industries and move towards the digitalisation of their economies. With an educated population, favourable demographics, and dynamic and ambitious neighbours such as China, Russia and India, the focus should be on developing technology in the 21st century.

As mentioned earlier, in addition to the region's geography, transport resistance depends not only on the quality of hard infrastructure, but also on the quality of soft infrastructure, which are internal barriers to cross-border flows of goods and services, the speed of customs procedures, and legislation, etc. It is also problematic that, along with underdeveloped transport infrastructure, the countries of Central Asia still have problems with the ease of doing business compared to other parts of the world.

Great opportunities lie ahead for Central Asia due to its proximity to large Asian markets, its location at the centre of the rapidly integrating Eurasian economic space, and the potential for greater intra-regional economic integration. However, overly "thick" borders, even after thirty years, remain severe obstacles to domestic and foreign trade and transit.

Business Environment and Investment Climate

The analysis we have presented in the previous sections of this chapter shows the critical importance of transport infrastructure for accelerated economic growth and domestic and foreign trade. But the economic development of any territory is determined not only by the presence of modern roads or railways, modern power plants or power lines, but also by the quality of the business environment and investment climate.

For a comparative analysis of the quality of doing business and the investment climate in different countries, it would be correct to refer to ratings determined by recognised international institutions. One such rating in this area is the Ease of Doing Business Index, compiled by the World Bank, which compares the ease of doing business in different countries (World Bank Group, 2019).

High scores in this index indicate the quality and ease of business regulation, as well as the quality of protection of property rights. The purpose of the index is to provide research data on the impact of government regulation of business on economic growth. Research findings indicate a strong relationship between better business practices and economic growth. These Ease of Doing Business Indices compare the laws, regulations and rules relating to doing business. This index does not consider infrastructure, inflation, crime, or business profitability (World Bank, 2021c).

In the most recent 2020 Ease of Doing Business ranking, out of 190 countries, the four Central Asian countries ranked as follows: Kazakhstan ranked 25th, Uzbekistan 69th, the Kyrgyz Republic 80th, Tajikistan 106th, and, for comparison, Afghanistan ranked 173rd (World Bank Group, 2019). Figures 3.40–3.41 show the performance achieved in this ranking and the corresponding positions taken by the Central Asian countries compared to a few other countries.

There are several points to mention from the data. Firstly, according to the integral indicator, the region's countries occupy quite different rankings. Therefore, in the region, there are countries from which one can take an example. Secondly, in the Trading across Borders indicator, the region's countries perform poorly. Thirdly, and according to this same indicator, all countries showed some progress compared to similar data in 2014. This is

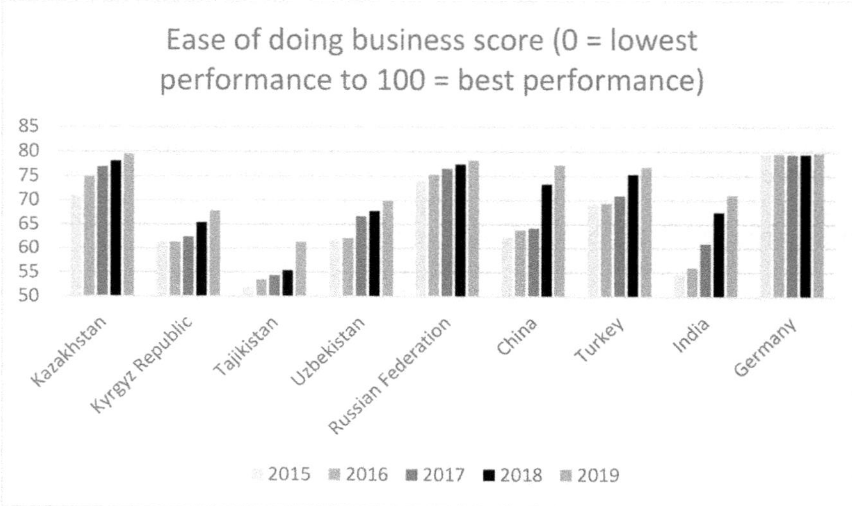

Figure 3.40 Ease of Doing Business score in Central Asia and a few select countries (2015–2019)
Source: World Bank (2021c).

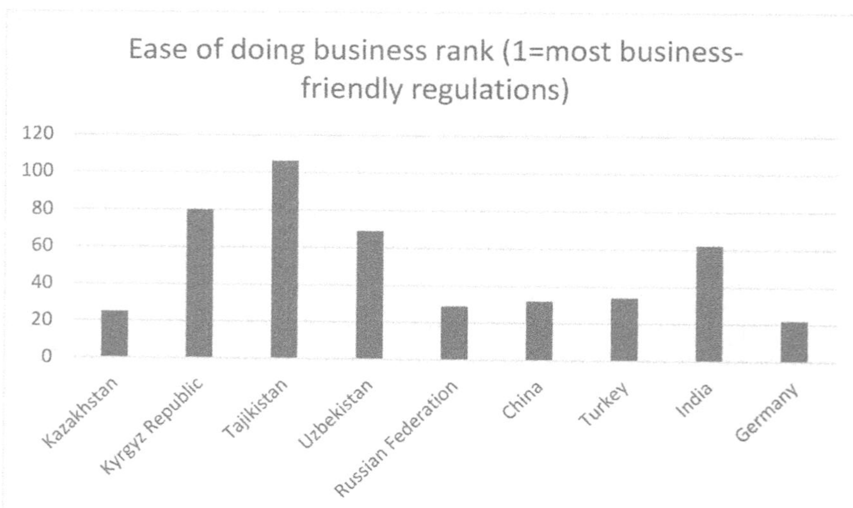

Figure 3.41 Ease of Doing Business ranking in Central Asia and a few select countries (2015–2019)
Source: World Bank (2021c).

largely due to the new policy of the leadership in Uzbekistan to open trade with its neighbours.

Interestingly, on 16 September 2021, the World Bank decided to stop publishing the annual Doing Business ranking. The bank clarified that it decided to do so in connection with the appearance in June 2020 of information about violations in the preparation of past reports. In December 2020, following an internal investigation, the World Bank reported that its governors pressured staff directly involved in preparing the ranking to manipulate data for some countries, incorrectly changing their positions in the ranking. In the future, the World Bank promised to develop a new approach to assessing the business and investment climate (World Bank Group, 2021).

It is only a regret that the critical studies carried out since November 2001, on which more than 800 scientific papers have been published, have been suspended by the World Bank for purely political reasons. At the same time, these actions prove how important the publication of such ratings was since they were recognised at the highest political level.

Other popular ratings do not cover every Central Asian country, a fact alone which indicates the region's insufficient integration into the world economy. In the latest World Economic Forum report on global competitiveness in 2020, Kazakhstan ranked 55th, the Kyrgyz Republic 96th and Tajikistan 104th out of a list of 141 countries (World Economic Forum, 2020). The report mentioned the imminent inclusion of a rating for Uzbekistan in future reports. The 2014 ranking mentioned only Kazakhstan and the Kyrgyz Republic, which ranked 50th and 121st out of 148 countries surveyed.

A breakdown of the ratings by component shows that the countries of Central Asia have had relatively good trade policies for a long time. Still, their implementation is weak, with corruption being the main obstacle in both countries. The report cites the main barriers to exports as being informal barriers, lack of knowledge about foreign markets, delays at border crossings and underdeveloped national financial systems. These data indicate the need to improve the institutional infrastructure related to international trade. The World Economic Forum publishes studies on the quality of various types of infrastructure in various countries. The quality of infrastructure is critical for everyone, but it is vital for the development of landlocked regions. That is why a separate chapter is devoted only to the analysis of the quality of infrastructure.

The World Economic Forum's data show that the costs of corruption, bribery, theft and tax evasion, and other illicit financial flows (IFF) for developing countries amount to $1.26 trillion annually. Even EU members lose $132 billion annually due to corruption (Fleming, 2019). According to various estimates, the losses associated with corruption in the global economy are incredibly high. According to the UN data (United Nations, 2018), they amount to $2.6 trillion, or 5 per cent of global GDP.

Such corruption is corroborated in the Corruption Perceptions Index compiled by the international non-governmental organisation Transparency International to reflect the level of corruption perception by analysts and entrepreneurs. The 2021 index, published in January 2022, ranks 180 countries based on the situation between May 2020 and May 2021 (Transparency International, 2021). Kazakhstan was in 102nd place, Uzbekistan 140th, the Kyrgyz Republic 144th, Tajikistan 150th, and Turkmenistan in 159th place out of 180 countries included in the rating. The situation has changed for the better compared to 2014, but not much. Then Kazakhstan was in 140th place, the Kyrgyz Republic – 150th, Tajikistan – 154th, Turkmenistan and Uzbekistan – 168th place, out of the 176 countries included. To create a favourable investment climate, the region's governments must demonstrate their commitment to fighting corruption. In this regard, the development of modern institutions should be a priority, and the sooner, the better.

Along with active trade, the effective economic transformation of any country requires foreign investment. Investments create jobs, fill public budgets with direct and indirect taxes, and strengthen national currencies. Investments fall into two categories – direct investment, which bypasses state institutions and goes directly to the private sector, and public investment, which goes straight to government budgets. They can be grants or loans from public institutions – the governments of donor countries or international financial institutions. How investments are attracted to the countries of Central Asia will be discussed in the following section.

Foreign Direct Investment

The two main reasons for the inflow of foreign direct investment (FDI) into the region are that it is rich in natural resources and has promising markets. The rise in world prices for energy and other commodities over the past twenty years has been a critical driving force behind these investments. Currently, FDI creates opportunities for more active development of the extractive industries and services sector, and it increases exports. All these investments are essential sources of government revenue.

FDI stocks rose rapidly in all five countries that benefitted directly or indirectly from the commodity boom. Central Asian producers are limited mainly to the supply of natural resources and labour in the current global supply chains. Labour-intensive manufacturing industry and infrastructure received a much smaller share of FDI, and the agricultural sector received almost nothing. Commodity-rich countries of Central Asia have considerable national savings, so they attract FDI mainly to master new technologies and learn from investors' experiences. It is worth emphasising that with an educated population, the countries of Central Asia are more interested in investments in the innovative economy, as well as in the technologies and professional knowledge offered by investors, than indirect financial benefits. However, investment in high tech is still minimal. There are only a few examples of high-tech investments which manufacture final products, such as in the automotive industry. The impact of FDI on employment is limited as well.

The volume of accumulated FDI in the countries of Central Asia in 2019 reached $378.2 billion (Yergaliyeva, 2020). Among the countries of Central Asia, Kazakhstan is a leader in attracting FDI, with the extraction of natural resources accounting for more than 70 per cent (Cohen, 2019). FDI inflows to Kazakhstan in 2019 decreased by 17 per cent compared to the previous year and amounted to $3.1 billion. Statisticians estimate FDI stock at about $150 billion (United Nations, 2020).

Thanks to the aforementioned economic reforms in Uzbekistan, FDI inflows in 2019 more than tripled from the previous year to $2.3 billion, while the FDI total stock amounted to $9.5 billion (United Nations, 2020). Companies from Russia and China invested in the oil and gas sector, a French company invested in uranium exploration and production, and companies from Singapore, the UK and the US invested in chemical processing projects.

FDI inflows to Turkmenistan increased by $2.2 billion in 2019, which means that the FDI stock in the country reached $38 billion (United Nations, 2020). According to the OECD report, China is the largest foreign investor in the country. Between 2003 and 2017, almost half of the foreign investment was in oil and natural gas, followed by transport (24 per cent) and metals (10 per cent) (OECD, 2019).

FDI inflows to Kyrgyzstan in 2019 increased compared to the previous year, reaching $209 million, and the total FDI stock amounted to $5.6 billion (United Nations, 2020). Most of the foreign investment goes to mining and primarily gold mining. The leading investors in Kyrgyzstan are Canada, China, the UK, Russia, and Kazakhstan (Santander Trade, 2020a). Kyrgyzstan directs China Eximbank loans for transport and energy projects, and these loans have improved the access of Chinese and other foreign investors to the market (United States Department of State, 2020a).

In 2019, FDI inflows to Tajikistan amounted to $213 million, and FDI stock reached $3 billion (United Nations, 2020). In 2019, Chinese foreign investment, mainly in the mining sector, accounted for almost 76 per cent of all FDI, followed by Russia, the UK and Turkey (United States Department of State, 2020b). Chinese firms that invested in Tajikistan continued to enjoy tax benefits (Santander Trade, 2020b).

Figure 3.42–3.44 shows the FDI dynamics of the countries of Central Asia, both in absolute figures and as a percentage of GDP. It is indeed easy to see a significant share of investments in the oil and gas sector of Kazakhstan and Turkmenistan. Turkmenistan's gas reserves are estimated to be the fourth largest in the world, accounting for around 10 per cent of world reserves. In 2015–2016, FDI in Kazakhstan's oil and gas industry accounted for 17 per cent of global investments in the sector (Samruk-Kazyna, 2018).

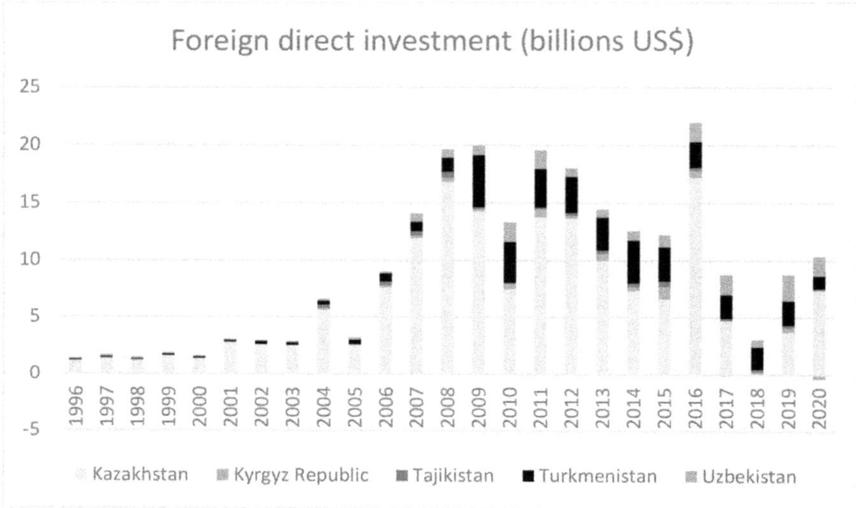

Figure 3.42 FDI in Central Asian countries by year (1996–2020)
Source: United Nations (2020).

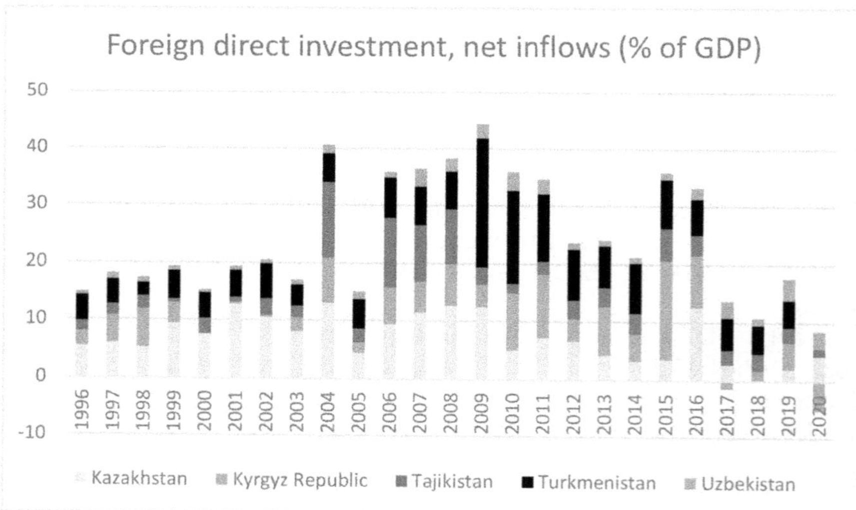

Figure 3.43 FDI net inflows as a percentage of GDP in Central Asian countries (1996–2020)
Source: United Nations (2020).

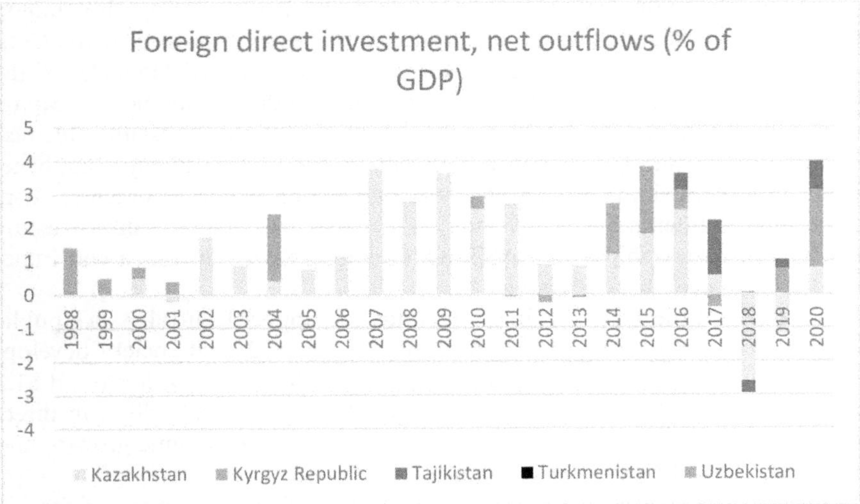

Figure 3.44 FDI net outflows as a percentage of GDP in Central Asian countries (1998–2020)
Source: United Nations (2020).

Financial Resources and Foreign Assistance

There are several other external economic relations between Central Asia and the economic centres of the modern world. These include financial flows, official development assistance, transport and transit, migration and remittances, and institutional linkages. In general, financial markets in the region are underdeveloped, and in most countries, the state has a significant role in them. The global financial crisis of 2008–2009 exposed the region's financial sector's vulnerability as well. It has become particularly acute in Kazakhstan, where it has weakened the state's budgetary position and diverted resources that could be used to promote economic growth.

In addition to external flows related to trade and FDI, another type of financial flow is portfolio investment, carried out by the National Fund of the Republic of Kazakhstan or a similar institution in Turkmenistan.

Except for the financial sector in Kazakhstan, similar institutions in other countries have little or no connection with the global financial markets. In that respect, it is appropriate to mention Astana International Financial Center (AIFC), a dedicated territory in the capital of Kazakhstan with a particular legal regime (AIFC, 2022). The government of Kazakhstan conceived the AIFC project back in 2015 to link the economies and financial structures of the countries of Central Asia, the Caucasus, the EAEU, Western China, Mongolia, the Middle East and Europe. In July 2018, its official opening took place, and in July 2020, the government approved its development strategy until 2025. Its uniqueness lies in the fact that the AIFC operates based on English common law, and the legal status of the financial centre is even enshrined in the Constitutional Law of the Republic of Kazakhstan. The official language of the AIFC is English. Its main strategic objectives include the development of capital markets, asset management, financial technologies (fintech), Islamic finance, private banking, and green finance. Residents of the centre will enjoy tax benefits for fifty years, simplified currency, visa, and labour regimes. The centre's core is the Astana International Exchange (AIX) stock exchange. Its infrastructure was built in partnership with NASDAQ, Goldman Sachs, the Silk Road Fund, and the Shanghai Stock Exchange.

The EU and the US provide grant funds to support Central Asia's public and political institutions, environmental projects, and civil society development. Between 2014 and 2020, the EU provided the region with around $1.2 billion in financial aid. The US has provided more than $9 billion in direct assistance to the region to support democratic reform, economic growth, and humanitarian aid (Yergaliyeva, 2020).

Official Development Assistance (ODA), a considerable source of foreign exchange earnings for these countries in the 1990s, has become less important. However, it remains significant for implementing expensive and technically complex infrastructure projects. To date, donor assistance continues to be provided only to low per capita income countries such as the Kyrgyz Republic, Tajikistan and Uzbekistan. Kazakhstan has now become a donor to various international development institutions.

Sovereign Debt

The situation with the sovereign debt of the post-Soviet countries deserves special attention. Figures 3.45–3.47 show impressive sovereign debt-to-GDP dynamics from the 2000s to the present day and a forecast till 2027 for twelve post-Soviet countries (IMF, 2022). We compared the data with other countries to demonstrate general borrowing patterns for all post-Soviet countries, specifically Central Asia.

In the 1990s, almost all countries were forced to take loans from international development institutions such as the World Bank and the International Monetary Fund. Some countries issued sovereign debt, such as government bonds. In a few countries, the situation with their obligations reached a critical level. Their sovereign debts to GDP ratio have greatly exceeded sustainable levels. For example, in 1998, it reached 160 per cent in Moldova, 125 per cent of GDP in the Kyrgyz Republic in 2000, and 110 per cent of GDP in Tajikistan in 2000. Simply put, these countries in the 1990s could not independently maintain the balance of payments and stability in the socio-economic development of their countries. In this regard, by applying to the Paris Club of creditor countries, the Kyrgyz Republic and Moldova achieved a partial write-off and restructuring of their sovereign debts – the Kyrgyz Republic in March 2005, and Moldova in May 2006.

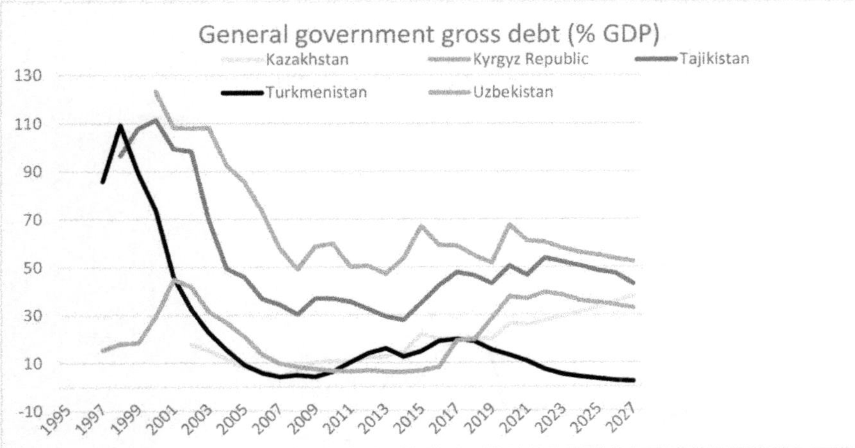

Figure 3.45 Sovereign debt as a percentage of GDP in Central Asian countries (1995–2027)
Source: IMF (2022).

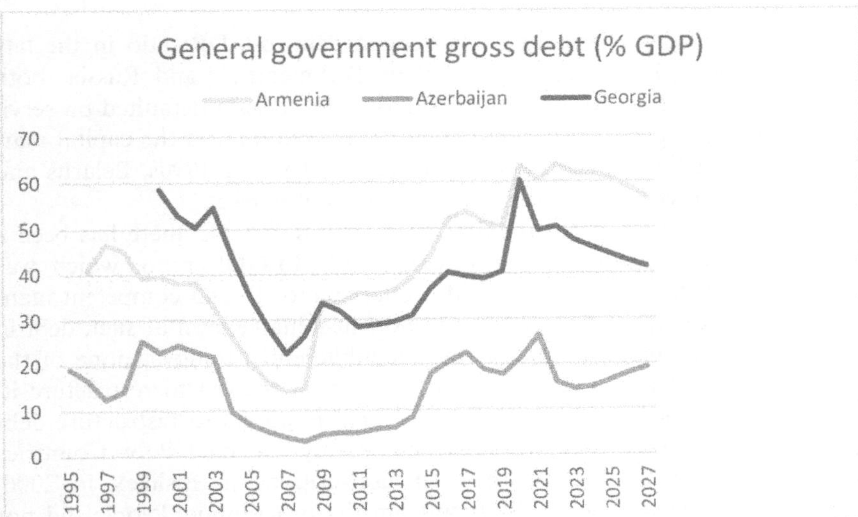

Figure 3.46 Sovereign debt as a percentage of GDP in South Caucasus countries (1995–2027)
Source: IMF (2022).

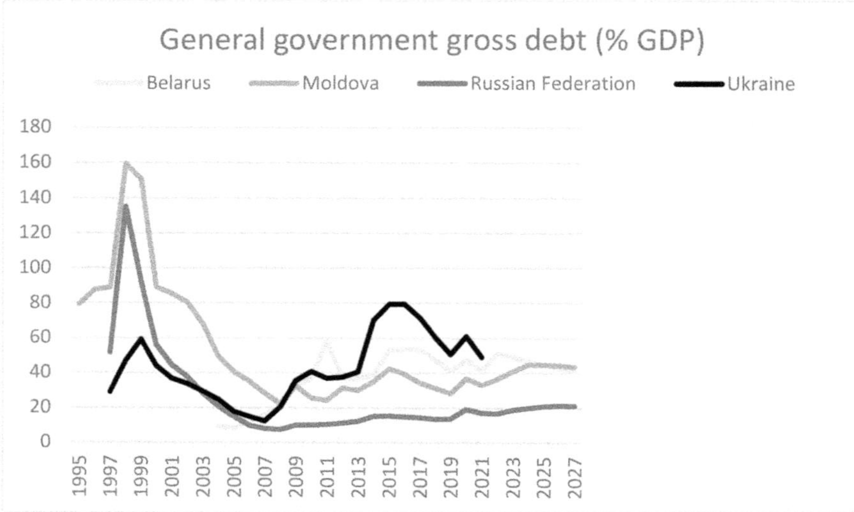

Figure 3.47 Sovereign debt as a percentage of GDP in Belarus, Moldova, Russia and Ukraine (1995–2027)
Source: IMF (2022).

But even more surprisingly, the sovereign debt-to-GDP ratio in the late 1990s exceeded 110 per cent of GDP in Turkmenistan and Russia, both heavy exporters of hydrocarbons. In August 1998, Russia defaulted on servicing its domestic public debt, undermining its reputation in the capital markets for a long time. It is also worth noting that in the 1990s, Belarus and Uzbekistan refused to enter the international debt market.

From the figures, one can see that from the early 2000s, there has been a healthy and sharp drop in the sovereign debt-to-GDP ratio, which was associated with these countries' rapid economic growth and competent management of sovereign debt. Despite the non-sustainable level of such debt in the early 2000s, except for the Kyrgyz Republic and Moldova, none of the post-Soviet countries approached creditors with a request to restructure it. An attempt by the government of the Kyrgyz Republic to restructure debt again under the IMF and World Bank's Highly Indebted Poor Countries (HIPC) initiative even led to mass demonstrations in Bishkek in 2006, demanding the government withdraw from the programme. People did not want the country to be on the list of hopeless jurisdictions that could not pay its debts. Mindful of this reaction, the government of the Kyrgyz Republic introduced a legislative norm under which the sovereign debt-to-GDP ratio should not exceed 60 per cent, which is in line with the IMF recommendations.

The structure of external loans in Central Asian countries varies considerably. The structure of sovereign debt of the Kyrgyz Republic and Tajikistan, the low-income countries of the region, is dominated by obligations to international financial institutions (IFIs) as they offer concessional financing. They provided 40 and 36 per cent of the total loan portfolio, respectively (Bashkatova, 2021).

China remains the primary source of credit in the region, providing loans with a preferential rate of around 2 per cent. Its share in the external debt of Kyrgyzstan and Tajikistan in 2020 was 45 and 52 per cent respectively or more than 20 per cent of GDP. The situation is different in countries rich in natural resources. Loans from China account for 16–17 per cent of the GDP of Turkmenistan and Uzbekistan. Kazakhstan's figure is the lowest at 6.5 per cent (Eurasian Research Institute, 2020). The debt of Kyrgyzstan and Tajikistan to China has stabilised over the past few years and even began to decline (Umarov, 2020). There is a dominance of external debt obligations in these two countries, which make up 77 to 86 per cent of all commitments correspondingly (Bashkatova, 2021). It is still more lucrative to attract funds on international markets than internally. In recent years, the government of Uzbekistan has also begun to attract external loans. According to its Central Bank, the country's total external debt as of 1 July 2020, reached $27.6 billion and compared to the beginning of 2020, the volume had increased by 12.7 per cent (UzDaily, 2020). Turkmenistan currently refrains from attracting external loans, except for from China. Unlike the Kyrgyz Republic and Tajikistan, Kazakhstan mainly attracts financing from private investors in foreign markets. Its leading investors are the US, Russia, Switzerland, and China.

Interestingly, in September 2017, Tajikistan raised $500 million from its first sovereign 10-year international bonds for the first time, at a coupon rate of 7.125 per cent. This deal was designed to finance the Rogun Dam Hydro Power Plant construction since the country could not attract loans from international financial institutions for these purposes (Nelthorpe, 2017).

So far, the countries of the region have been able, on the one hand, to attract significant funds but, on the other hand, to maintain their debt at a sustainable level. The World Bank has conducted a systematic Country Policy and Institutional Assessment (CPIA) for many years. The system assesses the ability of a country's policies and institutions to contribute to poverty reduction, sustainable growth, and the effective use of development assistance. The debt management performance of the governments of the three Central Asian countries compared to other low- and middle-income countries are shown in Figure 3.48 (World Bank, 2022d). High numbers mean better debt management. It can be seen from the presented graph that, apart from Tajikistan, the quality of debt management in two other Central Asian countries is recognised as de facto exemplary.

All Central Asian countries expect accelerated economic growth in the coming years. Correct or erroneous management of public finances can

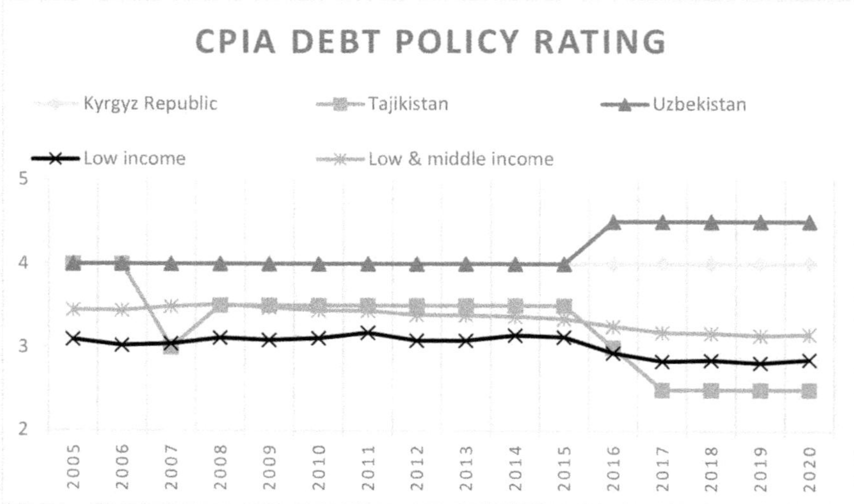

Figure 3.48 CPIA debt policy ratings in Central Asia, low- and middle-income countries (1=low, 6=high), 2005–2020.
Source: World Bank (2022d).

accelerate or slow down such a process, and all the recipients and their donors should pay special attention to this problem.

Conclusion

During the years following independence, the countries of Central Asia began a dynamic process of renewal and growth, determined by a combination of internal and external factors. In domestic politics, the most significant event was the political and economic reforms carried out in Uzbekistan, the most populated country in the region, which borders all the countries of Central Asia. Over the past seven years, President Shavkat Mirziyoyev has been actively reforming domestic and foreign policy. As one of the first steps, he declared improving relations with all Central Asian neighbours his main foreign policy priority, and these initiatives received full support from the leaders of neighbouring states. At the initiative of the President of Uzbekistan, regular summits of the Central Asian countries' heads of state were held, which had not happened for many years. In addition, bilateral meetings of the presidents of Central Asian countries are held regularly. Naturally, such summits strengthen the atmosphere of trust in the region. There is hope for genuine regional cooperation for the first time in many years and the borders between states cease to be walls of mistrust and hostility but become boundaries of interaction and cooperation. In 2019, *The Economist* declared Uzbekistan country of the year for the most improved economy (The Economist, 2019).

Since 2015, two regional initiatives have begun to play an essential role in the region's development. The Eurasian Economic Union (EAEU), including Kazakhstan, the Kyrgyz Republic, Russia, Belarus, and Armenia, is gaining strength. Uzbekistan, which views the role of the EAEU in developing its economy positively, recently joined as an observer state.

First announced in 2013 by the Chinese President while in Kazakhstan, the Belt and Road Initiative, originally called the New Silk Road Initiative, has had a visible economic impact on the development of Central Asia. The Shanghai Cooperation Organization (SCO) is essential in strengthening regional stability and security and includes all the region's countries except Turkmenistan. The SCO has established itself as an influential organisation on the Eurasian continent. These processes will bring clear social and economic benefits to the people of Central Asia, contributing to a more active movement of labour, capital, and goods. However, the same drivers of change can generate geopolitical challenges and intra-country and regional conflicts, such as persistent problems on the border between countries in the Fergana Valley or the civil unrest in January 2022 in Kazakhstan. In the coming years, the region's governments need further efforts to strengthen the atmosphere of trust and must carry out more active reforms to harmonise economic and humanitarian ties and eliminate trade barriers.

The accelerated development of the region's economy will require expanding and deepening economic ties with the centres of world economic power, among which are China, Russia, and Europe. There is vast untapped potential in strengthening various ties with other neighbours – the countries of South Asia – India and Pakistan, as well as with the region's Western neighbours – the countries of the South Caucasus and Turkey. Expanding economic ties will require adapting their economies to each other, the redistribution of human and financial resources between sectors of the economy and shifts in employment and production.

The countries of the region face several key challenges. Among them are the problems associated with population growth, transport and energy infrastructure development, the harmonisation of trade procedures, and the availability of human resources with the necessary qualifications. Additional challenges associated with internal and external migration, the quality of the business environment and investment climate, and access to modern financial services, may hinder the expansion and deepening of economic ties and socio-economic development. Issues related to managing the flow of goods and services, digital connectivity and the improvement in the structure of foreign direct investment between Central Asia and major centres of economic power are not well understood. These include features of production networks, technology transfer, barriers to further market integration, and the future of economic cooperation and division of labour. Underestimating such features might complicate the region's inclusive and sustainable economic growth prospects.

References

AIFC, 2022. Astana International Financial Centre. [Online] Available at: https://aifc.kz/ [Accessed July 2022].

Asian Development Bank, 2020. Strengthening support for labor migration in Tajikistan: assessment and recommendations. [Online] Available at: https://www.adb.org/sites/default/files/publication/681666/support-labor-migration-tajikistan.pdf [Accessed July 2022].

Asiaplustj.info, 2018. Ezhednevno tadzhiksko-uzbekskuju granicu peresekajut svyshe 10 tys. chelovek. [Online] Available at: https://www.asiaplustj.info/ru/news/tajikistan/society/20180402/ezhednevno-tadzhiksko-uzbekskuyu-granitsu-peresekayut-svishe-10-tis-grazhdan [Accessed July 2022].

Avesta, 2020. Iz Dushanbe v Tashkent otpravilsja pervyj za 30 let passazhirskij poezd. [Online] Available at: http://avesta.tj/2022/06/20/iz-dushanbe-v-tashkent-otpravilsya-pervyj-za-30-let-passazhirskij-poezd/ [Accessed July 2022].

Baier, S. & Standaert, S., 2020. Gravity models and empirical trade. In: *Oxford Research Encyclopedia of Economics and Finance.* London: Oxford University Press.

Barro, R. & Lee, J.-W., 2013. A new data set of educational attainment in the world, 1950–2010. *Journal of Development Economics*, Volume 104, pp. 184–198.

Bashkatova, A., 2021. Postsovetskie strany pogruzhajutsja v dolgovuju jamu. [Online] Available at: https://www.ng.ru/economics/2021-09-01/1_8240_economics2.html [Accessed July 2022].

Bhutia, S., 2019. Eurasianet: Uzbekistan's trade with neighbors rises sharply. [Online] Available at: https://eurasianet.org/uzbekistans-trade-with-neighbors-rises-sharply [Accessed July 2022].

Cohen, A., 2019. *The Need for Soft Infrastructure Development in Central Asia: Pathway to Growth*, Berlin: Dialogue of Civilizations Research Institute.

Cutler, D. M. & Summers, L. H., 2020. The COVID-19 pandemic and the $16 trillion virus. *JAMA: The Journal of the American Medical Association*, 324 (15), pp. 1495–1496.

Data Commons, 2022a. Place explorer - Kyrgyzstan. [Online] Available at: https://datacommons.org/place/country/KGZ?utm_medium=explore&mprop=amount&popt=EconomicActivity&cpv=activitySource%2CGrossDomesticProduction&hl=en [Accessed July 2022].

Data Commons, 2022b. Place explorer - Tajikistan. [Online] Available at: https://datacommons.org/place/country/TJK?utm_medium=explore&mprop=amount&popt=EconomicActivity&cpv=activitySource%2CGrossDomesticProduction&hl=en [Accessed July 2022].

Degot'kova, I., 2022. Eksperty VEBa predlozhili privlekat' migrantov finansovymi nadbavkami. [Online] Available at: https://www.rbc.ru/economics/10/05/2022/62742d169a7947331f5f9a40?from=from_main_1 [Accessed July 2022].

Doing Business, 2019. Trading across borders. [Online] Available at: https://archive.doingbusiness.org/en/data/exploretopics/trading-across-borders [Accessed July 2022].

Eurasian Research Institute, 2020. The risks of the high government debt for Central Asia. [Online] Available at: https://www.eurasian-research.org/publication/the-risks-of-the-high-government-debt-for-central-asia/ [Accessed July 2022].

European Commission, 2021. DG trade statistical guide - August 2021. [Online] Available at: https://trade.ec.europa.eu/doclib/docs/2013/may/tradoc_151348.pd [Accessed July 2022].

Finprom, 2017. "Utechka mozgov" narastaet - Kazahstan aktivno pokidajut tehnari, jekonomisty, pedagogi. Ottok kvalificirovannyh kadrov za poslednie 4 goda uskorilsja na 34–88%. [Online] Available at: http://finprom.kz/ru/article/utechka-mozgov-narastaet-kazahstan-aktivno-pokidayut-tehnari-ekonomisty-pedagogi-ottok-kvalificirovannyh-kadrov-za-poslednie-4-goda-uskorilsya-na-34-88 [Accessed July 2022].

Fleming, S., 2019. Corruption costs developing countries $1.26 trillion every year – yet half of EMEA think it's acceptable. [Online] Available at: https://www.weforum.org/agenda/2019/12/corruption-global-problem-statistics-cost/ [Accessed July 2022].

Gazeta.uz, 2018. Bolee 40 mln chelovek peresekli punkty propuska granicy za god. [Online] Available at: https://www.gazeta.uz/ru/2018/12/29/border/ [Accessed July 2022].

Hashem, M. K. et al., 2022. The burden of COVID-19 pandemic on tuberculosis detection: a single-center study. *Egyptian Journal of Bronchology*, 16 (1).

IMF, 2022. General government gross debt. [Online] Available at: https://www.imf.org/external/datamapper/GGXWDG_NGDP@WEO/CAQ/ARM/AZE/BLR/GEO/KAZ/KGZ/MDA/RUS/TJK/TKM/UKR/UZB [Accessed July 2022].

Isa, D., 2018. Granica s Uzbekistanom: ljudskoj potok, stihijnaja torgovlja. [Online] Available at: https://rus.azattyq.org/a/kazahstan-uzbekistan-post-zhibek-zholy/29239431.html [Accessed July 2022].

Jakab, M., Akkazieva, B. & Habicht, J., 2018. *Can People Afford to Pay for Health Care?*, Copenhagen: World Health Organization.

Jeraliev, S., 2018. KPP «Dostuk»: Beskonechnye ocheredi, zhaloby na vzjatki. [Online] Available at: https://rus.azattyk.org/a/kytgyzstan-uzbekistan-border/29246935.html [Accessed July 2022].

Kaiser, M., 1997. *Informal Sector Trade in Uzbekistan*, Bielefeld: Universität Bielefeld.

KG Analytics Intellectual Fund, 2022. School education. [Online] Available at: https://kganalytics.org/wp-content/uploads/2022/06/18-apr-2022_kg-analytics_obzor-shkolnogo-obrazovaniya-v-kr.pdf [Accessed July 2022].

Kommersant.ru, 2022. Trudovye migranty poekhali na record. [Online] Available at: https://www.kommersant.ru/doc/5503251 [Accessed August 2022].

Kunafin, D., 2020. Zakon.kz: Skol'ko oralmanov pribyli v Kazahstan. [Online] Available at: https://www.zakon.kz/5003829-skolko-oralmanov-pribyli-v-kazahstan.html [Accessed July 2022].

Kurnosova, A. & Lisicyna, M., 2020. RBK: V MVD soobshhili o snizhenii chisla migrantov v Rossii. [Online] Available at: https://www.rbc.ru/rbcfreenews/5fd974b79a79476744e0063f [Accessed July 2022].

Lenin, V., 1900. Lenin V. I. Zajavlenie Redakcii «Iskry». *Iskra*, 5 September.

Lord, M., 2015. Regional economic integration in Central Asia and South Asia. [Online] Available at: https://mpra.ub.uni-muenchen.de/66436/1/MPRA_paper_66436.pdf [Accessed July 2022].

Murat, A., 2021. «Bolashak»: kak pervye studenty obuchalis' za rubezhom i kakie izmenenija preterpela programma. [Online] Available at: https://www.inform.kz/ru/bolashak-kak-pervye-studenty-obuchalis-za-rubezhom-i-kakie-izmeneniya-preterpela-programma_a3859756 [Accessed July 2022].

Murzakulova, A., Omorova, G. & Shibkov, E., 2019. Reconsidering the meaning of neighbourship: The transformation of Uzbekistan-Kyrgyzstan border areas after 2016. [Online] Available at: https://www.researchgate.net/publication/335161251_Reconsidering_the_meaning_of_neighbourship_the_transformation_of_Uzbekistan-Kyrgyzstan_border_areas_after_2016 [Accessed July 2022].

Nelthorpe, T., 2017. Inside Tajikistan's baffling Rogun bond issue. [Online] Available at: https://www.proximoinfra.com/articles/6695/inside-tajikistans-baffling-rogun-bond-issue [Accessed July 2022].

OECD, 2018. PISA - Programme for International Student Assessment. [Online] Available at: https://www.oecd.org/pisa/ [Accessed July 2022].

OECD, 2019. *Investment in sustainable infrastructure in Turkmenistan. In: Sustainable Infrastructure for Low-Carbon Development in Central Asia and the Caucasus: Hotspot Analysis and Needs Assessment*. Paris: OECD Publishing.

Popov, V., 2013. *Economic Miracle of Post-Soviet Space: Why Uzbekistan Managed to Achieve What No Other Post-Soviet State Achieved*, Moscow: New Economic School.

Pravo i Status, 2020. Kak bystro oformit' VNZh grazhdanam Respubliki Kazahstan v 2020 godu. [Online] Available at: https://mmc.msk.ru/oformit-vnzh/kak-oformit-vnzh-grazhdanam-respubliki-kazaxstan [Accessed July 2022].

Ratha, D., 2021. World Bank Blogs: Global Remittance Flows in 2021: A Year of Recovery and surprises. [Online] Available at: https://blogs.worldbank.org/peoplemove/global-remittance-flows-2021-year-recovery-and-surprises [Accessed July 2022].

Ratha, D. & Kim, E. J., 2022. Russia-Ukraine conflict: Implications for remittance flows to Ukraine and Central Asia. [Online] Available at: https://blogs.worldbank.org/peoplemove/russia-ukraine-conflict-implications-remittance-flows-ukraine-and-central-asia [Accessed July 2022].

RBK, 2021. V MVD nazvali kolichestvo migrantov v Rossii. [Online] Available at: https://www.rbc.ru/rbcfreenews/615481a49a7947237a4aa621 [Accessed July 2022].

Samruk-Kazyna, 2018. *Overview of Investment Attractiveness of Central Asian Countries*, Nur-Sultan: Sovereign Wealth Fund "Samruk-Kazyna".

Santander Trade, 2020a. Establish Overseas - Kyrgyzstan: Foreign investment. [Online] Available at: https://santandertrade.com/en/portal/establish-overseas/kyrgyzstan/investing-3 [Accessed July 2022].

Santander Trade, 2020b. Establish Overseas - Tajikistan: Foreign investment. [Online] Available at: https://santandertrade.com/en/portal/establish-overseas/tajikistan/investing-3 [Accessed July 2022].

Tazabek, 2022. Denezhnye perevody iz Rossii v Kyrgyzstan v iyune vyrosli do rekordnykh $303 mln. [Online] Available at: https://www.tazabek.kg/news:1798052 [Accessed August 2022].

The Astana Times, 2022. Kazakhstan and Uzbekistan have both observed growth in Bilateral trade, $661 million in agreements already signed. [Online] Available at: https://astanatimes.com/2022/02/kazakhstan-and-uzbekistan-have-both-observed-growth-in-bilateral-trade-661-million-in-agreements-already-signed/ [Accessed July 2022].

The Economist, 2019. Which nation improved the most in 2019?. [Online] Available at: https://www.economist.com/leaders/2019/12/21/what-nation-improved-the-most-in-2019 [Accessed July 2022].

TheGlobalEconomy, 2020a. Remittances, percent of GDP - Country rankings. [Online] Available at: https://www.theglobaleconomy.com/rankings/remittances_percent_gdp/ [Accessed July 2022].

TheGlobalEconomy, 2020b. Exports, percent of GDP - Country rankings. [Online] Available at: https://www.theglobaleconomy.com/rankings/exports/ [Accessed July 2022].

TheGlobalEconomy, 2020c. Imports, percent of GDP - Country rankings. [Online] Available at: https://www.theglobaleconomy.com/rankings/imports/ [Accessed July 2022].

Transparency International, 2021. 2021 Corruption perceptions index. [Online] Available at: https://www.transparency.org/en/cpi/2021 [Accessed July 2022].

Turaeva, R., 2018. Border and road regimes in Central Asia: ordering disorder at Uzbek-Kazakh checkpoint. In: A. Horstmann, M. Saxer & A. Rippa, eds. *Routledge Handbook of Asian Borderlands.* London: Taylor & Francis, p. 462.

Umarov, T., 2020. China looms large in Central Asia. [Online] Available at: https://carnegiemoscow.org/commentary/81402 [Accessed July 2022].

United Nations, Department of Economic and Social Affairs, 2019. World population prospects 2019: Highlights. [Online] Available at: https://population.un.org/wpp/Publications/Files/WPP2019_Highlights.pdf [Accessed July 2022].

United Nations, 2018. Global cost of corruption at least 5 per cent of world gross domestic product, secretary-general tells security council, citing world economic forum data. [Online] Available at: https://www.un.org/press/en/2018/sc13493.doc.htm [Accessed July 2022].

United Nations, 2020. *World Investment Report 2020*, New York: United Nations Publications.

United States Department of State, 2020a. 2020 investment climate statements: Kyrgyz Republic. [Online] Available at: https://www.state.gov/reports/2020-investment-climate-statements/kyrgyz-republic/ [Accessed July 2022].

United States Department of State, 2020b. 2020 investment climate statements: Tajikistan. [Online] Available at: https://www.state.gov/reports/2020-investment-climate-statements/tajikistan/ [Accessed July 2022].

UzDaily, 2020. The total external debt of Uzbekistan makes up US$27.6 billion. [Online] Available at: https://uzdaily.uz/en/post/60195 [Accessed July 2022].

Wagstaff, A., Eozenou, P. & Smitz, M., 2019. *Out-of-Pocket Expenditures on Health: A Global Stocktake*, Washington, DC: World Bank.

WHO, 2021a. Global tuberculosis programme. [Online] Available at: https://www.who.int/teams/global-tuberculosis-programme/tb-reports [Accessed July 2022].

WHO, 2021b. Tuberculosis. [Online] Available at: https://www.who.int/news-room/fact-sheets/detail/tuberculosis [Accessed July 2022].

WHO, 2022a. Global health expenditure database. [Online] Available at: https://apps.who.int/nha/database [Accessed July 2022].

WHO, 2022b. Time: Nearly 15 million deaths are linked to COVID-19. [Online] Available at: https://time.com/6173831/who-covid-19-deaths/ [Accessed July 2022].

Wickham, C., Borowitz, M. & O'Dougherty, S., 1999. *Kazakhstan Health Reform Overview*, Almaty: ZdravReform.

World Bank Group, 2019. *Doing Business 2020: Comparing Business Regulation in 190 Economies*, Washington, DC: World Bank Publications.

World Bank Group, 2021. World Bank Group to discontinue Doing Business report. [Online] Available at: https://www.worldbank.org/en/news/statement/2021/09/16/world-bank-group-to-discontinue-doing-business-report [Accessed July 2022].

World Bank, World Health Organization, 2019. Hospital beds (per 1,000 people). [Online] Available at: https://data.worldbank.org/indicator/SH.MED.BEDS.ZS [Accessed July 2022].

World Bank, World Health Organization, 2020. Incidence of tuberculosis (per 100,000 people). [Online] Available at: https://data.worldbank.org/indicator/SH.TBS.INCD [Accessed July 2022].

World Bank, World Health Organization, 2022. Out-of-pocket expenditure (% of current health expenditure). [Online] Available at: https://data.worldbank.org/indicator/SH.XPD.OOPC.CH.ZS [Accessed July 2022].

World Bank, 2014a. *Kyrgyz Republic Public Expenditure Review Policy Notes: Education*, Washington DC: World Bank.

World Bank, 2014b. Central Asia: Development through trade. [Online] Available at: https://www.worldbank.org/en/region/eca/brief/central-asia [Accessed July 2022].

World Bank, 2018. The human capital project. [Online] Available at: https://openknowledge.worldbank.org/handle/10986/30498 [Accessed July 2022].

World Bank, 2020a. DataBank: Education statistics - All indicators. [Online] Available at: https://databank.worldbank.org/source/education-statistics-%5e-all-indicators# [Accessed July 2022].

World Bank, 2020b. Government expenditure per student, secondary (% of GDP per capita). [Online] Available at: https://data.worldbank.org/indicator/SE.XPD.SECO.PC.ZS [Accessed July 2022].

World Bank, 2021a. Population ages 0–14, total - Kazakhstan, Kyrgyz Republic, Turkmenistan, Uzbekistan, Tajikistan. [Online] Available at: https://data.worldbank.org/indicator/SP.POP.0014.TO?locations=KZ-KG-TM-UZ-TJ [Accessed July 2022].

World Bank, 2021b. Population ages 65 and above (% of total population) – Uzbekistan, Turkmenistan, Kazakhstan, Kyrgyz Republic. [Online] Available at: https://data.worldbank.org/indicator/SP.POP.65UP.TO.ZS?locations=UZ-TM-TJ-KZ-KG [Accessed July 2022].

World Bank, 2021c. Business Enabling Environment (BEE). [Online] Available at: https://www.worldbank.org/en/programs/business-enabling-environment [Accessed July 2022].

World Bank, 2022a. Metadata glossary: DataBank. [Online] Available at: https://databank.worldbank.org/metadataglossary/gender-statistics/series/SP.POP.DPND [Accessed July 2022].

World Bank, 2022b. DataBank: Health nutrition and population statistics. [Online] Available at: https://databank.worldbank.org/source/health-nutrition-and-population-statistics [Accessed July 2022].

World Bank, 2022c. DataBank: World development indicators. [Online] Available at: https://databank.worldbank.org/source/world-development-indicators# [Accessed July 2022].

World Bank, 2022d. DataBank: WDI database archives. [Online] Available at: https://databank.worldbank.org/source/wdi-database-archives# [Accessed July 2022].

World Bank, 2022e. Remittances to reach $630 billion in 2022 with record flows into Ukraine. [Online] Available at: https://www.worldbank.org/en/news/press-release/2022/05/11/remittances-to-reach-630-billion-in-2022-with-record-flows-into-ukraine [Accessed July 2022].

World Economic Forum, 2020. Global competitiveness report 2020. [Online] Available at: https://www.weforum.org/reports/the-global-competitiveness-report-2020 [Accessed July 2022].

Worldometer, 2022a. Central Asia population. [Online] Available at: https://www.worldometers.info/world-population/central-asia-population/ [Accessed July 2022].

Worldometer, 2022b. COVID Live - Coronavirus statistics. [Online] Available at: https://www.worldometers.info/coronavirus/ [Accessed July 2022].

Yergaliyeva, A., 2020. The Astana Times: FDI to Central Asia reached 378.2 billion over past 13 years. [Online] Available at: https://astanatimes.com/2020/12/fdi-to-central-asia-reached-378-2-billion-over-past-13-years/ [Accessed July 2022].

4 Leading Economic Players

Introduction

One of this book's aims is to show that the level of future growth of Central Asia will be related to its level of cooperation with the centres of world economic power. In Soviet times, the opportunities for diverse collaboration were almost exclusively domestic, developed in a single country and oriented towards the north. After gaining independence, countries began to look to connect to external markets. What have they achieved in their thirty years of independence? Who began developing trade and investing in the region, and for what reasons? In the previous chapter, we examined the leading economic indicators related to the development of foreign trade and investment. However, we did not look at which countries are the most active in the region.

Various analysts often view Central Asia in the context of the Great Game – a 19th-century rivalry between Great Britain and Russia in Central Asia. Then, like now, they view Central Asia in terms of a bid for regional dominance between Russia, China and the collective West. Many argue that a rapidly growing China is using its economic power to drive out other competitors and become a major economic and political player in this strategically important region. But an answer to the question of who is most active in the region can only be found by comparing economic and financial data, not mere speculation. Which big powers have the most trade and make the most investments in the region? In this chapter we will examine and compare the data from five of the most influential global powers – China, Russia, the US, the EU and India.

The final part of the chapter discusses the dominant role of the Russian ruble in the economic development of Central Asia. Although there are historical reasons for understanding this phenomenon, given the trends in the economic relations of the countries of the region with other influential powers, the dominance of the ruble should be reconsidered.

DOI: 10.4324/9781003360728-7

China

Trade

We begin our analysis with China, the region's eastern neighbour, which has been working in cooperation with the Central Asian countries for the last thirty years. The results of this cooperation can perhaps best be summarised by looking at the presentation made at the China-Central Asia Trade and Economic Cooperation Forum in January 2022, an event attended by the Economy and Commerce ministers of all five Central Asian nations. At the forum, China's Minister of Commerce said: "In the past three decades, China and the five Central Asian countries have been deepening pragmatic cooperation in economics and trade. We have established comprehensive, energetic, mutually beneficial economic and trade ties" (Liu, 2022). Perhaps the most important result of the forum was the announcement of a joint initiative for the qualitative and sustainable development of Central Asia–China trade and economic cooperation. The parties agreed to expand trade and mutual investment, as well as to boost collaboration in the field of green growth. The parties will actively develop cooperation in the digital economy and energy, oil and gas trade, petrochemical processing, and carbon emissions control.

The ministers underlined that over the past thirty years, trade between China and the countries of Central Asia had increased more than 100 times. China's Ministry of Commerce data shows that trade between China and the five countries grew 25 per cent year on year to $44.6 billion in the first 11 months of 2021, an increase of $6.3 billion from the previous year (Liu, 2022). For Kazakhstan, China's largest trading partner among the five countries, this figure rose by 15 per cent to $23 billion (Liu, 2022).

Figures 4.1–4.3 show the dynamics of exports and imports as well as the total trade volume between China and the countries of Central Asia over the past ten years. Data was taken from UN Comtrade (UN Comtrade, 2022) and the Ministry of Commerce of China (data for 2021 are given for the first eleven months) (Liu, 2022). From the graphs presented, one can note that trade has been at a stable level in the last decade with two periods of slight decline. The decline in trade turnover in 2014–2015 was associated with sanctions imposed by Western countries on Russia, which resulted in the weakening of both the Russian ruble and the currencies of Central Asia, which are closely related to the ruble. The decline observed in 2020 was caused by the coronavirus pandemic, which quickly bounced back the following year. Note that total trade turnover in 2020 and 2021 in Figure 4.3 is presented without a country breakdown.

The growing Chinese market has become increasingly essential for Central Asia producers. From 2015 to pre-pandemic 2019, exports from Central Asia to China grew by about 35 per cent, from $15,054 million to $20,276 million, with Kazakhstan, Tajikistan, and Uzbekistan reporting the fastest growth of over 50 per cent (UN Comtrade, 2022). China's share in total exports from

Figure 4.1 Exports from Central Asia to China (2011–2019)
Source: UN Comtrade (2022).

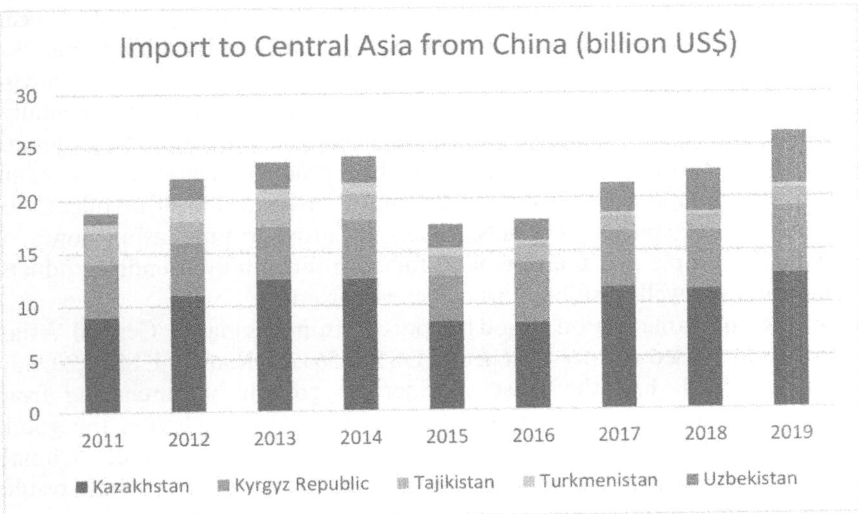

Figure 4.2 Imports to Central Asia from China (2011–2019)
Source: UN Comtrade (2022).

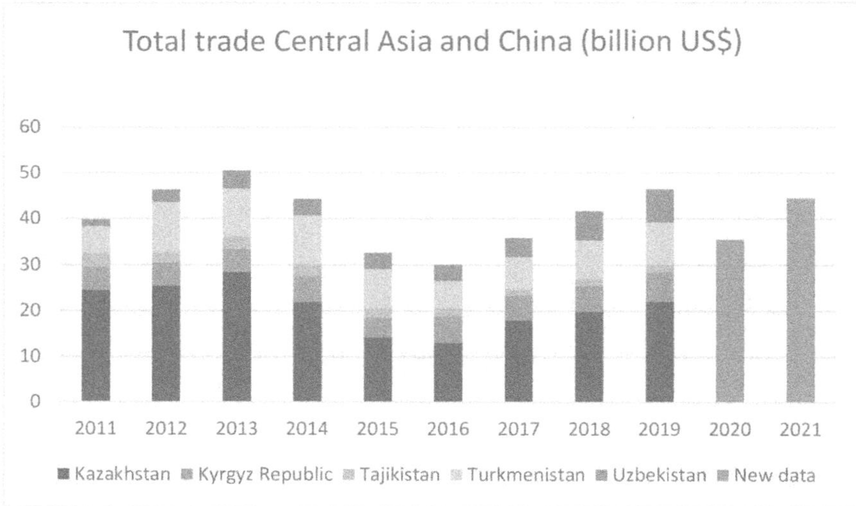

Figure 4.3 Total trade between Central Asia and China (2011–2021)
Source: UN Comtrade (2022) and Liu (2022).

Central Asia grew from 17 per cent in 2013 to an impressive 23 per cent in 2020. Once again, we must note that exports remain one-sided and fall almost exclusively in crude oil and gas sales. Central Asian nations have been discussing options for diversifying their exports to China for a long time. For example, they would like to not only supply raw materials to the vast Chinese market but also products for the processing industry and environmentally-friendly agricultural products. To achieve these goals, Central Asian manufacturers need to improve the quality of their products, increase the volume of deliveries and complete work on the mutual recognition of certificates of conformity for exported products. Given the growing purchasing power of the Chinese people and their demand for environmentally friendly products, such efforts are well-positioned to achieve their goals.

During the same period, goods exported from China to Central Asian countries increased 49 per cent from US$17,563 million to US$26,207million. Uzbekistan had the most considerable growth in purchasing from China, which rose by 126 per cent from 2015 to 2019, whereas the goods exported from China to Tajikistan and Turkmenistan decreased. China's share in the region's total imports fell from 28 to 21 per cent. These results can be attributed to increased competition in the markets and the rising costs of Chinese exports of consumer goods, driven by higher production costs, wages and logistics costs. Another possible factor is the introduction of new tariffs and duties in the Eurasian Economic Union (EAEU) and these countries' economic transformations. Negotiations on creating free trade zones between China and the EAEU countries are currently ongoing.

Table 4.1 China's role as Central Asia's most important trading partner

China's role as Central Asia's most important trading partner				
Countries	Import from China		Export to China	
	China's ranking	Share in total imports	China's ranking	Share in total exports
Kazakhstan	2	17.0%	2	13.6%
Kyrgyzstan	1	35.4%	6	4.1%
Tajikistan	3	18.2%	5	5.0%
Turkmenistan	3	14.3%	1	80.2%
Uzbekistan	1	23.1%	3	12.3%

According to the official statistics of each country in 2019, China was the largest trading partner of the Kyrgyz Republic and Uzbekistan in terms of imports and has been Turkmenistan's largest trading partner in terms of exports. China also ranks high as a destination for exports from all other Central Asian countries. More details can be found in Table 4.1 (Dezan Shira & Associates, 2021).

Not surprisingly, China has a positive trade balance with all Central Asian countries, except for Turkmenistan, from which China receives significant volumes of natural gas. The parties will need great efforts to achieve a more favourable balance of trade and also to diversify the number of commodity groups.

The spectrum of trade with China varies significantly between countries. The data refers to the pre-Covid year of 2019, giving one the latest trade landscape undistorted by various domestic and cross-border restrictions (Dezan Shira & Associates, 2021).

China–Kazakhstan

In 2019, Kazakhstan's total exports amounted to 66.198 billion US dollars, and total imports – to 51.629 billion US dollars (World Bank, 2022). As shown in Table 4.1, China was Kazakhstan's second-largest trade partner. Trade between the two countries has grown steadily over the past five years, increasing by 16 per cent. Kazakhstan exports crude oil, petroleum gas, refined copper, ferroalloys, and organic and inorganic chemicals to China. Since 2012, China has been the largest buyer of Kazakh uranium. Since the mid-2010s, Kazakhstan has increased exports of non-hydrocarbon and metal goods to China. Exports of ore, slag, and ash from Kazakhstan to China rose 58 per cent between 2015 and 2019. Imports from China are constantly growing and mainly consist of supplies of electrical machinery and equipment, clothing, and clothing accessories.

China–Uzbekistan

The total export volume of Uzbekistan in 2019 was 17.027 billion US dollars, and the total volume of imports was 26.621 billion US dollars (World Bank, 2022). This makes China Uzbekistan's largest trading partner, accounting for 23.1 per cent of Uzbekistan's total imports and its fastest-growing import market over the past decade. In terms of exports, China is Uzbekistan's third-largest trading partner, accounting for 12.3 per cent of Uzbekistan's total exports. The main export items from Uzbekistan to China are mineral fuels and mineral oils, cotton, and copper. In recent years, Uzbekistan has increased imports of machinery and mechanical appliances, electrical machinery and vehicles from China.

China–Turkmenistan

In 2018, exports from Turkmenistan amounted to 9.239 billion US dollars, while total imports amounted to 5.094 billion US dollars (World Bank, 2022). In terms of exports, China is Turkmenistan's largest trading partner. China is Turkmenistan's third-largest trading partner overall (Table 4.1). Turkmenistan's main exports are petroleum gas, refined oil, crude oil, non-retail pure cotton yarn and nitrogen fertilisers. In 2017, Turkmenistan exported 94 per cent of its natural gas to China, 50 per cent more than it did in 2012. China financed the construction of the entire pipeline infrastructure to deliver gas from Central Asia to China. Turkmenistan's main imports from China are machinery and mechanical appliances and equipment.

China–The Kyrgyz Republic

In 2019, total exports from Kyrgyzstan amounted to 3.126 billion US dollars, while total imports amounted to 5.690 billion US dollars. In terms of imports, China is Kyrgyzstan's largest trading partner. China has also been the fastest-growing import market for Kyrgyzstan over the past ten years. As for exports, China was Kyrgyzstan's sixth-largest trading partner in 2019, accounting for four per cent of total exports. Kyrgyzstan exports ores, slag and ash, rawhides, and skins to China, and mainly imports apparel and clothing accessories, footwear and cotton.

China–Tajikistan

In 2019, Tajikistan's total exports amounted to 1.243 billion US dollars, while total imports amounted to 3.409 billion US dollars. In terms of imports, China is Tajikistan's third-largest trading partner. Regarding exports, China is Tajikistan's fifth-largest trading partner, accounting for five per cent of total exports. Although China is not Tajikistan's leading trading partner, in 2019, China became the country's fastest-growing export market (up 10.5 per cent on the previous year) and import market (up 13.1 per cent on the previous year). Tajikistan's main exports to China are ores, slag and ash, raw hides and skins. Tajikistan's main imports from China are machinery, mechanical appliances, footwear, and vehicles.

Foreign Direct Investment

How have economic relations between China and Central Asian countries changed since the Belt and Road Initiative came into existence in 2013? China's foreign direct investment (FDI) in Central Asia has grown rapidly since then. Figure 4.4 shows the dynamics of FDI according to the China FDI Statistical Bulletin for 2019 (Zhang, 2021). Real direct investment has been growing rapidly since 2011. In pre-pandemic 2019, China's FDI to Central Asia reached approximately $14 billion, up 3.5 times from $4 billion in 2011. However, the distribution of this investment was highly homogeneous and Chinese investors mainly financed the exploration, development and export of Kazakh oil, which accounted for at least 50 per cent of all investment. Starting in 2018, investments in Uzbekistan began to grow rapidly as well.

The UN Conference on Trade and Development World Investment Report focuses on FDI trends globally and at the regional and country level. The report classifies FDI motives into four main categories: market seeking, resource seeking, efficiency-seeking and technology-seeking. China's FDI in the Central Asian countries has been pragmatic and falls into the market and resource-seeking categories. These two categories have stimulated China's

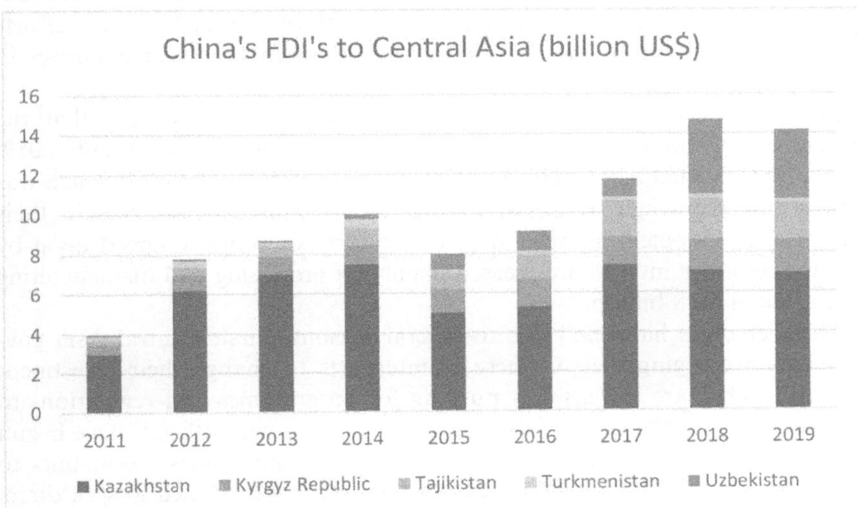

Figure 4.4 FDI to Central Asia from China (2011–2019)
Source: Zhang (2021).

imports of much-needed energy and mineral resources from Central Asia and increased Chinese exports of consumer goods, machinery, and equipment to the region.

Since establishing trade and economic relations with Central Asia, China has had several priorities. First, considering country requests, China began financing and building infrastructure – roads, power plants, and electrical transmission lines under sovereign guarantees from recipient governments. The impact on infrastructure development was particularly noticeable in the Kyrgyz Republic and Tajikistan. Secondly, Chinese corporations began actively investing in hydrocarbon assets, acquiring promising oil and gas fields, building pipelines in Kazakhstan, Uzbekistan, and Turkmenistan, and transporting hydrocarbons to China. Consequently, crude oil and natural gas exports to China have increased dramatically since the early 2000s. And thirdly, China began to import moderate amounts of raw metals from Kazakhstan, cotton from Uzbekistan, and ores and concentrates from the Kyrgyz Republic and Tajikistan.

Hydrocarbons still dominate Central Asia's exports to China. But in recent years, in response to requests from its governments, Beijing's focus has shifted to supporting the industrialisation of the region's economy and investment in value-added manufacturing industries. Given the sovereign over-crediting of the Kyrgyz Republic and Tajikistan and the critical size of their debt to GDP ratio, the volume of Chinese investment in their infrastructure has dropped. To prevent debt levels from becoming unsustainable, the parties decided to no longer be primary recipients of any new sovereign loans several years ago. Instead, Chinese companies are now trying to build factories, develop raw material processing capacities and modernise local agricultural operations to further export processed agricultural products. These efforts are integral to China's strategic desire to assist Central Asian countries in developing their export-oriented industries.

Both the public and the respective governments acknowledge that the structure of Chinese investment in the region is improving. As of July 2019, China had invested $2.16 billion in Kazakhstan's industrial sector, which was zero a few years ago. Uzbekistan prioritises Chinese investments in their industrial development as well. Most of the forty-six projects agreed upon by the two countries in 2018 are focused mainly on processing and manufacturing at a value of $6.8 billion.

These changes happened due to several reasons. First, Central Asia governments are urging their Chinese counterparts to change their investment priorities. They are increasingly pushing for programmes and regulations to hire and improve the skills of local workers. Government officials have begun to coordinate better with the Chinese government and Chinese companies to work out joint plans. Unlike in the past, they are more inclined to seek direct investment than sovereign loans. Secondly, China's central government and its two leading state-owned banks, the China Development Bank (CDB) and the China EximBank, encourage investing on commercial terms and moving away from large infrastructure projects funded by sovereign debt. And thirdly, an increasing number of Chinese companies are investing abroad due to the relocation of excess production capacity and access to foreign markets. It allows many of them to avoid fierce domestic competition, a sharp increase in domestic wages, and tightening domestic environmental legislation.

Russia

After getting acquainted with the details of China's economic cooperation with the countries of Central Asia, it is interesting to compare how its other influential neighbour, Russia, interacts with the region.

Trade

Figure 4.5 shows that Russia and China provide most of the imports that go to the countries of Central Asia (UNCTAD Stat, 2020). At the same time, it is clear that the share of imports from Russia is declining while the share of supplies from China is growing (Polivach, 2019). This trend is associated with the better competitiveness of Chinese products.

Industrial goods make up the bulk of Central Asian imports from Russia. Compared with the 1990s, their share has decreased to about 65 per cent. However, this is still noticeably higher than the share of these goods in total Russian exports, which does not even reach 20 per cent (UNCTAD Stat, 2020). At the same time, the share of imports of food and chemical products

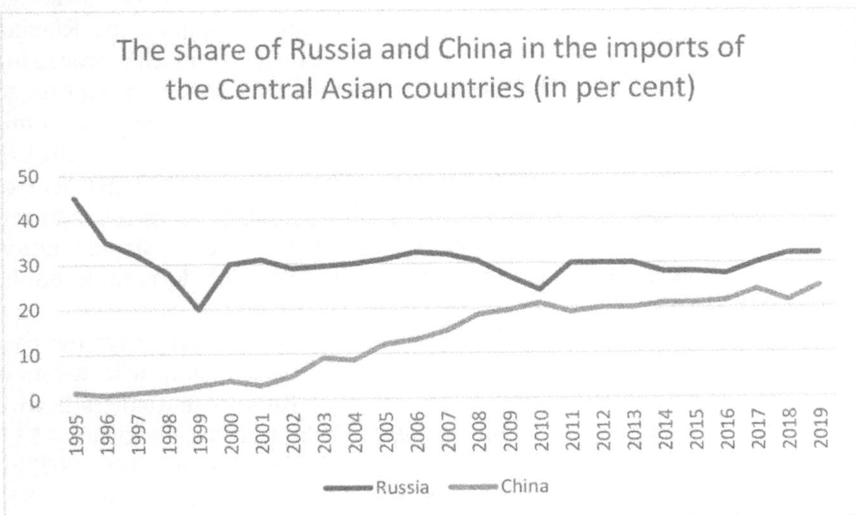

Figure 4.5 The share of Russia and China in the imports of the Central Asian countries (in per cent)
Source: UNCTAT Start (2020).

increased, and machinery and equipment remained stable in the range of 20–23 per cent, although this is still lower than in the 1990s (Polivach, 2019).

It is critical to understand the prospects for Russia and China as export markets from Central Asia. Figure 4.6 shows that over the past twenty-five years, the importance of the Russian market for the region's countries has decreased by about three times, while the volume of the Chinese market has increased by about the same amount (UNCTAD Stat, 2020). Since 2010, the Chinese market has become the most important for exports from Central Asia. Due to stagnation in the Russian economy, the demand for imported goods in Russia has grown weakly. In those years, the Chinese economy developed rapidly, and the country's consumption of raw materials and other goods increased. The growth of China's exports from the region is associated with a significant increase in the supply of hydrocarbons from Kazakhstan and Turkmenistan. After a sharp rise in 2009–2013, the share of China in exports from the region decreased slightly, which was associated with a fall in world prices for oil and natural gas. The share of Russia in the exports of some Central Asian countries, particularly the Kyrgyz Republic and Uzbekistan, has increased in recent years.

The structure of Central Asian states' exports to Russia is changing for the better. For example, over the past 25 years, the share of commodities peaked at 68.8 per cent in 2005 and has been gradually declining since then. In 2018, it accounted for less than 50 per cent of total exports (Ushkalova, 2018).

As for imports, countries' exports have a different structure. For example, exports of Tajikistan and Turkmenistan are dominated by raw materials, while Uzbekistan mainly exports manufactured goods. Thus, although exports from Central Asia to Russia are lower than to China, the Russian market remains more critical in supplying products from the processing industries. The growth in the share of manufactured goods in exports to Russia is evident in countries that are members of the Eurasian Economic Union (EAEU). Kazakhstan's share increased from 36.3 per cent in 2013 to 41.6 per cent in 2018, and the Kyrgyz Republic rose from 45.3 per cent to 55.2 per cent (Ushkalova, 2018). In the coming years, the garment industry, fruit and vegetable processing, dairy, grain and innovative instrumentation will have the most significant export potential for the Kyrgyz Republic (Kurasheva & Limareva, 2019).

In absolute terms, trade with Russia has grown substantially over the past two years. Russia is the largest trading partner of Kazakhstan, with whom it shares the 6,846 kilometres-long border. In 2020, Russia's mutual trade with Kazakhstan amounted to \$21.2 billion (OEC, 2022a), with Uzbekistan – \$5.7 billion (Stat.uz, 2022), with the Kyrgyz Republic – \$1.8 billion (OEC, 2022b), with Tajikistan – \$780 million (OEC, 2022c) and with Turkmenistan – \$76 million (OEC, 2022d). Thus, in 2020 the total trade volume with Russia reached 27.4 billion dollars.

In 2021 the trade volume between Kazakhstan and Russia increased, reaching \$24.2 billion (Kapital.kz, 2022), trade volume between Uzbekistan

Figure 4.6 The share of Russia and China in the exports of the Central Asian countries (in per cent)
Source: UNCTAT Start (2020).

with Russia grew the same year to 7.5 billion dollars (Latipov, 2022). The volume of trade of Kyrgyzstan, Tajikistan and Turkmenistan with Russia also increased significantly, amounting to \$2.5 billion (Kudrjavceva, 2022), \$1.35 billion (Tajtrade.tj, 2022) and 970 million dollars (Akulov, 2022), respectively. The total trade volume in 2021 between Russia and Central Asia reached \$36.5 billion, up 33 per cent from the previous year.

FDI

According to official statistics, in 2020, the volume of accumulated Russian investments in the economy of Kazakhstan reached \$16.9 billion, and Kazakhstani investments in Russia – \$4.3 billion. However, the Kazakhstani Embassy in Russia claims that the actual acquisition of Russian business in their country is much higher and, taking into account the activities carried out through European divisions of Russian firms, amounts to about \$42 billion (Rfembassy.kz, 2022). Russia has accounted for 30–40 per cent of all Kazakh imports for quite some time (Mazorenko & Kajsar, 2022).

From 2016 to 2020, Russia increased investments in post-Soviet countries by a factor of 1.3. Investments in Uzbekistan grew the most – by a factor of 2.1. Uzbekistan has become the second most popular investment destination among Russian investors after Kazakhstan, accounting for just under a third of Russia's

FDI. At the end of 2020, Kazakhstan and Uzbekistan occupied the top two places in accumulated FDI from Russia, 11.4 billion dollars and 9.1 billion dollars respectively (Degot'kova, 2021). The Russian FDI to the other countries of the region is insignificant. For instance, accumulated FDI in the Kyrgyz Republic is stable at $2 billion, and in Tajikistan at $642 million (Kuznetsov, et al., 2021). According to various sources, Russia has not made any significant investments in the economy of Turkmenistan. Thus, the total volume of accumulated Russian FDI in the countries of Central Asia is 23.1 billion dollars.

There are also other signs of increasing investment in the region by Russian companies. In Central Asia, many investments seemingly come from countries such as Cyprus or the Netherlands. However, several Russian companies, including large ones, are using these jurisdictions to optimise their tax payments. With such investors in mind, Russia's investment is getting even larger than the official statistics show. In an article dedicated to the 30th anniversary of the establishment of diplomatic relations between Russia and the republics of Central Asia published in May 2022, Russian Foreign Minister Sergey Lavrov stated that "for the period 2010–2021 alone, the volume of accumulated Russian investments amounted to about 30.5 billion dollars. More than 10 thousand Russian and joint-ventures operate in the Central Asian countries, creating 900 thousand jobs" (RG.ru, 2022). Given these estimates, we can safely assume that the volume of FDI from Russia to the countries of Central Asia is about double that of China.

EU

Trade

Immediately after the independence of the Central Asian republics, European oil companies began to show interest in the development of Kazakhstani oil fields. As a result, they achieved their goals of extracting and transporting Caspian oil to their markets. Central Asian exports to the EU peaked in 2012, exceeding $46 billion due to the record prices for crude oil observed this year. The global financial crisis, falling oil prices and the depreciation of national currencies against the US dollar have negatively affected export numbers. As a result, Central Asian exports to the EU market dropped to $18.6 billion in 2016; in 2020, this figure was $18.2 billion, the lowest level in the last decade, which was proportional to the fall in crude oil prices during these years. In 2020, Kazakhstan provided 97 per cent of all exports from Central Asia to the EU. But 90 per cent of this amounted to just one trade item – the export of hydrocarbons. The remaining exports of Central Asia consist of inorganic chemicals, metals, fertilisers, and agricultural products. Thus the export of other trade items from the region to the EU countries is uncompetitive.

In 2020, imports to Central Asia from EU countries amounted to $10.2 billion. The share of Kazakhstan in the region's total imports was 57 per cent in 2020. Uzbekistan's share of total imports increased from 22 per cent in 2001 to almost 33 per cent in 2020. The shares of other countries remain insignificant. In 2020, the allocation for Turkmenistan was nearly 6 per cent, while the value for Kyrgyzstan and Tajikistan was three and two per cent, respectively. Imports to Central Asia from the EU countries are fairly diversified and mainly consist of manufactured goods. In 2020, the share of mechanical engineering in the total volume of imports from the EU to Central Asia was 32 per cent, pharmaceutical products – 14 per cent, and electrical machinery and equipment – 7 per cent. Thus, the total trade volume between Central Asia and the EU in 2020 amounted to $28.4 billion, or 81 per cent of China's.

FDI

Collectively, the countries of the European Union remain the leading investors in the countries of Central Asia. The volume of their accumulated FDI is more than 42 per cent of the total. For comparison, the volume of American FDI in Central Asia was around 14.2 per cent, Russian FDI was about 8 per cent, and Chinese FDI was approximately 3.7 per cent. Over the past decade, EU member states have invested more than $160 billion in Central Asia (Nurmaganbetova, 2021).

Although investments from European businesses have focused on the exploration and development of hydrocarbon deposits, in its future interaction with the countries of the European Union, Kazakhstan proposes to focus on accelerated technological modernisation of the economy, improving the quality of human capital, and institutional reforms.

The US

Trade

American oil companies have also shown interest in developing promising Kazakhstani oil fields together with their European colleagues. Currently, exports from Central Asia to the US consist almost entirely of crude oil. The other American trade with the countries of Central Asia is modest, mainly due to geographical distance when compared to Europe, Russia or China. Imports from the US to Kazakhstan in 2019 amounted to $740 million (United States Trade Representative, 2020a), and Uzbekistan – $506 million (United States Trade Representative, 2020b). Imports from the US to other countries were insignificant. For example, in the Kyrgyz Republic, importers, among whom were sellers of used American cars, bought goods worth a tiny $21 million (United States Trade Representative, 2020c). The main imports were cars, aircraft, and electrical equipment. Exports of goods from Kazakhstan to the US in 2019 amounted to $1.2 billion in 2019, and from Uzbekistan – to $34 million. The primary export commodities were hydrocarbons, metals, and inorganic chemicals. Thus, in 2019, the total trade volume amounted to just 2.5 billion dollars.

FDI

Kazakhstan remains an essential destination for direct investment by American businesses. The USA's cumulative investment in Kazakhstan's economy amounted to 53.7 billion US dollars. If in the first years of independence, investments were mainly in hydrocarbons, in recent years, there has been an increase in the interest of American business in agribusiness, engineering, transport and logistics. In 2019, the US' direct investment reached a record high of $5.5 billion, accounting for a quarter of all investment inflows into the country (Satubaldina, 2021). Of the other countries in the region, American companies show particular interest in investing in Uzbekistan. However, the volume of such investments is still low – the US' FDI in Uzbekistan in 2019 amounted to $82 million, which is however 15.5 per cent more than the previous year (United States Trade Representative, 2020b).

India

Relations between Central Asia and India have deep historical roots. Historians believe that Buddhism came from India to China through Central Asia. Babur, the founder of the Indian Mughal dynasty, was born in the Ferghana Valley. Indo-Aryan languages are spoken by most Indians, and Turkic languages have many words in common. But complicated geographical features separate Central Asia and South Asia and make developing trade and other ties difficult. In ancient times, the territory of modern Afghanistan was a bridge between South and Central Asia, but now this 'bridge' is not working because the current Taliban government is not recognised by the international community. This can explain the regions' modest figures for mutual trade and investment.

However, this situation may yet change. In January 2022, Indian Prime Minister Narendra Modi hosted India's first-ever virtual summit with all five Central Asian presidents. As a major regional power, India seeks to balance Russian and Chinese influence in Central Asia and increase its presence. Initially, it was planned for the presidents of the five Central Asian countries to personally visit India and attend the Republic Day celebration on 26 January as chief guests, but the coronavirus pandemic prevented this (Dikshit, 2022) and the summit took place online instead.

In recent years, India has increased its interaction with some countries in Central Asia. A significant achievement was creating a trilateral ministerial working group between India, Uzbekistan and Iran on the port of Chabahar, just days after the President of Uzbekistan put forward this proposal during a conversation with the Indian Prime Minister in December 2020. India provided a $1 billion credit line and approved four investment projects in Uzbekistan worth $450 million. The campuses of several Indian universities, such as Sharda, Amity and Sambhroom, and the Medanta Medical Institutes, will be the centres for important joint educational projects. The pharmaceutical firm Cadilla is investing $50 million in a drug manufacturing plant in the country (Dikshit, 2022). In the Kyrgyz Republic, India has set up five Alpine Telemedicine Centers, provided a $200 million credit line, and conducts annual military exercises. There are at least 15,000 students in the country, mostly at medical universities (Manas.news, 2021). India established an IT centre in 2011 and a manufacturing training centre in 2002 (Ministry of External Affairs of India, 2013) in the Kyrgyz Republic. Kazakh troops are participating in the Indian UN peacekeeping battalion in Lebanon.

Trade and economic relations are at a stable, albeit relatively modest level. Among the countries of Central Asia, the leaders in trade relations are Kazakhstan and Uzbekistan, whose trade with India in 2021–2022 amounted to $1 billion and approximately $400 million, respectively. The trade with the three other Central Asian countries does not exceed $100 million in total (Department of Commerce, 2022). Therefore, as of 2020–2021, India's dealings with the countries of Central Asia was thirty times less than China's and twenty times less than Russia's.

Like many other countries, India's trade is centred on an eastward and westward shift, emphasising the Indian Ocean countries. Thus, trade with the countries of the Cooperation Council for the Arab States of the Persian Gulf (GCC) and the Association of Southeast Asian Nations (ASEAN) accounts for 12.7% and 11.5% of India's total trade, respectively. A similar indicator with the five Central Asian republics is only 0.2% (Shhedrov, 2022).

Why is the Ruble too Dominant in Central Asia? China Versus Russia

While observing the trends in Central Asia's GDP development, it is easy to see visible declines in 2008, 2015 and 2020. What are the reasons for those declines? Figure 4.7 shows the changing exchange rate of the Russian ruble against the US dollar from 1996 to 2022 (Investing.com, 2022). When comparing Figure 3.2 and Figure 4.7, it is easy to see that the drops in the Central Asia GDP have happened at almost the same time as the depreciation of the ruble against the world's major currencies at key historical moments: firstly, during the world's financial crisis in 2008, then when Western countries introduced economic sanctions against Russia in 2014, and later at the onset of the Coronavirus pandemic in 2020.

The depreciation of the national currencies in the Central Asian countries against the US dollar showed similar trends. For example, Figure 4.8 shows the exchange rate of the Kazakh tenge against the Russian ruble. For more than twenty years before the key events mentioned above, the rate had been at a stable level however, since the Kazakh currency is pegged to the Russian ruble, the ruble's volatility against major currencies automatically affects the behaviour of the tenge. The ruble's devaluation pushed the Kazakh monetary authorities to weaken the tenge to prevent an increased demand for Russian products and protect local producers. The currencies of other Central Asian countries have similar trends to the tenge. Comparing two graphs in Figure

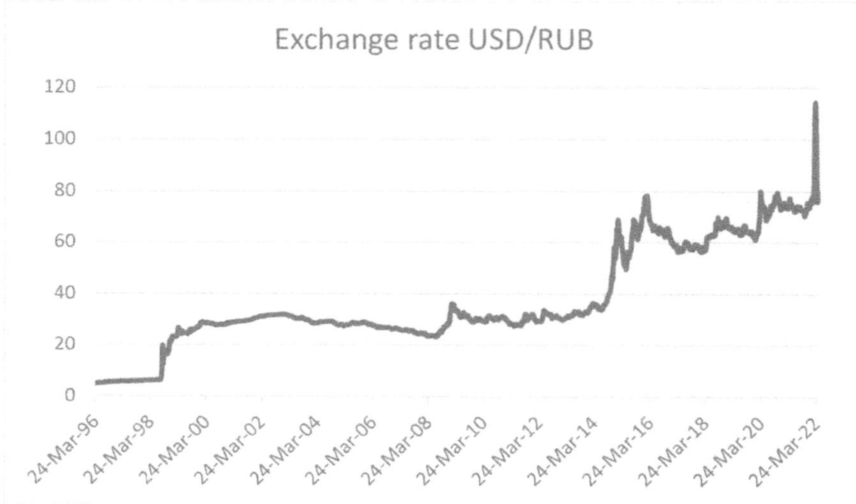

Figure 4.7 Exchange rate of the Russian ruble against the US dollar
Source: Investing.com (2020).

4.8 and Figure 3.2 illustrates the direct correlation of regional economies with the Russian one.

But why is the standard of living in Central Asia determined by what happens to the Russian currency? Indeed, the role of the Russian economy is essential, but it is far from owning a monopoly.

Large remittances from migrants who work in Russia support the importance of the Russian ruble for the Central Asian economies. Uzbekistan, Tajikistan, and the Kyrgyz Republic are Russia's largest recipients of remittances. The fall in remittances during the Russian crisis in 2014–2015 hit these countries hardest (Trilling, 2015). By the end of 2014, the reduction in US dollar transfers from Russia was 7.6% to Tajikistan and 15.5% to Uzbekistan (Trilling, 2015). According to the latest data, the strong remittance growth in 2017 continued into 2018. Data from the Russian Central Bank (Cbr.ru, 2022) shows that, of the $13.99 billion sent in 2018 by individuals from Russia to other countries of the former Soviet Union, about 68.1% went to these three countries. For comparison, in 2016, these figures were $10.1 billion and 63.3%, respectively, and in 2017 – $12.9 billion and 67%.

For the balance of payments remittances are essential, but they are not everything. Traditional economic theory argues that the interdependence of countries depends on the concentration of their trade and investment relationships. However, Russia has not occupied a dominant role in these areas of Central Asia for a long time, and China has already replaced Russia in many vital areas of the economy.

In 2020, China's trade with the countries of Central Asia amounted to $35 billion or 128% of Russia's (UN Comtrade, 2022). In the first eleven months

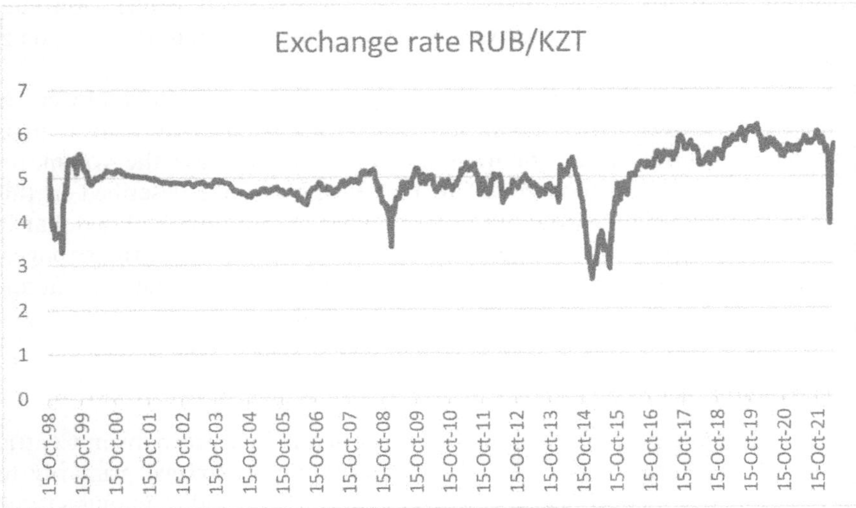

Figure 4.8 Exchange rate of the Kazakh tenge against the Russian ruble
Source: Investing.com (2022).

of 2021, the trade volume increased to $44.6 billion, and the expected trade volume between Central Asia and China in 2021 should exceed $48.5 billion, which is 133% of Russia's (Dezan Shira & Associates, 2021).

In addition, when considering the balance of payments of the Central Asian countries with China, it should be taken into account that China provides them with significant soft loans under government guarantees, again in hard currency. In total, sixty-one infrastructure projects worth $17.58 billion were started (Malik, et al., 2021). These data demonstrate that Central Asian countries' trade with China exceeds that of Russia. How and why, then, does the Russian ruble remain so dominant?

The impact of fluctuations of the Russian currency against the US dollar, dictated by geopolitics, remains disproportionately dominant. Therefore, in the years to come, it is the position of policymakers and national regulators of the region to give attention to reforming the system of interactions of national currencies. The new principles should not bring uncertainty and nervousness to economic relations, but rather become a source of development and stability.

China and the countries of Central Asia have begun negotiations for the first time on deals involving currencies other than the US dollar and the Russian ruble. In August 2019, the National Bank of Uzbekistan signed a loan agreement with China's Development Bank to attract the first credit line in the Chinese yuan. The total loan amounted to 500 million yuan (around $75 million). As noted in the Bank's press statement, the main advantage of attracting financing in the Chinese yuan is that it is not dependent on fluctuations in the global financial system, such as the Libor rate (Podrobno.uz, 2019).

On January 25, 2022, during a virtual summit between China and Central Asia leaders, President Xi Jinping said that China is ready to open its markets to the Central Asian countries and wants to increase the volume of mutual trade to $70 billion by 2030. For all the reasons described in this chapter and given that it would be unwise to continue to use the US dollar in financial transactions in the region, using the Chinese yuan as the strongest regional currency will be essential for a more stable and predictable economic and trade relationship between China and Central Asia.

Conclusion

Since the beginning of 2000, all the countries rich in hydrocarbons in Central Asia began to supply raw materials to international markets, primarily to Europe, the US and China. Exports of higher value-added manufactured goods and services are low. Imports to the countries of the region consist mainly of industrial goods, transport, engineering products and construction services. With an educated population and favourable demographics and an educated population, countries must refocus their trade priorities on high-tech and digital industries.

The EU remains the leading investor in Central Asia, accounting for more than 42 per cent of the total FDI stock (Nurmaganbetova, 2021). US FDI stock in Central Asia is about 14.2 per cent, Russian approximately 8 per cent, and Chinese around 3.7 per cent. In recent years, there has been an upsurge in FDI from India, South Korea and Japan and a slight increase in Asia's role as investment resources and expertise.

Despite investment growth, the share of FDI to GDP remains lower compared to other developing areas. Boston Consulting Group estimates showed that between 2008 and 2016, total FDI in Central Asia was only 18.2 per cent of the region's average annual GDP. At the same time, FDI in North Africa amounted to 26.8 per cent, Central America – to 35.9 per cent and the Balkan region – to 47.2 per cent (Boston Consulting Group, 2019).

It is easy to notice that the North African and Balkan territories are near the borders of the EU, and Central America is close to the US. These two centres of global economic power carry out the bulk of their FDI in their neighbouring regions. The Chinese economy is almost on par with the EU and the US. The question arises – can China invest more in their adjacent area, as others have done in their respective regions, and become a leader in FDI in Central Asia? The analysis of FDI in other parts of the world shows that there are ample opportunities.

Getting acquainted with the book, it is easy to see that we have paid disproportionate attention to the prospects for economic cooperation between Central Asia and China. There are several explanations for this. First, compared to other major economic players, China only began to develop cooperation quite recently – only thirty years ago. Secondly, China has enormous economic power. And thirdly, through its Belt and Road Initiative, China is making it clear that its economic interests will extend far beyond its borders for the first time in history. The geographic and geo-economic reasons for cooperation between Central Asia and China, even in the medium term, are apparent and deserve attention.

References

Akulov, A., 2022. Chto mozhet poterjat' i priobresti Rossija posle smeny vlasti v Turkmenii. [Online] Available at: https://www.gazeta.ru/business/2022/02/14/14534509.shtml [Accessed July 2022].

Boston Consulting Group, 2019. Overview of investment attractiveness of Central Asian countries over next decade. [Online] Available at: https://www.consultancy.asia/news/2078/bcg-outlines-170-billion-fdi-potential-for-central-asia-over-next-decade [Accessed July 2022].

Cbr.ru, 2022. Central'nyj bank Rossijskoj Federacii. [Online] Available at: https://www.cbr.ru/ [Accessed July 2022].

Degot'kova, I., 2021. Rossijskie investory pereorientirovalis' na Kazahstan i Uzbekistan. [Online] Available at: https://www.rbc.ru/newspaper/2021/11/18/6194f9809a79475080bec69f [Accessed July 2022].

Department of Commerce, 2022. Export import data bank. [Online] Available at: https://tradestat.commerce.gov.in/eidb/iecntq.asp [Accessed July 2022].

Dezan Shira & Associates, 2021. China and Central Asia: Bilateral trade relationships and future outlook. [Online] Available at: https://www.china-briefing.com/news/china-and-central-asia-bilateral-trade-relationships-and-future-outlook/ [Accessed July 2022].

Dikshit, S., 2022. PM Modi to host India's first-ever summit with Central Asian leaders later today. [Online] Available at: https://www.tribuneindia.com/news/nation/pm-modi-to-host-indias-first-ever-summit-with-central-asia-later-today-364673 [Accessed July 2022].

Investing.com, 2022. USD/RUB - US Dollar Russian Ruble. [Online] Available at: https://www.investing.com/currencies/usd-rub-historical-data [Accessed July 2022].

Kapital.kz, 2022. Tovarooborot Kazahstana so stranami EAJeS vyros na 28% za god. [Online] Available at: https://kapital.kz/economic/103557/tovarooborot-kazakhstana-so-stranami-yeaes-vyros-na-28-za-god.html [Accessed July 2022].

Kudrjavceva, T., 2022. Tovarooborot mezhdu Kyrgyzstanom i Rossiej vyros pochti v 1,5 raza. [Online] Available at: https://24.kg/ekonomika/223405_tovarooborot_mejdu_kyirgyizstanom_irossiey_vyiros_pochti_v15_raza/, [Accessed July 2022].

Kurasheva, N. & Limareva, I., 2019. EAES i Kirgizskaya Respublika - itogi i perspektivy ekonomicheskogo razvitiya. *Finansovaya Zhizn'*, Issue 2, pp. 36–40.

Kuznetsov, A. *et al.*, 2021. *Monitoring vzaimnyh investicij EABR (EDB Monitoring of Mutual Investments)*, Moscow: Eurasian Development Bank.

Latipov, S., 2022. Chem Uzbekistan torguet s Rossiej i Ukrainoj. [Online] Available at: https://www.gazeta.uz/ru/2022/03/09/uzb-rus-ukr/. [Accessed July 2022].

Liu, Z., 2022. Trade with Central Asia to expand. [Online] Available at: http://english.www.gov.cn/statecouncil/ministries/202201/19/content_WS61e76106c6d09c94e48a3e1c.html [Accessed July 2022].

Malik, A. A. *et al.*, 2021. *Banking on the Belt and Road: Insights from a New Global Dataset of 13,427 Chinese Development Projects*, Williamsburg, VA: AidData at William & Mary.

Manas.news, 2021. Studentov iz kakih stran v KR uchitsja bol'she vsego. [Online] Available at: https://manas.news/infografika/studentov-iz-kakih-stran-v-kr-uchitsja-bolshe-vsego/ [Accessed July 2022].

Mazorenko, D. & Kajsar, A., 2022. Kak mogut izmenit'sja torgovye otnoshenija Rossii i Kazahstana?. [Online] Available at: https://vlast.kz/kz/jekonomika/48997-kak-mogut-izmenitsa-torgovye-otnosenia-rossii-i-kazahstana.html [Accessed July 2022].

Ministry of External Affairs of India, 2013. *India-Kyrgyzstan Relations*, New Delhi: MEA of India.

Nurmaganbetova, Z., 2021. Kassym-Jomart Tokayev and European Council President Charles Michel hold talks. [Online] Available at: https://www.inform.kz/en/kassym-jomart-tokayev-and-european-council-president-charles-michel-hold-talks_a3867165 [Accessed July 2022].

OEC, 2022a. Russia (RUS) and Kazakhstan (KAZ) trade. [Online] Available at: https://oec.world/en/profile/bilateral-country/rus/partner/kaz [Accessed July 2022].

OEC, 2022b. Russia (RUS) and Kyrgyzstan (KGZ) trade. [Online] Available at: https://oec.world/en/profile/bilateral-country/rus/partner/kgz [Accessed July 2022].

OEC, 2022c. Russia (RUS) and Tajikistan (TJK) trade. [Online] Available at: https://oec.world/en/profile/bilateral-country/rus/partner/tjk [Accessed July 2022].

OEC, 2022d. Russia (RUS) and Turkmenistan (TKM) trade. [Online] Available at: https://oec.world/en/profile/bilateral-country/rus/partner/tkm [Accessed July 2022].

Podrobno.uz, 2019. Uzbekistan i Kitaj perehodjat na raschety v juanjah. GBRK vydal Nacbanku pervyj juanevyj kredit. [Online] Available at: https://podrobno.uz/cat/uzbekistan-i-kitay-klyuchi-ot-budushchego/uzbekistan-i-kitay-perekhodyat-na-raschety-/?mc_cid=dad6e5a73a&mc_eid=[4b516b0c01] [Accessed July 2022].

Polivach, A., 2019. Torgovlya stran Tsentral'noi Azii s Rossiei i Kitaem. [Online] Available at: https://www.imemo.ru/files/File/magazines/rossia_i_novay/2019_04/17-Polivach.pdf [Accessed July 2022].

Rfembassy.kz, 2022. Torgovo-ekonomicheskie svjazi. [Online] Available at: http://www.rfembassy.kz/lm/dvustoronnie_otnosheniya/torgovo-ekonomicheskie_svyazi/ [Accessed July 2022].

RG.ru, 2022. Sergej Lavrov: Rossija - Central'naja Azija. 30 let na puti druzhby i sotrudnichestva. [Online] Available at: https://rg.ru/2022/05/05/sergej-lavrov-rossiia-centralnaia-aziia-30-let-na-puti-druzhby-i-sotrudnichestva.html [Accessed July 2022].

Satubaldina, A., 2021. American companies invest nearly $54 billion in Kazakhstan over 30 years. [Online] Available at: https://astanatimes.com/2021/06/american-companies-invest-nearly-54-billion-in-kazakhstan-over-30-years/ [Accessed July 2022].

Shhedrov, I., 2022. Pervyj sammit Indija – Central'naja Azija: nachalo novoj politiki v regione?. [Online] Available at: https://www.imemo.ru/publications/relevant-comments/text/perviy-sammit-indiya-tsentralynaya-aziya-nachalo-novoy-politiki-v-regione [Accessed July 2022].

Stat.uz, 2022. Vneshnetorgovyj oborot Respubliki Uzbekistan (za janvar' 2022 g). [Online] Available at: https://stat.uz/ru/press-tsentr/novosti-goskomstata/17060-o-zbekiston-respublikasi-tashqi-savdo-aylanmasi-2021-yil-yanvar-dekabr-2 [Accessed July 2022].

Tajtrade.tj, 2022. Torgovye partnery Respubliki Tajikistan. [Online] Available at: https://tajtrade.tj/menu/28?l=ru [Accessed July 2022].

Trilling, D., 2015. Kak sil'no sokrashhenie denezhnyh perevodov iz Rossii udarilo po stranam Central'noj Azii?. [Online] Available at: https://russian.eurasianet.org/node/61951 [Accessed July 2022].

UN Comtrade, 2022. UN Comtrade Database. [Online] Available at: https://comtrade.un.org/ [Accessed July 2022].

UNCTAD Stat, 2020. UNCTAD Data Centre. [Online] Available at: https://unctadstat.unctad.org/wds/ReportFolders/reportfolders.aspx [Accessed July 2022].

United States Trade Representative, 2020a. Kazakhstan. [Online] Available at: https://ustr.gov/countries-regions/south-central-asia/Kazakhstan [Accessed July 2022].

United States Trade Representative, 2020b. Uzbekistan. [Online] Available at: https://ustr.gov/Uzbekistan [Accessed July 2022].

United States Trade Representative, 2020c. Kyrgyzstan. [Online] Available at: https://ustr.gov/countries-regions/south-central-asia/Kyrgyzstan [Accessed July 2022].

Ushkalova, D., 2018. Evolutsiya spetsializatsii Rossii vo vzaimnoi torgovle so stranami EAES. *Mir Novoi Economiki*, 12 (4), pp. 57–66.

World Bank, 2022. DataBank: World development indicators. [Online] Available at: https://databank.worldbank.org/source/world-development-indicators [Accessed July 2022].

Zhang, L., 2021. Research on import and export trade based on China's FDI to Central Asian countries. *International Journal of Innovation and Economic Development*, 7 (1), pp. 7–15.

5 Infrastructure

Introduction

As this book focuses on Central Asia's economic development and links to external markets, it is essential to understand the impact of its infrastructure on economic performance. Good infrastructure connects markets, facilitates trade, and supports economic growth. In contrast, a lack of infrastructure destroys markets, increases poverty, and slows the development of nations (Donaubauer, et al., 2018). Economists have calculated that in developing countries, a 10 per cent reduction in transport costs increases trade by 6 per cent, and a 10 per cent increase in total infrastructure investment contributes to export growth of 5 per cent (Hoekman & Nicita, 2008).

Experience shows that prioritising infrastructure development is particularly important for landlocked countries. Landlocked countries with a developed infrastructure, such as Switzerland or Liechtenstein, perform better in economic development and trade than their large maritime neighbours (Portugal-Perez & Wilson, 2012). There is therefore no reason why the landlocked nations of Central Asia cannot also be successful.

Several reputable global institutions assess the quality of infrastructure in various countries. One of the most authoritative ratings is compiled by experts from the World Economic Forum (WEF), which has been assessing the quality of infrastructure worldwide for many years. Their latest 2019 pre-Covid Global Competitiveness Index shows that Central Asia's infrastructure development rating remains low. Figure 5.1 compares infrastructure from the Global Competitiveness Score for three of the five Central Asian countries (World Economic Forum, 2019). According to the data, Kazakhstan performed the best, but its infrastructure index is still only average. Out of 141 countries, Kazakhstan ranked 67th with a general infrastructure index of 68.3 points, Tajikistan ranked 91st, and the Kyrgyz Republic had the worst performance out of the Central Asian countries, ranking 103rd. Figure 5.1 shows that despite the relatively low index scores, they have noticeably risen in recent years.

To comply with the best practices, for example, those in China or Europe, the region's countries need to pay more attention to their infrastructure. For

DOI: 10.4324/9781003360728-8

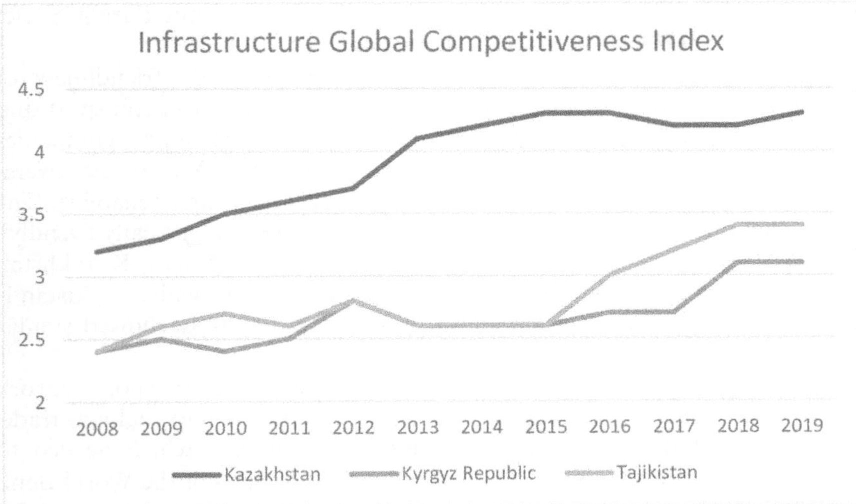

Figure 5.1 Infrastructure score for the Global Competitiveness Score in three Central Asian countries (2008–2019)
Source: World Economic Forum (2019).

this reason, China's Belt and Road Initiative has been received with great enthusiasm in the Central Asian region as it prioritises infrastructure development. This chapter will give an overview of the current state of infrastructure in the various sectors of the Central Asian economy and suggest key areas for further development.

Roads

The countries of Central Asia inherited highly integrated transport networks from their Soviet past built without regard to their administrative boundaries and mainly oriented toward Russia. After independence, the countries sought to improve their transport links with other (non-Soviet) neighbours. Still, the lack of financial resources and expertise slowed the integration of their transport systems into international networks.

Road and rail transport plays a particularly unique role in sustaining economic activity in landlocked countries. Efficient networks connect markets and lower the cost of exchanging goods. The transport sector has so far played a relatively minor role in the economic development of Central Asia in terms of its contribution to total output and employment. Transport accounts for 3–8 per cent of GDP and 2–5 per cent of total employment in the region (ADB, 2006). Table 5.1 shows the characteristics of roads in the five countries of Central Asia (Yoshino, et al., 2021). The average road density in Central Asia is only 28 kilometres per 100 square kilometres, which is much lower than in many developing countries such as those in South and

East Asia. In addition, many of these highways were built during Soviet times, and are currently in a state of disrepair.

The Asian Development Bank analysed the so-called "friendliness of logistics" as part of a wider study on regional cooperation in transport and transit in Central Asia (ADB, 2006). As part of the study, companies involved in international transportation and trade were asked to rate several countries regarding logistics services' availability, speed, and reliability. The results showed that the region's countries are much less "logistically friendly" than the US, EU, or Russia. Among the countries in the area, Kazakhstan and the Kyrgyz Republic are the most logistically friendly, while Tajikistan is the least friendly (Ojala, et al., 2004). A World Bank study showed similar results (Arvis, et al., 2012).

The collapse of the Soviet Union meant that the unified transport network became fragmented. These changes created severe barriers to regional trade. It was particularly detrimental to landlocked countries, which needed to trade across multiple borders. Figure 5.2 shows the results of the World Bank Logistics Performance Index for the countries of Central Asia, as well as for its closest neighbours – China and Russia – for comparison. From Figure 5.2, it becomes clear that the countries of Central Asia and Russia are experiencing serious transportation difficulties (World Bank, 2022a). According to this indicator, the region also lags far behind the advanced countries and countries of Eastern Europe, Turkey and East Asia. The bottlenecks in facilitation and logistics are significant, and these countries are generally lagging behind their competitors in developing both hard and soft road infrastructure.

Table 5.1 Road Infrastructure in Central Asian Countries, 2018

General Road Data	*Kazakhstan*	*Kyrgyz Republic*	*Tajikistan*	*Turkmenistan*	*Uzbekistan*
Total road network size (km)	96,718	34,810	26,767	58,592	18,3724
Trunk road network size (km)	23,485	18,810	14,067	13,644	42,530
Rural/urban road network size (km)	73,233	16,000	12,700	44,948	141,194
Land area (km^2)	2,699,700	191,800	138,786	469,930	425,400
Road density (km/100 km^2)	3.6	18.1	19.3	12.5	43.2

Source: Yoshino, et al. (2021).

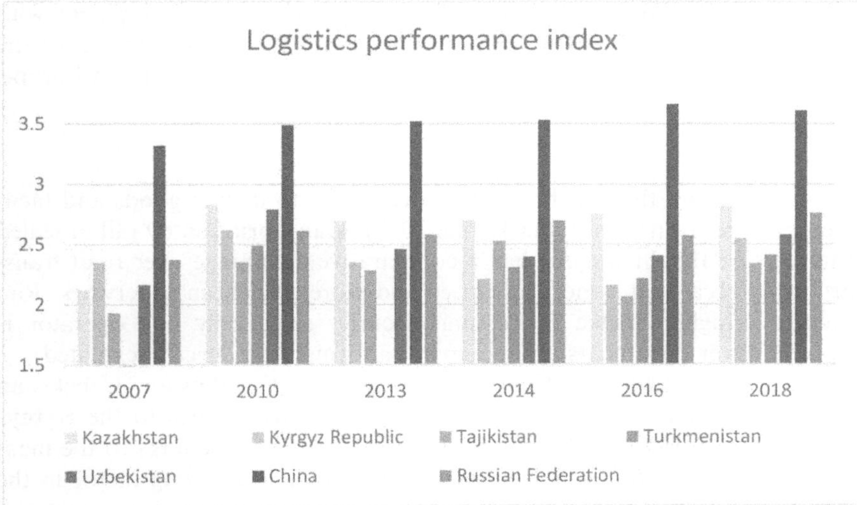

Figure 5.2 Logistics Performance Index in Central Asia and a few select countries (2007–2018)
Source: World Bank (2022a).

To understand some of the key developments in the region's roads, we can look at examples from the Kyrgyz Republic and Kazakhstan. After gaining independence, the Kyrgyz Republic took a large Chinese loan and constructed two high-speed highways connecting the south and north of the country with the western part of the Xinjiang Uygur Autonomous Region of China. The Kashgar-Irkeshtam-Osh road provides China's only direct connection to the Ferghana Valley. The second road, Kashgar–Torugart–Bishkek, has the possibility of further connection with the road network in Kazakhstan and Russia.

A few ambitious road transport projects are underway, linking the region to centres of economic power. Among these projects is the recently completed construction of the Kazakh section of a modern four-lane asphalt concrete road, 2,787 kilometres long, connecting Khorgos on the Chinese border with a point on the border with Russia in the Orenburg region. This section will be an essential part of the 8,445 km Western Europe-Western China (WE-WC) Expressway, which will soon stretch from Lianyungang port on the Yellow Sea in China to the port of St. Petersburg on the Baltic Sea in Russia. The cost of this new highway in the Kazakh segment is an impressive $5.6 billion. The World Bank is the main sponsor of the project and has invested $2.125 billion through the IBRD programme, making it the most expensive project it has ever invested in. Other major sponsors of the Expressway are the Asian Development Bank with investments of $700 million, the Inter-American Development Bank with its contribution of $414 million and the European Bank for Reconstruction and Development with $197 million (Shepard, 2016). Highways like these hold great promise for the rapid cargo transportation between China, Central Asia, Russia and Europe.

Rail

Rail networks are the backbone of any economy to deliver goods and facilitate passenger transportation (Aritua, 2019). Transportation by rail in sealed containers or freight wagons has a comparative advantage over road transport partly because it is more advanced and more efficient in paperwork. Rail provides a higher degree of customs security since only one operator is involved, fewer documents are required, and routes are strictly regulated.

The railway network in Central Asia connects Kazakhstan, Uzbekistan and Turkmenistan, and although there are no transit routes to the Kyrgyz Republic and Tajikistan, these two countries do have some links to the main network. In Soviet times, rail transport was the main unifying factor in the economic activity of a single country, which accounted for 70, and sometimes 85 per cent of all its freight traffic (Strong, et al., 1996). Today, the market share of transport by rail ranges from 60 per cent of all freight in Kazakhstan (including domestic transport) to 80–90 per cent in Tajikistan and Uzbekistan (Rastogi & Arvis, 2014).

Figure 5.3 shows the evolution of the rail networks in Central Asia (World Bank, 2022a). The main networks are located in Kazakhstan, which connects the region with the European part of Russia and Europe in the north, China and East Asia in the southeast. All other countries are currently connected to the rest of the world through Kazakhstan. Uzbekistan Railways has built a railway to Mazar-i-Sharif in Afghanistan to run through Afghanistan to Pakistani ports. Turkmenistan's railways have linked up with the Iranian railway network to connect beyond to Iran's ports, such as Bandar Abbas and Chakhabar, as well as to the countries of the South Caucasus, Turkey, and Europe. The Kyrgyz Republic and Tajikistan have small segments of railways on their territory, connecting them with Kazakhstan and Uzbekistan. The total length of Kazakhstan's railways in 2017 amounted to 16,040.3 kilometres. Over the previous decade, this had grown by 12.9 per cent. Significantly, the size of the rail network in Turkmenistan more than doubled from 3,181 kilometres in 2007 to 7,680 kilometres in 2017.

With the growth of economic activity in the early 2000s, the volume of rail traffic in the region began to increase, carrying both goods and passengers. Figures 5.4–5.5 show the corresponding dynamic of traffic (World Bank, 2022a).

One significant development in the rail network apart from the increase in size is high-speed railways, which began to operate in Central Asia. The first express train, Afrosiyob, began carrying passengers between Tashkent and Samarkand in Uzbekistan in 2011. It was the second high-speed railway in a post-Soviet country after the Moscow–St. Petersburg line opened in 2009.

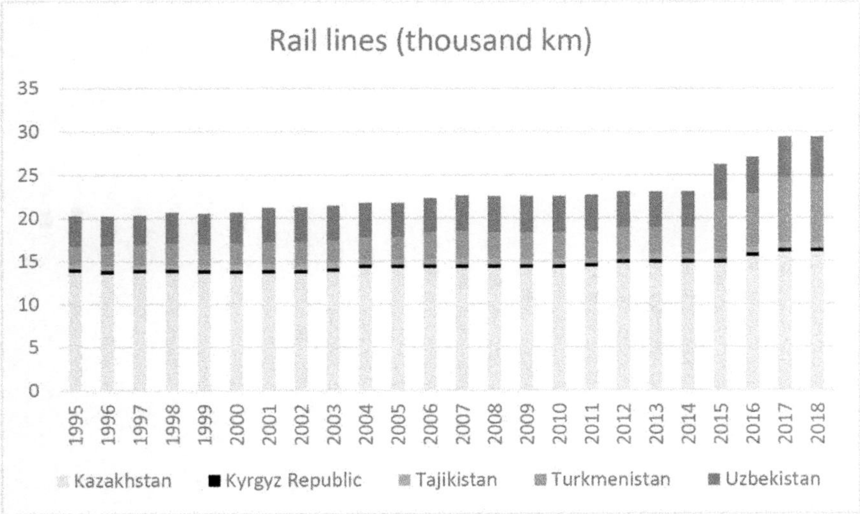

Figure 5.3 Evolution of the rail networks in Central Asian countries (1995–2018)
Source: World Bank (2022a).

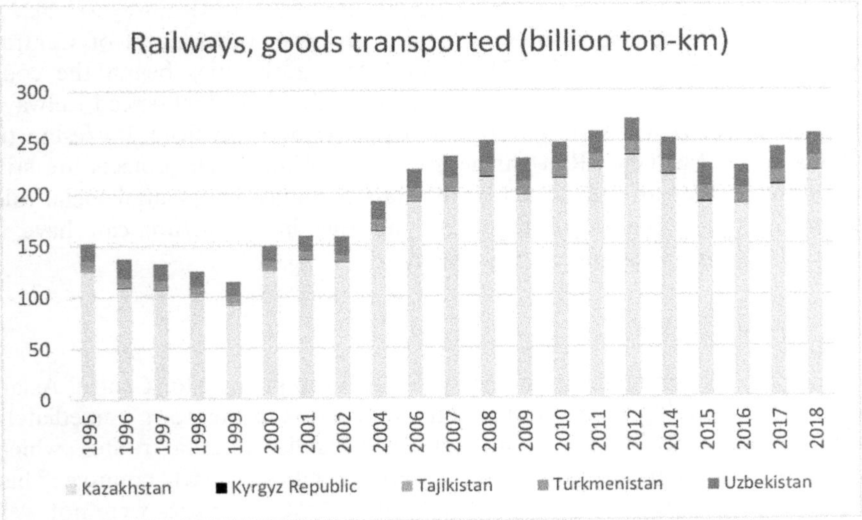

Figure 5.4 Goods transported by rail transport in Central Asian countries (1995–2018)
Source: World Bank (2022a).

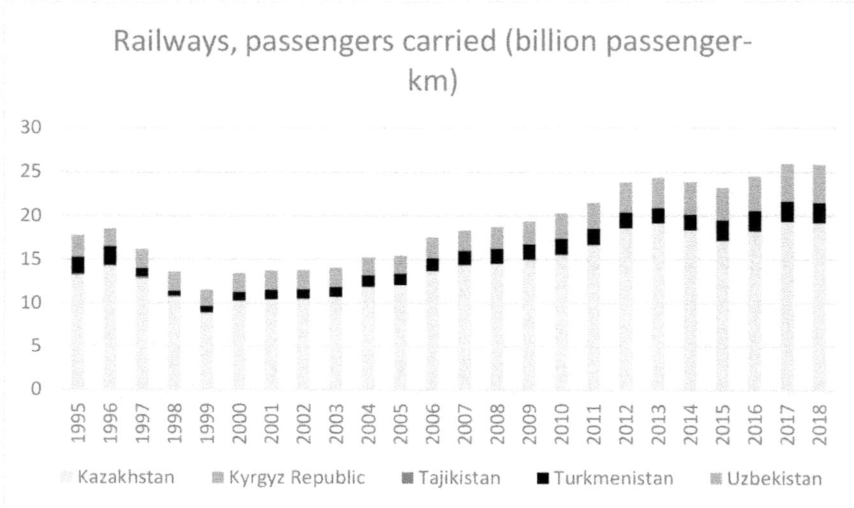

Figure 5.5 Passengers carried by rail in Central Asian countries (1995–2018)
Source: World Bank (2022a).

Now this high-speed passenger railway extends 741 kilometres and connects Uzbekistan's largest cities – Tashkent, Samarkand, Bukhara, Karshi and Navoi. Soon this line will reach the ancient city of Khiva (Railway.uz, 2022). It is hoped that a similar network will soon cover other parts of Central Asia. At the beginning of 2021, Kazakhstani authorities began the construction and connection of their high-speed railways to high-speed railways in Uzbekistan. It will soon be possible to travel by train from Turkestan to Chimkent to Tashkent (Rzd-partner.ru, 2021). While such projects are still unprofitable, they are subsidised by the state and play an essential social role in connecting populated settlements, and this infrastructure can have a positive effect on economic development.

Air

Developing air communication networks was a top priority for Central Asian countries to develop their internal communications in the years immediately after independence. Governments actively subsidise internal routes, which provide fast and reliable connections between cities in each country. That said, until recently, the capitals of the Central Asian countries were not well connected – a reflection of the lack of regional cooperation. Additionally, there are no direct flight paths between non-capital cities of neighbouring countries, which are the types of routes that are very popular in Europe.

In many cases, there are virtually no natural alternatives to air travel since many places are surrounded by mountains or lakes, making traditional land transport expensive. Air transportation within Central Asia has significant potential, determined by its geography, as its area is comparable to the size of Europe. The population is spread over vast areas, and the distances between regional centres often exceed thousands of kilometres. For example, a trip between the capitals of two neighbouring republics, Nursultan and Bishkek, takes about twenty hours by car and only an hour and a half by plane. These cities are further away than Amsterdam and Warsaw or Washington and Chicago. Realising the prospects of such a business in Kazakhstan, the government created two low-cost airlines in 2019, which both focus on local and nearby markets. Air Astana began Kazakhstan's first low-cost airline FlyArystan based in Almaty. The company operates budget flights to thirteen cities in Kazakhstan, the Kyrgyz Republic, Uzbekistan, Azerbaijan, Georgia and Turkey. Qazaq Air, owned by the state sovereign fund Samruk Kazyna, is based in Nursultan. It serves over twenty cities in Kazakhstan and flies to the Russian cities of Novosibirsk and Omsk.

Figure 5.6 shows the number of passengers travelling by air over the last three decades. As a result of economic growth and active aviation policy in the region, there has been a significant increase in passenger air transportation. In 1999, airlines in the five Central Asian countries carried 3.64 million passengers, but only twenty years later, in the pre-COVID year of 2019, this was 14.830 million passengers, which amounts to a 407 per cent increase (World Bank, 2020a). A significant drop in the number of passengers carried in 2020 was due to the coronavirus pandemic.

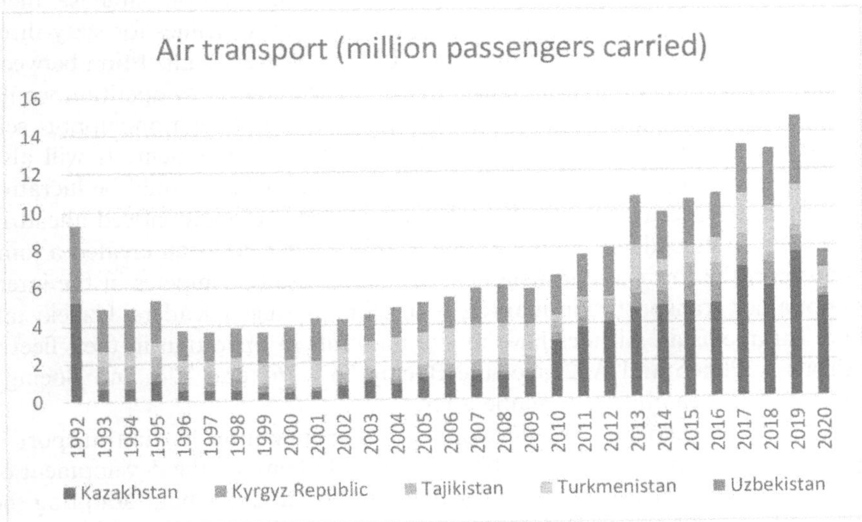

Figure 5.6 Passengers travelling by air in Central Asian countries (1992–2020)
Source: World Bank (2022a).

According to some aviation experts, Central Asia's geographic location makes it ideal for an aviation hub. The region is better positioned between the West and East than the Middle East (Clayton, 2015), which is currently the world leader in transit air transportation (Cummins, 2020). For those who want to fly from Southeast Asia to Europe, passing through Central Asia is quicker and cheaper. In addition, many major airlines fly to the countries of Central Asia today – Lufthansa, KLM, British Airways, Turkish Airlines, Austrian Airlines, Aeroflot, Qatar Airways, Etihad Airways, China Southern Airlines, Hainan Airlines, Ariana Airlines, and others.

Some airlines have benefitted from the quicker flying times via Central Asia. For example, Turkmenistan Airlines operates non-stop flights to European cities such as Moscow, St. Petersburg, Birmingham, London, Frankfurt, and Paris. From Ashgabat, passengers can continue to Amritsar, Bangkok, and Beijing. Other destinations with Turkmenistan Airlines include Istanbul, Abu Dhabi, and Kyiv (Turkmenistan Airlines, 2022). Another airline that had the same idea was Pegasus, an established low-cost airline which wanted to open a regional hub in Bishkek. They planned to connect it with their central hub in Istanbul. Through this hub, passengers from Bishkek would have been able to reach all Central Asian capitals and the nearest Asian markets, including China, Southeast Asia, India, Pakistan and the Arab countries. Unfortunately, this project has come to a halt, but other air carriers will undoubtedly build on this idea.

How competitive is the region in attracting foreign investment in the aviation industry? According to the CAPA – Center for Aviation database, there is almost one airline per airport in Central Asia (sixty airlines for sixty-three airports) (CAPA – Centre for Aviation, 2022). However, competition between airlines exists only on international routes. An increase in competition would help the aviation market to develop more actively, and aviation support services will also receive incentives to support their development. It will also support a healthy emerging market for newcomers, which would be lucrative for the right international partner. Kazakhstan has already moved ahead in this race. In its collaboration with BAE Systems, Kazakhstan created a joint venture in the form of Air Astana, which successfully competes in the international air transportation markets with global industry leaders. Uzbekistan and Turkmenistan Airlines have modern aircraft in operation in their fleet – Airbus A320neo and A321neo, the Boeing 757, 767 and 777, and Boeing's newest 787 Dreamliners, to name a few.

One major barrier to the development of competition in air transport is posed by problems with market liberalisation. Judging by the development of aviation regulatory policy in the region, there are doubts about adopting the free-market aviation model. This does not necessarily mean that there are no opportunities for competition but it does mean there are various hurdles for potential investors entering this lucrative market to overcome. The IATA forecast for 2019 indicates world aviation passenger traffic will double by 2037, and that there will be an expected shift of the global economic axis from west to east (Russian Aviation Insider, 2019). Consequently, passenger traffic in Central Asian countries will grow, and closer regional cooperation will be more and more crucial.

Another hurdle to overcome is the quality of air transport infrastructure. The World Economic Forum's classification of the quality of air transport infrastructure shows that the efficiency of air transport is on par with other developing countries. However, air transport links lag far behind economically developed regions such as East Asia and the EU. Given the direct relationship between GDP per capita and the frequency of air travel, one cannot expect a sharp increase in air travel anytime soon. However, the air travel market is still sure to grow.

Ports

Although there are no seaports in Central Asia, the quality of port infrastructure in Central Asia is still important to consider in this analysis, both in terms of the ports on the Caspian Sea and so-called dry ports (ESCAP, 2018). In recent years, inland intermodal facilities or dry ports have received more attention due to their potential to meet supply chain requirements by consolidating highway and rail access. The concept of a dry port originated from the idea of a seaport directly connected to a road or railway with inland terminals. It was in response to the problems caused by the increase in container traffic, the corresponding lack of space at seaport terminals, and the

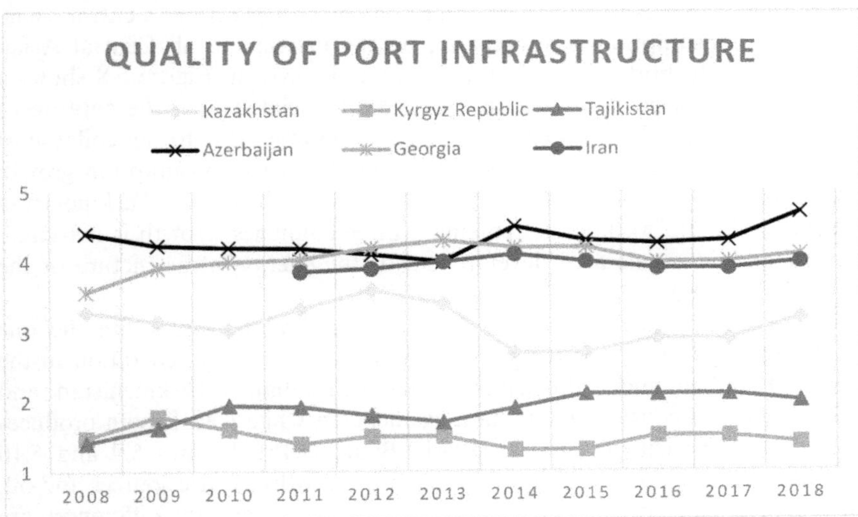

Figure 5.7 The quality of port infrastructure in Central Asia and a few selected countries

Source: World Bank (2022b).

growing congestion of the sidings serving their terminals. Dry ports can also play a key role in the customs processing of goods, storage and distribution along internal and cross-border economic corridors.

Figure 5.7 demonstrates the quality of port infrastructure in the three countries of Central Asia, as well as in Azerbaijan and Iran, which are neighbours on the Caspian Sea, and Georgia, which has access to the Black Sea. Data from the WEF is listed in the World Bank database (World Bank, 2022b). Here, a higher rating indicates better infrastructure.

It is not surprising that Georgia and Iran show the best results since they have access to the sea with developed port infrastructures. But here, it is more critical to evaluate the quality of the Azerbaijani ports, which is also a landlocked country with a port infrastructure on the Caspian Sea. In this regard, Azerbaijan is an excellent example for Kazakhstan and Turkmenistan, which also have ports on the Caspian Sea. It is clear from the ratings that these countries could do far more to develop their ports. With no access to the Caspian Sea, the Kyrgyz Republic and Tajikistan unsurprisingly received the lowest scores. Considering the future development of the southern railway routes between Asia and Europe, including through the Caspian Sea, all littoral countries should pay special attention to the development of their ports (ESCAP, 2019).

Energy

Energy is a core part of the infrastructure of any nation and a vital piece of the puzzle when examining the development prospects of Central Asia. Electricity consumption is, in general, on the increase in all Central Asian countries due to both population and economic growth. Figure 5.8 shows a fall in per capita consumption in the 1990s associated with the rupture of economic ties and the fall of the countries' economies due to the collapse of the Soviet Union. Since the 2000s, per capita electricity consumption growth has been continuously increasing especially in Kazakhstan and Turkmenistan (World Bank, 2022a). For the remaining three countries, growth is marginal. In light of this, accelerated development of the energy infrastructure of the region is required.

Nature has endowed the region with rich natural resources. On the one hand, clean hydropower is the primary source of electricity generation in the Kyrgyz Republic and Tajikistan. On the other hand, Turkmenistan and Uzbekistan have considerable natural gas deposits while Kazakhstan produces most of its electricity from coal (World Bank, 2015). Figures 5.9 and 5.10 show the dynamics of electricity production from hydroelectric sources and oil, gas and coal as a percentage of total generation. Significant differences are seen in the methods of electricity generation, with environmentally friendly hydroelectric power plants and natural gas being used for its production.

In addition, Kazakhstan, Turkmenistan and Uzbekistan actively export their energy resources, mainly crude oil and natural gas. Kazakhstan also

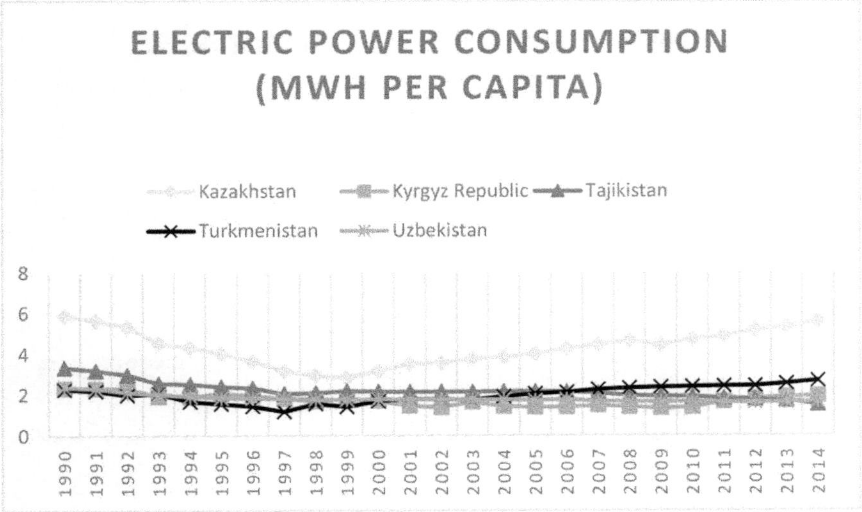

Figure 5.8 Electricity consumption per capita in Central Asian countries (1990–2014)
Source: World Bank (2022a).

exports coal and uranium from its large world-class deposits. The findings of a study by the World Bank suggest that the volume and quality of electricity generation in the region compared to other parts of the world are at a satisfactory level (World Bank, 2015).

According to the World Economic Forum's ranking of electricity infrastructure, Kazakhstan currently ranks 19th out of 144 countries, the Kyrgyz Republic ranks 94th and Tajikistan 107th. All countries in the region scored over 90 out of a possible 100 points for their electricity supply infrastructure. A similar picture occurs with the quality of transmission and distribution of electricity, and the countries of Central Asia rank between 19th (Kazakhstan) and 115th (Kyrgyz Republic) (World Economic Forum, 2019). Therefore, as in many other countries, apart from perhaps Kazakhstan, there are significant losses in delivering electricity to consumers.

In Soviet times, the coordination of energy flows in the region was carried out through Central Asia's specially designed Unified Energy System (UES). Eighty-three different power plants provided uninterrupted electricity to all five republics. The control centre for the entire system was in Tashkent (Smirnov, 2018). Considering seasonal fluctuations in generating capacity, this system supported a stable regional electricity supply. During the winter, Kazakh and Uzbek thermal power plants fed energy into the grid to supply Kyrgyzstan and Tajikistan, which returned electricity to the grid through their hydroelectric plants in the summer. The system also connected northern Kazakhstan to the Russian power grid, from which additional energy was taken by regulators when needed.

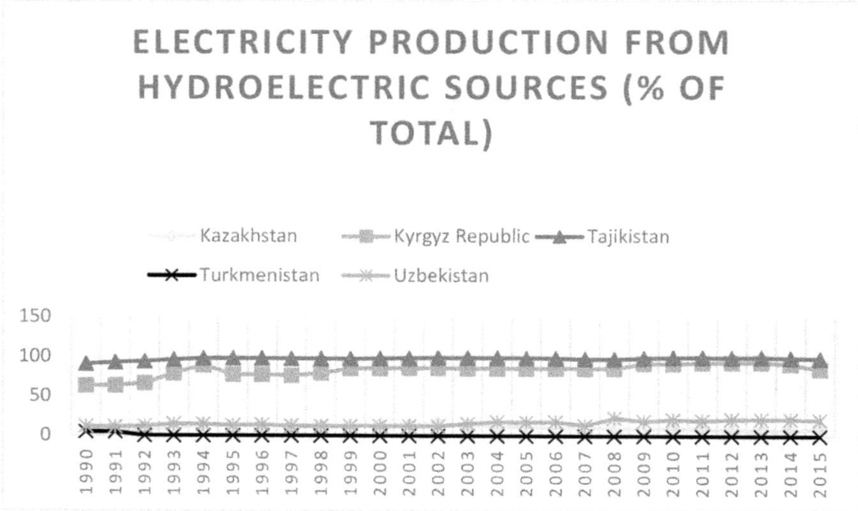

Figure 5.9 Electricity production from hydroelectric sources in Central Asian countries (1990–2015)
Source: World Bank (2022a).

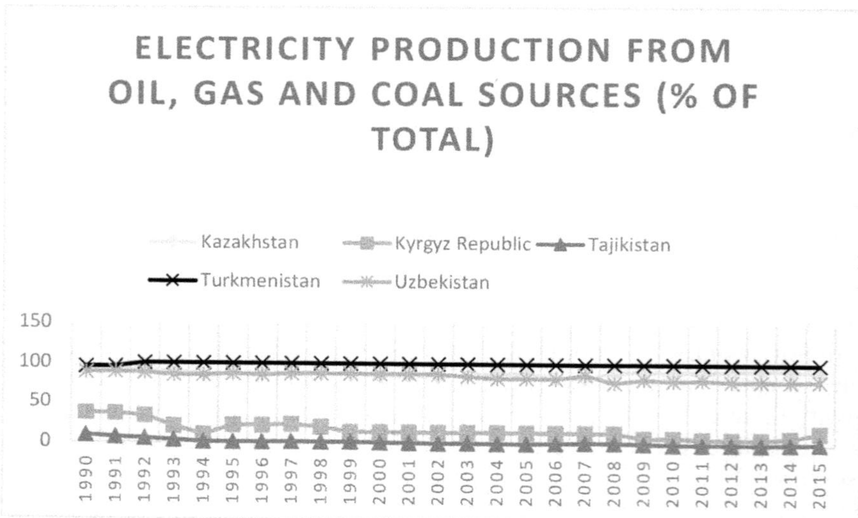

Figure 5.10 Electricity production from oil, gas and coal in Central Asian countries (1990–2015)
Source: World Bank (2022a).

This energy infrastructure has, since the 1990s, declined considerably, mostly because of its age. Many power plants, distribution and transmission lines were built many years ago by Soviet engineers using old technologies. Outdated equipment cannot work effectively, and significant losses occur in networks during operation. For example, in its report on Kazakhstan produced in September 2016, the Asian Development Bank noted that 70 per cent of its electricity production infrastructure needs rehabilitation (PwC, 2016). It is striking that this is the situation even in Kazakhstan, which is compared more favourably in the World Economic Forum ranking.

Here are a few notable examples of ageing infrastructure. The first part of the largest power plant in Central Asia, the Syrdarya Coal Handling Preparation Plant in Uzbekistan (CHPP), was commissioned in 1972. The first section of the Bishkek Combined Heat and Power (CHP) station, which provides electricity to most of the northern regions of the country, came into operation in 1961. In comparison, the Ekibastuz CHPP in Kazakhstan, whose first unit went into operation in 1980, is still considered to be relatively new. A similar problem plagues the region's power lines. In the wealthiest country in the region, Kazakhstan, electricity losses, mainly due to old transmission lines, are estimated at 16 per cent (ADB, 2013). In other countries, the situation with losses is even worse (OSCE, 2022).

Pipelines

In Russian, the saying goes that all roads lead to Moscow, not to Rome. In Soviet times, this was certainly the case. Not only oil and gas pipelines but all other infrastructure networks, including all transport connections, power lines and even water arteries from Central Asia were designed and built, and strictly directed toward the European parts of the Russian Federation. After countries gained independence in 1991, they began to diversify their investment priorities in energy infrastructure in search of new markets and self-development prospects. It quickly became apparent that global players were interested in supporting such a policy, especially concerning the transportation of hydrocarbons.

Russia was among these global players, keen to maintain its regional political and economic hegemony. For example, the supply of natural gas to Russia from Turkmenistan, which has existed since Soviet times, continued. However, Western countries and China quickly built massive oil and gas pipeline networks to export Central Asian hydrocarbons to sustain their economic growth and meet their energy needs. In an increasingly tense political climate, pipelines have become integral to developing the new Silk Road. Energy export controls have become associated with pragmatic economic interests and the desire to help countries diversify their economies. Energy was also the means to increase outsiders' political influence in Central Asia.

Oil Pipelines

To meet the growing demand and bring crude oil to their markets, major American and European energy companies such as Exxon Mobil, Chevron, ConocoPhillips, Eni, and Royal Dutch Shell began to make considerable investments in the region's energy infrastructure. Western oil companies invested in designing and constructing the Caspian Pipeline Consortium (CPC) pipeline, which opened in October 2001. It transports Kazakh oil 1,580 kilometres, from the Tengiz Field in Kazakhstan via Russian territory to its terminal in Novorossiysk on the Black Sea. The CPC was the first and only oil pipeline inside Russia not controlled by Transneft, which is the state oil pipeline monopoly.

The construction of the first oil pipeline between China and Kazakhstan was agreed upon in 1997. It was China's first direct oil import pipeline from Central Asia. Owned jointly by China National Petroleum Corporation (CNPC) and Kazakh oil company KazMunayGas, the 2,228-kilometre pipeline runs from the Kazakh coast of the Caspian to Xinjiang in China. Besides, Kazakhstan is developing a trans-Caspian barge system that can deliver crude oil from the port of Aktau by barge to the Baku-Tbilisi-Ceyhan (BTC) pipeline. Ceyhan is a Turkish deep-water port on the Mediterranean that opened in July 2006.

Gas Pipelines

In the post-Soviet era, the emergence of Gazprom as Russia's state gas monopoly maintained Russia's dominance in Central Asia. The Central Asia Center (CAC) pipeline connected Kazakhstan, Turkmenistan, and Uzbekistan to distribute gas within the region and export it to Russia. Gazprom continued to dominate this system, entering into contracts with three countries to purchase all available capacity in the CAC system. Due to this contract, Gazprom maintained its monopoly over Central Asian gas for a long time.

After thorough preparations, in the mid-2000s, China began an ambitious project to import natural gas from Turkmenistan. The Chinese National Petroleum Corporation (CNPC) acted as the operator of the gas pipeline construction project and started pumping gas in August 2007. In a record 2.5 years, CNPC built three channels of its 1,833-kilometre Central Asian Gas Pipeline from its Bagtyyarlyk concession in northern Turkmenistan – through Uzbekistan and Kazakhstan to the Xinjiang Uygur Autonomous Region (XUAR) of China.

If the political situation in Afghanistan begins to stabilise, Turkmen gas may be able to find its way to consumers in South Asia. In that case, it will be possible to implement the construction of the TAPI gas pipeline with a total length of 1814 kilometres, named after the first letters of the countries it should pass through – Turkmenistan, Afghanistan, Pakistan, and India. It can be argued that the oil and gas pipeline construction projects from Central Asia have become the most ambitious and successful infrastructure projects in the post-Soviet period. They provide a large share of exports and bring a large share of foreign exchange earnings to the exporters. They provide a large share of exports and bring a significant share of foreign exchange earnings to the region. The region retains the potential to export hydrocarbons to other markets as well.

Telecommunications

Despite its strategic location at the crossroads of Europe and Asia, Central Asia has long been poorly connected to the rest of the world. Several factors objectively hinder the establishment of reliable and fast communications. The region is remote, landlocked, and cut off from many centres of modern civilisation by deserts, steppes, and high mountains. The area has a harsh climate, and long distances separate settlements. During the Soviet period, Central Asia was fenced off from the rest of the world by a rigid border. Even today, the transport and energy infrastructure of the region reflects Soviet needs, rather than modern ones. In addition to physical barriers, political and regulatory barriers still hinder the free movement of goods, services, and ideas. To overcome these many barriers, high-quality communication is critical.

In today's world, affordable, up-to-date, secure, and reliable digital connectivity that empowers users is essential. Calculations and practice prove that a 10 per cent increase in broadband Internet speed can add at least one per cent to economic growth, and just a 1 per cent increase in Internet connectivity can increase exports by 4.3 per cent (Grzegorczyk, 2020). Experts have suggested that countries with robust communications infrastructure can mitigate up to 50 per cent of the negative economic impact caused by the pandemic (Katz, 2020).

Almost half of the population of Central Asia is still not connected to digital technologies, and many live in rural and remote areas with poor connectivity (World Bank, 2020b). Table 5.2 presents the results of a study on the number of individuals using the Internet and broadband subscriptions per 100 inhabitants in the countries of Central Asia compared to the global average (United Nations, 2020). Three of the five countries in Central Asia still lag behind the world average regarding the number of people using the Internet. Only Kazakhstan has achieved the average for broadband subscriptions per capita. But lack of access is not the only problem. Internet connection in Central Asia is generally still expensive and of poor quality.

Figures 5.11 and 5.12 show the distribution of fixed telephone lines and the number of subscriptions to broadband internet in the region. As expected, there is a direct correlation between the number of telecommunications connections and GDP per capita, with Kazakhstan leading the way and the Kyrgyz Republic and Tajikistan trailing behind (World Bank, 2022a).

Table 5.2 Percentage of individuals using the Internet and broadband subscriptions per 100 inhabitants in Central Asian countries (2020)

	Percentage of individuals using the Internet	*Broadband subscriptions per 100 inhabitants*
Kazakhstan	79%	13.44
Uzbekistan	55%	12.70
Kyrgyz Republic	38%	5.64
Tajikistan	22%	0.07
Turkmenistan	21%	0.09
Global average	54%	13.26

Source: United Nations (2020).

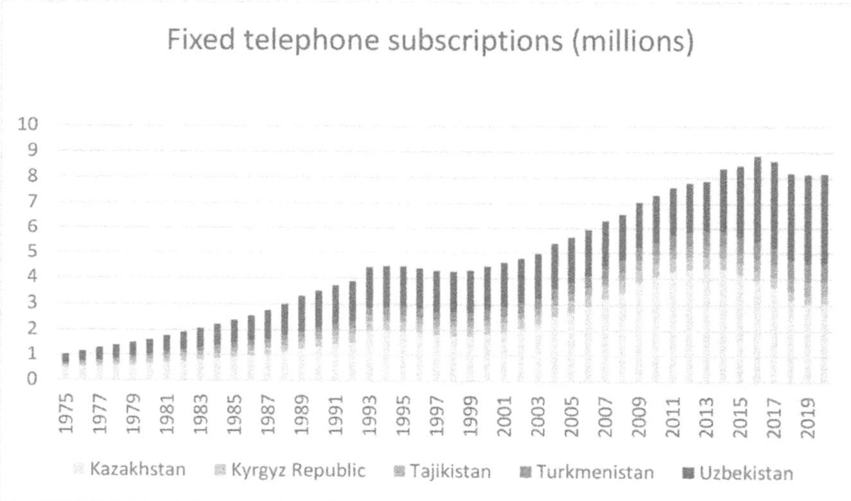

Figure 5.11 Fixed telephone subscriptions in Central Asian countries (1975–2019)
Source: World Bank (2022a).

This trend is especially noticeable in Figure 5.13, which shows the share of the region's population using the Internet compared to the OECD average. According to this indicator, Kazakhstan has practically caught up with the OECD countries. Particularly noteworthy is Internet development in Uzbekistan, which has approached the level of OECD countries despite a modest GDP per capita. The Kyrgyz Republic, where there are no restrictions on Internet use, is also quickly approaching this level.

In Central Asia, the population actively uses mobile communications (Figure 5.14). Rapid growth in the number of users in all countries was particularly observed in the 2000s when it slowed down and reached from 100 to 150 per cent of penetration in various countries.

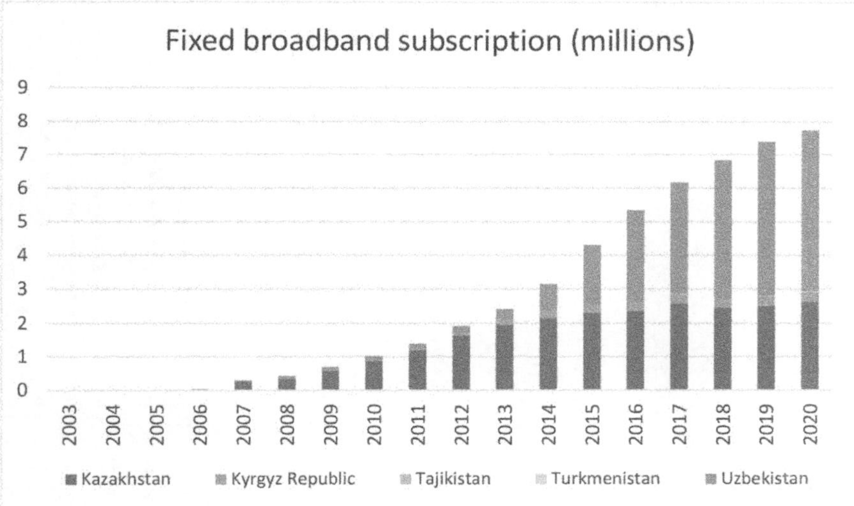

Figure 5.12 Fixed broadband subscriptions in Central Asian countries (2003–2020)
Source: World Bank (2022a).

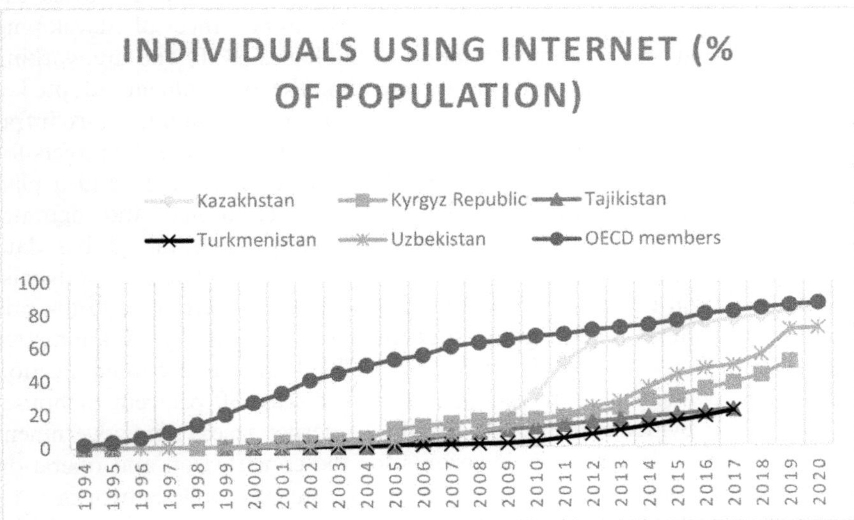

Figure 5.13 Percentage of individuals using the Internet in Central Asian countries
Source: World Bank (2022a).

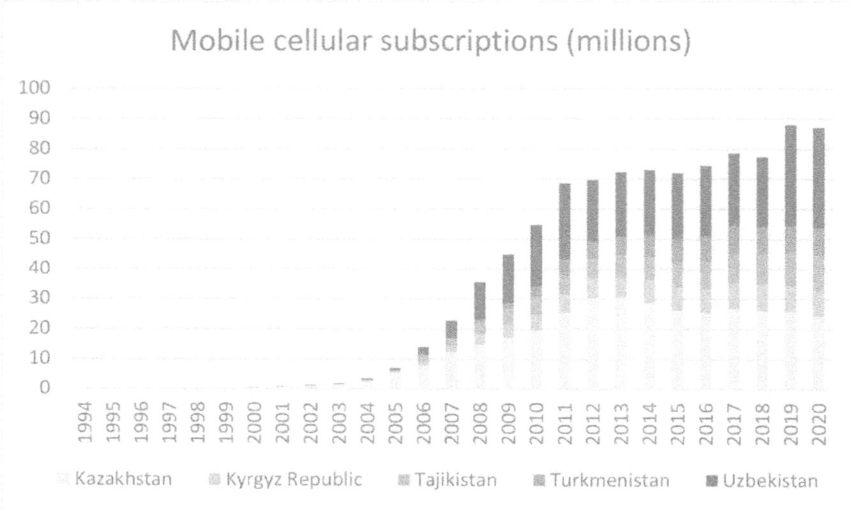

Figure 5.14 Mobile cellular subscriptions in Central Asian countries
Source: World Bank (2022a).

Those positive results are explained by the fact that in some countries, the governments have recognised the exceptional importance of developing modern information and communication technologies (ICT) and are working in this direction. For example, in Uzbekistan, the government adopted a resolution "on measures to develop further the telecommunications infrastructure of Uzbekistan" (Huquqiy axborot, 2021). It approved the targets for developing the telecommunications infrastructure for 2022–2024 and a plan to provide mobile coverage on highways of international and national importance. The government has decided that by 2023, the global data transmission channel capacity will be increased 3.5 times. The data transmission network will be expanded by building 150,000 kilometres of fibre-optic communication lines. The length of these networks was just 36,600 kilometres in 2019 and already 68,600 kilometres in 2020. Fibre-optic communication lines will be connected to all settlements, and at least 80 per cent of households will be provided with broadband wired Internet access. The government plans to simplify the issuance of permits for the construction and operation of cell towers, which will accelerate the deployment of mobile networks.

By the end of 2021, all police departments, buildings in the *mahallas* (neighbourhoods or local communities in Uzbek), penitentiary institutions, offices of preventive inspectors of law enforcement agencies, public education institutions, state archives and organisations had broadband Internet access. According to the resolution, the government will establish international backbone channels on Uzbekistan-Afghanistan-Pakistan, Uzbekistan-Kyrgyzstan-China, and Uzbekistan-Turkmenistan-Azerbaijan-Turkey routes through the existing border checkpoints. The government will take joint measures at the Chinese border to establish new connections and mutual Internet traffic exchange points.

It is estimated that the countries of the region will need to invest at least $6 billion to connect the remaining half of their populations to the Internet by 2030 (ITU, 2020). It will require political will and an unprecedented effort, including a massive influx of private investment to deploy infrastructure alongside public sector efforts to develop digital skills and policy reforms.

Given this ambitious plan and the current trends in the global market, the Central Asian telecommunications sector should seek to attract private and primarily foreign investment to meet infrastructure needs, especially in rural and remote areas. However, since these areas are often commercially unprofitable for private operators, there will be a need to encourage infrastructure sharing, apply public assistance mechanisms and develop public–private partnership models.

Which foreign investors are most interested in such investments? So far, there is no interest on the part of Western companies. On the other hand, the closest neighbours of the region, both China and Russia, are showing interest in investments in digital technologies and communications.

Chinese and Russian digital relations are a complex ecosystem of imitation and cooperation, as well as competition and suspicion. China acts primarily as a supplier, exporting technological products and services and models of Internet control and surveillance to countries in Central Asia. Russia manufactures products, tries to implement its regulatory policy in local markets, and competes with China to sell digital goods. Central Asian states have adopted part of the Russian systems, standards, and digital communications legislation. At the same time, the Russian government has signed lucrative contracts for Chinese ICT and surveillance equipment. It is increasingly implementing aspects of Chinese digital control techniques too.

Chinese companies dominate the supply of telecommunications equipment to governments and mobile operators in Uzbekistan, Kazakhstan, Tajikistan and the Kyrgyz Republic. For example, Huawei in 2008 upgraded the countries' telecommunications network. Later, the company included the 5G service in Uzbekistan's state-owned companies, Uzmobile and Ucell. In Kazakhstan, Huawei supports Kazakhtelecom, Kcell, Beeline and Tele2, and in the Kyrgyz Republic, it produces about 90 per cent of technologies for Sky Mobile and 70 per cent for Alfa Telecom, the two biggest telecom companies (Yan, 2019). Before leaving the market, the Tajik telecom operator TK Mobile had the majority of ZTE ownership (Asia-Plus, 2018).

However, China is planning an even more significant investment in Central Asia's digital and communications technologies through its Digital Silk Road (DSR) programme, announced in 2015 as part of the Belt and Road Initiative (BRI). DSR intends to cover the digital economy, artificial intelligence, nanotechnology, quantum computing, big data and cloud computing, and smart cities. While infrastructure, such as new railways and ports, is visibly changing the geography and economies of BRI countries, the impact of the "Chinese Internet", which extends from infrastructure to hardware, software, and services, is less visible. Is China creating a separate China-centric Internet among its neighbours and BRI customers? Will the world be divided into different Internets? Do DSRs and BRIs generally represent a single strategy, or are they a series of ad hoc projects that fall under the same ideological umbrella but with very different scopes, actors, and goals? We will know the answers to these questions quite soon.

Currently, at the level of services such as e-commerce, the typical strategy of Chinese companies is to partner with local partners and use the existing digital ecosystem to enter the market and establish their presence. An example of this is the entry of AliExpress, first into the Russian market and then into Central Asia. This is a prime example of the flexible nature of the outward expansion of the Chinese ICT industry, both inside and outside the Digital Silk Road. The rapid advancement of telecommunications and digital solutions shows how important these are for their development in the region. Both the governments and the private sector understand that to be leaders in the latest technologies, activities like these must continue at an even faster pace.

Water Supply and Sanitation

Water is vital for life itself. To maintain a constant flow of water to and in any country, a vast network of water infrastructure must be maintained: manmade irrigation networks, numerous reservoirs, dams, pumping stations and artificial channels. All these facilities serve multiple purposes, such as drinking, industrial and agricultural water supply, irrigation and hydropower, fisheries and shipping, recreation and environmental sustainability (CAWater-Info, 2022). Notable examples of water infrastructure facilities in Central Asia include the Nurek Dam, the highest dam in the world, located on the Vakhsh River in the mountains of Tajikistan; and, the Karakum Canal, built in the deserts of Turkmenistan, which is one of the longest artificial canals on the planet.

Due to the lack of finance, the safety of most hydraulic structures in the region is assessed by experts as unsatisfactory. Central Asia's government agencies and water utility companies face outdated infrastructure, inefficiency, and low productivity, and they urgently need to reform their water and sanitation sectors. Recently, the provision of drinking water has improved somewhat, but many still do not have access to piped water in their homes. This problem is most common in rural areas. The construction of new water supply systems and the maintenance of existing ones require significant financial resources, which, as always, are scarce.

Experts estimate that for about 22 million people, or about a third of the entire population of Central Asia, primarily rural residents, clean water is still a luxury (Burunciuc, 2019). In Uzbekistan and Tajikistan, only 31 per cent of the rural population can access safely managed water, compared to 86 per cent and 57 per cent in urban areas. The percentage of residents of

Kyrgyz villages who had access to drinking water in 2017 was about 54 per cent, which was considerable progress for the country (Burunciuc, 2019).

One study by the World Bank found that it makes more sense for the countries of Central Asia to actively invest in water supply and sanitation than to deal with the consequences of underinvestment. It is estimated that insufficient water and sanitation services cost Central Asia about $2 billion annually. Tajikistan suffers the most from this, with losses of up to 4 per cent of the country's GDP (Burunciuc, 2019).

Efforts by the World Bank and government agencies have helped more than 1.1 million people in Uzbekistan, 400,000 people in rural areas of the Kyrgyz Republic, and about 70,000 people in Tajikistan gain access to water (Burunciuc, 2019).

The World Economic Forum assessed water quality in terms of infrastructure, reliability of water supplies, and exposure to unsafe drinking water. The quality of water infrastructure and water quality in Central Asia, ranked among 141 countries in the world, are presented in Table 5.3 (World Economic Forum, 2019). Even in comparison with the republics of the South Caucasus, the situation of providing the population with quality water is at an unsatisfactory level.

A World Bank study showed that the dominant use of water in all countries is in the agricultural sector (World Bank, 2022a). Water consumption for domestic and industrial needs is incomparably less. For example, in the Kyrgyz Republic, less than 5 per cent of total water consumption is used for household needs (Russell, 2018).

When it comes to sanitation infrastructure in Central Asia, the urban population is provided with basic services, but rural residents still have insufficient access to sewerage connections, and septic tanks are often not available. Inadequate hygiene conditions not only pollute the environment but also endanger the health of the population. Figure 5.15 presents data which represents the share of the population in the Kyrgyz Republic using safely managed sanitation services (World Bank, 2022b). It can however be

Table 5.3 Water Infrastructure Indicators in Central Asia and the Caucasus, 2018–2019

	Water Infrastructure	*Reliability of Water Supply*	*Exposure to Unsafe Drinking Water*
Kazakhstan	68	78	59
Kyrgyz Republic	85	110	70
Tajikistan	80	75	85
Armenia	49	59	34
Azerbaijan	56	58	60
Georgia	58	63	58

Source: World Economic Forum (2019).

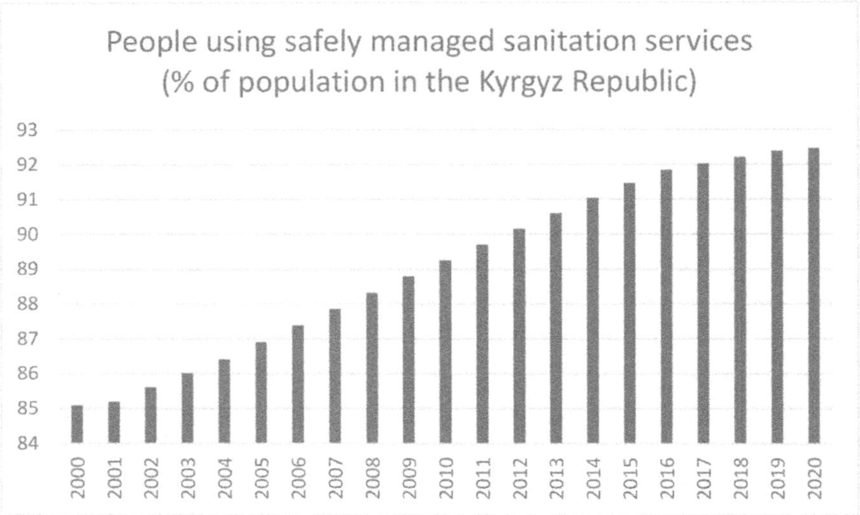

Figure 5.15 Percentage of people using safely managed sanitation services in the Kyrgyz Republic (2000–2020)
Source: World Bank (2022b).

seen that a growing number of the population has access to sanitation services, a figure that has already exceeded 92 per cent.

Conclusion

Despite the difficult economic situation after independence, the countries of Central Asia, understanding the role of developing their infrastructure, have implemented a few large-scale infrastructure projects. Governments have invested heavily in building pipelines to export energy resources, laying new electrical networks, building roads, and expanding the highways and rail networks. In recent years, they have invested heavily in developing digital infrastructure too.

It is imperative to underline that physical (or hard) infrastructure, which includes roads, railways, seaports and airports, energy, telecommunications, water supply, and sanitation, cannot contribute to economic development unless accompanied by so-called soft infrastructure. This refers to the effectiveness of regulatory measures and is weakened by excessive bureaucracy, lack of transparency, lengthy administrative procedures, delayed payments, favouritism, and corruption. The good infrastructure reduces production costs and improves transport connectivity through efficient transport networks and telecommunications. Its development expands market links and creates efficient markets, reducing time and price discrepancies and creating

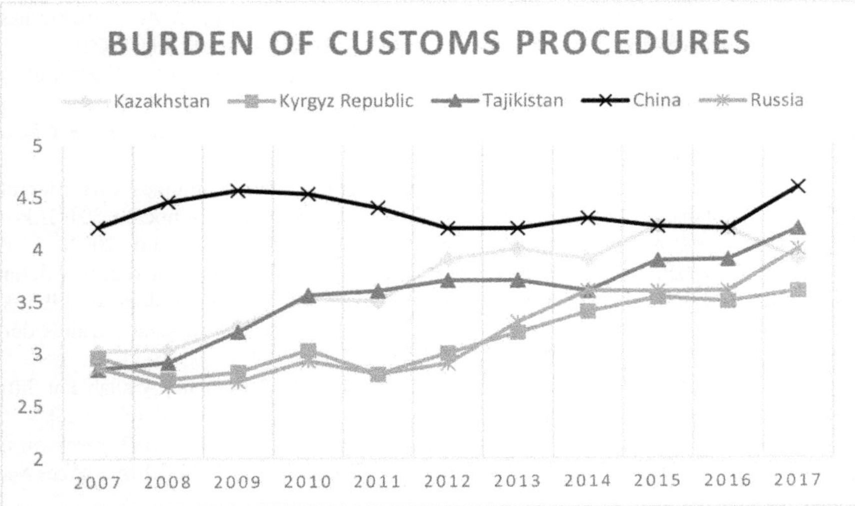

Figure 5.16 The burden of customs procedures in Central Asia and a few selected countries
Source: World Bank (2022c).

more jobs and public revenues. Both hard and soft infrastructure is equally important for optimal impact (Ismail & Mahyideen, 2015).

The countries of Central Asia understand the importance of improving soft infrastructure and are trying to simplify their regulatory framework. One example of this is shown in Figure 5.16, which represents the burden of customs procedures calculated by the experts of the World Economic Forum (WEF) for three countries in the region and for comparison for its closest neighbours, China and Russia (World Bank, 2022c). Higher numbers indicate more accessible customs procedures at borders.

In recent years, the countries of Central Asia have made progress in simplifying customs procedures, and this indicator has come close to the best practices in China. This practice of reducing bureaucratic barriers should continue. To reduce costs and increase their competitiveness, landlocked countries need to improve all of their hard and soft infrastructure at an even faster rate than others. The future of the region depends on how quickly this happens.

References

ADB, 2006. *Increasing Gains from Trade Through Regional Cooperation in Trade Policy, Transport, and Customs Transit*, Philippines: ADB.

ADB, 2013. Proposed Loans Akmola Electricity Distribution Company and Central-Asian Electric Power Corporation Akmola Electricity Distribution Network Modernization and Expansion Project (Kazakhstan). [Online] Available at: https://www.adb.org/sites/default/files/project-document/78750/46933-014-kaz-rrp.pdf [Accessed July 2022].

Aritua, B., 2019. *The Rail Freight Challenge for Emerging Economies*, Washington, DC: World Bank.

Arvis, J.-F. *et al.*, 2012. *Connecting to Compete 2012: Trade Logistics in the Global Economy*, Washington, DC: World Bank.

Asia-Plus, 2018. TK Mobile withdraw from country's telecommunications market. [Online] Available at: https://asiaplustj.info/en/news/tajikistan/economic/20180411/tk-mobile-withdraw-from-countrys-telecommunications-market [Accessed July 2022].

Burunciuc, L., 2019. Improving water and sanitation in Central Asia requires determination and shared commitment. [Online] Available at: https://blogs.worldbank.org/europeandcentralasia/improving-water-and-sanitation-central-asia-requires-determination-and-shared [Accessed July 2022].

CAPA – Centre for Aviation, 2022. Central Asia Region Profile. [Online] Available at: https://centreforaviation.com/data/profiles/regions/asia-central-asia [Accessed July 2022].

CAWater-Info, 2022. Safety of large hydraulic structures (dams, HPP, reservoirs). [Online] Available at: http://www.cawater-info.net/bk/1-1-1-1-4_e.htm [Accessed July 2022].

Clayton, E., 2015. *Airport infrastructure in Asia: Coping with the demand surge*, London: PwC.

Cummins, N., 2020. Why Central Asia Is The Next Big Opportunity In Aviation. [Online] Available at: https://www.eways-aviation.com/blog/why-central-asia-is-the-next-big-opportunity-in-aviation [Accessed July 2022].

Donaubauer, J., Glas, A., Meyer, B. & Nunnenkamp, P., 2018. Disentangling the impact of infrastructure on trade using a new index of infrastructure. *Review of World Economics*, 154 (4), pp. 745–784.

ESCAP, 2018. Regional framework for the development of dry ports of international importance for north and central Asia capacity building workshop. [Online] Available at: https://www.unescap.org/events/regional-framework-development-dry-ports-international-importance-north-and-central-asia [Accessed July 2022].

ESCAP, 2019. Infrastructure connectivity for integrated intermodal transport and logistics in Asia and the Pacific. [Online] Available at: https://unece.org/DAM/trans/doc/2019/wp24/II.5-_Ms._Azhar_Jaimurzina_UNESCAP.pdf [Accessed July 2022].

Grzegorczyk, M., 2020. The importance of connecting Central Asia. [Online] Available at: https://emerging-europe.com/news/the-importance-of-connecting-central-asia/ [Accessed July 2022].

Hoekman, B. & Nicita, A., 2008. *World Bank Policy Research Working Paper Series no. 4797*, Washington, DC: World Bank.

Huquqiy axborot, 2021. Kўp kvartirali ujlar kamida 1 Gbit/s ўtkazuvchanlik кobilijati bilan Internetga ulanadi. [Online] Available at: https://t.me/huquqiyaxborot/10740 [Accessed July 2022].

Ismail, N. W. & Mahyideen, J. M., 2015. *The Impact of Infrastructure on Trade and Economic Growth in Selected Economies in Asia*, Tokyo: Asian Development Bank Institute.

ITU, 2020. New ITU study estimates US$ 428 billion are needed to connect the remaining 3 billion people to the Internet by 2030. [Online] Available at: https://www.itu.int/en/mediacentre/Pages/PR16-2020-ITU-publishes-Connecting-Humanity-study.aspx [Accessed July 2022].

Katz, R., 2020. *Economic Impact of COVID-19 on Digital Infrastructure*, Geneva: ITU.

Ojala, L., Naula, T. & Queiroz, C., 2004. *Transport Sector Restructuring in the Baltic States Toward EU Accession*. Washington, DC, Logistics, The Turku School of Economics and Business Administration.

OSCE, 2022. Advancing Energy Security in Central Asia. [Online] Available at: https://www.osce.org/files/f/documents/8/8/513787_0.pdf [Accessed July 2022].

Portugal-Perez, A. & Wilson, J. S., 2012. Export Performance and Trade Facilitation Reform: Hard and Soft Infrastructure. *World Development*, 40 (7), pp. 1295–1307.

PwC, 2016. CAREC: Study for power sector financing road map mobilizing financing for priority projects Kazakhstan. [Online] Available at: https://www.carecprogram.org/uploads/CAREC_TA8727_CountryReport_Kazakhstan.pdf [Accessed July 2022].

Railway.uz, 2022. Istorija razvitija zheleznyh dorog v Uzbekistane. [Online] Available at: https://railway.uz/ru/gazhk/istoriya_zheleznykh_dorog/ [Accessed July 2022].

Rastogi, C. & Arvis, J.-F., 2014. *The Eurasian Connection: Supply-Chain Efficiency along the Modern Silk Route through Central Asia*. Washington, DC: World Bank.

Russell, M., 2018. Water in Central Asia: An increasingly scarce resource. [Online] Available at: https://www.europarl.europa.eu/RegData/etudes/BRIE/2018/625181/EPRS_BRI(2018)625181_EN.pdf [Accessed July 2022].

Russian Aviation Insider, 2019. Central Asian aviation industry faces up to new challenges. [Online] Available at: http://www.rusaviainsider.com/central-asian-aviation-faces-new-challenges/ [Accessed July 2022].

Rzd-partner.ru, 2021. Kazahstan i Uzbekistan soedinit skorostnaja zheleznaja doroga. [Online] Available at: https://www.rzd-partner.ru/zhd-transport/news/kazakhstan-i-uzbekistan-soedinit-skorostnaya-zheleznaya/. [Accessed July 2022].

Shepard, W., 2016. The Western Europe-Western China Expressway To Connect The Yellow Sea With The Baltic. [Online] Available at: https://www.forbes.com/sites/wadeshepard/2016/07/10/the-western-europe-western-china-expressway-to-connect-the-yellow-sea-with-the-baltic/?sh=25a2d1ac6c95 [Accessed July 2022].

Smirnov, S., 2018. Energosistema Central'noj Azii: v odnom hore, no s raznymi partiturami. [Online] Available at: https://www.ritmeurasia.org/news–2018-04-29–energosistema-centralnoj-azii-v-odnom-hore-no-s-raznymi-partiturami-36236 [Accessed July 2022].

Strong, J., Meyer, J. R., Smith, G. & Harral, C., 1996. *Moving to Market: Restructuring Transport in the Former Soviet Union*. Cambridge, MA: Harvard University Press.

Turkmenistan Airlines, 2022. Turkmenistan Airlines. [Online] Available at: https://turkmenistanairlines.tm/en [Accessed July 2022].

United Nations, 2020. 2020 United Nations E-Government Survey. [Online] Available at: https://www.un.org/development/desa/publications/publication/2020-united-nations-e-government-survey [Accessed July 2022].

World Bank, 2015. World Development Indicators: Electricity production, sources, and access. [Online] Available at: http://wdi.worldbank.org/table/3.7 [Accessed July 2022].

World Bank, 2020a. Air transport, passengers carried - Europe & Central Asia. [Online] Available at: https://data.worldbank.org/indicator/IS.AIR.PSGR?locations=Z7 [Accessed July 2022].

World Bank, 2020b. COVID-19 Prompts Urgency of Bridging Digital Divide in Central Asia. [Online] Available at: https://www.worldbank.org/en/news/press-release/2020/12/02/urgency-of-bridging-digital-divide-in-central-asia-increases-as-a-result-of-the-covid-19-pandemic [Accessed July 2022].

World Bank, 2022a. DataBank: World Development Indicators. [Online] Available at: https://databank.worldbank.org/source/world-development-indicators# [Accessed July 2022].

World Bank, 2022b. DataBank: WDI Database Archives. [Online] Available at: https://databank.worldbank.org/source/wdi-database-archives# [Accessed July 2022].

World Bank, 2022c. DataBank: WDI Database Archives. [Online] Available at: https://databank.worldbank.org/reports.aspx?dsid=57&series=IQ.WEF.CUST.XQ# [Accessed July 2022].

World Economic Forum, 2019. *The Global Competitiveness Report*, Geneva: World Economic Forum.

Yan, Y. T., 2019. Smart Cities or Surveillance? Huawei in Central Asia. [Online] Available at: https://thediplomat.com/2019/08/smart-cities-or-surveillance-huawei-in-central-asia/ [Accessed July 2022].

Yoshino, N., Huang, B., Azhgaliyeva, D. & Abbas, Q., 2021. *Developing Infrastructure in Central Asia: Impacts and Financing Mechanisms.* Tokyo: Asian Development Bank Institute.

6 Transport Resistance and Logistics

Introduction

> If you want to become rich, build yourself a road.
>
> (Chinese proverb)

Every great civilisation in history has developed because of favourable logistics. All the most critical advances in the economic development of the natural environment are associated with the availability and development of transport communications. This reality can be seen in all ancient river and sea civilisations.

Historians have long proven that the first human civilisations formed on the banks of rivers. The most striking examples are the ancient Egyptians who lived on the Nile, the Mesopotamians on the Tigris and Euphrates, the ancient Chinese on the Yellow River, and the ancient Indians on the Indus. Rivers were attractive sites for early civilisations because they provided a constant supply of drinking water and made the land fertile for growing crops. It is easy to transport people and commercial cargo along rivers. People in these civilisations could fish in the rivers or hunt animals that came to drink there. Those who were lost in the wilderness could return to society by travelling along the course of the rivers, where the main centres of human habitation were concentrated.

Access to the sea can have a similar effect on civilization building. A striking example of a marine civilisation is the Aegean archipelago in the Mediterranean. In the days of the Roman Empire, transporting grain by sea to the other side of the Mediterranean Sea was much cheaper than overland transportation over a distance of more than 100 kilometres (Finley, 1973).

The development of powerful empires, other critical political unions and influential states has always been associated with decreased transport costs between territories. Countries or state unions at the intersection of efficient transport routes have achieved an upsurge in their economic, social and cultural development. An analysis of historical events shows that each achievement in the improvement of logistics supply chains has had a positive change in the standard of living of the communities in question. The quality of

DOI: 10.4324/9781003360728-9

transport technologies used to overcome land and sea crossings has always determined the balance of geopolitical forces across the world.

The entire history of humankind has been shaped by changing logistics technologies. For example, in the Middle Ages, nomadic civilisations became more effective when they started to take full advantage of their horses. The nomads of central Eurasia, who invented stirrups, hard saddles for horses, and trousers for riders, began to dominate vast territories. These technological innovations allowed the rider to shoot arrows from a bow in any direction, and to be in the saddle all day. Thanks to these inventions, the nomads gained an incomparable advantage in speed and manoeuvrability over traditional troops using, for example, war chariots. With the extraordinary mobility of their cavalry, it was from the steppes of Central Asia that, starting from the 13th century, the Mongol and Turkic tribes spread their influence over Asia and a significant part of Europe. At one point, the Mongol empire spanned a territory the size of which is unprecedented in the history of humanity, amounting to about 33 million square kilometres. The rulers of this empire built a highly efficient logistics and postal system on this vast territory, allowing them to maintain control of state institutions. Even the volume of maritime trade between east and west declined as a result.

The development of the Navy led humanity in the 14th–16th centuries to an era of great geographical discovery. This meant that the balance of geopolitical forces shifted towards countries with access to the ocean and a strong fleet of sea-faring vessels. This period continued until the end of the 19th century when the second industrial revolution led to the creation of efficient rail transport. Land routes began to pull part of the traffic flow in their direction.

As a result of the industrial revolutions of the 19th century in modern society, accelerated growth in civilisations is no longer associated solely with the efficiency of trade along the seas, rivers or caravan routes. Now the development of railways, tunnels, bridges, and oil and gas pipelines play a vital role in the further growth of civilisation. History has shown that every big step in logistics has radically changed people's attitudes toward the geographical conditions of their life and existence. Countries or political associations at the intersection of active transport routes have achieved a rapid upsurge in their economic and cultural development. Logistics are just as important in the digital age as they were centuries ago.

Curse or Blessing?

Is the Central Asian region's unique geography a curse or a blessing? Experts disagree significantly on the problems of economic geography in their analysis of territories without ocean access. Most experts consider not having access to the sea to be a significant disadvantage, but not all. The historian Halford Mackinder called the central regions of Eurasia "Heart-land" (the core of the earth) and the "Pivot Area" (the axial region). Over a hundred years ago, he was convinced that Central Asia would become a significant economic power thanks to the development of rail transport. As early as 1900, Mackinder wrote that railroads gave land powers a commercial advantage over maritime forces, stating:

> A generation ago, it seemed that steam and the Suez Canal increased the mobility of maritime powers in comparison with land ones. Railroads played mainly the role of an appendage of ocean trade. But now the transcontinental railways are changing the position of the land powers, and nowhere do they work with such efficiency as in the closed central regions of Eurasia.
>
> (Mackinder, 1904: 434)

The famous work by the diplomat and political scientist Zbigniew Brzezinski brought Central Asia's existence to broader attention last century. In support of Mackinder's vision of the region's "untold riches", he directed the US "to help ensure a situation in which no power would control this geopolitical space, and the world community would have unhindered financial and economic access to it" (Brzezinski, 1997: 17).

Today, the primary mode of transport for world trade is by sea, accounting for about 80 per cent of all goods transported (UNCTAD, 2022). The oceans are therefore the main transport arteries of world trade. Analysts predict maritime trade will triple by 2050 as demand for global freight increases. Therefore in world trade, many are betting on marine transport.

The expert community generally pays much less attention to the problem of organising land transport. As economist Paul Krugman points out: "The analysis of international trade pays little or no attention to economic geography or the geographic location of states" (Krugman, 1993: 12). On the other hand, another influential economist, Ricardo Hausmann contrasts this by saying: "Economic development experts promise that with the right market policies, poor countries will eventually become prosperous. But it's not about politics - it's about geography" (Hausmann, 2001: 44). He further adds:

> Recent studies have shown that transporting goods an extra kilometre by land costs as much as transporting them seven extra kilometres by sea… Land transport is especially unaffordable for countries in the interior of the continent whose goods must cross the border. And this turned out to be much more expensive than hitherto thought.
>
> (Hausmann, 2001)

Conventional economic calculations show that the burden of ground transport costs is becoming too high to be profitable and that it slows economic growth. However, there are two significant differences between shipping within Central Asia and the more usual delivery of goods in landlocked areas.

The first difference is that the region is in the centre of Eurasia, centrally placed between the three most important growth centres of the world economy, China, South Asia, and Europe. The second difference is that the region sits on the new Silk Road, where there has been a recent massive increase in overland transport between China and Europe. These two circumstances indicate that the Central Asian region can turn the supposed curse of being landlocked into a blessing.

Transport Resistance

I believe that the concept of *transport resistance* is helpful when describing the efficiency of supply chains. I define transport resistance as the product of the time spent on the road and the material costs required to transport goods from point A to point B. In the history of humanity, it was always by such a criterion that optimal logistics routes were formed.

The most successful economically connected areas arose and existed in regions with minimal transport resistance. That is, where there was minimal transport resistance, effective trade and economic relations could form between territories, even if these were not within the framework of a single state. Such examples include the interaction and joint development of nations and nationalities, such as those living along the Rhine and Danube in Europe, or the Mekong River in Southeast Asia.

Here it would be appropriate to comment on the development of modern infrastructure within the framework of existing political entities. For a modern state, the priority of developing its transport corridors is no longer exclusively the traditional value of transport resistance between regions. Additional parameters come into play, such as transport links that ensure certain people's economic and cultural unity, and the preservation of their identity. A clear example is the creation of modern transport infrastructure in remote areas of China, such as Tibet and Xinjiang, to combat poverty and inequality there.

If in ancient times the availability of an adequate infrastructure determined the quality of the territory's economic development, in our time the situation has changed. Today, high-quality transport infrastructure development determines a particular territory's economic and social development. The management of transport resistance was made possible by constructing tunnels, bridges and viaducts. However, a real revolution in reducing transport resistance between territories has been and continues to be in the contributions made by rail transport.

Given the complex geography and lack of access to the sea, it is not difficult to guess that the countries of Central Asia are among the least interconnected economies in the world. For example, the region's connectivity score (World Bank, 2018) averages less than 60 per cent in terms of access to global GDP, which is the lowest in the world. The cost of foreign trade transactions in Central Asia remains exceptionally high, undermining the competitiveness of Central Asian products abroad and leading to a rise in the price of exports and imports. It is paradoxical but true – the cost of shipping a container from any of the countries of Central Asia to Shanghai is five times more expensive than to Shanghai from Poland or Turkey (World Bank, 2021).

Transport resistance within Central Asia is further increasing as the region suffers from weak infrastructure and bureaucratic barriers that hinder competitiveness and job creation. Over the past three decades, the countries of Central Asia have invested heavily in improving infrastructure. However, the region still lags behind middle-income countries in investment and infrastructure maintenance. Central Asia ranks low on key trade indicators such as the number of days to clear imports and exports and the Logistics Performance Index (World Bank, 2018). Figures 6.1–6.3 show indicators of the quality of logistics in the countries of the region in comparison with several other countries. Trends are presented in general logistics services and the level of logistics related to infrastructure and, in the case of customs clearance, the presence of bureaucratic barriers. The graphs presented show that transport resistance in Central Asia is very high, which makes the delivery of goods both from the region and to the area uncompetitive.

The graphs also show that despite some progress, logistics performance has not improved over the past ten years. Due to complex bureaucratic procedures, time savings in the delivery of goods due to improved infrastructure are all too often lost at the borders. The transport sector, especially rail transport, is still dominated by inefficient state-owned enterprises with little motivation to improve their performance.

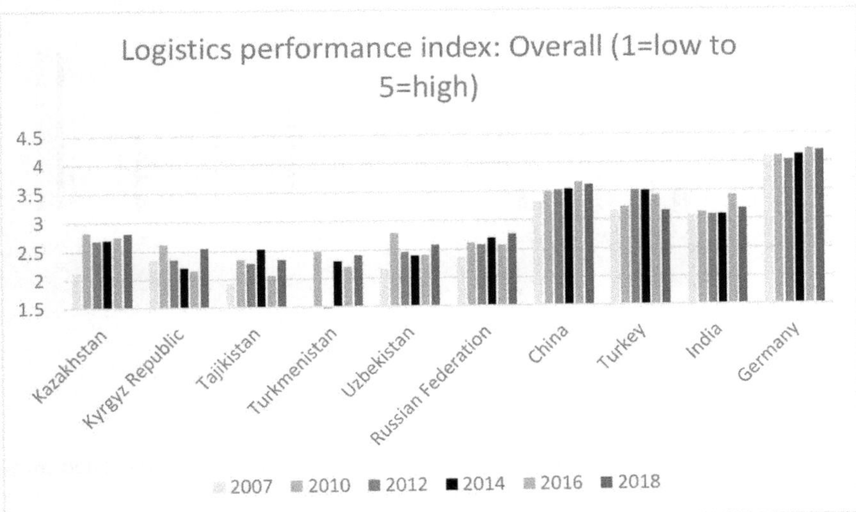

Figure 6.1 Overall logistics performance index in Central Asia and select countries
Source: World Bank (2018).

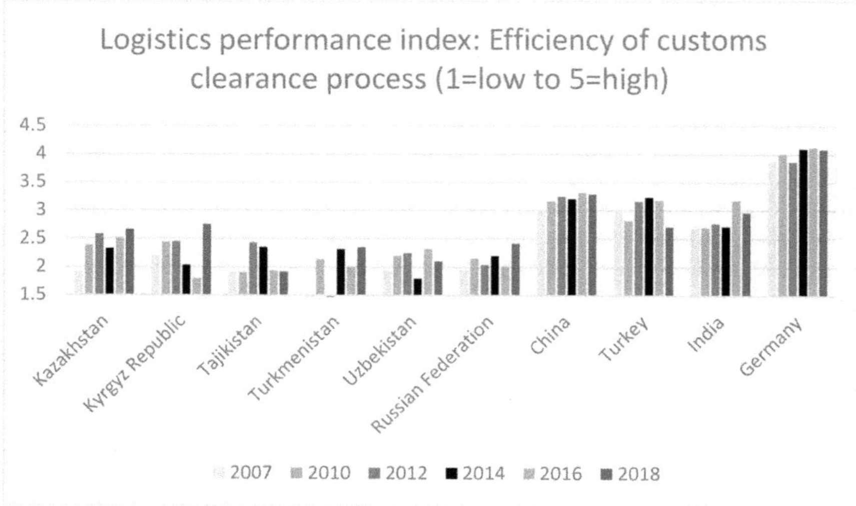

Figure 6.2 Logistics performance index: efficiency of customs clearance process in Central Asia and select countries
Source: World Bank (2018).

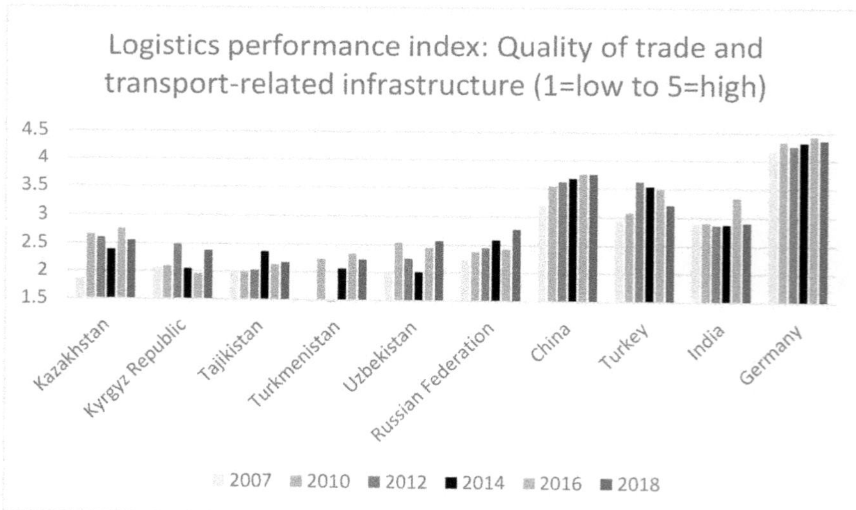

Figure 6.3 Logistics performance index: quality of trade and transport-related infrastructure in Central Asia and a few selected countries
Source: World Bank (2018).

Soviet Legacy: Cut Off From the South

Central Asia inherited integrated transport networks from Soviet times. These networks were built without considering the internal administrative borders and mainly focused on Russia. This meant that there were very few active connections with countries to the south, which were outside the sphere of influence of the Soviet Union.

On the one hand, being in the centre of the Eurasian continent, the Central Asian region is convenient for developing the shortest transcontinental communications. However, it has several fundamental drawbacks in contrast to overcoming the distance by waterways. The presence of significant mountain ranges determines the region's high transport resistance and low transit potential.

As elsewhere, the problem of transport resistance in Central Asia is determined primarily by its geography. First, not a single river in the region flows into the ocean. All rivers end their flows in inland waters – in the Caspian and Aral Seas. Consequently, the area has no natural water transport corridors with the outside world. In addition, the region is fenced off by mountain ranges from the main centres of economic power located to the southeast and southwest. The most favourable transport outlets to the outside world are in the north, connecting Kazakhstan with Russia.

Earlier it was noted that the region's high mountain ranges make a direct transport connection to several geographically close territories impossible. One pertinent example of this is that the Wakhan Corridor in Afghanistan is a 350 kilometre-long gorge located at the junction of four countries – Afghanistan, China, Pakistan and Tajikistan. It is also home to three of the world's major mountain ranges – the Hindu Kush, Karakoram and Pamir, known as the Pamir Knot. This corridor separates Tajikistan and Pakistan by less than 15 kilometres (Dunning, 2021), but because of these mountains, to deliver goods from Pakistan to Tajikistan, goods must first be transported through the Suez Canal and the Black Sea, and only then can they be delivered to Tajikistan by rail, crossing several countries' customs posts. It is therefore prohibitively expensive and takes several months, which is too long. Getting goods from South Asia to Central Asia is similarly difficult.

The history of the development of railways in Central Asia dates to 1874, when the government of tsarist Russia, to keep the territory of Central Asia under its control, decided to build the Orenburg-Tashkent railway line. Later the government decided instead that the first railway line would connect Tashkent with the eastern coast of the Caspian Sea – to ensure communication between the Turkestan and Caucasian regions. By the time of the disintegration of the Soviet Union in 1991, not only had the Central Asian Railway's network grown considerably, to a total length of 6,199 kilometres, but its potential was also huge.

Internal Logistics

Until 1991, Central Asia's entire transport and energy infrastructure lay within a single state – the Soviet Union – and functioned without regard to state borders. In the 1990s, when the "parade of sovereignties" began, the newly independent states focused on the "nationalisation" of their transport and energy networks. Each republic, trying to gain unilateral advantages, did not pay attention to close interdependence with its neighbours. Such a short-sighted policy led to the decline and often degradation of networks designed and built in the Soviet era.

Transport routes developed during Soviet times between settlements and often crossed international borders. For example, the Tashkent-Samarkand Road in Uzbekistan crossed the territory of Kazakhstan, and the Osh-Jalal-Abad and Bishkek-Balykchy roads in Kyrgyzstan passed through Uzbekistan and Kazakhstan, respectively. When goods crossed state and customs borders, disorder and conflicts regularly arose. These conflicts were associated with smuggling, illegal traffic, and the corruption of border guards and customs officers on both sides of the border. This confusion led governments to try their best to get out of the newly emerging international routes by building roads to bypass foreign sections. Priority has been given to the construction of national highways over international routes. For example, with the modernisation of roads from Bishkek to Osh, Ashgabat to Dashoguz and Dushanbe to Khujand, much longer routes have been chosen for the sole purpose of avoiding border crossings. These moves to consolidate national transport routes have diverted attention from more efficient international transport links.

The profound disintegration of relations between the Central Asian states in the 1990s can also be seen in air travel. To get from Bishkek to Dushanbe or Ashgabat, it was often necessary to fly through Moscow, Istanbul, or Urumqi, since there simply were no direct flights. Now, however, these flight paths are seeing some significant and positive changes. As a result of decisive reforms in Uzbekistan, after a twenty-five-year break, direct flights between Tashkent and Dushanbe resumed in 2017 (Radio Free Europe, 2017). On 20 June 2022, after a thirty-year break, the first train left on the Dushanbe-Tashkent route. The distance from Dushanbe to Tashkent is 916 kilometres, and the travel time is 21 hours. Tajikistan and Uzbekistan agreed to form new transit corridors and create a modern logistics infrastructure, increase air, rail and bus transportation, jointly create agricultural clusters and modern production facilities, organise the processing of fruits and vegetables and enter the markets of third countries (Avesta, 2020).

External Logistics

After the disintegration of the Soviet Union in 1991, the newly formed states of Central Asia began to explore the possibility of rail links with countries to the south of the region. Given the region's geographical features, two options came to the fore: Kazakhstan connecting to China through the Dzungarian Gate and Uzbekistan connecting to Afghanistan through Termez.

An additional northern branch from Urumqi to the Dzungarian Gate, 477 kilometres long, was built in the late 1980s. The westernmost station of the northern branch, Alashankou, is connected to Dostyk station in Kazakhstan. The connection with the Kazakhstan railway came into operation on 12 September 1990. Until 2013, the Dostyk (Druzhba)-Alashankou section was the only connection between the railways of Kazakhstan and China. In December 2013, another railway crossing was opened – Korgas (Kazakhstan) to Khorgos (China).

The shortest route to the ports of the Indian Ocean for the countries of Central Asia is through Afghanistan. In 2010, the construction of a railway line between Uzbekistan and the Afghan city of Mazar-i-Sharif began. The length of the Termez (Uzbekistan) Mazar-i-Sharif (Afghanistan) railway is 75 kilometres. The road was constructed in November 2010, and the first train passed through it on 21 December 2011.

It is worth noting that very soon, the ancient city of Mazar-i-Sharif in Afghanistan could become a real transport hub for the region. From there, it will be possible to build a new railway to Herat, located on the border with Iran. Such a corridor is also attractive because the Iranian side already has an established railway from the border checkpoint Khaf to Herat. Given the broad prospects for developing its transit potential, the Iranian government has begun constructing a double-track railway from Khaf to the port of Chabahar, a good point of access to the Indian Ocean.

Further projects for the construction of railways between Afghanistan, Tajikistan and Turkmenistan are also under discussion, but these projects have not yet come to fruition.

International Initiatives

Over the years, along with China's Belt and Road Initiative, which will be discussed in a separate chapter, several other countries and international organisations have put forward initiatives to improve transport communications between Central Asia and the outside world. Considering that in the 1990s, the countries of the region were still in the process of a "civilised divorce", there was sometimes an impression that arranging connectivity within the region was only in the interests of international organisations and not of Central Asia itself.

In 1997 the Asian Development Bank (ADB) initiated the Central Asia Regional Economic Cooperation (CAREC) programme to encourage economic cooperation among countries in Central Asia and nearby parts of Transcaucasia and South Asia (CAREC, 2022a). As of 2019, CAREC has invested more than $1.56 billion in China (CAREC, 2022b) and it is essential that China takes an active role in the project. The projects are improving transport and trade policies and infrastructure, which also promote connectivity between CAREC countries and global markets while harnessing the region's natural and human resources. China is also the main sponsor of the CAREC Institute, located in Urumqi, the capital of China's Xinjiang Uyghur Autonomous Region.

To this day, this programme is perhaps the most ambitious and successful. Since its inception in 2001 and as of June 2021, CAREC has attracted $40 billion covering 213 projects in investments that have helped build multimodal transport networks, increase energy trade and security, facilitate the free movement of people and goods, and lay the foundation for economic corridor development (CAREC, 2022c). Of this, almost $15 billion has been financed by ADB, more than $16 billion by other development partners, and nearly $9 billion from CAREC member governments (CAREC, 2022d). The programme involves other donor agencies, namely the World Bank (WB), the International Monetary Fund (IMF), the European Bank for Reconstruction and Development (EBRD), the Islamic Development Bank (IDB), and the United Nations Development Program (UNDP).

The second most important initiative of this kind was the TRACECA (Transport Corridor Europe-Caucasus-Asia) project, which came into existence in September 1998 at the international summit "Restoration of the historical Silk Road" in Baku. This was developed with the support of the EU and with the participation of the Central Asian and the South Caucasus governments (TRACECA, 2022). The programme's main goal was to develop a transport corridor from Europe to Central Asia through the Black Sea, the Caucasus, and the Caspian Sea. From a technological point of view, the programme focuses on transporting goods using a single transport document for the entire route using various modes of transport. The TRACECA programme totalled fifty-three projects (thirty-nine technical assistance and fourteen investment projects) amounting to €110 million (around $112 million) in multiple areas, including building border posts between Azerbaijan and Georgia, training logistics operators, and the modernisation of legislation (Jacobs Consultancy, 2003).

The UN Special Program for the Economies of Central Asia (SPECA) was launched in 1998 to strengthen subregional cooperation in Central Asia and its integration into the world economy. The SPECA countries are Azerbaijan, Afghanistan, Kazakhstan, Kyrgyzstan, Tajikistan, Turkmenistan, and Uzbekistan (UNECE, 2022). The United Nations Economic Commission for Europe (UNECE) and the United Nations Economic and Social Commission for Asia and the Pacific (ESCAP) jointly provide overall support for the work of this programme. This programme has not received large-scale development, most probably due to problems with its funding.

The US New Silk Road Initiative was launched in July 2011 in a speech by Secretary of State Hillary Clinton in India and aimed to integrate Afghanistan with Central Asia and promote the region's trade and economic development. However, it did not receive further development, remaining on paper since the

Pentagon stopped funding it, and the US State Department did not have enough funds to implement projects (U.S. Department of State, 2017).

Recently, a similar initiative to revive the new Silk Road was put forward by India, but no concrete steps have yet been taken. In this vein, it should be mentioned that under the auspices of the Connect Central Asia policy (Seethi, 2013), India is trying to establish economic ties with the region. For example, India is a major driver of the modernisation of the Iranian port of Chabahar, whose cargo volume is expected to increase fivefold to 12.5 million tons per year. Arranging logistics through this port and then through the territory of Iran, India hopes to enter the Central Asian market. The country is also co-financing a 218-kilometre road linking the centre of Afghanistan to the border with Iran.

It is notable that although the EU and the US were among the first to come up with such initiatives, they have since lost interest in further developing their programmes. Along with international organisations, initiatives regarding the outcome of transport corridors in Central Asia are currently supported mainly by Russia and China, which border the countries of Central Asia and conduct active trade with them.

References

Avesta, 2020. Iz Dushanbe v Tashkent otpravilsja pervyj za 30 let passazhirskij poezd. [Online] Available at: http://avesta.tj/2022/06/20/iz-dushanbe-v-tashkent-otpravilsya-pervyj-za-30-let-passazhirskij-poezd/ [Accessed July 2022].

Brzezinski, Z., 1997. *The Grand Chessboard: American Primacy and Its Geostrategic Imperatives.* New York: Basic Books.

CAREC, 2022a. CAREC program. [Online] Available at: https://www.carecprogram.org/ [Accessed July 2022].

CAREC, 2022b. People's Republic of China. [Online] Available at: https://www.carecprogram.org/?page_id=5 [Accessed July 2022].

CAREC, 2022c. About CAREC: CAREC program. [Online] Available at: https://www.carecprogram.org/?page_id=31 [Accessed July 2022].

CAREC, 2022d. CAREC project portfolio. [Online] Available at: https://www.carecprogram.org/projects/portfolio [Accessed July 2022].

Dunning, S., 2021. China is moving on Afghanistan's Wakhan corridor. [Online] Available at: https://foreignpolicy.com/2021/08/14/china-afghanistan-wakhan-corridor-imperial-ambitions/ [Accessed July 2022].

Finley, M. I., 1973. *The Ancient Economy.* London: Chatto & Windus.

Hausmann, R., 2001. Prisoners of Geography. *Foreign Policy*, Volume 122.

Jacobs Consultancy, 2003. *Evaluation of TRACECA Programme (1998–2002)*, London: Jacobs Consultancy.

Krugman, P., 1993. *Geography and Trade.* Cambridge, MA: MIT Press.

Mackinder, H. J., 1904. The geographical pivot of history. *The Geographical Journal*, 23 (4), p. 434.

Radio Free Europe, 2017. Uzbekistan to resume Tashkent-Dushanbe flights after 25-year break. [Online] Available at: https://www.rferl.org/a/uzbekistan-tashkent-dushanbe-flights-resume/28336240.html [Accessed July 2022].

Seethi, K., 2013. The diplomat: India's 'Connect Central Asia Policy'. [Online] Available at: https://thediplomat.com/2013/12/indias-connect-central-asia-policy/ [Accessed July 2022].

TRACECA, 2022. Home: TRACECA. [Online] Available at: http://www.traceca-org.org/en/home/ [Accessed July 2022].

U.S. Department of State, 2017. U.S. support for the New Silk Road. [Online] Available at: https://2009-2017.state.gov/p/sca/ci/af/newsilkroad/index.htm [Accessed July 2022].

UNCTAD, 2022. Review of maritime transport. [Online] Available at: https://unctad.org/topic/transport-and-trade-logistics/review-of-maritime-transport [Accessed July 2022].

UNECE, 2022. UNECE: SPECA. [Online] Available at: https://unece.org/speca [Accessed July 2022].

World Bank, 2018. Logistics performance index. [Online] Available at: https://lpi.worldbank.org/about [Accessed July 2022].

World Bank, 2021. Improving transport connectivity in Central Asia requires a coherent approach. [Online] Available at: https://www.worldbank.org/en/news/press-release/2021/04/02/improving-transport-connectivity-in-central-asia-requires-a-coherent-approach [Accessed July 2022].

7 Eurasian Railway Revolution

Introduction

Transport links have always played a crucial role in the economic unification of nation-states and geopolitical associations. The first examples of statehood arose along rivers which served as natural arteries for the emergence and development of ties between communities and trade. After that, communication across the oceans created new opportunities for rapid civilisational growth on all continents. As humankind developed, it also expanded the possibilities of land communication and trade between regions by constructing roads and railways, which quickly grew in the 19th century. In the 20th century, the practice of air transportation began to develop intensively. The 21st century has become particularly significant in the development of high-speed rail.

Paradoxically, the opposite is also true: the main reason for many ancient civilisations' degradation and even collapse was the decline of the internal transport systems that connected them. The Great Silk Road is perhaps the most famous example of such a decline. For several centuries, it had connected Asia and Europe via a Eurasian land bridge but, with the development of shipping, it all but ceased to exist.

Maritime shipping lanes developed rapidly, with overwhelming military and commercial superiority, first in Europe and then in North America. This left a landlocked region like Central Eurasia at a comparative disadvantage. The myth of Central Eurasia's "continental curse" is one of the most enduring reasons why landlocked countries are so eager to reach the nearest seas by developing transport links. For example, Russia, as a significant Eurasian power, spent most of its resources on the struggle for the seas for many a century, often to the detriment of the development of other areas of the country. This centuries-old scheme determined the inferiority of landlocked states and their inevitable dependence on territories with access to maritime trade routes. Simple economic calculations show that access to maritime trade routes is the key to successful international competitiveness, with all its advantages. Now it has become evident that the Central Asian nations need to somehow become part of globalisation through the organisation of new transport routes.

DOI: 10.4324/9781003360728-10

However, access to the sea does not guarantee effective inclusion in international economic relations or, indeed, exclusion from them. Sea trade routes are not open to everyone and can be unsafe. They can make users dependent on powers that have the military capability to control the seas. Such powers rely on their ability to control the sea rather than creating the conditions for peace on land. This can make them much less inclined to consider the interests of others. Therefore, any state needs the broadest possible choice of routes and access to world markets and trading partners to secure its interests. The development of overland trade routes depends on neighbouring countries working together. These countries have more reason to seek peace with their neighbours and more reason to negotiate consensus when discussing their political or economic priorities. The main conditions for this collaboration are the objective economic context, political circumstances and the respective governments' decision to unlock the potential of their economy through cooperation with their neighbours.

In today's land-based Eurasia, no single power has been able to establish and maintain control over the entirety of the continent. Bordering countries must negotiate with all their neighbours, given the increasingly apparent advantages of overland trade routes between East Asia, South Asia, Central Asia, Russia and Europe. Any agreements between neighbours should be an integral part of the global system of economic ties.

In recent years, the economic feasibility of cooperation between neighbouring countries can be seen in the consistent expansion of transit traffic. This has, in turn, contributed to the development of relevant infrastructure in different sectors of the economy. Today, the main Eurasian powers, China and Russia, particularly their interior provinces, have seen direct and clear benefits from the exponential growth in traffic on the route connecting Asia and Europe.

Strengthening their neighbours' sovereignty and economic viability is also a priority for both China and Russia. The Central Asian countries, seeking to emerge from the peripheral shadow of the dominant powers and take the opportunity to become a land bridge connecting the centres of economic power, are trying to diversify their foreign financial priorities and logistical capabilities to support such a policy. Therefore, both China and Russia, interested in developing the economy of Central Asia, should facilitate the connection of the countries of Central Asia to their national railway systems. Expanding transit links in the region will also contribute to the development of internal logistics systems, making the railway network the most important connectivity factor in Greater Eurasia, and making the continent more resilient to global challenges.

The five most important factors which support the economic feasibility of developing rail transport and logistics systems in Eurasia are as follows. Firstly, the region has been politically stable for a long time. Ukraine, the Middle East, South Asia, and Afghanistan are the only conflict zones in the region's periphery. Secondly, in the territory of the Eurasian Economic

Union (EAEU), there is a single customs space which facilitates the rapid transportation of goods between different countries without any bureaucratic barriers. Thirdly, China continues to be the world's most competitive economy, capable of pursuing the export-oriented and resource-importing policies that formed the basis of the Belt and Road Initiative launched in 2013. Fourthly, the new economic integration of Eurasia has dramatically simplified the regulation of land relations. Finally, new digital high-tech technologies open up additional opportunities to improve the efficiency of rail transport trade.

History

To better understand the importance of railways in Eurasia, we should start with a brief study of the history of their development. The industrial revolution began in the second half of the 18th century, first in England and then spread to other countries. Machine production arose and quickly replaced manual labour in handicraft workshops and the manufacturing industry. In 1773, James Watt built his first working steam engine. Then in 1774, together with industrialist Matthew Bolton, Watt opened a company to produce steam engines. The steam engine gave a powerful impetus to the development of transport. In 1769, French artillery officer Joseph Cugnot invented the first steam wagon to move heavy guns, and the first steam locomotive was built in 1804 by Richard Trevithick. However, iron was too expensive at the time, and cast-iron rails could not withstand a machine as heavy as a steam locomotive. With the development of steelmaking, this problem was solved. The first railway to offer a regular passenger service was the Swansea and Mumbles Railway in Wales in 1807. Since there were no workable steam locomotives, horses were often used as traction. The first railway in continental Europe was designed and built by engineers Pierre Simons and Gustave de Ridder. It opened on 6 May 1835 and started to operate between Mechelen and Brussels in Belgium. From then, the next fifty years saw rail transport go through a period of explosive growth, especially in Europe and North America.

The second half of the 1880s saw the highest level of growth in the world rail network in history. From 1880 to 1890, the railway network grew by 245,000 kilometres, reaching 617,300 kilometres. The US was ahead in terms of rates and absolute growth of railways. The gigantic scale of railway construction stimulated the intensive development of industrial production. Today, the railways have become a kind of the backbone of states.

Central Asia on the Eurasian map

Due to the region's unique history, the development of the railways in Central Asia has charted a somewhat different path, but there is still potential for a bright future. For a long time, the independent countries of Central Asia have maintained political stability. There has not been a major military clash since the end of the Cold War and the disintegration of the Soviet Union. The rapid growth of China's economy, especially its inland provinces, and the shift of international trade routes towards land transport have contributed to greater integration into the global and macro-regional transport and logistics system. Railway corridors were already functioning relatively effectively in Central Asia even when these countries were part of the Soviet Union. For example, the branched Turkestan-Siberian (Turksib) railway, part of the shared Soviet heritage, is in operation to this day. Built between 1927 and 1930, Turksib was one of the major construction projects of the first Soviet five-year plan. This project was designed to tie together the vast Soviet territory in the country's south. This railway was to play the same role as the famous Trans-Siberian Railway, which first connected the Eastern part of Russia with its centre at the end of the 19th century.

However, until recently, Central Asia had neither the opportunity nor the need to use its transit potential outside the region or to make the most of its logistical ties with Russia. After the collapse of the Soviet Union, various circumstances limited Central Asia's transport and logistics potential. This was mainly due to the difficulties of the transition period and the impossibility of reaching world trade routes dominated by maritime transport and the major coastal players – the US, Europe, and China. After gaining independence, the countries began to look for ways out of this disadvantageous situation imposed on them by their geographical and historical realities. But it was only recently that global transport and logistics processes have encouraged them to realise their aspirations.

It may seem too ambitious, but in recent years we have witnessed what could be called the beginning of the Eurasian railway revolution. Due to objective trends in world markets, Central Asia will improve communication between East and West through a highly efficient China–Central Asia–Europe rail route and will become a transit hub for new transport routes that run along all four sides of the horizon. The Central Asian governments are noticeably doubling their efforts to turn the region into a crossroads of transport corridors that connect East with West, North with South. They are joining together their future through the rapid development of collaborative regional actions, trying to bring the quality of their transit potential up to international standards.

The total length of the railway lines in the Central Asian countries exceeds 22,000 kilometres. Kazakhstan has the largest and most comprehensively operated railway system accounting for 66 per cent of the region's total railway route kilometres, and it handles 84 per cent of all freight traffic. About 18 per cent of regional railways cross Uzbekistan, accounting for about 11 per cent of all traffic. Turkmenistan has approximately 12 per cent of the region's railways and 4 per cent of all traffic (CIS portal, 2018).

If the ambitious projects in this area are successfully implemented, the prospects for turning Central Asia into a rapidly developing region will become real. This should also benefit China and Russia, which control Eurasia's major overland trade routes. Since Moscow and Beijing are not seeking to take more interest in their neighbours' survival, they should be interested in promoting opportunities for their neighbours' independent development.

Driving the railway boom in Eurasia

The explosive development of rail traffic from China to Europe began in 2011 when Russia, Kazakhstan and Belarus integrated customs procedures at the borders as part of their Customs Union. This move cut the costs of document management and logistics and significantly decreased shipping times between China and Europe. As a result, year on year, the volume of rail traffic between China and Europe through Kazakhstan and Russia has been setting new records, achieving double digit percentage growth every year. To understand this growth, we need to explore rail traffic figures for the last two years.

Even during the pandemic years, trans-Eurasian rail traffic grew considerably. In 2021, there were 22 per cent more trains on the China–Europe route than a year before, i.e. about 15,000 trains, carrying 1.46 million TEU (twenty-foot container equivalent units), up 29 per cent from one year previously (China.org.cn, 2022). This included sixty-one railway routes from Europe to China, and eighty-four from China to Europe (Tolstouhova, 2020). Goods shipped by rail from China to Europe reached customers in more than 160 cities in 22 countries.

Nowadays, transcontinental trains heading west leave almost every hour, and eastbound trains to China every two hours. According to reports from the Chinese shipping industry, more than 33,000 container trains crossed between China and Europe in 10 years, of which 53 per cent passed through the Dostyk-Alashankou and Altynkol-Khorgos border crossing points (Seanews.ru, 2021).

The Eurasian railway revolution continued into the pandemic year of 2021 when the China–Europe railway bridge set new records by providing stable, reliable and highly efficient logistics services as pillars of global supply chains. The China–Europe express train system has opened the door for mutual stimulation of supply and demand with additional benefits (Global Times, 2022a). Of fundamental importance is that the transportation of goods from China's western provinces in the European direction has grown even faster. In 2021, 570,000 TEU containers were shipped from there, 57.5 per cent more than a year earlier (Global Times, 2022b).

Today, railways directly connect 89 cities in China with 23 countries and 175 cities in Europe (Smith, 2022). It is easy to see that in the face of disruptions caused by the pandemic, the China–Europe freight trains have become the anchors of stability in the global supply chain. Meanwhile, the cost of international maritime and air transportation skyrocketed. According to London-based Drewry Shipping, as of 6 January 2021, the average cost of transporting a standard 40-foot sea container by sea between China and Europe on 8 significant routes was $9,408, 5 times more than before the start of the pandemic in early 2020 (John, 2022).

By comparison, transporting a similar container from China to Paris by rail was cheaper, or about $8,000, according to Xavier Wanderpepen, the director of China-Europe freight trains for France's national railway company SNCF. At the same time, transportation on the return route fell to about $2,000 due to subsidies from the Chinese authorities to encourage European companies to use the train to export to China (Xu, 2022). This is probably why the traffic from Europe to China in 2021 grew even faster than traffic from Europe to China. The existing problem of returning empty containers to China has become less acute. According to China Railways, in the first ten months of 2021, inbound traffic to China rose to an impressive 81 per cent of outbound (The Load Star, 2021). Since the journey to deliver containers between Europe and China takes up to seventy days, and the same journey takes less than twenty days by rail, railways are an attractive option for transporting even relatively cheap goods.

Another major trend in the Chinese government's support for international rail transport has recently come to light. For the first time, China has begun to improve the railway infrastructure not only in its own country but also in other countries. The China Development Bank (CDB) said it would support the construction of inland port stations abroad with bonded warehouses and international projects with multimodal transport functions. The CDB will also provide financing to accelerate the development of new technologies and equipment upgrades, which will help reduce transportation costs and improve efficiency. Last year, China invested in the construction of several foreign railway stations, for example, in Russia's Kaliningrad (Nulimaimaiti, 2021).

But the reverse process is also taking place. Given the significant increase in rail traffic, well-known international logistics companies have invested in China too. Europe's largest rail freight company, the German Deutsche Bahn, has established a full subsidiary in Shanghai. "DB Cargo Eurasia is repositioning itself to bring even more freight transport onto the rails between Europe and China long term," said a Deutsche Bahn representative in describing the initiative (DB Cargo, 2021).

Experts have begun to discuss the possible abolition of subsidies for railway transportation made by China's central and regional authorities given the significantly increased traffic on the railways. The potential reduction or abolition of subsidies shows that the overland is already commercially viable. According to media reports, the participants at the European Silk Road Summit in Amsterdam actively discussed this very topic in 2021 (Yeping, 2021). Given that the authorities cut subsidies before, there is a possibility that they will continue to do so again or even eliminate them this year.

"The intensity of market demand for trains is already far greater than the intensity of subsidies. For example, the freight rate of a 40-feet container used to be $10,000, but it has now reached about $20,000. The subsidy is only a few thousand dollars," Kang Shuchun, director of the China Logistics and Procurement Federation, told (Yeping, 2021).

According to Jackie Yan, founder and CEO of New Silk Road Intermodal, the authorities originally planned to replace subsidies by 2022, but due to COVID-19, they extended the deadline by a year (Yeping, 2021). At its peak, subsidies were $3,000-$5,000 per container but now, according to media reports, they have dropped to only $1,000 (Yeping, 2021). It is not difficult to see that even with the removal of subsidies, goods with a relatively high added value will still be profitable to deliver by rail. It should be noted however that low-value-added and heavy goods will likely continue to be transported by sea.

Ten years after the boom in railway trade due to the EAEU Customs Union, the Eurasian railway bridge connecting China and Europe has confirmed its high profitability and continues to hold great promise. Apart from Europe, the primary beneficiaries of this new trade route are the western provinces of China and the countries of Central Asia, which have suffered from their landlocked situation for centuries. They have become natural land bridges between global centres of economic power, and the future holds even better prospects. The real revival of the New Silk Road is at hand.

Rail freight traffic set records because it is cheaper than air freight and faster than shipping by sea. The cost of rail transport from China to Europe is about 80 per cent less than by air and 75 per cent faster than by sea (Hillman, 2018). Using rail transport for high-value goods that do not require ultra-fast delivery is especially attractive. These goods are heavily insured and need a certain quality of transport, while sea transport requires freezing working capital for a longer time, resulting in additional costs to consumers.

In addition to cost, surface transport, particularly railway transport, has a natural advantage over the sea. Sea air and high oceanic humidity could harm most high-value goods such as electronics and food, a problem which can be circumvented by using overland routes from China to Europe via Kazakhstan and Russia. In comparison to air, trains emit significantly less carbon dioxide. For example, according to Fujitsu and Siemens, their green trains produce 95 per cent less carbon dioxide, nonmethane hydrocarbons and nitrogen oxide emissions than air transport. Considering that the fight against climate change is only likely to intensify worldwide and that advanced countries are likely to introduce new taxes on carbon emissions, the cost of air cargo is set to grow even higher soon.

Ten years ago about 98 per cent of all shipping between China and the EU was by sea. Air and rail accounted for only 1.5–2 per cent and 0.5–1 per cent respectively (Utlc.com, 2021a). However, the exponential growth of rail traffic in the last decade, which has doubled every two years, has completely changed the accepted norms of world transportation. Considering that the annual traffic between China and Europe is about 20 million TEU, the share of rail traffic in 2021 was already 6–8 per cent of the total (Utlc.com, 2022).

These figures seemed incredible in the mid-2010s when the countries of the EAEU decided to merge with China's Belt and Road Initiative. Shipping by sea has ceased to dominate world trade. The Eurasian railway bridge has changed this situation, and hopefully forever.

Development of new transport routes

Here we will analyse the developments in the three major routes across Eurasia one by one: East–Northwest, East–Southwest, and North–South. The East-Northwest route goes from China to the countries of the EU. The East–Southwest route heads towards the Caucasus and the Middle East, while the North–South route passes from Russia through Central Asia to South Asia. Figure 7.1 shows those key rail corridors.

East–Northwest

On 19 March 2011, just eleven years ago, the first train left Chongqing for Duisburg in Germany. At the time, many considered this experiment a joke but little did many know that it would prove to be the start of the Eurasian railway revolution. By 2020, transport companies had broken yet another record in rail traffic between China and Europe through Kazakhstan and Russia (Utlc.com, 2021b). According to the Chinese state railway operator China Railway Express, 12,400 trains have been sent on this route, 50 per cent more than a year earlier. They transported 1.13 million 20-foot container equivalent units (TEU), up 56 per cent from one year previous (Li, 2021). Of that amount, 800,000 TEU went directly to the European market, and the remaining 313,000 TEU, to the Middle East, including Afghanistan and Pakistan.

It is noteworthy that about half of this vast cargo flow passed through railway routes only relatively recently built by Kazakhstan. According to the national railway company Kazakhstan Temir Zholy (KTZ), freight traffic through the border crossings between China and Kazakhstan increased by almost 50 per cent and exceeded 20 million tons last year. The volume of transported goods reached nearly half a million TEU. On average, 30 trains and approximately 2,000 wagons pass daily through border stations on the Kazakh–Chinese border.

In 2021 this volume of transported goods was also surpassed. According to a Chinese customs report, Alatau Pass, a major railway port in northwest China's Xinjiang Uygur Autonomous Region, handled 2,388 freight trains as of 29 May 2021, up 46.9 per cent from last year (Regnum, 2021). China–Europe trains transported over 1 million tonnes of goods, up 67.3 per cent over the same period in 2020.

As many as twenty-two destination routes cross Kazakhstan, connecting thirteen countries, including Germany, Poland, Belgium and Russia. Vehicles and auto components, household appliances and consumer goods are mainly exported through Kazakhstan, while imports to China include cars and auto parts, cotton yarn and timber.

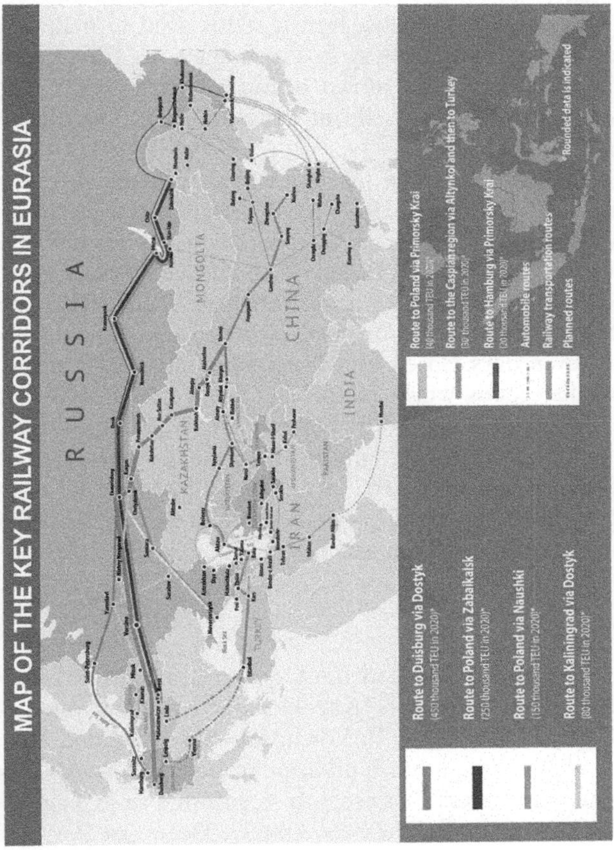

Figure 7.1 Eurasia's key rail corridors.

This explosive traffic growth is now starting to exceed the capacity of the two border checkpoints between China and Kazakhstan: Dostyk–Alashankou and Altynkol–Khorgos. On 1 March 2021, Kazakhstan had to suspend traffic at the border with China to free up capacity for China–Europe trains. KTZ released a special statement reporting that “the number of empty trains at the ports is increasing, and it is negatively impacting the operational capacity of Kazakhstan’s rail network” (Kapital.kz, 2021).

With the number of trains between China and Europe now exceeding the Kazakh rail system’s capacity, Russia will soon face the same problem of congestion. All this is to say that the transit states need to make additional efforts to further develop their railway system connecting China and Europe via Central Asia and Russia. As shown below, all participants in the Eurasian railway revolution have carried out active work in this direction, and this must continue.

Even non-specialists can recognise that the record volumes of transportation by rail from east to west point to the fact that it is much cheaper than air transportation and much faster than sea transportation. To be more specific, the cost of rail transport from China to Europe is about five times cheaper than air travel and four times faster than shipping (Hillman, 2018). For example, in November 2020, a shipment from Amazon’s warehouse in Shanghai arrived in Duisburg in just eleven days. Speed of delivery is essential for China’s growing exports of high-value goods which require a much faster delivery time than traditional ocean shipping can provide. Until February 2022, the East–Northwest corridor was the most popular among logistics companies, through which the bulk of rail cargo was transported. The East–Southwest route may become more important for the delivery of goods between East and West due to the conflict in Ukraine and anti-Russian sanctions.

East–Southwest

In recent years, the countries around the Caspian Sea have invested billions of dollars in developing their ports. Kazakhstan has significantly expanded the capacity of the Aktau port, Turkmenistan has upgraded the port at Turkmenbashi, and Azerbaijan has built a major new port at Alyat, south of Baku. In addition, major work has recently been done to expand the Georgian ports of Poti and Batumi. The new Anaklia Deep Sea Port will be the first Georgian deep-water container port with state-of-the-art infrastructure and equipment (Anaklia Development Consortium, 2022). These projects align with the strengthening railway networks which connect the western shore of the Caspian Sea to Turkey and Europe.

Thanks to exceptional support and significant investments from Kazakhstan and Turkmenistan, new railway routes have been developed from Central Asia, running through Iran and near the Caspian Sea to the South Caucasus and the Black Sea and the Mediterranean Sea, Turkey and Europe. Two new routes from Central Asia to western seaports are being used, albeit with restrictions – the first via Azerbaijan and Georgia to the Black Sea, and the second via Iran and Turkey to the Mediterranean and Black seas. But the traffic on this southern route via Iran and Turkey is not yet comparable to the northern route via Russia.

In the late 1990s, Turkmenistan and Iran connected their railways, which allowed the countries of Central Asia to enter the seas for the first time in history and begin transporting goods through the Iranian port of Bandar Abbas. Furthermore, the cutting-edge Kazakhstan – Turkmenistan – Iran line was completed and opened for service in 2014. Known as the North-South Transnational Corridor, the 677-kilometre railway line connects Central Asia with the Iranian rail network, which is predominantly in the north of the country. Kazakhstan, Turkmenistan and Iran co-financed this $620 million project.

At the same time, the Central Asian countries also invested in developing the South Caucasus transport corridor. The new Baku–Tbilisi–Kars (BTK) railway officially opened in October 2017. Its total length is 826 kilometres, and the line is to carry 1 million passengers and over 15 million tonnes of cargo annually. The freight volume has been growing steadily since the new line came into operation. By the beginning of 2021, a total of 21,260 TEUs had already been transported on the line (Azertag.az, 2022). In 2020 alone the number was 10,779 TEUs. The project is part of a broader plan to link Central Asian railway systems to the South Caucasus and Europe via Turkey. This route connects with the Turkish railway network through Iranian railways, facilitating onward transportation to the Mediterranean and Black seas.

In addition, an Uzbekistan–Turkmenistan–Iran–Oman route could offer Central Asia another option to access the Indian Ocean. This corridor could connect Central Asia with Iranian ports in both the Persian Gulf and the Gulf of Oman. It looks likely that Kazakhstan and India will soon join the project as collaborators, further increasing its significance as traffic along this route will increase. In addition, these countries can become new investors in the project.

Uzbekistan is very interested in building a China–Kyrgyzstan–Uzbekistan railway, which could become an essential link in the East–West and North–South corridors. It would open new markets for manufacturers from all three countries, transport goods from China to Eastern Europe and the Middle East via Kyrgyzstan and Uzbekistan, and provide the landlocked states in Central Asia with access to international seaports.

Uzbekistan considers cooperation with the Caspian states one of its strategic priorities and this provides a new impetus for multilateral relations. Tashkent included joining the BTK in its comprehensive programme to improve the country's infrastructure and diversify foreign trade routes to transport goods for 2018–2022. A Navoi–Turkmenbashi–Baku–Tbilisi–Kars railway corridor would connect the railway systems in Uzbekistan, Turkmenistan, Azerbaijan and Georgia with that of Turkey and would help goods from Central Asia countries to reach the Mediterranean coast. This route would also become essential for transporting goods between China and Europe. Since it is shorter than the northern routes, analysts believe delivery times from China to Southern Europe could be reduced to a mere twelve–fifteen days (Yılmaz & Çakır, 2017).

Considering the possibility of reaching Central Asia and China, Turkey has shown great interest in using this route. The Marmaray railway tunnel beneath the Bosporus strait in Istanbul, designed to connect Asia with Europe, has already been built and is in operation. It directly links the Asian part of the country and the European rail network. The first container train from Xi'an, China, to Prague via BTK and Istanbul's Marmaray tunnel arrived in Prague on 6 November 2019. The average speed of transportation was 40 km/h. According to China Railway Express, the train reached Prague from central China in 18 days. The number of containers sent from China on this route reached 2,343 TEU in January–October 2020, 35 per cent more than in 2019. However, almost all goods were moving in one direction, from China to Europe.

Recently though, trains have also started running in the opposite direction. On 4 December 2020, the first container train left Istanbul for China (Interfax.az, 2020). The total length of this route is 8,693 kilometres, and the train covered it in just 12 days. However, the main problem with this route is the cost. This route includes shipping across the Caspian Sea, which currently costs approximately $2,000 per container. However, logistics companies believe that the cost of ferry shipments in the Caspian Sea will decrease with higher traffic. In general, building up the transport and transit capabilities of the BTK corridor will help develop trade and economic cooperation between Central Asia and the Caspian region. In addition, it will accelerate the Central Asian states' integration into international transport corridors.

Turkish President Recep Tayyip Erdogan stated that Turkey is actively working on using the Navoi–Turkmenbashi–Baku–Tbilisi–Kars railway transport corridor during his official visit to Uzbekistan on 28 March 2022. This railway line will allow the Central Asian countries to provide access to the Mediterranean Sea through the Turkish port of Mersin. In addition, with Beijing, Ankara intends to implement a trans-Caspian transport route project, effectively connecting all the countries of the "Turkic world" with a railway bridge. Turkey will provide a direct, efficient connection to China and Central Asia through this corridor.

North–South

One of the most problematic areas for implementing infrastructure projects as part of the North–South corridor is Afghanistan, both in terms of its political situation and its geography. Nevertheless, Uzbekistan has started an initiative to develop transport and logistics routes through Afghanistan. The so-called Kabul corridor will link Termez in Uzbekistan with Mazar-i-Sharif and Kabul in Afghanistan, and Peshawar in Pakistan. It is estimated that the new railway will reduce goods transportation times from Central Asia to Pakistan from 30 days to 15 and cut transportation costs by 30–35 per cent (Kun.uz, 2021).

Even in the first years, the annual cargo volume could reach 10 million tons and this could potentially increase to 20 million tons in the near future.

The Termez–Mazar-i-Sharif line, built by Uzbekistan, opened several years ago. The further 573-kilometre stretch to Peshawar will have to cross the Hindu Kush with its mountain passes of 3,500 meters and higher. As well to the mountainous terrain, another problem is that all 537 kilometres of the railway through Afghanistan will use a track gauge of 1520 mm, which is used in the railway networks of Central Asia, although in Pakistan, the gauge used will be 1676 mm. The geographical terrain of Afghanistan is very complex, and many sophisticated technical solutions will need to be implemented. Among them are 912 unique structures, 18 kilometres of bridges and seven tunnels with a total length of more than 70 kilometres, as well as 27 railway stations (Yousafzai, 2022).

Implementing the first phase of the Mazar-i-Sharif-Kabul project worth about $5 billion will require the support of international financial institutions. At the end of last year, Uzbekistan, Afghanistan and Pakistan sent a joint request to donor organisations to support the project. China, the US and many international organisations, notably the World Bank, the Asian Development Bank, the European Bank for Reconstruction and Development, the European Investment Bank, the Islamic Development Bank and the Asian Infrastructure Investment Bank, all agreed to join the project.

At the end of 2020, Russia and Kazakhstan also announced their desire to join the construction of this railway. Five interested countries formed a financial consortium for its construction in Tashkent, including Uzbekistan, Afghanistan, Pakistan, Russia and Kazakhstan. The project began to develop rapidly, and by February 2021, Uzbekistan, Pakistan and Afghanistan had signed a plan for the project implementation, with construction to begin in September 2021. These plans were however thwarted due to the withdrawal of American troops and their allies from Afghanistan and the Taliban's seizure of power in August 2021. The international community, including various international financial institutions, has not yet recognised the new government of Afghanistan, so it is impossible now to expect early funding for the construction of the railway.

Unlike many others, Uzbekistan's government quickly established relations with the Taliban government. A month after the seizure of power by the Taliban, they delivered humanitarian supplies by rail from Termez to Mazar-i-Sharif. In December 2021, the Minister of Foreign Affairs in the Taliban government, Amir Khan Muttaki, and the Minister of Transport of Uzbekistan, Ilkhom Makhkamov, signed an agreement that in the spring of 2022, the Uzbek side would begin work on the construction of the Trans-Afghan Railway (MFA Afghanistan, 2021).

In March 2022, during his visit to Pakistan, Uzbek President Shavkat Mirziyoyev agreed with Prime Minister Imran Khan to speed up the implementation of the project. But a new problem arose with the change of government in Pakistan in April 2022, and it is unclear to what extent the new Pakistani government will keep their promises.

Further development of this and other infrastructure projects will depend on Afghanistan's political situation and the international community's recognition of the Taliban government. Stabilisation in Afghanistan is a condition that will determine the future of infrastructure projects and the chances of achieving connectivity on the southern branch of the Eurasian railway system. When stability happens, the time will come for the ancient city of Mazar-i-Sharif to again become a major regional logistics hub for Central Asia (Peacenexus.org, 2019). It will also be possible to build a new railway from Mazar-i-Sharif to Herat, located on the border with Iran. This corridor is also attractive because the Iranians have already made a railway from the Khaf border checkpoint to Herat.

Upon completion of the project, Uzbekistan and other countries of Central Asia will have access to the deep Pakistani ports of Karachi and Gwadar on the coast of the Arabian Sea. It will be the shortest route to South Asia's oceans as well as its promising markets. The commissioning of the new railway will shorten the delivery time of goods between Pakistan and Uzbekistan from thirty-five to five days. Currently, the countries of Central Asia only have access to the Indian Ocean via rail and road routes passing through Iranian territory, which is much longer and more complicated.

The Iranian government, realising the development opportunities for the country's transit potential, in 2016 began the construction of a doubletrack line from Khaf to the port of Chabahar, a promising outlet to the Indian Ocean in Iran (Rogers, 2022). India is showing great interest in the port's development. Indian businesses consider it a perfect transhipment hub for the overland transit of goods from India to Central Asia, Russia, and Europe. In 2002, India and Iran signed an agreement on using Chabahar as a joint deep-water port.

The port of Chabahar is also attractive because ships do not have to pass through the dangerous Strait of Hormuz, which will allow them to reduce transit costs. The current shipments to world markets from Bandar Abbas, which now accounts for 85 per cent of Iran's maritime trade, require the payment of significant insurance premiums due to the risks involved. Another 730 kilometres of track between Mazar-i-Sharif and Herat should complete the corridor from Central Asia to Chabahar.

The China–Pakistan Economic Corridor (CPEC) stretches from Xinjiang to the Pakistani port of Gwadar and incorporates several major infrastructure projects financed by the Chinese government. Pakistan predicts the CPEC will create over 2.3 million jobs between 2015 and 2030, adding between 2 and 2.5 per cent to the country's annual economic growth. The countries of Central Asia will also be able to access Pakistani ports via this route. The shortest access to this new transport infrastructure would be to build an additional railway section between Uzbekistan and China across the Kyrgyz Republic. The project holds as much promise as the already operational highway, Kashgar–Irkeshtam–Osh–Andijan–Tashkent, the first route that enabled Central Asian carriers to reach China.

The North–South transport corridor has other promising development prospects, heading from Europe through Russia to Central Asia or the Caspian Sea, and then to Iran and India. It can go in three different directions. By building a railway from the Azerbaijani city of Astara to the Iranian cities Rasht and Qazvin, railway communication between Iran, Azerbaijan and Russia will be accelerated and expanded. The second transport corridor will pass from Iran to Russia through the Caspian Sea, and the third through Kazakhstan, Uzbekistan and Turkmenistan. Then cargo can be delivered to Indian ports from the Iranian ports of Chabahar and Bandar Abbas. In this way, India and the rest of Southeast Asia will have an alternative to the Suez Canal. A study prepared by the Shipping Corporation of India showed that the transport corridors under discussion would save one-third of the cost of passage through the Suez Canal and more than half of its duration, i.e. twenty-three days instead of forty-five–sixty at present (Middleeastmonitor.com, 2022).

The role of major regional institutions and players

In light of the many different routes across the continent that will connect Central Asia with its neighbours and beyond, it is vital to also understand the major regional institutions and players that will determine the success – or failure – of the Eurasian Railway Revolution.

China

The Chinese policy of advancing towards the North and West prioritises relocating production capacities deep inside the continent. Both labour and materials in inland provinces cost less than in coastal areas. As a result, more enterprises are relocating to the country's landlocked inland provinces. These companies have realised that promoting direct railway traffic to Europe would create additional opportunities for expediting shipping and reducing logistics expenses. Delivery by sea from the interior provinces of the country first requires the transport of goods to a seaport, then the reloading of these goods onto ships, followed by the time-consuming transportation of goods by sea. After receiving them at the European port, these goods will need to be reloaded onto other transport again. Only after delivery to the final destination can the end-user receive the goods. All of these steps increase freight delivery costs and shipping times. The pandemic seriously disrupted air and sea shipping, so the railways gained an extra chance to expand their market share. Now, this process is happening before our eyes.

Most of China's landlocked provinces subsidise domestic railway rates to encourage cheaper freight deliveries to Europe. The Chinese authorities realise that this situation cannot last long. The sustainable development of ties with Europe should hinge solely on market mechanisms, and the subsidies will gradually end. Chinese media outlets report that state subsidies for railway traffic to Europe totalled about 50 per cent of shipping costs in 2018 and dropped to 40 and 30 per cent in 2019 and 2020 (Fedorenko, 2020). According to current expectations, all subsidies should be abolished by 2022. Experts believe this will happen when annual railway traffic volumes between China and Europe reach approximately 1.5 million TEUs.

This strategy appears feasible with a substantial increase in traffic volumes and declining shipping costs. Most logistics companies estimate that the cost of delivering one 40-foot container from terminal to terminal by rail from China to Europe was about \$9,000–\$10,000 in 2018. This cost had dropped by almost half in 2021 to about \$4,500–\$5,500 (Otorbaev, 2020).

No official data on the total subsidies are published. We estimate that total railway subsidies since early 2021 from the various Chinese provinces were about \$800 million. However, this substantial sum is negligible compared to the \$100 billion that China annually spends on railway development projects (Otorbaev, 2020).

China has several ambitious long-term projects underway to develop railway transiting routes. The latest Chinese priorities for developing international railways under the Belt and Road Initiative deserve special mention. Chinese engineers have developed new trains with variable-gauge wheelsets. Some of these new trains are already being used, allowing Chinese trains to run with a minimal delay into Russia, Mongolia or Kazakhstan with their broader track gauge compared to China's standard gauge (1,435 mm track). It will also be important to develop automated gauge-changing wheelsets for trains going to India and Pakistan via Myanmar and Bangladesh. Unlike similar equipment, for example, in Europe, this technology will need to operate in hostile climates, with temperatures ranging between minus 50 and 50 degrees Celsius.

Russia and EAEU

The significant increase in the volume of transit rail traffic from China to Europe achieved in recent years has positively impacted the development of the entire Russian transport system. Currently, the Russian government has set the task of increasing the share of transit traffic through Russia along the China–Europe route. By 2025, it plans to bring traffic volume to 10–15 per cent of the total cargo. The government plans to achieve this by increasing the competitiveness of land transport over sea transport through special subsidies.

To this end, on 21 August 2021, Russian Prime Minister Mikhail Mishustin signed a government decree on subsidising the transit rail transportation of containers across the territory of the Russian Federation. The subsidies will amount from 25,000 to 77,000 rubles per container, depending on its type and the direction of transit. The government plans to further reduce rail transportation tariffs in its territory to bring prices closer to maritime container transportation.

Oleg Belozyorov, CEO and Chairman of the Board of Russian Railways (RZD), recently stated, "We can reach 2 million TEUs per year or more" when transporting goods between China and Europe (Atlas Network, 2019). To do this, Russian Railways plans to reduce the time for transporting containers from the Far East to the western border of Russia to just seven days. In addition, Russian Railways plans to implement large-scale projects to reconstruct the Baikal–Amur Mainline (BAM) and the Trans–Siberian Mainline, which will increase container trains' speed. Trains will cover 1,500 kilometres daily instead of the current 1,150 kilometres per day.

Additionally, Russia plans to allocate up to $30.8 billion for the development of railway infrastructure in China, Kazakhstan and Mongolia by 2030. With these funds, three railway checkpoints on the borders of Russia will be established. They will also build 369 km of railway track in Russia and 3,000 km in Kazakhstan, Mongolia and China. The largest of these projects may involve the creation of a transport corridor Russia–Mongolia–China (Potaeva & Il'yushenkov, 2022).

The EAEU has a ramified transport network that can provide direct transcontinental connections across the continent. Cooperation with the EAEU will expand transit volumes and help boost trade between all states on the Eurasian continent. For example, 80 per cent of foreign-trade shipments of Uzbekistan are delivered via the EAEU's member countries, especially Russia, Kazakhstan, and Kyrgyzstan (Hasanov, 2021). Through cost-effective cooperation, Uzbekistan can reduce freight transit costs by up to $220 million via the EAEU's member countries' railway systems. Moreover, it is possible to expand Uzbekistan's transit potential from 7 million to 16 million tons (Nematov, 2020) through simplified customs clearance procedures, transparent tariffs, prices, and rates, and by opening new routes.

But the fact is that the EAEU's member countries lack container trade. According to various estimates, the EAEU countries need over 1.5 million 20-foot equivalent units (TEUs) to justify expanded transiting. The comprehensive containerisation of EAEU trade will require about 60 million tons or 4 million TEU (Eurasian Economic Commission, 2021). It is essential to develop more container technology and capacity in the EAEU to eliminate the current deficiencies.

These steps would make it possible to convert the freight volume of up to 3 or 4 million TEUs into containers. More specialised containers, including refrigerated containers, are also needed to expand the container handling infrastructure, as is the introduction of digital management and upgrading the container traffic tariff system.

Simplification and synchronisation of soft infrastructure are critical for establishing a common transport infrastructure. This includes the creation of standardised shipping documents and agreements on standard railway technical requirements. Pursuing the standardisation of railway traffic requirements under the Convention on International Carriage by Rail (COTIF) provisions is required. EAEU member states understand the need for these changes, which is why a plan for the implementation of the transport policy of the EAEU for 2021–2023 was approved in February 2021 (Eurasian

Economic Commission, 2021). The document stipulates the coordination of the regulations in the EAEU states to expand mixed and container traffic and ensure the comprehensive development of Eurasian transport corridors, including transport and logistics centres.

Domestic upheaval in the EAEU member countries was however an alarming trend for the union as a whole, and the transportation sector in particular. In connection with the imposition of anti-Russian sanctions, Russia and Kazakhstan in particular have faced severe consequences. In addition, the pandemic hit their economies especially hard. Kazakhstan saw massive protests in the tragic events of January 2022 that shook the country (see Chapter 13 for a description of these events). Meanwhile, the Kyrgyz Republic experienced a revolution and a regime change in October 2020, Belarus went through a domestic political crisis in 2020, and Armenia experienced the consequences of a painful defeat following the armed conflict with Azerbaijan in the autumn of 2021.

Although these events are not necessarily related, they have distracted and continue to distract the union's attention and resources from solutions to topical integration problems. The EAEU has ambitious short-term plans. During the pandemic, officials called to launch the Eurasian import substitution policy in all key sectors, promote its digital agenda, achieve greater financial independence, strengthen anti-crisis mechanisms at the EAEU level, and make the association more stress-resistant.

Domestic political unrest does not add credibility to the Eurasian integration project nor makes the EAEU more attractive for investment. From the first days of the approval of the strategy for the implementation of the transport policy, the union has been implementing a new integration model in unfavourable conditions. In particular, the participating countries have not fully formed an atmosphere of trust. There are traces of long-term internal political upheavals and a protracted global socio-political crisis. These problems and challenges might prevent the Union from implementing its initial plans. More clear priorities are expected in advancing integration into the EAEU and understanding the current opportunities and limitations of the union. This includes expanding the Eurasian transport and infrastructure system as a vital aspect of the overall development of the EAEU and the Eurasian states for the next five to ten years. Realising the transport and transit potential of EAEU countries is not just a way to increase the income of the population, economic entities and the budget but is also of important geopolitical significance.

Europe

Despite expanding trade volumes between China and the Central Eurasian countries and Russia, the EU market still receives the bulk of all Chinese freight shipments by all means of transport. Europe's huge consumer market is the main objective in expanding Eurasian transport and logistics systems.

China contributes its export potential, and the EAEU works to create a convenient regulatory framework to facilitate trade.

Collectively, the countries of the EU are the second-largest importer of Chinese goods after the US and one of the most attractive partners. Paradoxically, Europe has not made a worthy contribution to developing its transport and logistics systems to expand trade with China. Today, almost all rail transportation from China to Europe passes through the Brest–Malashevichi border on the Belarusian–Polish border. The lack of reliable railway traffic between Russia and Ukraine, due to the political situation since 2014, is a problem. For now though, we cannot expect the number of EU points handling incoming cargo to increase anytime soon. Russian transshipment seaports for delivering railway consignments to major Western European ports are an available alternative.

Shortly after freight volumes began to increase in the mid-2010s, the European countries faced considerable cargo handling problems. This is because the European railway network is seriously outdated, and its capacity is severely limited. The greatest transportation problems arose in Eastern European countries. It was identified that their railways were designed for transporting goods internally only. Europe was unprepared for large-scale railway transit of goods from Asia. The remoteness of Poland and other countries of Eastern Europe from the main centres of international trade in the European Union, including major ports in Germany, the Netherlands and on the Atlantic coast of France, did not facilitate the active development of domestic trade. Hamburg and Rotterdam trans-shipped most of the Asian goods for the European market. The "old" EU members were not interested in encouraging competition from the countries of the former socialist bloc.

Consequently, logistics restrictions at Poland's Małaszewicze on the border with Belarus became the main bottleneck along the route between China and Europe. Seeing the potential for developing this border crossing point, with the financial contribution from the European Union, the Polish government has now begun to invest in the modernisation of the facilities. Its capacity, including the transit of goods from China, will increase significantly as a result of these upgrades. In 2020 the facility handled 14 pairs of trains daily, and in 2021, following a large overhaul, the number was set to reach 55 pairs. The expenses, financed by the Polish government and the EU budget, are estimated at 700 million euros. The new Małaszewicze hub will be upgraded, covering an area of 30 square kilometres. The project will rehabilitate the railway infrastructure of the transit hub, which will significantly increase the speed of trains and modernise the railway tracks to withstand heavy loads.

Regulations on the maximum length of container trains on European railways are another restriction on freight traffic volumes and delivery times, with high operational costs. The average container train can consist of seventy-one standard carriages in Russia and fifty-seven–sixty-five carriages in Belarus, while EU regulations limit train lengths to only forty-three carriages. Therefore, trains entering Europe via Małaszewicze can have just forty-three carriages with eighty-six TEUs. Due to restrictions on the number of carriages across European territory, a container train arriving at the Polish border must be stopped and divided roughly in half. Practically, this means that when reloading containers in Brest, the train must be limited to a maximum of forty-three carriages, and the remaining carriages must wait for the next train.

Eliminating bureaucratic barriers is another factor of great importance in boosting the speed of delivery of goods. This includes the optimisation of customs standards, the minimisation of administrative procedures for clearance of goods and acceleration of border procedures. Implementing such changes is difficult because the streamlining of bureaucratic processes must be carried out by signing international agreements. The lack of dialogue between the European Union and the EAEU on these matters also hampers the expansion of transit on the territory. Some EU authorities believe that surface routes will not offer long-term competition and that investing in upgrading the eastern EU railway system is pointless. Unfortunately, the situation with transportation between East and West through Russian territory has become uncertain due to the war in Ukraine and the imposition of anti-Russian sanctions by Western countries.

Challenges for trans-Eurasian connectivity

In addition to geopolitical problems, the development of Eurasian railway transportation faces a few technical challenges. One of these challenges, discussed previously, relates to track gauge – the distance between the two tracks of a railway. Russia, Kazakhstan, Belarus, and Mongolia use a track gauge of 1,520 mm, while Europe and China use a standard gauge track (1,435 mm). As it stands today, containers must be reloaded onto different trains twice on the route between China and Europe. Alternatively, as mentioned earlier, new automated wheel-set gauge change equipment will need to be used.

Some believe the differing track gauge widths are the main obstacle to shipping times and volumes. In our opinion, this barrier is not critical. For example, it takes several hours to reload a train from one gauge to another in Khorgos. But when automated wheel gauge technology is applied, there is only a forty-five-minute delay. The Chinese have been working hard on rolling stock with variable gauge wheelsets, which will minimise the impact of the wheel gauge issue.

Given the impressive growth in freight rail traffic on the Eurasian route between China and Europe and the prospects it holds, the governments of the countries through which this route passes and the transport companies involved must reconsider their traditional plans. It is essential to identify the bottlenecks on the route and other factors that potentially hinder traffic growth. Most analysts agree that there are two main mid-term challenges. First, it is necessary to balance Chinese traffic to and from Europe. Second, resolving the capacity problem at the Belarusian–Polish border is required.

In 2020, about 66 per cent of all railway traffic was headed west, and the remaining 33 per cent, east. This situation is unlikely to change anytime soon. A rapid increase in Chinese domestic consumption could be the most promising development, as it would boost China's demand for high-quality European imports. The Chinese market must also be opened up for goods from the EAEU and Uzbekistan, and traditional and non-tariff trade restrictions from China must be eliminated.

Another problem is a critical shortage of containers in connection with the coronavirus pandemic. The lack of containers causes a chain reaction along all supply chains and disrupts the international trade system. The shortage of containers also increases prices for new containers. According to goods producers, shipping costs jumped from $1,500 to $6,000–$9,000 per container in February 2021. Chinese container manufacturers, who now dominate the market, are charging $2,500 per container, compared to $1,600 last year. During 2021, container lease rates increased by nearly 50 per cent. Experts do not doubt that the increase in the volume of rail traffic, will also contribute to the solving of any emerging technical problems.

Growth potential for rail traffic

Most analysts believe container traffic volumes between China and Europe will continue to grow. Analysts from the Eurasian Development Bank estimate that, given the existing infrastructure, annual railway traffic volumes between China and Europe can reach about 2 million twenty-foot equivalent units (TEUs) (Japan International Freight Forwarders Association Inc., 2020). In order to achieve this target, it is necessary to strive for lower rates and tariffs to increase traffic volumes further. This growth will also require significant investments in physical infrastructure, the development of transport and logistics centres, an increase in the efficiency of locomotives, the automation of border crossing procedures, the introduction of processes using blockchain and smart contracts, the standardisation of the regulatory framework, and an improvement in the formation procedures tariffs, along with many others actions.

In early 2022, Russian Railways announced even more ambitious targets. The company expected to increase annual transit traffic between China and Europe to 4 million TEUs. This figure will be reached within five years, and possibly earlier. It was stated by the Deputy General Director of Russian Railways, Alexei Shilo (Korenjako, 2022) that "this is an ambitious task; we want to fight for this figure [4 million TEU]. We would like to achieve it in 2025". Now Russian Railways is preparing a programme of measures to achieve this goal. In 2021, the annual transit of containers through Russia increased by 43 per cent to 1.1 million TEU. In 2021, Russian Railways transported a total of 6.5 million TEU, including domestic traffic. During the past five years, the volume of container traffic has doubled.

A single company transported more than 62 per cent of all transit containers – UTLC ERA, owned on parity by Russian, Belarusian and

Kazakhstan Railways. In total, the company transported 692,500 TEU in 2021. Of these, 439,500 TEU (63 per cent) were transported from China to Europe, and 253,000 TEU (37 per cent) proceeded in the opposite direction (Korenjako, 2022). The volume of container traffic has reached a record in the history of Russian Railways. This is associated with high rates on the sea and air routes between Asia and Europe and pandemic restrictions in the seaports of Europe and China. Shippers are actively shifting to land routes as they are cheaper, faster and safer. As market participants note, Japan and South Korea are beginning to demonstrate an interest in the inland transit to Europe through Russia, which is creating the additional potential for further growth in transit. Russian experts believe that transit traffic between East and West will continue with double-digit growth in the coming years.

On average, the transit of one container through the territory of Russia has about a $10,000 effect on the Russian economy and budget, said Sergey Shishkarev, co-owner of the largest container operator TransContainer (RBK, 2021). According to his calculations, Russia accounts for only about 6 per cent of container traffic between Europe and Southeast Asia, the majority being delivered by sea. Therefore, both the government and private carriers should be interested in growing domestic and transit container traffic through Russia.

The experience of transit traffic in 2021 "revealed many bottlenecks", acknowledges Mr Shilo. Dealing with these bottlenecks will require additional investments. These will primarily come in the form of creating specialised container terminals in Kazakhstan and China. Shilo said modern checkpoints in Russia, Kazakhstan, and China need to be developed and new exit points for European routes need to be identified.

From the analysis presented, it is clear that producers, recipients of goods, logistics companies and transit countries maintain interests in developing container transportation along the Eurasian land bridge. Rail transport has already shown a few clear advantages over sea transport, which until recently dominated global international transit. Achieving a traffic target of 4 million TEU per year means that every 10–15 minutes, a fully loaded train will have to depart and arrive from Asia to Europe and back.

All the above allows us to make an optimistic forecast on the prospects for the expansion of railway transportation between Asia and Europe. Building modern railways along new routes will likely become necessary in new geographical areas along the shorter but slightly more complicated southern way, crossing the mountain ranges. But what was technologically tricky or even impossible just a few years ago, with the help of modern technologies, is becoming much easier. Everything points to the fact that the day is not far off when an increasing number of modern trains will cross the Eurasian continent, connecting the current centres of economic power. As before in its history, Central Asia could become a backbone of transit trade, again connecting East and West, but this time along a technologically advanced and modern Silk Road.

However, it should be emphasised here that such grandiose plans are now subject to very high risks. These plans were formulated before Russia launched a special military operation in Ukraine in February 2022, that poses a severe threat to the very existence of the Eurasian Railway Bridge. Currently, transportation of goods by rail continues, delivering Russian oil, metals and wheat to the West and goods in transit between China and Europe. However, the risks are growing every day with the large-scale sanctions imposed by Western countries. The most dangerous scenario would be the imposition of sanctions against Russian Railways. This would put an immediate end to all transit. Such a development would be a big shock to Chinese and European companies accustomed to fast and efficient transportation by rail. At a briefing on 5 January 2022, Chinese Foreign Ministry spokesman Wang Wenbin called the Eurasian railway bridge an "anchor of stability" in global supply chains (Global Times, 2022a). Now there is a risk that this will not be the case.

Will the Eurasian rail route survive anti-Russian sanctions?

Sanctions against Russia imposed by Western countries due to its invasion of Ukraine pose a massive threat to the development and existence of the Eurasian railway route connecting China with Europe. All countries along the route are analysing the potential negative consequences of restrictions and the possible suspension of operations. A global rethinking of regional development, security and investment strategies has been triggered. Many agree that Kazakhstan will feel the most severe long-term consequences of a restriction or suspension in the logistics chain as a large amount of rail traffic passes through its territory.

Rail traffic across Russia proceeded on schedule during the first few weeks after the outbreak of hostilities in Ukraine, as the operators had placed orders for transport in advance. Moreover, while transit using the state-owned Russian railway company, which is subject to sanctions, is still technically possible, many Western logistics companies are effectively suspending their operations on the overland rail route (Leijen, 2022).

Russian Railways is on the EU and the US sanctions list as a state-owned company, but so far the company is only subject to financial sanctions related to the capital markets. Legally, doing business with the company is still possible, so logistics companies can still use its services. However, the point is not in legal restrictions but the moral and reputational motives of the participants in the transportation market. The Western world is focusing now on ethical decisions and values.

For example, on 9 March 2022, the large German logistics company Hapag-Lloyd confirmed that it no longer accepts orders where Russia, Belarus and Ukraine are involved (Hapag-Lloyd, 2022). The next day, DB Schenker, a major logistics provider, announced that it was temporarily suspending land, air and sea transportation to and from Russia (DB Schenker, 2022). However, the most severe threat to the very existence of the land bridge was the statement by the administration of the dry port of Duisburg, which is the leading European hub for transportation from Asia (Hutson, 2022). It noted that, in all likelihood, international insurers would stop insuring goods in transit through Russia or Belarus.

The economic and financial impact of sanctions and traffic restrictions will hurt all countries along this route. For example, the joint Chinese-Belarusian industrial park Great Stone (Great Stone Industrial park, 2022), with a Chinese investment of about two billion dollars, may find itself without markets for its products.

Similar risks associated with sanctions and restrictions on transit traffic exist in China's interaction with the countries of Central Asia. China's 13th Five-Year Development Plan specifically noted that the task of Xinjiang Province, which borders Central Asia, was to "strengthen infrastructure development along the main routes and main ports of entry" and that it was necessary to "work on the development of Xinjiang as the core region of the Silk Road Economic Belt" (National Development and Reform Commission, 2020). China's strategy also emphasised greater economic integration with Central Asia, thus promoting confidence, security and stability along China's northwestern borders.

Kazakhstan is the leading country in Central Asia in terms of the massive volume of goods that pass through on their way from China to Europe. The government has included strengthening transit trade in all recent development strategies. The significant growth in this trade in recent years has dramatically impacted the development of its economy and brought about an increase in budget revenues.

The Kazakh economy has already been hit hard by Western anti-Russian sanctions since Kazakhstan and Russia are in a single economic bloc - the Eurasian Economic Union and Kazakhstan has a significant trade turnover with its northern neighbour. At one point, the value of the Kazakh currency, the tenge, fell 22 per cent against the US dollar. The inflation rate in March 2022 exceeded 12 per cent, twice the pre-sanction level (Smajyl, 2022). In March 2022, the Central Bank of Kazakhstan spent more than $990.5 million from its gold and foreign exchange reserves to support the tenge (Diasov, 2022). The government also imposed restrictions on the export of foreign currency and gold.

The country had not yet recovered from the sanctions strike on Russian oil when it faced another big problem. An accident occurred on the main oil pipeline in Kazakhstan. Deputy Prime Minister of Russia Alexander Novak reported on 23 March 2022 that due to the failure of mooring facilities at the terminal in the Russian port of Novorossiysk, the Kazakhstan Pipeline Consortium (KPC) completely stopped loading its oil and transporting this oil through its pipeline (RIA Novosti, 2022). This could be a considerable problem for Kazakhstan's budget revenues, as approximately 80 per cent of Kazakhstan's oil is sent abroad via this pipeline. In 2021, 53 million tons of oil passed through the pipeline, while the total capacity of CPC was 63 million tons per year (Kazistaev, 2022).

According to experts' preliminary estimates, if the CPC operation shutdown drags on for two months, then the budget of Kazakhstan may lose about $500 million. Energy Minister Bolat Akchulakov was quick to coolly add that the accident will not affect budget revenues, since oil prices are high this year (Sputnik.kz, 2022). The Minister also stated that it would take three weeks to a month to repair CPC's berthing equipment. It is unclear whether the post-invasion surge in global energy prices can help offset the financial turmoil by generating additional revenue for the country. But Kazakh officials are concerned, especially as the country has yet to recover from a painful period of instability in January 2022. By the end of July 2022, the operation of the pipeline was restored, but it is not known how long its stable operation will last (Radio Azattyk, 2022).

What alternatives for rail transport between China and Europe through Russia's territory? Many experts believe these cargo flows will switch to other routes (Dreissen, 2022). Using the railway corridors outside Russia such as the Trans-Caspian International Transport Route (TITR) via Kazakhstan, Turkmenistan, Azerbaijan, Georgia, and Turkey is a possible but rather expensive solution. Admittedly, traffic on the TITR has been growing steadily since its launch in 2017. In the year of the route's start, about 300 containers have used the corridor. But only in the first half of 2021 did this number increase to more than 7,000 containers (Kumenov, 2022). The main contributors to traffic volume growth were Chinese companies, which consider TITR a profitable and faster transportation option than crossing oceans (Russian.news.cn, 2016). Recently, Turkey has been paying particular attention to this direction, bearing in mind the increase in trade volumes with China and the fraternal Central Asian countries.

In the medium term, the current situation around restrictions on transportation through Russian territory may increase interest in constructing the shortest, southern Eurasian railway route from China through the Kyrgyz Republic and Uzbekistan and further through the countries of the South Caucasus and Turkey to Europe.

Southern route

Another scenario related to the military-political situation in Afghanistan is the southern branch of the Eurasian railway system. Uzbekistan is the most active supporter of this idea, including expanding capacity on existing routes, laying new tracks, and constructing new infrastructure on this shorter "southern" route from China to Europe via the Kyrgyz Republic, Uzbekistan, Turkmenistan, Iran, and Turkey. Construction of this route would strengthen the Eurasian railway network and increase Russia and China's interest in developing Central Asia. Building about 268 kilometres of new railways from China to Uzbekistan via the Kyrgyz Republic would be necessary to open this new transport corridor.

Using this new corridor, Russia and China could become more actively involved in current and planned railway lines in Uzbekistan, Turkmenistan, and Afghanistan. The shortest railway route via Kyrgyzstan could link China and Russia with three good courses: 1) India and Pakistan, including reaching the Indian Ocean; 2) Azerbaijan and Georgia, including the Black Sea; and, 3) Iran and Turkey, the Mediterranean Sea and the Black Sea to reach Europe beyond. Estimates show that such a rail route between China and southern Europe would be about 900 kilometres shorter than current routes. This corridor would reduce delivery times between Asia and Europe by another seven to eight days. According to calculations by Uzbek experts, an annual freight volume of just 5 million tonnes would compensate for railway construction expenses (Podrobno.uz, 2019).

Unfortunately, after the events of August 2021 in Afghanistan, it has become much more difficult to predict the prospects for the development of transport and other infrastructure projects involving the country. Potential stakeholders can only consider projects as long-term strategic prospects. Despite the ambitions and interests of various parties, the practicality and feasibility of opportunities directly depend on the stabilisation of the political situation in this country, the readiness of the legitimate Afghan government to be a civilised member of the world community, and the recognition of this readiness by the international community.

At the virtual summit of the presidents of China and the countries of Central Asia, held in January 2022, the presidents of China, the Kyrgyz Republic and Uzbekistan confirmed their interest in building a southern railway route. In particular, the Chinese leader said that the Chinese side would speed up the process of designing a railway along the new southern route China–Kyrgyzstan–Uzbekistan. It will be necessary to agree on its optimal path, determine the project's financial and economic model, and agree on a project management method.

It is likely that financing schemes and further management of the southern railway route will form a type of international agreement between the partners. To find the optimal mechanism for financing, operating, and managing the project, using the experience of building similar international projects is critical.

Other examples of international rail routes in Asia

When discussing the prospects for the further development of rail transport in Eurasia, it is crucial to focus on successful examples of the development of similar projects in other parts of Asia. Here, the recently commissioned railway between China and Laos comes to the fore. This first section of the unique China–Singapore international railway (Figure 7.2) will be an important landmark project in South–East Asia of high-quality Belt and Road cooperation.

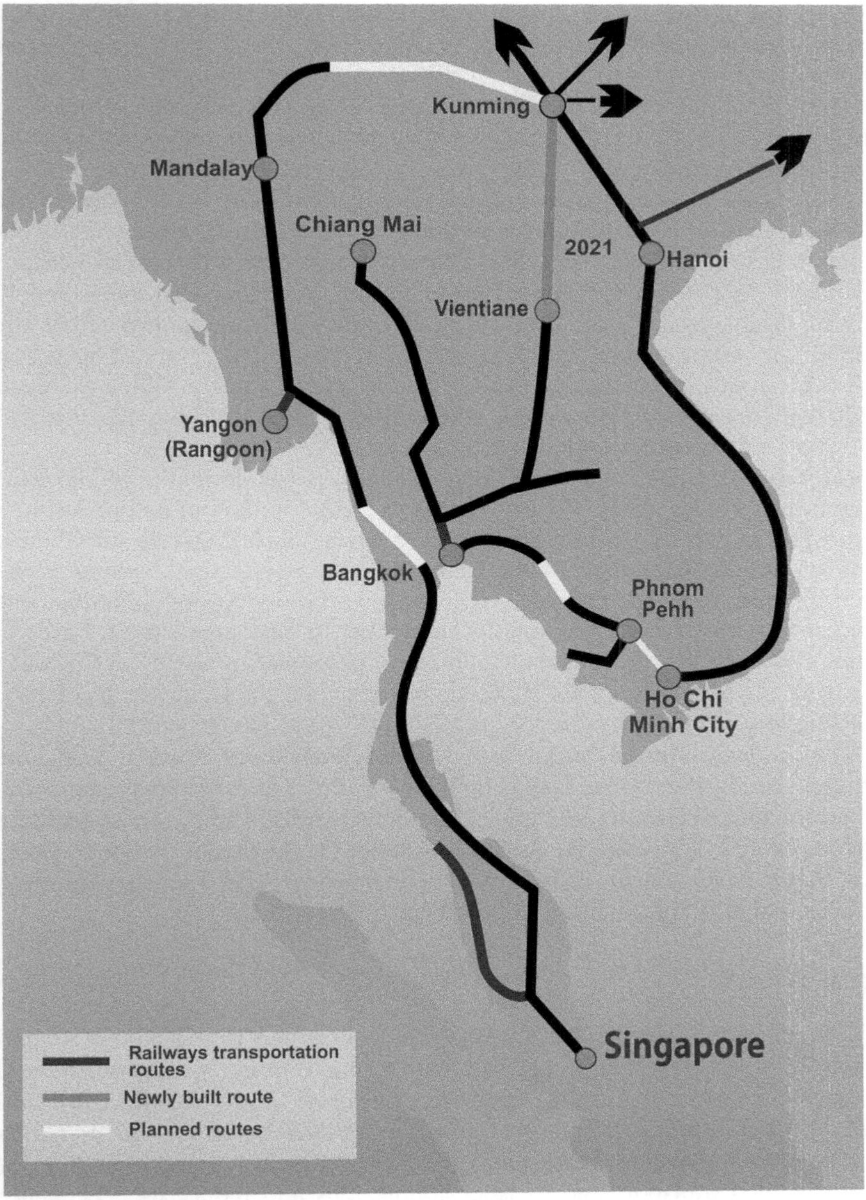

Figure 7.2 Rail map of Southeast Asia

Opening to traffic on 3 December 2021, the China–Laos Railway stretches over 1,000 km and links Kunming, the capital of southwest China's Yunnan Province, to the Laotian capital Vientiane. According to the China Railway Kunming Group Co., Ltd., thirteen provinces and municipalities, including Beijing, Shanghai, and Sichuan, have opened freight train services on the railway (Xinhua, 2022a).

Naturally, an active trade in goods began along this route immediately. "The China-Laos Railway saves us about 30 per cent of logistics cost from Kunming to Vientiane. The rail transport is more punctual and can reduce damages to the goods," said Yang Jie from Shanghai Rencheng Supply Chain Management Co., Ltd. "We are more confident in expanding the Southeast Asian market" (Xinhua, 2022b). In the first 100 days of operation of this railway, the volume of exports of goods from Laos to China exceeded 120,000 tons, worth more than 500 million yuan, while imports reached 70,000 tons, worth more than 1.7 billion yuan.

However, it is also remarkable that this railway has dramatically increased the transportation of passengers. Within the first 100 days of its operation, it transported over 1.8 million passengers (Xinhua, 2022a). During the Chinese New Year, the Kunming Chinese Railway Group operated 32.5 pairs of passenger trains daily and carried 33,000 passengers daily. At the same time, one bullet train ran every 30 minutes. The number of passengers in the Lao section also grew steadily. The daily number of passengers reached 2,600 people. During the Spring Festival, 78,000 passengers used the train (Global Times, 2022c).

The railway also contributed to the development of tourism along the route. During the tourist boom, bookings in Pu'er and Xishuangbanna Dai Autonomous Prefecture in Yunnan Province increased by 92.4 per cent and 59.9 per cent, respectively, further boosting the province's previous year's economic development. This example clearly shows that Eurasian Railways also has significant potential in passenger transportation.

Conclusion

The exploration of various examples and scenarios has suggested that a rapid increase in freight volume between China and Europe is likely for several reasons. Firstly, the Chinese economy has become more competitive and continues to increase exports to European markets. In the mid-2010s, China attained impressive production and growth rates, making it possible to invest in expanded transport and logistics connections and reduce its dependence on sea routes. China's greater economic presence abroad and expanding commercial ties will play the most crucial role. Secondly, China exports higher-value goods that must be delivered more quickly to consumers than sea shipping. This increases the significance of surface routes, increases traffic volumes and will help drive the expansion of the Eurasian railway network. Thirdly, the Chinese policy to relocate production facilities inland prioritises the development of the country's landlocked central and western provinces, where it is possible to develop cheaper and faster railway traffic to Europe. Fourthly, the Chinese population is becoming more affluent and more Chinese citizens want high-quality and expensive European goods, including wines, certain foods, and cars. This, once again, increases demand for the fastest but cost-effective delivery of these goods to the Chinese market.

Fifth, the stabilisation of the Russian economy, the expansion of rail links within Russia, and the country's growing network of seaports support long-term political stability and economic development in Central Asia and the development of their interstate relations. Finally, establishing the Customs Union in Eurasia ensured the free movement of goods, and transport companies gained access to a reliable, fast, and cost-effective railway service. Members of the union will continue their efforts to reduce costs and tariffs for the transportation of goods. In addition, further steps can be made to subsidise rail transport tariffs.

Over the past ten years, the Eurasian railway bridge linking economic powerhouses in Asia, the largest continent, has confirmed this expansion policy's high profitability and promising nature. In addition to global players, including Russia, China, and Europe, China's inland provinces and the Central Asian countries would be the primary beneficiaries of these commercial routes. For centuries, the latter has suffered from their landlocked position and now see new opportunities in land transport and logistics corridors.

By expanding its transiting potential, Central Asia has every opportunity to become part of the macro-regional transport and logistics system and integral to the leading global economic centres. Establishing a diversified transport and communications system will make it possible to realise transport and transit potential, provide a multiplier effect for the sustainable development of the most dynamic and stable (in the military-political context) region, and turn it into a logistics hub.

References

Anaklia Development Consortium, 2022. Anakliadevelopment.com. [Online] Available at: http://anakliadevelopment.com/info/ [Accessed July 2022].

Atlas Network, 2019. Container shipping by rail from China to Europe may exceed 2 million TEU/Year. [Online] Available at: https://atlas-network.com/container-shipping-by-rail-from-china-to-europe-may-exceed-2-million-teu-year/ [Accessed July 2022].

Azertag.az, 2022. Poslednie novosti - Azertag. [Online] Available at: https://azertag.az/ru/xeber/ [Accessed July 2022].

China.org.cn, 2022. China-Europe freight train services surge in 2021. [Online] Available at: http://www.china.org.cn/business/2022-01/04/content_77969503.htm [Accessed July 2022].

CIS portal, 2018. Central Asia in the system of international transport corridors: A view from Uzbekistan. [Online] Available at: https://e-cis.info/news/566/62962/?sphrase_id=22646 [Accessed July 2022].

DB Cargo, 2021. DB Cargo goes Transasia. [Online] Available at: https://www.dbcargo.com/rail-de-en/logistics-news/db-cargo-goes-transasia-subsidiary-china-eurasia-6981698 [Accessed July 2022].

DB Schenker, 2022. Ukraine crisis update. [Online] Available at: https://www.dbschenker.com/de-en/meta/ukraine-crisis-update [Accessed July 2022].

Diasov, O., 2022. Bolee 990 mln dollarov potratil Nacbank v marte na podderzhanie kursa tenge. [Online] Available at: https://online.zakon.kz/Document/?doc_id=37202168 [Accessed July 2022].

Dreissen, F., 2022. Nieuwe Zijderoute op dood spoor; containertransport per trein door Rusland raakt ook Limburgse bedrijven. [Online] Available at: https://www.limburger.nl/cnt/dmf20220321_95138577 [Accessed July 2022].

Eurasian Economic Commission, 2021. Soglasovana «dorozhnaja karta» po realizacii transportnoj politiki na 2021–2023 gody. [Online] Available at: http://www.eurasiancommission.org/ru/nae/news/Pages/19-02-2021-4.aspx [Accessed July 2022].

Fedorenko, R. V., 2020. Problems of developing the customs and logistics infrastructure of the East-West International Transport Corridor. *RUDN Journal of Economics*, 28 (3), p. 499.

Global Times, 2022a. China-Europe freight train service bolsters continental supply chain stability: Foreign Ministry says. [Online] Available at: https://www.globaltimes.cn/page/202201/1245139.shtml [Accessed July 2022].

Global Times, 2022b. China-Europe freight train trips reach 15,000 in 2021, a y-o-y jump of 22%. [Online] Available at: https://www.ciie.org/zbh/en/news/exhibition/news/20220106/31136.html [Accessed July 2022].

Global Times, 2022c. China-Laos Railway sees major progresses. [Online] Available at: https://www.globaltimes.cn/page/202202/1253352.shtml [Accessed July 2022].

Great Stone Industrial park, 2022. Industrial'nyj park «Velikij kamen'». [Online] Available at: https://industrialpark.by/ [Accessed July 2022].

Hapag-Lloyd, 2022. An FAQ for our customers on the war between Russia and Ukraine. [Online] Available at: https://www.hapag-lloyd.com/en/services-information/news/2022/03/mar09-russia-ukraine-conflict-faq-frequently-asked-questions.html [Accessed July 2022].

Hasanov, U., 2021. Uzbekistan rasschityvaet na uglublenie promkooperacii v EAJeS – uzbekskij jekspert. [Online] Available at: https://eurasia.expert/uzbekistan-rasschityvaet-na-uglublenie-promkooperatsii-v-eaes/ [Accessed July 2022].

Hillman, J. E., 2018. The Rise of China-Europe Railways. [Online] Available at: https://www.csis.org/analysis/rise-china-europe-railways [Accessed July 2022].

Hutson, N., 2022. War in Ukraine is hamstringing China's 'Belt and Road Initiative'. [Online] Available at: https://responsiblestatecraft.org/2022/03/22/beltandroadchinarussia [Accessed July 2022].

Interfax.az, 2020. Zheleznaja doroga Baku-Tbilisi-Kars nachala rabotat' v dvustoronnem rezhime. [Online] Available at: http://interfax.az/view/821745 [Accessed July 2022].

Japan International Freight Forwarders Association Inc., 2020. The EDB: Container transit along the China – EAEU – EU axis is guaranteed to grow up to 500,000 TEU, by 2020. [Online] Available at: https://www.jiffa.or.jp/en/news/entry-5264.html [Accessed July 2022].

John, 2022. From crisis to opportunity: why companies return to using long-distance trains. [Online] Available at: https://www.worldstockmarket.net/from-crisis-to-opportunity-why-companies-return-to-using-long-distance-trains/ [Accessed July 2022].

Kapital.kz, 2021. Kazahstan snjal zapret na jeksport gruzov v Kitaj. [Online] Available at: https://kapital.kz/economic/94081/kazakhstan-snyal-zapret-na-eksport-gruzov-v-kitay.html [Accessed July 2022].

Kazistaev, E., 2022. Kak avarija na terminale KTK povlijaet na jeksport kazahstanskoj nefti. [Online] Available at: https://ru.sputnik.kz/20220325/kak-avariya-na-terminale-ktk-povliyaet-na-eksport -kazakhstanskoy-nefti-23724465.html [Accessed July 2022].

Korenjako, A., 2022. RZhD sprognozirovali rost tranzita kontejnerov v chetyre raza. [Online] Available at: https://www.rbc.ru/business/28/01/2022/61f2a8c19a79470d73b3dbab [Accessed July 2022].

Kumenov, A., 2022. Russia sanctions prompt Kazakhstan to increase exports via Caspian. [Online] Available at: https://eurasianet.org/russia-sanctions-prompt-kazakhstan-to-increase-exports-via-caspian [Accessed July 2022].

Kun.uz, 2021. Uzbekiston, Afgoniston va Pokiston temir yol kurilishi buicha «Yol kharitasi“ imzoladi. [Online] Available at: https://kun.uz/news/2021/02/09/ozbekiston-afgoniston-va-pokiston-temir-yol-qurilishi-boyicha-yol-xaritasini-imzoladi [Accessed July 2022].

Leijen, M. v., 2022. Sanctions or not: these companies stop transit through Russia. [Online] Available at: https://www.railfreight.com/railfreight/2022/03/03/sanctions-or-not-these-companies-stop-transit-through-russia/ [Accessed July 2022].

Li, Z., 2021. China railway express. [Online] Available at: https://zhuanlan.zhihu.com/p/354338082 [Accessed July 2022].

MFA Afghanistan, 2021. Afghan Foreign Minister Mawlawi Amir Khan Muttaqi met this evening with Uzbek delegation led by Minister of Transport Mr. Ilkhom Makhkamov. [Online] Available at: https://mfa.gov.af/en/afghan-foreign-minister-mawlawi-amir-khan-muttaqi-met-this-evening-with-uzbek-delegation-led-by-minister-of-transport-mr-ilkhom-makhkamov/ [Accessed July 2022].

Middleeastmonitor.com, 2022. Russia and Iran are accelerating their project to rival the Suez Canal. [Online] Available at: https://www.middleeastmonitor.com/20220624-russia-and-iran-are-accelerating-their-project-to-rival-the-suez-canal/ [Accessed July 2022].

National Development and Reform Commission, 2020. *The 13th Five-year Plan for Economic and Social Development of the People's Republic of China*, Beijing: Central Compilation & Translation Press.

Nematov, A., 2020. Detal'no izuchit', prezhde chem prinjat' «pravila igry». [Online] Available at: https://xs.uz/ru/post/detalno-izuchit-prezhde-chem-prinyat-pravila-igry [Accessed July 2022].

Nulimaimaiti, M., 2021. China-Europe rail trade set for infrastructure upgrade, with container traffic up 30 per cent. [Online] Available at: https://www.scmp.com/economy/global-economy/article/3161588/china-europe-rail-trade-set-infrastructure-upgrade-container [Accessed July 2022].

Otorbaev, D., 2020. Eurasian railway breakthrough. [Online] Available at: https://valdaiclub.com/a/highlights/eurasian-railway-breakthrough/ [Accessed July 2022].

Peacenexus.org, 2019. Razvitie transportnyh koridorov v Central'noj Azii i effekt Iniciativy «Pojas i Put'». [Online] Available at: https://peacenexus.org/wp-content/uploads/2020/01/%D0%9E%D1%82%D1%87%D1%91%D1%82_DSC_PN_2019.pdf [Accessed July 2022].

Podrobno.uz, 2019. Kitaj predlozhil neskol'ko variantov marshruta novoj zheleznoj dorogi "Uzbekistan-Kyrgyzstan-Kitaj". [Online] Available at: https://www.podrobno.uz/cat/uzbekistan-i-kitay-klyuchi-ot-budushchego/kitay-predlozhil-neskolko-variantov-marshruta-novoy/?sphrase_id=4414088 [Accessed July 2022].

Potaeva, K. & Il'yushenkov, D., 2022. Rossiya mozhet vydelit' $31 milliard na zh/d proekty v Kazakhstane, Mongolii i KNR. [Online] Available at: https://www.vedomosti.ru/business/articles/2022/07/28/933568-rossiya-videlit-zhd-proekti [Accessed July 2022].

Radio Azattyk, 2022. Kaspiiskii truboprovodnyi konsortsium: pabota nefteprovoda vosstanovlena posle avarii. [Online] Available at: https://rus.azattyq.org/a/31966405.html [Accessed July 2022].

RBK, 2021. Vladelec gruppy «Delo» — RBK: «Do Maersk nam kak do sirenevoj zvezdy». [Online] Available at: https://www.rbc.ru/business/07/12/2021/61ade07c9a79473f30f9c146 [Accessed July 2022].

Regnum, 2021. Pereval Alatau v Sin'czjane propustil na 47% bol'she poezdov Kitaj — Evropa. [Online] Available at: https://regnum.ru/news/3283359.html [Accessed July 2022].

RIA Novosti, 2022. Postavki nefti po truboprovodu KTK mogut prekratit'sja, zajavil Novak. [Online] Available at: https://ria.ru/20220323/truboprovod-1779654069.html [Accessed July 2022].

Rogers, D., 2022. Iran and Afghanistan meet to plan completion of vital rail link to Herat. [Online] Available at: https://www.globalconstructionreview.com/iran-and-afghanistan-meet-to-plan-completion-of-vital-rail-link-to-herat/ [Accessed July 2022].

Russian.news.cn, 2016. Transkaspijskij mezhdunarodnyj transportnyj marshrut sozdaet uslovija dlja stroitel'stva "Pojasa i puti" (peredaetsja povtorno s popravkoj v zagolovke). [Online] Available at: http://russian.news.cn/2016-10/30/c_135791597.htm [Accessed July 2022].

Seanews.ru, 2021. Zheleznodorozhnye perevozki Kitaj – Evropa. [Online] Available at: https://seanews.ru/2021/07/07/zheleznodorozhnye-perevozki-kitaj-evropa/ [Accessed July 2022].

Smajyl, M., 2022. Infljacija v Kazahstane vyrosla do 12 procentov. [Online] Available at: https://tengrinews.kz/kazakhstan_news/inflyatsiya-v-kazahstane-vyirosla-do-12-protsentov-465481/ [Accessed July 2022].

Smith, K., 2022. China-Europe express traffic up 23% between January and November. [Online] Available at: https://www.railjournal.com/freight/china-europe-express-traffic-up-23-between-january-and-november/ [Accessed July 2022].

Sputnik.kz, 2022. Skol'ko poterjaet bjudzhet Kazahstana ot sokrashhenija jeksporta nefti iz-za avarii na KTK. [Online] Available at: https://ru.sputnik.kz/20220324/skolko-poteryaet-byudzhet-kazakhstana-ot-sokrascheniya-eksporta-nefti-iz-za-avarii-na-ktk-23708028.html [Accessed July 2022].

The Load Star, 2021. China-Europe rail freight grows. [Online] Available at: https://www.maritimegateway.com/china-europe-rail-freight-grows/ [Accessed July 2022].

Tolstouhova, N., 2020. Problemy i perspektivy kontejnernyh perevozok. [Online] Available at: http://www.morvesti.ru/analitika/1685/86587/ [Accessed July 2022].

Utlc.com, 2021a. Ob"em perevozok OTLK ERA v 1 kvartale 2021 goda vyros bolee chem v dva raza. [Online] Available at: https://www.utlc.com/news/obem-perevozok-otlk-era-v-i-kvartale-2021-goda-vyros-bolee-chem-v-2-raza-/ [Accessed July 2022].

Utlc.com, 2021b. Rekordnyj tranzit. [Online] Available at: https://utlc.com/smi/rekordnyy-tranzit/?PAGEN_2=5 [Accessed July 2022].

Utlc.com, 2022. OTLK ERA. [Online] Available at: https://www.utlc.com [Accessed July 2022].

Xinhua, 2022a. China-Laos railway puts freight transport on fast track. [Online] Available at: https://english.news.cn/asiapacific/20220312/c42c9a6b3dbc471d930322f67209f046/c.html [Accessed July 2022].

Xinhua, 2022b. China-Laos railway puts trade on fast track. [Online] Available at: http://www.xinhuanet.com/english/20220303/01148fc9205f4c3683d7a27086a7609b/c.html#:~:text=Opening%20to%20traffic%20on%20Dec,who%20benefit%20from%20the%20railway [Accessed July 2022].

Xu, X., 2022. 6,000 miles through 7 countries. Why companies are turning to long-haul trains. [Online] Available at: https://edition.cnn.com/2022/01/06/business/trains-europe-china-pandemic-shipping/index.html [Accessed July 2022].

Yeping, Y., 2021. China-Europe freight train services expect manageable impact despite subsidy speculation: insiders. [Online] Available at: https://www.globaltimes.cn/page/202112/1243314.shtml [Accessed July 2022].

Yılmaz, M. & Çakır, M. Ö., 2017. BTK sdadut v jekspluataciju vesnoj. [Online] Available at: https://www.aa.com.tr/ru/загёлёвки-дня/дё-завершения-рабёт-в-рамках-бтк-ёсталёсь-2-месяца-министр/732303 [Accessed July 2022].

Yousafzai, S., 2022. Taliban give nod to Pakistan-Afghanistan rail link. [Online] Available at: https://tribune.com.pk/story/2339289/taliban-give-nod-to-pakistan-afghanistan-rail-link [Accessed July 2022].

8 The Future of Rail

Lessons from China

Introduction

Considering the promising prospects of the use of rail transport in further strengthening transit trade between Asia and Europe and, consequently, its impact on the development of Central Asia, it is impossible not to dwell on the impressive results of new technological solutions in this area. The absolute leader here is China, as we will explore in this chapter. We can reasonably conclude that our southeastern neighbour has outperformed all its competitors for quite a long time and in quite remarkable ways. Will we see the results of the railway technological revolution in the region of Central Asia? Considering China's tremendous achievements in developing its domestic rail transport network and its ambition to keep pace, the answer to this question is probably yes, and this chapter will explore why this is the case.

Development of High-speed Railway in China

One of Central Asia's close neighbours is taking steps that could contribute to the expansion of the Eurasian railway network. China is investing significantly in developing a high-speed rail (HSR), a technological factor that could play a major role in the future of communications.

It seems that China's achievements in the field of innovating in technology are turning the country into something of a rival in the field. In the US, Congress is so concerned that the country is lagging behind China in their development of modern technologies that, on 27 May 2021, the US Senate approved an extensive package of legislation specifically to improve the US's ability to compete with Chinese technology. Senators ended their debate by voting for the $250 billion US Innovation and Competition Act (USICA) of 2021 (Zengerle & Shepardson, 2021). This move by lawmakers was an essential addition to an unprecedented $2.3 trillion infrastructure plan initiated by President Biden in February 2020, which provides $80 billion to improve American rail services (Committee for a Responsible Federal Budget, 2021). As the global economic competition between the two

DOI: 10.4324/9781003360728-11

countries deepens, investment in transport infrastructure is becoming an area in which Washington is seeking to catch up with Beijing. Experts argue that allocating such funds is the most significant government investment in rail transport over the past several decades (McFarland, 2021).

President Biden, sometimes referred to as "Amtrak Joe" for his love of rail travel, seems to be living up to his name. At a meeting with Republican senators on the upcoming infrastructure proposal, the US president warned China is ready to "eat our lunch" with infrastructure investments, explicitly highlighting China's ambitious high-speed rail initiatives (Silk & Kunz, 2021).

But, how real are American ambitions to get ahead of China in developing modern, high-speed rail transportation? This question can only be answered through an examination of Beijing's latest plans for the further development and improvement of both national and regional railway infrastructure.

It is hard to believe that a mere twenty years ago China did not have any high-speed rail service. The country's first high-speed rail line, the Qinhuangdao-Shenyang Passenger Railway, was built in 1999 and opened to commercial operation in 2003. In 2008, Beijing approved an unprecedented investment package to the tune of 4 trillion yuan (or $590 billion) to further develop the existing railway networks. Many now agree that these measures proved decisive in overcoming the consequences of the global financial crisis, and then achieving rapid economic growth and accelerating the progress of urbanisation.

China created its network with great attention to detail, relying on high-speed technologies imported from Europe and Japan. Global railway engineering giants such as Alstom, Bombardier, Siemens, and Kawasaki Heavy Industries were understandably eager to cooperate, given the size of the new market and China's ambitious plans. However, over the past decade, it is domestic Chinese companies that have become world leaders in high-speed train technology and design, thanks to the talents and astounding skills of Chinese scientists and engineers and unprecedented support from their government.

Growth was fast. By the end of 2020, China National Railways played host to more than 9,600 high-speed trains daily, including the first-ever high-speed overnight sleeper services on selected longer-distance routes. Seventy-five per cent of Chinese cities with populations of 500,000 or more now have direct access to high-speed rail services (Jones, 2022). New technological solutions such as autonomous train control (driverless trains), as well as modern signalling and control technologies, were developed and are currently in use. However, this success was not unaffected by world events. China National Railways reported a total of 2.166 billion passenger journeys in 2020, down 39.4 per cent from 3.578 billion in 2019, due to the Covid-19 pandemic restrictions (Benton, 2021).

China's performance in constructing high-speed railways stands out, especially when compared to other developed countries. In Spain, which ranks second in the world for high-speed rail with its extensive high-speed network, the total length of high-speed rail is about 3,200 kilometres, which is only 8 per cent of the entire length of the Chinese network. The UK currently has only 107 kilometres of rail capable of operating at speeds of more than 250 kilometres per hour. In Germany, there were also high hopes. On 28 May, Deutsche Bahn board member Ronald Pofalla enthusiastically told the media group Funke that they are aiming to expand high-speed rail lines by 50 per cent from 1,000 kilometres to 1,500 kilometres. Pofalla also said that this will take at least ten to twelve years since protests and negotiations always accompany infrastructure projects (Hachatrjan, 2021). The US has only one high-speed rail route, which is the Amtrak Northeast Corridor. The Acela Express achieves a maximum speed of 240 kilometres per hour in three areas totalling approximately 54 kilometres of the 370-kilometres segment, with an overall average speed of roughly 100 kilometres per hour.

As well as outperforming other countries in the length of its high-speed rail network, Chinese scientists and engineers have also achieved significant savings in the cost of building high-speed railways. The cost of building 1 kilometre of high-speed railway in Spain ranges from 9 million euros (Madrid–Andalusia) to 22 million euros (Madrid–Valladolid). In Italy, the cost was between 24 million euros (Roma–Napoli) and 68 million euros (Bologna–Firenze). In the 2010s, costs per kilometre in France ranged from 18 million euros (BLP Brittany) to 26 million euros (Sud Europe Atlantique) (Beria, et al., 2017). At £309 million per mile, the UK's High Speed 2 line, which is currently under construction, is the most expensive high-speed line globally (Pratley, 2020). The World Bank estimated in 2019 that currently, the average cost of the Chinese high-speed rail network was from 17 to 21 million dollars per kilometre, which is one-third less than the cost in other countries (Lawrence, et al., 2019).

China's achievements do not stop there. In 2008, the first high-speed trains began running on the Beijing–Tianjin intercity railway, which opened during the 2008 Summer Olympics in Beijing. Similarly, new technical "surprises" were made for the Beijing 2022 Winter Olympics. Crewless "bullet trains" were introduced linking Beijing and Zhangjiakou in the northern Hebei province, capable of speeds of up to 350 km per hour, making them the world's fastest autonomous trains. The new route opened in December 2019 and has already cut the 174-kilometre journey from the traditional 3 hours to less than 60 minutes. The fastest trains cover this distance in just 45 minutes. The line was built in just four years and has ten stations, as well as serving two of the main Winter Games venues and another station in Badaling Changcheng, providing quicker access for tourists to the Great Wall of China. The latter is the deepest high-speed railway station in the world, located 102 metres underground. At the end of 2020, the Chinese state-owned company CRRC unveiled a prototype for a high-speed electric train for international routes, capable of speeds of up to 400 km per hour.

In twelve short years, China has made high-speed rail the preferred means of transporting people over long distances. In addition, the emergence of these railways has become an important social phenomenon, a source of pride for the country's citizens. Like the Japanese Shinkansen in the 1960s, they have become a shining symbol of the country's economic strength, an example of accelerated modernisation, and growing technological power. They have increased the population's self-awareness. If this was achieved in just twelve years, what do we have to look forward to?

Future of HSR

Even China's impressive current high-speed rail performance pales into insignificance compared to the targets set for the next fifteen years. The document released jointly by the Central Committee of the Communist Party and the State Council in February stated that the national high-speed rail network would expand to 70,000 kilometres by 2035, up 84 per cent from the current 38,000 kilometres. Standard rail is also expanding. In just fifteen years, standard railway lines are expected to reach 200,000 kilometres, a 37 per cent increase from the current 146,000 kilometres (Railway Technology, 2020).

The newest priorities set by China in developing international high-speed railways as part of the Belt and Road Initiative deserve special attention. Chinese engineers have developed new special trains with variable-width wheelsets. They are already in use, allowing them to travel non-stop to Russia, Mongolia, and Kazakhstan, all of which use a broader gauge than the standard gauge of 1,435 mm in China. These trains can operate in extreme climatic conditions and at a unique temperature range – from -50 to +50 degrees Celsius (Jones, 2022). To maximise this breadth of train travel, it will be vital for automatic gauge changes to be introduced for trains going to India and Pakistan via Myanmar and Bangladesh too.

Expansion to neighbouring countries is already underway. A $5.3 billion Lao–China railway has recently opened. The new 411-kilometre line provides stable links between the southern provinces of China and Laos, including Vientiane (the capital of Laos). The construction of a railway to Bangkok in Thailand and Singapore is also in progress. In November 2020, a $48 billion 965-kilometre railway opened between Chengdu, the capital of Sichuan province, and western Tibet near the Indian border. The extension of the existing Lhasa–Xigaze railway, which opened in 2014, is expected to be the forerunner of the planned line to Kathmandu in Nepal and beyond. The construction of these new railways will be completed by attracting new investment, and they will reach India and Pakistan through the Himalayas, as well as to the countries of Central Asia and Russia (Jones, 2022).

On 25 May 2021, the groundbreaking ceremony for a test line project in Datong (Yangao) for a high-speed train in Shanxi province was successfully held (EqualOcean, 2021). Ma Tiehua, Dean of the School of Electrical Engineering and Control Systems, North China University, announced that the high-speed flying train uses superconducting Magnetic Levitation (Maglev) technology to eliminate contact with surfaces and avoid frictional resistance. Trains will move along special pipelines, where conditions close to vacuum will be created to minimise air resistance. In this way, trains can reach speeds of more than 1000 km per hour. Ma Tiehua said that the high-speed train would reach 300 meters per second, approximately equal to the speed of a bullet fired from a gun. Last year, the American Virgin Hyperloop tested its ultra-fast transportation system based on a similar model with great success.

China has invested billions of dollars in improving Maglev technology and has tested magnetically levitated trains at speeds of up to 620 kilometres per hour. Similar studies are underway in other countries such as Japan and the US. Two lines with a total length of about 270 kilometres, which use this technology, are currently under construction on the Shanghai-Hangzhou route in Zhejiang province and a 110-kilometre underground route connecting Guangzhou and Shenzhen, the two largest cities in the densely populated Pearl River Delta region, is also on its way. Authorities are planning for this route to reach Kowloon in Hong Kong too.

These new developments build on the first experience installing a magnetic suspension line at Shanghai Airport, which opened in 2003 and is currently the only publicly owned line of its type.

Returning to the point raised earlier in the chapter, it can be assumed that it will be a challenge for any country to catch up with China in developing high-speed railways. One option for an early solution to constructing such railways in other countries such as Central Asia is holistic cooperation with China from the outset. Looking at the development of high-speed rail, China's proposal to establish a high-speed rail link that allows passengers to travel from Shanghai to Berlin via Nursultan in two days is no longer an impossibility. How far could China go?

What is the Future of Maglev Trains?

Current status

On 19 July 2021, China's first high-speed magnetic suspension train with a top 600 kilometres per hour speed rolled out of Qingdao, Shandong province (Wan, 2021). It was developed entirely by CRRC Qingdao Sifang, a state-owned China Railway Rolling Stock Corp. subsidiary.

It could be said that English novelist Jonathan Swift first described Maglev technology in 1726 when Gulliver's Travels described Laputa Island as a land capable of floating several kilometres in the air using magnets to levitate. Maglev (derived from magnetic levitation) is a train transportation system that uses two sets of magnets: one to repel and push the train off the track and another to move the elevated train ahead, taking advantage of the lack of friction. The train travels along a guideway of magnets with maglev technology, which controls the train's stability and speed (Hyung-Suk Han and Dong-Sung Kim, 2016).

Magnetic levitation technology, first developed in the 1940s by British engineer Eric Laithwaite, is still not widely used in transportation (Kingsland, 2018). Shanghai Maglev Train (Reuters, 2021) is the fastest commercial passenger train globally, reaching 600 kilometres per hour in operation today. The only Maglev systems currently serving the public are Linimo in Japan (Linimo, 2022) and Daejeon in South Korea (Railway Gazette International, 2008). In 2015, an experimental maglev train in Japan broke the record for the fastest train globally, travelling at 603 kilometres per hour (Lo, 2017).

Those involved with the Chinese project are optimistic it will completely transform China's travel landscape, filling the gap between high-speed rail and air transportation. "Take Beijing to Shanghai as an example - counting preparation time for the journey, it takes about 4.5 hours by plane, about 5.5 hours by high-speed rail, and [would only take] about 3.5 hours with [the new] high-speed maglev," said CRRC Deputy Chief Engineer Ding Sansan, head of the train's research and development team, in a statement (Hood, 2019).

It is worth emphasising that few technologies are as controversial as Maglev. After being developed eighty years ago, magnetic levitation technology has so far failed to reach the transportation mainstream. Therefore, it is essential to determine whether the application of this technology in transportation will have a future.

The benefits of maglev trains are hard to dispute. Hovering trains can reach high speeds by replacing wheels and supporting mechanisms with electro- or superconducting magnets. Preventing contact between wheels and rails also means less noise, no vibration, and no mechanical damage. It is highly efficient in maintenance and encounters fewer problems in bad weather. It uses 30 per cent less energy than conventional trains. At a speed of 420 kilometres per hour, maglev trains use half the primary thermal energy per passenger-kilometre used by a car going at 100 kilometres per hour, and only a quarter of what is used by aeroplanes (The New York Times, 1990). The trains use only electricity, which can come from renewable energy sources, which in turn reduces pollution and carbon emissions, enables greater and safer mobility at lower costs, and reduces dependence on hydrocarbons (The New York Times, 1990).

The main problem facing the development of maglev technology has always been high costs (Kingsland, 2018). It requires an exceptional and dedicated infrastructure, including substations and power supplies. Unlike traditional high-speed trains, new technologies do not integrate into existing transport systems. Maglev can operate only on its unique tracks, unable to switch to thousands of miles of conventional railway lines already in existence.

"There was already a rail network between the two cities," says (Kingsland, 2018) Roger Goodall, a professor at Loughborough University. "When they started to analyse it, they realised that it was much cheaper to upgrade this line than to build an entirely new line with completely new technology. This is the problem with the Maglev."

"There are three criteria you need to fulfil," says Goodall, "The first is a large megacity at both ends; the second is a distance of about 500 miles because if the cities are too close, it's not worth going fast, and if they are too far air travel comes into its own; and the third is having no existing railway. There are a very limited number of cases where all these criteria obtain" (Kingsland, 2018).

Maglev Trains also lack clear support in the transportation and investment community. With this fact, Lawrence Blow, founder of the Maglev Transport consulting group, has struggled in his thirty-plus years as an advocate in the US. "Maglev is a competitor to cars, trains, and planes, as well as buses and subway systems," says Blow. "It has many natural enemies but no natural friends. It was a product of the scientific community, and, by and large, scientists do not dominate transport." For his part, Blow remains convinced that the most significant benefit of using magnetic suspension is "connecting cities" but doubts that this technology will gain widespread acceptance anytime soon. "In the current environment, it is doubtful that it will ever enter the mainstream of transportation technology," he says, adding that the Maglev will have to "fight for whatever it gets."

It seems problematic to develop the new Maglev technology, entirely relying on such a purely capitalist calculation. What will ultimately win – the brilliant prospects of new technology or short-term cold mathematics?

Ambitious Plans

China is not stopping in its quest to create a unique, modern railway network, virtually unparalleled worldwide. According to the Ministry of Transport, China has the most extensive high-speed rail network globally, covering 95 per cent of cities with more than a million inhabitants (Xinhua, 2021a). Directives jointly published in February 2021 aim to expand the country's transportation network even further by 2035. 200,000 kilometres of railways, 460,000 kilometres of roads, and 25,000 kilometres of sea routes will be constructed. In addition, 27 major coastal ports and 36 inland ports, approximately 400 civil airports, and about 80 express mail hubs will be built (Xinhua, 2021b).

The directive emphasises that the network aims to support the so-called National 123 transportation circle. This means achieving a maximum of a one-hour journey within a city, a two-hour journey between urban clusters, and a three-hour journey between major cities. The maglev system will become one of the essential components of this network.

According to China Railway Rolling Stock Corp (CRRC), the Maglev project in China kicked off in October 2016. After optimising the system in January 2021, the system began experimental testing. The trains can include 2 to 10 cars, each of which can accommodate more than 100 passengers.

According to a CRRC report (Global Times, 2021), it is the fastest ground transportation method for distances up to 1,500 kilometres.

In the process, Chinese scientists and engineers have introduced numerous innovations in Maglev technology. Among them are the latest electrical, anti-vibration, and information systems. The braking mechanism used will be 30 per cent more efficient than the magnetic suspension train in Shanghai, which means that the braking distance of the train will be reduced from approximately 16 to 10 kilometres. Engineers have created a unique power-supply system especially for this train whereby the power supply becomes contactless when the train's speed exceeds 100 kilometres per hour. 5G will ensure uninterrupted high-speed internet connectivity, and passengers will be able to charge their mobile phones wirelessly (Global Times, 2021).

A real breakthrough is the new train's active use of "high-temperature superconductivity" technology (Yi, et al., 2021). It uses two unique properties of high-temperature superconductors: the "Meissner effect," which allows the superconductor to repel magnetic fields around it to achieve complete levitation, and "flux pinning," which keeps the superconductor steady above its magnetic tracks, so it never falls off. It took researchers over twenty years to take this concept from a university laboratory to a full-fledged industrial application.

China ranks first in terms of the number of newest patents related to Maglev technology, according to a study by intellectual property service provider PatSnap (Global Times, 2021). Their patent filings in this field stood at 43.52 per cent by 2021, well above Japan's 20.57 per cent, which came in second. However, Japanese patents were mainly related to the scientific properties of materials. In contrast, the Chinese patents focused more on practical applications, including permanent magnets, rail beams, transportation technology, suspension frame, etc. Undoubtedly, the research and development of Maglev technologies will contribute to the growth of other high-tech industries in China and worldwide.

Demand for such services already exists on the railways between Beijing and Shanghai, Chongqing and Chengdu, and Guangzhou and Changsha, according to Feng Hao, a researcher at the Integrated Transport Institute of the National Development and Reform Commission (Nan & Chuanjiao, 2021). A few provinces and cities have already included the development of high-speed Maglev lines in their development plans. Among such lines will be the Shanghai-Hangzhou and Chengdu-Chongqing routes.

When completed in 2030, the new magnetic suspension lines will cut travel times from Guangzhou to Shanghai to a mere two and a half hours. Travel time from Guangzhou to Beijing will be just over three hours (Yang, 2021), halving the high-speed rail's current travel time.

Combining Maglev technology with a vacuum tube would hugely reduce air resistance, further increasing the train's speed. Elon Musk's Hyperloop uses a similar idea (O'Malley, 2022). Hyperloop is currently under development, but it will revolutionise overland travel if it becomes a reality. With a speed of 1200 kilometres per hour, it will be possible to get from Los Angeles to San Francisco in an incredible 35 minutes.

But we can also dream bigger. ET3 (Evacuated Tube Transport Technologies) (Et3.com, 2020) combines Maglev with a complete vacuum tube system. Passengers will be sitting in capsules the size of a car, and unique gateways at stations will allow the movement of people and goods without letting any air into the system. For long journeys, speeds of up to 6500 kilometres per hour would make it possible to get from New York to Beijing in 2 hours. The developers call it "space travel on Earth."

All of this means China is getting closer to bringing more travellers by air down to earth. Professor of Beijing Jiaotong University Zhao Jian is doubtful that Chinese Maglev trains and related technologies will be in commercial demand abroad any time soon. Other countries will lack the scale to develop large-scale projects and will struggle to make magnetic suspension lines profitable. "Maglev lines can only make money when a high-speed network with huge passenger flows is formed," Zhao said.

It means that Chinese scientists and engineers' current breakthrough in applying Maglev technology in future transportation has excellent prospects. Once again, it turns out that China is not thinking years – but decades – into the future.

Some may feel that this book focuses too much on the future of rail transport, especially in China. However, the previous chapter shows that China is building modern railroads in neighbouring regions, such as Southeast Asia. Central Asia also neighbours China, so its countries must understand the current trends in railway transport to conduct an equal dialogue with their southeastern neighbour on the development of joint regional transport systems.

References

Benton, A., 2021. China National Railways' passenger numbers down in 2020, freight up. [Online] Available at: https://www.railjournal.com/passenger/main-line/china-national-railways-passenger-numbers-down-in-2020-freight-up/ [Accessed July 2022].

Beria, P., Albalate, D., Grimaldi, R. & Bel, G., 2017. Delusions of success: costs and demand of high speed rail in Italy and Spain. [Online] Available at: https://re.public.polimi.it/retrieve/handle/11311/1015984/186783/Beria%20Bel%20et%20al%20-%20Mismatches%20HSR%20Italy%20n%20Spain%20-%20PAPER%2013%20%5BSENT%5D.pdf [Accessed July 2022].

Committee for a Responsible Federal Budget, 2021. What's in President Biden's American Jobs Plan?. [Online] Available at: https://www.crfb.org/blogs/whats-president-bidens-american-jobs-plan [Accessed July 2022].

EqualOcean, 2021. Construction of 1000 km/h high speed Maglev test line. [Online] Available at: https://equalocean.com/briefing/20210526230048994 [Accessed July 2022].

Et3.com, 2020. ET3 global alliance inc. [Online] Available at: http://www.et3.com/ [Accessed July 2022].

Global Times, 2021. World's speediest 600 km/h maglev rolls off assembly line in China's Qingdao. [Online] Available at: https://www.globaltimes.cn/page/202107/1229097.shtml [Accessed July 2022].

Hachatrjan, K., 2021. Poezda Deutsche Bahn poedut bystree. [Online] Available at: https://ru.euronews.com/2021/05/28/germany-high-speed-railway [Accessed July 2022].

Hood, B., 2019. China's New 373-Mile-Per-Hour Bullet Train Will Be the World's Fastest. [Online] Available at: https://www.yahoo.com/lifestyle/china-373-mile-per-hour-163314866.html [Accessed July 2022].

Hyung-Suk Han and Dong-Sung Kim, 2016. *Magnetic Levitation: Maglev Technology and Applications*. Berlin: Springer.

Jones, B., 2022. Past, present and future: The evolution of China's incredible high-speed rail network. [Online] Available at: https://edition.cnn.com/travel/article/china-high-speed-rail-cmd/index.html [Accessed July 2022].

Kingsland, P., 2018. Will maglev ever become mainstream? [Online] Available at: https://www.railway-technology.com/features/will-maglev-ever-become-mainstream/ [Accessed July 2022].

Lawrence, M., Bullock, R. & Liu, Z., 2019. *China's High-Speed Rail Development*, Washington, DC: International Bank for Reconstruction and Development/The World Bank.

Linimo, 2022. Linimo. [Online] Available at: http://www.linimo.jp/language/en/ [Accessed July 2022].

Lo, A., 2017. Can megafast maglev revive Japan's rail reputation?. [Online] Available at: http://edition.cnn.com/travel/article/japan-record-breaking-maglev-train/index.html [Accessed July 2022].

McFarland, M., 2021. This is Amtrak's new dream map after Biden's infrastructure push. [Online] Available at: https://edition.cnn.com/2021/04/02/economy/biden-amtrak-infrastructure/index.html [Accessed July 2022].

Nan, Z. & Chuanjiao, X., 2021. High-speed maglev train to be rolled out. [Online] Available at: http://www.chinadaily.com.cn/a/202107/20/WS60f60cb6a310efa1bd662eb2.html [Accessed July 2022].

O'Malley, J., 2022. Hyperloop: 9 years later, Elon Musk's biggest pipe dream may finally come true. [Online] Available at: https://www.inverse.com/innovation/hyperloop-horizons [Accessed July 2022].

Pratley, N., 2020. At £307m per mile of track, can the cost of HS2 be justified? [Online] Available at: https://www.theguardian.com/uk-news/2020/feb/03/at-307m-per-mile-of-track-can-the-cost-of-hs2-be-justified [Accessed July 2022].

Railway Gazette International, 2008. Urban maglev opportunity. [Online] Available at: https://www.railwaygazette.com/news/urban-maglev-opportunity/33261.article [Accessed July 2022].

Railway Technology, 2020. China unveils plans to expand railway network to 200,000km by 2035. [Online] Available at: https://www.railway-technology.com/news/china-railway-network-200000km/ [Accessed July 2022].

Reuters, 2021. China unveils 600 kph maglev train - state media. [Online] Available at: https://www.reuters.com/world/china/china-unveils-600-kph-maglev-train-state-media-2021-07-20/ [Accessed July 2022].

Silk, E. & Kunz, A., 2021. Commentary: To compete with China, Biden must launch national rail mobilization. [Online] Available at: https://www.desertsun.com/story/opinion/2021/02/20/commentary-biden-must-launch-all-out-national-rail-mobilization/4511336001/ [Accessed July 2022].

The New York Times, 1990. Opinion: Magnetic trains offer environmental benefits. *The New York Times*, 26 December.

Wan, L., 2021. World's first 600km/h high-speed maglev train to make public debut in Qingdao. [Online] Available at: https://www.globaltimes.cn/page/202107/1228998.shtml [Accessed July 2022].

Xinhua, 2021a. China's high-speed rail lines top 37,900 km at end of 2020. [Online] Available at: http://www.xinhuanet.com/english/2021-01/09/c_139654709.htm [Accessed July 2022].

Xinhua, 2021b. China unveils guidelines on developing comprehensive transport network. [Online] Available at: http://english.www.gov.cn/policies/latestreleases/202102/24/content_WS6036593dc6d0719374af9866.html [Accessed July 2022].

Yang, J., 2021. Guangdong plans Shanghai-Guangzhou maglev. [Online] Available at: https://www.shine.cn/news/metro/2102224928/ [Accessed July 2022].

Yi, D., Xiao, Y. & Zhao, Y., 2021. Tech It Out: What is the future of high-speed maglev? [Online] Available at: https://news.cgtn.com/news/2021-03-11/Tech-It-Out-China-to-set-a-new-speed-record-in-ground-transportation-YxvOSRLko8/index.html [Accessed July 2022].

Zengerle, P. & Shepardson, D., 2021. Sweeping tech bill to counter China advances in U.S. Senate. [Online] Available at: https://financialpost.com/pmn/business-pmn/sweeping-tech-bill-to-counter-china-advances-in-u-s-senate [Accessed July 2022].

9 Energy

Introduction

Central Asia has significant oil, gas and water reserves and great potential for solar and wind energy (Hydropower Sustainability Council, 2022). However, these resources are distributed unevenly across the region with fossil fuels in abundance in Turkmenistan, Kazakhstan and to a lesser extent Uzbekistan, and water resources mainly concentrated in the Kyrgyz Republic and Tajikistan. As of 2017, Turkmenistan holds 265 trillion cubic feet (Tcf) of proven gas reserves, ranking 6th in the world and accounting for about 4.3 per cent (Reuters, 2012) of the world's total natural gas reserves of 6,923 trillion Tcf (Worldometers, 2015). Kazakhstan has the world's 12th-highest oil reserves (IEA, 2020a), about 3.2 per cent of the world's proven oil reserves of 30 billion barrels (Economic Times, 2009). It currently produces around 1.5 per cent of the global crude oil supply (Falakshahi, 2022). The Kyrgyz Republic and Tajikistan have huge hydropower potential. The latter has 4 per cent of the world's and 53 per cent of Central Asia's hydropower resources.

How can energy be provided for the region's economy and its rapidly growing population? How can institutions capable of effectively developing the energy potential of the territory be created, ensuring that energy efficiency is improved, and principles of a green economy can be introduced? Can countries increase their income by supplying excess energy resources to vast neighbouring markets? All these challenges will be crucial for the accelerated development of Central Asia in the coming years and decades and will be discussed in this chapter.

At the beginning of this chapter, we will analyse the historical milestones of energy development in Central Asia. We will pay special attention to the unique work of the Unified Energy System of Central Asia (UES), created in the 1960s and 1970s by Soviet scientists and engineers. The Central Asian principles of electricity exchange developed back in the Soviet era, can still benefit all states. The most rational choice for all countries would be to maintain the UES and resume electricity trade on a regional scale.

The most pressing problem with Central Asia's energy infrastructure is that it is physically outdated. Many power plants, distribution and

DOI: 10.4324/9781003360728-12

transmission lines were built many years ago by Soviet engineers. At the same time, countries forecast a significant increase in electricity consumption in the coming years, driven by economic development and population growth, putting further pressure on the system. For example, the government of Kazakhstan predicts that by 2030 its annual volume of energy consumption will increase by 26 per cent. Similar forecasts were made by the government of Uzbekistan, predicting that energy consumption will almost double by 2030. What is the current state of energy infrastructure, and what plans are in place to increase generation and transmission capacity in their countries? These issues are also discussed in this chapter.

Two of the countries of Central Asia, the Kyrgyz Republic and Tajikistan, have significant potential to generate electricity using their vast hydropower potential. However, almost all existing hydroelectric power plants (HPPs) were built in Soviet times about half a century ago. The development of the economy and the growing population of these countries led to generating capacities that were no longer sufficient to meet domestic needs. Both countries had to attract credit resources from China to build new thermal power plants (TPPs) in their capitals, powered by local coal. Despite this, these two countries still need to purchase additional electricity from abroad.

Since independence and for a long time before, these countries could not find sufficient investments to make better use of their hydropower potential. Disagreements also hampered the attraction of investment from the downstream countries for constructing new hydropower plants, as they feared water blackmail from the Kyrgyz Republic and Tajikistan. For twenty-five years, mistrust has persisted between the upstream and downstream countries. This abnormal situation changed after President Mirziyoyev came to power in Uzbekistan. Unexpectedly for many, he quickly announced that Uzbekistan would not, any longer object, to constructing new hydroelectric power plants in the Kyrgyz Republic and Tajikistan, but would also be ready to enter into equity capital and to co-finance those projects. There is light at the end of the tunnel in developing green hydropower in Central Asia.

If new hydro-generating capacities appear in the region, it should be possible to export electricity. Deliveries to the countries of South Asia which are experiencing an acute shortage of electricity, especially in their northern territories, show particular promise. With this in mind, a few years ago, the implementation of the CASA-1000 project for the seasonal export of Central Asian electricity to Afghanistan, Pakistan and India began. Western countries and leading international financial institutions are actively supporting this project.

Nature has rewarded Kazakhstan, Turkmenistan, and Uzbekistan with rich oil and gas deposits. In Soviet times, only modest extraction of hydrocarbons was carried out exclusively for local markets and Russia. But after independence and the discovery of significant new oil and gas fields, promising opportunities arose for supplying oil and gas to new markets. The two giants at either end of Eurasia – Europe and China – became the primary recipients of these hydrocarbons. With the attraction of large-scale investments, oil and gas pipelines were laid, delivering them to these seemingly limitless markets. The region's leading supplier of crude oil to foreign markets is Kazakhstan, and the leading natural gas supplier is Turkmenistan.

The proactive supply of hydrocarbons to outside markets and the rapid price growth in the 2000s led to accelerated economic development for the entire region. But producers are exploring additional opportunities for the export of hydrocarbons. Here we should note the project for constructing the TAPI gas pipeline, named after the countries involved: Turkmenistan will supply natural gas to Afghanistan, Pakistan, and India. By implementing this project, Central Asia will become a place connecting all the main centres of Eurasia – Europe, China and India – with modern energy corridors.

Given the energy sector's critical importance for Central Asia's future development, it is vital to understand the future global trends in this sector. Key among these trends is a need to understand what will happen to the worldwide energy market in connection with developing a green economy and transitioning to low-carbon technologies. Therefore, the following section of the chapter discusses trends in the global energy market, including fossil fuels, nuclear power, and green technologies.

History

During Soviet times, when the region was part of a single country, its energy system was uniquely designed. It had a powerful synergy and worked successfully for many decades. In this setup, the five countries of Central Asia were conditionally divided into two clusters. One cluster consisted of downstream countries with low hydropower potential but significant hydrocarbon resources – Kazakhstan, Uzbekistan, and Turkmenistan. These countries were in dire need of water for irrigating crops in the summer. The other cluster, the Kyrgyz Republic and Tajikistan did not have ample hydrocarbon resources, yet their upstream location meant that they had vast water reserves in their glaciers and rivers and significant hydroelectric potential.

The system worked as follows: during the winter, downstream countries supplied surplus energy to upstream countries, and in the summer, the reverse process took place. Namely, the water accumulated during the winter in the upstream countries was used to generate electricity at hydroelectric power stations. At the same time, the water flowing downstream through the dams was used to irrigate crops in downstream countries (Figure 9.1).

In the 1960s and 1970s, the so-called Unified Energy System of Central Asia (UES) was created and successfully operated. Approximately 30 per cent of the total energy production came from hydroelectric power plants (HPPs) in upstream countries and 70 per cent from thermal power plants (TPPs) in downstream countries. Although UES was part of the Unified Energy System of the Soviet Union, it was physically isolated from the Russian power grid. After the disintegration of the Soviet Union, the system began to operate independently.

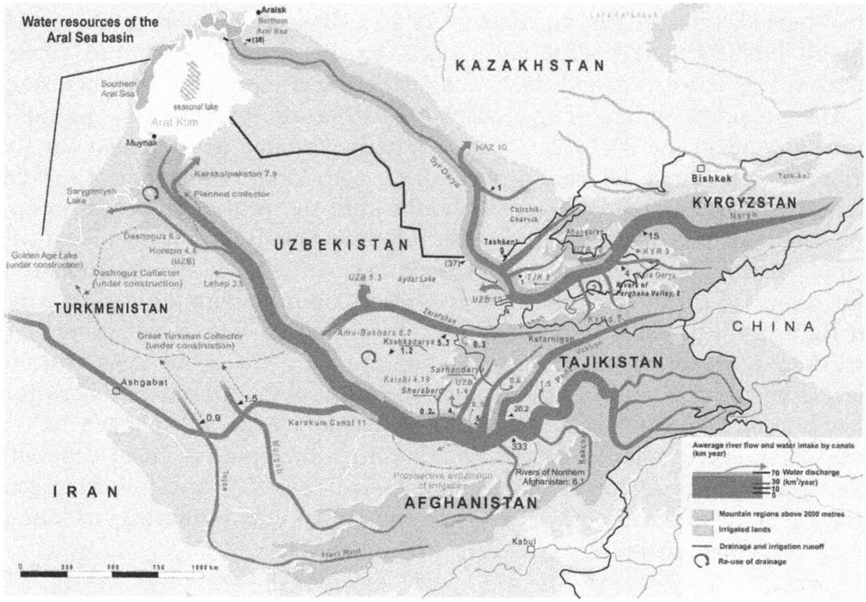

Figure 9.1 Water resources in Central Asia
Source: CAWater-Info (2022).

By 1991, the UES, also called the Central Asian "electric ring", connected all eighty-three power stations, including twenty-nine thermal and forty-eight hydro units, and was controlled from a single centre in Tashkent. Approximately 51 per cent of the total electricity was produced in Uzbekistan, 13.8 per cent in Kyrgyzstan, 9.1 per cent in southern Kazakhstan, 15 per cent in Tajikistan and 10 per cent in Turkmenistan (Aminjonov, 2016).

After gaining independence, due to the lack of trust, endless disputes began between countries from different clusters. Who benefits more and less from functioning in such a water-energy system? What is more critical, gas or water, or what is more expensive, water or electricity? Such disputes eventually led countries to stop coordinating their activities and the well-functioning UES began to fall apart. For purely pragmatic reasons, the states revived it in 1997, but not for long. The chain quickly started to break apart again. Turkmenistan left the system in 2003, and Tajikistan left after disagreements with Uzbekistan in 2009. A few years ago, Tajikistan decided to re-join the system. Now, with the support of the Asian Development Bank, work is underway to connect the Tajik energy system to the UES. Tajikistan's energy network is expected to be restored to the UES in 2023.

The forces that caused the disintegration of the UES, determined by hostile political actions, endless disputes over non-payments and other financial problems, and intractable regional water problems, are now beginning to weaken. Many positive developments are happening thanks to the political will of Uzbekistan's new leadership, which prioritised restoring trust with neighbours and strengthening regional cooperation.

Traditionally, downstream countries, especially Uzbekistan, have opposed the construction of new hydroelectric power plants in the Kyrgyz Republic and Tajikistan. They feared water blackmail, whereby the two upstream countries could threaten to turn off the water during the irrigation season to extract concessions. Again, this lack of trust between the neighbours served as a cause of tensions.

Therefore, when in 2017, the President of Uzbekistan Mirziyoyev announced his country's readiness to participate in constructing the Kambarata hydroelectric power stations in the Kyrgyz Republic, it came like a bolt out of the blue. The projects of these stations on the Naryn River were approved in the Soviet Union as early as 1988 and construction began the same year. However, in 1994 it was suspended due to a lack of funding. At that time, 25 per cent of the work had been completed. In this statement on the matter, the President of Uzbekistan said: "We will build the Kambarata station together because we need it. Because history will not forgive us, we must do it in a balanced way, reasonably, so that it is beneficial for both sides. And this is beneficial" (Hydropower Central Asia and Caspian, 2017).

Earlier, officials in Tashkent openly opposed the construction of this HPP, adhering to the opinion that the Kyrgyz Republic should not own the drainage of its rivers alone but should consider its neighbours' views. Experts have assessed the rapprochement of the two countries' positions on constructing hydropower facilities differently, but everyone has noted the countries' leaders' important political decision to take a significant step towards restoring trust.

More trusting relations emerged between the countries when working on the exchange of various water and energy resources. An example was the events of 2014 when an extreme drought happened in the Kyrgyz Republic. That year, too little water accumulated in the reservoir of the Toktogul hydroelectric power station, and its volume was not enough to provide the country with electricity during the winter months. For the first time in many years, the Kyrgyz Republic started to import electricity from abroad. In December 2014, the governments of Kazakhstan and the Kyrgyz Republic signed agreements to supply Kazakh electricity to Kyrgyzstan in exchange for natural gas that Kyrgyzstan purchased from Russia and delivered to northern Kazakhstan. In addition, during the summer, the Kyrgyz Republic committed to supplying Kazakhstan with electricity and water for irrigation. This problematic situation of the supply of electricity to the population and industrial enterprises also made it possible for the government to raise electricity tariffs for the first time in many years. But even so, electricity was supplied to the domestic market below cost value and was subsidised by the state.

This analysis shows that the Central Asian principles of energy exchange, developed back during the Soviet times, would still benefit all states. In this regard, perhaps the most rational choice for all countries would be the restoration of the UES and the resumption of electricity trade on a larger scale.

To this end, the World Bank commissioned a study to estimate the unrealised benefits of regional electricity trading for four Central Asian countries between 2010 and 2014. AF Mercados, a consulting and transaction advisory firm based in Madrid, conducted the study from October 2015 to June 2016 (World Bank, 2016). The analysis focused on the benefits of electricity trading in the aggregate at the regional level and the benefits for specific countries. The firm handled three cases, namely (i) benefits including fuel savings at historical energy prices, (ii) benefits including both fuel savings and the economic value of forgoing lost energy at historical fuel prices, and (iii) benefits, which include both fuel savings and the economic value of eliminating lost energy at fuel costs estimated at market prices for energy. The report's conclusions in Figure 9.2 show that the benefits to the region could be close to $1.5 billion if only fuel savings were considered in the calculations. In the case that the economic value of avoiding unmet electricity demand is added to the benefits, the benefits will reach nearly $5.2 billion in historical energy prices and about $6.4 billion in market energy prices.

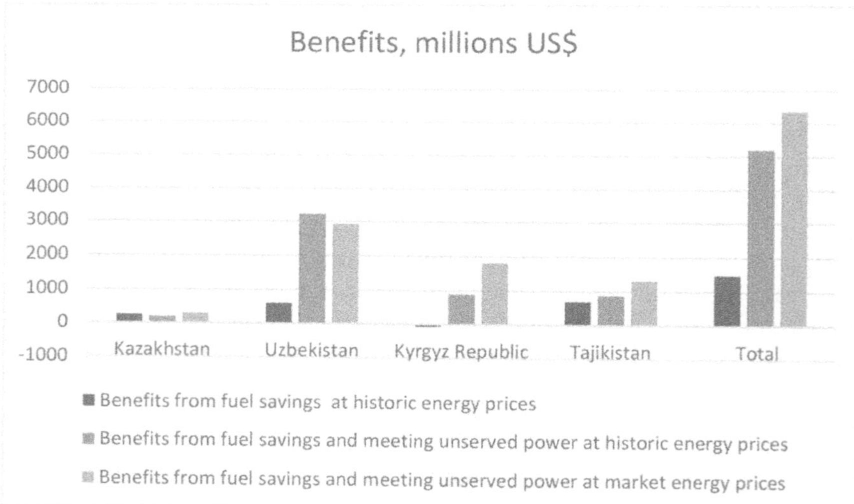

Figure 9.2 Potential benefits from fuel savings in Central Asian countries
Source: World Bank (2016).

Central Asia's Energy Needs

The urban and rural populations of the countries of Central Asia are almost universally provided with electric energy (Figure 9.2). This feat was achieved back in the days of the Soviet Union; however, even after gaining independence, despite a significant increase in energy consumption, all countries in the region managed to maintain and even increase already high indicators. Figure 9.3, taken from the World Bank data, shows the area's level of electricity access. It can be seen that at almost every point, electricity coverage exceeded 98–99 per cent (World Bank, 2020a), although many settlements in the region are difficult to access and remote from the main centres. How did the Central Asian countries maintain such high performance in generating, transmitting and distributing electricity?

Kazakhstan is the largest electricity producer in Central Asia (Energo-cis.ru, 2017). As of 2022, the total capacity of the 190 power plants installed in Kazakhstan was about 24 GW (Kegoc.kz, 2022). Thermal power plants generate about 85 per cent of the energy, with about 70 per cent of electricity generated by burning coal. Since the largest deposits of coal are in the north of the country, it is there that most coal-fired power plants operate. The rest of the energy is generated by hydroelectric power plants or by burning other

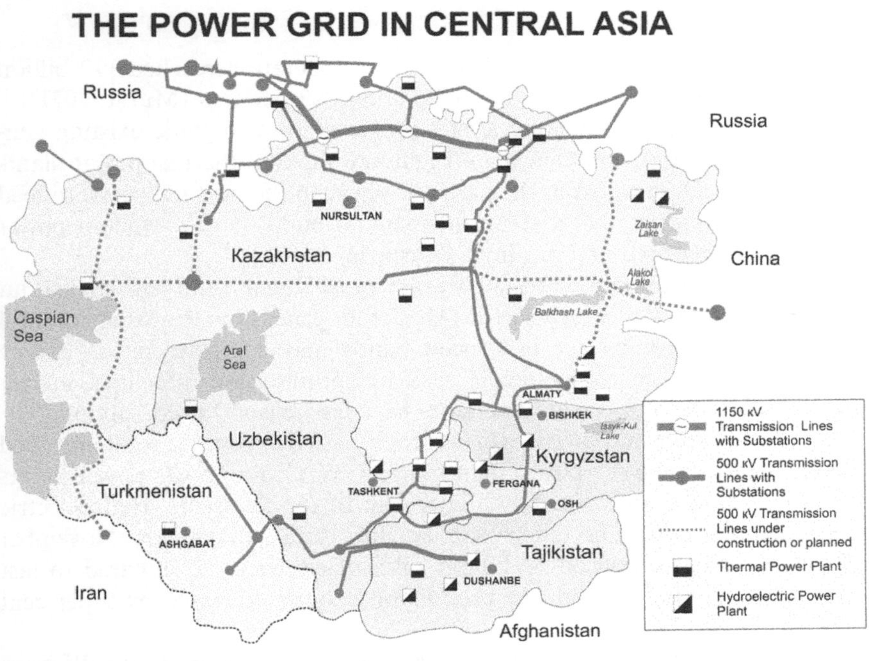

Figure 9.3 Power distribution in Central Asia
Source: World Bank (2020a).

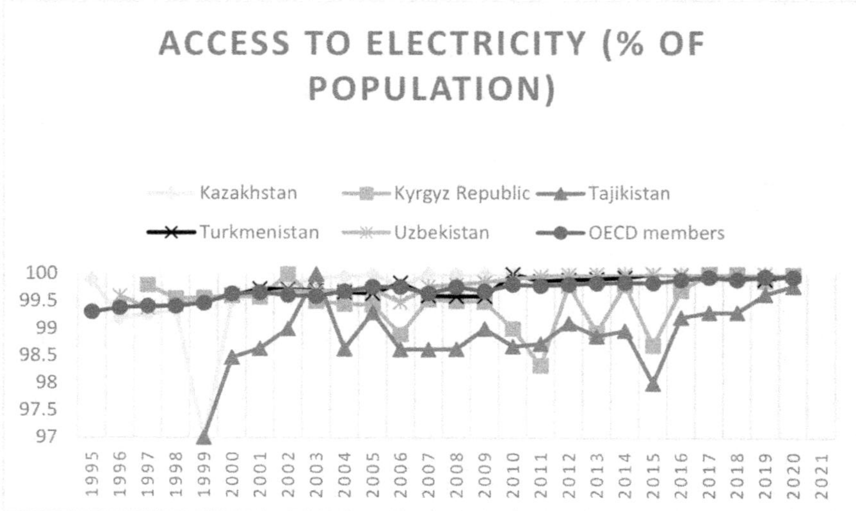

Figure 9.4 Percentage of population with access to electricity in Central Asian countries
Source: World Bank (2020a).

hydrocarbons. By the end of 2021, electricity generation reached 112 billion kWh, an increase in the 2020's figure by about 6.3 per cent (Murat, 2021).

The country is implementing a vast programme to upgrade existing generating facilities and build new ones. Eight new modern thermal power plants (TPPs) have been installed in the past two years. In the next ten years, to feed its growing economy, the government plans to build 36 new modern power plants, both coal-fired and gas-fired (Nurtazin, 2019).

It is important to note that the government of Kazakhstan has carried out drastic reforms in the energy sector. Almost all generating, transmission and distribution companies are in private hands and compete in the energy market. This has led companies to seek to optimise their activities, attract new technologies, and private operators have less reason for corruption.

Uzbekistan fully meets its own electricity needs. Today's total installed capacity of the country's power plants is 15 GW. Coal and gas power plants currently generate approximately 85 per cent of the electricity. Hydroelectric power plants produce the rest (Asiaplustj.info, 2021). In January–November 2021, Uzbekistan produced 63 billion kWh of electricity. Compared to last year's corresponding period, the production volume increased by 9 per cent (UzDaily.uz, 2022).

In 2021, nine new power plants with a total capacity of 1.39 GW were commissioned in Uzbekistan (Minenergy.uz, 2021). By the end of 2022, seven new stations with a total capacity of 1.47 GW will be operational, of which six are thermal and one solar. In just two months of 2022, three new thermal power plants with a total capacity of 684 MW came online in three country regions (Energyland.info, 2022). As a result, by the end of 2022, the total capacity of the energy system of Uzbekistan will exceed 16 GW.

In the 2000s, eight thermal power plants were in operation in Turkmenistan and now the total installed capacity of its twelve power plants is about 5.2 GW. The Ministry of Energy does not publish official data on electricity production. But earlier, the authorities announced that they plan to generate over 20 billion kWh in 2020, of which 6 billion kWh will go for export. According to their development plan, by 2024, the government plans to commission new generating facilities, and electricity production should reach 33 billion kWh per year. Turkmenistan has found a new market for its electricity in the Iranian market, with the energy system of which it works in parallel. A unique fact about the country is that until 1 November 2017, Turkmenistan was the only country whose citizens used electricity for free. Currently, the population pays $0.7 per kWh (Asiaplustj.info, 2021).

The total installed capacity of power plants in Kyrgyzstan is around 4 GW. Hydroelectric power plants produce about 85 per cent of the country's electricity. The country has fifteen hydroelectric power plants, but the five largest ones make about 75 per cent of the electricity. Almost 15 billion kWh of electricity is generated in Kyrgyzstan annually. The country's largest electricity producer is the 1,200 MW Toktogul HPP, which generates about a third of all electricity. Its reservoir holds 19 billion cubic meters of water, regulating the Naryn River's flows and influencing water distribution throughout all Syr Darya river basins. There are six other large hydroelectric power stations – Kurpsaiskaya, Shamaldysayskaya, Tash-Kumyrskaya, Uch-Kurganskaya, Kambarata-2 and At-Bashinskaya (Azattyk, 2020). The depreciation of the equipment of these HPPs is about 80 per cent. With the financial support of the ADB, the energy sector has almost completed the rehabilitation of the Toktogul HPP. They replaced its main elements and thus increased the efficiency of the essential equipment.

In the country's north, the largest electricity producer is the Bishkek TPP, which covers about 15 per cent of the country's needs. It runs on coal, so it is one of the primary sources of smog in the capital. Until recently, the total depreciation of this TPP stays at 60 per cent. Therefore, the government decided to reconstruct it and double its capacity. Reconstruction was completed in 2017, and the station's capacity is now 812 MW (Azattyk, 2020).

The total installed capacity of the electricity system in Tajikistan is about 5.8 GW. Hydroelectric power plants generated about 91 per cent of all electricity in 2021, and the rest of the electricity comes from thermal power stations. The leading producer is the Nurek HPP, which produces more than half of all electricity in the country even when individual units are being modernised. By 2033 the Rogun HPP will come into operation, becoming the largest HPP in Central Asia, with an installed capacity of 3.6 GW. Currently, two out of six units of this station are in operation.

A peculiarity of the Tajik electric power industry is that just one company – the Tajik Aluminium Company (TALCO), consumes about 40 per cent of the total generated volume. The plant provides about a third of exports and 75 per cent of foreign exchange earnings to the country's budget. With the assistance of the World Bank, an international consortium led by the Norwegian company, Norsk Energi, is reconstructing the plant, which will save about 20 per cent of the electricity used there (Tajikta.tj, 2013).

An essential step in providing the country's capital with electricity and heat was the launch at the end of 2016 of a thermal power plant with 400 MW. It offers more than 80 per cent of Dushanbe's daily electricity needs. Completing the project made it possible to significantly relieve the country's entire energy system (Bankwatch.org, 2020).

Hydropower

The Kyrgyz Republic

Originating in the Tien Shan mountains, the Naryn River flows through the whole Kyrgyz Republic, emptying into the vast Toktogul reservoir and powering several downstream hydroelectric power stations. The volume of the Toktogul reservoir located in the Jalal-Abad region is 19.5 cubic kilometres, and the surface area is 284 square kilometres (CAWater-Info, 2022).

The country has many large and medium-sized rivers with significant hydropower potential, estimated at 140–170 TWh, of which only 10 per cent is currently being used (International Trade Administration, 2021). Hydropower provides about 90 per cent of all electricity produced in the country. However, its production and consumption are subject to seasonal fluctuations. Kyrgyzstan supplies water resources to downstream nations in spring and summertime when Kyrgyzstan does not need large amounts of electricity.

Five of the Kyrgyz Republic's seven main hydroelectric power stations were built during the Soviet era and are over thirty years old. As a result, there are severe risks in ensuring the reliability of the energy supply. To keep pace with its growing economy, attracting investment in this sector is necessary. It is especially true in winter when generation becomes limited and demand rises, putting pressure on the power grid. Energy companies have calculated that by 2030 the winter supply gap will increase to 900 GWh. It dictates the need for significant capital investments in the industry, both in generation and distribution. A sign of this growing electricity consumption was when the country turned from an electricity exporter to an importer in 2015.

In 2014, the government decided that the Toktogul HPP, which has been in operation since 1975, must be fully rehabilitated. It generates about half of the country's electricity and provides multi-year and regional storage grid regulation services. The programme of work includes the modernisation of Toktogul HPP equipment and an increase in generating capacity from 1200 MW to 1440 MW, as well as support for the modernisation of all five hydroelectric power plants along the Naryn cascade (800 MW Kurpsai, 450 MW Tashkumyr, 240 MW Shamaldy-Sai and 180 MW Uch Kurgan). For this, the government attracted investments from development partners, primarily from the Asian Development Bank.

Regarding additional generating capacity, work has already begun constructing the remaining two 120 MW units at Kambarata-2. Plans for the development of Kambarata-1 with a total of 1860 MW and the Upper Naryn cascade of HPPs (more than 200 MW), providing an additional 5 TWh of electricity generation, were repeatedly postponed due to a lack of financial resources. However, at the end of 2017, the governments of Uzbekistan and the Kyrgyz Republic agreed to cooperate in constructing Kambarata-1. Other proposed projects include the cascades of the Kazarmanskaya and Suusamyrsko-Kokomerenskaya HPPs, with a combined capacity of over 2,465 MW.

Recently, there has been an important trend in investment in medium-sized hydropower by private local investors in Kyrgyzstan. Private investors have implemented small hydropower projects, such as the 3.0 MW Tegermentinskaya HPP commissioned in 2017 in Chon-Kemin. This interest has been fuelled recently due to the low costs of generating electricity from mountain rivers, especially for mining cryptocurrency. Due to their profitability, interest in such projects is growing throughout the country.

Backed by a loan from the Chinese government, a highly important project was recently completed to build a 405 kilometre Datka-Kemin 500 kV transmission line linking the main generating facilities in the country's south with its northern regions. Before this, electricity was transmitted along a much longer route passing through the territories of Uzbekistan and Kazakhstan, which caused significant losses and additional payments.

Since 2014, the government has taken significant legislative steps to reform the energy sector. The government formed an independent regulator and introduced a new revenue settlement mechanism. In addition, for the first time in many years, the government raised tariffs for electricity consumption, which are still below the cost of production. This was a step that the previous authorities did not dare to take for political reasons. Tariffs are still subsidised, making cost recovery a major issue for electricity producers. Although the measures implemented under the Medium Term Tariff Policy (MTTP) for 2014–2017 have led to some improvements, according to a recent World Bank report, the country will need to make further reforms, including in tariff policy, to attract investment in hydropower (International Hydropower Association, 2022a).

Tajikistan

Although Tajikistan has a vast hydropower potential and has 4 per cent of the world's hydropower, the country constantly experiences electricity shortages. About 94 per cent of electricity generation capacity comes from hydropower, although only about 5 per cent of the total potential is used. Hydroelectric power generates about 17 GWh per year. Still, the country faces a power shortage of 3.0 to 3.5 GWh each year, resulting in regular power outages, mainly from October to April. Power outages also affect the population directly. The shares of primary energy in 2008 were: oil 21.6 per cent, gas 18.3 per cent, hydropower 56.4 per cent and coal 3.7 per cent (Tajikistan Mission, 2009).

Tariffs vary, and residents typically pay 1.5 US$ cents per kWh. Uniquely, the Tajik Aluminium Company (TALCO) is the largest consumer in Tajikistan and uses about 40 per cent of the total electricity consumption.

Many components of the transmission and distribution system were built during the Soviet era and are in poor condition. Network and commercial losses lead to losses of up to 17 per cent. The rural population is experiencing great difficulties in accessing electricity due to the poor state of the system, voltage instability and significant losses (IEA, 2021a).

The complex history of relations between the region's countries in the energy sector perhaps most clearly manifested itself in the example of the Rogun hydroelectric power station construction in Tajikistan. The project was approved during Soviet times as early as 1974, and work began at the facility in 1976. The disintegration of the Soviet Union and the civil war in Tajikistan in the late 1980s stopped construction. In addition to economic problems, the completion of the Rogun HPP was also hampered by a political factor. Uzbekistan, for a long time, categorically opposed its construction, fearing that the construction of a power plant and a reservoir on the Vakhsh, one of the tributaries of the Amu Darya, would reduce the filling of this river, a river which the Uzbek irrigated agriculture depends on (EIU Digital Solutions, 2016). At times, it even came to direct forceful threats (Putz, 2015).

Since October 2016, the Italian company Salini Impregilo has been participating in the completion of the Rogun HPP. The initial contract was worth $3.9 billion (Cabar Asia, 2020). The government of Tajikistan used all possible means to raise funds for the facility's construction, for example placing an internal loan on the country's population. It even issued Eurobonds on international markets at relatively high-interest rates, making it possible to raise an additional $500 million.

After the new president of Uzbekistan, Shavkat Mirziyoyev, came to power Tashkent changed its attitude towards this project. In March 2018, following his first visit to Dushanbe, Uzbekistan supported the completion of the construction of the Rogun HPP and even expressed its readiness to take part in its creation.

In January 2018, the media reported on Uzbekistan's intention to reconnect its energy systems with Tajikistan. The parties took the first steps to unify their energy systems at the beginning of April 2018, when, after a nine-year break, electricity from the Regar power plant in Tajikistan began to flow again to Uzbekistan. The parties agreed that Tajikistan would resume imports of Uzbek natural gas, which had stopped in 2012.

Upon completion of the project, the dam of the Rogun HPP, with a height of 335 meters, will become the highest in the world, and the plant will reach a capacity of 3600 MW and become the largest hydroelectric power plant in Central Asia (BBC, 2016).

Most of Tajikistan's other hydroelectric power plants were built during the Soviet era and installed along the Vakhsh River downstream of Rogun. It includes the 3,000 MW Nurek Dam (World Bank, 2020b), currently the highest in Central Asia. In 2018, to improve the quality of the equipment, a contract was awarded to replace all nine power units of the power plant with new 380 MW turbines and generators, which will increase its capacity. The first unit of the Golovnaya HPP was also put into operation in 2018 as part of the ongoing modernisation programme aimed at expanding the station's capacity.

Further north, in the Sughd region, the 127 MW Kayrakkum hydroelectric power plant on the Syr Darya, built in the 1950s, has also attracted investment to replace and repair equipment. Financing provided by development partners will help increase the station's capacity to 174 MW and will include measures to improve climate resilience.

Tajikistan is prioritising programmes for the development of small and medium hydropower stations. For example, in the remote Gorno-Badakhshan Autonomous Oblast (GBAO), the Aga Khan Fund for Economic Development (AKFED) has established a public–private partnership to repair existing and build new hydroelectric power plants. As a result, about 96 per cent of households gained access to a reliable and environmentally friendly energy supply.

Along with the development of generating capacities, the government is investing in the development of electricity networks. Thanks to improved relations between Tajikistan and Uzbekistan in recent years, transmission lines were restored in April 2018, allowing up to 1.5 TWh to be sold annually to Uzbekistan (International Hydropower Association, 2022b). In addition, the CASA-1000 project is underway, which, when completed, will enhance regional electricity trade with Afghanistan and Pakistan.

CASA-1000

Central Asia and South Asia Power Project, commonly known by its acronym CASA-1000, is a $1.2 billion project currently under construction that will allow the export of surplus hydroelectric power from the Kyrgyz Republic and Tajikistan to Afghanistan and finally to Pakistan (World Bank, 2022). It will be a significant new source of revenue in the regional electricity market, transmitting 4.6 billion kWh per year (CASA 1000, 2021). The project started in May 2016 with the leaders of all four countries present (Daily Times, 2016). The entire project is to be completed in 2023. The project will export about 1,300 megawatts of electricity during the summer months when both the Kyrgyz Republic and Tajikistan experience excess electricity production from the release of water from hydroelectric dams.

It is planned that the project will include high voltage direct current (HVDC) converter stations and a 477 km 500 kV AC transmission line between Datka, the Kyrgyz Republic and Khujand, Tajikistan. Under the project, the parties will build a 1300 MW AC/DC converter station in the city of Sangtuda, Tajikistan, and a 300 MW converter station in Kabul, Afghanistan. A 750 km high voltage DC line will be made between Sangtuda and Peshawar in Pakistan via the Salang Pass and Kabul. A 1,300 MW converter station will be built in Peshawar and connected to the Pakistani power grid. The transmission lines will carry 1,300 MW of electricity, of which 300 MW will go to Afghanistan and 1,000 MW to Pakistan (CASA 1000, 2021).

An essential feature of CASA-1000 is that Western countries, led by the US, initiated and actively supported the project (USAID.gov, 2022). It is also primarily funded by international financial institutions such as the World Bank, the European Investment Bank (Jona, 2015), the European Bank for Reconstruction and Development (Pyrkalo, 2015), the Islamic Development Bank, and several other organisations.

From planning to completion of CASA-1000, it will take at least ten years. Meanwhile, the Kyrgyz Republic's and Tajikistan's economies and the population of these countries have grown significantly, and much more electricity is required to meet their needs (Biibosunov, 2021). They have now begun to purchase electricity in neighbouring countries (World Bank, 2014). Countries are forced to import electricity from neighbouring countries, especially in dry years when insufficient water reserves accumulate in their hydroelectric reservoirs (Pannier, 2021) (Najibullah, 2021). The question is, can these two countries, which had electricity surpluses ten years ago, once again have surplus energy to export? The answer to this question is not apparent. To generate additional electricity, Kyrgyzstan and Tajikistan require the construction of new large-scale hydropower plants, which will require significant capital expenditures, which are unavailable in these countries. It does not seem that foreign investors have the appetite for building new hydroelectric power plants in these countries either. Thus, the large-scale export of electricity to Afghanistan and Pakistan under the CASA-1000 project in the coming years may become a big problem.

Initially, the CASA-1000 project envisaged the completion of the construction of the Rogun HPP and the Sangtuda HPP and, in addition, the building of new HPPs on the Vakhsh cascade in Tajikistan, and the Toktogul cascade, including the Kambarata HPPs in Kyrgyzstan. However, now it is unclear who will invest in the construction of these stations.

Oil

The most notable infrastructure projects in the energy sector have been the laying of oil and gas pipelines across Central Asia. Kazakhstan, with oil reserves accounting for 95 per cent of the total reserves in the region, and Turkmenistan, which has 83 per cent of regional gas reserves on its territory, are leaders in the extraction of these hydrocarbons. As of 2019, total proven reserves were 31.4 billion barrels of oil and 825.8 trillion cubic feet of gas (Dwivedi & Turaga, 2022).

To the west

As part of the Soviet legacy, the entire logistics infrastructure of Central Asia was built in the direction of the European part of Russia. This likewise applies to all oil and gas infrastructure. Central Asia was isolated even from its closest neighbours outside the Soviet space. Refineries in eastern Kazakhstan pumped crude oil from western Siberia, while crude oil from western Kazakhstan was shipped to Samara in the Russian Federation.

Shortly after the independence of the Central Asian states, major Western oil companies became interested in exporting oil from the region. Western companies saw the existing Soviet pipeline system as the easiest way to bring their initial volumes to external markets and defer capital expenditures on new transportation infrastructure. Chevron, the first major player in Central Asia, proposed that production from their Tengiz field in Kazakhstan be shipped first to Samara, Russia. The company offered the Russian oil pipeline monopoly Transneft to invest in modernising this oil pipeline for delivery to the Russian Black Sea port of Novorossiysk. Tengiz's daily production was only 90,000–180,000 barrels at the time.

Chevron's proposals went unnoticed by its regulators, and Russia lost the opportunity to earn money from the transit of Kazakh oil through its territory. Chevron then began to look for other ways to transport oil. It developed a complex process of transporting crude oil by rail and barge from Tengiz to the Black Sea via Georgia, Ukraine, Finland and China. Transneft did not make money on this, but Russian Railways did.

Ultimately, Chevron decided to create the Caspian Pipeline Consortium (CPC) project and build a pipeline to transport crude oil produced by Western oil companies in Kazakhstan and deliver oil to its terminal on the Russian Black Sea coast. It runs from the Tengiz fields through Atyrau (Kazakhstan) and Astrakhan to Novorossiysk (Russia). The construction of the 1,580 kilometre long CPC gas pipeline cost $2.6 billion and was completed in 2003. Its initial daily capacity was 450,000 barrels, and its final capacity was 1.35 million barrels. The CPC terminal handles roughly 80 per cent of Kazakh crude and condensate loadings (CPC, 2022). Thus, with the unconscious assistance of Russia, Western oil companies began to own and transport oil from Central Asia to world markets without using the Russian pipeline network.

Additional opportunities for the transportation of Kazakh oil to foreign markets arose in 2005 in connection with the work of the Baku-Tbilisi-Ceyhan (BTC) oil pipeline. In this case, ships deliver oil to the Baku terminal through the Caspian Sea. The possibility of transporting oil along this route was associated with modernising the port of Aktau. BP and its partners completed the $4.2 billion and 1,768 kilometres long BTC pipeline to Turkey's Mediterranean coast in May 2006.

China

Unlike Western oil companies that signed their first oil concessions in the Caspian region immediately after the disintegration of the Soviet Union in the early 1990s, Chinese companies only signed their first deal in 1997. At that time, the China National Petroleum Corporation (CNPC) acquired the rights to the Aktobe oil deposit in Kazakhstan. Following this, Chinese companies have acquired additional oil assets in Kazakhstan.

As noted earlier, Kazakhstan is a leading producer of crude oil and, along with Turkmenistan, has become China's top energy partner in Central Asia. China currently produces and exports about 20 per cent of the total oil in Kazakhstan. CNPC owns a significant stake in the Kashagan oil field in the Caspian Sea, and Chinese companies own several large oil fields near Aktobe in the country's west (Bin, 2014). In 2006, China built a pipeline linking the Caspian oil fields of Kazakhstan with the Chinese network. The oil pipeline, with a length of 2,228 kilometres, connected the Kazakh city of Atyrau and the city of Alashankou in the Xinjiang Uygur Autonomous Region of China. This oil pipeline's capacity is, however, insignificant and amounts to only a few hundred thousand barrels daily.

Given that the Kyrgyz Republic has the lowest electricity prices in the region, Chinese companies have invested in constructing two modern oil refineries in Kara-Balta and Tokmok. Initially, Chinese investors expected that these refineries would receive crude oil from CNPC-owned fields in neighbouring Kazakhstan and produce up to 1.35 million tons of modern petroleum products annually. However, these plants do not operate at total capacity due to disagreements between countries on oil purchases.

Kashagan

Many experts agree that the next chapter in the history of the distribution of Central Asian hydrocarbons will determine which direction the enormous resources of the Kashagan oil field will go. This field was the largest oil discovery in the world in over thirty years. Potentially, Kashagan's production will reach 1.5 to 3 million barrels per day, justifying hopes that the Caspian will become a world-class oil region on par with the Middle East and the North Sea.

The Kashagan field is developed and operated by the North Caspian Operating Company (NCOC), which has brought together a unique composition of shareholders. It includes the Kazakh state company KazMunayGas (KMG, 16.9 per cent), as well as Shell (16.8 per cent), Total (16.8 per cent), Eni (16.8 per cent), ExxonMobil (16.8 per cent), CNPC (8.3 per cent) and Inpex (7.6 per cent). Investment in the first phase of Kashagan is estimated at

$55 billion and is the most significant international investment in Kazakhstan. Developed in harsh offshore conditions, the project is considered one of the world's most technically challenging oil and gas projects. The first phase of Kashagan, also known as the Pilot Program, reached its maximum design capacity of 380,000 barrels per day (bpd) in the first half of 2019. The shareholders plan to develop the offshore field in subsequent stages under the Full Field Development Program, increasing production at the site to at least 1.5 million barrels per day. Oil will be transported onshore by a 92-kilometre (57 mi) long pipeline (Eni.com, 2022).

Russia's Oil Transit to China via Kazakhstan

At the end of March 2022, Russia and Kazakhstan agreed to create a working group on the issue of increasing the transit of oil to China through Kazakh territory, Deputy Prime Minister of the Russian Federation Alexander Novak told reporters. He recalled that the previous contract for oil transit to China through Kazakhstan had been extended (Interfax.ru, 2022a). Speaking in the Russian parliament, Novak said that given the West's preparations for a ban on the purchase of Russian oil, the issue of increasing the supply of Russian energy resources to the East is becoming urgent. In early February, Rosneft and CNPC signed an agreement until 31 December 2033, on the supply of 100 million tons of oil for refineries in northwest China. Russia will supply oil via the Kazakh oil pipeline. The capacity of the existing oil pipeline in the direction of China through Kazakhstan is about 10 million tons. Several years ago, the parties discussed the possibility of increasing supplies to 17 million tons. Given the embargo on the export of Russian oil to Western countries, this volume will be achieved and will continue to grow (Gazeta.ru, 2022).

Gas

China

The history of Turkmen's gas supplies abroad dates back to the 1990s when a small gas pipeline from Turkmenistan to Iran came into operation. However, due to low energy prices in those days, investors were not particularly enthusiastic about expensive pipeline projects. Central Asian gas exporters continued to depend on the Russian natural gas transportation monopoly, Transneft.

As a result of a sharp rise in energy prices in the early 2000s and the need to supply additional energy to its domestic market, China began financing the large-scale construction of three strings of a new gas pipeline along the Turkmenistan–China route through the territories of Uzbekistan and Kazakhstan. The first line was constructed in November 2009, the second line – at the end of 2010, and the third line – in May 2014. The total gas pipeline cost with a design length of 1833 kilometres outside China is more than $7.3 billion (Hydrocarbons Technology, 2022). The diameter of each pipeline is 1067 mm. Lines A, B and C are three parallel lines and, as of 2015, have a total capacity of 55 billion cubic meters per year. The gas fields of South Iolotan-Osman and Dovletabad in Turkmenistan became the resource base of these lines.

The project proved to be a clear demonstration of China's technological and financial capabilities. It was able to design and implement the project in a short time, unlike the previously proposed Russian pipeline from Turkmenistan along the Caspian coast or the EU-backed Nabucco pipeline, which remained unrealised.

Over the past decade, China has overtaken Russia as the leading importer of Central Asian gas. Total exports in 2018 amounted to 46.8 billion cubic meters (bcm) to China, 16.1 bcm to Russia and 5.7 bcm of intra-regional trade. Due to the high demand for gas in China, the Central Asia–China pipeline corridor will be used at a level close to its capacity of 55 bcm per year. The fourth pipeline – line D, 966 kilometres outside China – will connect the Galkynysh field with western China through Kyrgyzstan, Tajikistan, and Uzbekistan. Its design capacity is 30 bcm per year. When transporting gas, all transit countries get the opportunity to receive transit payments and additional export volumes of their gas through this pipeline. After the commissioning of line D of the Central Asia-China gas pipeline, the capacity of gas supply from Central Asia to China will reach up to 85 bcm per year. China signed memorandums with all parties along the D-line route in September 2013. However, this project has not started yet.

Uzbekistan produces the same volumes of gas as Turkmenistan, which is about 55–60 bcm per year, but most of this gas is consumed domestically. The largest foreign investor in gas production in Uzbekistan is the Russian company Lukoil, which produced 13.4 bcm in 2018 out of a total of 57.4 bcm of gas produced in the country. Uzbekistan plans to increase exports to China from 6.5 bcm in 2018 to at least 10 bcm (Pirani, 2019).

China's energy market experts believe that gas demand will increase in the coming years. Gas consumption in China in 2018 amounted to 283 bcm. By 2024 CNPC expects that it will grow by another 130 bcm, and according to the IEA - by another 160 bcm. Both CNPC and BP forecast Chinese demand in 2035 at 610 bcm. China's own natural gas reserves are limited, and experts agree that its dependence on imported gas will continue to grow. Recently, Russia and China decided to launch a new source of imported gas through Russia's Power of Siberia gas pipeline. By 2025, its capacity will reach 38 billion cubic meters per year.

For years, the European Commission has nurtured plans to build a Trans-Caspian Gas Pipeline that would bring Turkmen gas to Azerbaijan to join the expanded southern gas corridor to Europe. So far, the European Commission has not made an agreement with Turkmenistan on this issue. It is awaiting a final investment decision to expand production at the Shah Deniz-

2 field in Azerbaijan and complete a transit corridor through Azerbaijan, Georgia and Turkey. The project will now be implemented without Turkmen gas, based on 16 billion cubic meters of gas exported from Azerbaijan annually – 10 bcm for European markets and 6 bcm for Turkey. The Malaysian company Petronas, which produces gas in the Turkmen sector of the Caspian Sea, has studied the possibility of implementing a project in the western direction and said it would support Turkmenistan's policy of diversifying energy exports (Pirani, 2019). Many experts agree that, based on economic and political realities, the realisation of large-scale gas exports to Europe is unlikely.

Central Asian natural gas exporters are working on deep processing to produce modern petrochemical products. The recent launch of the Shurtan complex in Uzbekistan (Sgcc.uz, 2022) and Kiyanly in Turkmenistan (Oilgas.gov.tm, 2021) carried out with financial and engineering support from both Japanese and other Asian companies should prove a critical turning point in this regard. The ability of Central Asian countries to export advanced petrochemicals to expanding but volatile markets has yet to be demonstrated.

TAPI Project

Turkmen gas can also find its way to consumers in South Asia if the TAPI gas pipeline is constructed. TAPI is named after the first letters of the countries through which it will pass – Turkmenistan, Afghanistan, Pakistan, and India. This gas pipeline, with a capacity of 33 billion cubic meters per year, should run from the Turkmen Galkynysh field through the Afghan cities of Herat and Kandahar, Pakistan's Quetta and Multan to the city of Fazilka in western India. Its total length should be 1814 kilometres, of which 207 kilometres will pass through the territory of Turkmenistan, 774 kilometres through Afghanistan and 826 kilometres through the territory of Pakistan to the border with India.

The first discussions on the TAPI project took place in 1991. Since the interested parties announced the creation of the gas pipeline consortium at the end of 2014, the construction has faced numerous delays. The work on the Turkmen section started in December 2015. In February 2018, the laying of the Afghan section of the gas pipeline took place. The parties assumed that the gas pipeline would be put into operation in 2021. However, a year later, after the workers carrying out preparatory work on the gas pipeline route in Afghanistan were killed by unidentified people, its construction was stopped (Reuters, 2018). In addition, the parties did not review the cost estimate of $10 billion for ten years. Its actualisation could lead to another delay in construction financed by the Asian Development Bank with the European Bank for Reconstruction and Development, the Islamic Development Bank (Bhutta, 2016), the Saudi Development Fund, and several other investors. Russia, the US and several other countries also supported the project.

After August 2021, power in Afghanistan passed to the Taliban, and several Taliban officials expressed their interest in implementing the TAPI gas pipeline and other major infrastructure projects, promising safety guarantees for their construction. "The work on power supply, the TAPI project and the expansion of the railway will be opened and started in March 2022," the Taliban Foreign Ministry said in a tweet in January 2022 (Interfax.ru, 2022b).

After a meeting in October 2021 with Turkmen Foreign Minister Rashid Meredov, Mawlawi Muhammad Yaqub, the Taliban interim Defence Minister in the Afghan interim administration (and son of Taliban founding leader Mullah Omar), said that he had taken direct responsibility for the security of the multibillion-dollar TAPI gas pipeline project. The meeting took place when Meredov was in Kabul for talks. (Khan, 2021).

Completing the TAPI project will allow Turkmenistan to reduce its dependence on China. In 2021, Turkmenistan doubled its gas exports to Russia, which was once the largest importer until China replaced it in 2010. For Afghanistan, the TAPI project can provide gas transit revenues of about $500 million per year and annual supplies of 500 million cubic meters of gas during the first 10 years, with a further increase to 1.5 billion cubic meters per year (Zhunisbek, 2020).

Of equal importance, the success of the TAPI project will demonstrate that the Taliban government can be a reliable partner in major infrastructure initiatives. Of course, Afghanistan has yet to decide what to do with this gas since it already has reserves estimated at 1.75 trillion cubic feet (U.S. Energy Information Administration, 2021). The US Development Plan for Afghanistan emphasised renewable energy sources, such as solar and wind power, but it is not yet clear whether the Taliban will follow this plan. The 59 MW gas-fired power plant in Mazar-i-Sharif, funded by the International Finance Corporation, would increase the country's electricity generation by 30 per cent, provided the Taliban can secure the project.

However, TAPI may have competition. For example, Iran, Azerbaijan and Turkmenistan have recently signed a trilateral gas swap agreement for up to 2 billion cubic meters per year (Reuters, 2021). This is a relatively small amount, given that Turkmenistan exports about 40 billion cubic meters to China annually, but this is another source of income that should be managed with an eye on future growth.

In addition, there is the possibility of connecting Turkmenistan to the long-discussed Trans-Caspian Gas Pipeline (TCP) project to supply Europe through the Southern Gas Corridor (SGC) (Fuhrmann, 2019). Getting Turkmen gas to the SGC would require the construction of a 200-mile underwater pipeline between Baku and Turkmenbashi (EIA, 2013), however, this project may face opposition from Iran and Russia for political and environmental reasons. But once the parties resolve the political issues, the TCP project is likely to be cheaper and less burdened by security concerns than the TAPI land route. Its additional resource base may be the agreement signed in January 2021 between Baku and Ashgabat on the joint development of the Dostluk ("Friendship") oil and gas field in the Caspian Sea (Morning Express, 2021).

As for Pakistan, TAPI will help solve its chronic energy shortage problem, particularly by closing the gap between its current gas production of 4 billion cubic feet per day and demand of 6 billion cubic meters (Xu, 2020a). In addition, by 2025, Pakistani gas production is expected to fall to less than 1 billion cubic feet per day due to the depletion of fields, and demand will increase by at least a third (Petroleum Institute of Pakistan, 2011). Due to insufficient reserves of gas and electricity, Pakistan has already lost a large part of its textile industry, which has mainly relocated to Bangladesh. Since Pakistan believes that the Taliban government has obligations to it, TAPI will help solve this problem by becoming an independent source of income for Afghanistan.

Finally, thanks to TAPI, India can increase the share of gas in its energy balance from 6.5 to 15 per cent. Perhaps the appearance of the gas pipeline will also become an incentive to increase its trade with Afghanistan (Lopes, 2021).

India is already the world's third-largest energy consumer, having doubled its consumption since 2000, yet 80 per cent of the demand is still met by coal, oil and solid biomass. According to the International Energy Agency, TAPI will allow India to use less coal (Steiner, 2019) and help the country achieve carbon targets and meet the expected 25–35 per cent energy demand growth by 2030 (Gnana, 2021).

The Future of Energy

Fossil Fuels

Given the energy sector's importance for Central Asia's future development, understanding the global trends in this sector is critical. It is especially important to understand what will happen to the global energy market in relation to developing a green economy and transitioning to low-carbon technologies.

By 2050, the world will look vastly different. By this time, the global economy will have doubled, and the world's population will have increased by two billion people. At the same time, according to the estimates made by the International Energy Agency (IEA), the total world electricity generation will reach nearly 45 trillion kWh by 2050, almost 20 trillion kWh more than the 2018 level, while energy demand should decrease by around 8 per cent. Nearly 90 per cent of electricity will come from renewable sources, with almost 70 per cent from wind and solar power plants, while the rest will come from the generation of nuclear power. Fossil fuel use will fall from nearly 80 per cent of the total energy supply today to just over 20 per cent in 2050 (IEA, 2021b). Fossil fuels will mainly find applications in manufacturing products such as plastics, facilities equipped with carbon capture systems, and sectors with no alternative to replacing carbon technologies.

Nearly 200 countries ratified the Paris Climate Agreement in 2015 (CNBC, 2015), agreeing to continue efforts to keep the planet's temperature rise to 1.5 degrees Celsius. However, some scholars believe that achieving these goals is "virtually unattainable" (Australian Academy of Science, 2021). A recent UN analysis showed that commitments to reducing greenhouse gas emissions are "very far" from the serious action (Meredith, 2021) required to prevent the devastating effects of climate change. Most experts agree that the energy market will increasingly electrify under the 2050 fast-track energy transition scenario, displacing the most polluting hydrocarbons such as oil (McKeever, 2021).

In May 2021, the International Energy Agency announced that the world no longer needs new developments in oil and gas. Global oil demand will fall by 75 per cent under the scenario required to put the world on the path to zero emissions by 2050 (Perkins, 2021).

According to the IEA, due to the suspension of new oil exploration and production projects and the expected reduction in the price of oil, the so-called Net-Zero Emissions (NZE) scenario should be realised. It will balance the whole amount of greenhouse gas released and the amount removed from the atmosphere. According to their estimates, oil demand will never again reach its historic peak in 2019 and should decrease from about 90 million barrels per day in 2020 to 24 million barrels per day by 2050. Natural gas demand will also decline 55 per cent from its 2020 amount to 1,750 billion cubic meters. Oil prices will fall from \$75 to about \$35 a barrel by 2030 and then further down to \$25 a barrel by 2050. Estimates by consulting firm Wood Mackenzie indicated an even more radical decline, suggesting that by 2040, oil prices may drop to \$28–32 per barrel, and in 2050 they will fall to \$10–18 per barrel (McKeever, 2021).

Of the total volume of 100 million barrels of oil per day, approximately 60 per cent is accounted for by transportation. The rest is used in petrochemicals (10 per cent), electricity (5 per cent), heating (6 per cent), and other industries (19 per cent) such as construction, lubricants, agriculture, etc. (Malik, 2019).

Under the Net-Zero Emissions scenario, most countries will ban the sale of conventional passenger cars from 2035. According to the plan, about 60 per cent of global car sales in 2030 should be electric vehicles, and 85 per cent of heavy trucks will be electric by 2040. Refiners estimate that between 2020 and 2050, average oil production will fall by 85 per cent, leading to multiple plant closures. Oil demand for petrol and diesel for cars will fall to less than 15 per cent in 2050, down from about 55 per cent now (Perkins, 2021).

While the demand for crude oil has increased by about 15 per cent over the past ten years, the need for oil for use in the petrochemical industry has increased by about 50 per cent, driven by economic growth, urbanisation, and increased consumer demand. Given the optimistic target of recycling 75 per cent of the world's plastic by 2050, experts estimate that petrochemical companies' demand for crude oil will drop to about 14 million barrels per day by 2050 (Malik, 2019).

The IEA's underlying assumption for global oil demand is that it will continue to recover from the 2020 lows over the coming years rather than immediately enter a structural downturn. In March, the IEA said it expects global demand for liquid hydrocarbons, including biofuels, to rise to 103.2 million barrels per day in 2025, up from 90 million barrels per day in 2020. S&P Global Platts Analytics expects, in the "most likely" scenario, that global consumption of liquids, including biofuels, to return to pre-pandemic levels in 2023 and to about 114 million barrels per day in 2040 (IEA, 2021c).

In the absence of the need to develop new oil and gas fields, the supplies will mainly be provided by small producers at low costs. As a result, the IEA has estimated that OPEC's share of global oil supplies will grow from about 37 per cent in recent years to 52 per cent in 2050, the highest in the history of oil markets. If global demand drops to 25 million barrels a day by 2050, even the oil revenues of cheap OPEC producers will be severely affected. IEA claimed that rising clean and renewable energy consumption would also pose critical risks for states that rely heavily on oil revenues to ensure social and political stability in their countries (Perkins, 2021).

The IEA estimates that, even outside the oil and gas producing countries, the Net-Zero Emissions scenario will result in a sharp drop in oil and gas tax revenues by about 40 per cent between 2020 and 2030, requiring careful financial planning and budgetary reforms to offset the deficits.

The hydrocarbon-producing countries are serious about the prospects of reducing production and a drop in income from their exports. Speaking at the International Financial Congress, the Head of Russian Sberbank, Herman Gref, said that the price of Urals Oil (a reference to the oil brand used for the Russian export oil mixture) may fall to $26 per barrel by 2050. At the same time, the price of gas will halve. The volume of oil production in Russia at the current rate of decarbonisation in the next thirty years will drop threefold, and oil exports may fall four–six times (Mazina, 2021).

Bloomberg reported that the United Arab Emirates (UAE) might become the first country among the OPEC to set a target to reach Net-Zero Emissions, a move that would not require them to produce and sell less oil. Although the government has been working to diversify its economy since the 1980s, fossil fuels remain its most significant source of revenue, providing about 30 per cent of its GDP. According to people familiar with the discussions, the country plans to achieve this goal by 2050 by investing more than $160 billion in green technologies. If the UAE decides to do so, it will be the first major oil and gas nation to set such an ambitious climate target (Rathi, et al., 2021).

China is one of the largest countries in terms of carbon dioxide emissions, accounting for 10 billion tons per year, or 30 per cent of the total emissions on earth, but the country is determined to change this situation radically. Jiang Xuefeng, Deputy Director of the Institute of Economic and Technical Research, said that according to his institute's research, the demand for oil in China, including petroleum products, will peak at 5.37 billion barrels per year in 2025 decline to 2.28 billion barrels annually by 2050. According to the study, demand for natural gas in China will peak at 550 billion cubic meters per year in 2050, up from 306 billion cubic meters last year. Under the carbon-neutral scenario, China will reduce its dependence on crude oil imports to less than 40 per cent and natural gas to about 30 per cent, down from 70 per cent and 40 per cent in 2020, respectively. The main gas demand drivers are electricity generation and commercial and residential use, accounting for 72 per cent of total gas demand between 2020 and 2050. The study also shows that annual coal demand will decline to 2.9 billion tons in 2030 and 900 million tons in 2050, down from 4 billion tons last year (Xu, 2020b).

Ding Zhimin, former deputy director of the National Energy Administration's Policy and Law Department, said that a massive 100 to 130 trillion yuan ($15.4 to $20 trillion) would be required to achieve carbon neutrality. Those numbers are much higher than the $5 trillion previously predicted by consulting firm Wood Mackenzie (Xu, 2020b).

Severe risks exist for oil and gas companies, which will need to radically reorientate their activities (Perkins, 2021). These companies started investing in renewable technologies a long time ago and are becoming broad-based energy companies. Of the six "supermajors" – BP, Shell, Chevron, Total, Eni, and Exxon – many have invested billions of dollars in clean energy projects, although the question remains whether they are doing enough. Despite the rise in renewables, major oil companies' budgets in 2018 spent only one per cent of their total on green energy schemes (Murray, 2020a). Among the most prominent companies developing detailed plans to achieve NZE are BP, Shell, Total, Repsol, and Equinor (Murray, 2020b).

BP recently announced that it is time to wind down its core business. It plans to produce 30–40 per cent less oil and gas than it does now by 2030. The company has promised to stop hydrocarbon exploration in new countries and increase its low-carbon investment tenfold by then (Parnell, 2020).

A joint analysis by the IEA with the International Monetary Fund showed that under the Net-Zero Emissions scenario, total annual energy investment would rise to $5 trillion by 2030, adding 0.4 percentage points per year to global GDP growth annually. The jump in private and public investment will create millions of clean energy jobs, including mechanical engineering, manufacturing, and construction. It will increase global GDP by 4 per cent by 2030 (IEA, 2021b).

Growing challenges to energy security arising from the rising importance of electricity (IEA, 2020b) include the volatility of its supply due to the risks associated with the nature of renewable energy generation and cybersecurity issues (IEA, 2020b). In addition, the growing dependence on essential minerals (IEA, 2021d) requires critical technologies, and clean energy infrastructure carries risks of price volatility and supply disruptions that could impede an efficient and rapid transition to renewables (IEA, 2021b).

Nuclear Energy

The accident at the Fukushima Daiichi nuclear power plant in Japan on 11 March 2011, was a severe shock for the nuclear power industry. At that time, many predicted the decline and even a complete ban on the use of nuclear reactors. What is happening to the nuclear industry ten years after Fukushima?

As expected, a devastating blow to nuclear power generation occurred in Japan. Authorities suspended forty-six of the country's fifty operating power reactors. The generation of nuclear power, which provided nearly a third of Japan's electricity before the accident, was suspended. In 2019, nuclear power provided only 7.5 per cent of Japan's electricity (Paillere & Donovan, 2021). Up until 2011, Japan was generating some 30 per cent of electricity from its reactors and this was expected to increase to at least 40 per cent by 2017. The plan is now for at least 20% by 2030 (World Nuclear Association, 2022a).

The echo of the accident had the most significant impact on Europe. Less than three months after the accident, Germany decided to phase out nuclear power entirely by 2022. Since then, of the country's 17 nuclear reactors, 11 have been shut down. In 2019, nuclear power produced only about 12 per cent of the country's electricity, compared with about 25 per cent before the accident. Belgium has also confirmed plans to end the use of nuclear power by 2025. Spain and Switzerland decided never to build new nuclear power plants again. From 2011 to 2020, 65 reactors across the world, which generated about 48 GW of nuclear power globally, were shut down (Paillere & Donovan, 2021).

Although the events of ten years ago had a massive impact on the development of nuclear power throughout the world, they could not stop its growth. The statistics of recent years show positive growth in its development. Today, nuclear power plants operating in 31 countries boast more than 18,000 reactor years of experience. Thanks to regional power grids, many other countries are also reaping the benefits of nuclear power. For example, Italy and Denmark get nearly 10 per cent of their electricity from nuclear imports.

In 2019, 440 operating nuclear power plants produced 2,657 TWh of electricity compared to 2,563 TWh in 2018. About 50 more reactors were under construction, equivalent to 15 per cent of the existing capacity. Twelve countries currently produce at least a quarter of their electricity from nuclear power plants. France receives about three-quarters of its electricity from nuclear power, Slovakia and Ukraine more than half. South Korea, Hungary, Belgium, Sweden, Slovenia, Bulgaria, Switzerland, Finland, and the Czech Republic receive one-third or more. The US, UK, Spain, Romania, and Russia generate about one-fifth of their electricity from nuclear energy.

The global fight against climate change requires a decisive rejection of energy from fossil fuels. Those sources still account for a dominant 84 per cent of global energy consumption today (Rapier, 2020). For example, in the US in 2018, they provided about 80 per cent of the country's needs, slightly lower than 84 per cent a decade earlier (Desilver, 2020). Fossil fuels generate about 85 per cent of energy in China (Ritchie & Roser, 2020). The annual consumption of fossil fuels has increased over the past ten years from 116,214 to 136,761 TWh in 2019. The current consensus among experts is that wind and solar cannot yet meet our energy needs. Their main disadvantage is high cost and low reliability as wind and sun are not constantly available, and they also need some form of storage and regulation (Ballinger, 2022). Thus, it has become evident that the development of nuclear energy will be necessary along with obtaining low-carbon energy from solar and wind power plants.

It must be said that the world has seen a significant increase in electricity generation from renewable energy sources. The countries of the European Union have achieved particularly substantial success. European solar and wind power plants generated 38 per cent of electricity last year, according to Ember and Agora Energiewende, surpassing, for the first time in history, the 37 per cent generated from fossil fuels (Twidale, 2021). However, things are not yet so impressive elsewhere. A vast 64 per cent of the world's electricity was generated last year from fossil fuels. Even with a significant increase in electricity generation from renewable sources, fossil fuels have remained virtually unchanged over the past fifteen years. For instance, it was broadly similar in 2005 at 66.5 per cent (World Nuclear Association, 2022b).

The World Energy Outlook 2020 contains an ambitious Sustainable Development Scenario that, among other things, is in line with providing clean and reliable energy and reducing air pollution (IEA, 2020c). In this scenario, electricity production at nuclear power plants by 2040 should increase by 55 per cent and amount to 4,320 TWh. The generated capacity should increase to 599 GW. The World Nuclear Association has put forward an even more ambitious scenario. Their Harmony programme (World Nuclear Association, 2018) envisions an increase in new nuclear capacity to 1,000 GW by 2050. The total volume of electricity generated worldwide will be about 10,000 TWh. This scenario will require an annual capacity increment of 25 to 33 GW starting this year. These figures differ from the yearly average increase of 31 GW achieved in 1984 (World Nuclear Association, 2022b).

Meeting the rapidly growing demand for low-carbon energy will require the accelerated development of nuclear power, which should provide up to 25 per cent of electricity by 2050 (World Nuclear Association, 2018). It all means that nuclear energy production in the world should triple within the next thirty years. Instead of shrinking, the generation of nuclear power will dramatically increase. Fukushima's effect is gradually fading away.

Nuclear Energy in China

Great strides forward in the introduction of green energy are observed in neighbouring China. Its peculiarity is that using hydropower as an alternative low-carbon energy source often becomes economically and environmentally disadvantageous. Most new dams are to be built in the ecologically sensitive southwestern regions. For the population living there, their construction is becoming a big problem. The construction of barrages will result in flooding of fertile land and increase the risk of flooding. As many river ecosystems have been damaged, environmentalists have called for a ban on major hydropower projects.

The country is now turning to large-scale use of renewable energy sources. Considerable investments are being made to construct solar and wind power generators, but their use is also limited. Such generators have low power, occupy valuable land, and depend on weather conditions. Significant losses are incurred when deployed in the western desert regions and transmitting solar and wind power over long distances. Experts argue that solar and wind power can only play an auxiliary role and be used to supply urban and rural enterprises and households but will not be able to provide enough power to newly developed industrial areas. The further development of nuclear power has become economically justified.

Meeting the rapidly growing global demand for low-carbon energy will require the rapid development of nuclear power, which should provide up to 25 per cent of electricity produced worldwide by 2050. It means that over the next thirty years, global nuclear energy production will need to triple. As mentioned, instead of declining, nuclear power production will skyrocket, and the Fukushima effect will continue disappearing. But what will happen in the future development of nuclear power in neighbouring China?

As of the end of 2020, the top three nuclear-generating countries based on installed capacity were the US, which produced 98.2 GW (which was 20 per cent of the country's total capacity), France – 63.1 GW (70 per cent of the total capacity), and China – 47.5 GW (5 per cent of the total capacity) (Kumar, 2021). These numbers show that to approach or exceed the global average nuclear power generation rate of 25 per cent by 2050, China must accelerate its production of this type of low-carbon energy. What is the situation today, and what are the plans for the future?

Between 2016 and 2020 twenty new commercial nuclear power units were commissioned with an additional installed capacity of 23.45 GW. These figures show that the volume of commissioned capacities has doubled in just five years (Global Times, 2021). Secretary-General of the China Nuclear Energy Association (CNEA) Zhang Tingke said in his interview in April 2020 that 17 nuclear power units with a total capacity of 18.53 million kilowatts are currently under construction (Global Times, 2021).

The China Nuclear Power Development Center estimates that nuclear capacity will more than double to 130 GW by 2030, reaching 170 GW by

2035 and 340 GW by 2050. By 2030, nuclear power will account for only 10 per cent of national electricity generation, but it will have a significant impact globally due to the country's huge energy sector (Zheng, 2021). According to GlobalData Plc, China will quickly rise in the ranking of the world's leading nuclear energy producers, overtaking France as the world's second nuclear power producer by 2022 and ranked first in the world by 2026 (GlobalData, 2020).

The country must have its most modern nuclear reactors to implement such ambitious plans. In 2015, China began constructing a new block of the Fuqing nuclear power plant for the first time, based on its technologies. The historic power-up of China's first Hualong One Reactor, the result of thirty years of research and development, took place on 27 November 2020. Commissioned by the National Energy Administration (NEA), these reactors were jointly designed by two nuclear companies – China General Nuclear Power Group (CGN) and China National Nuclear Corporation (CNNC). They solved the problem of combining two reactor designs – ACP1000 and ACPR1000, based initially on the French M310 reactor (Petushkova, 2021).

Thus, at the end of last year, China became the fourth country to develop its technology of third-generation nuclear reactors after the US, France, and Russia. This remarkable achievement means that China has broken the foreign monopoly on nuclear technology and has become one of the leading countries in this area. The installed capacity of each Hualong One power unit is about 1.2 GW, and the reactor can generate about 10 billion kWh of electricity annually. One Hualong One power unit will reduce carbon dioxide emissions by 8.16 million tons and carbon consumption by 3.12 million tons annually. CNNC chairman Wang Shoudun said that "China is capable of mass production of its third-generation Hualong One reactor, which can be seen as China's newest business model". Work in this direction is one of the sixteen key national scientific and technical projects (Petushkova, 2021).

In the next thirty years, the total power generated by Chinese nuclear reactors must grow more than sevenfold. The world has never seen projects of this magnitude. It will take significant efforts from the state, scientists, engineers, and technologists to achieve such an ambitious goal, but without such unprecedented-scale work, the global challenge of tackling climate change will not be possible.

Future of Energy in Central Asia

Nuclear

Economic recovery and population growth are the main factors influencing energy consumption growth. The countries of Central Asia are forecasting significant growth in electricity consumption and are planning significant investments to increase their generating capacity. The government of Kazakhstan has predicted that by 2030 the annual volume of energy consumption in the country should be approximately 141 billion kWh, thus increasing by 26 per cent (Peretok.ru, 2021). Similar estimates were released by the government of Uzbekistan, predicting that consumption will almost double to 117 billion kWh by 2030 (Cameron, 2019).

Both countries have decided to build nuclear power plants in their territories to achieve such goals. The President of Kazakhstan, Kassym-Jomart Tokayev, made it clear when addressing a Russian business forum in September 2021: "I believe that it's time to consider this issue substantially since Kazakhstan needs a nuclear power plant" (Tengrinews.kz, 2021). Kazakhstan has the world's largest uranium reserves and, therefore, has every opportunity to build a nuclear power plant. In all likelihood, the nuclear power plant will be built in the village of Ulken on Lake Balkhash. The new capacities will be able to cover the required amount of electricity generation, which is estimated at 150 billion kWh in 2035, which is one-third higher than the current level. According to the forecast of the Ministry of Energy, today in Kazakhstan there are about thirty-seven thermal power plants that are outdated and in critical condition (Tazabek, 2022a). According to the ministry, the future nuclear power plant will have a capacity of about 2.4 GW. The project may take 10 years to complete, the cost of 1 power unit should be $5 billion, and the general contractor will be selected in 2023 (Neft i Kapital, 2022).

Uzbekistan signed an agreement to construct a nuclear power plant with the Russian corporation Rosatom in 2018 (Spot.uz, 2018). In 2019, the parties decided on a construction site in the Jizzakh region (Spot.uz, 2019a). Currently, the authorities have completed the development of project documentation and have estimated the necessary funding at $11 billion (Spot.uz, 2019b). According to the preliminary plan, the power plant will be fully operational by 2030, and the first reactors will be commissioned by 2028. The facility, with four reactors, is expected to provide just under 20 per cent of the country's electricity needs (IAEA, 2021c). Uzbekistan is in the top ten uranium producers, so it would benefit from switching from hydrocarbons to nuclear power (Spot.uz, 2021).

Meanwhile, the Kyrgyz Republic has also announced its plans to build nuclear power plants. The Russian State Corporation Rosatom and the Ministry of Energy of the Kyrgyz Republic signed a memorandum of cooperation to construct several small nuclear power plants. They signed the document on 20 January 2022, on the side-lines of the Expo 2020 World Exhibition in Dubai, where a presentation of Russian low-power nuclear technologies took place (Azattyk, 2022).

Solar and Wind

Like more than 190 countries worldwide, which have signed the Paris Agreement on Climate Change, the region's governments aim to become carbon neutral by 2060. The geography of Central Asia favours the active use of green technologies, yet it has a long way to go. According to the Global Carbon Atlas platform for 2019, Kazakhstan ranks 21st among 221 countries for carbon dioxide emissions, 11th in terms of emissions per capita, and 5th for carbon intensity to GDP (Globalcarbonatlas.org, 2021) and is therefore still far off achieving carbon neutrality. The scale of the planned green transition will be massive. In 2017, fuel and energy together comprised 54 per cent coal, 24 per cent oil and 22 per cent gas. Calculations showed that by 2060 the share of fossil energy resources would drop 3.4 times to just 29 per cent, while the share of renewable energy will increase to 70 per cent (Nurbay, 2021).

The first concrete steps are already being taken. Over the past six years, the installed capacity of renewable energy sources has grown almost ten times – from 178 MW in 2014 to 1,635 in 2020. In 2020, Kazakhstan reached 3 per cent of its energy total from green sources ahead of schedule. One hundred and sixteen renewable energy facilities operate in the republic with an installed capacity of 1685 MW. At the end of 2020, its consumption level amounted to 3.24 billion kWh. Twenty-three renewable energy facilities with a capacity of 381.1 MW began operating in 2021. Kazakhstan intends to increase the share of renewable energy in total electricity production from 6 per cent in 2025 to 10 per cent by 2030. By 2050, renewable and alternative energy sources should account for at least half of all energy consumption (Bogatova, 2021).

Calculations showed that to achieve carbon neutrality over the next 40 years, the country needs to invest about 650 billion US dollars in developing low-carbon technologies. Ecology Minister Serikkali Brekeshev explained the emergence of such a colossal figure: "The sectors requiring the largest amount of investment in 40 years are the production of electricity and heat - $305 billion, transport $167 billion, mining and manufacturing $65 billion, housing and communal services $57 billion, agriculture $49 billion" (Nurbay, 2021).

Uzbekistan intends to move to carbon-neutral electricity production ten years ahead of its neighbour Kazakhstan, by 2050. A consortium of international experts set out this goal and developed a specific roadmap (Gazeta.uz, 2021). According to the highest estimate, the government noted that the demand for electricity in Uzbekistan in 2050 will be 400 GW. At the same time, the technical potential of wind energy is 1000 GW, and solar energy is 3000 GW (Sidorovich, 2021).

By 2030, Uzbekistan plans to receive more than a quarter of electricity from renewable energy sources. By 2030, according to the plan of the Ministry of Energy, 45 per cent of electricity in the country will be generated at thermal power plants from natural gas, 17 per cent from solar and wind stations, 13 per cent from hydroelectric power plants, 8 per cent will come from nuclear energy and only 6 per cent from coal-fired thermal power plants (Astrasheuskaya, 2021).

At the end of August 2021, the first large Nur-Navoi photoelectric power plant with a capacity of 100 MW started its operation in the Navoi region of Uzbekistan, built by Masdar, a company from the United Arab Emirates, with the involvement of funds from the European Bank for Reconstruction and Development and the Asian Development Bank. It became the first of nineteen renewable energy projects planned for the next five years. In addition to Navoi, Masdar intends to create three solar energy facilities – in the regions of Surkhandarya, Jizzakh and Samarkand. The Ministry of Energy is holding tenders for three more solar power plants. The total investment will reach $6.5 billion.

Other types of renewable energy sources will also develop. The company ACWA Power will build the largest wind farm in Central Asia in Uzbekistan, while Masdar is working on another wind farm in the Navoi region. Sixty-two hydropower projects will receive additional funding to create new and upgrade existing facilities.

In April 2022, at a meeting in the government of the Kyrgyz Republic, representatives of Masdar announced plans to build a 200 MW solar power plant, which will be the first stage in a few future large-scale investments in the country (Tazabek, 2022b; Tazabek, 2022a).

Conclusion

In their ambitious energy programmes, all Central Asian countries are following the global trend of developing green energy and achieving carbon neutrality either by 2050 or 2060. The geography of the region favours the proactive use of green technologies. Two countries are already getting their electricity from green hydropower, and three others have significant natural gas reserves. Soon, nuclear power plants will start operating in the region for the first time in history. Three countries have announced their ambitions to develop nuclear technologies. There are ample opportunities for this – Kazakhstan has the world's largest uranium reserves, and Uzbekistan is in the top ten uranium producers globally. The region has at least 300 sunny days annually, favouring solar energy development. There are broad prospects for wind energy development in its steppe and desert expanses. But the planned green transition will not be easy. Governments and local and foreign investors will require significant and synchronised efforts to achieve such ambitious goals. For example, to achieve carbon neutrality over the next forty years, Kazakhstan needs to invest about $650 billion in developing low-carbon technologies. The road of green transition which lies ahead is bright if the right people, experts and attitudes are involved, but it will almost certainly not be a simple journey.

References

Aminjonov, F., 2016. Central Asian countries' power systems are now isolated, but not everyone is happy!. *Asya Avrupa: Haber-Yorum*, Issue 4.

Asiaplustj.info, 2021. Elektroenergeticheskij rynok Central'noj Azii. Kto est' kto?. [Online] Available at: https://www.asiaplustj.info/news/tajikistan/economic/

20210116/elektroenergeticheskii-rinok-tsentralnoi-azii-kto-est-kto [Accessed July 2022].

Astrasheuskaya, N., 2021. Uzbekistan pins hopes on renewable energy. [Online] Available at: https://www.ft.com/content/c317f58c-ef31-4b1c-8c7d-9ff94896cdf2 [Accessed July 2022].

Australian Academy of Science, 2021. The risks to Australia of a 3°C warmer world. [Online] Available at: https://www.science.org.au/supporting-science/science-policy-and-analysis/reports-and-publications/risks-australia-three-degrees-c-warmer-world [Accessed July 2022].

Azattyk, 2020. Gordost' i pozor strany. Chto iz sebja predstavljaet energetika Kyrgyzstana. [Online] Available at: https://rus.azattyk.org/a/30649740.html [Accessed July 2022].

Azattyk, 2022. Rosatom nameren postroit' maluyu AES na territorii Kyrgyzstana. [Online] Available at: https://rus.azattyk.org/a/kyrgyzstan-i-rosatom-namereny-stroit-atomnuyu-stantsiyu-na-territorii-kr/31664380.html [Accessed July 2022].

Ballinger, J., 2022. Are wind and solar power really more expensive and less reliable?. [Online] Available at: https://news.climate.columbia.edu/2022/02/10/are-wind-and-solar-power-really-more-expensive-and-less-reliable/ [Accessed July 2022].

Bankwatch.org, 2020. TEC Dushanbe-2 - ugolnaya stantsia v cherte tadzhikskoi stolitsy. [Online] Available at: https://bankwatch.org/wp-content/uploads/2018/01/dushanbe-brief.pdf [Accessed July 2022].

BBC, 2016. Tajikistan's Rogun: Building the world's tallest dam. [Online] Available at: https://www.bbc.com/news/world-asia-37929367 [Accessed July 2022].

Bhutta, Z., 2016. Islamic Development Bank offers $500m for TAPI pipeline. [Online] Available at: https://tribune.com.pk/story/1226125/loan-islamic-development-bank-offers-500m-tapi-pipeline [Accessed July 2022].

Biibosunov, A., 2021. Opechatannye obogrevateli. Pomozhet li mera preodolet' energeticheskij krizis?. [Online] Available at: https://rus.azattyk.org/a/31568932.html [Accessed July 2022].

Bin, H., 2014. Oil and gas cooperation between China and Central Asia in an environment of political and resource competition. *Petroleum Science*, Issue 11, pp. 596–605.

Bogatova, E., 2021. K 2025 godu dolya VIE v Kazakhstane dostignet 6%. [Online] Available at: https://kapital.kz/economic/93292/k-2025-godu-dolya-vie-v-kazakhstane-dostignet-6.html [Accessed July 2022].

Cabar Asia, 2020. Construction of Rogun hydroelectric power plant in Tajikistan: workers have not been paid since summer. [Online] Available at: https://cabar.asia/en/construction-of-rogun-hydroelectric-power-plant-in-tajikistan-workers-have-not-been-paid-since-summer [Accessed July 2022].

Cameron, R., 2019. Uzbekistan plans to sell most of its power plants to private investors. [Online] Available at: https://www.sustainable-carbon.org/uzbekistan-plans-to-sell-most-of-its-power-plants-to-private-investors/ [Accessed July 2022].

CASA 1000, 2021. CASA 1000 power transmission and trade project. [Online] Available at: https://www.casa-1000.org/ [Accessed July 2022].

CAWater-Info, 2022. Vodohranilishha Kyrgyzstana. [Online] Available at: http://www.cawater-info.net/bk/1-1-1-1-3-kg.htm [Accessed July 2022].

CNBC, 2015. Paris climate agreement: All you need to know. [Online] Available at: https://www.cnbc.com/2015/12/13/paris-climate-agreement-all-you-need-to-know.html [Accessed July 2022].

CPC, 2022. CPC terminal operating at full capacity. [Online] Available at: https://www.argusmedia.com/en/news/2325030-cpc-terminal-operating-at-full-capacity [Accessed July 2022].

Daily Times, 2016. Casa-1000 formally inaugurated. [Online] Available at: https://dailytimes.com.pk/81955/casa-1000-formally-inaugurated/ [Accessed July 2022].

Desilver, D., 2020. Renewable energy is growing fast in the U.S., but fossil fuels still dominate. [Online] Available at: https://www.pewresearch.org/fact-tank/2020/01/15/renewable-energy-is-growing-fast-in-the-u-s-but-fossil-fuels-still-dominate/ [Accessed July 2022].

Dwivedi, P. & Turaga, U., 2022. Regional spotlight: Oil & Gas in Central Asia. [Online] Available at: https://adi-analytics.com/2021/05/28/regional-spotlight-oil-gas-in-central-asia/ [Accessed July 2022].

Economic Times, 2009. OMEL eyes Kazakh block. [Online] Available at: https://economictimes.indiatimes.com/industry/energy/oil-gas/omel-eyes-kazakh-block/articleshow/4262562.cms?from=mdr [Accessed July 2022].

EIA, 2013. International - U.S. energy Information Administration (EIA). [Online] Available at: https://www.eia.gov/international/analysis/regions-of-interest/Caspian_Sea [Accessed July 2022].

EIU Digital Solutions, 2016. Uzbekistan issues warning on Rogun dam plans. [Online] Available at: http://country.eiu.com/article.aspx?articleid=1524460736 [Accessed July 2022].

Energo-cis.ru, 2017. Elektroenergetika Respubliki Kazakhstan. [Online] Available at: http://energo-cis.ru/wyswyg/file/news/%D0%AD%D0%BD%D0%B5%D1%80%D0%B3%D0%BE%D1%81%D0%B8%D1%81%D1%82%D0%B5%D0%BC%D0%B0_%D0%9A%D0%B0%D0%B7%D0%B0%D1%85%D1%81%D1%82%D0%B0%D0%BD%D0%B0.pdf [Accessed July 2022].

Energyland.info, 2022. Uzbekistan v 2022 godu vvedet v ekspluataciju 7 novyh elektrostancij. [Online] Available at: http://www.energyland.info/news-show-tek-electro-225879 [Accessed July 2022].

Eni.com, 2022. Kashgan: offshore oil and gas in Kazakhstan. [Online] Available at: https://www.eni.com/en-IT/operations/kazakhstan-kashagan.html [Accessed July 2022].

Falakshahi, H., 2022. What's at stake for oil and gas markets in the Kazakhstan protests?. [Online] Available at: https://www.kpler.com/blog/whats-at-stake-for-oil-and-gas-markets-in-the-kazakhstan-protests [Accessed July 2022].

Fuhrmann, M., 2019. *European union keen on Trans-Caspian Pipeline development - improvement of relations with Russia and Turkey a key hurdle*, Tokyo: Mitsui & Co. Global Strategic Studies Institute.

Gazeta.ru, 2022. Tranzit rossiiskoi nefti v Kinai cherez Kazakhstan v aprele uvelichilsya na 9% k martu. [Online] Available at: https://www.gazeta.ru/business/news/2022/05/24/17800430.shtml [Accessed July 2022].

Gazeta.uz, 2021. Uzbekistan planiruet pereyti k uglerodno-neytral'noj energetike k 2050 godu. [Online] Available at: https://www.gazeta.uz/ru/2021/02/02/carbon-neutrality/ [Accessed July 2022].

Global Times, 2021. China takes global lead in rolling out nuclear power generators. [Online] Available at: https://www.globaltimes.cn/page/202104/1221064.shtml [Accessed July 2022].

Globalcarbonatlas.org, 2021. Global Carbon Atlas. [Online] Available at: http://www.globalcarbonatlas.org/en/content/welcome-carbon-atlas [Accessed July 2022].

GlobalData, 2020. China set to overtake US in nuclear capacity by 2026, says GlobalData. [Online] Available at: https://www.globaldata.com/china-set-overtake-us-nuclear-capacity-2026-says-globaldata/ [Accessed July 2022].

Gnana, J., 2021. India's energy demand to surge 25–35% by 2030, IEA says. [Online] Available at: https://www.thenationalnews.com/business/energy/india-s-energy-demand-to-surge-25-35-by-2030-iea-says-1.1166745 [Accessed July 2022].

Hydrocarbons Technology, 2022. Central Asia-China Gas Pipeline, Turkmenistan to China. [Online] Available at: https://www.hydrocarbons-technology.com/projects/centralasiachinagasp/ [Accessed July 2022].

Hydropower Central Asia and Caspian, 2017. Bishkek and Tashkent to construct a hydropower plant. [Online] Available at: https://hydropowercongress.com/en/news-en/bishkek-tashkent-construct-hydropower-plant/ [Accessed July 2022].

Hydropower Sustainability Council, 2022. Hydropower capacity building in Tajikistan. [Online] Available at: https://www.hydrosustainability.org/capacity-building-tajikistan [Accessed July 2022].

IAEA, 2021c. IAEA reviews Uzbekistan's nuclear power infrastructure development. [Online] Available at: https://www.iaea.org/newscenter/pressreleases/iaea-reviews-uzbekistans-nuclear-power-infrastructure-development [Accessed July 2022].

IEA, 2020a. *Kazakhstan energy profile*, Paris: IEA.

IEA, 2020b. *Power Systems in Transition*, Paris: IEA.

IEA, 2020c. *World Energy Outlook 2020*, Paris: OECD International Energy Agency.

IEA, 2021a. IEA launches cross-border electricity trading roadmap for Tajikistan to fully benefit from its unique hydropower potential. [Online] Available at: https://www.iea.org/news/iea-launches-cross-border-electricity-trading-roadmap-for-tajikistan-to-fully-benefit-from-its-unique-hydropower-potential [Accessed July 2022].

IEA, 2021b. Pathway to critical and formidable goal of net-zero emissions by 2050 is narrow but brings huge benefits, according to IEA special report. [Online] Available at: https://www.iea.org/news/pathway-to-critical-and-formidable-goal-of-net-zero-emissions-by-2050-is-narrow-but-brings-huge-benefits [Accessed July 2022].

IEA, 2021c. Net Zero by 2050: A Roadmap for the Global Energy Sector. [Online] Available at: https://iea.blob.core.windows.net/assets/20959e2e-7ab8-4f2a-b1c6-4e63387f03a1/NetZeroby2050-ARoadmapfortheGlobalEnergySector_CORR.pdf [Accessed July 2022].

IEA, 2021d. *The Role of Critical Minerals in Clean Energy Transitions*, Paris: IEA.

Interfax.ru, 2022a. Rossia i Kaza⊠hstan sozdadut rabochuyu gruppu po uvelicheniyu tranzita nefti v Kitai. [Online] Available at: https://www.interfax.ru/business/830382 [Accessed July 2022].

Interfax.ru, 2022b. Vozobnovlenie rabot po stroitel'stvu gazoprovoda TAPI nameсheno na mart. [Online] Available at: https://www.interfax.ru/world/815692 [Accessed July 2022].

International Hydropower Association, 2022a. Kyrgyzstan. [Online] Available at: https://www.hydropower.org/country-profiles/kyrgyzstan [Accessed July 2022].

International Hydropower Association, 2022b. Tajikistan. [Online] Available at: https://www.hydropower.org/country-profiles/tajikistan [Accessed July 2022].

International Trade Administration, 2021. Kyrgyz Republic - Energy. [Online] Available at: https://www.trade.gov/country-commercial-guides/kyrgyz-republic-energy#:~:text=Hydropower,Kyrgyz%20Republic%20 (nearly%2090%25) [Accessed July 2022].

Jona, T., 2015. EIB supports power interconnection between Tajikistan and Kyrgyzstan. [Online] Available at: https://www.eib.org/en/press/all/2015-130-eib-supports-power-interconnection-between-tajikistan-and-kyrgyzstan [Accessed July 2022].

Kegoc.kz, 2022. Elektroenergetika Kazahstana: kljuchevye fakty. [Online] Available at: https://www.kegoc.kz/ru/electric-power/elektroenergetika-kazakhstana/ [Accessed July 2022].

Khan, S. K., 2021. Taliban pledge mega gas pipeline project's security in Afghanistan. [Online] Available at: https://www.aa.com.tr/en/asia-pacific/taliban-pledge-mega-gas-pipeline-projects-security-in-afghanistan/2407241 [Accessed July 2022].

Kumar, H., 2021. The top ten nuclear energy-producing countries in 2021. [Online] Available at: https://www.power-technology.com/features/top-ten-nuclear-energy-producing-countries/ [Accessed July 2022].

Lopes, F., 2021. How natural gas could thwart or support India's renewables progress. [Online] Available at: https://www.business-standard.com/article/ current-affairs/how-natural-gas-could-thwart-or-support-india-s-renewables-progress-121101900140_1.html [Accessed July 2022].

Malik, V., 2019. The future of oil in 2050. [Online] Available at: https://energy.economictimes.indiatimes.com/energy-speak/the-future-of-oil-in-2050/3866 [Accessed July 2022].

Mazina, M., 2021. «Sber» predskazal neft' Urals po $26 za barrel' k 2050 godu. [Online] Available at: https://quote.rbc.ru/news/article/60dc69fe9a7947ee375b9076 [Accessed July 2022].

McKeever, V., 2021. Oil could plummet to $10 by 2050 if Paris climate goals are achieved, energy consultancy says. [Online] Available at: https://www.cnbc.com/2021/04/15/oil-could-plummet-to-10-by-2050-if-paris-climate-goals-are-achieved.html [Accessed July 2022].

Meredith, S., 2021. What 'energy transition'? Global fossil fuel use is accelerating and set to get even worse. [Online] Available at: https://www.cnbc.com/2021/04/14/climate-global-fossil-fuel-use-accelerating-and-set-to-get-even-worse.html [Accessed July 2022].

Minenergy.uz, 2021. Minenergo: kak obespechivaetsja rastushhee energosnabzhenie v Uzbekistane. [Online] Available at: https://minenergy.uz/ru/news/view/1063 [Accessed July 2022].

Morning Express, 2021. Ashgabat and Baku are negotiating on joint development of the Dostluk field in the Caspian. [Online] Available at: https://morningexpress.in/ashgabat-and-baku-are-negotiating-on-joint-development-of-the-dostluk-field-in-the-caspian/ [Accessed July 2022].

Murat, A., 2021. 6,3% sostavil rost potreblenija elektroenergii v Kazahstane po itogam 2021 goda. [Online] Available at: https://www.inform.kz/ru/6-3-sostavil-rost-potrebleniya-elektroenergii-v-kazahstane-po-itogam-2021-goda_a3876871 [Accessed July 2022].

Murray, J., 2020a. How the six major oil companies have invested in renewable energy projects. [Online] Available at: https://www.nsenergybusiness.com/features/oil-companies-renewable-energy/ [Accessed July 2022].

Murray, J., 2020b. Which major oil companies have set net-zero emissions targets? [Online] Available at: https://www.nsenergybusiness.com/features/oil-companies-net-zero/ [Accessed July 2022].

Najibullah, F., 2021. Tajikistan Faces Crippling Electricity Shortages, But Officials In Denial. [Online] Available at: https://www.rferl.org/a/tajikistan-energy-shortages-official-denials/31544068.html [Accessed July 2022].

Neft i Kapital, 2022. Kazakhstan khochet postroit' vtoruyu AES na Irtyshe. [Online] Available at: https://oilcapital.ru/news/companies/05-08-2022/kazahstan-hochet-postroit-vtoruyu-aes-na-irtyshe [Accessed August 2022].

Nurbay, R., 2021. Uglerodnaya neytral'nost': ozvuchen scenariy po dostizheniyu nulevyh vybrosov v Kazakhstane. [Online] Available at: https://strategy2050.kz/ru/news/uglerodnaya-neytralnost-ozvuchen-stsenariy-po-dostizheniyu-nulevykh-vybrosov-v-kazakhstane/ [Accessed July 2022].

Nurtazin, A., 2019. Ugol'noj generacii Kazahstana prorochat horoshee budushhee. [Online] Available at: https://kapital.kz/economic/76502/ugol-noy-generatsii-kazakhstana-prorochat-khorosheye-budushcheye.html [Accessed July 2022].

Oilgas.gov.tm, 2021. The products of the Kiyanly Polymer Plant are in demand in the domestic market and abroad. [Online] Available at: https://www.oilgas.gov.tm/en/posts/news/3081/the-products-of-the-kiyanly-polymer-plant-are-in-demand-in-the-domestic-market-and-abroad [Accessed July 2022].

Paillere, H. & Donovan, J., 2021. Nuclear Power 10 Years After Fukushima: The Long Road Back. [Online] Available at: https://www.iaea.org/newscenter/news/nuclear-power-10-years-after-fukushima-the-long-road-back [Accessed July 2022].

Pannier, B., 2021. Power Outage: Winter Is Starting To Look Colder And Darker For Kyrgyzstan. [Online] Available at: https://www.rferl.org/a/kyrgyzstan-power-outage-winter-colder/31572858.html [Accessed July 2022].

Parnell, J., 2020. BP Aims to Build 50GW of Renewables by 2030, Cut Fossil Fuel Output by 40%. [Online] Available at: https://www.greentechmedia.com/articles/read/bp-to-invest-5b-a-year-on-low-carbon-and-cut-fossil-fuel-output-by-40-percent-by-2030 [Accessed July 2022].

Peretok.ru, 2021. Kazakhstan zhdet rosta vyrabotki energii na 26% k 2030 godu i dumaet o stroitel'stve AES. [Online] Available at: https://peretok.ru/news/trading/24375/ [Accessed July 2022].

Perkins, R., 2021. World needs no new oil, gas projects under path to net-zero emissions by 2050: IEA. [Online] Available at: www.spglobal.com/platts/en/market-insights/latest-news/natural-gas/051821-world-needs-no-new-oil-gas-projects-under-path-to-net-zero-emissions-by-2050-iea [Accessed July 2022].

Petroleum Institute of Pakistan, 2011. Pakistan Energy Outlook (2010/11 to 2025/26). [Online] Available at: https://www.pip.org.pk/images/Outlook_Executive_Summary.pdf [Accessed July 2022].

Petushkova, V., 2021. Kitayskie atomshhiki zapuskayut «Drakona». [Online] Available at: https://www.fondsk.ru/news/2021/04/27/kitajskie-atomschiki-zapuskajut-drakona-53459.html [Accessed July 2022].

Pirani, S., 2019. *Central Asian Gas: Prospects for the 2020s*, Oxford: Oxford Institute for Energy Studies.

Putz, C., 2015. Uzbekistan Still Hates the Rogun Dam Project. [Online] Available at: https://thediplomat.com/2015/08/uzbekistan-still-hates-the-rogun-dam-project/ [Accessed July 2022].

Pyrkalo, S., 2015. EBRD invests in energy reform and transmission system upgrade in Tajikistan. [Online] Available at: https://www.ebrd.com/news/2015/ebrd-invests-in-energy-reform-and-transmission-system-upgrade-in-tajikistan-.html [Accessed July 2022].

Rapier, R., 2020. Fossil Fuels Still Supply 84 Percent Of World Energy — And Other Eye Openers From BP's Annual Review. [Online] Available at: https://www.forbes.com/sites/rrapier/2020/06/20/bp-review-new-highs-in-global-energy-consumption-and-carbon-emissions-in-2019/?sh=49bb421a66a1 [Accessed July 2022].

Rathi, A., Ratcliffe, V. & Paola, A. D., 2021. UAE Eyes First Net Zero by 2050 Goal Among Major Petrostates. [Online] Available at: https://www.bloomberg.com/news/articles/2021-06-24/uae-eyes-first-net-zero-by-2050-goal-among-major-petrostates [Accessed July 2022].

Reuters, 2012. Turkmen leader sacks oil and gas minister. [Online] Available at: https://www.reuters.com/article/uk-turkmenistan-gas-idUKBRE84O13620120525 [Accessed July 2022].

Reuters, 2018. Sixth member of gas pipeline clearance team killed in Afghanistan. [Online] Available at: https://www.reuters.com/article/us-afghanistan-tapi-idUSKCN1IO0SE [Accessed July 2022].

Reuters, 2021. Iran, Turkmenistan and Azerbaijan sign gas swap deal. [Online] Available at: https://www.reuters.com/markets/commodities/iran-turkmenistan-azerbaijan-sign-gas-swap-deal-2021-11-28/ [Accessed July 2022].

Ritchie, H. & Roser, M., 2020. Energy mix. [Online] Available at: https://ourworldindata.org/energy-mix [Accessed July 2022].

Sgcc.uz, 2022. Shurtan gas chemical complex - official website. [Online] Available at: https://sgcc.uz/en/ [Accessed July 2022].

Sidorovich, V., 2021. Pravitel'stvo Uzbekistana opublikovalo plan perehoda k uglerodno-neytral'noy elektroenergetike. [Online] Available at: https://renen.ru/pravitelstvo-uzbekistana-opublikovalo-plan-perehoda-k-uglerodno-nejtralnoj-elektroenergetike/ [Accessed July 2022].

Spot.uz, 2018. RIA Novosti: Uzbekistan i Rossia dogovorilis' o stroitel'stve AES. [Online] Available at: https://www.spot.uz/ru/2018/06/21/atom/ [Accessed July 2022].

Spot.uz, 2019a. Stoimost' stroitel'stva AES v Uzbekistane opredelyat k koncu goda. [Online] Available at: https://www.spot.uz/ru/2019/10/22/nuclear/ [Accessed July 2022].

Spot.uz, 2019b. V «Uzatome» podtverdili vybor prioritetnoy ploshhadki dlya AES v Dzhizakskoy oblasti. [Online] Available at: https://www.spot.uz/ru/2019/05/31/atom/ [Accessed July 2022].

Spot.uz, 2021. Kak i zachem Uzbekistan delaet stavku na zelenuyu energetiku. [Online] Available at: https://www.spot.uz/ru/2021/09/14/renewable-energy/ [Accessed July 2022].

Steiner, C., 2019. A Pipeline as Lifeline: The Environmental Benefits of TAPI. [Online] Available at: https://thediplomat.com/2019/08/a-pipeline-as-lifeline-the-environmental-benefits-of-tapi/ [Accessed July 2022].

Tajikistan Mission, 2009. Tajikistan Mission - Energy. [Online] Available at: https://www.tajikistanmission.ch/all-about-of-tajikistan/energy.html#:~:text=Tajikistan%20has%20enormous%20hydro%20power,its%20potential%20is%20in%20use. [Accessed July 2022].

Tajikta.tj, 2013. Tadzhikskaya alyuminievaya kompanija TALCO raspolagaet znachitel'nym potencialom po energosberezheniyu - Norsk Energi. [Online] Available at: https://tajikta.tj/ru/news/tadzhikskaya-alyuminievaya-kompaniya-talco-raspolagaet-znachitelnym-potentsialom-po-energosberezheniyu-norsk-energi [Accessed July 2022].

Tazabek, 2022a. U Kazakhstana net drugogo varianta, krome ctroitel'stva atomnoi electrostantsii, - Minenergo RK. [Online] Available at: https://www.tazabek.kg/news:1797261 [Accessed August 2022].

Tazabek, 2022b. Kompaniya iz OAE gotova postroit' v Kyrgyzstane solnechnuyu stanciyu moshhnost'yu 200 MVt. [Online] Available at: https://www.tazabek.kg/news:1775391?from=portal&place=last&b=2 [Accessed July 2022].

Tengrinews.kz, 2021. Kazakhstanu nuzhna atomnaya stanciya - Tokaev. [Online] Available at: https://tengrinews.kz/kazakhstan_news/kazahstanu-nujna-atomnaya-stantsiya-tokaev-447558/ [Accessed July 2022].

Twidale, S., 2021. Renewables overtook fossil fuels in EU electricity mix in 2020: Report. [Online] Available at: https://www.reuters.com/article/us-eu-renewables-idUSKBN29T0T8 [Accessed July 2022].

U.S. Energy Information Administration, 2021. U.S. energy Information Administration - EIA - independent statistics and analysis. [Online] Available at: https://www.eia.gov/opendata/v1/qb.php?sdid=INTL.3-6-AFG-TCF.A [Accessed July 2022].

USAID.gov, 2022. The USAID CASA-1000 secretariat activity fact sheet. [Online] Available at: https://www.usaid.gov/central-asia-regional/fact-sheets/secretariat-casa-1000-power-transmission [Accessed July 2022].

UzDaily.uz, 2022. Proizvodstvo elektroenergii v Respublike Uzbekistan. [Online] Available at: https://www.uzdaily.uz/ru/post/66292 [Accessed July 2022].

World Bank, 2014. Energy imports, net (% of energy use) - Tajikistan. [Online] Available at: https://data.worldbank.org/indicator/EG.IMP.CONS.ZS?locations=TJ [Accessed July 2022].

World Bank, 2016. *Central Asia: Enhancing Regional Power Trade in Central Asia*, Washington, DC: The International Bank for Reconstruction and Development/The World Bank.

World Bank, 2020a. Access to electricity (% of population). [Online] Available at: https://data.worldbank.org/indicator/EG.ELC.ACCS.ZS?view=chart [Accessed July 2022].

World Bank, 2020b. World Bank Provides Additional Resources for the Rehabilitation of the Nurek Hydropower Plant in Tajikistan. [Online] Available at: https://www.worldbank.org/en/news/press-release/2020/06/26/world-bank-provides-additional-resources-for-the-rehabilitation-of-the-nurek-hydropower-plant-in-tajikistan [Accessed July 2022].

World Bank, 2022. Central Asia South Asia Electricity Transmission and Trade Project (CASA-1000). [Online] Available at: https://projects.worldbank.org/en/projects-operations/project-detail/P145054 [Accessed July 2022].

World Nuclear Association, 2018. The Harmony Programme. [Online] Available at: https://world-nuclear.org/our-association/what-we-do/the-harmony-programme.aspx [Accessed July 2022].

World Nuclear Association, 2022a. Nuclear Power in Japan. [Online] Available at: https://world-nuclear.org/focus/fukushima-daiichi-accident/japan-nuclear-power.aspx [Accessed July 2022].

World Nuclear Association, 2022b. Nuclear Power in the World Today. [Online] Available at: https://world-nuclear.org/information-library/current-and-future-generation/nuclear-power-in-the-world-today.aspx [Accessed July 2022].

Worldometers, 2015. Turkmenistan Natural Gas. [Online] Available at: https://www.worldometers.info/gas/turkmenistan-natural-gas/#:~:text=Turkmenistan%20holds%20265%20trillion%20cubic,gas%20reserves%20of%206%2C923%20Tcf [Accessed July 2022].

Xu, Y., 2020a. Pakistan mulls major gas infrastructure expansion as demand set to spike. [Online] Available at: https://www.upstreamonline.com/lng/pakistan-mulls-major-gas-infrastructure-expansion-as-demand-set-to-spike/2-1-908731 [Accessed July 2022].

Xu, Y., 2020b. CNPC says China's emissions and oil demand to peak in 2025. [Online] Available at: https://www.upstreamonline.com/energy-transition/cnpc-says-chinas-emissions-and-oil-demand-to-peak-in-2025/2-1-933609 [Accessed July 2022].

Zheng, X., 2021. N-power in new phase of high quality. [Online] Available at: http://epaper.chinadaily.com.cn/a/202104/16/WS6078d0eea31099a23435576a.html [Accessed July 2022].

Zhunisbek, A., 2020. Prospects and Challenges in Realizing the TAPI Project. [Online] Available at: https://www.eurasian-research.org/publication/prospects-and-challenges-in-realizing-the-tapi-project/ [Accessed July 2022].

10 Water

History

Historians rightly pronounce Ancient Egypt as the most ancient river civilisation which, thanks to the mighty Nile, retained its power for 3,000 years. There are dozens of other examples of historical riverine civilisations. For example, the presence of the great Tigris and Euphrates rivers allowed Babylon to become the world's leading city and hold this position for 2000 years. The great Chinese civilisation, dating back 4,000 years, originated and actively developed along its great rivers, the Yellow River and the Yangtze. Waterways could be described as the backbone of many ancient civilisations, but even today they are as important as ever; access to water resources is critical to modern civilisations as well. Currently, more than 2.8 billion people worldwide suffer from water scarcity (Xingcai Liu, 2022). Experts predict that by 2050, the number of countries facing water scarcity or shortages could rise to 54, affecting a total population of 4 billion, or about 40 per cent of the projected global population of 9.4 billion by then (Rekacewicz, 2006). What is the picture in Central Asia?

Rivers in Central Asia – Then and Now (Water and Employment)

Water has been a principal means of connecting the peoples of Central Asia for centuries: physically, economically, and culturally. Due to its natural features and geographical location, Central Asia is one of the most extensive regions on earth with water resources and these are often of the highest quality, for example being used for drinking water. However, despite this, most of the region's rivers flow into inland lakes or disappear into the desert because of filtration and evaporation. For the entire region, where the dominant share of water has always been directed to the fields since ancient times, the history of water relations is mainly the history of irrigation. The region's climatic conditions determined the appearance of the first centres of civilisation in the fertile land of the river basins.

The most important rivers in Central Asia are the Amu Darya (formerly called the Oxus) and the Syr Darya (formerly called the Yaksart), whose

DOI: 10.4324/9781003360728-13

sources are in the Pamir and Tien Shan mountains. They flow through the deserts of the Karakum and Kyzylkum, respectively, before entering the Aral Sea in the middle of the desert. The annual flow of the Amudarya is 73.6 km^3 (Menga, 2020). More than 35 reservoirs regulate almost 80 per cent of the Amu Darya, with a capacity of more than 10 million m^3. The annual runoff volume reaching the Syr Darya's trunk is 30.8 km3 (Menga, 2020), and these waters are used for irrigation. Nevertheless, Central Asia has long been a territory where the climate is changing, and the rivers are one of the most affected areas. The current runoff volume at the mouth of this river has decreased more than ten times, from 400 m^3 per second to 30 m^3 per second, compared with the period before 1960. Once upon a time, our two largest rivers, the Amu Darya and the Syr Darya flowed into the Caspian Sea, but now they hardly reach the Aral Sea, which is contributing to this sea's own sad story.

The Tragedy of the Aral Sea

Back in 1960, the Aral Sea area was the fourth-largest lake in the world, with a surface area of 66,000 km^2 (Streshnev, 2001). Since then, the volume of water in the Aral Sea and its overall volume have been in rapid decline. In 1989, the ever shallower waters of the sea split it into two separate bodies of water. In 2014, the southeastern section completely dried up, with overall levels reaching a historical minimum area of just 7,297 km^2 that year. The shrinking Aral Sea poses a more serious yet less obvious additional threat to climate change, specifically the disappearance of glaciers. As the settled salt from the bottom of the sea rises into the atmosphere, it later falls on glaciers, contributing to their accelerated melting.

However, the story of the Aral Sea is not completely bleak. Thanks to some environmental measures taken by the governments and the World Bank, the sea area has begun to stabilise and water levels have even slightly increased. Magzum Mirzagaliyev, Minister of Ecology, Geology and Natural Resources of Kazakhstan, said last year that as part of the programme to restore the Aral Sea, the water surface area has increased by as much as 40 per cent. The important work to restore the Aral Sea will continue, for example, in projects where agronomists will actively plant trees in dry areas (Ogurtsov, 2021). But, why is the Aral Sea receiving so much attention?

Irrigation and Environment

During the Soviet period, Moscow managed the Aral Sea basin as a single economic project, and the Ministry of Land Reclamation and Water Resources determined the distribution and use of the waters of the Amu Darya and Syr Darya rivers, prioritising economic interests exclusively (International Crisis Group, 2005).

From the 1950s to the 1980s, the Soviet Planning Committee (Gosplan) developed and financed a complex system of canals, reservoirs, and pumping stations to grow cotton as the main crop in developing the region's economy. On the territory of Uzbekistan, engineers built about 170,000 kilometres of canals for irrigation of 4.2 million hectares of land (International Monetary Fund, 1992). As a result of these water distribution policies, 90 per cent of Soviet cotton was grown in the republics of Central Asia (CIA Historical Review Program, 1955). In addition, the largest-ever irrigation project was the construction of the Karakum Canal, which diverted water from the Amu Darya for 1,400 kilometres to the deserts of Turkmenistan. With this in mind, the rivers of the region could be understood as key players in the Soviet industrialisation drive.

Because of its geography, most of the cultivated land in Central Asia is in need of and subject to artificial irrigation. In Kyrgyzstan, 75 per cent of cultivated land is irrigated (AHT Group AG Management and Engineering, 2013), in Tajikistan 84 per cent (Sehring, 2006), in Uzbekistan 89 per cent (Agarwal, 2019) and in Turkmenistan, 100 per cent of cultivated land requires artificial irrigation (Lerman & Stanchin, 2010). Agriculture constitutes a fundamentally important aspect of Central Asia, economically as much as culturally.

Over half of Central Asia's population lives in rural areas. The rural population ranges from about half of the total in Kazakhstan and Turkmenistan, and two-thirds in Tajikistan and the Kyrgyz Republic. Agriculture employs about half of the Central Asian workforce, or over 15 million people (International Labour Organization, ILOSTAT database, 2022). Irrigated agriculture accounts for a significant percentage of GDP in the Central Asian states; in 2019, it was 15 per cent of GDP in Kazakhstan, 19 per cent in Kyrgyzstan, 21 per cent in Turkmenistan, 26 per cent in Uzbekistan, and 45 per cent in Tajikistan (International Labour Organization, ILOSTAT database, 2021).

Currently, out of the total land resources of Central Asia, which is about 154.9 million hectares, 32.6 million hectares are considered suitable for irrigation, and the actual area of irrigated land is about 7.9 million hectares. This means that only 2 per cent of Central Asia is irrigated. Non-irrigated areas (pastures, hayfields, meadows, perennial fallows) occupy about 54 million hectares. This area includes nearly 2 million hectares of non-irrigated arable land, but its productivity averages no more than 10 per cent of the productivity of irrigated lands (CAWater-Info, 2022).

Where does all the water come from? Glaciers play a crucial role in the water cycle in Central Asia. The melting of snow and glaciers in the Pamirs and the Tien Shan Mountain Range provides water for all of Central Asia. Glaciers can store water as ice for decades and carry winter precipitation into the summer months, releasing it as meltwater. This is an essential process in seasonally dry regions such as Central Asia, where there is often no rainfall for months. For this reason, meltwater fully determines the local and regional water supply. As discussed previously, due to climate change the glaciers are experiencing significant losses in mass and area. Along the Tien Shan, Central Asia's most extensive mountain range, glaciers have lost 27 per cent of their mass and 18 per cent of their area over the past 50 years. An international research team has calculated that almost 3,000 square kilometres of glaciers and an average of 5.4 gigatons of ice per year have been lost since the 1960s (Farinotti, et al., 2015). The authors calculated that by the 2050s, about half of the Tien Shan glaciers could be depleted (Kirby, 2015).

If ecologists' calculations are correct, then Central Asia will lose two-thirds of its glaciers and two-thirds of its water within a century. How can agriculture, which employs more than half of the population of Central Asia, develop under these conditions? And with such a disappointing forecast, is there a need to build the giant hydroelectric power plants discussed in the previous chapter if they will relatively quickly become inefficient and unprofitable? The problem of climate change in Central Asia is not just a distant theoretical task but a hazardous reality, and the countries of the region should start addressing this global threat now.

The management of water and its nations, though, is not something that the countries of Central Asia are unfamiliar with. During Soviet times, the five Central Asian republics managed to develop water management projects that significantly changed the geographical map and the living conditions of people in a short time. There were never any disputes between the countries around water issues. However, the sudden "parade of sovereignties" from 1991 not only threw back the level of socio-economic development of the young states by a few decades but also awakened the symptoms of separatism and a struggle for leadership in the region. It took the countries of Central Asia twenty-five years to realise the undoubtable advantage of the Soviet cooperation model in water and energy matters, compared to senseless separatist ideas. The reality that faces Central Asia now, is that although there are many unresolved problems in the region, water problems play and will continue to play a primary role in economic and social development and are essential for maintaining peace and harmony in the area. The question is how to channel the water for these purposes.

Tensions Between Upstream and Downstream Countries

The dissolution of the Soviet Union destroyed the economic basis of the highly centralised water management system that had existed for more than half a century. Now, regular disputes on water resources arise between two clusters of countries. Three 'downstream' countries – Kazakhstan, Turkmenistan, and Uzbekistan, which consume vast amounts of water for growing various crops; and two 'upstream' countries – Kyrgyzstan and Tajikistan. The downstream countries are increasingly demanding more water for their expanding agricultural sectors and growing populations. Meanwhile, the economically weaker upstream countries are trying to manage their water resources and want more water to generate electricity and cultivate the land. Tensions are building around the region's two main rivers that empty into the Aral Sea, the Syr Darya, which originates in the Kyrgyz Republic and flows through Uzbekistan and Kazakhstan, and the Amu Darya, which flows from Tajikistan through Uzbekistan and Turkmenistan.

Uzbekistan does not control the sources of the three main rivers – the Syr Darya, Amu Darya and Zarafshan (which in ancient times was a tributary of the Amu Darya, but now does not reach it due to water withdrawals for irrigation). Yet its irrigated crop production depends on these rivers because 91 per cent of the water sources are outside its territorial borders (Smith, 1995). Similarly, 98 per cent of Turkmenistan's water sources originate outside its borders (Smith, 1995). Additionally, 43 per cent of Kazakhstan's average annual river flow originates outside the country. The sudden end to the central management of the region's water and energy resources from Moscow in 1991 quickly exposed the issue of whose territory on which water sources are located. The downstream states, water consumers for irrigated agriculture, found themselves in a weaker position than the upstream countries, and there was no longer any authority which had the legal right to resolve conflicts over the allocation and use of water.

Not surprisingly, shortly after independence, the five states agreed to maintain the Soviet principle of water quotas. In 1992, the five republics signed the Almaty Agreement to maintain the status quo and continue the Soviet-era water-sharing arrangement. However, this system quickly fell apart when the civil war in Tajikistan and political unrest in the Kyrgyz Republic led to the collapse of the water monitoring system. The control mechanisms stopped working, and countries began to accuse each other of exceeding quotas. It was alleged that Turkmenistan consumed too much water to the detriment of Uzbekistan, which in turn accused Kazakhstan of exceeding water consumption norms. Kyrgyzstan and Tajikistan considered that all three downstream countries systematically exceeded their allocated quotas. Even within the downstream countries, different regions accused each other of using too much water.

As might have been expected, the greatest controversy has developed around barter transactions. Following agreements, the upstream countries supplied water to Uzbekistan and Kazakhstan in exchange for energy resources – gas, coal, or electricity. For example, under the original barter agreements, Kyrgyzstan supplied Uzbekistan and Kazakhstan with water during the summer months in exchange for gas and coal, respectively, during the winter months (Protocol of the Meeting of Representatives of Fuel-Energy and Water Management Complexes of Kazakhstan, Kyrgyzstan, and Uzbekistan on Problem of the Toktogul Cascade Water-Energy Resources Use in 1996, 1996). Kyrgyzstan sold its surplus electricity generated from hydroelectric power plants during the summer months to Uzbekistan and Kazakhstan as part of these barter agreements. These first barter agreements were still based on the Soviet Protocol No. 413 of February 7, 1984. According to this protocol, Uzbekistan receives 46 per cent of the river's total surface runoff of 22.7 billion cubic meters, Kazakhstan gets 44 per cent, Tajikistan receives 8 per cent, and Kyrgyzstan 2 per cent (World Bank, 2004).

However, because energy supplies were unreliable, the upstream countries were forced to release more water through their hydroelectric dams in the winter to generate electricity. This resulted in flooding downstream land and less irrigation water in the summer months. Attempts by upstream countries to demand water payment resulted in resistance from downstream countries. As countries began to view the problem as a zero-sum game, each took steps to increase their control over water resources, often to the detriment of others. Until 2016, there was growing uncertainty in Central Asia about plans to build new reservoirs and dams or expand irrigated areas.

Regional Water Security

Tensions over water and energy resources became a fundamental factor in regional security and contributed to an increasingly tense political climate in the region in the 1990s and 2000s. Things went as far as hostile statements that countries were ready to defend their interests forcefully if needed and some countries conducted military exercises near borders, leading their neighbours to suspect that the drills were training for raids to seize water reservoirs. Cuts in gas supplies during cold periods and winter floods had a severe moral and psychological impact on the inhabitants of neighbouring countries. They increased ethnic tensions, especially in the densely populated Ferghana Valley.

Such dangerous incidents eventually led the neighbouring countries to recognise the need to develop mutually beneficial agreements on the use of border water and energy resources. For example, in 1998, Uzbekistan and the Kyrgyz Republic signed the first cooperation agreement on using energy and water resources in the Syr Darya basin. However, this agreement did not put an end to the problems.

The primary sources of tension between the countries of Central Asia are seasonal competition for the flow of major rivers and the high cost of maintaining reservoirs upstream, and climate change has done nothing but exacerbate these tensions. All available data on precipitation and river flows due to climate change indicate that severe weather events will become more powerful and more frequent. Data from national meteorological agencies indicate an increase in annual precipitation in winter and a decrease in summer, which determines the increase in floods and droughts. The unpredictability of water flows makes it more important to coordinate flood and reservoir management within a joint regional structure without fail. But unfortunately, until recently, the risk of climate shocks to water security was hardly part of the regional dialogue.

However, the situation gradually began to change in 2012 due to the conflict between Tajikistan and Uzbekistan regarding the construction of the Rogun hydroelectric power station. The World Bank was invited to participate in the debate as a referee and found itself in a rather difficult situation due to the two countries' opposing positions on the practicalities of construction. The Bank's analysis showed the benefits of additional water conservation considering the increasing risks of drought and flooding. However, Uzbekistan's concerns about building a large reservoir upstream seriously hampered effective high-level dialogue on regional water management. A general discussion initiated in 2014 with mid-level government representatives and civil society generated interest in climate-related risks to the region's water security, but agreements and policies on the way forward in light of ongoing climate-related and political developments have not yet been forthcoming.

Conclusion

Throughout Central Asia's history, managing its water resources has been critical to its economic, social, and political survival, and this will continue to be the case in the future. The water in the region is not only the most crucial component in climate change, energy policy or agricultural development, but a condition for the peaceful coexistence of its people and nations. Currently, scarce and threatened water resources are being used inefficiently, resulting in low agricultural productivity and environmental damage. Despite some progress, upstream and downstream countries do not trust each other and are not willing to cooperate in managing water resources. Climate change, and the associated rapid melting of glaciers, threaten to undermine not only the entire water and energy balance of the region, but leave vast agricultural lands without irrigation, potentially leading to mass displacement of people.

As discussed in the chapter on energy security in Central Asia, the situation with the region's water problems changed in 2016 when the President of Uzbekistan launched initiatives to jointly build large hydropower plants in the Kyrgyz Republic (Hydropower Congress, 2017) and Tajikistan (Eurasianet, 2018). This is one significant step forward, and now is truly the time for such creative solutions to the pressing water problems. Here, the task of strengthening trust between countries through practical dialogue and mutual incentives comes to the fore.

References

Agarwal, A., 2019. ORF: Water woes in Central Asia: Can SCO offer a solution? [Online] Available at: https://www.orfonline.org/expert-speak/water-woes-in-central-asia-can-sco-offer-a-solution/ [Accessed 2 July 2022].

AHT Group AG Management and Engineering, 2013. *Kyrgyz Republic: Developing Water Resources Sector Strategies in Central and West Asia*, Bishkek: Asian Development Bank.

CAWater-Info, 2022. CAWater-Info: Land resources of the Aral Sea basin. [Online] Available at: http://www.cawater-info.net/aral/land_e.htm [Accessed 2 July 2022].

CIA Historical Review Program, 1955. *Soviet Cotton Production in the Postwar Period*, s.l.: Princeton Collection.

Eurasianet, 2018. Eurasianet: Uzbekistan gives backing to Tajikistan's hydropower project. [Online] Available at: https://eurasianet.org/uzbekistan-gives-backing-to-tajikistans-hydropower-project [Accessed 2 July 2022].

Farinotti, D. *et al.*, 2015. Substantial glacier mass loss in the Tien Shan over the past 50 years. *Nature Geoscience*, Issue 8, p. 716–722.

Hydropower Congress, 2017. Hydropower Congress: Bishkek and Tashkent to construct a hydropower plant. [Online] Available at: https://hydropowercongress.com/en/news-en/bishkek-tashkent-construct-hydropower-plant/ [Accessed 2 July 2022].

International Crisis Group, 2005. *The Curse of Cotton: Central Asia's Destructive Monoculture*, Bishkek/Brussels: International Crisis Group.

International Labour Organization, ILOSTAT database, 2021. World Bank: Employment in agriculture (% of total employment) (modeled ILO estimate) - Europe & Central Asia. [Online] Available at: https://data.worldbank.org/indicator/SL.AGR.EMPL.ZS?locations=Z7 [Accessed 2 July 2022].

International Labour Organization, ILOSTAT database, 2022. World Bank: Labor force, total - Europe & Central Asia. [Online] Available at: https://data.worldbank.org/indicator/SL.TLF.TOTL.IN?locations=Z7 [Accessed 2 July 2022].

International Monetary Fund, 1992. *Uzbekistan*. Washington, DC: International Monetary Fund.

Kirby, A., 2015. The Energy Mix: Central Asia's glaciers may lose half their ice by mid-century. [Online] Available at: https://www.theenergymix.com/2015/08/21/central-asias-glaciers-may-lose-half-their-ice-by-mid-century/ [Accessed 2 July 2022].

Lerman, Z. & Stanchin, I., 2010. Water in Turkmenistan II. In: M. Arsel & M. Spoor, eds. *Water, Environmental Security and Sustainable Development: Conflict and Cooperation in Central Eurasia*. Abingdon: Routledge, pp. 250–266.

Menga, F., 2020. *Power and Water in Central Asia*. Abingdon: Routledge.

Ogurtsov, I., 2021. Liter. [Online] Available at: https://liter.kz/108185-2/ [Accessed 2 July 2022].

Protocol of the Meeting of Representatives of Fuel-Energy and Water Management Complexes of Kazakhstan, Kyrgyzstan, and Uzbekistan on Problem of the Toktogul Cascade Water-Energy Resources Use in 1996, 1996. *Protocol of the Meeting of Representatives of Fuel-Energy and Water Management Complexes of Kazakhstan, Kyrgyzstan, and Uzbekistan on Problem of the Toktogul Cascade Water-Energy Resources Use in 1996*, s.l.: ICWC Bulletin 11.

Rekacewicz, P., 2006. GRID-Arendal. [Online] Available at: https://www.grida.no/resources/5625 [Accessed 2 July 2022].

Sehring, J., 2006. The politics of irrigation reform in Tajikistan. *Discussion Papers / Zentrum für internationale Entwicklungs- und Umweltforschung*, Issue 29.

Smith, D., 1995. Environmental security and shared water resources in post-Soviet Central Asia. *Post Soviet Geography*, Issue 36, pp. 351–370.

Streshnev, R., 2001. OrexCA. [Online] Available at: https://www.orexca.com/rus/uzbekistan/aralsea.htm [Accessed 2 July 2022].

World Bank, 2004. *Water Energy Nexus in Central Asia: Improving Regional Cooperation in the Syr Darya Basin (English)*, Washington, DC: World Bank Group.

Xingcai Liu, e. a., 2022. Global agricultural water scarcity assessment incorporating blue and green water availability under future climate change. *Earth's Future*.

11 Governance and Institutions

Most policymakers, academics, donors, and recipients recognise that good governance and efficient public administration are critical components of sustainable economic growth. Initially based on a limited set of empirical indicators, this growing understanding has sparked interest in developing more accurate and detailed indices. This demand has led to impressive growth in the sources of indicators used to measure governments' performances, institutional quality, and citizens' perceptions. Some well-known institutions calculate and publish respective data for different countries and regions (UNDP & European Commission, 2004). One of the most recognised is the World Governance Indicators (WGI) produced by the World Bank (World Bank, 2021a). These indicators combine the opinions of the companies, experts and citizens who participated in the surveys. They are based on over thirty data sources from research organisations, think tanks, NGOs, international financial institutions, and private sector firms (World Bank, 2021b).

The definition of governance by the World Bank is as follows (World Bank, 2021c):

> Governance consists of the traditions and institutions by which authority in a country is exercised. This includes the process by which governments are selected, monitored, and replaced; the capacity of the government to effectively formulate and implement sound policies; and the respect of citizens and the state for the institutions that govern economic and social interactions among them.

The annual World Bank report covers six aspects of governance – voice and accountability, political stability and absence of violence, government effectiveness, regulatory quality, the rule of law, and control of corruption. These indicators aggregate quite a few data sources and combine the views of businesses, citizens, and expert survey respondents.

Figures 11.1–11.6 illustrates these indices from 1996 to 2020 for all five Central Asian countries. WGI reports note that the countries of Central Asia still rank in the bottom 35 per cent of the list, indicating that the quality of

DOI: 10.4324/9781003360728-14

governance and public administration is at a low level, and that these countries, though to differing degrees, must work to improve them.

The figures presented are the sum of all five countries combined. Each column is the product of the contributions of all countries to a specific indicator, and one can see both the individual contribution of the country and, most importantly, how the situation with each indicator changes throughout Central Asia. To get an idea of the indicator compared to the ideal case of 100, the y-axis score needs to be divided by five since we have summed the scores of all five countries.

The results presented must be taken with a degree of caution. There are shortcomings and biases in collecting information, processing, and calculating the final ranking. But one essential feature of this approach is that the same methodology has been used for twenty-five years. Therefore, if the quantitative parameters can be subjected to fair criticism, then the patterns and trends of the indicators deserve more trust. Thus, one can draw several conclusions on the dynamics of governance indicators in Central Asia.

According to the first aspect of governance – Voice and Accountability, shown in Figure 11.1 – the countries were at about the same low level as a quarter of a century ago. The Kyrgyz Republic remains the undisputed leader in voice and accountability, although its rating has not improved over the years. Kazakhstan, which follows, shows the same trend of non-improvement. A specific increase in the rating of Uzbekistan has become a new trend associated with a new policy of openness. It is generally understood that overly rapid changes in such a society are not advisable since a whole

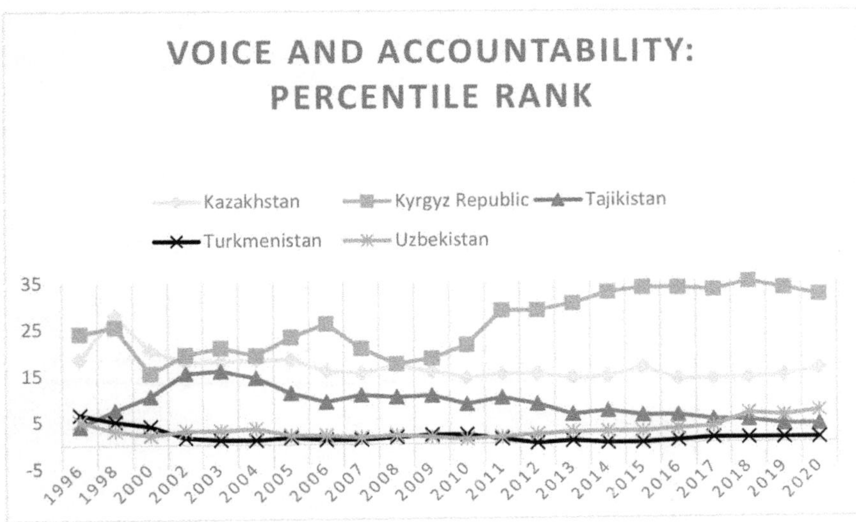

Figure 11.1 Voice and Accountability indices in Central Asian countries
Source: World Bank (2021c).

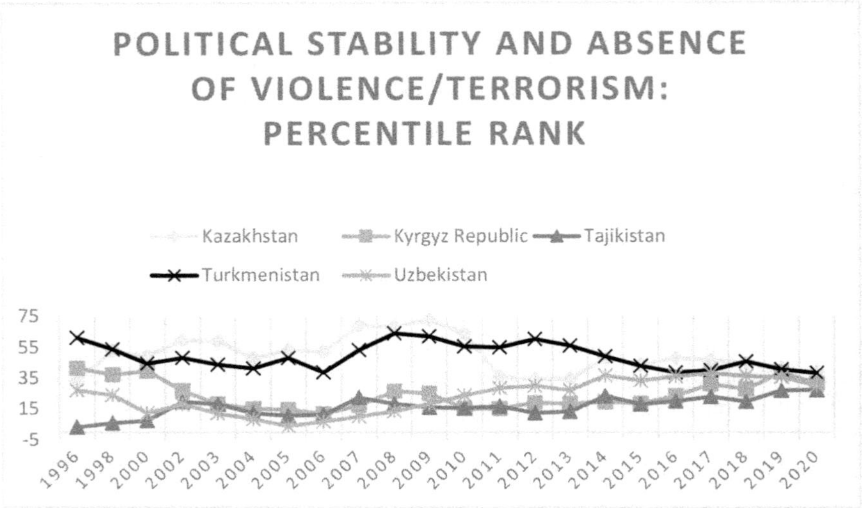

Figure 11.2 Political Stability and Absence of Violence/Terrorism indices in Central Asian countries
Source: World Bank (2021c)

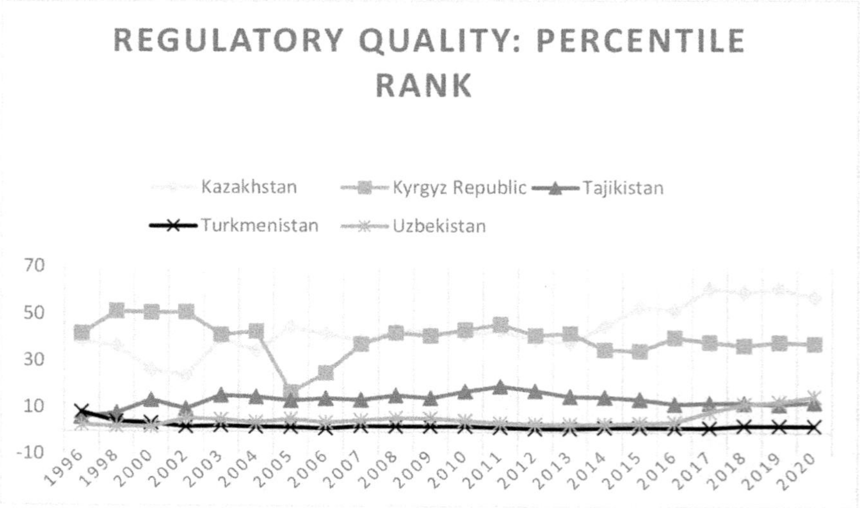

Figure 11.3 Regulatory Quality indices in Central Asian countries
Source: World Bank (2021c)

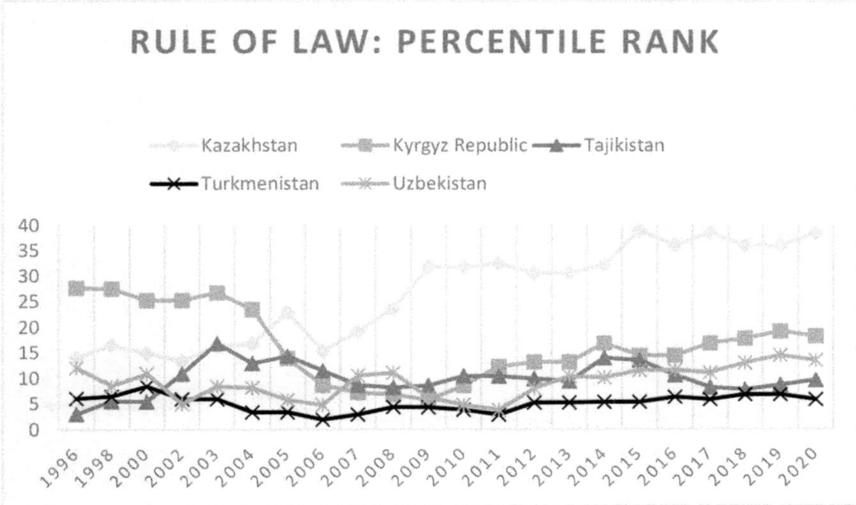

Figure 11.4 Rule of Law indices in Central Asian countries
Source: World Bank (2021c)

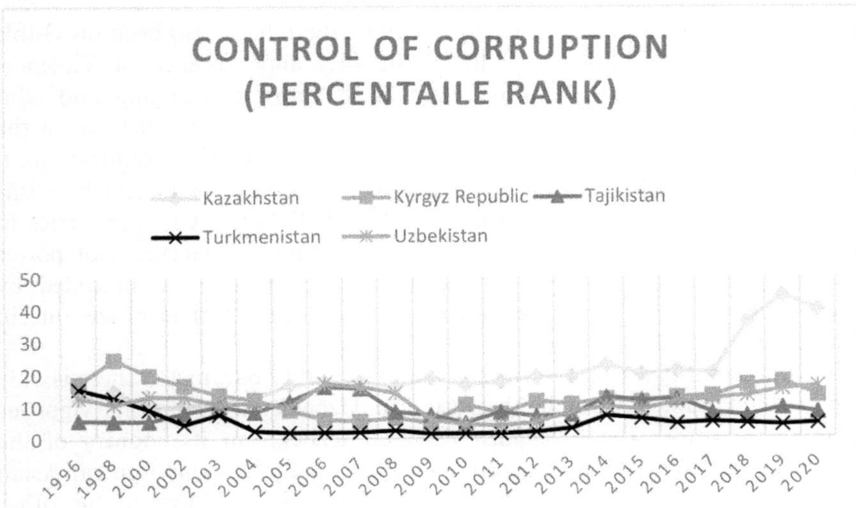

Figure 11.5 Control of Corruption indices in Central Asian countries
Source: World Bank (2021c)

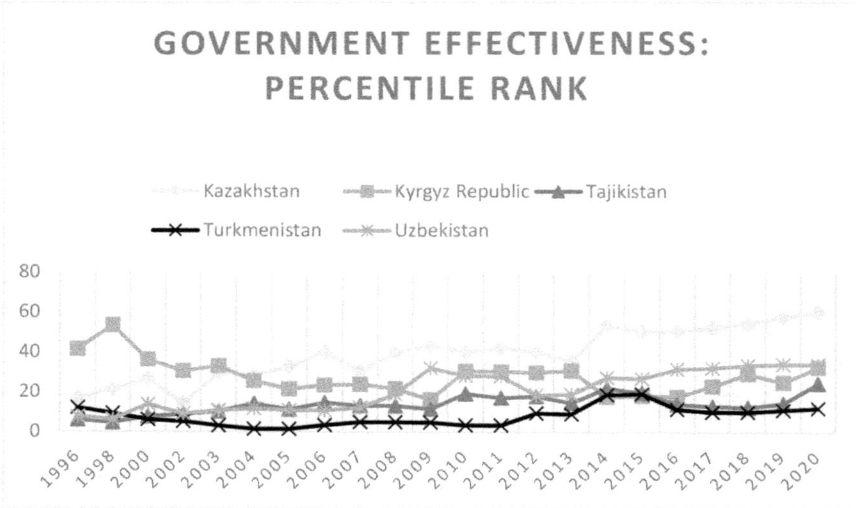

Figure 11.6 Government Effectiveness indices in Central Asian countries
Source: World Bank (2021c)

generation of its citizens grew up in a different and rather specific ideological environment. Therefore, a country with a population of many millions will require more gradual adaptation to the new political environment and the realities of life.

Since the publication of the ratings in 1996, there have also been no visible changes in the indicator for Political Stability and Absence of Violence/Terrorism (Figure 11.2). This indicator is the most challenging and controversial of all the governance indicators, which is especially relevant for the new states in transition. However, as far as the Central Asian countries go, it could be argued that this data is not entirely accurate. It is unclear how this rating could be approximately the same for all Central Asian countries in 2020, especially when we know that a revolutionary replacement of power occurred in the Kyrgyz Republic in 2020 and that this data also preceded, by just a few years, the unprecedented large-scale unrest that broke out in Kazakhstan in 2022.

As shown in Figure 11.3 in the Regulatory Quality parameter, there is only a very slight improvement in the rating in Uzbekistan despite its vigorous economic reforms. *The Economist* declared Uzbekistan its country of the year, arguing that "no other country travelled as far" as this Central Asian nation in 2019 regarding economic and other reforms. Most of the other reputable rating agencies have also recognised this fact. Therefore, the growth of this indicator in 2020, at least for Uzbekistan, should be much higher.

There are notable positive upward trends concerning the Rule of Law indicator (Figure 11.4). The overall numbers have doubled since 2006.

Moreover, in all countries except for Tajikistan, one can see growth. National governments are trying to ease business environments and improve the investment climate. Indeed, many positive laws have been written and approved, although there is no reliable supervision of the execution of the new legislation, and many agree that the judicial system remains the weakest link in the Rule of Law indicator. Judges in Central Asian countries have not become independent even after thirty years. Although almost the entire generation has changed, the current judges cannot get used to the fact that they can make decisions independently without looking back at the respective presidential administrations. Thus, the citizens remain unprotected by the judicial and executive branches of government. Weak protection of property rights and enforcement of contracts particularly undermine the trust of citizens and investors in public institutions. Civil society's faith in the judiciary is still at its lowest point, which means that the government will still be unable to create and maintain a reliable business environment and a predictable investment climate.

Figure 11.5 shows the Control of Corruption indicator. After some deterioration until the mid-2000s, the rates began to improve, although they are still at an unsatisfactory level. It is very difficult, and almost impossible, to hide anything in Central Asia. People meet in teahouses, cafes, and rallies and if someone knows something exciting today, thousands will know about it tomorrow. A person offended by one bureaucrat surely will tell dozens of others about it. However, this knowledge is not always reflected in official sources, as many do not trust the authorities. Since this indicator mainly shows corruption perception, citizens note less corruption at the household level. The volume and frequency of informal payments and bribes received by low-level officials – inspectors, police officers, as well as doctors and teachers – have decreased with the growth of the population's income. Figure 11.5 shows that this trend is noticeable in Kazakhstan and Uzbekistan, where wages have increased in recent years in both the public and private sectors. As for corruption in the highest echelons of power, the general population still considers it high. The main reason for large-scale political unrest in the Kyrgyz Republic in 2020 and Kazakhstan in 2022 was suspicions of corruption at the top of political leadership.

Real progress can be seen in the Government Effectiveness indicator (Figure 11.6). This observation inspires optimism for the region's future, as the quality of the work of a state's institutions and civil servants determines its progress. Our southeastern neighbour can serve as an example here to this day. In China, for centuries, nationwide examinations have selected the most talented and ambitious young people for the most prestigious civil service, regardless of their social status.

Due to the instability in the 1990s after the collapse of the Soviet Union, the indicator for Government Effectiveness was low throughout that decade. Many government officials did not know how to run an independent country and how a market economy differed from a planned one. But as each country's political situation stabilised with time, the picture began to change. The past quarter of a century has seen a brand-new generation of civil servants, and the indicator now shows that there is progress in government effectiveness in all five countries. All this has happened despite well-known economic laws, which state that higher salaries attract higher-quality staff. Because government budgets were insufficient to raise civil servants' wages, they remained low (except for in Kazakhstan). The most significant reasons for the interest of talented youngsters in public service were its social prestige and the chances of acquiring the right connections. The governments of all Central Asian countries should make every effort to increase remuneration for their civil servants, which will improve the quality of work of all governments and reduce corruption.

The analysis presented shows that further systematic work is required to strengthen Central Asia's current political and economic institutions, which are still weak. Institutional development will have to be based on the following fundamental principles – the rule of law, the fight against corruption, building a responsible public administration, ensuring transparency of the state apparatus and democratisation of society and the state. Creating such institutions will undoubtedly not be easy or quick, but the work must not stop.

References

UNDP & European Commission, 2004. Governance indicators: A users' guide. [Online] Available at: https://www.un.org/ruleoflaw/files/Governance%20Indicators_A%20Users%20Guide.pdf [Accessed July 2022].

World Bank, 2021a. WGI 2021 Interactive > Documentation. [Online] Available at: http://info.worldbank.org/governance/wgi/Home/Documents [Accessed July 2022].

World Bank, 2021b. WGI 2021 Interactive > Home. [Online] Available at: http://info.worldbank.org/governance/wgi/ [Accessed July 2022].

World Bank, 2021c. Worldwide governance indicator - DataBank. [Online] Available at: https://databank.worldbank.org/source/worldwide-governance-indicators# [Accessed July 2022].

Part III

Political Challenges

12 The Fergana Valley and Its Conflicts

Introduction

The Fergana Valley is a unique place. Located in the southeastern part of Central Asia and surrounded by the Tien Shan mountains to the north and the Gissar-Alai Range to the south, the triangular-shaped valley covers an area of 22,000 square kilometres, roughly the size of the State of Israel. It boasts one of the highest population densities in the world thanks to its strong agricultural base and mild climate. Almost 17 million people, or nearly a quarter of Central Asia's total population of 76 million, live there, in just 5 per cent of Central Asia's total area. While the average population density of Central Asia is only 19 people per square kilometre, in the Fergana Valley, it is almost 800 people per square kilometre. It is also the fastest-growing region of Central Asia, experiencing population growth of about 40 per cent over the past twenty years (Temirov, 2021). The dense population of the Fergana Valley makes the region easily identifiable on satellite images taken at night as the numerous lights of the villages contrast against the sparsely populated steppes and mountains of other parts of the region.

The mountain ranges and plains in the Fergana Valley are distributed among three countries – the Kyrgyz Republic, Tajikistan, and Uzbekistan. Observers often compare the bizarrely drawn Soviet-era borders, some of which enclose exotic enclaves, to a patchwork quilt. Rumour has it that Stalin himself drew the final versions. Citizens of different countries and people of various nationalities have lived in the same villages on neighbouring streets for hundreds of years, often in a checkerboard pattern (Muratalieva, 2019). They speak several languages, adhere to the traditions of various nationalities, and usually start interethnic families.

The Fergana Valley includes some of the most productive irrigated oblasts of the region, such as Andijan, Namangan, Kokand and Fergana in Uzbekistan; Jalal-Abad, and Osh in the Kyrgyz Republic; and Khujand in Tajikistan. As such, this region is the primary source of food for all of Central Asia. In addition, agricultural producers actively export their produce to other countries, primarily Russia. The main crops from the Fergana include wheat, cotton, rice, vegetables and fruit. All districts, regardless of international

DOI: 10.4324/9781003360728-16

borders, depend on the tributaries of the Syr Darya for the irrigation of their exceptionally fertile lands, with approximately 45 per cent of the entire irrigated portion of the Syr Darya basin located within the Fergana Valley.

For millennia, people have found ways to negotiate the sharing of pastures and use water, regardless of nationality. They moved freely, traded, and forged friendships with each other.

Data from the census of 1897 – the only census conducted in the Russian Empire before 1917 – provided in the 1911 *Encyclopædia Britannica* indicates that the population of the Fergana Valley at the time was just 1,571,243, of which 707,132 were women and 286,369 were living in cities (Rakhmatillaev, 1988). The figures show that the valley's population has increased more than a hundred times over the past century. Due to subsequent population pressure and potential conflicts over water and land resources, the valley has become one of the most volatile regions in Central Asia.

The first state borders established by the Soviet government resulted from the so-called national-territorial delimitation that began in the country in the 1920s and 1930s. The authorities decided to divide the then united Turkestan Republic into five parts – the Kazakh, Kyrgyz, Tajik, Turkmen, and Uzbek Soviet Socialist republics – with the present national borders being the product of this more recent history.

The Soviet authorities carried out procedures for clarifying state borders in the valley many times. The most significant changes occurred in the 1920s, 1930s, 1950s, and 1980s. Early maps quickly became obsolete due to population growth and the displacement of residents. In Soviet times, the state authorities preferred to obscure the exact location of the borders since this was not a priority in a then unified country. As a result, neither central nor local authorities fully ratified the numerous maps of the areas, and significant territories were not delimited and demarcated. These have continued to be sources of dispute and conflict.

In Central Asia, Turkmenistan is the only country without any enclaves. While Kazakhstan has no enclaves within the country, there are two Kazakh exclaves in Uzbekistan. Tajikistan likewise contains no enclaves within its borders, but there are two Tajik exclaves in the Kyrgyz Republic and one in Uzbekistan. In the Kyrgyz Republic, there are two Tajik enclaves plus four Uzbek enclaves, while Uzbekistan has one Tajik, one Kyrgyz, and two Kazakh enclaves.

The reality is that dividing the disputed territories into different republics was extremely difficult. The basic principle of national-territorial demarcation used was a population census to determine which parts of a region were inhabited by the majority of a particular nationality. Given the multilingualism and multi-ethnicity of the area and the nomadic lifestyle that the local population led, living in one place in summer and another in winter, for instance, population censuses were often inaccurate and not representative. Such difficulties in delimitation did not arise only in the Fergana Valley, but also slightly further afield in some of the Central Asian republics.

Examples of some of the most complex historical drawings of borders can be found in the current Samarkand and Bukhara *oblasts* of Uzbekistan. The mostly Tajik-speaking cities of Samarkand and Bukhara were surrounded by rural areas where the majority of the population spoke Uzbek. In the end, both cities became part of the Republic of Uzbekistan. Another example can be found in the Tashkent and Shymkent oblasts, where Uzbeks lived in the regions' main cities and Kazakhs lived in the territories around these. Yet once the census was in and the borders were drawn, Tashkent became part of Uzbekistan and Shymkent became part of Kazakhstan. Such complexities and contradictions were the norms in the delimitation and demarcation of smaller settlements in other territories.

Inter-ethnic clashes in the Fergana Valley began soon after the appearance of these borders and regularly flared up throughout the Soviet era, in the 1960s, 70s and 80s.

The growing scarcity of resources, namely the lack of water, land, and pastures, combined with the rapid population growth in the Fergana Valley and the border disputes, have all contributed to the development of tensions and regional instability.

Conflicts During the Soviet Period

The Fergana Valley experienced several severe local conflicts during Soviet times. The last of these during this period was the so-called Osh events, which began on 4 June 1990, with a dispute over the thirty-two hectares of cotton fields of the Lenin collective farm near the city of Uzgen in the Kyrgyz Republic. Without prior consultations with the inhabitants, the district authorities had decided to reallocate the land used by rural producers for housing construction. This ill-conceived plan led to a confrontation between local Kyrgyz and Uzbeks, swiftly turning into an armed clash. Bloody riots quickly spread throughout the south of the Kyrgyz Republic and the neighbouring regions of Uzbekistan. A few days later, the authorities quashed the problem by force.

Most of the clashes during the Osh events took place in Osh, Uzgen, Kara-Suu, Jalal-Abad and other settlements of the Osh and Jalal-Abad *oblasts* of the Kyrgyz Republic. According to the investigative group of the USSR Prosecutor General's Office, about 1,200 people died in conflicts in the cities of Uzgen and Osh and the villages of the Osh *oblast*. Experts argue that the events in Osh were a direct result of the *perestroika* era policy of the Soviet government and were one of the most tragic events in the lead-up to the disintegration of the Soviet Union. The main reasons for the conflict were the short-sighted policy of the leadership of the Soviet Union in delimiting the republican borders, the rise of nationalist sentiments in the republics associated with growing poverty, and the lack of land and water resources (Globalsecurity.org, 2016).

Conflicts Post-independence

The disintegration of the Soviet Union had a particularly strong effect on the inhabitants of the border regions and enclaves. Relatives became citizens of different independent countries, and their usual stomping grounds turned into neighbouring independent republics.

During independence, conflicts that had previously had an internal and local character within a single country quickly turned from being classified as interethnic to interstate. With the emergence of new frontiers, many of the canals that were previously built on economic expediency began crossing the borders of newly formed states, over time becoming a source of interstate tensions. Such conflicts have continued to arise in the border areas throughout the thirty years of the existence of independent Central Asian states, especially where water is in insufficient supply.

Uzbekistan, which borders all other Central Asian countries, has the region's largest and most well-equipped army. Given this, the country's former leadership often resorted to force to resolve border disputes. In some instances, the Uzbek military introduced armed troops to undefined sections of the borders with its neighbours such as the Kyrgyz Republic (Geyne, 2016). Such cases immediately heightened tension between the countries, but fortunately, these actions did not lead to armed conflicts.

Another issue came about when Uzbekistan unilaterally set mines along the borders with Tajikistan (Lenta.ru, 2000) and the Kyrgyz Republic (Jumagulov, 2005), fearing the penetration of Islamic extremists into the country in 2000 (Pannier, 2018). Since the border remained unmarked in many places, civilians, including children, were killed by these mines. Authorities in neighbouring countries have never made public the number of mine-related incidents at the borders, but experts say more than 90 civilians were killed and 100 injured. Nearly 90 per cent of the victims were citizens of Tajikistan, with most of the victims being shepherds, women collecting firewood, or children herding cows (The New Humanitarian, 2004).

Tajikistan and Uzbekistan

The Tajik and Uzbek peoples have lived in the same neighbourhoods for thousands of years, connected by a common historical and cultural heritage. These two peoples are so close that many historians, not without reason, argue that Tajiks and Uzbeks are people who share one ethnicity but speak two different languages. After the disintegration of the Soviet Union, however, relations between Tajikistan and Uzbekistan remained tense. Many experts have termed these relations a Cold War. For twenty-five years, there was no direct air communication between the countries, visa regimes were employed, and state borders were closed and, in some places, even mined. Close relatives who lived on either side of the border could not see each other for decades.

For two decades, the presidents of the two countries, Emomali Rahmon and Islam Karimov, could not come to a mutual understanding on several fundamental issues, mainly those related to history and territory. This is even though President Rahmon came to power in Tajikistan in the early 1990s precisely because of Uzbekistan's military and financial support.

The cooling of relations can primarily be attributed to the fact that, since President Rahmon came to power with the active assistance of Uzbekistan, the Uzbek leadership counted on significant influence on the domestic and foreign policy of the new Tajik administration. President Rahmon began to pursue an independent policy, which did not please his northern neighbour.

Dushanbe accused Tashkent of waging a hybrid war with the country, replacing those in power with politicians more loyal to Uzbekistan. According to the Tajik authorities, this also involved the organisation of a transport blockade and a trade war.

The geographical position of Uzbekistan, located in the centre of Central Asia, made it possible for the country to have absolute control over the transport arteries – the railway and highway leading to Tajikistan. Dushanbe repeatedly highlighted how the Uzbek authorities detained rail cargo at the border for weeks and months without explanation. It forced the Tajik authorities to build alternative roads that did not have access to Uzbekistan. Many of the planned transport projects bypassing Uzbekistan have now been implemented.

Uzbekistan was aggressively opposed to all water and energy initiatives taken by Tajikistan in terms of the construction of large hydroelectric power plants. Tajikistan reasonably believed that launching new power units would allow the country to achieve energy independence without detriment to neighbouring countries. After all, the country experienced huge problems with electricity supply which left most of the republic without electricity for many winters. On the other hand, Tashkent expressed concern that the construction of large-scale hydropower plants would lead to a shortage of water for consumption and irrigation in Uzbekistan and Kazakhstan and cause serious environmental problems in the region. This complicated relations between neighbours and contributed to disputes over the use of transboundary rivers.

The length of the Tajik–Uzbek border is 1,312 kilometres. The border of Tajikistan with Afghanistan is approximately the same length at 1,357 kilometres. It is telling that Uzbekistan's borders with Tajikistan and Afghanistan are almost the same length, yet no border conflicts happened on the Uzbek–Afghan border, perhaps because this border was delineated.

The Kyrgyz Republic and Uzbekistan

In June 2010, a conflict broke out between ethnic Kyrgyz and Uzbeks in the south of Kyrgyzstan, which caused numerous casualties and led to great destruction. According to the Independent International Commission, 470 people died and more than 2,000 people were injured because of the tragedy (Regnum.ru, 2011). Entire blocks of Osh, the second largest city, in Kyrgyzstan were destroyed, more than 1,500 houses burned down, and more than 100,000 people were forced to flee the pogroms to Uzbekistan, fearing for their lives. It was only through great efforts by the governments of the Kyrgyz Republic and Uzbekistan that this conflict was stopped.

The latest conflict between residents of the Kyrgyz Republic and Uzbekistan occurred in May 2022, again over water use. Residents of the Uzbek village of Chashma and the Kyrgyz village of Chechme quarrelled over a spring in a disputed area between the villages and, as in other cases, the conflict turned into throwing stones at each other. In Uzbekistan, they announced 187 injured victims, and in the Kyrgyz Republic – about 25 (Eraliev, 2020).

With the new president coming to power in Uzbekistan in 2016, border negotiations with the Kyrgyz Republic got off the ground. The intergovernmental agreement of 2017 delimited and ratified 1,170 kilometres of the state border between the two countries, which is 85 per cent of the total length of the border of 1,378 kilometres. In 2019, the governments delimited and ratified another 10 per cent. It was significant that the agreement was concluded without external intermediaries, such as Russia or Kazakhstan. This positive precedent shows that, given the parties' political will, even such acute problems as the drawing of borders can be resolved through peaceful bilateral negotiations.

The process of resolving the remaining 5 per cent of the Kyrgyz–Uzbek border has begun (Currenttime.tv, 2021). It is not a big surprise that the most challenging sections of the border for delimitation and demarcation are within the Fergana Valley itself. On 26 March 2021, the Chairman of the State Committee for National Security of the Kyrgyz Republic, Kamchybek Tashiev, stated that the parties had resolved all disputed issues (Azattyk, 2021a). According to him, a preliminary protocol was signed, and no disputed areas were left between the countries. He stated that the parties agreed to conduct a site description on the territory of the Kempirabad (Andijan) reservoir and leave the dam in the territory of Uzbekistan, provided that both countries jointly manage the water resources of the reservoir, and the Uzbek side undertakes not to install restrictive structures around the water's edge. Mr Tashiev said that Uzbekistan is giving the Kyrgyz Republic 1,000 hectares of land between border points in the Andijan region.

However, after his statement, Mr Tashiev received a flurry of criticism on social networks and on the streets. Residents of the border areas, who would be forced to relocate as a result of the agreement, came out to protest. As a result, he retracted his words (Azattyk, 2021b) and the Kyrgyz Republic and Uzbekistan have not yet succeeded in resolving all border disputes.

The Kyrgyz Republic and Tajikistan

The most complex border delineation processes in the Fergana Valley are between the Kyrgyz Republic and Tajikistan. Kyrgyzstan and Tajikistan's problems with the distribution of land and water resources have been ongoing since the 1920s from the very first attempts to delimit the borders. The only skirmishes officially documented in Soviet times between Kyrgyz and Tajiks occurred in 1936, 1938, 1969, 1975 and 1989, but there were many more. For example, in the areas of Ak-Sai and Vorukh (1975, 1989), Uch-Dobo, and Khoja Alo (1989), people used stones, agriculture and firearms to fight each other (Matveeva, 2017), although these were not officially documented.

After gaining sovereignty as independent nations, the new authorities could only agree to 519 kilometres of their 971 kilometre border. The rest remains disputed and there are about seventy unsettled conflict areas, especially on the border between Batken and Sughd oblasts in Kyrgyzstan and Tajikistan respectively, which includes conflicts around the enclave of Vorukh in Tajikistan. During certain years, for example, in 2014, there were over thirty border clashes. Over the past 15 years, more than 200 conflicts have occurred with victims, both injured and killed, on both sides. Every year there are more skirmishes in the border areas and seven clashes have even occurred since 2020 despite the pandemic and lockdowns.

Conflicting parties regularly attempt to resolve conflicts themselves as they create big problems for each of them. For example, the authorities have long discussed resolving tensions by exchanging several territories along some 144 kilometres of the shared border. But unfortunately, official procedures for exchanging land have not yet taken place (Cabar Asia, 2020).

Conflicts between residents of border areas are a regular occurrence. However, the bloodiest example in recent years were the events of late April–early May 2021 near the borders of the two countries. Not only were residents involved, but also the two countries' militaries used mortars and heavy equipment. As a result, dozens of people on both sides were killed, and hundreds were left injured. About a dozen villages were also affected, and houses burned down. More than 50,000 people were evacuated from the conflict zone. Fortunately, despite numerous casualties, the parties held negotiations, putting an end to the conflict. This armed conflict brought mutual hostility which had previously been mainly at the local level to the national level in both countries, which is a dangerous trend.

Another source of conflict is international highways that cross borders. People from both sides often block these roads to express their dissatisfaction and to protest. During disputes, the Kyrgyz often blocked the Tajik Vorukh-Isfara highway, which crossed the territory of the Kyrgyz Republic three times through the villages of Kok-Terek, Tash-Tumshuk and Ak-Sai. In turn, Tajik citizens blocked the Batken-Razzakov road on the bridge across the Ak-Suu River at the exit from Kok-Tash village (Akipress, 2020). To avoid crossing that bridge, the Kyrgyz side decided to build an alternative Kok-Tash – Ak-Sai – Ravat road through the outskirts of Kok-Tash village, which is also a hotbed of conflict since the route passes through disputed territories.

The border zone's economy is wholly dependent on agriculture. The economy accounts for 74 per cent of employment in the Batken oblast of the Kyrgyz Republic (Unep.org, 2009) and 75 per cent in the Sughd oblast of Tajikistan (FAO, 2016). Unemployment is extremely high on both sides of the border, and Batken has the highest unemployment rate in the country.

It is worth emphasising that in the public consciousness of both countries, there is a significant demand for the settlement of border issues and the building of stable, conflict-free, good-neighbourly relations. In one of the latest studies by the International Republican Institute (IRI), citizens of the Kyrgyz Republic, mainly due to border problems, marked Tajikistan as the country with which they have the worst relations (Center for Insights in Survey Research, 2019).

The Primary Sources of Conflict: Water and Land

Yet the main cause of current conflicts is not borders but the distribution of water resources. As already noted, most cultivated land in Central Asia requires irrigation. Seventy-five per cent of cultivated land in the Kyrgyz Republic is irrigated (AHT Group AG Management and Engineering, 2013), 84 per cent in Tajikistan (Sehring, 2006), and 89 per cent in Uzbekistan (Agarwal, 2019).

Therefore, many rely on water in border negotiations, an invaluable resource in this arid region. For example, the Kyrgyz Republic and Tajikistan share about forty water channels (Cabar Asia, 2021). This is because water infrastructure, including hydroelectric power stations, water intakes and canals, was all held in common by the five Central Asian republics during the Soviet period.

The leading cause of conflict is when an upstream Kyrgyz or Tajik village blocks a canal or uses more water than it should, which results in less water reaching downstream villages (Kurmanalieva, 2019). Most often, conflicts and clashes occur near the Tortgul reservoir from which the Ak-Tatyr (Machai) Canal, the Big Fergana Canal, and the Ravat Hydroelectric Complex originate. It was built in the 1970s to expand crop areas for Kyrgyz and Tajik residents.

The next critical issue is the tense demographic situation, especially in Tajikistan. A striking example of land shortage due to high overpopulation is the border region of Chorkuh in Tajikistan, where there are only 240 square meters of land per capita. In contrast, the neighbouring Isfana region of the Kyrgyz Republic has 800 square metres of land per capita (Cabar Asia, 2021). The local authorities of Tajikistan tried to solve the problem by reducing the transfer of household plots to the population but, despite their efforts, by 2011 no such lands remained. Each of the three municipalities of the Isfara region of Tajikistan – Vorukh, Chorkuh and Surkh – has approximately 100,000 inhabitants. The neighbouring Kyrgyz municipalities of Ak Tatyr, Ak-Sai and Samarkandek in the Batken region have a much smaller population of only around 20,000 people each. From these Kyrgyz municipalities, there is significant internal and external migration of the population. People fear for their lives and do not see prospects in their homeland. It is particularly alarming that many young people see no opportunity of staying and working in their home countries (Public Association "Vorukh Jamoat Support Center", 2011). The rapid population growth in the border areas, especially in the Tajik part, increases the risk of recurrence of conflicts. The political will of the leaders of neighbouring countries is needed to bring order to the border.

How Can Peace Be Brought to the Valley?

The region's two poorest countries, the Kyrgyz Republic and Tajikistan should not divert their meagre human and financial resources to purchasing weapons and disproportionate funding for their armies and border troops. But how can the current tension at the border be defused? How can peace be maintained, and what is required to build trust between people in the border areas?

In the short term, it is necessary to focus on maintaining peace and building trust. The primary task is to prevent the outbreak of armed conflict, for which the authorities need to maintain a constant dialogue both at the central and local government levels. The leadership of the internal affairs bodies and the border troops must be in continuous contact and communication. The border areas' population should hold joint events, such as festivals, holidays, concerts, and sports competitions, especially with the involvement of young people. With a short and mid-term focus on maintaining peace and building trust, at a later stage, it might be possible to launch joint infrastructure projects and develop disputed territories currently not in use.

One of the medium-term options for maintaining peace could be introducing joint power of the two states over the Batken and Isfara regions. Countries may need to grant special administrative status to such territories when border posts are temporarily removed to their outer perimeter. To maintain public order, the parties could use joint unarmed police patrols, which could focus on preventing minor crimes such as cattle theft or illegal logging.

Countries should request assistance from reputable international organisations to rapidly implement such plans, drawing on the best practices in border conflict resolution from other parts of the world. Meanwhile, all required work on delimitation and demarcation of the border should continue.

The delimitation and demarcation of borders is an exceedingly long and painful process. It requires patient negotiations and mutual concessions between states and local communities. In international practice, there are several ways to resolve issues of state borders. They can be conducted both at the bilateral level and through the involvement of a third "neutral" party. Most experts and researchers offer several solutions to border delimitation, considering the economic and political characteristics of the regions. Among them are the following: exchange of neutral territories; strengthening of the capacity of existing institutions in resource management, coordination, and monitoring; the introduction of agreements on the joint use of water and land resources; improvements in the infrastructure of water channels and reservoirs; and access to social and economic benefits.

The problem requires a comprehensive and systematic solution. In clarifying the borders, both countries' governments should work to improve the infrastructure of border areas and activities to improve the socio-economic benefits reaped by residents of neighbouring states.

With President Shavkat Mirziyoyev coming to power in Uzbekistan, relations in Central Asia are being reset, which is also affecting the situation in the Fergana Valley. It is important to note that under the new president, Tashkent has made relations with its closest neighbours a foreign policy priority. Uzbekistan has shown the political will to normalise relations on border issues with Tajikistan and the Kyrgyz Republic, not just in word but also in deed. Uzbekistan cleared the border with Tajikistan of mines and resumed the two countries' air and rail links. The parties agreed to open checkpoints on the border and made a decision on the disputed Farhad hydroelectric power station. Of the 1,312 kilometres of the Uzbek–Tajik border, 20 per cent remain disputed. In March 2018, the Presidents of Tajikistan and Uzbekistan signed an agreement on separate border sections. Since then, the Joint Border Demarcation Commission has met regularly which, just a few years ago, would have been impossible.

Positive changes can also be seen in relations between Uzbekistan and the Kyrgyz Republic. In September 2019, Tashkent and Bishkek exchanged equal plots of land for the first time. Since the resumption of negotiations, the percentage of borders agreed has increased from eighty-four to ninety-two.

The focus now is for the neighbours to resolve sensitive issues through negotiations alone which is the only way to create a favourable environment for discussing and solving other vital problems in the valley, primarily water and land resources management.

References

Agarwal, A., 2019. Water woes in Central Asia: Can SCO offer a solution?. [Online] Available at: https://www.orfonline.org/expert-speak/water-woes-in-central-asia-can-sco-offer-a-solution/ [Accessed July 2022].

AHT Group AG Management and Engineering, 2013. *Kyrgyz Republic: Developing Water Resources Sector Strategies in Central and West Asia*, Bishkek: Asian Development Bank.

Akipress, 2020. Karta-skhema konfliktov vokrug anklava Voruh v Batkenskoy oblasti. [Online] Available at: https://kg.akipress.org/news:1591004 [Accessed July 2022].

Azattyk, 2021a. Glava GKNB Tashiev zajavil o reshenii voprosa granicy s Uzbekistanom «na 100 procentov». [Online] Available at: https://rus.azattyk.org/a/tashiev-vopros-s-kyrgyzsko-uzbekskoy-granitsey-reshen-na-100-protsentov/31170879.html [Accessed July 2022].

Azattyk, 2021b. Tashiev: Peredachi uchastka Kempirabadskogo vodohranilishha Uzbekistanu ne budet. [Online] Available at: https://rus.azattyk.org/a/tashiev-peredachi-uchastka-kempirabadskogo-vodohranilischa-uzbekistanu-ne-budet/31221849.html [Accessed July 2022].

Cabar Asia, 2020. Nereshennyi vopros: smozhet li obmen territoriyami pomirit' kyrgyzstancev I tadzhikistancev?. [Online] Available at: https://cabar.asia/ru/nereshennyj-vopros-smozhet-li-obmen-territoriyami-pomirit-kyrgyzstantsev-i-tadzhikistantsev [Accessed July 2022].

Cabar Asia, 2021. Kyrgyzsko-tadzhikskie pogranichnye spory: prichiny i puti resheniya. [Online] Available at: https://cabar.asia/ru/kyrgyzsko-tadzhikskie-pogranichnye-spory-prichiny-i-puti-resheniya?pdf=44169 [Accessed July 2022].

Center for Insights in Survey Research, 2019. Public opinion poll: Residents of Kyrgyzstan. [Online] Available at: https://www.iri.org/wp-content/uploads/legacy/iri.org/final_kygyzstan_slides.pdf [Accessed July 2022].

Currenttime.tv, 2021. V Kyrgyzstane ob"yavili, chto posle 30 let peregovorov dogovorilis' s Uzbekistanom o demarkacii granicy. [Online] Available at: https://www.currenttime.tv/a/kyrgyzstan-uzbekistan-border/31171146.html [Accessed July 2022].

Eraliev, S., 2020. «Problema s rodnikom v Chechme reshitsya posle utochneniya granic». [Online] Available at: https://rus.azattyk.org/a/30645939.html [Accessed July 2022].

FAO, 2016. *Nacional'nyi gendernyi profil' sel'skogo hozyaystva i sel'skih domohozyaystv– Tadzhikistan*, Ankara: Prodovol'stvennaya i sel'skohozyajstvennaya organizaciya Ob"edinennyh Naciy.

Geyne, H., 2016. Specreportazh: Kak uzbekskie bronetransportery obnazhili prigranichnyeroblemy. [Online] Available at: https://kloop.kg/blog/2016/03/29/spetsreportazh-kak-uzbekskie-bronetransportery-obnazhili-prigranichnye-problemy/ [Accessed July 2022].

Globalsecurity.org, 2016. Osh conflict of 1990. [Online] Available at: https://www.globalsecurity.org/military/world/war/osh-conflict.htm [Accessed July 2022].

Jumagulov, S., 2005. Uzbeksko-Kyrgyzskaya granitsa po-prezhnemu zaminirovana. [Online] Available at: https://iwpr.net/ru/global-voices/uzbeksko-kyrgyzskaya-granica-po-prezhnemu-zaminirovana [Accessed July 2022].

Kurmanalieva, G., 2019. *Kyrgyzstan and Tajikistan: Endless Border Conflicts*, Berlin: EUCACIS Online Paper No. 4.

Lenta.ru, 2000. Uzbekistan taykom zaminiroval granicu s Tadzhikistanom. [Online] Available at: https://lenta.ru/news/2000/10/23/border/ [Accessed July 2022].

Matveeva, A., 2017. Divided we fall … or rise? Tajikistan–Kyrgyzstan border dilemma. *Cambridge Journal of Eurasian Studies*, 1 (1).

Muratalieva, N., 2019. O pogranichnom konflikte mezhdu Kyrgyzstanom i Tadzhikistanom – kyrgyzskiy politolog Alibek Mukambaev. [Online] Available at: https://www.caa-network.org/archives/17728/o-pogranichnom-konflikte-mezhdu-kyrgyz [Accessed July 2022].

Pannier, B., 2018. Putting an end to 20 years of death along the Tajik-Uzbek border. [Online] Available at: https://www.rferl.org/a/putting-an-end-to-20-years-of-death-along-the-tajik-uzbek-border/29541805.html [Accessed July 2022].

Public Association "Vorukh Jamoat Support Center", 2011. *Potential for Peace and the Threat of Conflicts: Development Analysis Border Communities of Isfara Region of Tajikistan and Batken Region of The Kyrgyz Republic*, Isfara: UNDP project "Conflict Prevention and Mitigation in the Fergana Valley".

Rakhmatillaev, H., 1988. Dinamika etnicheskoi kultury selskogo naseleniya Fergans-koi doliny. *Sovetskaya Etnographiya*, 18 (6).

Regnum.ru, 2011. Kiljunen: Mezhdunarodnoe soobshestvo priznalo otchet po iyun'skim besporyadkam v Kirgizii sbalansirovannym. [Online] Available at: https://regnum.ru/news/1409627.html [Accessed July 2022].

Sehring, J., 2006. The politics of irrigation reform in Tajikistan. [Online] Available at: https://www.researchgate.net/publication/45130097_The_Politics_of_Irrigation_Reform_in_Tajikistan [Accessed July 2022].

Temirov, Z., 2021. Reconstruction of the population in the Fergana Valley regions and its territorial characteristics. *New York Science Journal*, 14 (1), pp. 26–31.

The New Humanitarian, 2004. Tashkent moves to de-mine borders with Kyrgyzstan and Tajikistan. [Online] Available at: https://www.thenewhumanitarian.org/news/2004/06/24/tashkent-moves-de-mine-borders-kyrgyzstan-and-tajikistan [Accessed July 2022].

Unep.org, 2009. Social'no-ekonomicheskoe issledovanie po vozdeystviyu proizvodstva pervichnoy rtuti na okruzhayushhuyu sredu v Kyrgyzskoy Respublike. [Online] Available at: https://wedocs.unep.org/bitstream/handle/20.500.11822/11477/socio-econ-r.pdf?sequence=1&isAllowed=y [Accessed July 2022].

13 Political Upheavals

Introduction

It should be understood that thirty years of independence of the Central Asian countries has not been enough to build harmonious communities and effective state institutions. These structures include a wide range of organisations that support society, including the political systems that govern parliaments and governments. There must be institutions that regulate economic and financial stability, such as a central bank, and institutions that protect property rights, such as the judiciary. The state must have institutions that protect the security of the citizen and the state, such as the army and the police.

The presence of state institutions is a primary contributor to social and economic development. These institutions can be the main source of welfare for citizens. Effective institutions contribute to the development of education, and investment in physical and human capital, scientific and technical innovations, and technologies. Properly functioning institutions are essential for economic development. Higher growth rates and lower borrowing costs give governments the resources to meet social needs and invest in infrastructure, health, and education. The reverse is also true. Failed institutions undermine public confidence, increase the cost of doing business, limiting the possibilities of state and local budgets. Weak state institutions have been a major cause of the political turmoil seen since independence in some Central Asian countries.

Civil War in Tajikistan

The civil war was a tragic page in the modern history of Tajikistan. The conflict reached its climax from July 1992 to July 1993, when the country was divided in two between government forces and the United Tajik Opposition (UTO). Between 35,000 and 157,000 people were killed as a result (Sobiri, 2017). The number of internally displaced people reached 1 million, and about 250,000 people became refugees. The war also dealt a severe blow to Tajikistan's industry, almost completely wiping it out.

Some sources posited that external forces had a significant impact on the development of the civil war. On the one hand, Russia and Uzbekistan were

DOI: 10.4324/9781003360728-17

in a coalition that supported President Rahmon. On the other hand, influential Tajik warlords from Afghanistan, who traditionally received financial support from Iran, backed the UTO (Iji, 2005). For example, in 1993, Uzbek aviation took part in the battles, which supported the Rahmon government with airstrikes on opposition positions in the Karategin Valley. Conversely, the opposition received weapons and training from the Hezb-i Islami led by Gulbuddin Hekmatyar and the Northern Alliance led by Ahmad Shah Massoud, supporting the UTO (Epkenhans, 2016).

The war lasted for more than five years and finally ended because of international efforts, primarily on the part of Russia, Iran, and neighbouring Uzbekistan. An Agreement on Peace and National Unity was signed on 27 June 1997 in Moscow. The signers were the People's Front, an alliance of those from the south and parts of the north, and the United Tajik Opposition (UTO), which represented the democratic and Islamic forces in the centre and east of the country. It provided for peace and security, elections, and a multi-party system, and was designed to ensure freedom of religion, freedom of speech and the independence of the media. The agreement suited all parties including the UTO armed military group, which by that time numbered about 5,000 well-armed soldiers and officers. The UTO agreed to lay down their arms and integrate into the state armed forces.

The guarantors for implementation of the widely publicised Inter-Tajik Agreement with Russia and Iran, were the UN and the OSCE. In return for complete disarmament and renunciation of supreme power, the UTO received 30 per cent of the posts in the government of Tajikistan, constitutional guarantees for the activities of religious parties, primarily the Islamic Renaissance Party, the main backbone of the UTO, the promise of free parliamentary and presidential elections, and a general amnesty.

Time passed and, on 29 September 2015, the Supreme Court of Tajikistan recognised the Islamic Renaissance Party of Tajikistan (IRPT) as a terrorist group and banned its activities on the territory of the republic. Before the ban, it was the only legally operating Islamic political party in the post-Soviet space.

During the war, over sixty medical institutions, dozens of schools and other educational institutions, as well as dozens of social and cultural facilities were destroyed. According to the most conservative estimates, the civil war cost Tajikistan more than 7 billion dollars (International Crisis Group, 2001). If before the collapse of the Soviet Union, the country was the poorest union's republic, then because of the civil war, Tajikistan became one of the poorest countries in the world.

Three "Revolutions" in the Kyrgyz Republic[1]

In the early days of October 2020, Bishkek was calm. It was as if there had been no emotionally driven rallies of young people clashing with the police deploying tear gas and stun grenades against them. Latent tension was only revealed in the windows of shopping centres, covered with heavy curtains. Such a landscape strikingly resembles similar pictures of the city that followed the previous Kyrgyz revolutions in March 2005 and April 2010.

Kyrgyzstan's latest revolution began in a typical fashion. Following a parliamentary election on 4 October 2020, protesters and rioters took to the streets seeking to annul the result, triggering a full-scale political crisis. By 6 October, demonstrators had occupied the White House – the government building that houses the president's office and Parliament. In the following days, a peaceful power struggle unfolded. In the end, the Central Election Commission annulled the election results, President Sooronbai Jeenbekov resigned, and Sadyr Japarov, a politician who had just been released from prison, became the acting president. In just one day, a country's entire political system was completely dismantled. How did it all happen, and why so quickly?

As a result of the 2020 elections, four parties were elected to the Parliament. Among them were three pro-government parties, which had at their disposal huge official and unofficial financial resources by Kyrgyz standards. According to the protesters, it was the bribery of voters that had helped them to achieve a constitutional majority in Parliament. The composition of the new Parliament was such that 107 out of 120 deputies were pro-government, which according to the opposition, is entirely implausible. Only one opposition party got into Parliament, barely breaking the seven per cent threshold. That party and twelve other parties that took part in the elections refused to recognise the results of the elections. And so, the opposition brought its supporters to the central square of Bishkek.

Curiously, the opposition had no complaints about the vote-counting process thanks to the use of modern electronic ballot boxes. The main reason for the mass discontent was namely the bribery of voters. Specific figures were also cited, 2,000 KGS (US$25) per vote, not a small amount for a poor voter. Once again, by its example, the country has demonstrated that democracy cannot function without solid institutions and a reliable legal system.

Additional reasons for the protests were the presence in the electoral lists of the "pro-government" parties of representatives of criminal groups and a "corrupted elite", as well as the widespread use of administrative pressure by the local authorities. All such facts were straightforwardly recorded and publicly covered both in the opposition press and on social media.

The country was in real danger of sinking into the abyss of confusion and chaos. Both Kyrgyz citizens and neighbouring states showed concern about the situation in the country. "We hope that a normal democratic political process will be restored", said Russian President Vladimir Putin (Xinhuanet.com, 2020). The Presidents of Kazakhstan and Uzbekistan talked on the telephone about the situation in Kyrgyzstan. "China sincerely hopes that all parties in Kyrgyzstan can resolve the issue … as soon as possible", China's foreign ministry spokeswoman Hua Chunying said (Anadolu Agency, 2020). China joined the European Union and the US in calls for a peaceful resolution to the situation, and both Beijing and Washington warned that there should be no foreign interference in the country.

Why is it that the people of the small state of Kyrgyzstan, which few know about, so clearly show their desire to live in a just society and be a democratic country? In my opinion, there are several explanations for this. In the past, the Kyrgyz, the ancient nomadic nation, always had a particular craving for freedom and justice. Power was not inherited, because the ruler simply had to have popular support.

If the ruler could not ensure the security and economic prosperity of his fellow tribesmen, families simply migrated to another place, and the ruler was left on his own. This is the big difference between a nomadic culture and a sedentary one, in which the ruler ruled over the people, simply owning the land on which his subjects lived and fed.

The cause of all three recent Kyrgyz revolutions was not poverty and unemployment but injustice. Since the earliest days of the country's independence, public trust in the government has been repeatedly undermined by systemic corruption, falsified election results, and the state's reliance on informal institutions including criminal entities and other actors. The country is not rich in natural resources, unlike most of its neighbours in Central Asia with their vast hydrocarbon deposits. The main contributor to the country's economy is the development of several gold mines, Kumtor being the main one, run by Canadians. The tourism sector is also a significant contributor to the economy. The country has always had high unemployment and this situation is partially rescued because more than a million citizens work abroad, mainly in Russia. The country is one of the leading destinations in the world for the size of migrant remittances, reaching up to 30 per cent of the country's GDP.

Naturally, the coronavirus pandemic has further exacerbated the plight of most of the population. In the International Monetary Fund's 2020 report, the Kyrgyz Republic is included in the list of countries whose economies would be most affected by the pandemic. The country's GDP fell 8.6 per cent in 2020. This is the worst indicator among the Central Asian countries.

"Why did the Kyrgyz succeed in one night that the Belarusians did not succeed in two months in 2020?", many ask. Mentality, customs, and experience differ. Perhaps the Kyrgyz do not have that law-abidingness that Belarusians have in their blood. Therefore, 10,000 Kyrgyz, in one night, can accomplish what hundreds of thousands of Belarusians attending peaceful rallies could not do in 2 months. Each of the rebellious Kyrgyz jumped straight to the end and overthrew the government. But what will the next government be? After staging three revolutions in two decades, one could argue that the people of Kyrgyzstan have accumulated a unique knowledge of how to do it. Then again, because new problems have emerged each time, there are clearly limits to what this experience can offer.

After a few days in October, the Kyrgyz Republic quickly "disappeared" from the editorials of mass media, apparently because the country continued to move on peacefully, and the situation smoothly morphed into an evolutionary channel. Meanwhile, as the country's only remaining independent political body, the parliament continued to work throughout the protests, enacting legislation to hold a presidential election and a vote on a new constitution on 10 January 2021. This reform was initiated by Mr Japarov himself, prompting his opponents to accuse him of attempting to usurp power and divert the country from the path of democracy.

Mr Japarov's vivid biography, the determination of his supporters on the streets, and the backing of MPs were three key reasons that got him into power. Despite all the criticism of his actions, it must be admitted that during those critical days he became an influential leader who did not allow the country to slide into chaos. In Japarov, people saw a political outsider who could finally unite the country and carry out the necessary reforms. Mr Japarov announced that he wanted to fight corruption, crime, and the shadow economy, and to renew the political establishment. He wanted to see a new generation of young and clean professionals in power and to change the long-suffering constitution again.

Issues related to the form of government have been raised throughout the country's history. The current constitution is the tenth since the Kyrgyz Republic produced its first one in 1991. There is a persistent myth in Kyrgyzstan that changing the constitution will suddenly make life better. But, of course, constitutional changes yield real-world results only when there is a deep public understanding and acceptance of constitutionalism.

The Kyrgyz people recognise and appreciate the fact that they have barely avoided falling into the political abyss. During the revolution, law-enforcement agencies seemed paralysed, unable to ensure the security of either state institutions or private property. The only force capable of maintaining a degree of legality was the self-organised "people's guards" who had cut their teeth during previous periods of unrest.

The official law-enforcement agencies were hampered by their leaders' incompetence, corruption, and lack of professionalism. During the days of rioting, many division chiefs (those with a rank above a colonel) simply vanished, no longer even answering calls from their subordinates. The whereabouts of the former ministers of internal affairs and national security are still unknown. After one and a half years it is safe to assume that they are on the run. State institutions and civil society have once again functioned completely on their own.

The gap between private and public income is one of the main sources of systemic corruption in the country. The Kyrgyz do not expect anything from the state and ask only that it does not take too much from them in bribes and kickbacks. Indeed, the revolutionary impulse stems not from poverty and unemployment but from perceived injustice.

Famous conspiracy theories claim that the first Kyrgyz "tulip" revolution in 2005 was organised by the US. For example, the first president of the country, Askar Akaev, still asserts (Smith, 2005) this. According to some media, the second revolution of 2010 was provoked by Russia, unhappy with the policies of the second President Kurmanbek Bakiev (Kirchick, 2010). As for the current third revolution, its "external organiser" has not yet been found or is still to be appointed. So far, no one can find them.

The popular theories of "colour revolutions" should be rethought. Most people believe that revolutions should always have external organisers or puppeteers. Few believe that they happen only for internal reasons. The latest revolutionary experience in the country demonstrates that the latter point of view has a chance to exist.

What kind of preliminary conclusions can be drawn from the events of October 2020? An astute observer can conclude that Kyrgyzstan has found its statehood "hanging by a thread". During the unrest, the law enforcement agencies were completely paralysed and unable to ensure the security of either state institutions or private property. Only the effective self-organisation of the "people's guards", which had the experience of self-organising during previous periods of unrest, made it possible to preserve elements of legality in the country. With that, no one was entirely sure that the arsenals of weapons in police and military storage facilities were properly guarded.

Many things happen so quickly in Kyrgyzstan, especially the overthrowing of corrupt regimes. But the Kyrgyz must learn not only how to destroy but also how to build, or the risks of plunging into the abyss of fear and chaos will only grow. The country's transition to failed state status would be a disastrous, but real, prospect.

What Happened in January 2022 in Kazakhstan?[2]

The protests that erupted across Kazakhstan on 2 January 2022 quickly turned into riots in all of the country's major cities. What did the protesters want, and what will be the outcome of the country's most severe civil unrest since independence in 1991? Although the initial trigger was a doubling of fuel prices, the protesters soon demanded the dissolution of parliament and new elections. Moreover, they wanted former President Nursultan Nazarbayev to exit the political scene for good.

The protesters, who did not have any of the opposition leaders on their side, represented a wide range of views, and their demands varied widely. Among them were relatively well-organised oil workers in Zhanaozen, Aktau, Aktobe and Atyrau, miners in Karaganda, copper smelters in Zhezkazgan, and liberal activists in Almaty. Young people across the country joined them. Some were dissatisfied with rising prices, and others were bothered by unemployment. But most protesters were frustrated with corruption and injustice, inequality, lack of support for families, fuel prices and low wages.

Indeed, the gap between the elite and the majority of Kazakhs is striking. It has been estimated that less than 160 people from the Kazakh elite own half of the total wealth of Kazakhstan (KPMG, 2019). Like many other post-Soviet states, most of this wealth has been hidden abroad. For example, Chatham House data shows that Kazakhstani oligarchs have invested half a billion British pounds in luxury real estate in London and its immediate surroundings (Cooley, et al., 2021).

Nazarbayev, the country's ruler for the first thirty years of independence, gave up the presidency in 2019, but not before having himself proclaimed "leader of the nation", thus ensuring that he would maintain a tight grip on the country's politics. In 2022, protesters toppled a statue of him in Taldykorgan, the capital of the Almaty region, with chants of "*Shal ket!*" ("Old man, go away!").

By 7 January, clashes had killed dozens of law-enforcement officials and demonstrators, and Nazarbayev's successor, President Kassym-Jomart Tokayev, had declared a state of emergency. Official sources claimed that during the state of emergency, the bodies of 225 people were delivered to morgues, including 19 law enforcement officers and military personnel. The Ministry of Health said more than 2,600 people had sought medical attention in hospitals (The Guardian, 2022).

President Tokayev requested assistance from Russia and other members of the Collective Security Treaty Organization (CSTO), which includes Russia, Armenia, Belarus, Kazakhstan, Kyrgyzstan, and Tajikistan. Russian President Vladimir Putin quickly answered the call, deploying Russian troops to help quell the protests. Tokayev gave the security forces permission to "fire without warning" on protesters. The CSTO deployed approximately 4,000 troops, most of them from Russia. It was the first operation of this kind in the almost thirty-year history of the alliance.

What preliminary conclusions can be drawn by analysing the Kazakh events? For a start, the authorities clearly panicked when the protests erupted. How else to explain Tokayev's frantic call for foreign troops to enter the country to impose order? Instead of recognising that the demonstrations were an angry – and predictable – response to the government's policies, he has conjured up the spectre of an external aggressor. Tokayev claims that the rioters received extensive training abroad. In his appeal to the members of the CSTO, he insisted that his government needed help to overcome a "terrorist threat". But the rationale for appealing to the CSTO remains in question: Why would any other country bother to offer "serious training" to "bandit formations" to disrupt Kazakhstan's regional centres?

By calling on CSTO, Tokayev took a gamble. What would happen if foreign paratroopers mowed down Kazakhstani women or children or a military helicopter crashed in a densely populated area? Any such event would deepen the crisis and the scale of intervention. It is hard to see how the presence of CSTO "peacekeepers" could do anything other than inflame the situation and awaken anti-Russian and nationalist sentiment in Kazakhstan.

Obviously, the real issue concerns the government's own competence and legitimacy. With well-trained police and security forces and a fully equipped army, why couldn't the authorities manage the protests on their own? Most likely, they could have done so. But by seeking external assistance, Tokayev hoped to shape the internal situation in ways that will buttress his own rule vis-à-vis rival factions.

Although the protests and rallies were relatively peaceful at the start, mainly comprising young men and women, organised groups showed up on 4 January 2022 and started seizing warehouses and weapons. The government's official line was that these groups were foreign mercenaries, but that claim does not withstand scrutiny. Kazakhstan has an effective border service, and the idea that several thousand foreigners could suddenly appear in the country, undetected, is strange.

It is far more likely that these quasi-military groups received special training and funding from local oligarchs seeking to influence events in their favour. According to former Kazakhstani officials, some of this support has come from officials in power. "The National Security Committee of Kazakhstan (KNB) for years hid information about the training camps of militants in the country", said the former Minister of Information and ex-adviser to Nursultan Nazarbayev, Yermukhamet Yertysbayev (Kalyukov, 2022). Besides, there are well-founded rumours that the Nazarbayev family, which was ousted from power during the protests, was trying to use them to regain influence (BBC News, 2022). These oligarchs, they argue, want to be able to mobilise paramilitary groups to influence elections. Their preparations often take place under the cover of oligarch-sponsored "sports clubs", where young people gather, train, and receive cash allowances.

While these informal groups have been deepening their roots in Kazakhstan for many years, the current crisis seems to have brought them to the surface. Several organised-crime figures "unexpectedly" returned to Kazakhstan from abroad. The Kazakh Interior Ministry said that "six members of the organised criminal group, led by Dikii (Wild) Arman (Arman Dzhumageldiev), were detained during a special operation by the Almaty police department" (Interfax.ru, 2022). People here know that these "thieves in law" – a typical phenomenon in post-Soviet politics – hold real authority, especially among unemployed youth. The question, then, is whose interests they were serving.

If these shadow groups fuel the riots and more violent forms of protest, there are no legal grounds for introducing CSTO troops into Kazakhstan. What started as a protest over socio-economic issues quickly escalated into a chaotic battle among oligarchs for political influence. In addition, because the demonstrations were driven not by the organised opposition but by ordinary citizens, the authorities can conveniently dismiss participants as opportunistic bandits, hooligans, and looters, rather than seeking a settlement through dialogue.

According to some experts, the political crisis into which the protests in Kazakhstan have grown was caused by the people's fatigue with Nazarbayev's family domination in both power and business, the immovability of power, oligarchic rule, the lack of political institutions and honest elections, a free press, and the absence of political competition (Gunkel', et al., 2022). Judging by the fact that the protests took place in several parts of the country, people accumulated discontent, and the increase in gas prices was only a pretext for the start of the unrest.

Obviously, the socio-economic problems in the country were the most important reasons for the protests. Energy prices were soaring due to the pandemic, but wages have not risen, and working conditions remain poor. Kazakhs were angry with the authorities because in an exceptionally rich country in raw materials, the bulk of the people still live in poverty. People at the protests said that export earnings were distributed unfairly, and the average monthly salary in Kazakhstan of 250,000 KZT ($575) shows that some get everything while others cannot buy LNG at 120 KZT ($0.27) per litre.

What lessons did the Kazakhstan protest teach us about the evolving post-Soviet space? In the past, political upheavals mainly occurred in relatively poor states such as Georgia, Ukraine, Armenia, Moldova, and Kyrgyzstan. For the first time in history, nationwide protests took place in a country that is prosperous by post-Soviet standards. Among those countries, Kazakhstan is in joint first place with Russia in terms of GDP and purchasing power parity per capita. Thus, it was not only poverty and desolation but mainly injustice that brought the people to the streets.

For the first time, protests began in the absence of political leaders. It was not the opposition that took to the streets but ordinary people. This is convenient for the current authorities, who call the protesters bandits, hooligans, and looters. Considering the Kyrgyz experience, it should be emphasised that the absence of a systemic opposition will complicate the process of stabilising the socio-political situation since it will not be easy to stabilise the case without a serious political dialogue.

The protests in Kazakhstan confirm that no transition of power will take place either in Belarus or in Russia, according to the Kazakhstan scenario. In these countries, the top officials either must completely withdraw from power or stay put and hold on to absolute power by any means.

Uzbekistan's Good Crisis[3]

In the summer of 2022, protests erupted in Uzbekistan's autonomous Republic of Karakalpakstan after the government announced plans to strip the region of its constitutional status. Viewing the move as a blow to their identity, the people of Karakalpakstan, especially ethnic Karakalpaks, took to the streets and clashed with the police and security forces, leaving 21 dead and 243 injured (Gazeta.uz, 2022).

This episode is simultaneously horrific and a notable improvement from 2005, when Uzbek government forces killed hundreds of unarmed protesters in the city of Andijan. The official death toll was 189, but witnesses say the real figure is much higher. Not only were there far fewer casualties this time around, but Uzbek authorities were quick to share sensitive details of the event.

Moreover, President Shavkat Mirziyoyev swiftly agreed to the protesters' demands, declaring that Karakalpakstan would retain its autonomous status (Özdemir, 2022). This brought the unrest to a rapid end. In fact, Mirziyoyev lifted the month-long state of emergency he declared on 2 July after less than three weeks (Reuters, 2022).

This is no small feat, especially given the region's history of ethnic conflict. To appreciate it, one need only recall the clashes between Uzbeks and Meskhetian Turks in Uzbekistan in 1989, and between ethnic Uzbeks and Kyrgyz in the Osh region of Kyrgyzstan in 1990 and 2010.

The Karakalpaks ("black hats") are formerly nomadic Turko-Muslim people who migrated to the area south of the Aral Sea from the 16th to the 18th centuries. They received the status of an "autonomous republic", first as part of Kazakhstan from 1925 to 1930, then as part of the Russian Federation, and since 1936 – part of Uzbekistan. Karakalpakstan occupies about 40 per cent of Uzbekistan's territory, although its population of 2 million makes up less than 6 per cent of the country's total population of 34 million. The population is divided almost equally into three ethnic groups – Karakalpaks, Uzbeks and Kazakhs. Linguistically, Karakalpaks are closer to the Kazakhs, given that their language belongs to the Kypchak branch of the Turkic family, like Kazakh, and the Uzbek language belongs to the Karluk branch.

The Uzbek authorities' success in restoring stability drew praise from the leaders of Uzbekistan's Central Asian neighbours (President.uz, 2022). Russian President Vladimir Putin also weighed in (Kremlin.ru, 2022), as did China's foreign ministry (Fmprc.gov.cn, 2022). The United States and the European Union, however, expressed (State.gov, 2022) concern over the violence and called (EEAS Press Team, 2022) for a full, credible, and transparent investigation into the events.

The prospect of losing autonomous status clearly spurred on the protests in Karakalpakstan. But on 6 July, Mirziyoyev's press secretary, Sherzod Asadov, suggested that the upheaval was "prepared for years by foreign forces", whose "main goal is to encroach on the territorial integrity of Uzbekistan and create an inter-ethnic conflict" (Uz.sputniknews.ru, 2022).

This might call to mind accusations made by then-President Islam Karimov after the Andijan violence in 2005: western powers, he claimed, were attempting to orchestrate a "colour revolution". The episode upended Uzbekistan's relations with the West for at least a decade. But Mirziyoyev is no Karimov.

Since coming to power in 2016, Mirziyoyev has promoted regional cooperation, released political prisoners, introduced measures to ban forced labour, improved media freedom, and implemented many more positive reforms. In 2019, foreign direct investment in Uzbekistan increased by more than 150% (UNCTAD, 2020), and *The Economist* named Uzbekistan the world's "most improved country" in 2019 (Economist, 2019).

Mirziyoyev wants to be taken seriously as a progressive and trustworthy leader, so could his government's claims about the protests be true? One should first consider which outside force could possibly orchestrate such large protests. Uzbekistan is no fledgling state: unlike its Central Asian neighbours, statehood preceded the arrival of the Russian Empire. And, since not just anyone can undermine the unity of a mature country, the most likely culprit would be a major foreign power, even a global superpower.

But regional destabilization is not in the interest of Uzbekistan's giant neighbours, Russia and China. Both would prefer a prosperous and confident Central Asia to a poor and volatile region, which could become a source of extremism, terrorism, poverty, and mass migration.

The same is true of the West, which has always supported Central Asian countries' independence and development, and thus has no reason to oppose Mirziyoyev. In fact, the US and Europe are the leading foreign investors (Otorbaev, 2022) in the region, by a large margin. With Russia and China also holding major stakes in Uzbekistan's economy, it seems unlikely that any of the world's biggest powers would be eager to sow instability there.

It is far more likely that the recent protests were mainly driven by widespread poverty, high unemployment, and climate change. While recent reforms are undoubtedly a step in the right direction, economic development will take time.

The good news is that Uzbekistan has significant economic potential, not least owing to its considerable primary energy resources. The country's proven reserves are estimated at about 1.8 trillion cubic meters of gas, 600 million barrels of oil, and 1.9 billion tons of coal (World Bank, 2013). Karakalpakstan, in particular, is home to substantial natural-gas fields, the development of which would create jobs and fill the regional government's coffers.

But, as neighbouring Kazakhstan's experience shows, hydrocarbon-rich countries are hardly immune to protests. And the people of Karakalpakstan have plenty of other grievances. The desiccation of the Aral Sea has caused widespread land degradation and desertification and also resulted in the release of toxic chemicals that had accumulated in the lake (once the world's fourth largest) during Soviet times, when upstream farmers used pesticides intensively to increase crop yields. As a result, the people of Karakalpakstan suffer from water shortages and poor health. Climate change will exacerbate these trends. It is estimated (Kirby, 2015) that, by 2050, Central Asia will have lost two-thirds of its glaciers – and thus its water – relative to 1960 levels.

But, aside from natural resources, Uzbekistan stands to benefit from a population that understands what it means to be a unified people under a single government. Importantly, it also has leaders who are committed to preserving their country's independence and advancing its development. One hopes that, far from being a harbinger of further unrest, the recent violence stimulates more positive reforms.

Notes

1 Part of the section was published in the *Project Syndicate* [https://www.project-syndicate.org/commentary/kyrgyzstan-third-political-revolution-root-causes-by-djoomart-otorbaev-2020-10], and [https://www.project-syndicate.org/commentary/kyrgyzstan-third-revolution-what-happens-next-by-djoomart-otorbaev-2020-11]; copyright: Project Syndicate, 2020.

2 Part of the section was published in the *Project Syndicate* [https://www.project-syndicate.org/commentary/kazakhstan-protests-opportunities-for-russia-and-oligarchs-by-djoomart-otorbaev-2022-01]; copyright: Project Syndicate, 2022.

3 Part of the section was published in the *Project Syndicate* [https://www.project-syndicate.org/commentary/uzbekistan-karakalpakstan-protests-fueled-by-poverty-climate-change-by-djoomart-otorbaev-2022-08]; copyright: Project Syndicate, 2022.

References

Anadolu Agency, 2020. China calls for stability in Kyrgyzstan amid protests. [Online] Available at: https://www.aa.com.tr/en/politics/china-calls-for-stability-in-kyrgyzstan-amid-protests/1998479 [Accessed July 2022].

BBC News, 2022. Kazakhstan: Prezident Tokaev prikazal strelyat' na porazhenie, protesty v strane stihayut. [Online] Available at: www.bbc.com/russian/new-59906874 [Accessed July 2022].

Cooley, A. *et al.*, 2021. The UK's kleptocracy problem. [Online] Available at: www.chathamhouse.org/2021/12/uks-kleptocracy-problem [Accessed July 2022].

Economist, 2019. Which nation improved the most in 2019? [Online] Available at: https://www.economist.com/leaders/2019/12/21/which-nation-improved-the-most-in-2019 [Accessed July 2022].

EEAS Press Team, 2022. Uzbekistan: Statement by the spokesperson on the latest developments. [Online] Available at: https://www.eeas.europa.eu/eeas/uzbekistan-statement-spokesperson-latest-developments_en [Accessed July 2022].

Epkenhans, T., 2016. *The Origins of the Civil War in Tajikistan: Nationalism, Islamism, and Violent Conflict in Post-Soviet Space.* Lanham, MD: Lexington Books.

Fmprc.gov.cn, 2022. Foreign ministry spokesperson Zhao Lijian's regular press conference on July 4, 2022. [Online] Available at: https://www.fmprc.gov.cn/mfa_eng/xwfw_665399/s2510_665401/2511_665403/202207/t20220704_10715130.html [Accessed July 2022].

Gazeta.uz, 2022. Chislo pogibshikh vpri volneniyakh v Nukuse vyroslo na 3 cheloveka. [Online] Available at: https://www.gazeta.uz/ru/2022/07/18/victims/ [Accessed July 2022].

Gunkel', E., Sosnickaya, O. & Prokopenko, A., 2022. Eksperty o Kazakhstane: Tranzit vlasti Nazarbaeva byl "fiktivnym". [Online] Available at: www.dw.com/ru/jeksperty-o-kazahstane-tranzit-nazarbaeva-provalilsja/a-60341424 [Accessed July 2022].

Iji, T., 2005. Cooperation, coordination and complementarity in international peacemaking: The Tajikistan experience. *International Peacekeeping*, 12 (2), pp. 189–204.

Interfax.ru, 2022. V Alma-Ate zaderzhan kriminal'nyi avtoritet "Dikii Arman". [Online] Available at: www.interfax.ru/world/814231 [Accessed July 2022].

International Crisis Group, 2001. Tajikistan: An uncertain peace. [Online] Available at: https://www.crisisgroup.org/europe-central-asia/central-asia/tajikistan/tajikistan-uncertain-peace [Accessed July 2022].

Kalyukov, E., 2022. Eks-sovetnik Nazarbaeva obvinil specsluzhby Kazahstana v predatel'stve. [Online] Available at: www.rbc.ru/politics/07/01/2022/61d863399a7947dc8c6e8e6c [Accessed July 2022].

Kirby, A., 2015. *Central Asia's Glaciers May Lose Half their Ice by Mid-century*, Ottawa: The Energy Mix.

Kirchick, J., 2010. Russia rises while Kyrgyzstan burns. [Online] Available at: www.wsj.com/articles/SB10001424052748704009804575308773623569614 [Accessed July 2022].

KPMG, 2019. *Private Equity Market in Kazakhstan*, Almaty: KPMG in Kazakhstan and Central Asia.

Kremlin.ru, 2022. Telefonnyi razgovor s Prezedentom Uzbekistana Shavkatom Mirzieevym. [Online] Available at: http://kremlin.ru/events/president/news/68821 [Accessed July 2022].

Otorbaev, D., 2022. Who is the biggest investor in Central Asia? It is not China or Russia. [Online] Available at: https://news.cgtn.com/news/2022-05-02/Who-is-the-biggest-investor-in-Central-Asia-It-is-not-China-or-Russia-19HRnQhtnrO/index.html [Accessed July 2022].

Özdemir, S., 2022. Republic of Karakalpakstan retains autonomy in Uzbekistan. [Online] Available at: https://www.dw.com/en/republic-of-karakalpakstan-retains-autonomy-in-uzbekistan/a-62357018 [Accessed July 2022].

President.uz, 2022. Lidery Uzbekistana i Kazakhstana rassmotreli aktual'nye voprosy dvustoronnei povestki. [Online] Available at: https://president.uz/ru/lists/view/5310 [Accessed July 2022].

Reuters, 2022. Uzbekistan lifts state of emergency in Karakalpakstan after protest deaths. [Online] Available at: https://www.reuters.com/world/asia-pacific/uzbekistan-lifts-state-emergency-karakalpakstan-after-unrest-2022-07-20/ [Accessed July 2022].

Smith, C. S., 2005. U.S. helped to prepare the way for Kyrgyzstan's uprising. [Online] Available at: www.nytimes.com/2005/03/30/world/asia/us-helped-to-prepare-the-way-for-kyrgyzstans-uprising.html [Accessed July 2022].

Sobiri, B., 2017. The long echo of Tajikistan's civil war. [Online] Available at: https://www.opendemocracy.net/en/odr/long-echo-of-tajikistan-s-civil-war/ [Accessed July 2022].

State.gov, 2022. Protests in the Karakalpakstan autonomous region in Uzbekistan. [Online] Available at: https://www.state.gov/protests-in-the-karakalpakstan-autonomous-region-in-uzbekistan/ [Accessed July 2022].

The Guardian, 2022. Kazakhstan authorities raise death toll from unrest to 225. [Online] Available at: www.theguardian.com/world/2022/jan/16/kazakhstan-authorities-raise-death-toll-from-unrest-to-225 [Accessed July 2022].

UNCTAD, 2020. *World Investment Report 2020*, New York: UNCTAD.

Uz.sputniknews.ru, 2022. Шавкат Мирзиёев: за беспёрядками в Нукусе стёяли инёстранные силы. [Online] Available at: https://uz.sputniknews.ru/20220706/shavkat-mirziyoev-za-besporyadkami-v-nukuse-stoyali-inostrannye-sily-25955347.htm [Accessed July 2022].

World Bank, 2013. *Uzbekistan Energy/Power Sector Issues Note*, Washington DC: World Bank.

Xinhuanet.com, 2020. Putin hopes for peaceful settlement of crisis in Kyrgyzstan. [Online] Available at: http://www.xinhuanet.com/english/2020-10/07/c_139424385.htm [Accessed July 2022].

Part IV

Neighbourhoods

14 Eurasian Economic Integration

Introduction

Currently, the only economic union operating in the Central Asian region is the Eurasian Economic Union (EAEU), which includes Kazakhstan and the Kyrgyz Republic. The agreement, signed in Astana, Kazakhstan, on 29 May 2014, marked the launch of the Union. There are five member countries – the Russian Federation, Kazakhstan, Belarus, Armenia, and the Kyrgyz Republic – and three observer states – Moldova, Uzbekistan and Cuba.

The EAEU is an international economic union for the free movement of goods, services, and financial and labour resources. The Union has become the successor to the previously established customs union but represents the next, higher level of supranational integration. Under the Charter of the Union, its member countries jointly develop and implement a unified strategy in key sectors and contribute to the modernisation and strengthening of the competitiveness of national economies.

The main governing body of the Union is the Supreme Eurasian Economic Council (SEEC), which includes the heads of its states. It meets at least once a year and takes major decisions on the development goals and strategy of the union. The Eurasian Economic Commission (EEC) is the executive body of the EAEU, headquartered in Moscow. The EEC adopts decisions of a legal nature, the execution of which are mandatory for all participating countries. The Union has a judicial body – the Court of the EAEU, located in Minsk. The organisation's governing bodies are financed based on the budget agreed by the member states. The EAEU is open to new members who share its principles and primary goals.

The customs union created in 2011, which included Russia, Belarus and Kazakhstan, and then its legal successor – the EAEU, is the first post-Soviet initiative with the characteristics of a supranational political institution. Until 2010, the post-Soviet countries achieved close economic cooperation only in a few select areas, such as rail transportation, aviation security standards and electrical networks. On the one hand, the EAEU is not a flawless success story. After an initial rapid growth phase in 2009–2015, progress slowed down and became largely formal. On the other hand, the EAEU can boast a few

DOI: 10.4324/9781003360728-19

achievements in functioning institutions, common goods and labour markets, several dozen standard technical regulations and its first free trade zones.

History

A formal proposal for economic integration in the post-Soviet space was made in a speech by the President of Kazakhstan, Nursultan Nazarbayev, in March 1994 in a lecture at the Moscow State University. The crux of his thesis was that breaking economic ties between the republics of the former Soviet Union had been a mistake. Natural geographic proximity, deep cultural ties, shared transport and energy infrastructure, similar legal and regulatory frameworks, and the absence of language barriers are a solid basis for restoring economic ties that will benefit everyone. In his speech, President Nazarbayev presented the idea of a union, emphasising the importance of establishing the EAEU with a focus on restoring and developing historic economic ties. From the very beginning, the idea received Russia's support. Russia lost its former imperial greatness and influence over the former Soviet republics, and its economy suffered the most from the rupture of economic ties. Naturally, together with Russia, the idea was supported by Belarus, which has close relations with its eastern neighbour. However, it took a long twenty years before the member countries managed to turn this idea into reality.

As a result of initial discussions, several international treaties aimed at restoring lost economic ties were prepared and signed. In 1995, Belarus, Kazakhstan and Russia signed an agreement on establishing the Customs Union. This tool was designed to remove barriers to economic interaction, promote the free exchange of goods and ensure fair competition. In 2000, the Kyrgyz Republic and Tajikistan joined the Customs Union, and these five states created the so-called Eurasian Economic Community (EurAsEC). More than 100 additional agreements have been signed under the auspices of this structure, and the Customs Union Commission has become the executive body of the community. The EurAsEC was officially dissolved on 1 January 2015, due to the creation of the EAEU.

There were also other, less successful attempts at the economic integration of the post-Soviet countries. For example, in 2003, the Presidents of Belarus, Kazakhstan, Russia and Ukraine signed an agreement on creating the Common Economic Space. However, Ukraine's Orange Revolution of 2004 put an end to this endeavour.

Trade

The volume and dynamics of trade between union members and other partners are particularly important economic indicators. The foreign trade volume of the EAEU member states with countries outside the EAEU in 2021 reached a record of $844.2 billion, 35.1 per cent more than in 2020. There was an increase in exports of goods, which reached $525.7 billion with a rise of 44.1 per cent (Figure 14.1), and imports, which amounted to $318.5 billion, with an increase of 22.6 per cent (Figure 14.2). The foreign trade surplus amounted to $207.2 billion against $105 billion in 2020 (Eurasiancommission.org, 2022a). A low base partly drove this strong growth in trade compared to 2020 due to the coronavirus pandemic. At the same time, the trade balance increased due to a favourable ratio of prices for exported and imported goods with countries that are not members of the EAEU.

Exports from the EAEU member states to countries outside the EAEU grew in 2021 by 46.3 per cent due to an increase in prices for exported goods. At the same time, the physical volume of supplies of goods decreased by 1.5 per cent. In 2021, compared to 2020, exports from Belarus increased by 47.8 per cent, from Russia by 47 per cent, and from Kazakhstan by 25.8 per cent. The physical volume of imports increased by 13.9 per cent, and their cost – by 22.6 per cent. Imports increased due to the growth of import of goods to the Kyrgyz Republic – by 60.6 per cent, Russia – by 26.5 per cent and Armenia – by 14.8 per cent (Eurasiancommission.org, 2022b).

The European Union has become the primary buyer of goods exported by the EAEU member states. The share of exports to these countries amounted to 42.2 per cent (in 2020 – 37.6 per cent); 24.7 per cent of all goods were exported to Asian countries (26.5 per cent in 2020), of which 15.1 per cent (16.4 per cent) were exported to China and 3.6 per cent (3.7 per cent) to South Korea. Exports to the US were only 3.6 per cent (3.2 per cent).

Import deliveries mainly came from Asian countries – 41.5 per cent (in 2020 – 40.1 per cent) and the European Union – 33.8 per cent (35.5 per cent).

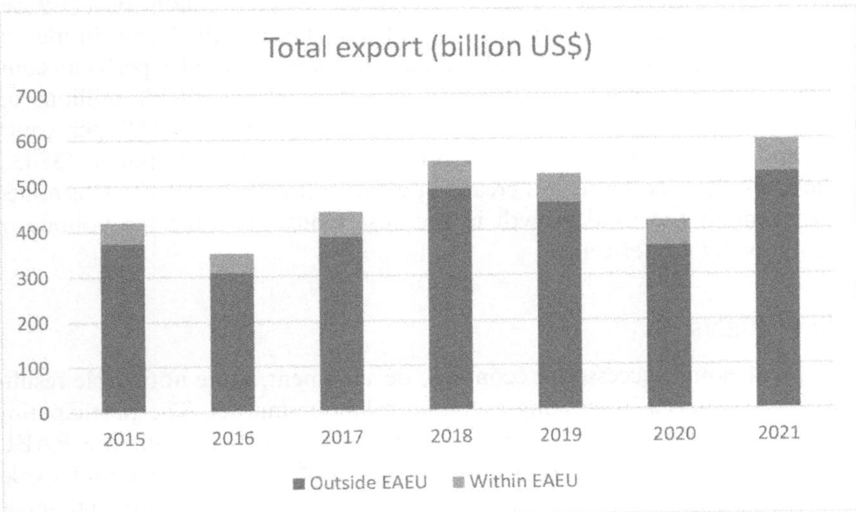

Figure 14.1 Total exports of EAEU countries
Source: Eurasiancommission.org (2022).

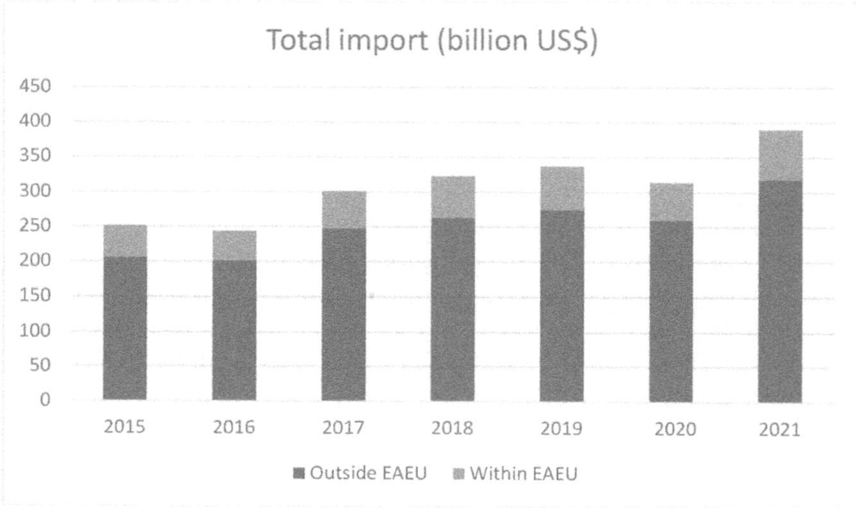

Figure 14.2 Total imports of EAEU countries
Source: Eurasiancommission.org (2022).

Of the Asian countries, the largest volumes of imports were accounted for by China – 27.4 per cent (in 2020 – 25.5 per cent), and South Korea – 4.4 per cent (4.7 per cent). Imports from the US accounted for 6 per cent (5.7 per cent).

The volume of mutual trade between the EAEU member states in 2021, calculated as the sum of the value of export operations of the EAEU member states in mutual exchange, amounted to $72.6 billion, or 131.9 per cent of the 2020 level (Figure 14.1–14.2). Russia became the leader in mutual trade with a volume of $45,806.4 million (an increase of 34.3 per cent compared to 2020). Russia was followed by Belarus ($17,464.0 million, an increase of 24.7 per cent), Kazakhstan ($7,648.9 million, 34.9 per cent), Armenia ($888.8 million, 25.2 per cent) and the Kyrgyz Republic ($803.2 million, 44.9 per cent). The increase in average prices for goods determined 58 per cent of the total growth in the cost indicator, while the volume of goods grew by 42 per cent.

Labour Rights

Along with some successes in economic development, quite noticeable results have been achieved in creating a common labour market. The participating countries have removed all barriers that prevent citizens from the EAEU countries from finding work in other countries of the union. Migrant workers and members of their families receive the same labour rights and social guarantees as citizens of the host countries. Employers from member countries could hire workers from other countries without restrictions in their national labour markets and no licensing or quota obligations remain.

Workers from member countries are not required to obtain work permits. If labour migrants are officially employed, their children can freely attend kindergartens and schools, and all family members get health insurance. The problem of pension provision – where each country has its own national pension legislation – for labour migrants has also been resolved.

During the accession of the Kyrgyz Republic to the EAEU, public opinion paid particular attention to the rights of its labour migrants. It could be suggested that EAEU membership has dramatically improved the work and life of Kyrgyz labour migrants. It is especially noticeable when they are compared to migrants from Tajikistan and Uzbekistan, non-EAEU states. The differences have been discerned to the extent that the citizens of these countries want to obtain citizenship of the Kyrgyz Republic en masse to enable them to enjoy the same labour and social rights in Russia and Kazakhstan as the citizens of the Kyrgyz Republic. Comparing the dynamics of the volume of remittances to the countries of Central Asia in recent years, which is described in detail in Chapter 3, one can notice a more stable growth in remittances from Kyrgyz migrants compared to migrants from other countries.

Public Opinion

It is imperative that, on the whole, the public in the EAEU countries and Tajikistan (which is seen as the next potential member of the union) support Eurasian integration for the project to be a success. According to public opinion monitoring conducted by the Eurasian Development Bank (EDB) since 2012, the public approval rating of the Eurasian integration project ranges from 50 to 83 per cent. In Tajikistan, it reaches 69 per cent. At the same time, the positive attitude towards Eurasian integration is slightly decreasing (Zadorin, et al., 2017).

In the first three years of the EAEU's existence (2015–2017), the most visible decline in public support for participation in the union occurred in Russia (from 78 to 68 per cent of the population) and Armenia (from 56 per cent of the population to 50 per cent). In other EAEU countries, public support for Eurasian integration has also declined – in Kazakhstan from 80 to 76 per cent, in Belarus from 60 to 56 per cent. Since 2015, the Kyrgyz population has shown the most positive attitude toward EAEU membership and has only changed slightly over this time – from 86 to 83 per cent. Compare this to 2014, when only 50 per cent of the country's population supported its entry into the union, and 30 per cent opposed it.

One of the reasons for the decline in public confidence in Eurasian integration is the slowdown in economic growth, high inflation and the devaluation of national currencies, which were associated, among other things, with economic sanctions imposed by Western countries against Russia in 2014–2015.

The EDB's report's authors consider the high level of social ties between the countries and trust in each other "phenomenally", which is regarded as indispensable integration capital. Answering the question of which entities are friendly and able to support their country in difficult times, the majority, as in the last five years of observations, spoke in favour of the Commonwealth of Independent States (CIS) region (which, until recently, included all former republics of the Soviet Union). The highest confidence in neighbours is expressed by the population of Tajikistan, the Kyrgyz Republic, and Kazakhstan (in 2017–95, 94 and 90 per cent, respectively). At the same time, Russia continues to be the leader in perceiving all respondents as a friendly state. Seventy-six per cent of citizens from all six countries surveyed named it the friendliest. In second place was Kazakhstan with 31 per cent, and in third was Belarus with 21 per cent.

The countries of the EAEU and Tajikistan showed the highest result in the penetration of mutual social ties. 51 to 80 per cent of their population (excluding Russia) stated that they regularly keep in touch with relatives, friends, and colleagues from the CIS countries. This is the highest level of social connections in the world. In 2017 the highest rates were recorded in the Kyrgyz Republic with 80 per cent, Armenia with 79 per cent and Tajikistan with 66 per cent. Thirty-one per cent of the Russian population also maintains social contacts in neighbouring CIS countries. Given the very different cultural, educational and social statuses of the people of these countries, these figures are also relatively high.

A business community survey conducted by EDB experts among 337 commercial companies operating in the EAEU countries also showed positive results (Chimiris, et al., 2022). On average, 73 per cent of companies believe Eurasian integration makes it easier to do business in the EAEU. This opinion was shared by 79 per cent and 78 per cent of respondents in Kazakhstan and Belarus, respectively, 75 per cent each in Russia and Armenia, and 60 per cent in the Kyrgyz Republic.

The EAEU and the BRI

When analysing the prospects for developing Eurasian economic cooperation, it is not possible to ignore its interaction with the Belt and Road Initiative (BRI), promoted by China. This topic has become more actively discussed since 2014 due to the deterioration of relations with Western countries. Russia has intensified the development of its economic ties with Asian countries and, above all, with China, which has become Russia's closest ally in many areas of activity, from joint investments in hydrocarbon development projects in Siberia and the Far East to the laying of new sea transportation along the Northern sea route in the Arctic. Evidently, the Sino–Russian partnership should have some effects on the cooperation between China's BRI and the EAEU, where Russia plays a leading role.

In May 2015, Vladimir Putin proposed to "coordinate" or match the BRI through economic integration within the EAEU (The Kremlin, 2015a). Russia and China signed a special agreement, which describes the initiative of cooperation between these projects (The Kremlin, 2015b). Under this agreement, China and the EAEU decided to work on joint infrastructure and trade facilitation projects. Interestingly, this document was signed by the Russian President himself, not by the representative chairing the EAEU, which directly indicates the Russian interest in developing such cooperation. This fact is not however crucial since, in 2013, all EAEU member countries supported the BRI.

The first Russian proposals for coordinating the BRI and the EAEU, especially in Central Asia, have undergone a few changes over time. First, in his speech at the 70th session of the UN General Assembly, President Putin proposed to involve the EU in this cooperation, which he called an "integration of integrations" (The Kremlin, 2015c). Then the idea was further developed and included in the collaboration of ASEAN and the Shanghai Cooperation Organization (SCO) while excluding the EU (The Kremlin, 2015d). Another iteration of the Eurasian partnership occurred in 2016 when in his speech at a meeting of the St. Petersburg International Economic Forum, President Putin presented the concept of a "Greater Eurasian Partnership" that would include the EAEU, China, India, Pakistan, Iran, and the CIS countries (The Kremlin, 2016). In his speeches, President Putin stated that other members of the EAEU fully supported the idea of partnership since all members share a common vision of what Eurasian integration should look like (The Kremlin, 2017). Indeed, in their statements, the presidents of the EAEU member states have repeatedly supported the idea of an "integration of integrations" (Belta, 2015).

The countries of Central Asia welcome economic interaction with their powerful neighbours, Russia and China, aimed at developing the entire region and individual countries alike. Although there are speculations about a rivalry between the two countries for dominance in the area, they are probably exaggerated. It is unprofitable for either of these two influential neighbours of Central Asia to have weak and poor neighbours complaining about their fate and asking for help. This is even more the case with neighbours who pose security threats in the form of terrorism, nationalism, or extremism. On the contrary, it is beneficial for both Russia and China to have predictable and prosperous neighbours pursuing effective domestic and foreign policies. It is not a short-sighted competition between influential neighbours but effective interaction that will bring beneficial and fruitful results to our region.

Uzbekistan and the EAEU

Regarding the prospects of the EAEU, full membership of Uzbekistan in the union would be a real breakthrough. In 2020, the country received observer status; since then, it has been analysing the pros and cons of joining the union as a full member. Uzbekistan is the most populous country in Central Asia, with a population exceeding 34 million (or 18 per cent of the EAEU countries' population) (Worldometer, 2022), and the second-largest economy in Central Asia, with a GDP exceeding $60 billion (World Bank, 2021). The country is rich in natural resources and has a developed industrial base. The GDP of Uzbekistan is equivalent to about 3 per cent of the total GDP of the EAEU countries and is comparable to that of Belarus. Until 2017, even the most optimistic predictions did not consider the country's membership in the EAEU possible. However, that year President Mirziyoyev started a policy of openness, structural transformation and economic reforms and soon announced the need to study the issue of joining the EAEU. In his address to the nation in January 2020, Mirziyoyev made it clear that the government was looking to cooperate with the EAEU. He also stressed that, apart from investment and broader economic benefits, "integration means better conditions for our migrants in Russia and Kazakhstan".

According to calculations by the EDB, the potential annual volume of infrastructure investments from the EAEU to Uzbekistan could amount to $1–1.5 billion. This would provide an additional annual GDP growth of 0.3–0.4 per cent (Vinokurov, et al., 2021). Access to the common labour market of the EAEU will bring an additional inflow of remittances to Uzbekistan of $1.5–2 billion per year. According to the report's authors, the additional contribution to GDP growth from a greater flow of remittances could be around 0.3–0.4 per cent. In addition, labour migration will mitigate potential socio-economic tension caused by unemployment. An essential advantage of deepening integration for Uzbekistan will be the chance to increase exports to EAEU countries by an additional $1.2 billion. In 2020, exports to the EAEU member states amounted to $3 billion (Vinokurov, et al., 2021).

In addition to the direct benefits of Uzbekistan's accession to the EAEU, the economy of Central Asia will also receive an additional impetus for regional development. There will be additional funding for transport and energy infrastructure and the implementation of new cross-border projects. Existing components of the transport infrastructure, which have a predominantly latitudinal orientation (West-East), will be supplemented by new meridional branches (North-South), which are currently underdeveloped. According to estimates, the necessary annual financing for transport infrastructure in Uzbekistan until 2030 may reach about 2.1 per cent of its GDP.

Not yet a full member of the EAEU, Uzbekistan has still begun to promote initiatives to involve the countries of the Union in joint infrastructure projects. "We are ready to cooperate with partners in the EAEU in the implementation of the construction project of the Trans-Afghan railway from Termez to Pakistani Peshawar, which will provide the shortest access to South Asia with a market of two billion consumers", President of Uzbekistan Shavkat Mirziyoyev said during a speech on the video link at a meeting of the Supreme Eurasian Economic Council on 27 May 2022 (Rambler/finansy, 2022).

The entry of Uzbekistan into Eurasian structures would contribute to the harmonisation of Central Asia's water and energy balance. Considering the complementary architecture of the power grid economy, the design of generating capacities and the water resources management system, the development of the region's water and energy complex has broad development prospects. Uzbekistan and other countries of Central Asia need modern integration approaches to the formation and regulation of the regional water and energy market based on modern technological and digital solutions. If Uzbekistan does become a full member of the EAEU, Tajikistan may be encouraged to follow suit to avoid isolation.

Criticism of the Union

It is worth recognising that many experts still express fair criticism regarding the formation and functioning of the Eurasian Economic Union, especially when compared to the development of the EU. But, as discussed, we must recognise that the history of each of the unions, the time of their formation, the economic scale and the quality of their members differ greatly. One union includes developing economies, and the backbone of the other is made up of the most developed countries. Therefore, it is more appropriate to compare the EAEU with similar unions that include developing countries such as ASEAN, Mercosur, the Gulf Cooperation Council, or the South African Customs Union.

The most common criticism of the EAEU is that its members are unequal and economically and politically dominated by Russia. But firstly, the union is not called 'economic' for no reason, and secondly, all decisions are made by consensus, with each country having a veto. Secondly, if we are talking about the dominance of one nation over others, the role of the US and South Africa in successful associations such as NAFTA and the South African Customs Union, is no smaller than Russia's in the EAEU.

Moreover, various studies show that it is small economies have benefitted the most from their memberships. The Kyrgyz Republic is benefitting greatly from the increase in remittances from migrant workers and the growth of foreign investments and exports. Starting in 2016, exports from the Kyrgyz Republic to the EAEU countries greatly increased. In 2019, exports reached \$621 million, 48.8 per cent higher than in 2016, which was \$417 million. After joining the EAEU, Armenia more than tripled its exports to the countries of the Union – from \$236.5 million in 2015 to \$746.1 million in 2019. Russia was the primary sales market, but an increase in exports was observed in all EAEU countries. As a result, after accession, the weight of Armenian exports to the EAEU countries in total exports increased from 16 per cent in 2015 to 28.5 per cent in 2019 (Vinokurov.info, 2020).

Conclusion

What can we already note from these early stages? Public opinion towards the union in member countries is positive, and its institutions have been established and are functioning. A common labour market is being successfully formed, and the social protection and pension systems are starting to bear fruit. There is progress in technical regulation and the development of unified technical norms. The EAEU is a single market for foreign investors: a single market with quite different characteristics on the territory of five countries. Also noteworthy are specialised initiatives, such as scientific and educational cooperation, unification of norms in construction, infrastructure, energy and more. The new economic reality of the post-Soviet space is just being born.

References

Belta, 2015. Vystuplenie Lukashenko v obshhey diskussii 70-y sessii General'noy assamblei OON. [Online] Available at: https://www.belta.by/president/view/vystuplenie-lukashenko-v-obschej-diskussii-70-j-sessii-generalnoj-assamblei-oon-164411-2015/ [Accessed July 2022].

Chimiris, E. *et al.*, 2022. *EDB Integration Business Barometer*, Moscow: Eurasian Development Bank.

Eurasiancommission.org, 2022a. Statistika vneshney i vzaimnoy torgovli tovarami. [Online] Available at: http://www.eurasiancommission.org/ru/act/integr_i_makroec/dep_stat/tradestat/Pages/default.aspx [Accessed July 2022].

Eurasiancommission.org, 2022b. Dinamicheskie ryady po razdelam statistiki. [Online] Available at: http://www.eurasiancommission.org/ru/act/integr_i_makroec/dep_stat/union_stat/Pages/series/sections.aspx [Accessed July 2022].

Rambler/finansy, 2022. Tashkent priglashaet strany EAES k uchastiyu v stroitel'stve Transafganskoy zheleznoy dorogi. [Online] Available at: https://finance.rambler.ru/business/48733559-tashkent-priglashaet-strany-eaes-k-uchastiyu-v-stroitelstve-transafganskoy-zheleznoy-dorogi/ [Accessed July 2022].

The Kremlin, 2015a. Russian-Chinese talks. [Online] Available at: http://en.kremlin.ru/events/president/news/49430 [Accessed July 2022].

The Kremlin, 2015b. Sovmestnoe zayavlenie Rossiyskoy Federacii i Kitayskoy Narodnoy Respubliki o sotrudnichestve po sopryazheniyu stroitel'stva Evraziyskogo ekonomicheskogo soyuza i Ekonomicheskogo poyasa Shelkovogo puti. [Online] Available at: http://kremlin.ru/supplement/4971 [Accessed July 2022].

The Kremlin, 2015c. 70th session of the UN General Assembly. [Online] Available at: http://en.kremlin.ru/events/president/news/50385 [Accessed July 2022].

The Kremlin, 2015d. Presidential address to the Federal Assembly. [Online] Available at: http://en.kremlin.ru/events/president/news/50864 [Accessed July 2022].

The Kremlin, 2016. Plenarnoe zasedanie Peterburgskogo mezhdunarodnogo ekonomicheskogo foruma. [Online] Available at: http://kremlin.ru/events/president/news/52178/videos [Accessed July 2022].

The Kremlin, 2017. Belt and Road international forum. [Online] Available at: http://en.kremlin.ru/events/president/news/54491 [Accessed July 2022].

Vinokurov.info, 2020. Evgeniy Vinokurov. Rol' Kazakhstana kak predsedatelya v EAES vazhna dlya dal'neyshey integracii. [Online] Available at: https://vinokurov.info/ru/rol-kazahstana-kak-predsedatelja-v-eajes-vazhna-dlja-dalnejshej-integracii/ [Accessed July 2022].

Vinokurov, E. *et al.*, 2021. *Uzbekistan i EAES: perspektivy i potencial'nye effekty ekonomicheskoy integracii*, Moskva: Evraziyskiy bank razvitiya.

World Bank, 2021. GDP (current US$) - Uzbekistan. [Online] Available at: https://data.worldbank.org/indicator/NY.GDP.MKTP.CD?locations=UZ [Accessed July 2022].

Worldometer, 2022. Uzbekistan population (2022). [Online] Available at: https://www.worldometers.info/world-population/uzbekistan-population/ [Accessed July 2022].

Zadorin, I. *et al.*, 2017. *Integracionnyi barometr EABR — 2017*, Almaty: Eurasian Development Bank Centre for Integration Studies.

15 The Belt and Road Initiative in Central Asia

Introduction: "Great History is Behind Us"

As far back as the 3rd century BC, the ancient trade route that is the Silk Road attracted merchants who, until the 16th century, travelled thousands of kilometres around the Eurasian continent in caravans in all directions. They carried exotic goods like porcelain, silk, spices, linen, amber, paper, jewellery, and many more. Travelling from China to the Roman Empire and back through the vast space of "unknown and exotic territories" was hard if not perilous. Conflicts often arose due to internal disputes and various militant groups operated along paths that cut through the mountains and deserts.

In those days, it took several months or even years due to the distances and difficulties involved. This long transit time was still cost-efficient due to the considerable trade turnover. For example, the city of Kashgar was the largest trading centre of the Silk Road, where many nations – Persian, Turkish, and Afghan tribes to name a few – were continuously exchanging goods. The Roman historian Gaius Pliny Secundus (23 AD – 25 August 79 AD) wrote that before about 100 AD, China sent at least twelve convoys a year to Europe. The volume of goods transported along the route was so high that direct taxes on these sales alone accounted for up to 30 per cent of the Han Dynasty's tax revenue.

Travelling in multiple directions, hard-working merchants with their goods, travellers, explorers and missionaries simultaneously exchanged ideas, scientific discoveries, inventions, and technological innovations. Forming links between many civilisations, these people spread and exchanged religions, beliefs, sciences, cultures, and languages. As a result of the immense flow of goods, capital and human resources along this route, the peoples found and practised new forms of cooperation between nomadic communities and the settled population. The mutual influence of communities located thousands of kilometres away contributed to the establishment of ancient globalisation.

Marco Polo was not the first European to reach China, but he was the first to leave behind a detailed chronicle of his experience. In 1271 Marco Polo, just seventeen years old, set off for Asia on a series of adventures that he

DOI: 10.4324/9781003360728-20

later documented in his travel memoirs. He returned to Venice in 1295, 24 years and 24,000 km later.

The wilting of the Great Silk Road in the 16th century was directly related to the development of shipbuilding by maritime powers. Shipping of goods by sea became much more cost-efficient and attractive than by land.

Much of the Great Silk Road has been lost in the mists of time. Most of the great cultural values, temples and shrines have disappeared, swallowed up by deserts, destroyed by atmospheric phenomena, as well as by looting and numerous wars. Today on the historic Silk Road, highways and railroads are to be seen in place of caravan routes. Very few traces are left of that era, but the ancient ruins and historical chronicles that have survived are charming, yet vivid evidence of the ancient cultures that have long since disappeared.

Indeed, the German geographer Ferdinand von Richthofen would surely not imagine that the term "Silk Road" which he coined in 1877 would be reborn in the 21st century. The maritime routes' cheaper logistics costs have slowly but surely transformed the world into what it is today. The population living in areas within 100 km of the nearest ocean coast generate about 80 per cent of the world's GDP. Because of complicated and expensive overland trade routes, only a tiny group of people – around 7 per cent of the world's population – live in landlocked countries and, as it has been said, if you are coastal, you should please the world; if you are landlocked, you should please your neighbours.

Back to the "Good Old Days"

The simple reality and the current consensus among scholars is that our century will be the "Asian century". By 2050, Asian countries will generate more than half of the world's GDP. Yet many have forgotten that, apart from in the last two centuries, it always was that way.

It is only in the past 200 years, that the share of the world's GDP shifted to Europe and North America, thanks to the chain of three successful industrial revolutions there. History books reasonably objectively chart the state of the world's development over the last twenty centuries, and during this period, the world has changed significantly. Until the 18th century, the world's economy was imbalanced, with a definite leaning in Asia's direction, and it is specifically the 19th century that appears to be the critical juncture when Asia declined and the West rose. Before China was "opened up" in 1842 during the First Opium War, it accounted for a dominant share of the world's wealth, but within just one century, China's share of the world's GDP reduced from 32 per cent to just 5 per cent. With the modern rise of Asia, the world is simply returning to the "good old days". It could be suggested that China is not only the biggest story of the past but of the present and the future. The country already is and will be in the future at the centre of transformation on a historic scale.

Let's examine the reality of the modern world. The role of China as the engine of the Asian economy will benefit the entire world, especially the

Eurasian continent. It is only a matter of time before this growth fundamentally influences China's neighbouring regions, including modern Eurasia. But when and how will it happen? Quickly or slowly, sooner or later, painfully or easily, this is inevitable. We should all do everything to make this historic transformation a success.

What is happening in China now is not a standalone miracle but the natural product of its extraordinary history. It is simply a return to its former glory. Currently, the country's economy is like a coiled spring, exploding with its people's accumulated energy and wisdom, civilisational and political customs, culture and history, traditions and pride. The Belt and Road Initiative (BRI) is the ideological umbrella that attempts to cover, shape, and harmonise the new world's order around China's growth. Before going forward, one must realise where we are now and that we all live in an increasingly complex world.

The Complexity of Our World

The modern world is currently in the middle of a dramatic increase in complexity: both vertically and horizontally. These complexities sometimes link and sometimes divide the world. "Vertical" links do not recognise geography and borders. These are our world's common characteristics and qualities, independent of continents, countries, etc. Knowledge, education, science, and technology all count as vertical connections. Meanwhile, "horizontal" links are the connections between countries or ideologies.

The Vertical Complexity of the World and the Fourth Industrial Revolution

What is happening with vertical connectivity right now? One common characteristic of the modern world is that we currently find ourselves in the middle of the "fourth industrial revolution".

So far, the world has had three industrial revolutions. The first was related to a shift from production by hand to machines, along with the inventions of the steam engine, machine tools and factory systems (at the beginning of the 19th century in Britain and Europe). The second industrial revolution was related to mass production, electricity usage, and rapid industrialisation (at the end of the 19th century in Europe and the US). The third industrial revolution was related to digital computerisation technologies (in the middle of the 20th century, in the US and Japan).

A commonly accepted fact is that the fourth industrial revolution is upon us with newly invented bio- and nanotechnologies, quantum computers, artificial intelligence, 3D printers, and global connectivity. This revolution is approaching us like a giant tsunami with unprecedented speed. The pace of this fourth industrial revolution is so great that the political and legal arrangements and *status quo* cannot match its speed with normative and legislative acts. Importantly, a fundamental difference from previous industrial revolutions is that it encompasses the entire world.

Asia lost its historic superiority because of previous industrial revolutions which happened in other parts of the world. But now, it is unlikely that future innovations will take place without Asia's active participation. Asia still lags in research and innovation, but the gap is closing fast. The critical issue is that China, Asia's largest country by population, is taking the lead in the fourth industrial revolution and is likely to continue to lead in future industrial revolutions too.

History teaches us that Asia in general, and China in particular, only prospered and had periods of sustainable growth when they were open. Conversely, Asia and China declined during periods of isolation. These lessons of history should be well noted.

The Horizontal Complexity of the World and Ideologies in Competition

As we all know, during the economic boom of the 18th and 19th centuries, European thinkers invented a so-called European identity "the West against the rest", but for the last two decades, a new variety of actors have challenged the eurocentric concept of the international order. These actors include, for instance, states such as Russia, Brazil, India, China, and Turkey, who are raising their voices and developing their own ideas about the future international order.

As always in times of uncertainty, our world is currently going into crisis mode – concerns about the global economy, the refugee crisis, instability in Ukraine, Afghanistan, the Middle East, and more. Confidence seems to be at a low ebb when it comes to resolving the troubles the world is facing right now, and maybe the most significant crisis is politicians' inability to provide authentic leadership and offer long-lasting solutions.

Our challenges are firstly global and secondly long-term, and perhaps these two most fundamental features of horizontal complexity in our century can be condensed into one word: globalisation. Conversely, the two most fundamental shortcomings of our times are nationalism, which is the lack of respect for others, and short-termism, which is the lack of care for the future. Both are misguided practices with purely political motivations.

Why is it, to start with, so hard to agree with interdependence? Whether it is global warming, terrorism, pandemics, migration, or the global economy, serious problems are connected globally. There are no sustainable solutions that any nation alone can find. Policies pursued at one end of the globe affect the other end. But looking at climate change, our resource and energy consumption level, recent security policy woes, or some of today's monetary and fiscal policies, it is clear that we continue to finance our present with loans. We borrow from the future, paying for our present with natural resources without leaving them to future generations. Of the many conclusions that we need to draw from the current horizontal complexity of the modern world, two are very important.

First, cooperation is not a nice-to-have extra, but the only solution. The simple truth is that humankind is on one ship and has only one planet.

Pursuing national interests by confrontation is, in the end, self-destructive. Interdependence urgently calls for new thinking in international politics, a new push for efficient partnership, and a new spirit of cooperation for mutual benefit, solidarity and accountability.

Cooperation, of course, is not just some philosophical embrace we give each other but has real political consequences. A paradigm of cooperation means recognising and respecting this world's multi-polarity institutionally. Many more countries are now competing for the leading role in the international order – and the modern world is hugely influenced by its vertical links and interconnectedness. The old-world order has already fundamentally changed.

The second conclusion is about growth and wellbeing. Politicians love growth, especially before elections; economists love growth as well. And they have good reasons to do so: growth is a measure of human progress, a sign of creativity and inventiveness, an enabler, and a creator of prosperity and wellbeing. But growth is a means, not an end, and our admiration of growth must not blind us. We need to ask ourselves: what is it that should grow? And where should it grow? Yes, in those places where people still live in extreme poverty, we need more schools, hospitals, energy plants, roads, services, and IT. But do we need more cars in China or Europe or more second homes in the US?

What should Asia, and growing China more specifically, do in this quickly changing world? Wait, think, or act? The answer is simple. It should not wait, but it should act to help others. And do it soon, take the initiative and assume the leadership.

An Alternative Concept of International Order?

It is crucial to observe and analyse what is happening now. In early September 2013, in his speech in Kazakhstan, President Xi Jinping first announced the "Silk Road Economic Belt" to deepen cooperation and expand development in the Eurasian region. What was the external world's reaction to this initiative? How have other countries received it, especially China's neighbouring countries?

Crucially, the Chinese authorities have never officially announced the geographic boundaries of the Belt and Road Initiative (BRI). The maps published represent only an unofficial interpretation of their authors. Most maps do not even show national borders but various corridors, regions, and cities, and some are puzzled about when the map appeared. But the absence of any geographical allocation or association with any territory was the right approach – China does not impose cooperation but invites to it.

China is moving fast. Since Xi Jinping's speech, thousands of Silk Road events have been organised all over China, and many Chinese universities and scientific institutions have established specialised research institutes for the BRI. In late March 2015, the government even set up a "special leading group" under the National Development and Reform Commission (NDRC) to oversee the coordination and implementation of different projects under the framework of the BRI. There are three main aspects of the initiative.

Firstly, emphasis is placed on inclusivity and the chance to create win-win cooperation between countries along the Silk Road. The primary goal is to strengthen connectivity.

Secondly, the recommendations refer to many recently announced multilateral investment banks or funds like AIIB, the New Development Bank (formerly known as the BRICS Development Bank), the Silk Road Fund, and the future Shanghai Cooperation Organization Development Bank. National development institutions such as the Export-Import Bank or the China Development Bank will provide significant financial support for the entire initiative.

Thirdly, the BRI has a prominent domestic socio-economic dimension through increased focus on China's borderland regions, such as Xinjiang, Fujian, Guangxi and Yunnan, by strengthening these provinces' cooperation with neighbouring countries. These are not new elements of Chinese policy. What is new is that all these policy areas – domestic, foreign and regional – will interact within the framework of a single initiative. For the Central Asians, it is essential to understand what has happened after almost ten years since the announcement of the BRI.

As part of the initiative, China plans to create the world's longest economic corridor, which will cover the territory, where 4.4 billion people live. By the end of 2021, 138 countries and 31 international organisations have signed documents on cooperation with China under the project (Komrakov, 2022). According to China's Ministry of Commerce, trade with the initiative's partners hit a record $1.8 trillion in 2021. Wang Xianju, Deputy Director of the Center for Russian Studies at the People's University of China, said that despite the restrictions associated with the pandemic, China's investment in countries that joined the BRI in 2020 increased by 20.6 per cent to $22.5 billion, and in 2021 this volume increased by another 8 per cent. According to him, in 2020, thanks to BRI investments, more than 50 large new projects were implemented (Komrakov, 2022).

Prospects, Challenges, and Achievements

Without a doubt, the Belt and Road Initiative initially known as the "new Silk Road", or "One Belt One Road", will be the global phenomenon of the modern world. Its sheer scale shows that a new, China-led economic and political cooperation framework will be genuinely geopolitical.

The BRI will form a vast network of highways, railways, airways, oil and gas pipelines, power grids, transmission, and communication networks. Along with the active development of infrastructure projects, the Chinese government will stimulate direct investments to develop industrial clusters and service networks. Ideally, they will form an integrated land area stretching from the Pacific to the Atlantic oceans and establish a direct land link between the two major global economic powers, China and Europe. The construction of this intercontinental infrastructure will be the basis for solid regional economic integration to strengthen the free flow of goods, labour, and capital, which in the long run is likely to create a single Eurasian market. This unprecedented China-led free trade cooperation will undoubtedly impact global economic development, forming the foundation for a new and more predictable political and economic order.

North America, Europe, and Southeast Asia, including China, currently produce 90 per cent of the world's GDP. Speaking pragmatically, these world power centres should strengthen trade and economic ties to achieve sustainable economic growth. Since two of these centres, China and Europe, are located on the Eurasian continent, it is possible and necessary to develop land trade relations along with maritime ones. The inner provinces of China and the countries of Central Asia are being presented with new opportunities. It is not just a win-win situation for China and Europe. Since it is through Central Asia that a new land bridge will pass, it is a "triple win", with China, Europe and Central Asia all standing to benefit. We presented a detailed analysis of the Eurasian transport bridge in Chapter 7.

Admittedly, because of the global scale of the BRI, it will encounter significant challenges along its way. The most considerable risk in the Eurasian continent will be the enormous differences between the economic, political, cultural, social, and legal systems found in the countries along its routes. As the historian Alexis de Tocqueville put it, "the interests of the big" must be considered. China must deal with Russian interests on the Eurasian course due to its historically strong links with Central Asia and the Caucasus region. The initiative will be an additional challenge for the current global leader, the US.

It makes no sense to consider the BRI initiative as China's new "grand strategy". This initiative is China's proactive response to the growing complexity of our world. With a favourable development of events, this example may become a new concept in the organisation of the international order.

Firstly, the BRI involves building and strengthening cooperation between countries. It should be a joint "belt and road to peace and prosperity". Its goal is to create collaboration networks in many areas and at all political levels.

Secondly, the BRI must be flexible, inclusive, and open. The geographic scope of the initiative is still to be determined. Those willing to join will join; those who do not join will have time to think. The Chinese government has not published an "official" BRI map, further underscoring its global openness and inclusiveness, and this is correct. Every country interested in one of the institutions related to the BRI initiative can become part of it. The success of creating the AIIB was associated with the same method of inclusiveness. Despite its inclusive orientation, the BRI and its related institutions' success relies on the diversity of the countries that participate in it. Taking part in the BRI is not by pressure or enforcement: it is a grand invitation.

Thirdly, the main task would now be to build a comprehensive economic and political network to promote various connections between the countries along the Silk Road. On the one hand, the BRI comprises all actors outside and within China. Central, provincial, and city governments, private sector players, NGOs, expert communities, academia, and universities can all be part of the initiative.

One of the main reasons for initiating the BRI was security concerns. Take the example of energy security: China imports about half of its crude oil needed from abroad. More than half of this amount is delivered from the Middle East by sea. Almost 40 per cent of all world cargo passes through the South China Sea, and more than 60 per cent of cargo from the Persian Gulf goes to China (Schrag, 2017). With that, it becomes clear that maritime transportation safety from this potentially unstable region is a critical national security issue. All existing risks can significantly worsen in a global or regional conflict. For example, the great maritime powers could simply block the delivery of hydrocarbons by sea to China. Thus, China needs to diversify oil imports and here the obvious alternative is to import it by land from Eurasia.

Experts estimate that China's dependence on foreign oil will rise from 65 per cent in 2016 to more than 80 per cent in 2030 (Wang, et al., 2018). Naturally, imports from Central Asia and Russia could contribute to this growth. By 2022, these countries additionally supplied to China up to 20 per cent of all crude oil, and by 2030 this number could grow to up to 35 per cent of additional energy (Pang, 2022).

Building a Demand-driven Approach

The Chinese government has outlined the BRI in a handful of official documents alongside numerous unofficial books, papers, and comments. It must be said that research on the BRI has mostly been published by scholars from either China or Western Europe. Due to a lack of capacity and resources, Eastern European, Central Asian, and Russian scholars have produced less by way of analysis and publications. It is easy to see that this is not a unilateral but a multilateral initiative. This fact reflects the fact that we live in a multipolar world and that the initiative happened to arise from just one of these poles.

Not so long ago, China imported knowledge, technology, and capital. But now the country is successfully achieving development on its own soil. Now the time has come to deliver those qualities beyond its borders, which will be much more complicated. Successful outward foreign investments require money and knowledge of foreign laws, regulations, and business practices. They also involve understanding and recognising diversity, appreciating cultural differences, ethics, habits, and customs.

The BRI's thoughtful acknowledgement of these differences is an absolute must. Chinese mentality and business practices differ from their Western or Islamic counterparts, for example. Habitual standards and norms cannot be automatically applied to a new political and economic environment. One cannot automatically insist on deploying previously known norms, rules, or principles in new contexts. Practical steps must be flexible and compatible with different backgrounds. Any action should foster trust, build bridges, and construct a sense of joint ownership. It should unite people and nations, rather than divide them.

How will others, such as the neighbouring countries of Central Asia, receive the Belt and Road Initiative? It is of critical importance to know what should and should not be done while planning, acting, and communicating between potential partners during the project implementation. The key advice here is that countries and their communities should consider the BRI a responsible demand-driven process, which can build a profound sense of local ownership. As Confucius famously said: "I wouldn't know what to do with someone whose word cannot be trusted". Building trust between new partners should become the highest priority.

Building trust will not be an easy task. For example, the Soviet Union tried to harmonise its multi-cultural and multi-ethnic societies inside its country for almost seventy-five years. In some cases, this was successful, but in others, it failed. China itself recognises that this is no easy process.

One barrier the initiative may come up against is so-called "resistance groups" within the recipient countries, whose interests contradict the principles of globalisation and the ideas and goals of the BRI. Among such resistance groups could be nationalist, populist, ethnic, environmental, and other lobbyist forces. These groups currently benefit politically or economically from their nationalistic, populist, and isolationist policies and rhetoric. Only openness, inclusiveness, and effective communication will improve exchanges and mutual understanding between different people and ethnic groups, lowering the "temperature" of historical, economic, environmental, and political disputes. As the BRI drives countries towards prosperity, and ordinary people's wellbeing continuously improves, these lobbying groups will find it more and more challenging to influence the population, since the initiative will undermine the very principles of resistance groups' support and threaten their existence. With the success of the BRI, their social influence will decline.

It is therefore vital to avoid any careless steps on foreign soil, to avoid igniting nationalistic, ethnic, or environmental hysteria under the predictable slogan of "Chinese takeover". The lack of information about China's real plans and intentions in Central Asia creates fertile ground for speculation and provocation by various interest groups. Several cases of unrest in Central Asia have already been motivated by completely outlandish, fabricated reasons. Controversial nationalist groups' mere speculations and fact falsification were the main reasons for all of these cases.

A few years ago, Kyrgyz villagers entered a mine site operated by a Chinese company to fight with Chinese workers. The source of the conflict was minor and artificial, but the fact that it occurred caused significant damage to the country's investment climate. Another source of conflict is frequent speculations that Chinese workers are marrying Kyrgyz women in large numbers. How large are those numbers? From 2010 to 2018, the state recorded only six such marriages.

Many critics of China speculate about a large influx of Chinese immigrants to Kazakhstan, although the actual numbers are pretty low. According to official data, between 1995 and 2014, the Kazakhstani government granted citizenship to 73,800 individuals from China, of whom only 13 were Han Chinese, the dominant ethnicity in China which represents 92 per cent of the total population. At the end of May 2016, Kazakhstan experienced spontaneous protests sparked by proposed amendments to the Land Code adopted in 2014 to enter into force in June 2016. The changes would have allowed foreigners to rent agricultural land for twenty-five years instead of ten. Following protests, the Kazakh government postponed the introduction of this amendment. But how large was the size of land rented by Chinese citizens? According to Kazakhstan's Ministry of Regional Development, only 32 Chinese citizens have leased 4,750 hectares of land: 0.0002 per cent of the country's agricultural area.

There was a general misunderstanding, coupled with false propaganda put out by interest groups, based on an assumption that the amendments which, the officials had not adequately explained, would allow foreigners to own land. Then protests erupted. It was generally recognised that these Land Code amendments were not the real cause of the protests, which reflected an underlying discontent with the state of the national economy, dwindling income, shrinking social benefits, and widespread fear of growing Chinese economic influence in the country. Naturally, the primary blame for this case should lie with central and local governments and the intelligence services, which were unable to explain the basic ideas of this proposal. The authorities did not disseminate correct information, and the "opposition" capitalised on this. The result of all of this was that interest groups and political forces artificially but skilfully used amendments to the national law, made in the interest of the country, to build resistance to this valuable initiative.

Another example recently heard in the local Kazakh press relates to intergovernmental consultations on transferring factories from China to Central Asia. These factories are part of excess capacity in the Chinese manufacturing sector. Mass media publicised these consultations without describing what this really meant or informing the public about what enterprises China would offer. Immediately after that announcement, a few lobbying groups and media outlets spread disinformation about "these environmentally dirty, dangerous and unhealthy excessive" industries. In the end, due to the government's idleness or ignorance, public opinion turned against this initiative. After these unpleasant events, even Kazakh officials started to call their country the "buckle" in the Chinese "belt" of the Belt and Road Initiative.

Many similar examples have harmed Chinese companies' status and image in Central Asia and worldwide. There are several conclusions to draw from these cases: a disregard for the real problems, a lack of transparency, and an ignorance of key details all create an atmosphere of mistrust and suspicion.

In these cases, the public did not understand what ownership means, and it was as if someone was forcing it on them. The authorities planned their information campaign poorly, which took the guise of a demand-driven process. Good intentions led to the opposite result, and at the end of the day, public opinion turned against these healthy investment propositions. These cases also show how easy it is in some quarters to heighten dangerous anti-Chinese sentiments, leading to potentially destructive consequences. Sometimes the projects in question were destroyed and the relationships between the countries involved were harmed.

Can these "artificially created tensions" be avoided? Surely yes, but only by applying complete and transparent public consultation in advance. Firstly, governments should launch transparent public debates on each subject. Secondly, they should organise tailor-made, private-public dialogues on what is required by the countries involved and their economies. They should consult with society on what potential benefits and challenges each project would bring to the country or the region. Finally, only upon reaching complete public consensus on a specific matter, the respective government should register an open request for specific and targeted investment. That way, these "artificial problems" can be outmanoeuvred.

It could be suggested that it would be good to create educational institutions to teach and train businesspeople to work in foreign countries with different political and economic environments. In fact, this is already happening in China.

"Think globally but act locally" is an apt business slogan in these cases. Local people and society at large must be fully involved from initial planning to implementation. Every step of every action should be planned well with carefully considered tactics, precise strategies, and well-planned implementation steps. Of course, each step must include transparent communication with total inclusivity and connectivity. The fundamental goal of these steps is to build a sense of local ownership. Again – fully responsible demand-driven, rather than supply-driven, actions are required.

All parties involved must work deeper and closer on matters of "what to do and what not to do". In official BRI documents, the Chinese government clearly states that it will promote cultural, academic, and individual cooperation and exchange, building public trust and mutual understanding, and reducing the risks of public discontent. Work is planned both at the official level and at the "experts to experts" (E2E) level, to offer scientific advice and deliver straight-to-the-point recommendations to the policymakers. Such an approach is required to build trust and avoid what are sometimes costly mistakes and errors, leading to opposite results.

Each policy discussion should have input from both researchers and practitioners. That is why it is essential to comment on connections between fundamental and applied research and development. As a professor of physics, I was an active scientist in the former Soviet Union, during which time, the country was strong in fundamental research. The country survived the arms race with the US despite their military budgets being vastly different. However, it could be suggested that the Soviet Union lost economic competitiveness with the West partly because of the poor practical and commercial application of this fundamental research.

Although this subject belongs not to natural or social science, we must first acknowledge that such a problem exists and work to avoid this trap. We have an enormous number of fundamental studies here and in the outside world, creating excellent foundations for the following practical application. It is critically important to focus on the practical details of implementing these recommendations – the devil is in the detail. Actual processes will always be more complex than general, mostly theoretical studies. Our goal is not merely generating papers, but in making practical, pragmatic, and "straight-to-the-point" policy recommendations, which politicians and practitioners will actively use in their daily work. It is now time to focus on challenges for executing the idea of better cooperation and connectivity.

Politicians and policymakers everywhere are broadly the same. As a rule, they do not read papers, even brilliant ones. However, they do sometimes listen. Let's get them to listen. More multi-cultural debates between expert communities and policymakers, with the direct involvement of Eurasian, Chinese and European scholars, thinkers, and politicians, should target the creation of particular "road maps" from the initial planning of various projects to their final implementation.

Bridges, roads, and pipelines should not be the priority; human beings must be at the centre of the BRI. The initiative will only be a success if we understand this. The success of international endeavours will require a deep understanding of individual and family values, traditions, and national characteristics in different and diverse cultures. This understanding is an absolute "must" in making friends and friendships.

Soft Power

From the inception of the Belt and Road Initiative, China rightly stated that it would not force anyone to participate in it. On the contrary, China invited interested parties to join in this endeavour, considering its partners' interests. Thus, the BRI is essentially an intertwining of China's hard power, consisting of the ability to develop and finance projects, and soft power, consisting of trust in the true intentions of partners to develop mutually beneficial cooperation. While well-known commercial patterns apply to hard power, here we provide more details about the lesser-known soft power. It will later become clear that China, like most developing countries, will need to put much more effort into developing its soft power. This section will define and describe the basic principles of soft power. We will pay particular attention to best practices in developing and applying soft power in countries that have succeeded in this regard.

Definition and History of Soft Power

Soft power is the ability to attract and persuade. While hard power is the ability to coerce and grows out of military or economic might, soft power arises from the attractiveness of a country's culture, ideals, and policies. In general, power is the ability to affect others, to get what one wants, and this goal can be achieved through coercion, payment or attraction.

History shows that the most effective empires and their leaders always recognised the necessity to balance and skilfully use military and non-military force. Take the Roman Empire's providing "bread and circuses" to appease those who depended on them. Or take Genghis Khan, who paid particular attention to ideology, efficient communication, and diplomacy. It was he who invented, for instance, the concept of diplomatic immunity. Joseph Nye, a former US assistant secretary of defence and a professor at Harvard University, first coined "soft power" in the late 1980s and pointed to three primary sources of soft power: culture, political values, and foreign policy (Nye, 2005).

Hard power continues to be critical in a world of states trying to protect their security and independence and other groups willing to resort to violence to achieve their goals. For example, in modern history, hard power formed the core of the George W. Bush administration's national security strategy. According to Joseph Nye, the neo-conservatives who advised the President made a fundamental mistake (Nye, 2005). They focused too heavily on using America's military power to force other nations to do their will and paid too little attention to soft power. American politicians likely overestimated the importance of hard power because, in those years, the world turned into a unipolar world, where the US had no worthy opponents in terms of economic and military power. For many years to come, America's use of force against and disregard for countries' national dignity will affect its image worldwide. The world's strongest country neglected the need to maintain its soft power and has since incurred enormous costs to its reputation.

It is soft power that will help prevent terrorists from recruiting supporters from among the moderate majority. And it is soft power that will help deal with critical global issues that require multilateral cooperation among states. That is why it is essential that all nations better understand and apply soft power. Another pertinent example lies in with Israel, where in its Middle East policy, it relies too heavily on military strength and firing power rather than working with Palestinians and other Arab nations to improve their soft power. Let us analyse the development of soft power in several influential countries that have achieved success. Their methods differed greatly, but some techniques have become universally recognised.

The US

Undoubtedly, the primary beneficiary of the effective use of soft power in foreign policy has become the US. Such a policy did not develop spontaneously, and developing it became a vital priority and state task for American foreign policy many years ago. In the late 1930s, the Roosevelt administration made it clear that: "America's security depended on its ability to speak to and to win the support of people in other countries" (Pells, 1997). The American Marshall Plan in post-war Europe was based on "hard" economic resources and financial support. But few in those years noted its critical soft power component. Later it turned out that creating a favourable image of support and vision was just as important as direct financial assistance, and it was this that became especially attractive to ordinary Europeans. As Norwegian political scientist Geir Lundestad rightly argued, America's role in post-war Europe may have resembled an empire, but it was an "empire by invitation" (Lundestad, 2002).

In the mid-1960s, former American diplomat Edmund Gallion first introduced the definition of public diplomacy, designed to rid the US government's information activities abroad of the term "propaganda", with all its negative connotations (USC Center on Public Diplomacy, 2014). Instead, he articulated that the overall goal of strategic US communications efforts was to understand, engage, inform, and influence the attitudes and behaviour of global audiences in support of US strategic interests. A recent example of this in practice shows that some prominent figures in the American government understand the great role of soft power in modern politics. General James Mattis, the secretary of defence in Trump's administration, warned Congress, "if you don't fund the State Department fully, then I need to buy more ammunition" (Lamothe, 2017).

The US has become the primary beneficiary of this policy by systematically employing soft power in its domestic and foreign policies. American ideologists quickly realised the need to move from aggressive rhetoric to mass propaganda of the American way of life or the American Dream. Power often depends on whose army or economy wins, but it can also depend on whose story wins. Becoming a soft power superpower depends on two factors. The first is to create national stories. The second is to understand how to tell these stories and deliver them to the audiences. Thanks to the pop culture industry, displayed in phenomena such as Hollywood and the National Basketball Association, many people from all over the world not only want to buy American goods but also to be part of the American way of life, filled with freedom, civic institutions, and equal opportunities. Instead of forcing people to do things by violence or through economic pressure, America wins them over with its power of attraction.

Japan

Asia's renaissance began with the growth of Japan's post-war economy. By the end of the last century, Japan's remarkable performance had made the Japanese people wealthy and enhanced the country's soft power. As the first non-Western country in modernity to successfully compete with the West while showing that it could maintain its unique culture, Japan accumulated more potential soft power resources than any other Asian country. Like in the US, the leading role in promoting Japanese soft power was played by state institutions. In 2005, the Japanese Ministry of Foreign Affairs introduced the term "soft power" into its annual Diplomatic Blue Book, defining the term as "gaining respect and attracting others in the direction that Japan wants to move using Japan's philosophy and culture, rather than by military and economic coercion" (Melissen & Lee, 2011: 29). Shortly after, further actions to promote Japanese soft power by other government agencies followed. In 2010, the Ministry of Economy, Trade and Industry of Japan established a dedicated office to fund creative industries' content creation to promote a pleasant and attractive image of the country. Even the secretariat of the Cabinet of Ministers joined in, forming a special fund to promote the image of "Cool Japan" (Iwabuchi, 2019). Since then, soft power has become synonymous with national prestige and attractiveness. In Japan, creating a positive image at the international level has become a task at the national level.

Today Japan ranks first in the world in the number of patents, third in expenditure on research and development as a share of GDP, second in book and music sales, and it has the highest life expectancy. It is home to several top multinational brands, such as Toyota, Honda, and Sony. The decade-long economic slowdown of the 1990s tarnished Japan's reputation, but did not erase Japan's soft-power resources (Iwabuchi, 2019). Japan's global cultural influence grew in fashion, food, and pop music as well as consumer electronics, architecture and art. Japanese manufacturers rule the roost in home video games. In short, Japan's popular culture still produced potential soft-power resources even after its economy slowed down.

South Korea

South Korea is another Asian "success story" in developing and using its soft power. Kim Dae-jung, who won the presidential election in 1998, immediately styled himself "president of culture". The following year, the government passed a law on developing the culture industry and allocated an additional $149 million for this purpose, which was a considerable sum in those days. From that moment on, South Korea expanded its soft power worldwide. According to a book published in 2019 (Kim, 2020: 86), South Korea's government "targeted the export of popular media culture as a new economic initiative, one of the major sources of foreign revenue vital for the country's economic survival and advancement".

State support for developing soft power through cultural initiatives soon bore fruit. The first of these cultural initiatives are soap operas known as Korean dramas, which although initially intended for domestic audiences, gained popularity in other parts of Asia, such as the Arab countries and beyond. The triumph of Korean pop music followed the great success of

Korean soap operas. Years of investment in training and management in this industry fully paid off in terms of the care and rigorous selection of performers and their repertoire. For example, pop group EXO was promoted as a Korean Chinese group performing in Korean and Chinese and was hugely successful in both China and Korea. In 2012, Psy's Gangnam Style song became the first YouTube video to reach 1 billion views. Even UN Secretary-General Ban Ki-moon appreciated the song, calling this art a path to cultural understanding. In 2017, South Korean President Moon Jae-in announced that his goal was to spread Korean films, music and television to 100 million people within 5 years.

The popularity of Korean music and television series among young people worldwide has stimulated a general interest in Korean history and culture. People have become more interested in other aspects of the culture, such as language and cuisine. There is a widespread belief that this popularity has translated into an increase in interest in the "Made in Korea" label, including Korean cosmetics. In 2021, South Korea exported cosmetics worth $9.19 billion (Cochrane, 2022). Statistics show record sales in predominantly Muslim countries such as Indonesia, Kazakhstan, and Malaysia, as well as in the Arab nations. These countries became the main export markets for Korean halal-certified food and pharmaceuticals. It became evident that South Korea's soft power brought more commercial success to Korean exports and raised the country's prestige in the international arena.

China and India

China and India are the new giants of Asia, with their vast populations and rapid economic growth rates. Not only are their military, or "hard power", resources growing; there are signs that their soft-power resources are on the rise too. In 2000, Chinese novelist Gao Xingjian won China's first Nobel prize for literature, followed by the Indian diaspora writer V.S. Naipaul a year later. The Chinese film "Crouching Tiger, Hidden Dragon" became the highest-grossing non-English film, and Indian movies like "Monsoon Wedding" were global box-office successes. Indeed, "Bollywood" produces more movies every year than Hollywood.

The list goes on. The Chinese star of the National Basketball Association's Houston Rockets, Yao Ming, became a worldwide celebrity, and China successfully hosted the Summer Olympics in 2008. Large expatriate communities in the US – 2.4 million Chinese and 1.7 million Indians – have increased other Americans' interest in their home countries. Moreover, transnational ties in the information industry are tight, as Western high-tech companies increasingly employ affiliates in Bangalore and Shanghai to provide real-time services. But the real promise for China and India lies in the future. A country's soft power rests upon the attractiveness of its culture, the appeal of its domestic political and social values, and the style and substance of its foreign policies.

Conclusion

Of course, China's global rise is hardly a new phenomenon. Still, only recently has the context changed enough to give Beijing the space, conditions, and clout to push its ambitious designs for international development and cooperation. In 2014, President Xi Jinping said, "We should increase China's soft power, give a good Chinese narrative, and better communicate China's message to the world" (Biswas & Tortajada, 2018). The President formulated the ideology of implementing the "Chinese Dream", as an alternative and a competitor to the American Dream.

In his speech at the 19th Congress of the Chinese Communist Party in October 2017, President Xi proposed "socialism with Chinese characteristics for a new era" and the "realisation of the Chinese Dream of national rejuvenation". It will offer "a new option for other countries and nations who want to speed up their development while preserving their independence, and it offers Chinese wisdom and a Chinese approach to solving the problems of mankind".

Among the goals to be achieved in 2020–2035, Xi Jinping outlined the steps to strengthen China's soft power and make its culture more attractive. "We will improve our capacity for engaging in international communication so as to tell China's stories well, present a true, multi-dimensional and panoramic view of China, and enhance our country's soft power (Biswas & Tortajada, 2018)", he said.

China has great potential to enhance its soft power by informing people worldwide of its long history, culture, and philosophy. The ideologists of the party and the state need to supplement this by sharing its unprecedented economic and social achievements over the past four decades. For example, the country has lifted more than 800 million people out of poverty. The UN's Millennium Development Goals would not have been achieved without China's action.

China has also made remarkable improvements in its infrastructure. In 2002, it had no high-speed rail network, and by 2020, China National Railways served more than 9,600 high-speed trains daily, including the first-ever high-speed overnight sleeper services on selected longer-distance routes. Seventy-five per cent of Chinese cities with a population of 500,000 or more have direct access to high-speed rail (Jones, 2022). New technological solutions such as autonomous train control (driverless trains) and modern signalling and control technologies have been developed and are already in use.

High-quality Development is the Right Policy for Central Asia

Though moving unprecedently quickly, China faces severe challenges in modernising its economic model for the future. While the most powerful country on the planet, the US, has announced its policy of containing China through sanctions and tariffs, China is reorienting its policy towards high-quality economic growth. The model consists rapidly developing the high-tech sector and adopting modern digital ecosystems and platforms at an accelerated pace. How should China's foreign economic policy be modified in light of the new priorities? How would the new policy affect its cooperation with the Belt and Road nations?

Let's first consider the key internal challenges facing the country. China must now make a concerted effort to break the so-called middle-income trap when the growth of a national economy slows down and eventually stops after reaching a GDP per capita of around $10,000–12,000. Due to rising wages and declining price competitiveness, many emerging economies have been stuck in this state. On the one hand, they lose their ability to compete with other emerging nations' cheaper labour due to lower wages. On the other hand, they cannot compete with highly skilled and innovative advanced economies because they lag behind in technology and the ability to innovate and produce more sophisticated goods and services.

The best-known region which has fallen into the middle-income trap is Latin America. Why here? Experts point out that in Latin America, the share of industry in GDP has steadily declined over the years, while the service sector, which now exceeds 60 per cent of GDP, has grown at a faster pace (Statista, 2021a). It is known that the service sector is much less productive than the industry.

Over the past twenty years, the industry share in China's GDP declined to 37.8 per cent in 2020 from 45.5 per cent in 2000. During this period, the service sector increased its contribution to 54.5 per cent from 45.5 per cent (Bajpai, 2022). Many agree that the country's development strategy should be such that the share of industrial production does not fall below 33 per cent of GDP, which roughly corresponds to the structure of the South Korean economy (Statista, 2021b), which has been exceptionally successful in overcoming the middle-class trap. South Korea's successful experience shows that it is a high-tech rather than a traditional industry that needs to be developed at a faster pace.

China also now faces other, more complex problems, namely global competition with the US at almost all levels. This confrontation with the US compounds the threat of the middle-income trap. The US imposes various control measures and sanctions against China to slow economic growth and restrict its access to advanced technologies.

In this situation, the only correct solution is to prioritise qualitative economic growth. China intends to increase its research and development (R&D) spending by more than 7 per cent per year from 2021 to 2025, focusing on cutting-edge technologies (Kharpal, 2021). This includes nine key industries – next-generation information technology, biotechnology, new energy, materials, high-tech equipment, new energy vehicles, environmental protection, aerospace, and marine technology. The state resolved to provide significant tax breaks and credits on a large scale to companies encouraging and spending on R&D.

Another critical direction for China's development is the fight for control over big data. Big data is the most essential and irreplaceable resource for the present and the future. It fuels the work of artificial intelligence, corporations' economic power, and the state apparatus's national power. The source of this data is all human beings and everything they do, dream of, and desire – their medical records, internet habits, business value chains, and images consumed by phones. Eight years ago, Chinese President Xi Jinping said (Trkanjec, 2021): "The vast ocean of data, just like oil resources during industrialisation, contains immense productive power and opportunities. Whoever controls big data technologies will control the resources for development and have the upper hand". Many American experts have pointed out that Beijing is beating the US and its allies in this critical area (Pottinger & Feith, 2021).

How can China's efforts to modernise its economy affect the development of other countries? It is of fundamental importance that Chinese President Xi Jinping, on 19 November 2021, called for joint efforts to promote further quality development within the Belt and Road Initiative. He stressed that China should develop digital cooperation with the Belt and Road countries, promote e-commerce on the Silk Road and build a digital cooperation model. "We should carry out the 'Belt and Road' Science, Technology, and Innovation Cooperation Action Plan, strengthen international cooperation on intellectual property protection and create an open, fair, just, and non-discriminatory environment for scientific and technological development," he added (CGTN, 2021).

While achieving success in developing a high-quality digital economy, China can and should involve all countries that would like to participate in this process. China's closest neighbours, the Central Asian countries, have repeatedly expressed their desire to develop high-tech products jointly. With a highly educated population and ambitious youth, the Central Asian countries are well-placed to cooperate with China to develop the digital Belt and Road (Kley & Yau, 2021). There is, therefore, a strong argument that this is the right strategy for China in the immediate future.

A Future of Cooperation

On 25 January 2022, President Xi Jinping and the leaders of all Central Asian countries held a virtual summit dedicated to the 30th anniversary of the establishment of diplomatic relations between their countries. This summit highlighted the results of joint activities during this period and, most importantly, outlined ways for further cooperation. Next year will also mark the tenth anniversary of the announcement of the Belt and Road Initiative, which the Chinese President first announced in Kazakhstan. During the meeting in 2022, Xi Jinping presented five proposals (Xinhua, 2022). The first was related to the development of good neighbourly relations. To this end, participants in the discussion agreed to create mechanisms and develop relations based on principles of friendship, sincerity, mutual benefit, and inclusiveness. The Chinese President also said China opposes interference in countries' internal affairs under the pretext of human rights activities.

Secondly, the participants decided to continue the active development of economic relations and to strengthen ties between their countries. The Chinese President said that his country is ready to open its markets to Central Asia goods, and by 2030 he wants to bring the trade volume in the region to $70 billion. He stated that trade and logistics corridors would be built between China and Central Asia. For example, the process of designing and building a railway along the new China–Kyrgyzstan–Uzbekistan route will be accelerated.

The third thesis presented at this meeting was related to regional security, and special attention was paid to stabilising the situation in Afghanistan as part of a strategy to deepen cooperation in counterterrorism, radicalisation, separatism, and cyber threats. Because Afghanistan is a neighbour and a most important partner of both China and the countries of Central Asia, it is critically important to note that Afghanistan was first mentioned as part of greater Central Asia. The Chinese President stressed that China supports establishing an inclusive government in Afghanistan through dialogue and by completely cleansing the country of terrorism. The leaders of the Central Asian countries have repeatedly noted this as a crucial step toward achieving peace in Afghanistan.

The fourth recommendation was devoted to strengthening culture. To this end, the President proposed to open joint cultural centres and stated that China would like to make Central Asia a vibrant tourist centre for the Chinese people. He announced that China will provide more scholarships for youth from Central Asia. Finally, China's President announced that he had taken various initiatives within the UN 2030 Agenda for Sustainable Development and that his country would provide a grant of $500 million to the countries of Central Asia.

As previously described, the Boston Consulting Group estimated that between 2008 and 2016, total foreign direct investment (FDI) in Central Asia was only 18.2 per cent of the region's GDP. A similar figure in North Africa was one and a half times more, in Central America – twice as much, and in the Balkans - two and a half times more (Samruk-Kazyna, 2018). North African and Balkan territories are close to the EU, and Central America is close to the US. Correspondingly they carry out the dominant FDI in neighbouring regions. As the Chinese economy is almost on par with the EU and the US, it becomes clear that China has every opportunity to invest much more in Central Asia. This is also because China accounted for only 3.7 per cent of total FDI in the region and ranked fourth after the EU, US and Russia.

In August 2022, Bloomberg reported that companies in mainland China alone have raised a record $58 billion in initial public offerings this year, compared to $19 billion in the US and $9.9 billion in Europe (Bloomberg, 2022). Considering the economic power of China and its proximity to

Central Asia, the untapped potential for cooperation became clear. The implementation of the Belt and Road Initiative opens unlimited possibilities for this. China continues to move forward with confidence.

References

Bajpai, P., 2022. China's GDP examined: A service-sector surge. [Online] Available at: https://www.investopedia.com/articles/investing/103114/chinas-gdp-examined-servicesector-surge.asp [Accessed July 2022].

Biswas, A. K. & Tortajada, C., 2018. China's soft power is on the rise. [Online] Available at: https://www.chinadaily.com.cn/a/201802/23/WS5a8f59a9a3106e7dcc13d7b8.html [Accessed July 2022].

Bloomberg, 2022. China IPO market trounces the world with record $58 billion boom. [Online] Available at: https://www.bloomberg.com/news/articles/2022-08-07/china-ipo-market-trounces-the-world-with-record-58-billion-boom [Accessed August 2022].

CGTN, 2021. Xi Jinping urges continuous efforts to promote high-quality BRI development. [Online] Available at: https://news.cgtn.com/news/2021-11-19/Xi-Jinping-addresses-symposium-on-Belt-and-Road-construction-15jUcnDceeQ/index.html [Accessed July 2022].

Cochrane, P., 2022. Exports of South Korean cosmetics to OIC countries surge 28%. [Online] Available at: https://www.salaamgateway.com/story/exports-of-south-korean-cosmetics-to-oic-countries-surge-28 [Accessed July 2022].

Iwabuchi, K., 2019. *Cool Japan, Creative Industries and Diversity*, Jakarta: Economic Research Institute for ASEAN and East Asia.

Jones, B., 2022. Past, present and future: The evolution of China's incredible high-speed rail network. [Online] Available at: https://edition.cnn.com/travel/article/china-high-speed-rail-cmd/index.html [Accessed July 2022].

Kharpal, A., 2021. China spending on research and development to rise 7% per year in push for major tech breakthroughs. [Online] Available at: https://www.cnbc.com/2021/03/05/china-to-boost-research-and-development-spend-in-push-for-tech-breakthroughs.html [Accessed July 2022].

Kim, Y., 2020. *South Korean Popular Culture and North Korea*. 1st ed. Oxfordshire: Routledge.

Kley, D. v. d. & Yau, N., 2021. How Central Asians pushed Chinese firms to localize. [Online] Available at: https://carnegieendowment.org/2021/10/15/how-central-asians-pushed-chinese-firms-to-localize-pub-85561 [Accessed July 2022].

Komrakov, A., 2022. Zapad brosaet vyzov Shelkovomu puti. [Online] Available at: https://www.ng.ru/economics/2022-06-27/1_8471_silkway.html [Accessed July 2022].

Lamothe, D., 2017. Retired generals cite past comments from Mattis while opposing Trump's proposed foreign aid cuts. [Online] Available at: https://www.washingtonpost.com/news/checkpoint/wp/2017/02/27/retired-generals-cite-past-comments-from-mattis-while-opposing-trumps-proposed-foreign-aid-cuts/ [Accessed July 2022].

Lundestad, G., 2002. "Empire by invitation" in the American century. *Diplomatic History*, 23 (2), pp. 189–217.

Melissen, J. & Lee, S., 2011. *Public Diplomacy and Soft Power in East Asia*. New York: Palgrave Macmillan.

Nye, J., 2005. *Soft Power: The Means To Success In World Politics*. New York: PublicAffairs.

Pang, I., 2022. Gas and coal imports from Russia key to China's economic recovery. [Online] Available at: https://think.ing.com/articles/gas-and-coal-imports-from-russia-key-to-china-economic-recovery [Accessed August 2022].

Pells, R. H., 1997. *Not Like Us: How Europeans Have Loved, Hated, and Transformed American Culture Since World War 2*. New York: Basic books.

Pottinger, M. & Feith, D., 2021. Opinion. [Online] Available at: https://www.nytimes.com/2021/11/30/opinion/xi-jinping-china-us-data-war.html [Accessed July 2022].

Samruk-Kazyna, 2018. *Overview of Investment Attractiveness of Central Asian Countries*, Nur-Sultan: Sovereign Wealth Fund Samruk-Kazyna.

Schrag, J., 2017. How much trade transits the South China Sea? [Online] Available at: https://chinapower.csis.org/much-trade-transits-south-china-sea/ [Accessed July 2022].

Statista, 2021a. Share of value added by the services industry to gross domestic product (GDP) in Latin America and the Caribbean from 2010 to 2019, by region. [Online] Available at: https://www.statista.com/statistics/1070873/latin-america-caribbean-services-sector-share-gdp-region/ [Accessed July 2022].

Statista, 2021b. South Korea: Distribution of gross domestic product (GDP) across economic sectors from 2010 to 2020. [Online] Available at: https://www.statista.com/statistics/375580/south-korea-gdp-distribution-by-industry-of-economy/ [Accessed July 2022].

Trkanjec, Z., 2021. Editor's take: Intelligence, artificial intelligence. [Online] Available at: https://www.euractiv.com/section/politics/short_news/editors-take-data-centric/ [Accessed July 2022].

USC Center on Public Diplomacy, 2014. What is PD? [Online] Available at: https://uscpublicdiplomacy.org/page/what-is-pd [Accessed July 2022].

Wang, Q., Li, S. & Li, R., 2018. China's dependency on foreign oil will exceed 80% by 2030: Developing a novel NMGM-ARIMA to forecast China's foreign oil dependence from two dimensions. *Energy*, Volume 163, pp. 151–167.

Xinhua, 2022. Full text: Remarks by Chinese President Xi Jinping at the virtual summit to commemorate the 30th anniversary of diplomatic relations between China and Central Asian countries. [Online] Available at: http://www.xinhuanet.com/english/20220126/255aaf5820044c13a1de344745cac4cb/c.html [Accessed July 2022].

16 China's Loans to the World and Central Asia

Loans to the World

When analysing the volume and quality of loans provided by China to the countries of Central Asia, it is helpful to refer to a recent study by the international research centre AidData at the College of William and Mary in the US, published in September 2021. This report describes China's overseas project financing programme from 2000 to 2017 (Malik, et al., 2021). According to the study, China's Belt and Road Initiative has provided 165 developing countries with $385 billion in additional funding. Sometimes these figures are not reflected in recipient countries' balance sheets and do not qualify as sovereign debt. Therefore, the report's authors call these loans the hidden debt of these countries to China. Indeed, when signing agreements on such lending, the contracting parties voluntarily agree to their terms. No one persuades or forces anyone; as a rule, borrowers get real benefits from these concessional loans. In this case, there is a difference between the classic definition of public debt introduced by the Bretton Woods rules (Capie, 2013). In such cases, the recipient countries' governments do not reflect the loans in their balance sheets. After a while, they reclassify the funds received as additional debt outside their regular budgets. Some useful terms for this chapter include "first category loans", which are loans that are directly reflected in government balance sheets, and "second category loans", which refer to loans that are issued, not to governments, but to other public institutions subject to government obligations.

The AidData study covered 13,427 projects implemented between 2000 and 2017 worth more than $843 billion. Of these, 10,849 projects have been approved, implemented, and completed, while the remaining 2,577 projects have been suspended or closed. These projects were funded by more than 300 Chinese government agencies and non-governmental organisations. The data was collected based on information on grants and loan agreements officially published in government registries and bulletins. The analysis also used official reports from countries that receive aid and loans from China, information from Chinese state banks, and data from Chinese embassies and the Ministry of Commerce. The study shows that annual commitments to

DOI: 10.4324/9781003360728-21

international development finance are about $85 billion a year, and in this respect, China has long surpassed all major lenders, including international financial institutions.

The study showed that before the launch of the BRI, China provided loans exclusively to state institutions and under sovereign guarantees. Since the launch of the BRI, up to 70 per cent of loans have gone to other institutions, among which were state-owned companies, state-owned banks, joint ventures, and even private companies. Since some borrowers did not legally belong to the state, their debts were not reflected in government balance sheets, and they are therefore second category loans. In these cases, on the donors' requests, the actual legal agreements and contracts eliminated the distinction between public and private debt, and all obligations automatically qualify as sovereign. Since governments do not directly take on these debts, they were not formally subject to the rules of the reporting systems of Bretton Woods institutions, such as the International Monetary Fund or the World Bank.

Official aid flows fall into two categories, which correspond to the OECD definitions of "official development assistance" (ODA) and so-called "other official flows" (OOF). Since the early 2000s, following Beijing's "Going Out" strategy, which seeks to encourage its enterprises to invest overseas, China's spending on overseas development skyrocketed from $3.6 billion a year in 2000 to $114 billion a year in 2016. Even before the 2008 global financial crisis, China began to behave more like a banker than a benefactor. In 2000 Beijing issued 1.7 OOF dollars for every ODA dollar, and in 2007 this figure increased to 5.6. The sharp fall in global asset prices since the 2008 global financial crisis has further accelerated Beijing's transition from donor to banker status. Until 2008, China held most of its excess foreign exchange reserves in US Treasury bills. However, when the US Federal Reserve's quantitative easing weakened the US dollar, China decided to start investing its foreign exchange reserves in undervalued overseas assets. It deposited its surplus of hard currency in state-owned banks and instructed them to seek higher returns on investment through foreign currency lending. Between 2008 and 2013, the growth rate of Chinese OOF provision was almost double that of ODA and is currently at an impressive 9.25 OOF dollars for every ODA dollar.

China also increased its financing of ODA, further strengthening its position as the world's largest creditor to developing countries. African countries received 42 per cent of all Chinese ODA between 2000 and 2017, in line with Beijing's official stance that most of its foreign aid is for Africa. During the same period, Asia was the second-largest regional recipient of Chinese ODA, receiving 38 per cent of all. Of the Central Asian countries, only Uzbekistan was in the top 25 ODA recipient countries.

Loans to Central Asia

China is the main creditor of three Central Asian countries in the ODA category. Uzbekistan received $2.8 billion, about 20 per cent of its total sovereign debt (CAA Network, 2021). The sovereign debt of the Kyrgyz Republic to China is approximately $1.8 billion, or roughly 35 per cent of the country's total external debt (Akchabar, 2022), and Tajikistan has about $1.1 billion, which is about 35 per cent of its total external debt (Karaev, 2022). This means that the Kyrgyz Republic and Tajikistan have borrowed too much from China and that their debt levels may soon become unsustainable. That is, they will not be able to service their debts and will move towards default. For this reason, these countries stopped borrowing from China several years ago.

At the same time, Kazakhstan, with $39.01 billion or 23.4 per cent of the country's GDP, and Turkmenistan, with $8.52 billion or 14.4 per cent of the country's GDP, were in the top 25 recipients of Chinese OOF loans in 2017. The study's authors categorised Kazakhstan as a primary recipient of those loans, whose second category debt to China reached 16 per cent of GDP (Malik, et al., 2021). Here a difference in wording and definitions should be noted. For example, according to the National Bank of Kazakhstan, as of 1 April 2021, Kazakhstan's total debt to China amounted to $9.7 billion or 5.7 per cent of GDP, of which only $1.3 billion or 0.76 per cent of GDP billion was guaranteed by the state (Alimova, 2021).

Along with a few other countries with rich natural resources, Turkmenistan is in the top ten countries that have contracted the highest levels of collateralised debt from Chinese state-owned lenders. Lenders are willing to provide loans to countries with rich resources, as in many cases, they require borrowers to deposit a portion of their export revenues into accounts they control. If the borrower cannot meet its loan obligations, the lender can freeze its assets without going to court. Turkmenistan has chosen this path, pledging its current and future cash flows to secure loans.

Chinese loans have facilitated several infrastructure projects in Central Asia. In 2017, Kazakhstan had 21 projects worth $12.07 billion, Uzbekistan had fifteen projects worth $3.08 billion, there were twenty-one projects worth $2.11 billion in the Kyrgyz Republic and four projects in Tajikistan totalling $0.32 billion. China did not finance any infrastructure projects in Turkmenistan. In total, 61 infrastructure projects worth $17.58 billion are underway (Malik, et al., 2021).

Consequently, the countries of Central Asia have one of the highest ratios of their debt obligations to GDP to China. In 2017, the sovereign debt of the Kyrgyz Republic to China amounted to 30 per cent of GDP, while 1 per cent was attributed to second-category loans. The debt of Tajikistan was 24 per cent of GDP, of which 3 per cent was the second category, and in Turkmenistan debt was 2 per cent of GDP, while 23 per cent accounted for the second-category debt. Meanwhile, in Kazakhstan the debt was 2 per cent of GDP, with 16 per cent being the second category, and in Uzbekistan debt was 2 per cent of the GDP, while 9 per cent was the second-category debt.

These figures show that China is willing to provide loans without their complete formalisation as sovereign debt to countries with rich hydrocarbon resources, which export them to China. It willingly lends to Kazakh, Uzbek, and Turkmen state-owned enterprises, using its current and future contracts with these companies as collateral. At the same time, China is less willing to lend to countries that do not have liquid resources, as is the case for the Kyrgyz Republic and Tajikistan, which could be considered a logical and pragmatic strategy.

China's Role in Solving the World's Current Public Debt Problem

In April 2022, Sri Lanka announced a temporary default on its external debt amid the country's worst economic crisis in seventy years. Before this, Zambia, Argentina, Belize, Ecuador, Lebanon, and Suriname defaulted on their sovereign bonds. Others will probably follow. Fitch Ratings gives almost forty sovereign bonds a rating of B+ or worse, where B denotes a "material" risk of default (Trading Economics, 2022).

Debts are more prominent than ever, and the main creditor to emerging economies, China, is new to this business. In 2018, 72 developing countries owed $104 billion to Chinese creditors (World Bank, 2019) out of total debt of $514 billion. That amount includes direct loans from China's government "policy banks", such as China Export-Import (Exim) Bank and China Development Bank, and profit-seeking loans from state-owned commercial lenders. For comparison, these countries owed $106 billion to the World Bank and $60 billion to private holders of sovereign bonds (Horn, et al., 2020). According to Chinese government sources, the Chinese numbers are even higher. At the end of 2017, the People's Bank of China statistics showed that the country's outstanding international lending was $637bn (State Administration of Foreign Exchange, 2022). China is now in the driver's seat in controlling and managing the sovereign debt of developing countries, but does it know how to drive?

A broad consensus evolved after the outburst of the coronavirus pandemic, and the G20 forum seized on it. In April 2020, during the spring meetings of the International Monetary Fund (IMF) and the World Bank (WB), the finance ministers of the G20 agreed on a "time-bound suspension of debt service payments" for the seventy-seven poorest countries in the world as they fought an economic battle with the coronavirus. Within this Debt Service Suspension Initiative (DSSI), an estimated $12 billion due to be paid between 1 May 2020 and the end of 2020 was rescheduled.

China is a member of the G20 and fully implemented the DSSI while overcoming its own difficulties. President Xi Jinping told the other G20 leaders: "We should keep our support for developing countries and help them overcome the hardships caused by the pandemic" (Xinhuanet.com, 2020). China is by far the biggest bilateral creditor to low-income countries. It accounts for about 20 per cent of the total foreign debt owed by the seventy-seven governments eligible for the G20 initiative and about 30 per cent of their debt service. That is more than all other lenders combined, including the US, European countries, and Japan.

While this restructuring due to coronavirus was a good move, it was only a one-off for the poorest countries. Many countries that may default or call for debt restructuring are middle-income countries, requiring another approach. The G20 needs universal rules for various creditor groups on managing developing countries' debts. Fortunately, such an organisation already exists, the Paris Club of creditors, which maintains general practices for managing sovereign debt. It was created in 1956 when the first negotiation between Argentina and its public creditors occurred in Paris and is comprised of a group of finance ministry officials from important creditor countries whose role is to find solutions to debtors' payment difficulties.

Paradoxically, China, the largest lender in the world, is not a member of the Paris Club. Other creditors complain that Chinese loans and their conditions are not transparent. A common suspicion is that China is trying to make special deals, and debtor governments quickly feel like they are at the mercy of China. Yet, as default multiplies and the volumes of debt in arrears also mount, China might desire a different approach. After all, it has not regulated its credit very well, and its conditions are not standardised; China has little debt restructuring experience, and the experience they do have is mainly multilateral, with the IMF in a lead role. Everybody – debtor countries, other creditors, and China – all have an interest in China joining the Paris Club.

The experience of Russia after the collapse of the Soviet Union is enlightening. The Soviet Union had lent vast amounts to many developing nations. The conditions were complex and secret, and the interest rates were tiny. It was unclear whether they were loans or subsidies. In the mid-1990s, the Russian government decided to clean up its act. It revealed the conditions of the loans, and it turned to the Paris Club to work out how to reach reasonable settlements. In September 1997, Russia became a member of the Paris Club. Anatoly Chubais, then Finance Minister, claimed that the Paris Club accord would triple repayments to Moscow from debtor countries, increasing these to at least $500 million yearly from less than $200 million. However, Russia would apply a 30 to 80 per cent discount on about $37 billion of debt owed to it. In the end, the arrangement worked so well that it is now rare to hear anything about Russian loans and the Paris Club (The Washington Post, 1997). As defaults increase among the emerging economies, China could follow Russia's example and join the Paris Club for everyone's benefit.

Time to reform the public debt management system

The coronavirus pandemic and its effects were estimated to push as many as 150 million people into extreme poverty (World Bank, 2020). In all likelihood, poverty will rise for the first time in more than twenty years. Achieving the Sustainable Development Goals (SDGs) in the world's poorest countries may be delayed by a decade. The current system for reducing poverty and inequality does not work and requires fundamental reform.

Governments all around the world took unprecedented action to protect their citizens during the pandemic. Globally, an estimated $16 trillion has been spent on fighting the pandemic and restoring economies. As a result, in 2021, the global public debt level reached 98 per cent of the world's GDP, which is 14 per cent higher than it was at the end of 2019. Roughly the same high level of public debt existed in 1944, which led to the convening of the UN and the signing of the Bretton Woods agreement.

Unfortunately, the poorest and most disadvantaged countries suffer at both ends. Of the $16 trillion in stimulus and recovery funds, less than 20 per cent have gone to developing countries. Yet, many of them are now becoming overburdened by public debt. IMF Managing Director Kristalina Georgieva predicts that "2021 debt levels [will] go up significantly – to around 125 per cent of GDP in advanced economies, 65 per cent in emerging markets, and 50 per cent in low-income countries". However, developing countries must pay higher interest and have much less ability to manage a large debt.

In 2020 public debt increased by 20 per cent in developed countries, 9 per cent in middle-income countries, and only a few percentage points in low-income countries. The IMF says that "this reflects the limited fiscal space and financial capacity of these countries". So, one can now state that the "crisis response" has led to the opposite effect – an increase in existing inequality within countries and peoples. Why is this happening, and what should the international community do about it?

In 2020, the IMF made around $100 billion in financing available to over 80 member countries. At the end of November 2020, $11.8 billion went to 50 low-income countries, while $90.4 billion was available for emerging market economies. The IMF's debt sustainability assessments only look quite narrowly at a country's ability to pay its creditors, without considering how servicing debt might undermine its ability to meet its people's needs.

The main IMF initiative in 2020 adopted the DSSI, which was a step in the right direction. Its essence was that wealthy bilateral official creditors would suspend debt service payments for a limited period to seventy-three lower- and lower-middle-income countries that requested suspension. The support of the initiative from the G20 countries played a decisive role. For the first time, this Common Framework brought together the Paris Club and non-Paris Club creditors of the G20. It could be the first step towards a more universal and possibly permanent framework for efficient sovereign debt resolution.

However, the impact of this move was relatively small. According to the IMF, in 2020, just 43 countries benefitted from a total of $5.7 billion in debt service suspension. By June 2021, an additional $7.3 billion was suspended. These are tiny amounts and only reflect debt suspension, even though the DSSI is not yet complete. The thirty-three most indebted countries eligible for relief owe about a quarter of their public debt to China, the world's largest creditor. While China joined the initiative and provided some debt relief, it did so on different terms to other DSSI participants and, furthermore, private sector lenders did not sign up at all.

Times of crisis are ideal for bringing in sweeping reforms. The current situation calls for systemic reforms to the international debt architecture to ensure the effective restructuring of loans. First, the public response to global crises must be fair. More attention needs to be given to the weak and vulnerable countries, the opposite of which happened in 2020 and 2021. US Treasury Secretary, Janet Yellen, recently warned of the risk of a "permanent divergence" in the global economy in the years to come between high-income countries' prosperity and the debt-burdened, lower- and middle-income countries.

Given low inflation, developed countries can accumulate serious debt and finance their programmes with unusual ease, but developing countries cannot because they face far higher interest rates. Why is large debt permissible for developed countries but not for developing ones?

It could be suggested that the existing architecture of public debt management does not work. The role of the IMF and the WB should be to facilitate access to international finance for developing countries with decent economic policies, but this is not the case today. Developed countries are permitted far more significant public debt, or fiscal irresponsibility, than developing ones. The IMF and the WB should come to their rescue – they are both vital institutions that need reform.

A possible step forward, which has had input from some experts already, would be to create independent institutions and forums, such as the Sovereign Debt Forum or the Sovereign Debt Office. These could become international platforms for in-depth discussions between donors and recipients on public debt issues. Among their priorities would be formulating policy principles that support orderly debt restructuring. Such reforms should alleviate the debt burden of countries in need, which would benefit both these countries and the global financial system. These institutions should arguably include all the G20 countries.

What is the picture in this regard in Central Asia? Since the size of their external borrowings was small, the three countries of Central Asia that use external loans – the Kyrgyz Republic, Tajikistan and Uzbekistan – did not actively and regularly restructure them, for example, through the Highly-Indebted Poor Countries (HIPC) programme, unlike most African countries. The HIPC programme was launched in 1996 by the IMF and World Bank, to ensure that no poor country faces a debt burden it cannot manage. Isolated cases of restructuring were observed in the 1990s, and the last notable restructuring of debt took place in 2005. Figure 16.1 shows the total amount of debt rescheduled by donors for three Central Asian countries, including the debt stock, principal, interest, charges, and penalties rescheduled as shown in the International Debt Statistics database of the World Bank (World Bank, 2021). The most severe restructuring occurred in the late 1990s and 2005 in the Kyrgyz Republic, when the amount of sovereign debt exceeded critical levels. After that, the region's countries followed a moderate borrowing policy from international financial institutions. In 2020, Tajikistan and in 2021 the Kyrgyz Republic entered the DSSI programme and were granted deferrals in external debt payments. This data is not reflected yet in Figure 16.1.

Governments, not central banks, should use recent IMF assistance

It became clear that the coronavirus pandemic's impact on world affairs would be unprecedented from the very beginning. International financial institutions were among the first to realise the impending danger of the pandemic. The IMF and the WB urged G20 countries to establish the specially designed DSSI to help nations safeguard poor people's lives and livelihoods. Since it came into effect on 1 May 2020, the initiative has delivered over $5 billion in relief to more than 40 eligible countries (World Bank, 2022). A new chapter in the fight against economic and social challenges opened on 23 August 2021 when, to boost global liquidity, the IMF Governors approved a massive $650 billion allocation of Special Drawing Rights (SDRs) (Georgieva, 2021a).

Because of the pandemic, most countries have opted for significantly increasing their public debt. In middle-income countries, the debt increased by an average of 12 percentage points in 2020 to 65 per cent of their GDP, and in developed countries, by 17 per cent to 120 per cent of GDP (Vinokurov, 2021).

Issuing and distributing SDRs at record levels is the right and timely move. If the risk of debt volatility continues to rise, then monetary stimulus will decline. Similarly, if interest rates rise, so will the cost of servicing debt, which will become a massive problem for the stability of the global economy. This step will reduce the risks of imbalances in the countries' fiscal and debt policies.

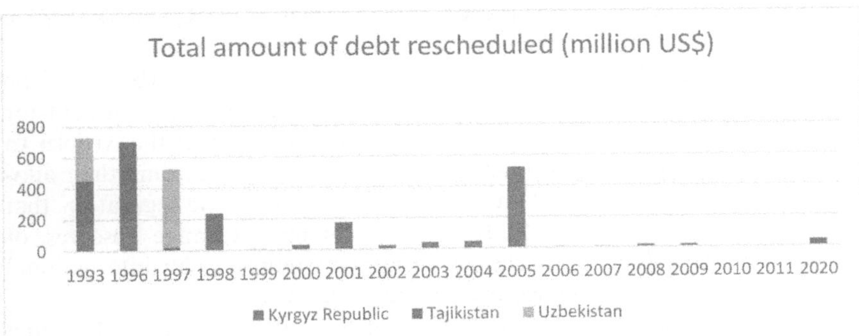

Figure 16.1 Total amount of debt rescheduled by donors for three Central Asian countries

Source: World Bank (2021).

SDRs are not traditional money nor a means of payment. Technically, these are potential claims of the holder of SDRs for the freely convertible currencies of other IMF members. The SDR exchange rate is determined daily based on exchange rates for major currencies – dollar, euro, yen, British pound, and yuan. Countries can use SDRs in different ways, but they are traditionally stored in reserves, providing a higher level of hard currency, and positively affecting the stability of national economies.

The last time the IMF issued SDRs was in 2009 to support the global economy after the global financial crisis. Until 23 August 2021, SDR 204 billion was in circulation and since then, this figure has grown to SDR 456 billion or $650 billion, which is an unprecedented volume comparable to the IMF's share capital (IMF, 2021a).

The critical question is how to best use the SDRs received by countries. Surprisingly, it is almost *a priori* assumed that SDRs should go to central banks' accounts to replenish states' foreign exchange reserves. However, it could be suggested that in the current situation, these funds need to be used by national governments, not central banks.

First, we should consider all the necessary legal grounds for this (Bedoya, et al., 2021). Under Articles XV and XVII of the IMF's Articles of Agreement, SDRs must be owned by "members", which are the governments and not central banks. A recent IMF manual explicitly states (IMF, 2021b: 1):

> Member countries can use their newly allocated SDRs unconditionally… Members enjoy a large degree of freedom in how to manage the SDRs allocated to them, including to what extent central banks are involved in their management and whether the budget can directly use them for budget support.

Additionally, footnote 13 says: "In some countries, authorities record the SDRs in the government balance sheet, and their domestic legislation specifies that a government agency is the ultimate owner of SDRs" (IMF, 2021b: 10).

Aside from this, the IMF's recent guidance says (IMF, 2021b: 11): "The Articles of Agreement do not prescribe a specific accounting treatment for SDR allocations. Accordingly, members are not obliged under the Articles to follow a specific accounting framework or methodology regarding their allocations." Even if the central banks have achieved domestic legislation that promotes the placement of SDRs in the foreign exchange reserves of countries, then the IMF's Articles of Agreement represent an international agreement that takes precedence over domestic legislation.

One of the direct proponents of a similar position is IMF Managing Director, Kristalina Georgieva, who notes that the distribution of the 2009 SDR was often primitively used to increase foreign exchange reserves. She hopes things will be different this time: "After the 2009 crisis, we issued $250 billion in SDRs. 90 per cent of those SDRs were used simply to boost reserves. This is necessary today, too. But we must do more. We must use this unique opportunity for strategic transformation of countries – a transformation that is going to be driven by this crisis. We call on you – on the leaders – to use these resources strategically, for top priorities. And, of course, self-resilience on health is a top priority", she underlined. (Georgieva, 2021b).

Sometimes, the new issue of SDRs also provides opportunities to lower debts. Experts estimate that, on average, the resources provided would cover about 10 per cent of the debt service of middle-income countries in the next 5 years and 20 per cent of the debt service of lower-income countries (Kharas & Dooley, 2021).

However, the most effective use of SDRs would be to restore economies, improve infrastructure, or provide loans to businesses in fragile countries. The direct beneficiaries of the new liquidity must be the normal people, and not the central bankers, who may want to sterilise and hide those funds in their vaults. It would be regrettable if, after all the international community's efforts invested in the unprecedented distribution of SDRs, the governments could not use these funds to help the real people in need, due to artificial bureaucratic obstacles.

References

Akchabar, 2022. Gosdolg Kyrgyzstana po itogam 2021 goda sostavil 60.33% k VVP. [Online] Available at: https://www.akchabar.kg/ru/news/gosdolg-kyrgyzstana-po-itogam-2021-goda-sostavil-6033-k-vvp/ [Accessed July 2022].

Alimova, E., 2021. «Skrytyi» dolg Kazakhstana pered Kitaem prevysil 10 procentov VVP. Chem jeto grozit?. [Online] Available at: https://rus.azattyq.org/a/31493325.html [Accessed July 2022].

Bedoya, C. *et al.*, 2021. *Handbook for the Use of Special Drawing Rights (SDRs) for Fiscal Purposes*, Lima: Latin American Network for Economic and Social Justice.

CAA Network, 2021. Kak Uzbekistan stanovitsya prioritetnym partnerom Kitaya v Central'noy Azii?. [Online] Available at: https://www.caa-network.org/archives/21445 [Accessed July 2022].

Capie, F., 2013. *Development and Evolution of International Financial Architecture. In: Handbook of Safeguarding Global Financial Stability.* Amsterdam: Academic Press, pp. 393–401.

Georgieva, K., 2021a. IMF managing director announces the US$650 billion SDR allocation comes into effect. [Online] Available at: https://www.imf.org/en/News/Articles/2021/08/23/pr21248-imf-managing-director-announces-the-us-650-billion-sdr-allocation-comes-into-effect [Accessed July 2022].

Georgieva, K., 2021b. Remarks of the managing director at the open session of the compact with Africa conference. [Online] Available at: https://www.imf.org/en/News/Articles/2021/08/27/sp08272021-remarks-of-the-managing-director-at-the-open-session-of-the-cwa-conference [Accessed July 2022].

Horn, S., Reinhart, C. & Trebesch, C., 2020. China's overseas lending and the looming developing country debt crisis. [Online] Available at: https://voxeu.org/article/china-s-overseas-lending-and-looming-developing-country-debt-crisis [Accessed July 2022].

IMF, 2021a. IMF governors approve a historic US$650 billion SDR allocation of special drawing rights. [Online] Available at: https://www.imf.org/en/News/Articles/2021/07/30/pr21235-imf-governors-approve-a-historic-us-650-billion-sdr-allocation-of-special-drawing-rights [Accessed July 2022].

IMF, 2021b. Guidance Note for Fund Staff on the Treatment and Use of SDR Allocations. *Policy Paper No. 2021/059*, 23 August, p. 44.

Karaev, S., 2022. Minfin: Dolg Tadzhikistana pered Kitaem prevyshaet $1 mlrd. [Online] Available at: https://asiaplustj.info/ru/news/tajikistan/economic/20220202/minfin-dolg-tadzhikistana-pered-kitaem-sostavlyaet-bolee-1-mlrd [Accessed July 2022].

Kharas, H. & Dooley, M., 2021. Debt service risks, special drawing rights allocations, and development prospects. [Online] Available at: https://www.brookings.edu/wp-content/uploads/2021/09/Debt-service-risks-SDRs.pdf [Accessed July 2022].

Malik, A. *et al.*, 2021. *Banking on the Belt and Road: Insights from a new global dataset of 13,427 Chinese development projects*, Williamsburg, VA: AidData at William & Mary.

State Administration of Foreign Exchange, 2022. The time-series data of international investment position of China. [Online] Available at: https://www.safe.gov.cn/en/2018/0928/1459.html [Accessed July 2022].

The Washington Post, 1997. Russia joins Paris club of creditors. [Online] Available at: https://www.washingtonpost.com/archive/politics/1997/09/18/russia-joins-paris-club-of-creditors/a81da42b-1f57-44d2-8c4c-b62c613ff017/ [Accessed July 2022].

Trading Economics, 2022. Credit rating - Countries - List. [Online] Available at: https://tradingeconomics.com/country-list/rating [Accessed July 2022].

Vinokurov, E., 2021. Privivka dlya mirovoy ekonomiki. [Online] Available at: https://ko.ru/articles/privivka-dlya-mirovoy-ekonomiki/ [Accessed July 2022].

World Bank, 2019. International debt statistics (IDS). [Online] Available at: http://datatopics.worldbank.org/debt/ids/ [Accessed July 2022].

World Bank, 2020. COVID-19 to add as many as 150 million extreme poor by 2021. [Online] Available at: https://www.worldbank.org/en/news/press-release/2020/10/07/covid-19-to-add-as-many-as-150-million-extreme-poor-by-2021 [Accessed July 2022].

World Bank, 2021. International debt statistics: DSSI - DataBank. [Online] Available at: https://databank.worldbank.org/source/international-debt-statistics:-dssi# [Accessed July 2022].

World Bank, 2022. Debt service suspension initiative. [Online] Available at: https://www.worldbank.org/en/topic/debt/brief/covid-19-debt-service-suspension-initiative [Accessed July 2022].

Xinhuanet.com, 2020. Full text: Remarks by Chinese President Xi Jinping at 15th G20 Leaders' Summit. [Online] Available at: http://www.xinhuanet.com/english/2020-11/21/c_139533609.htm [Accessed July 2022].

17 Afghanistan

Continuation of War or Revival of Greater Central Asia?

Introduction

Afghanistan is of particular interest to the five nations we have hitherto referred to as Central Asia since, until the middle of the nineteenth century, it was an integral part of greater Central Asia. Afghanistan's northern border was the line that divided the Russian and the British Empires. I have visited the Afghan capital Kabul twice. First in 2001, immediately after the entry of international coalition troops into the country, and then again in 2006. The main question for me was – what is Afghanistan? Does it look like a South Asian country like India or Pakistan, or is it Central Asia? When I arrived in Kabul, I immediately sensed that Afghanistan was just a part of Central Asia. I saw this by observing people's behaviour, the atmosphere on the streets, and the dialect spoken by Kabul's residents, which closely resembles Tajik.

In the past two years, Afghanistan and the Taliban have been among the most frequently used words in the world media, and not without reason. Yet Afghanistan is a developing country far from the main centres of world politics, and the Taliban movement has never intended to expand its activities outside the country. Afghanistan's closest neighbours – Central Asia, China, Iran, Pakistan, Russia, and India show particular concern. They pay particular attention to the Taliban because this movement won its twenty-year war with the US, a country with the strongest army in the world backed by immense financial capabilities, spending more than $2.313 trillion on the war (Debre, 2021).

So what did happen in Afghanistan during the summer months of 2021, weeks before the unexpected fall of Ashraf Ghani's government in August 2021 and the rise of the Taliban? Surprisingly, all major powers were greatly mistaken in their assessment of the situation in the country. Meanwhile, with their close cultural links to Afghanistan, the countries of Central Asia understood better than others what was happening there. There was a chance that the leading world powers would agree on a joint effort to restore stability, but they missed this chance. At this time, the leadership of the Central Asian countries remained surprisingly calm in the light of unpredictable developments in their southern neighbour.

DOI: 10.4324/9781003360728-22

The summit entitled "Central and South Asia: Regional Connectivity. Challenges and Opportunities" was organised by the Government of Uzbekistan and was held in Tashkent on 15–16 July 2021. Among the attendees at the conference were the Presidents of Uzbekistan and Afghanistan, Prime Ministers of India and Pakistan, Foreign Ministers, and high-ranking representatives of the countries of Central and South Asia, Russia, China, the US, the European Union, Israel, Malaysia, Saudi Arabia, the United Kingdom, Japan, and other states, international organisations, financial institutions, and some companies. Despite the broad representation at the event, the conference participants went home with different views of what would happen in the long-suffering country of Afghanistan.

In June 2021, the US intelligence community wrongly concluded that the Afghan government could be in place at least six months after the withdrawal of the US Army. However, the fall of the Ashraf Ghani government happened much faster, even before the departure of the American army and their allies (Lubold & Trofimov, 2021).

In early June 2021, the UN Afghanistan Sanctions Monitoring Team claimed that the Taliban exercised direct control over more than half of the country's regional capitals while controlling up to 70 per cent of the territory outside urban areas (Analytical Support and Sanctions Monitoring Team, 2021). At this point, Taliban officials were reporting that their militants had taken over 85 per cent of the territory. Subsequent events showed that the Taliban were correct.

In the summer of 2021, dramatic events began to unfold even in the country's north, close to the border with Central Asia and far from the main Taliban-controlled Pashtun territories in southern Afghanistan. There was fierce shooting just three hours away from the Tajik capital, Dushanbe. The Taliban quickly captured the territory to the south of the Pyanj River, which has separated Afghanistan from Uzbekistan and Tajikistan since the Anglo-Russian agreement in the late 19th century. At that time, there was a danger that fighting near the border could lead to a flow of refugees from Afghanistan to Central Asia and Russia, but this did not happen. The Taliban have always said that they will never threaten neighbouring countries, and a year after the Taliban took control over the country, it can be seen that they fulfilled their promises.

Russia was also seriously worried about the possible destabilisation of the situation in Central Asia, so decided to strengthen its military grouping in the region. Russian Defense Minister Sergei Shoigu said (Tass.ru, 2021): "By the end of this year [2021], the command of the Central Military District will have to re-equip two aviation regiments with modernised Su-34M fighter-bombers and MiG-31BM fighter-interceptors". To explain its policy to the Russian leadership, a delegation of the political office of the Taliban movement visited Moscow in early July 2021. The press secretary of Russian President Dmitry Peskov mentioned that "contacts [with Taliban] are necessary against the background of the tense situation in Afghanistan"

(Himshiashvili, 2021). China has also expressed fears that the withdrawal of US troops from Afghanistan could destabilise Central Asia. The collapse of state institutions in Afghanistan could lead to the growth of the three evils China is fighting – terrorism, separatism, and religious extremism.

Before leaving for Washington at the end of June 2021, Uzbek Foreign Minister Abdulaziz Kamilov gave an interview to American TV presenter Dennis Wholey. The Minister spoke about events in Afghanistan and stressed that the main elements of Uzbekistan's position had been agreed upon by the leadership of all Central Asian states (ThisIsAmericaTV, 2021).

The minister clarified that the Afghans should only resolve Afghanistan's problems based on a mutual compromise between the government and the military opposition – the Taliban and others. When asked what the Taliban wanted, the Uzbek Foreign Minister answered with a smile: "First of all, the Taliban wants the [US] troops to withdraw" (Gazeta.uz, 2021). Crucially, the Minister made an upbeat statement that Afghanistan would become an integral part of Central Asia in the nearest future. This could trigger the reconstruction of "Greater Central Asia", an area that existed as a single whole for many centuries. Throughout the Golden Age of Central Asia (1100–1600 AD), the region was a world leader in economic development, trade, technology, manufacturing, and intellectual life (Starr, 2015).

Mullah Abdul Ghani Baradar, Head of the Political Office of the Taliban in Doha, confirmed this assessment:

> In the future, we will not allow the emergence of a threat and danger from Afghanistan to Uzbekistan or other Central Asian countries… In the future, on Afghan soil, we will not allow the existence of radical groups and organisations, terrorist groups.
>
> (Gazeta.uz, 2020)

At that time, the governments of the Central Asian countries wanted to explain that Afghanistan would not pose a threat to its neighbours. Understanding such a position would contribute to forming a common strategy and converging Russian, Chinese and American regional policies. In the ideal case, Afghanistan could become a place for effective interaction between global powers to create an atmosphere of trust and cooperation, perhaps not only in Central Asia. But such a rapprochement, unfortunately, did not happen.

There is no silver bullet for Afghanistan to transform and become a faithful member of the international community. The country is still at a crossroads without an established direction for its development. According to observers, mass human rights violations are taking place in Afghanistan today. The Taliban introduced Sharia law into the daily life of citizens of the republic, and the government has infringed the rights of girls and women. Girls are banned from attending school beyond the sixth grade and women must be accompanied by a close male relative when travelling long distances. New regulations prescribed that women should cover their bodies from head to toe. The authorities will punish men responsible for violations if women do not comply. State and local administrations operate inefficiently, which is why the international community has refrained from recognising the current government of Afghanistan. Its closest neighbours, who are most interested in stabilising and developing the country, have not yet decided what to do in the current situation and what strategy of cooperation to follow.

To act in its people's interests, Afghanistan's government must embark on a policy of creating jobs and start to fill the state treasury as soon as possible. Then, the authorities must establish the rule of law, protect property rights and create a favourable investment climate for local and foreign entrepreneurs. There is no other way to develop societies and states. Unfortunately, no one has taken these steps yet. The citizens of this long-suffering country, especially the most creative and educated among them, are doing all they can to leave. At the same time, the top leadership of the Taliban has repeatedly called on the business world to start investment projects in Afghanistan. Which foreign investors could be the first to respond to these calls and get to work there? Based on geographic proximity, political vision, economic feasibility, financial capabilities, and practical benefits, it could be suggested that China is the only one who could lead the economic recovery of Afghanistan in the short term. Given this, the focus of the following sections of this chapter will focus only on what China can do in Afghanistan.

Who can stabilise Afghanistan?

A common characteristic of Afghanistan's neighbours – apart from India – is friendly relationships and even strategic partnerships with China and Russia. Here, we will highlight the role of China in the face of opportunities and risks that will arise in Afghanistan in connection with the withdrawal of American troops.

The universal recipe for rebuilding emerging countries, especially those coming out of a conflict, has never changed. It has at least two basic elements – jobs and education. As for creating jobs, the recipe has not changed here either – it is necessary to attract investment. Moreover, given Afghanistan's history of almost endless wars over many decades, it must attract foreign investment. Therefore, the government should do everything possible to create a favourable investment climate.

The list of potential investors is minimal. China, Russia, India, and perhaps some Western countries may be interested. It is likely that Chinese investments will be the most ambitious for several reasons. First, through its specific actions, China is decisively contributing to the speedy stabilisation of the situation in its neighbour. Secondly, it has sufficient human and financial resources. Thirdly, China has maintained good relations with all parties in the Afghan internal conflict. Finally, the government and the private sector have accumulated the expertise needed to create favourable conditions for the earliest possible start to the particular projects (Kaura, 2022).

With the price of natural resources skyrocketing globally, mining projects have gained new impetus. Afghan subsoil is rich in strategic resources, such as non-ferrous and rare-earth metals. For example, it has the world's largest unexploited reserves of copper, coal, iron, gas, cobalt, mercury, gold, lithium, and thorium, valued at over $1 trillion. Realistically speaking, only China has the chance and capacity to take tangible steps to extract them (Chew, 2021).

Qian Feng, research director at the National Strategy Institute at Tsinghua University, said China and Afghanistan show a solid political will to expand BRI cooperation. If the authorities bring stability to Afghanistan, it will "undoubtedly bring great convenience to cargo flow between China and Eurasia", said Qian Feng (News Quick24, 2021). Fan Hongda, a professor at the Institute for Middle East Studies at the Shanghai University of International Studies, said China would actively support efforts to bring political stability to Afghanistan. "Even though China has for a long time been extremely cautious about sending military forces overseas, if it is supported by a United Nations resolution, China might join an international peacekeeping team to enter Afghanistan", he said. "With continued turbulence, Afghanistan could quickly become a hotbed for growing Islamic extremism, which would to some extent affect stability in Xinjiang" (Shepherd, 2021).

According to several diplomats and analysts, Beijing has held talks with representatives of the Taliban. Details of the discussions have yet to be released but an anonymous Indian government spokesman said China's approach is to try to rebuild Afghanistan's destroyed infrastructure in cooperation with the Taliban, working through Pakistan, one of Beijing's staunchest allies in the region. "We can vouch that China will fund the rebuilding of Afghanistan through the Taliban via Pakistan", the official said. "China is Pakistan's wallet". Another regional diplomat said: "China, at the request of Pakistan, will support the Taliban" (Shepherd, 2021).

Alongside this, the Taliban views China as a "friend" of Afghanistan and hopes to talk to Beijing about investing in reconstruction "as soon as possible", said spokesman Suhail Shaheen on 7 July 2021. In an exclusive interview with *This Week in Asia*, he said that the Taliban would guarantee the safety of Chinese investors and workers if they return to the country. "We welcome them. If they have investments, of course, we ensure their safety. Their safety is essential to us. We have been to China many times, and we have good relations with them", Suhail said. "China is a friendly country that we welcome for reconstruction and developing Afghanistan" (Chew, 2021).

One of the most crucial additional measures in restoring the Afghan economy should be cooperation between Central and South Asian countries. Given that Afghanistan will be at the centre of such multilateral collaboration, China will also support such projects. Restoring close economic relations between Central and South Asia countries will undoubtedly contribute to the prosperity of these countries and Afghanistan. This happened before, during the golden period of the Great Silk Road when Greater Central Asia was the most prosperous region globally. Surely history can repeat itself in the region.

Potential projects

China currently has an almost ideal political and economic environment for implementing investment projects of various scales in Afghanistan. It has sufficient human and financial resources, has maintained good relations with all parties in the Afghan conflict, and has the expertise required as well as favourable conditions for the earliest possible start. But above all, China's main interest in Afghanistan is to maintain political stability.

Afghanistan has long been of significant interest to China as the wealthiest storehouse of natural resources. For example, in 2007, a consortium of Chinese companies won a tender to develop a copper mine at Mes Aynak in Logar province, some forty kilometres southeast of Kabul. The deposit has about 11 million tons of copper reserves and was discovered in the 1970s by Soviet geologists. Thirteen companies worldwide participated in the tender to develop the field, including the Chinese Zijin Mining and the China Metallurgical Group Corporation. In exchange for the right to mine copper ores for thirty years, the companies promised to invest about $3 billion in the main project and build the necessary power plant and a railway (Polyakov, 2021).

But exploration and subsequent development of the deposit became impractical due to the unstable political situation in Afghanistan and a sharp drop in copper prices, which fell to about $1.5 per pound. These days the energy market is undergoing a global transformation, and the cost of copper is skyrocketing. In June 2022, it was trading at around $4.3 per pound, and interest in the Mes Aynak deposit has grown significantly. Due to the lack of new major copper projects globally, experts also predict an ongoing shortage in the medium term (Northern Miner, 2021).

Afghan subsoil is rich in hydrocarbons as well. In 2011, China National Petroleum Corporation (CNPC) won a $400 million bid to drill three oil fields containing about 87 million barrels of oil over a period of twenty-five years (Chew, 2021).

Given the strong market demand for rare earth metals coupled with their high prices, the potential for extracting minerals such as praseodymium, cerium, lanthanum, neodymium, and gadolinium is exceptionally high. In 2014, based on the results of research conducted by the US Geological Survey, the Afghan authorities announced that their value was approximately $3 trillion. The physical volume of lanthanides alone was at least 1.4 million tons (Polyakov, 2021).

Recently China announced the start of a series of new projects in Afghanistan. At the end of May 2021, several Chinese companies planned to invest $400 million in constructing a 300 MW coal-fired power plant. The emergence of this facility will sharply reduce Afghanistan's dependence on electricity imports from neighbouring countries (Polyakov, 2021).

Developing these colossal resources again hinges on energy and transport infrastructure, which are lacking in Afghanistan. However, China's investments in African countries with a complete lack of infrastructure show that this is not an insurmountable problem. For this reason, concerns have already been voiced in the Western media that the American forces' withdrawal from Afghanistan would automatically mean that the country's resources would fall under Chinese control (Almond, 2021).

Back in 2016, Afghan President Ashraf Ghani signed a memorandum of understanding with China, and a year later, Afghanistan officially became a member of the Asian Infrastructure Investment Bank (AIIB). The Bank was supposed to help Afghanistan raise funds to construct solar power facilities, railways, and other infrastructure. According to a few analysts, in the short term, China is ready to invest about $62 billion in the development of Afghanistan (Tikhonova, 2021).

Given the potentially substantial economic benefits from developing Afghanistan's natural resources, China is likely to be highly interested in coming to the country. But witnessing the impasse that Britain, the Soviet Union, and the US have all been drawn into over the past centuries, Beijing knows that Afghanistan is a "graveyard of empires". Traditionally, Beijing believes it should avoid any political interference in Afghan affairs at all costs. Thus to steady the political situation in Afghanistan, the main direction of Chinese foreign policy towards Afghanistan should now be effective coordination with all of Afghanistan's immediate neighbours – Central Asian countries, Pakistan, Iran, and Russia.

On 16 July 2021, the President of Uzbekistan, Shavkat Mirziyoyev, proposed to finalise a multilateral agreement on economic cooperation between Central and South Asian countries. He also offered to develop effective measures for the free movement of investments, goods, and services, by forming an expanded transport communications and energy infrastructure (Regnum, 2021). The countries involved will likely mobilise all their political and economic resources and do their best to find practical solutions to bring peace to the region.

The current state of the Afghan economy

The Taliban's most urgent goals are to maintain public order, respect human rights and create an inclusive government that can take responsibility for the peaceful development of an Afghanistan devastated by war. Another critical goal is the development of the country's economy. Given the uncertainty and absence of a legitimate government, the international community has a wait-and-see attitude. What is the current status of the economy of Afghanistan? What is the likelihood that the country will fall apart? What will become of the Afghan people?

The Taliban inherited a country of 39 million people and an economy of less than $20 billion. In the period from 2003 to 2012, the growth of the Afghan economy averaged 9.4 per cent thanks to the influence of international aid and active development of the service sector, and from 2015 to 2020, the average annual growth dipped to 2.5 per cent (World Bank, 2022a). The Asian Development Bank (ADB) estimated that Afghanistan's GDP fell 5 per cent in 2020, mainly due to the coronavirus pandemic (ADB, 2021). The country's GDP per capita is just $520, lower than Sudan or Niger. The private sector is tiny, and around 75 per cent of the population is employed in agriculture (USAID, 2022).

A massive problem for the country is the enormous cost of maintaining security. The World Bank (WB) estimated this at 28 per cent of GDP, compared with an average of 3 per cent of GDP for other low-income countries (World Bank, 2021). Afghanistan's reliance on external aid is disproportionately large, and although international assistance had fallen from about 100 per cent of GDP in 2009 to 42.9 per cent in 2020, it remains dangerously high (World Bank, 2022a). Many donor agencies have left the country or are about to do so.

In 2021, the US administration announced that they prevented the Taliban from gaining access to Afghanistan's 22-ton gold reserve held at the Federal Reserve Bank of New York. Its value at London Bullion Market Association prices is approximately $1.25 billion. Sources said Treasury Secretary Janet Yellen prepared the resolution and the State Department and the White House were actively involved in this process (Daily Sabah, 2021).

It is believed that the country's central bank, Da Afghanistan Bank (DAB), stores foreign exchange, gold, and other treasures in its vaults, but the primary keepers of most of the country's assets are still foreign banks. The most recent financial report shows DAB's total assets are about $10 billion, including $1.3 billion in gold reserves and $362 million in foreign currency cash reserves (Daily Sabah, 2021).

According to various estimates cited by the Council on Foreign Relations in Washington, the Taliban annually earns from $300 million to $1.6 billion from activities in the informal economy, such as the cultivation of opium poppies, drug trafficking, extortions from commercial activities in territories they control, and illegal transfers from abroad (Findlay, 2021). For example, according to various estimates, about 90 per cent of the world's heroin comes from the Helmand River Valley, the Taliban stronghold in southern Afghanistan (Maizland, 2021). Moreover, according to the UN, the Taliban have earned about $460 million from unofficial mining (Tkachyov & Abramova, 2021).

Official statistics show that the country's exports in 2019 amounted to $870 million, including commodities of $719 million. At the same time, imports to Afghanistan were higher at about $8.6 billion, of which almost $2.5 billion was for consumer goods. The most significant imports were peat, petroleum products, and vegetable oils. The country's main trading partners were Iran, China, and Pakistan (Roma, 2021).

Economic development, investment attraction, and job creation are absolute priorities, given the critical social-economic and financial situation in the country. According to the ADB, more than 47 per cent of the country's citizens were living below the poverty line in 2020. For every 1,000 babies born in Afghanistan in 2019, 60 die before their fifth birthday (ADB, 2022). WB data show that the unemployment rate had been growing over the past ten years, and in 2020 it amounted to 11.2 per cent (Trading Economics, 2022). Official statistics vastly underestimate such numbers since these data contain only enterprises that officially report their activities, of which there are very few in the country.

The humanitarian situation in the country is close to catastrophic. The head of the European Parliament's Development Committee, Tomas Tobe, said on 19 August 2021 (Kovalenko & Tarasenko, 2021): "As a result of the drought, the coronavirus pandemic and the fighting in Afghanistan, almost half of the population of this country – 18 million people – need urgent humanitarian assistance, (and) almost 4 million have become internally displaced persons." UN World Food Program Executive Director David Beasley said a food crisis was brewing in Afghanistan (Cornwell, 2021), and 14 million people might face hunger. Beasley called on the world community to "act fast". According to him, to prevent a humanitarian catastrophe, it is necessary to provide at least $200 million in urgent assistance to help the country. Against this backdrop, as the UN coordinator for humanitarian affairs in Afghanistan, Ramiz Alakbarov told RIA Novosti on 19 August 2021 that the Taliban called on the UN not to stop providing humanitarian aid to fellow citizens (RIA, 2021).

The socio-economic situation in Afghanistan is at a dangerously low level, and a humanitarian disaster associated with food shortages, the spread of infectious diseases, and dangerous epidemics is likely. Despite the absence of a legitimate government in the country, the international community urgently needs to assist the Afghan people.

The future of the Afghan economy

Afghanistan's most critical economic challenge is to find a sustainable source of growth. The Taliban have already called on other countries to help Afghanistan "at a critical juncture in history" to create jobs and secure investment. Taliban spokesman Suhail Shaheen called on the international community to invest in Afghanistan's development, Ariana News reported on 13 August 2021: "We have just emerged from the stage of war and destruction and entered a new phase when the people of Afghanistan need help from other countries. They can come and develop our natural resources," he said, noting that the Taliban "appreciate the help of any state at such a critical moment in the history of Afghanistan" (Kovalenko & Tarasenko, 2021).

Afghan subsoil is indeed exceptionally rich in strategic resources, but there is one chemical element that has incredibly unique potential for development – lithium. This alkali metal is used in almost all batteries for mobile devices and electric vehicles. In 2010, a senior US general told the *New York Times* (Risen, 2010) that Afghanistan's mineral potential was "stunning", and the paper also later reported that an internal US Defence Department memo had said the country could become "the Saudi Arabia of lithium".

The leaders of the G7 countries met for a virtual meeting on 24 August 2021 to discuss the situation in Afghanistan. In the future, the leaders said they would "judge the Afghan parties by their actions, not words". The announcement confirms their previous warnings to the Taliban not to return to the harsh Islamic form of government they adhered to when in power from 1996 to 2001: "In particular, we reaffirm that the Taliban will be held accountable for their actions on preventing terrorism, on human rights, in particular, those of women, girls and minorities and on pursuing an inclusive political settlement in Afghanistan," the G7 leaders stated (Lee, et al., 2021).

With better relations with the Taliban than the Western powers, Russia, China, and Afghanistan's neighbours could benefit from investment in the country if the new regime stays in control. On 19 August 2021, Russian Foreign Ministry spokeswoman Maria Zakharova noted (Kovalenko & Tarasenko, 2021) that it was too early to comment on trade and economic relations between Moscow and Kabul. However, she added that "we have no reason to believe that they will not receive an impetus for further development after establishing the system of functioning of state structures and the restoration of tranquillity in Afghan society".

China, it seems, does not intend to wait long. Just a few hours after the Taliban seized Kabul Chinese Foreign Ministry spokesman Hua Chunying announced that Beijing was ready for "friendly cooperation" with Afghanistan. Many reports show that China is keen to stabilise the situation as soon as possible (Mfa.gov.cn, 2022).

Two large infrastructure projects with Afghanistan's direct neighbours – Central Asian countries, India, and Pakistan, could become especially important. Among them, the project for constructing the Kabul Corridor railway from Termez in Uzbekistan to the Pakistani city of Peshawar through Mazar-i-Sharif and Kabul is of particular relevance. The railway could carry up to 20 million tons of cargo per year. The section from Termez to Mazar-i-Sharif, built by Uzbekistan, has already been commissioned. The new government has yet to build the remaining 573 km to Peshawar. According to preliminary estimates, the railway line from Mazar-i-Sharif to Kabul has a budget of $5 billion and is supposed to be built mainly with loans (Ollard, 2021).

The second critical large infrastructure project looking promising for the region, as discussed in Chapter 9, is the TAPI gas pipeline, named after the four countries it will pass through – Turkmenistan, Afghanistan, Pakistan, and India. The 1,814 km pipeline is to run from the Galkynysh gas field in Turkmenistan to the Indian city of Fazilka, through Herat and Kandahar in

Afghanistan, and the Pakistani cities of Quetta and Multan. It would have an annual capacity of 33 billion cubic meters of gas, and experts estimate it would cost $8–10 billion (Konyrova, 2020). Even in the early stages of discussions around these projects, senior Taliban representatives expressed direct support for these initiatives through security guarantees for their construction and further operation (Otorbaev, 2021).

However, it cannot yet be said that the Afghan government is acting effectively enough to convince the international community and institutional investors that the situation in the country is improving. The ADB recently announced that the bank's assistance in constructing the gas pipeline has been suspended (Mustafa, 2022), and that it will not be resumed until the de facto authorities receive legitimacy from the UN and the world community. As the project facilitator and coordinator, this move by the ADB puts the pipeline's fate in limbo. This information was reported on 31 January 2022 by Turkmen officials during a meeting of the official delegation of Turkmenistan, headed by Deputy Foreign Minister Vepa Hajiyev, and Pakistani officials headed by Energy Minister Hammad Azhar, in Islamabad.

However, Afghan Ministry of Finance spokesman Ahmad Wali Khakmal said that the TAPI project would continue and that the ADB's suspension of its support would not stop the project. "The project is mainly owned by Turkmenistan, and the ADB played the role of a financial advisor," he said (TOLOnews, 2022).

Despite the uncertain political environment in the country, the government intends to act decisively to attract investment. As reported by Al-Mayadeen TV on 15 April 2022, the Ministry of Mines and Petroleum of the Taliban government announced tenders to develop two significant mineral deposits (Rambler.ru, 2022) – an iron ore deposit in Herat province and a lead deposit in Ghor Province – saying the tender announced "belongs to the category of major national projects".

Regarding the development of the Afghan economy and infrastructure, any potential investor, regardless of citizenship, would want to be confident in maintaining security in the country, observing civilised legislation and the rule of law. Investors will come if they do not see that the authorities are in tight control of the problems of security and corruption. A key question for any potential investor will be whether the Taliban can more effectively create a business environment and investment climate than the previous government did. As in many other cases, the ball is now in the Taliban's court.

The only sustained dialogue with the Taliban has been with Afghanistan's neighbours, including Russia, China, Iran, Pakistan, and the three Central Asian countries of Tajikistan, Turkmenistan, and Uzbekistan. The group's first meeting was held on 20 October 2021 in Moscow, and the second was a week later in Tehran. However, after a quick start, there was a pause of almost six months. The group's third meeting at the level of foreign ministers was held on 30–31 March 2022 in the city of Tunxi in the eastern Chinese province of Anhui.

The conference programme included a meeting of the expanded "troika" on Afghanistan: Russia, China, the US and Pakistan. The tension over the Russian military operation in Ukraine has made the interaction between these four participants discussing the Afghan problem even more complicated. After the US and its allies left the country, Moscow and Beijing played the leading role and become the guarantors of Afghanistan's stability. According to the Chinese Foreign Ministry, the meeting of the expanded "troika" on the side-lines of the main conference was to remind Washington of its responsibility to the country, whose isolation threatens a humanitarian catastrophe.

The increasingly difficult situation in the Taliban's relations with the world community did not prevent the meeting organisers from initiating a restart of multilateral negotiations. The organisers invited a Taliban delegation to the talks in Tunsi, including the interim government's deputy head, Abdul-Ghani Baradar, and the country's Foreign Minister, Amir Khan Mottaki.

Politicians continue to deal with the status of their relationships, but life continues. On 5 June 2022, Turkmen railway workers resumed construction work on the section of the Akina-Andkhoy railway in Afghanistan (Turkmenportal, 2022). The laying of this branch is being carried out under an earlier agreement between the Turkmen Railways Agency and the Afghan Railways Organization. The section will become part of the first trans-Afghan railway corridor Turkmenistan-Afghanistan-Tajikistan, the construction of which began on 25 July 2019.

On 13 April 2022, World Bank released a report entitled "Towards Economic Stabilization and Recovery" (World Bank, 2022b). It shows that per capita income in Afghanistan is likely to have fallen by about one-third in the last months of 2021, which will reverse the economic progress made since 2007, and will lead to a further deterioration in the financial situation of households. This economic collapse was caused by a sharp decline in international aid, the loss of access to foreign central bank assets, the disruption of international banking relationships, and a lack of investment. The report noted that the economy of Afghanistan anticipates a catastrophic scenario. The country's economy is expected to continue to contract throughout 2022, with real GDP per capita declining by about 30 per cent between the end of 2020 and the end of 2022. The economy will be unable to achieve growth at a pace capable of employing the estimated 600,000 Afghans who reach working age each year. At the same time, the report emphasises that Afghanistan has significant economic potential, should the Taliban government take the necessary measures to "sensibly" manage the economy.

The primary beneficiary of the war

According to the Costs of War Project at Brown University, the US spent $2.313 trillion on the war in Afghanistan between 2001 and 2021 (Debre, 2021), although experts from the American independent think tank Security Policy Reform Institute (SPRI) consider these figures an underestimate

(Prohvatilov, 2021). Regardless, the amount spent on the war is enormous. How was this huge amount of American taxpayer money spent? Who were the primary beneficiaries of these colossal costs? How much of this vast pie did the average Afghan get? After President Biden's unexpected decision to withdraw American troops from Afghanistan, understanding the effectiveness of using these funds is of interest to everyone.

The SPRI recently released a list of the top beneficiaries of the war in Afghanistan: who took the biggest share of the $2 trillion that America threw into the Afghan war. Many were not surprised that it turned out to be five of the best-known American military corporations – Lockheed Martin, Raytheon, General Dynamics, Boeing, and Northrop Grumman (Semler, 2021).

The SPRI report cites Julian Assange as saying back in 2011 that the US-Afghan war "is to have an endless war, not a successful war", to "wash money out of the tax bases of the United States…into the hands of the transnational security elite" (The Global Herald, 2021). Similar thoughts that the reconstruction of Afghanistan has never been the primary goal of the US are expressed in the Swiss newspaper *Neue Zürcher Zeitung*: "Trillions of dollars out of the pockets of American taxpayers were spent on the war, and only a fraction of the money went to rebuild the country" (Spalinger, 2021).

Massachusetts Democrat Senator Elizabeth Warren expressed concern about the Pentagon's expenditures, suggesting that payments were partly spent by the giants of the American military-industrial complex on "buy-backs of shares, to pay higher dividends and pay management salaries". There are serious reasons for this American senator's scepticism, one being that it transpired that in 2015–2019, the combined salaries of the CEOs of the five leaders of the American military-industrial complex exceeded half a billion dollars (Prohvatilov, 2021). Is this corruption or fundamental institutional failure?

According to official sources, since 2001, the US has allocated more than $144 billion to rebuild Afghanistan. However, most of that money went to private contractors and nongovernmental organisations: US government-commissioned programmes and projects to build Afghan security forces, improve governance, promote economic and social development, and combat illegal drugs. The most severe and costly failure of these efforts from May 2002 to March 2021 was the $88.3 billion spent on training and equipping the Afghan army (Sabga, 2021). US lawmakers channelled this large sum of money to train Afghan soldiers, fight drug trafficking, and "keep the peace" against counter-insurgencies. The fact that Afghanistan is still the world's largest opium producer (Malyshev, 2021) and the Taliban returned to power shows that this was all to no avail.

Due to suspicions that taxpayer money was being used ineffectively in Afghanistan, in 2008 the US Congress even created an institution – the Special Inspector General for Afghanistan Reconstruction (SIGAR) – the primary purpose of which was to test and evaluate the government's actions to rebuild Afghanistan. Now it is becoming clear that this institute's possibly corrupt activities turned out to be useless since the effectiveness of using those funds has proved to be virtually zero.

SIGAR published its 10th "Lessons Learned in Afghanistan" report in August 2021, just before the withdrawal of the Americans. Inspector General John F. Sopko wrote in his summary: "In unpredictable and chaotic environments such as Afghanistan, poor oversight or improper implementation can threaten relationships with local communities, endanger the lives of the US and Afghan government personnel and civilians, and undermine strategic goals" (Sabga, 2021). In this typically bureaucratic report, the Inspector General acknowledged that everything was going well and that there were only minor risks to the American mission in Afghanistan. It has now become clear that SIGAR did not fulfil its mission. The American taxpayer has the right to ask: who is to blame and what next?

The media was flooded with material analysing the consequences of America's withdrawal from Afghanistan. Almost all experts believe that the American move will mostly benefit the US's geopolitical rivals, primarily Russia and China, who gloat (which boast) over the failure of the American mission, however, this is not an opinion that is easy to agree with. In the globalisation era, Russia, China, and the whole world need a strong and confident, not a weak and aggressive, America. No one is interested in weakening the country, but unfortunately, the latest actions of this great power suggest that the US itself is metaphorically "cutting off the very branch it is sitting on". Over the past twenty years, America has made mistakes on a historic scale, leading to significant human and material sacrifices in various parts of the globe. Of fundamental importance is that these faults were not associated with external reasons, but with the very functioning of political institutions within the US.

Almost two centuries ago, the French historian and political writer Alexis de Tocqueville wrote in his book *Democracy in America* (1835–1840): "The greatness of America lies not in being more enlightened than any other nation, but rather in her ability to repair her faults". Let's hope that the US will learn the right lessons from these events. Maybe Afghanistan can become something of a Rubicon, which the American elite will cross to enter new normality, which they will understand and come to accept. The US should continue to take a leading role, but perhaps Afghanistan will help them to formulate a more realistic concept of this role in the future. Surely America will correct its recent flaws – the question now is how long it will take.

Conclusion

Wherever you look in Afghanistan, there is a crisis. Terrorist attacks occur regularly, human rights are abused, the rule of law is not respected, the economy does not function normally, taxes are left unpaid and drugs are still being produced. What should the government do first to start rebuilding the country? In my opinion, providing security is of utmost importance for the country to develop in a civilised direction, because only by ensuring the safety of the people can Afghanistan's economy be developed, jobs created and a decent quality of life provided for its citizens.

However, a recently released twenty-seven-page report issued by the Monitoring Team under the Taliban Sanctions Committee of the UN (Analytical Support and Sanctions Monitoring Team, 2022), reveals worrisome threats emerging from Afghanistan for its neighbours. The report highlights three of the most troubling aspects. Firstly, there is an increased presence of terrorist groups in Afghanistan after August 2021, including Al-Qaeda, Jaish-e-Mohammed and Lashkar-e-Taiba. Secondly, there has been a growing flow of drugs from the country. The report states that the smuggling of "drugs of Afghan origin increased significantly in the second half of 2021", by up to 50 per cent (p. 5).

Thirdly, and even more troubling, "the Taliban's victory in Afghanistan inspired terrorists worldwide". The report says the Taliban are "still close" to Al-Qaeda, which has now "increased freedom of action" in Afghanistan. Al-Qaeda's core has continued to be active in Afghanistan since August 2021. The report also states that the central leadership of Al-Qaeda, led by its head Ayman al-Zawahiri, remains in Afghanistan, in the "eastern region from Zabul province north towards Kunar and along the border with Pakistan. He has "released more frequent recorded messages" (p. 6), appearing in eight videos since the Taliban took over Afghanistan in August 2021. Al-Qaeda has reaffirmed its pledge of allegiance to the Taliban leader. The report also notes that forty-one Taliban members on the UN sanctions list have been appointed to the Afghan government and other high-ranking positions. Among them is Sirajuddin Haqqani, leader of the Haqqani Taliban network, which, according to the UN, now controls key Afghan ministries, such as the interior ministry and the intelligence, passport and migration departments. In a previous UN report, Haqqani, Afghanistan's acting interior Minister, was listed as a member of the Al-Qaeda leadership. He is also on the FBI's most-wanted list.

The report went on to say that "Central Asian embassies based in Afghanistan reported with concern the appearance of several leaders of foreign terrorist groups moving freely around Kabul from August onwards" (p. 11). There is some good news in the UN report, concluding that the Afghan branch of ISIS and Al-Qaeda are not yet strong enough to be "capable of organising international attacks until at least 2023". More positive news from Afghanistan, and not only of this kind, is needed by everyone, and above all by its neighbours.

References

ADB, 2021. Afghanistan's economy to rebound in 2021 despite challenges — ADB. [Online] Available at: https://www.adb.org/news/afghanistan-economy-rebound-2021-despite-challenges-adb [Accessed July 2022].

ADB, 2022. Poverty data: Afghanistan. [Online] Available at: https://www.adb.org/countries/afghanistan/poverty [Accessed July 2022].

Almond, M., 2021. Mark Almond: Days after we leave Afghanistan, China is moving in to gain a direct route to the riches of the Middle East. And with billions in their war chest, where will their ambitions end?. [Online] Available at: https://www.dailymail.co.uk/debate/article-9762955/MARK-ALMOND-Days-leave-Afghanistan-China-moving-gain-direct-route-Middle-East.html [Accessed July 2022].

Analytical Support and Sanctions Monitoring Team, 2021. *Twelfth report of the Analytical Support and Sanctions Monitoring Team Submitted Pursuant to Resolution 2557 (2020) Concerning the Taliban and Other Associated Individuals and Entities Constituting a Threat to Peace Stability and Security of Afghanistan*, New York: United Nations.

Analytical Support and Sanctions Monitoring Team, 2022. *Thirteenth Report of the Analytical Support and Sanctions Monitoring Team Submitted Pursuant to Resolution 2611 (2021) Concerning the Taliban and Other Associated Individuals and Entities Constituting Threat to Peace Stability and Security of Afghanistan*, New York: United Nations.

Chew, A., 2021. China a 'welcome friend' for reconstruction in Afghanistan: Taliban spokesman. [Online] Available at: https://www.scmp.com/week-asia/politics/article/3140399/china-welcome-friend-reconstruction-afghanistan-taliban [Accessed July 2022].

Cornwell, A., 2021. Afghanistan 'marching towards starvation' - UN Food Chief. [Online] Available at: https://www.reuters.com/article/afghanistan-conflict-aid/update-1-afghanistan-marching-towards-starvation-un-food-chief-idINL1N2PV1AT [Accessed July 2022].

Daily Sabah, 2021. US reportedly freezes Afghan govt reserves in American banks. [Online] Available at: https://www.dailysabah.com/business/finance/us-reportedly-freezes-afghan-govt-reserves-in-american-banks [Accessed July 2022].

Debre, I., 2021. Counting the costs of America's 20-year war in Afghanistan. [Online] Available at: https://apnews.com/article/asia-pacific-afghanistan-middle-east-business-5e850e5149ea0a3907cac2f282878dd5 [Accessed July 2022].

Findlay, S., 2021. Taliban finances swelled by proceeds of Afghanistan's shadow economy. [Online] Available at: https://www.ft.com/content/25b48967-2d8c-4acd-8699-e0cbdf164cb8 [Accessed July 2022].

Gazeta.uz, 2020. «My ne dopustim vozniknoveniya ugrozy dlya Uzbekistana» — glava ofisa «Taliban». [Online] Available at: https://www.gazeta.uz/ru/2020/09/15/taliban/ [Accessed July 2022].

Gazeta.uz, 2021. SShA nachnut vyvod vojsk iz Afganistana s 1 maja. [Online] Available at: https://www.gazeta.uz/ru/2021/04/15/us-troops/ [Accessed July 2022].

Himshiashvili, P., 2021. Zachem v Moskvu priezzhala delegaciya zapreshhennogo v Rossii «Talibana». [Online] Available at: https://www.rbc.ru/politics/09/07/2021/60e82fc69a7947693f4f9c91 [Accessed July 2022].

Kaura, V., 2022. China draws closer to the Taliban as regional foreign ministers prepare to meet in Beijing. [Online] Available at: https://www.mei.edu/publications/china-draws-closer-taliban-regional-foreign-ministers-prepare-meet-beijing [Accessed July 2022].

Konyrova, K., 2020. Turkmenistan offers Saudi to invest in TAPI pipeline. [Online] Available at: https://www.neweurope.eu/article/turkmenistan-offers-saudi-to-invest-in-tapi-pipeline/ [Accessed July 2022].

Kovalenko, M. & Tarasenko, P., 2021. Talibskiy pritok. [Online] Available at: https://www.kommersant.ru/doc/4955065 [Accessed July 2022].

Lee, M., Lawless, J. & Madhani, A., 2021. G-7 Leaders can't sway Biden to delay Afghanistan withdrawal. [Online] Available at: https://apnews.com/article/europe-afghanistan-g-7-summit-13631be5beba847935719ec4d8a4d5ce [Accessed July 2022].

Lubold, G. & Trofimov, Y., 2021. Afghan government could collapse six months after U.S. withdrawal, new intelligence assessment says. *Wall Street Journal*, 23 June.

Maizland, L., 2021. The Taliban in Afghanistan. [Online] Available at: https://www.cfr.org/backgrounder/taliban-afghanistan [Accessed July 2022].

Malyshev, V., 2021. Geroin stal krov'yu «Talibana» i Afganistana. [Online] Available at: https://www.fondsk.ru/news/2021/08/27/geroin-stal-krovju-talibana-i-afganistana-54327.html [Accessed July 2022].

Mfa.gov.cn, 2022. Ministry of Foreign Affairs of the People's Republic of China. [Online] Available at: https://www.fmprc.gov.cn/mfa_eng/xwfw_665399/s2510_665401/2511_665403/t1899785.shtml [Accessed July 2022].

Mustafa, K., 2022. Dead winds for TAPI as ADB stops work till recognition of Taliban regime. [Online] Available at: https://www.thenews.com.pk/print/939687-dead-winds-for-tapi-as-adb-stops-work-till-recognition-of-taliban-regime [Accessed July 2022].

News Quick24, 2021. China watches Afghanistan anxiously as the US withdraws. [Online] Available at: https://newsquick24.com/business/china-watches-afghanistan-anxiously-as-the-us-withdraws/ [Accessed July 2022].

Northern Miner, 2021. Copper supply expected to move into deficit in 2021, says StoneX. [Online] Available at: https://www.mining.com/copper-supply-expected-to-move-into-deficit-in-2021-says-stonex/ [Accessed July 2022].

Ollard, H., 2021. What's behind the planned Uzbekistan-Afghanistan-Pakistan railway?. [Online] Available at: https://thediplomat.com/2021/02/whats-behind-the-planned-uzbekistan-afghanistan-pakistan-railway/ [Accessed July 2022].

Otorbaev, D., 2021. Central Asia's Afghan route to prosperity. [Online] Available at: https://www.japantimes.co.jp/opinion/2021/05/04/commentary/world-commentary/afghanistan-kyrgyzstan-asia-europe-china-russia-global-economy-taliban/ [Accessed July 2022].

Polyakov, O., 2021. Pekin na hvoste u NATO: dostanutsya li Kitayu bogatstva nedr Afganistana? [Online] Available at: https://eadaily.com/ru/news/2021/07/08/pekin-na-hvoste-u-nato-dostanutsya-li-kitayu-bogatstva-nedr-afganistana [Accessed July 2022].

Prohvatilov, V., 2021. Kto zarabotal na voyne v Afganistane?. [Online] Available at: https://www.fondsk.ru/news/2021/08/28/kto-zarabotal-na-vojne-v-afganistane-54338.html [Accessed July 2022].

Rambler.ru, 2022. SMI: taliby ob"yavili dva tendera na razrabotku rudnyh mestorozhdeniy v Afganistane. [Online] Available at: https://finance.rambler.ru/markets/48493129-smi-taliby-obyavili-dva-tendera-na-razrabotku-rudnyh-mestorozhdeniy-v-afganistane/ [Accessed July 2022].

Regnum, 2021. Mirziyoev prizval vozrodit' svyazi stran Turkestana i Yuzhnoy Azii. [Online] Available at: https://regnum.ru/news/polit/3323870.html [Accessed July 2022].

RIA, 2021. Taliby poprosili OON ostat'sya v Afganistane. [Online] Available at: https://ria.ru/20210819/oon-1746473667.htm [Accessed July 2022].

Risen, J., 2010. U.S. identifies vast mineral riches in Afghanistan. [Online] Available at: https://www.nytimes.com/2010/06/14/world/asia/14minerals.html [Accessed July 2022].

Roma, G., 2021. Afghanistan's trade balance. [Online] Available at: https://www.barrons.com/news/afghanistan-s-trade-balance-01629201909 [Accessed July 2022].

Sabga, P., 2021. The US spent $2 trillion in Afghanistan – and for what?. [Online] Available at: https://www.aljazeera.com/economy/2021/8/16/the-us-spent-2-trillion-in-afghanistan-and-for-what [Accessed July 2022].

Semler, S., 2021. The top 5 military contractors ate $2 trillion during the Afghanistan war. [Online] Available at: https://stephensemler.substack.com/p/the-top-5-military-contractors-ate [Accessed July 2022].
Shepherd, C., 2021. China watches Afghanistan anxiously as the US withdraws. [Online] Available at: https://www.ft.com/content/49d266c6-a6c2-4ab2-bf52-ed34d72b22c1 [Accessed July 2022].
Spalinger, A., 2021. Taliban's rapid advance due to Afghan elites' corruption. [Online] Available at: https://www.nzz.ch/english/talibans-rapid-advance-due-to-afghan-elites-corruption-ld.1639784 [Accessed July 2022].
Starr, S. F., 2015. *Lost Enlightenment: Central Asia's Golden Age from the Arab Conquest to Tamerlane.* Princeton, NJ: Princeton University Press.
Tass.ru, 2021. Dva aviapolka CVO perevooruzhat na Su-34M i MiG-31BM k koncu 2021 goda. [Online] Available at: https://tass.ru/armiya-i-opk/11755149 [Accessed July 2022].
The Global Herald, 2021. 'US goal is an endless war, not a successful war' – WikiLeaks co-founder Julian Assange. [Online] Available at: https://theglobalherald.com/news/us-goal-is-an-endless-war-not-a-successful-war-wikileaks-co-founder-julian-assange/ [Accessed July 2022].
ThisIsAmericaTV, 2021. YouTube: TIA&TW - the New Uzbekistan - foreign affairs. [Online] Available at: https://www.youtube.com/watch?v=EqJe1hCmcko [Accessed July 2022].
Tikhonova, P., 2021. China prepares to move into Afghanistan with $62 billion 'Belt and Road' Initiative as American troops leave. [Online] Available at: https://insiderpaper.com/china-belt-and-road-afghanistan-us-forces-leave/ [Accessed July 2022].
Tkachyov, I. & Abramova, A., 2021. Chto vazhno znat' ob ekonomike zakhvachennogo talibami Afganistana. [Online] Available at: https://www.rbc.ru/economics/17/08/2021/611a51009a7947d0272802ff [Accessed July 2022].
TOLOnews, 2022. Work on TAPI Project will continue: Islamic Emirate. [Online] Available at: https://tolonews.com/afghanistan-177052 [Accessed July 2022].
Trading Economics, 2022. Afghanistan unemployment rate. [Online] Available at: https://tradingeconomics.com/afghanistan/unemployment-rate [Accessed July 2022].
Turkmenportal, 2022. Turkmenistan vozobnovil stroitel'stvo zheleznoy dorogi Akina-Andhoy v Afganistane. [Online] Available at: https://turkmenportal.com/blog/48081/turkmenistan-vozobnovil-stroitelstvo-zheleznoi-dorogi-akinaandhoi-v-afganistane [Accessed July 2022].
USAID, 2022. Agriculture - Afghanistan. [Online] Available at: https://www.usaid.gov/afghanistan/agriculture [Accessed July 2022].
World Bank, 2021. Afghanistan development update. [Online] Available at: https://thedocs.worldbank.org/en/doc/e406b6f24c2b7fdeb93b56c3116ed8f1-0310012021/original/Afghanistan-Development-Update-FINAL.pdf [Accessed July 2022].
World Bank, 2022a. Afghanistan overview: Development news, research, data. [Online] Available at: https://www.worldbank.org/en/country/afghanistan/overview [Accessed July 2022].
World Bank, 2022b. Towards economic stabilisation and recovery. [Online] Available at: https://thedocs.worldbank.org/en/doc/5f01165822f3639224e0d483ba1861fc-0310062022/original/ADU-2022-FINAL-CLEARED.pdf [Accessed July 2022].

Conclusion

Opening mutually beneficial transport and energy routes to connect Europe and Asia via Central Asia will be one of the most decisive events in Eurasia this century. For Central Asia to survive, modern land routes crossing the Eurasian continent will be required to allow the rapidly developing Chinese economy to effectively trade with European partners, increasing the competitiveness of all territories involved, including transit zones. The countries of Central Asia have much to gain from this, including the prospects of new hard and soft infrastructure, job creation, increased tax and tariff revenues, and increasing access to markets in both the East and the West.

Understanding the prospects that are opening up for the region, the countries of Central Asia have begun to implement several initiatives to expand their existing external transport and energy ties. These include the construction of railways from China through the Alashanlou and Khorgos checkpoints in Kazakhstan and beyond, along the northern corridor to Russia, Belarus, and Europe or along the southern corridor to Central Asia, the South Caucasus, Turkey, and Europe; the building of a modern high-speed highway through Kazakhstan to Russia and on to Europe; and the creation of new oil and gas pipelines from Turkmenistan and Kazakhstan to both China and Europe. However, a real breakthrough in global connectivity could come about from China's potential interest in building new high-speed rail routes across Central Asia to Europe. China has largely already accomplished the task of providing high-speed rail service to its own country, and therefore the Chinese government can now use its considerable human potential and huge production capacities to develop similar projects in neighbouring countries.

China has begun implementing an ambitious railway project outside its borders in the ASEAN countries. Using modern technology, Chinese and Lao specialists have recently built a railway connecting Kunlun (China) and Vientiane (Laos). The designers plan to continue it all the way down the length of mainland Southeast Asia. The overall network will consist of three main routes – the central one from Kunming to Bangkok and on to Singapore, the eastern one through Vietnam and Cambodia, and the western one through Myanmar to Bangkok. The southern half of the network from Bangkok to Singapore has been operational since 1918.

DOI: 10.4324/9781003360728-23

If the European Union were to support initiatives like these, it would be a massive breakthrough. There are already commercial interests, as these days a fully loaded train departs from China to Europe every hour, and similar trains leave in the opposite direction every two hours. Logistics companies can see obvious benefits from opening additional rail services between China and Europe, but there is already congestion on the current rail links through Kazakhstan and Russia. New railway lines must be built, but projects of this magnitude should only be implemented with collaboration between national governments and the private sector, necessitating close coordination between all interested partners. Partner governments should take the lead in developing a comprehensive programme of joint activities based on shared interests, determined by close consultation with all parties involved. With the intensive use of Eurasian transport and energy corridors, partners should think beyond the boost in trade relations and consider other opportunities for broader cooperation that will open up as a result.

Potential partners have been conducting processes for a long time, but mainly on a bilateral basis. In our opinion, the ideal scenario would be the creation of a new multilateral advisory council, composed of Central Asia, China and the EU, to study the development of energy and transport corridors through Central Asia and make recommendations accordingly. In the future, such consultations could include the countries of the South Caucasus, Iran, Turkey, and possibly Afghanistan.

When designing transport routes in Eurasia, planners need to consider the inevitable growth within the Indian subcontinent. Recognising this reality, partners should join forces to promote direct and efficient transit corridors between Central and South Asia. In this process, the development of energy and transport corridors will be of great strategic importance. These southern routes should be an essential but distinct addition to the classic Silk Road corridor, reflecting the realities of the 21st century. The complete stabilisation of the situation in Afghanistan is required for the implementation of such plans.

When planning new logistics routes between China and Europe, it is of utmost importance to consider modern geopolitical realities. The use of existing road and rail links with Europe through Russian territory should continue, but this northern route will need to run alongside the emerging southern corridor to Europe via the South Caucasus and Turkey. If only one route is in operation, the Eurasian rail bridge is vulnerable to all kinds of disruption along its length. Failure to strike the balance between the use of northern and southern routes could therefore jeopardise the success of the entire project.

Setting up logistics routes through Central Asia from China to Europe will not only mean investment in hard infrastructures like railways or pipelines. All stakeholders need to pay close attention to developing modern, soft infrastructure too. Along the way, a mechanism like a customs union should come into effect. It is necessary to introduce modern electronic procedures for customs clearance, insurance, forwarding and storage of goods, and maintenance of equipment and consumables. The hospitality industry should operate along these routes. Systematic work to harmonise soft infrastructure will speed up delivery and reduce costs to the benefit of logistics, shippers, and final recipients alike. Transparent, fully functioning soft infrastructure will be necessary to gain local support in Central Asia and vital for the stable operation of new routes.

Naturally, the main priority of the consultative process between the countries of Central Asia, China and the EU will be to construct additional energy and transport routes between China and Europe. If the situation in Afghanistan stabilises, building a railway from Uzbekistan and laying a gas pipeline from Turkmenistan through Afghanistan to Pakistan and India are exciting prospects. If the partners can implement this plan, energy and transport routes will connect through Central Asia, the diverse regions of Southeast Asia, South Asia, the South Caucasus, Iran, Turkey, Russia, and Europe. Will it happen in our lifetime?

Index

Page numbers in italics refer to figures; Page numbers in bold refer to tables.

For Product Safety Concerns and Information please contact our EU representative GPSR@taylorandfrancis.com
Taylor & Francis Verlag GmbH, Kaufingerstraße 24, 80331 München, Germany

www.ingramcontent.com/pod-product-compliance
Ingram Content Group UK Ltd.
Pitfield, Milton Keynes, MK11 3LW, UK
UKHW020156200926
475702UK00016B/2731
* 9 7 8 1 0 3 2 4 1 9 8 9 3 *